The Network Migration Workbook

Zero Downtime Migration Strategies for Microsoft Networks

2nd Edition

Karl W. Palachuk
Manuel L. Palachuk

Published by

GLB

Great Little Book Publishing Co., Inc.

Sacramento, CA

www.GreatLittleBook.com

www.ZeroDowntimeMigration.com

Great Little Book Publishing
7485 Rush River Dr., #710
Sacramento, CA 95831

www.greatlittlebook.com

ISBN: 978-0-9819978-7-2

Library of Congress Control Number: 2012938693

Register This Book

This information is repeated at the end of the book. But we learned that many people never read the appendices. So we're putting it here in the hopes that you will register the book online and gain access to your electronic content.

First, you need to register to the book at www.zerodowntimemigration.com. On the front page, simply click on the Register the Book link. Note: This takes some time because we need to authenticate your purchase. Please allow up to 72 hours for us to process your request if it occurs over a weekend.

Once you register the book you will receive access to the ZDTM Registered Owners content. This includes electronic versions of the chapters and checklists, plus additional materials, such as:

- Excel Spreadsheets for quotes
- Visio diagram of common network configuration
- PowerPoint Presentation: Pre-Migration Introduction
- PowerPoint Presentation: Post-Migration Welcome

. . . and More! Check it out.

Warning About Used Books

When you register your book online, you agree that the book is no longer returnable for a refund. We simply have to assume that anyone who registers the book is going to download the electronic content and use it. Therefore, the book cannot be returned once the e-version has been downloaded.

That also means that the owner of a used copy of the book does not have access to the electronic version.

If you bought this book used, and you want electronic versions of the checklists, you need to ask the seller for a refund so you can buy a new copy of the book.

We are sorry that this policy is necessary, but we have had a few "bad apples" buy the book and then intentionally violate the copyright. As you can imagine, this book took thousands of hours of labor to produce. Even a casual user will save dozens of hours of labor by using these checklists and resources. So, while the price is not cheap, we believe it is fair.

Thank you for your support and understanding.

The Network Migration Workbook

Zero Downtime Migration Strategies for Microsoft Networks

2nd Edition

Karl W. Palachuk
Manuel L. Palachuk

Table of Contents

Foreword to the Second Edition

By Harry Brelsford,

The only constant is change but the one thing you can count on is that Karl Palachuk will get you to where you are going. And now he is joined by his brother Manuel to make it even better!

In this second edition of the acclaimed *The Network Migration Workbook*, the Palachuk brothers have refreshed the content to remain relevant and accurate in the fast moving field of technology. What's refreshing is that at every turn, the book provides evergreen business strategies in the technical migration realm. That is, this book could stand alone as a migration primer irrespective of your individual network configuration. Many of the conversations between these covers are general enough to benefit everybody.

At some level, a book is a book and based on 500+ year workflow. But books are changing and becoming more engaging. The Palachuk brothers didn't disappoint as they have delivered *The Network Migration Workbook* to include adjunct external content including Excel spreadsheets for quotes, a Visio diagram for common network configurations and PowerPoint presentations that include pre- and post-migration content and messaging (e.g. Pre-migration welcome). These resources are made available to you after you register your book.

The "flow" of this book is appropriately outlined to make the migration experience. You will find the high-level introduction is followed be a well-written project management primer to level set the conversation for you, the reader. Then the good stuff starts with section two on defining the migration project. It is here where well-positioned nuggets are shared. The Palachuks give a shout-out to "scope creep" as a gotcha in waiting. Because I completed my Master's in Business Administration with a concentration in Project Management, I concur completely with that sentiment.

Another nugget is the conversation on "Methods for Achieving Zero Downtime." Starting with "Intercept the Process" (which essentially means two simultaneous environments to achieve a real zero downtime migration) to "Flip the Big Switch" when you achieve completion and the line of business (LOB) application is writing to the database in the new environment, the Palachuks present this important content with high readability.

The reader's attention turns to cloud in Chapter 9, "Cloud Strategies, Cloud Migrations, and Hybrid Solutions" where four types of clouds are easily defined. Digging deeper, there is ample specificity on how and what to migrate to the cloud from the on-premises infrastructure.

So the "net-net" on the Palachuks' book is that it balances high-readability and proffers a friendly writing style with the type of in-depth content we "techies" demand. Great work Karl and Manuel on this updated version of your well-received original. Go ahead and take a vacation day to celebrate!

- Harry Brelsford

Harry Brelsford is the founder of SMB Nation (www.smbnation.com) from Bainbridge Island,

WA. He is a long-time SMB channel partner who has served customers and mentored other partners (SMB Nation has over 35,000 tribal members who are SMB technology consultants).

Harry oversees the popular SMB Nation world-wide events including webinars, workshops and multi-day conferences. He holds an MBA (and numerous certifications such as MCSE, MCT, CNE, et al) and is the author of 17-books. He is also the publisher of SMB Partner Community magazine. His 20-years of SMB technology experience were supplemented by teaching 12+ years at night as an adjunct professor at Seattle Pacific University and other higher-learning institutions. Harry is a frequent speaker at industry events. Harry's recent books include the Microsoft Response Point Primer and Microsoft Small Business Server 2008 Blueprint.

Foreword (Original)

By Philip Elder, MCTS. Co-Author: *Small Business Server 2008 Blueprint*

Experience, Knowledge, and Checklists

Having been around Small Business Server (SBS) since the Microsoft BackOffice product that was based on NT 4.x, I have had a lot of hands-on experience with the various SBS versions since that time. My interest in the SBS product as a part of the solutions designed for our SMB clients turned into a passion with the release of SBS 2003. The product rocked!

SBS, and now EBS, are complicated products. When it comes to SBS, Microsoft has worked very hard to make all of the various server components and applications work well together. The same can be said of EBS and its three or four server solution setup.

Critical in the midst of this knowledge building is the need to delve into understanding the way things work. We need to know the why too. If we do not know the underlying server components, how they work, why they work, and how Microsoft has made them work well together, then there is no checklist out there to help us with troubleshooting our way out of a server crash or a migration that has stalled.

However, with a product series as complex as SBS and EBS are, we do have a need to break down the various set up, maintenance, and migration procedures and document them. We need to build and maintain a checklist system to make sure we stay on top of the various procedures and especially not lose our way in the myriads of steps those procedures require.

A checklist is a tool in the SMB/SME I.T. professional's hand that helps them to be consistent.

Karl and Manual have done an excellent job compiling their business and technical procedures into a series of checklists. The checklists are awesome. The beauty of this book though, is the fact that they also took the time to explain in great depth the why things are done in the order they are done. The explanations found in the chapters that precede the actual checklists should be mandatory reading for anyone aspiring to build their own I.T. business and anyone employed in the industry.

Why mandatory? Because, the checklists, and their background, are also tools in the aspiring I.T. professional's training regimen. The checklist in this case provides a series of logical steps for the Trainee to delve deeper into their I.T. business operations, to become a strong member of a team, or getting to know products they sell. They provide directions for the I.T. Trainee to take when learning the business or a new product and its complexities.

With those directions in hand, the Trainee can then work with hands-on, in-person, online, and book based business and product training. After a few years of working on building the knowledge base, experience, and passing certificate exams the I.T. professional would become a valuable asset to any I.T. company's sales, sales engineer, or technical support positions.

- Philip Elder MCTS

Microsoft SBS MVP
(SBS Microsoft Most Valued Professional)

Co-Author: *Small Business Server 2008 Blueprint* (SMB Nation Press) along with Harry Brelsford

Blog: http://blog.mpecsinc.ca

About the Authors

Karl W. Palachuk is the founder and CEO of KPEnterprises Business Consulting* and other successful companies in the Sacramento area. He is the founder and, for eight years, president of the Sacramento SMB IT Professionals group. He is also the author of several books, including *The Network Documentation Workbook.*

Outside the world of technology, Karl is also the author of *Relax Focus Succeed, A Guide To Balancing Your Personal And Professional Lives And Being More Successful In Both.*

Karl has been a featured speaker at conferences and seminars over the last ten years. He is a Microsoft Certified Systems Engineer with a Bachelor's Degree from Gonzaga University and a Master's Degree from The University of Michigan. He is also a Microsoft Small Business Specialist, and is an original member of Microsoft's Small Business Specialist Advisory Panel.

Contact him at
karlp@greatlittlebook.com

Manuel L. Palachuk is the President of Conceptual Age Consulting of Boca Raton, FL.

Manuel has over 25 years of business, management, and training experience in the computer and electronics industries. He is an expert of process, systems and their efficiency who is driven toward continuous improvement in all aspects of the business. His goal and passion is to take your service-based business to the next level and he has the blueprint to do it.

He holds an Associate Degree in Electrical Engineering Technology and a Bachelor's Degree in Automated Manufacturing. He has been Microsoft Certified for more than ten years and is a Microsoft Small Business Specialist.

Manuel is the former President of KPEnterprises Business Consulting. Since then he has been coaching and working as an outsourced Chief Operating Officer for small business consultants in the SMB space.

Contact him at
manuel@conceptualageconsulting.net

---

* Note on KPEnterprises

For sixteen years, Karl owned and operated KPEnterprises Business Consulting, Inc. In 2011 this corporation was dissolved and now exists only as a brand name owned by Great Little Book Publishing Co., Inc.

All the experiences described in this book are real. Prior to 2011 these experiences occurred with KPEnterprises and its clients. During 2011, Karl became the Senior Systems Engineer at America's Tech Support in Sacramento, CA. At the same time, Manuel Palachuk served as a special Consultant and Business Coach to Network Technology Solutions of Pompano Beach, FL.

Experiences described in this book during 2011-2012 occurred with ATS or NTS.

Dedication

This book is dedicated to the SBS Community. That includes all the great people at Microsoft who conceived of the Small Business Server product line, who built the products, tested them, promoted them, and improved them in leaps and bounds with each new release. That community also includes Harry Brelsford, the founder of the SBS Community "in the wild," even though that community has grown and morphed beyond what he originally imagined.

The SBS Community also includes all the User Group Leaders, the MVPs, the bloggers, the product advisory councils, the folks who attend the events, the Yahoo Groupies, and everyone who jumps in with both feet and participates in the global SBS / SMB / SME / MSP Community.

We have enjoyed tremendous success selling, supporting and migrating the SBS family of products. We have also been blessed to have met so many dedicated, talented, hard-working, fun-loving consultants over the years. You the community that makes SBS much more than a piece of software have given us friends flung across the globe.

A very special dedication goes out to our friend and associate Scott Mallet who passed away during the writing of this second edition. Scott worked with Karl on a few projects here and there and was a member of his HTG 13 group. Manuel took a job with Scott's company, Network Technology Solutions and was COO there for all of 2011. We are honored to have called Scott our friend and we will miss him.

We hope that this book will contribute something to global SBS Community.

- Karl W. Palachuk and Manuel L. Palachuk
  Sacramento, CA / Boca Raton, FL

Thank you for purchasing this book. We hope you'll find it useful and we trust you'll give us feedback by emailing

Karl Palachuk at karlp@greatlittlebook.com

or

Manuel L. Palachuk at manuel@conceptualageconsulting.net

The Plan of the Book

This book has a decidedly practical bent. We start with a discussion of theory and approach, but that doesn't last long and we're into building checklists and working through the system.

Please refer to the "map" on the next page. The flow of the book is organized to take you through the entire migration process and finish with a "Big Checklist" to take with you.

Section I: Introduction and Overview

Chapters 1-2 are an overview of the process of migrating a Windows-based system from one machine to another. We understand that there are great tools out there to do this job, including the Active Directory Migration Toolkit and Jeff Middleton's Swing Migration Toolkit. But here we spell out the argument for using a more "manual" migration process. We also give a brief introduction to project management.

Section II: Defining the Migration Project

Chapters 3-4 talk about the specifics of managing a migration project and quoting the project so you can guarantee you'll make money.

(See the note below for technicians who argue that they don't need this section.)

Section III: The Big Checklist

Chapter 5 introduces the key element in our process: The SBS Migration Checklist. The Checklist is literally the core of our process and the core of this book. The Checklist will allow you to make spectacular promises to your clients – like a perfect migration, with zero company-wide downtime and less than one hour of downtime per user. Chapter 5 "explains" the checklist

Section IV: Bringing It All Together

Chapter 6 goes into some of the strategies of defining each migration. It also covers all the miscellaneous details of the migration project, particularly those not related to the technology of Windows Server or SBS. Finally, Chapter 6 discusses the finishing process for the migration: The human side, the cleanup, the documentation, and preparing for the next project.

Section V: Case Studies

Chapters 7-8 cover two examples of SBS migrations. One is extremely simple, straight forward, and "plain vanilla." The other is rather complicated and probably pushes SBS just a little beyond what it was intended for. <wink>

Section VI: Cloud and Other Non-SBS Migrations

Chapters 9-11 address migrations to cloud services and Foundation Server – a great little server alternative to SBS. Before we had SBS Essentials, Foundation server became a key offering for us.

Section VII: SBS 2011 and SBS Essentials

Chapters 12-13 address Microsoft's latest offering the small business space: SBS 2011 and SBS 2011 Essentials. As with all versions of SBS (and Windows Server generally), SBS 2011 has many of the same features, a few new ones, and a few gotchas to be aware of.

Appendices

The Checklists have been revised in this edition. In the earlier book, Appendix A was a checklist for migrating to SBS 2003. Appendix B was for migrating to SBS 2008.

First, the 2011 Checklist is really now a universal checklist. It can be used for all versions. This takes a little extra reading, but is well worthwhile. The universal checklist is now Appendix A.

Second, We've decided to save a few trees. The SBS 2003 and SBS 2008 Checklists are online in a downloadable format (Word format). We have printed the complete 2011 Checklist only because it's current, it's a GREAT resource tool to bookmark and use, and it's handy to have in front of you as we make several references to it in the text of the book.

Appendix B is a unique kind of index: It is a procedure-focused index of the SBS 2011 Checklist. In other words, it examines a specific topic within the checklist and gives you all the references you need for that specific process.

For example, if you are looking to move the exchange database without the whole migration project, you will need some pages regarding discovery and system build, some pages about the export process, some pages about the import process, etc.

Appendix C is very brief – VERY brief. But it's also very important. Appendix C contains the information you need to register this book and gain access to the online content at www.zerodowntimemigration.com.

To obtain your downloadable content:

First, you need to register to the book at www.zerodowntimemigration.com. On the front page, simply click on the Register the Book link.

Once you register the book you will receive access to the ZDTM Registered Owners content. Note: This takes some time because we need to authenticate your purchase.

Downloadable content includes electronic versions of the chapters and checklists, plus additional materials, such as:

- Excel Spreadsheets for quotes
- Visio diagram of common network configuration
- PowerPoint Presentation: Pre-Migration Introduction
- PowerPoint Presentation: Post-Migration Welcome

. . . and More! Check it out.

Warning About Used Books

When you register your book online, you agree that the book is no longer returnable for a refund. We simply have to assume that anyone who registers the book is going to download the electronic content and use it. Therefore, the book cannot be returned once the e-version has been downloaded.

That also means that the owner of a used copy of the book does not have access to the electronic version.

If you bought this book used, and you want electronic versions of the checklists, you need to ask the seller for a refund so you can buy a new copy of the book.

Thank you for your support and understanding.

The Network Migration Workbook

Overview and Flow

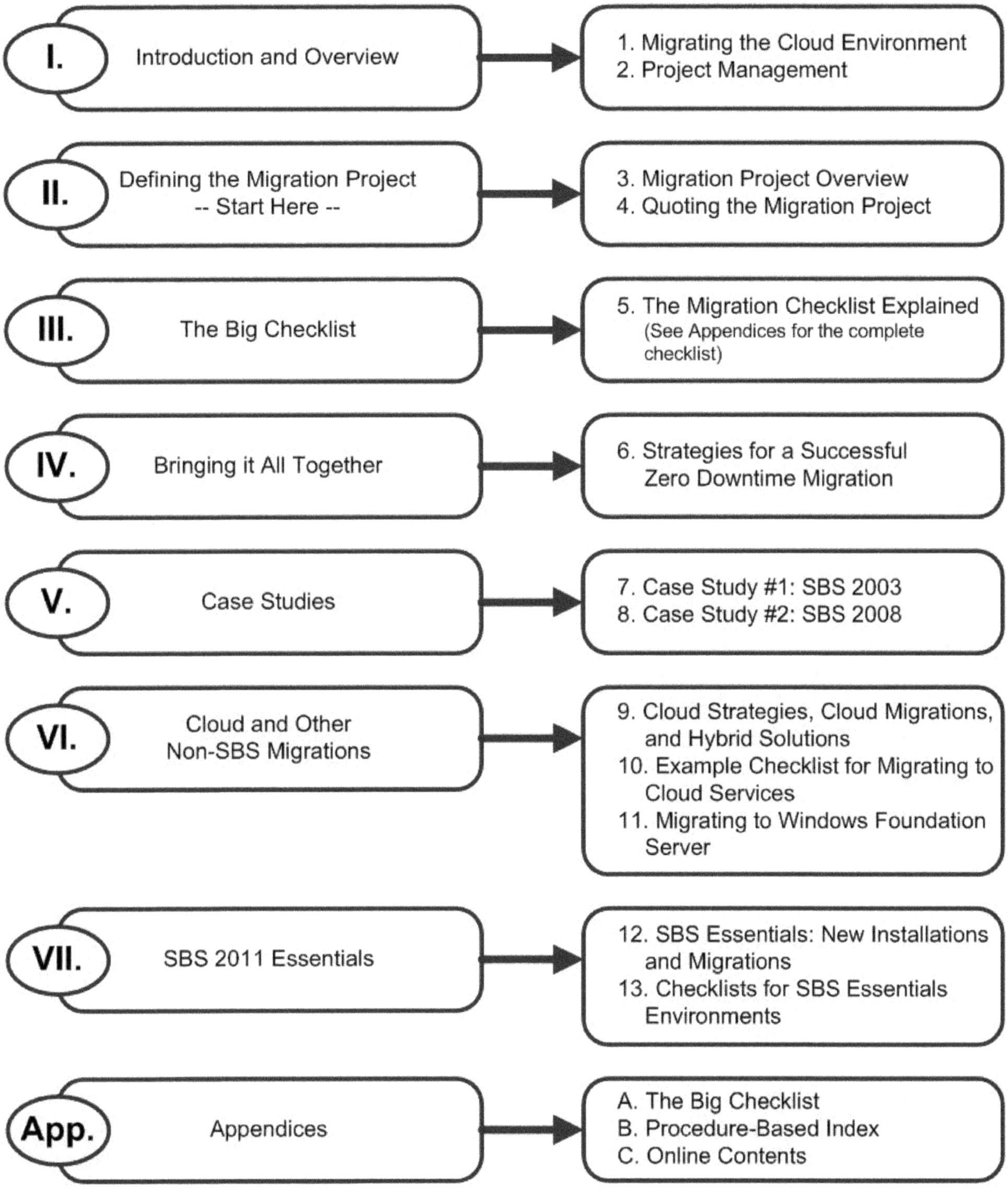

We'll come back to this map again and again so you always know where you are in the process.

In a sense, the "plan" of the book is to give a big overview, then focus in a bit. Then focus in some more. Then give you a massive amount of detail.

We honestly believe the that the parts of the book that precede the Big Checklist are very important because they represent our approach, our techniques, and the Best Practices that have allowed us to perform profitable Zero Downtime Migrations for several years.

Legal Disclaimer

Everything changes all the time. This information is for advice only. We make no representation about its completeness or suitability for any specific project.

Please note, also, that software products change all the time, including those described in great detail in this book. This book is not intended to describe an exact process that will not change.

Quite the opposite: this book is intended to give you an approach to network migrations that will allow you to build and maintain a big, complicated collection of checklists that change after every successful migration project.

And finally: You're responsible for what you do.

Who Should Read this Book?

This book is focused primarily on the Small Business environment. So, for the most part, it was written with the SMB Consultant in mind. But the concepts, tools, and techniques discussed here are not unique to SBS. 98% of this book is directly relevant to anyone who wants to gain a deeper understanding of all the processes and procedures needed to migrate Windows servers.

SBS is a great focus for this book because of the unique nature of the SBS product. With a collection of great products all packaged together – Windows, Exchange, SQL, SharePoint, etc. – SBS is necessarily complex enough that you can't just drop a new domain controller in the environment and drag over the active directory. But during the writing of this book, we participated on the beta programs for SBS 2008, the now-defunct Windows Essential Business Server (EBS) line, and the SBS 2011 Essentials product. Not surprisingly, we found many similarities in how we would migrate to and from these server systems.

What about users of the Swing Migration kit from Jeff Middleton over at www.sbsmigration.com? There is no denying that Swing Migrations are great, and that there's a place for Jeff's tools. But we also believe there is a large market for doing "manual" migrations. After all, what we do is pretty low-tech. It's sophisticated but very easy to do. And that means it is easy to train your employees to do. We're also convinced that this book goes into the details of some technologies that will be very beneficial to users of the Swing Migration Toolkit.

Hey, we're authors. What else can we say? Everyone who will ever migrate a Windows server can benefit from this book! ☺

What About the Microsoft Migration Process?

We must briefly address the Microsoft Migration process. Microsoft has put forth their best efforts to provide a clear and concise path for migrating from the previous version of Microsoft Small Business Server to the latest. Our experience and what we have heard from many others in the industry is very clearly that it is not consistent and not truly repeatable. At its best, it has problems!

And when the Microsoft Migration process goes bad, it goes pretty bad. We've rescued more Microsoft SBS migrations than we have had go seamless. Aside from this, the process is incomplete and provides no flexibility in migration of components to other locations such as email or SharePoint to the cloud.

Microsoft's new products, including SBS Essentials, have no choice but to provide some great migration tools for these components. But what do you do when you're moving from a Server with Exchange to SBS, or from SBS to a Server with Exchange?

Suffice to say we don't believe in the Microsoft migration because we have no control of the most critical components. This is of primary importance when attempting to attain Zero Downtime. The benefits of bypassing the Microsoft migration are countless in our opinion.

When engineers ask us, "But what about when I have 65 users and all those unique profiles and email addresses and groups?" We say: There is no system that is so complicated it cannot be broken down to a logical list of users, groups and permissions. And if it is well documented it can be recreated in a new environment.

Yes, at some point you may have to come up with some creative ways to document and recreate SMTP addresses or AD Groups etc. This is where you should realize that if you truly master your craft it is simply a matter of learning a new script or command for PowerShell or Exchange Command Shell.

Everything about these systems can be known, documented and reproduced. We believe our system of migrations represents the foundation and brick level. If you truly understand each of the components of the migration process, you can have full control of the entire migration and can easily design a zero downtime solution.

Where we stand apart is that we can always take a step back if something goes wrong, and we can always choose the best solution for each component independently. We will always have a cleaner end product, and most important, we can fix everything we break.

Technicians, Project Managers, and Sales People

Other than the client, there are three primary types of people involved in the migration process:

- Technicians
- Project Managers
- Sales People

The technicians are the folks "in the trenches" during a network migration. They actually put their hands on the hardware, go down the checklists, and make the migration happen.

Project managers are the strategic planners and the guides through sometimes choppy seas. They work more with the client's I.T. management (or owners). It is the project manager's job to make sure everything gets done, gets done in order, and that communications with the client are as good as they can be.

The Sales People have to figure out what the client needs, translate between the techno-speak and client (human) language, and put in all together in a package that everyone accepts. A Sales Person has to give the client a good value while giving the I.T. provider a reasonable margin.

One of our reviewers pointed out that technicians don't want to see anything intended for project managers or sales people. We considered dividing up the book and marking chapters as being most relevant to each of these groups. But the truth is that good technicians need to understand that other stuff too.

We hope that most good technicians want to be good enough someday to run a migration project. First, they will need to be a project lead, then eventually play the role of project manager.

With that in mind, reading about the higher-level management of a project should be very useful.

Sales are admittedly a little different. But we know from our own consulting business, we want technicians to be sensitive to the costs involved in delivering a project – on time and on budget.

It helps us a great deal with technicians begin to see the big picture and not just the small set of clicks in front of them.

In addition to all of that, we have a system that is "unified" in the sense that there are certain threads running through the project to bring consistency and profitability to the entire migration project.

For example, the quoting process assumes that there will be a clearly defined scope and that the desktops migrations will be carefully managed. The project manager is responsible for keeping the project within that scope and for managing the desktop migrations so they are in line with the original expectations.

At the same time, the technician needs to understand these elements and how they affect the big picture (the profitability of the project).

A technician will not be held personally responsible when a project is over budget, but he *should* be responsible for knowing where his role fits in that larger picture. And if too many projects are unprofitable because of the actions of a technician, he should be looking for a new job!

As you review the rules for success in Chapter One, note that we assume these are understood team-wide. These are literally mantras of success for a project management team. If technicians want to be part of a successful team, these apply to them as well as the sales people and project managers.

So, while many people will pick and choose the chapters they read, and the chapters they assign to various members of their staff, we believe everyone would be better off reading the entire book.

We believe you will have success with any of the material you find here. We also believe you will find greatest success by understanding all of the material you find here.

Acknowledgements (Revised for the 2nd Ed.)

As with all major projects, we owe a great deal to the people who have inspired us, promoted us, and helped us make it to the end.

More than anyone else, we thank our clients. KPEnterprises has been consulting with small businesses since 1995. In that time we've been grateful to work with some of the nicest people on earth. They have trusted us with their technology and their *business*. They made our migration process possible, and therefore this book.

Jeff Middleton (Microsoft MVP and author of the Swing Migration process) has been a friend to us and to the SMB community for many years. Jeff heard about this project almost exactly two years before it went to press. He has always been very supportive.

Jennifer Corry was the Office Manager at KPEnterprises and Great Little Book for six years. She kept us in line and is largely responsible for making sure we don't drop things while managing two businesses and many projects at once.

Connie Kong started as our Design Intern and jumped right in to make this the *Network Migration Workbook* a lot less "clunky" looking than our past books. Connie has been a constant help with all the little details.

Svetlana Shurayev was in charge of our Fulfillment and E-Commerce operations at GLB when the book was released. With this book she took a huge step up, formatting every chapter, every paragraph, and every page. She did a spectacular job with proofreading and copy editing. And she did all this on top of her regular work!

Of course we owe huge thank you for our reviewers: Chris Boyle, Amy Babinchak, James Wirth, Kyle Elworthy, and Michael Alligood. They gave us feedback on form, content, and overall look and feel. Chris Boyle, in particular, gave lengthy and detailed feedback that was integrated early in the review process and lightened the load for everyone else.

It is wonderful to have a true community of people to call on for a project like this.

Of course we also thank everyone who bought our previous books and the entire community that supports the efforts of independent authors!

Special Thanks

Michael Bayless of America's Tech Support. Michael evolved from being the Service Manager at KPEnterprises to running his own business. He generously gave us access to his resources and spent a lot of time digging into the new checklist. He gave us a lot of feedback and we appreciate it.

The Senior Engineering Team at network Technology Solutions, specifically Leo Nguyen, helped us in refining the 2011 checklist and proving new procedures.

Christian Johnston at Artisan Infrastructure not only let us test drive their excellent product but allowed us time to test our migration on an entirely virtual environment. (See Chapter Five on test environments.)

Finally, we thank all of our excellent technicians over the years. They helped us implement and fine-tune the checklists over the years.

-- Karl W. Palachuk

-- Manuel L. Palachuk

2009, 2012

Consulting Assistance

We hope you'll agree that you can complete every step in this book successfully. After all, you already have all the technical skills required to plan, sell, and execute a migration project. Virtually everyone who buys this book will have already migrated many networks.

Our "technique" is to tackle the job as a slightly longer-term, low stress project with zero downtime. To accomplish that, or come close, you need to have a process. This book attempts to provide that process.

But we all know that sometimes you can learn a lot faster if someone gives you a step up. So, if you would like some *migration consulting* assistance for your first zero-downtime migration, we can help. Or if you have a particularly complicated migration, we can help with that.

You can do this, too. You really can, with this workbook. But if, for whatever reason, you want some *migration consulting* assistance for your first zero-downtime migration, we can help.

But, guess what? A) It's expensive; B) It must be planned and scheduled; and C) The price is doubled outside of regular business hours (8 AM to 6 PM on whichever coast our technician is located).

Here's how our consulting package works:

- Standard hourly labor: Ten hour minimum
- Rate doubled after hours (outside 8AM – 6PM Monday-Friday)
  Four hour minimum
- All labor must be prepaid
- No last-minute assistance is available.
  If you engage us, we need to be involved at a minimal level and schedule ourselves to be available on the two-day period when you do the server switch-over.
- No refunds are given for unused hours. Unused hours expire after eighteen months.

Please contact us or see our web site for information on individual or group trainings.

For assistance, please contact one of us:

Karl W. Palachuk
(West Coast)
karlp@greatlittlebook.com

Manuel L. Palachuk
(East Coast)
manuel@conceptualageconsulting.net

The Network Migration Workbook

Overview and Flow

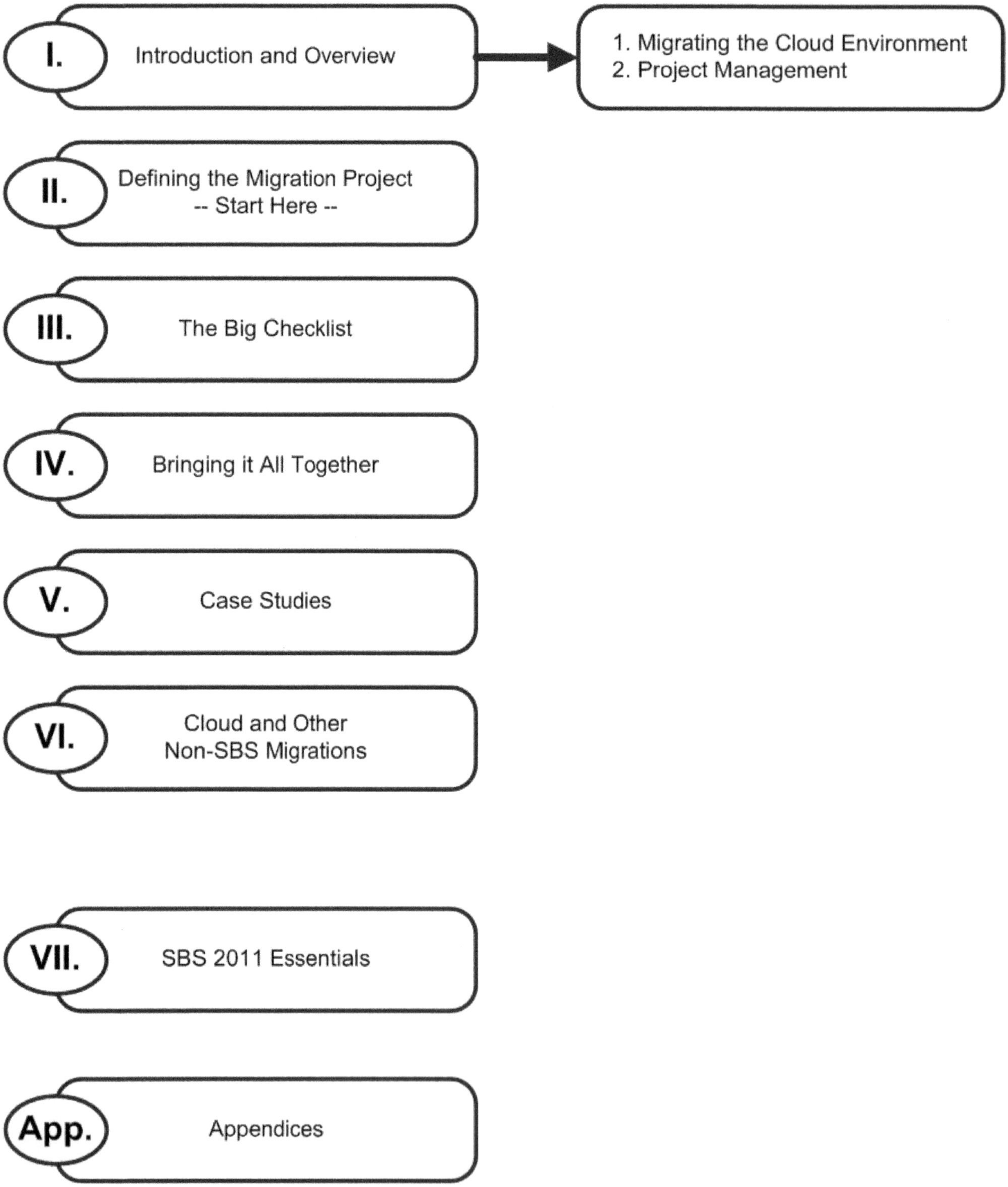

I. Introduction and Overview

Chapter 1

Migrating the Windows Environment

Introduction

This workbook is the product of our business. It is literally the "write up" of how KPEnterprises designs and executes network migrations. KPEnterprises has been doing this since 1995. Because these procedures are based on real-world experiences in the trenches of small business consulting, you'll find three things that stand out in this book:

First, we think you'll see a bit of your own business here. You'll find stories about clients you'll recognize and systems you've worked on.

Second, we have a real-world view about how small businesses work. We won't recommend solutions fit for "enterprise" customers. We will also give some advice about working with small business owners and their employees.

Third, we provide advice and guidance that really can be implemented by a small shop. KPEnterprises normally employs three or four technicians. Of those, one is Karl, who primarily plays the roles of salesman, elder statesman, and ultimate escalation point. Another is Manuel, the President, Service Manager, chief cook, and bottle washer.

In other words, we're very technical, but spend a lot of time doing non-technical chores. These network migration procedures have been developed by and for a small business consulting practice. We know you'll be able to implement them successfully.

As this book goes to press, Small Business Server 2008 has been released. If it lives for five years – as its predecessor did – you'll be fine-tuning and perfecting these procedures for some time to come.

It seems odd, but migrating entire computer operations from one system to another is almost unique to the small business market. Think about that.

Larger businesses replace a machine here, a "system" there. But they never replace all of their core operating equipment at once.

Small businesses, by contrast, perform this kind of wholesale upgrade every three or four years. It's just the way things are done in the SMB (small and medium business) space.

What's New in The Second Edition?

The obvious "new" material here is the SBS 2011 checklist and Chapters 9-13. But many other sections have been updated as well.

One of the big changes is our mindset on the SBS Family of servers. In 2008, Microsoft EBS or Essential Business Server product was new and ready to change the world. Now it has ceased to exist and is a distant memory. In the meantime, SBS 2011 Essentials has been released and brought a new little sibling to the family.

Of the core content, here's what's completely new:

The SBS 2011 Checklist. Now 270 pages! This is the ultimate resource guide to SBS, whether you use it for a Zero Downtime Migration or a reference guide.

Chapter Nine: Cloud Strategies, Cloud Migrations, and Hybrid Solutions. Here we cover moving services to the cloud. We introduce our "server lite" concept. And we discussion choosing between SBS 2011 Essentials and Windows Foundation Server.

Chapter Ten: Example Checklist for Migrating to Cloud Services. We talk about moving web site, hosted spam filtering, Exchange, and backups to the cloud. And, of course, all the details.

Chapter Eleven: Migrating to Microsoft Foundation Server. We introduce the "Windows Server 2008 R2 Foundation" edition and why it's so cool. Then we present a checklist for moving from an SBS or standard server to Foundation Server.

Chapter Twelve: SBS Essentials – New Installations and Migrations. We introduce the new SBS family member and talk about combining this product with cloud-based services. We present a two-part Technology Roadmap Questionnaire to get you started on a small server migration project.

Chapter Thirteen: Checklists for SBS Essentials Environments. The final chapter covers preparing the network for an SBS Essentials migration, and setting up a variety of network configurations. We also cover connecting workstations to the new SBS Essentials network.

Other new features . . .

Combined 2003, 2008, 2011 Checklists

The most important new feature of the Big Checklist (as we like to call it) is that we combined what would have been three checklists of well over 200 pages each into one comprehensive checklist.

Faced with the task of re-writing both the 2003 and 2008 checklists to accommodate moving to SBS 2011 was a daunting task to begin with.

As we reviewed what would have to be covered as "new content" we also had to consider what could be cut from the checklist. Unfortunately for us, we could not bring ourselves to drop anything from the checklist. What would we drop anyway? Office 2003? XP Pro? SBS 2003? After all SBS 2003 and Office 2003 are both over eight years old, XP Pro is eleven, and who uses any of these anymore anyway? Well these were pretty obvious choices so we dropped nothing.

As for additions we had no choice but to detail the use of Office 2010, Exchange 2010, and USMT 4.0. And then there are all the new features and changes of SBS 2011 itself, not the least of which is the Roles based Security that performs wonderful magic everywhere, but also makes the SQL migration require just a little more detailed in every aspect.

As we moved from section to section it became obvious that we needed to combine where we could and if possible condense down to one multifunction checklist. We will say: If we had tried this the first time around writing this book, we might just now be releasing the SBS 2008 checklist not the 2011 checklist. Luckily we did have two separate checklists for 2003 and 2008 to start from.

We set out to first complete the 2003 to 2011 checklist. Next we looked at it from a Source to Destination viewpoint. When we did it was obvious that all we needed to add or incorporate where the possibility of a different source than SBS 2003, SBS 2008, Exchange 2003, Exchange 2007, Office 2003, 2007, 2010, etc. existed.

What we have now are small checklist sections or subsections where the steps to perform in each subsection are relative to the migration source. If the source is Office 2003 do this, if its Office 2007 0r 2010 do this. If the source is Exchange 2003 do this, for Exchange 2007 do this and for Exchange 2010 do this. The checklist is now right about 270 pages. The end result is there is only one checklist that covers three generations spanning over 10 years of Small Business Server, Microsoft SQL Server, and Microsoft Office. It will make the Small Business Server 2014 checklist that much easier to build. ☺

Pre-Discovery and Discovery Highlighted

The Pre-Discovery and Discovery sections have always been a point of discussion when it comes to who should do which parts. It's not as simple as Technician's do the Pre-Discovery and Engineers do the full Discovery. There are decisions that need to be make in the Pre-Discovery that should only be made by a senior level engineer and conversely there are many things in the full Discovery that do not require a senior engineer.

It has always been intended that you should have the simple data collection performed by a technician of a sufficient level of knowledge that they can be relied upon to have collected the right information and to have covered all of the important aspects. It became obvious that all we need do is highlight the sections that are for a project lead or senior engineer in light Grey. Then we simply insert a statement in the General section of the Pre-Discovery and Discovery explaining the intent that these Grey sections, unless specifically directed otherwise, are for project leads or senior engineers only.

Much of the work load of the Discovery process can now be delegated to a technician (or even the Back Office) with minimal concern as a project lead or senior engineer is still required to review the most critical aspects. You may freely adjust the highlighting for sections based on your company's comfort with your technical staff. You may even choose to continue highlighting's into major checklist sections to help technicians understand what steps are intended only for senior engineers. This would be excellent for sections such as the DNS or firewall changes on migration day or even the informing the client checklist items.

Discussion of Test Environments and Virtual Test Environments

Whether you're new or seasoned, please check out the discussion of test environments in Chapter Five. We have always used test environments. They used to be physical machines we had lying around the office.

For this version of the book, tow big things changed. First, we make great use of virtual and cloud-based technology. Second, the authors were split between east and west coasts, 3,000 miles apart.

As a result, we took full advantage of virtual environments for testing, retesting, and running through the checklist. Just to write this book, Manuel has probably performed more end-to-end SBS 2011 migrations than anyone on earth, including Microsoft engineers.

Anyway, read the section on test environments in Chapter Five.

Index to the Checklist

This may be one of the most useful features we could have added to the checklist. We added it because even as we "wrote the book" we don't have perfect recall so even for one of us to say to another tech or engineer "It's in the checklist and I'm sure it's in the System Build section" doesn't usually work.

Suffice it to say, it is a simple index but it has already been hailed as a much needed feature by everyone we have worked directly with in the development of the 2011 edition.

If you have any desire you customize the index or expand upon it feel free to do so, knowing it was built as the most basic index possible in Word 2010. All you need to do is mark a new word, phrase or sentence for inclusion then rebuild the index.

What Does Migration Mean To You?

It only occurred to us after writing 300 pages and getting some early feedback that we need to define what we mean by migration.

Most people in our business talk about "migration" or "the migration process" in reference to moving active directory from one physical server to another. Certainly, this is the migration process that is made much simpler with Jeff Middleton's Swing Migration.

At the same time, we all know that it takes a lot more than moving active directory to migrate a network.

Karl has made several presentations about the Zero Downtime Migration process. Many people are surprised that so much time is spent discussing the business side of migrations. But the truth is that the basic technical process is not particularly complicated.

The complicate part of a migration comes with all the snags you run into. I'm sure you've seen your share:

- The unexpected 100 MB Exchange database in a company of ten people
- Profiles "from hell"
- Clients who think the migration to a new server is a great time to refresh office on every desktop and move to a new ISP
- The line of business vendor whose database breaks during the migration and can't be reached

It goes on and on.

Microsoft has developed some tools to help with the migration process. We call them out in the *Our Favorite Whitepapers* section of the checklist. But even their 100+ page explanation of the migration process stops short of addressing all these parts of a migration that don't involve moving the server's personality to its new home.

When a small business gets a new server, it is usually a major event. That client normally only has one or two servers. If the one you're replacing is the domain controller (or with SBS, domain, exchange, SQL, SharePoint, etc. all in one), then it affects every device and person on the network.

And you should treat this like a break/fix job. In other words, you can't just look at replacing a piece of hardware and not think about the bigger picture.

- How old is the UPS on the server?
- Are there any messed up profiles that should not be brought forward?
- Are profiles, user names, and security all set up exactly as you'd like them on the domain?
- Will all the line of business applications work well on the new hardware and software?
- Is the client getting maximum value from each of the subsystems on the network (e.g., printers, VPN, SharePoint)?
- Will the new backup system allow recovery from whatever media were used on the old backup system?
- How tolerant is this client of downtime?
- Are there troublesome components on the old system that should be separated out and not moved to the new system (e.g., faxing)?

We could go on, but we're sure you get the point. Migration means a lot more than moving active directory!

If you've ever compared your migration project proposal with other companies, then you've discovered two surprises.

First, it's amazing how different we all are, even when we're selling the same technology. We take very different routes to get to the same place.

The following are examples of simple migrations:

Old	New
Win NT 4.0	Server 2008 or SBS 2011 / New Hardware
Windows 2000 Server	Server 2008 or SBS 2011 / New Hardware
Windows Server 2003	Server 2008 or SBS 2011 / New Hardware
Windows Server 2008 on old hardware	Server 2008 or SBS 2011 / New Hardware

---

Second, the bottom line prices are not very far apart. The truth is, we all charge about the same for a five-user or a ten-user migration. And why is that? Because there's a certain amount of labor involved in all the stuff that's *not* related to moving the active directory.

Modern Migration Strategies

In the world of Windows, and particularly in the era of Windows 2008, we have a dizzying array of migration possibilities. In most cases, you will do a simple upgrade. "Simple" means moving from an old version of an operating system to a new version of the operating system, or moving the same system to new hardware.

In standard (non-Small Business Server or non-Essential Business Server) networks, migrations tend to be rather straight forward. You put the new server in place, install your applications, move the data, and take over the domain control function as needed.

You'll still want to go through the checklist, to guarantee a complete, zero-downtime migration, but the process is not very complicated because the environment is not very complicated.

SBS is another story altogether. SBS migrations are more complicated because, by design, there can only be one primary domain controller.

Yes, we know that Microsoft got rid of the terminology of Primary Domain Controller and Backup Domain Controller in 2003. But if you've ever migrated an SBS machine, you can't escape the fact that there's one machine that controls the domain, the global catalog server, and the global everything else server.

SBS is not very flexible when it comes to FSMO (Flexible Single Master Operations). The FSMO roles include the Relative ID Master role, the PDC Emulator role, the Infrastructure Master role, the Domain Naming Master role, and the Schema Master role.

You can add a second Domain Controller, but it can't take over these functions. It can't be simply promoted to PDC, let alone become the SBS PDC with all the FSMO roles.

So we're going to use the term PDC! ☺

In a nutshell, here's what happens in a simple network migration (See Figure 1-1). For example, you could do this with a Server 2003 to Server 2011 migration.

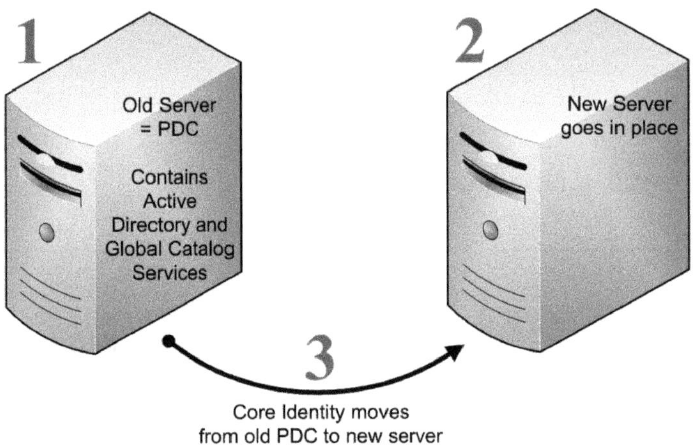

Figure 1- 1

You can't do this on an SBS network. You *can* drop a new SBS machine on the network, but the two SBS controllers will detect each other. After that, you have a limited time to unplug one of them. And you can't just suck over the active directory and global catalog services from one to the other.

In these days of easy disc imaging, you could image a machine and restore to dissimilar hardware (with Acronis, Storage Craft, or similar software).

But that doesn't help with an upgrade. After all, the image will have a server operating system and setup that is identical to the original. This is handy to have in case you need to "go back," but it doesn't ready advance you toward the goal of migrating your server.

One excellent option is the Swing Migration, developed by our friend Jeff Middleton (www.sbsmigration.com). The Swing Migration is great because it dramatically reduces downtime, allows you to do most of the work at *your* office and completely migrates the SIDs from the "old" domain. So you don't have to create all those users and computers again.

It's called a swing because you first copy the core identity to a temporary machine and then back to the new machine (or even an "in-place upgrade" of the old machine).

See Figure 1-2.

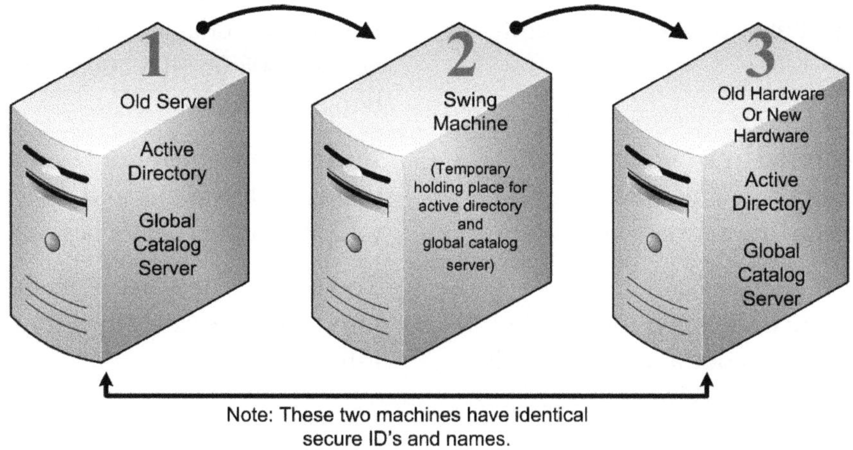

Figure 1-2

Now, is this a simple process or a complicated process? Let's be honest: Any process that requires a third party product to simplify it is a complicated process!

A Good Rule

What's the best for your client?

We have a handful of rules that simplify our lives when it comes to recommending updates. Microsoft may not like all of them, but as a consultant, we think most or all of them will ring true to you.

The first, and most important rule is: Don't waste the client's money. Please note: That doesn't mean we always chase after the cheapest solution today. We're interested in the best solution in the long run.

This rule results in some very specific behaviors:

1. Sell servers with three year warranties that will really last three years.
2. Don't sell the client a replacement server (hardware or software) before the three years is up.
3. Unless there's a compelling reason to do so, never do an in-place upgrade (always move to new hardware and the latest software).

Because of these rules, our clients can expect:

1. They will buy a new server every three years.
2. When they replace their server, they will replace the full operating system in most cases.
3. If a new operating system is available at the time of the new server installation, they'll get it.

And here's what we don't do:

1. Don't sell a client a new server just because Microsoft has released it.
2. Don't install a newer operating system on old server hardware.
3. Don't spend more on labor during the migration than would be saved on the cost of a new server license.

Let us take a little time to talk about some of the specific things we do at KPEnterprises. You might not agree with all of these, but it will make our reasoning clear.

First, we sell HP hardware. We sell machines that come with a three years next business day warranty. You can get the same thing from Dell.

Second, we replace those machines after three years. When clients try to drag this on, we explain that they are just making their I.T. spending more expensive.

Third, our managed service agreements require that all servers be covered by a manufacturer's warranty. That means those older machines either have to be replaced, or a service contract must be purchased.

Fourth, we always match the generation of the hardware to the generation of the software. This means that we only install software that was in release and designed for the hardware. Similarly, the hardware must be in release and designed for the software.

This means, for example, that we will not sell or install Server 2003 (or SBS 2003) on a brand new server today. Similarly, we won't install Server 2008 (or SBS 2008) on a server you bought in 2007.

Insisting on generational consistency will save you countless hours and dollars. And, truth be told, it's in the client's best interest.

Too many people in our business get themselves into trouble because they try to fit square pegs into round holes!

We can only speculate about the future (and we'll do that, for sure), but here's a rough timetable for what we did with the SBS 2003 generation of servers.

Q 1-3 2003	Q4 2003	2004	2005	2006	2007	Q 1-3 2008	Q 4 2008
SBS 2000	SBS 2003	SBS 2003	SBS 2003	SBS 2003	SBS 2003	SBS 2003	SBS 2008

Note: We never replaced a server before its third year. So if it came up for replacement, it got replaced. That means that some people got new servers in mid 2003 and didn't get SBS2003 until mid 2006.

The only exception to this is the client who needed a feature from SBS2003 that was not available in SBS2000. Or, if they had standard edition and needed to add an SQL server, we may have moved them to SBS2003 premium edition. Again, it depends on what's right for the client.

As for the future, we expect pretty much the same thing. Until the end of Q1 2008, we were installing SBS2003. But starting in early 2007, we sold SBS with software assurance so that clients would get the upgrade to SBS2008.

So, for example, if we installed a server in early 2008, it was SBS 2003. We replaced that machine in 2011 with SBS 2008 (because SBS 2011 was not yet released). If it's no in the clouds, we'll replace it again in 2016 with whatever's the latest version.

We can't stress enough: If the client needs something in the new operating system, we'll upgrade them. But an upgrade can easily cost 30-50 hours of labor, plus related hardware and software.

If you buy the argument that a client will buy new hardware every three years, that means one migration project every three years. If the client takes our advice and buys good quality hardware, we could see stretching a machine to 3.5 years, or maybe four for the right client. We might delay an upgrade of the hardware in order to wait for the operating system.

But scheduling client upgrades around Microsoft's operating system releases is more art than science. And we cannot justify adding a 30-50 hour migration project in the mix, given that they're already doing a migration every 36 months.

For a little perspective, consider which features your clients *really* need and use the most. For more than ninety percent of all small businesses, the "killer" features are:

- File sharing
- "Getting to the financials," however that's achieved
- Accessing email and other Outlook information

Let's assume you're working from an installed base of SBS2003 and not an older operating system. Many clients got addicted to remote web workplace. These clients will love RWW in SBS2008. Some clients still use VPN, although this is more from habit than need. Again, RWW in SBS2008 and 2011 is so good that VPNs are not really needed.

SharePoint is a killer feature in some companies. Version 3.0 lives somewhat happily alongside the old version in SBS2003. It is native in SBS2008.

We find that most client don't know or care about "features." They would be happy to just keep everything the same forever. So, while we – the nerd community – are eager to install the latest, greatest operating system, that doesn't mean it's in the client's best interest.

If your labor rate is in the range of $100 to $150 per hour, then a 30 hour migration will cost your client $3,000 - $4,500, *plus* any hardware or software costs. You need to consider that against the "disadvantage" of waiting another year or two to migrate on the normal three year cycle. Is it worth the extra cost?

(If you're not charging at least $100 per hour, raise your rates. If you're not worth $100 per hour, consider doing something else for a living.)

What's right for the client? Well, we're right back where we started. You need to balance needs, desires, and finances. And please don't make decisions on your client's behalf! Don't have both sides of the conversation about this stuff. No matter how well you think you know your client, you don't live in their head.

Your favorite client may have resisted every upgrade recommendation for five years. But don't assume nothing has changed. Maybe her son just graduated from college. (If so, it's none of your business.) And maybe she's planning to take on a new partner with an infusion of money. (If so, it's none of your business.)

The point is: Ask and don't assume. Because here's what *is* your business . . .

Talk to your client. Find out what they're planning in the years ahead. Is there a new line of business application on the horizon? Will they be adding staff? Remember our roadmap discussion. You're going to "right size" this server by looking at more than the amount of disc space used!

Of course our policies are not your policies. We're just laying out some of what we do. But you should take the time to formalize your policies and preferred upgrade strategies. Find something that works for you and your clients.

Zero Downtime?

For several years, our company has performed what we call the Zero Downtime Migration (ZDTM), primarily in the small business (under 100 desktops) environment.

Yes. That means no company-wide downtime of critical functions, and less than one hour of downtime on each desktop. Amazing? Spectacular? Impossible? No. No. No.

There are actually many ways to achieve this, if you put your mind to it. We describe how we do it. We use very common tools and procedures.

Most of the tools are available for free on the Microsoft web site.

There is an obvious comparison to the Swing Migration developed by Jeff Middleton (see www.sbsmigration.com). We do not use the Swing tools or procedures.

Why not swing?

The Swing Migration was designed to save labor, minimize downtime for the client, and to avoid re-joining the computers to the new domain, and re-creating all the users. Of all of these, minimizing client downtime is the most important.

In pursuit of minimizing downtime, you will need to swing the active directory out to a temporary machine. But before you do this, you need to make sure the active directory is as clean as it can be. For example, you want to spend time removing the remnants of half-deleted users. So some of the time you save in moving users is given back as time spent preparing the active directory.

And the Swing Migration does not eliminate downtime, it simply minimizes it.

We have achieved zero downtime migrations with what you might call a "manual" process. We do recreate users. Very often, we do re-join the new domain.

Overall, we believe we have a pretty lean process, even though we do many things manually. And, to be honest, we don't mind charging the client for a few more hours in order to deliver a perfectly new, clean active directory with zero company downtime.

We also place a very high premium on doing our work during normal business hours – 8 AM to 6 PM Monday through Friday. That means we save the client money by not having to charge after-hours rates.

Run the numbers in your own business (we'll show you how to do this later). What's the price difference between an evening/weekend migration and a completely manual migration with zero downtime for email and other critical services?

Assuming you track time and don't sell a flat-fee migration, we bet the after-hours migration costs your client more. If you do sell a flat-fee migration, the after-hours migration costs your company more!

Normal Hours

Since we've stumbled down this road, let's look at the argument for doing a migration during business hours.

First, you should *have* an after-hours rate (say, double the normal). This is just good business practice. We hear people talk about how "our industry requires evening and weekend work."

No, it doesn't!

This is very simple: Stop making yourself available and people will stop assuming you're available.

Second, your clients – even the big corporate ones – are people. They have families and personal lives. Yes, emergencies happen. But a network migration is rarely a crisis. Since there's no business or technical need to have your client give up part of their personal life, why do it?

Third, an orderly, non-disruptive "live" migration *can* take place, so why do it after hours? Again, zero downtime for critical functions and one hour per workstation.

Plus you have the advantage of having a technician be at the desk for each user at time of switchover. So you avoid a scenario where everyone comes to work at once and then all the glitches show themselves at the same time. Who needs the frustration?

Fourth, all the people you need to call in a true emergency are available during normal business hours. After hours, many members have lower or no availability. In some cases, they charge more for such support.

So, what excuses are left?

"Well, that's what we've always done."

Record that and play it back to yourself. It's not very convincing. You're more comfortable doing it the old way? Granted. But do you remember doing tech support before remote connectivity was universal? Do you remember when there was no active directory in Windows?

Change is good. Remember, all your growth takes place in areas of discomfort.

So commit to doing this during business hours and stop giving yourself an "out." You will soon discover that this is a selling point to prospects. Your competition is quoting a higher rate in order to do the migration after hours. You want to charge less and do the job during regular hours, with no disruptions in service.

The next conversation might be about rates: How can you charge $150 per hour when the competition is only charging $100 per hour?

Well, that's pretty obvious. The competition doesn't have the level of skill needed to perform a zero-downtime migration during business hours! You do. You're both more knowledgeable and better skilled. You'll solve problems more quickly . . . and save the client money in the long-run. You get the idea.

A Good Rule

Tools and Rules

The Zero Downtime Migration (ZDTM) is not like most technical procedures you're used to. While we have a checklist, you'll see that there really is no one, pure, universal checklist (but ours is close ☺).

Therefore, this is *not a procedure*. In fact, this is a *process* built around a set of procedures. For the process to be successful, you'll need to do more than tick through a technical procedure.

To get the most out of this, you'll need to adopt some of the rules and processes that have made us successful.

The most important rule is actually so important that we made a poster and put it on our wall. Here it is:

Rule Number One:

Slow Down, Get More Done

All too often, technicians find themselves in crisis mode. Always on the go-go-go. We love putting out fires and being the hero. We suspect this love for the fast-paced environment is partly responsible for the industry's general inability and unwillingness to plan ahead.

The term break/fix fits this behavior quite well. And even though we love to complain about clients who call us in at the last minute, we also behave in ways that encourage this behavior (whether intentionally or not).

Welcome to the brave new world.

This project will not be rushed. It won't be done at the last minute. It won't keep you working until midnight. With this project, you'll plan the hardware, plan the software, coordinate with the client, and organize third party vendors.

You'll eliminate re-work by doing things right the first time.

As you'll see, we put in several "control functions" to make sure that progress is being made. At the same time, these control functions allow you to put the project on hold until certain conditions are met.

For example, if you're doing an office upgrade as part of the migration project and the media arrives cracked, it is probably best to suspend the project until the new media arrives.

If you say you'll just push through without the media, and go and upgrade those desktops later, you'll either chew into your profits or get the client to agree to a change order that increases the cost of the project.

Don't be surprised if he asks "Why do I have to pay extra because you didn't plan to get the media here in time to make sure it was good?"

The thing about checklists is that they're a lot more than a collection of things to do. A "pre-flight" checklist is a very serious thing. Ask any pilot. You go through it carefully and thoughtfully.

- Port flaps
- Starboard flaps
- "Yeah, whatever. I'm sure they're fine."

Whoah. Who wants to fly on "Yeah, whatever" airlines? Not us!

If you hit a stop on your migration checklist, you need to stop. Every time you push on without completing the checklist, you're either losing some of your profit or costing the client more money.

Remember: There really aren't any emergency network migrations. So you won't schedule urgency into the project calendar. At the same time, the migration is absolutely not an *all at once* process. So you can usually make progress on some piece even if there's a delay on another piece.

Rule Number Two:

Do It Our Way First

As a technician and (most likely) an entrepreneur, you are very likely to be an inquisitive, smart, tinkerer. How do you fix a lot of stuff? You take the knowledge and experience that got you here, and you apply it to the problem in front of you.

You mentally pick up the problem in three dimensions and look at it from all sides. You plan with it, tinker a bit, take some notes, and work at it until your knowledge and experience deliver a resolution.

We know your tendency will be to take the broad outline of the ZDTM and tweak it for your organization. We ask you to *please* resist this tendency and do a migration our way at least once before you start making changes. There are two primary reasons for this.

First, the process really does work. We've done this for dozens of migrations over three generations of server software. So, as arrogant as it sounds, we know that you'll be successful if you do it our way.

If you make changes on the fly and create a hybrid process, we can't say how much success you'll have.

Second, we fully expect that you'll fine tune and make changes during your second or third migration project. But doing it our way the first time will give you a thorough understanding of why we do everything we do, in the order we do it, and in the manner we do it.

So, when you go to make changes, we want you to have first had a very successful experience. At least then, when you begin to tweak the process, you'll do so from a position of complete knowledge.

It's Okay to Start Slow

Please note that it's perfectly fine to "ramp up" to using the process outlined here. You can adopt one process and integrate it into your current migration process. Then add another and another as you feel comfortable.

For example, you might start by integrating the email templates found in the big checklist. This will give you a nice place to start, improve communication, and get your team used to SOPs – Standard Operating Procedures.

Next, you might start doing a regular pre-discovery process (as you'll learn about in a bit). Pre-discovery is extremely important to your profitability.

It's a little tedious, so you might not want to assign it to your lead engineer. But he should do it at least once so that he can help guide whoever is doing it.

As you go through the book, look for items like this that you can implement "today" – separate from the entire process. This is a huge process and can be overwhelming.

Take it at your pace to get the most out of this book.

Rule Number Three:

You WILL Use a Ticketing System to Track Time

Whether it's Autotask, ConnectWise, or some other product, we don't care. But you must have something that allows you to:

- Create the individual Service Requests that are required in the project.
- Keep track of exactly where you are within each of these SRs.
- Keep track of the time spent on each SR.
- Create additional SRs for things that come up and are outside the scope of the original project.
- Keep track of the labor hours you and your staff work on the project (whether billable or not).

If your PSA (Professional Services Administration) / ticketing system has a "project" module that works well enough for you to actually use it, you might want to try that. Or, if you can nest service tickets inside other service tickets, you might want to try that.

The key functionalities are those we listed above. That's what you need to define your project, track progress, report on progress, bill the client, and evaluate your profitability.

As we go through the project, you'll see just how important a good PSA tool is (and the reports you'll generate from it). For example, as we work through the estimation process, you'll see that actual time reports from previous jobs can be extremely valuable. Similarly, you'll need to report to your client about where you are with hourly estimates as the project moves along.

If you bill clients weekly, as we do, you need to be able to point out where estimated time translates to SR numbers and then to individual invoices. Even if you received full payment up front, the client will still want to see where it all went. A good PSA system is essential for this.

Karl likes to say, in his Relax Focus Succeed® seminars (www.RelaxFocusSucceed.com), that you are going to get better at whatever you put your attention on. This is a good example: When you put regular attention on tracking labor hours, progress, and profitability, you're going to get better at it. And that will lead to making every project profitable and efficient.

Rule Number Four:

You Are In Charge

There can only be one person whose opinion matters *the most.* That's going to be you. That may seem obvious, but there are a lot of people who need to have a say, and that can lead to confusion over who has the ultimate say.

You must be absolutely clear from the minute the project begins that you are the "foreman." Yes, the client is paying the bill. And the client is the *most important person* in the process. But the client's not in charge here.

The client hired you to make this happen on time, under budget, and as smoothly as possible. You'll work with the client to define goals and you'll do everything you can to reach those goals.

The toughest clients to deal with are the ones who know enough about technology to really understand a lot about what's going on. But even if the client understands *everything* that will happen, he hasn't done this project before. He doesn't do this for a living. He hasn't read this book. He's never performed a ZDTM.

One of our favorite clients is a former network administrator who changed careers. He now runs a very successful accounting firm. And he'll tell you that a large part of his success comes from the fact that he hires us to manage the computers.

More than any client we have, he is absolutely capable of managing the network, and even a major migration project. But one day he came to realize that he was either going to be at a high level of competence in technology or accounting, but not both. He picked accounting and pays us to be at the top of our game with technology.

There was once an old cartoon about a sign at an auto mechanic's shop:

Labor:	$25 per hour
If you watch:	$50 per hour
If you help:	$75 per hour

Update that for your clients! Let them be doctors and lawyers and accountants. You be the technical professional.

Now, attitude aside: No matter how much they want to be involved, your client simply can't run this project. And you need to be clear with them: Your quote is based on *you* running this project *your* way. If they meddle in the middle, or make changes on the fly, you're going to bill them. Yes, really.

A client can come up with an unlimited amount of changes once they get involved. Your financial success depends on sticking to your plan. When the client makes changes to that plan, he needs to pay for it. You depend on a specific profit for each project and the client has no right to chip away at that on a whim.

The second set of people who have a say in the project are "key people" at the client's office. These include the in-house I.T. person, the office manager, the SQL programmer, and anyone else that the client designates.

Some of these people are likely to believe they are in charge of the project. Others will want to be in control of some piece of the project. Your job is to simply assume command.

You will need to communicate very effectively with these folks, give them a good overview of the project stages that affect them, and engage them in the discovery process.

But *you* will decide whether to move SQL before or after the data are moved. *You* will decide whether adding memory to the desktops is done at the "desktop migration" stage or set aside as a completely separate project to be completed before (or after) the big network migration project.

The third group you need to work with are the end users. They know they're not in charge, but that doesn't mean they're unable to ruin your timeline and destroy the profitability of your project!

As you'll see when we get into the details, you're going to have the client determine whether each user's migration will be basic, moderate, or thorough. If the boss says that user will have a basic desktop migration, that means you're not going to pull over every little icon and shortcut on the desktop. You won't set their background picture, and you won't put every icon exactly where it was.

Some users don't care. They're happy to take an hour and play with colors and themes. Others will try to hijack you. You have to resist this. You *could* help them. After all, it's easy and quick. But remember your bid process.

You based the price of this project on the number of hours you estimated. If ten end-users add an extra 15-30 minutes each, that adds three to five hours to your project!

You went through a process with the boss. The boss determined the desktop migration levels. If they now wish to make a change, that's fine, but it means that you create a separate, billable service request. Why? Because this work is outside the scope of the project.

We could give a hundred other examples, but you work with end users every day. Most of your business probably revolves around making their systems work perfectly. So you've seen all the stuff they can try to throw on the pile.

Your role here is to create a service request for every little thing they want. Monitor's making noise? Outlook signature disappeared? Adobe update request keeps popping up? Create service requests.

All of these are either billable or covered by a managed services agreement. But they're all outside the scope of this project, and you need to 1) finish the migration project first, and 2) create a way to make sure all the problems get addressed and nothing gets dropped. That's what the service requests do for you.

The final group you need to worry about are third parties. These include line of business (LOB) application vendors and their support people, ISPs, hosting companies, and even the copier/scanner/fax machine people (if that's not you).

Basically, anyone who you might have to talk to or work with during the migration project will need to know that you are the key person.

We've got a whole section on working with technical support people for LOB applications. In the discovery process you'll rely on their expertise to educate you. On the day you move their application, you need to have quick access to the key support person in their organization.

And if that person's going to be on vacation? Then you need to reschedule the project date. That's why *you* are the one in charge. In a situation like this, a client might say, "Let's leave the LOB application on the old server, move everything else as planned, and just operate the two side by side for a week."

It's a perfect example of how they can lead you down the path to an un-profitable project. Again, remember that there are no migration emergencies. As long as you have a process to keep track of where you left off and where you'll pick up, it's pretty inexpensive to pause a project. Going off your planned route will always cost you money.

As you can see, being in charge is a lot less fun that it sounded at the beginning of this section.

As the one ultimate decision maker, you have to keep the client happy, keep your company profitable, keep all the other egos satisfied, and generally balance the needs of everyone involved in the whole process. You're the leader, diplomat, counselor, accountant, and more.

And if anything goes wrong, it's on you.

Somebody has to play this role or the project will be haphazard, un-planned, off schedule, over budget, and easily hijacked. And nobody is in a position to assume this role except you.

Congratulations: You're In Charge!

Rule Number Five:

Do Not Be Interrupt-Driven

We all know that computers are interrupt-driven. That means they work on whatever project is in front of them until they receive an interrupt, or request for action.

A computer will evaluate the priority of the interrupt and allocate processing time based on the importance of the request.

People don't behave that way.

When people are interrupted – especially technicians – they stop what they're doing and go do something else. This is particularly true at client offices.

Being interrupt-driven means that you or your staff have dramatically lower productivity because you are constantly interrupting the current job in order to chase after "something," even if that something is un-important or extremely low priority.

The client has every reason to ignore your process and make you less productive. Chances are very good that it won't cost them any extra. It will cost you time and money, but it probably won't cost them a nickel.

In exchange (for nothing) they get instant satisfaction.

Being interrupt-driven is much, much worse with a major project such as a network migration.

In a network migration, you're going to touch every desktop and talk to every user. The potential for going outside the scope of the project is tremendous.

In your daily operating environment, you should work very hard not to be interrupt-driven. And with a network migration, you need to re-dedicate yourself to this goal.

Later, we'll talk about the magic phrase "That's outside the scope of this project" and how it will keep you on track and under budget.

We'll also discuss the process for getting the client to buy-in to this approach and respect the need to stay focused.

Rule Number Six:

Know What You Know

Whenever you have a major project, you can be sure that something will go wrong. It might be major, it might be minor. The more discovery you do, the less severe the problems will be.

But the fact remains, something will go wrong.

And when it does, this rule will be extremely important. You'll be working on a problem, troubleshooting, taking notes, and working with third party vendors.

When you find yourself frustrated and confused, remember this rule. Stop. Think.

What do you know?

What do you know about this technology?

What do you know about the problem?

What have you done? What happened as a result?

You get the point. The most important incarnation of the rule "know what you know" is related to dealing with various tech support agents. They don't know very much about your situation.

They know a great deal about *their technology*, but not your implementation or environment. The most likely scenario is that you're talking to the lowest level tech support at that company. Remember that.

Don't let them make you second-guess what you know or forget that you are more familiar with this company than they are. They are doing what they can at their level of expertise.

While many such tech support incidents can be very helpful, don't let the technician talk you into or out of something you know to be true.

Of course you need to keep your ego in check. If they're right, and know the right thing to do, then you should follow their directive.

We have had more than one incident where a telephone tech recommended an action that would have destroyed all the data on a hard drive and required a labor-intensive rebuild.

Sometimes you need to do that. Sometimes you don't. Just remember to go slow and be very clear about what you know and what you don't.

Rule Number Seven:

Documentation Will Set You Free

There are two components to the miracle of documentation.

First, there's the complete and accurate description of how your systems work. Our company lives and breathes according to the documentation we keep. Our basic documentation is the basis of one of Karl's earlier books – *The Network Documentation Workbook*.

Second, there's the accurate record of all labor performed by your company, whether billable or not.

Both of these are assisted greatly by a professional services administration (PSA) program.

Network Documentation

- What's the external IP on that firewall? Did you look in Autotask?
- Where's the license file for [client's] new Office licenses? In Autotask.
- Who was the last person to work on that PC? Check Autotask.
- How many times have we had problems with that switch? Look in Autotask.

And most importantly . . .

- Where can I get a list of every single activity, project, and problem that needs attention by someone in my company? Autotask.

If it's not in the PSA system, it doesn't exist.

If you've bought a professional services tool and not yet implemented it, get your butt in gear.

Time Tracking

One of the most important concepts in managing the profitability of your service business is to track how you use your time. The only thing that comes close to that in importance is to make sure that nothing on your "to do" list gets dropped or forgotten.

We know we can't bill for everything we do. But we still need to make the client aware of all the things we do.

One of the really great things about Autotask, or any good PSA system, is that all your tech notes get printed on the invoices. So a client who cares can look through all these notes and see why they're getting billed. Or not billed. In either case they see the progression of each SR to completion.

Another great example of a PSA system setting you free is when a client comes to you and says "We have *this problem*. It's been going on for over a month. What have you done about it?"

You can answer, "Well, let's see. On your last invoice, SR 12345, we noted the problem, documented it, developed a plan to fix the problem, made a list of affected workstations, and fixed three of them. We are currently working on the other three."

Documentation will set you free in a hundred ways you can't foresee.

Documentation defines your business, your processes, your equipment, your clients' equipment, and all the work you do.

In a major project – such as a network migration – your documentation will make everything work better. It will make the job go faster. It will billing easier. It will make the whole project more profitable.

Give great attention to your documentation and it will make your migration projects and your business more profitable.

Rule Number Eight:

Over-Freakin' Communicate

We all know how important communications are. And yet we all fall short in some ways, at some times, in providing excellent communications.

Communicating within your company (server desk, administrative support, sales, etc.) and with your clients (owners, managers, users, vendors, etc.) are all critical. Each communication channel has the ability to make your company *more* profitable or *less* profitable.

And on the softer side, good communication can make work and relationships more enjoyable and rewarding. Bad communication can make work difficult and frustrating.

Some communication is easy to control. For example, one great way to communicate is to keep a complete list of every activity expected from every person in your company inside a ticketing system.

Other communications are more difficult. Karl likes to say "Technicians are from Mars, Clients are from Venus."

As technical people we have a specific view of the world, how it works, and even how we describe it. Clients may not share this view. In fact, they probably *don't* share it.

Here are two strategies for helping to improve communication with clients: Reflective Listening and Closed Loop Communication.

For in-person communication, nothing beats Reflective Listening. As the name suggests, this simply means repeating what the client has told you.

When you first start this, you'll be amazed at what people think they've said, or think they've heard.

For example, a client might say "I read the proposal and we're good to go." Uh. Does that mean the budget is approved? Should I schedule work? Were you going to go with the rack-mount or the tower?

Let's face it, Ms. Client: You've given me hope, but you haven't given me useful information!

Reflective listening simply means reflecting back to the client what you've heard. And if you haven't heard the message clearly, ask for more information.

"Okay. We're good to go. Thank you for putting faith in our company. Did you want to discuss the specific details now or make an appointment?"

We use Closed Loop Communication primarily online, but it can be used in person as well. It simply means that you don't commit to critical action steps without involving the client.

The best example of this is the completion of a service ticket. Never close a service ticket without the client's authorization.

In a phone call that means asking the question "May I close this service request?"

Within a service ticket, you should have a status of "Waiting on Client." When you think you've fixed a problem, have the client verify the fix. While waiting, put the ticket on "Waiting on Client."

We all know that most (99%) tickets don't need this kind of completeness. But beware the one percent that does!

We're sure you've seen the scenario. The client reports a problem inside MS Word. You go out, log on. You fix it, test it, and document it. You close the ticket.

But the client comes back to her office, logs on, and the problem is still there! How? Because you didn't do exactly what she did, in the exact order.

For whatever reason, you didn't replicate the problem exactly, so you couldn't verify the fix. Only the client can verify the fix.

You will never run out of communication problems as long as human beings are involved. Just be aware of them and commit your company to working on communication as a regular part of your business.

Now Let's Get Started

This chapter presented a general introduction to migrating Windows networks and an extremely brief introduction to the concept of Zero Downtime Migrations. We also covered our rules for success in project management and the consulting business generally.

We encourage you to follow Karl's blog – http://smallbizthoughts.blogspot.com – in order to keep up with his latest thoughts on all this.

Downtime's Okay

There's one more thing we need to cover before we conclude the chapter: You don't have to do a zero downtime migration. You can have all the downtime you want.

You might be afraid to attack the ZDTM right away. You might not have faith in us or in yourself. You might have a client who just doesn't believe it can be done.

Whatever the reason, you might choose to have downtime.

If that's the case, rest assured that this workbook is still extremely valuable.

We provide a series of true best practices with regard to domain migration, desktop preparation, project planning, client management, project estimation, and more.

We're biased, of course, but we believe you'll find this workbook to be filled with great advice and very practical considerations about the entire network migration process.

While you can certainly attack any chapter in any order, we encourage you to work through the chapters before you jump into the checklists. You'll find great value in the checklists, but we think you'll find even more value in the descriptions that accompany them!

We welcome your feedback at any time.

Please enjoy the book and let us know how your first ZDTM goes!

Chapter 2

Project Management

Introduction

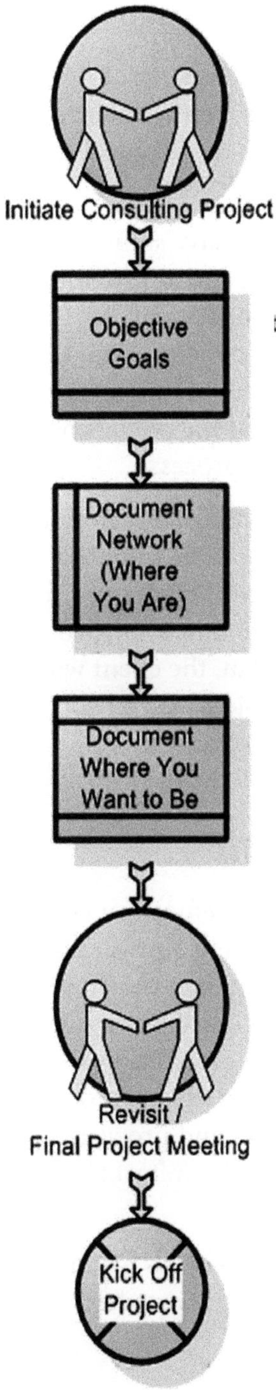

Before we get too far along on designing your project, we want to provide you with an overall structure and process for project management that will guarantee success. That sounds bold, but it's true. This process will guarantee your success in every network migration you do, and in a broader sense, with every project you undertake.

The first and most important key to your successful network migration is that you follow this process rigorously. This process is "closed loop" so nothing gets forgotten, and nothing gets dropped. This process is well-defined, so it has a definitive end and there is no un-billable labor or unexpected spin-off that lasts for weeks.

The more rigorous you are at following this process, the more success you will have on every measure. Your migration will be more profitable. Your migration will be more precisely defined.

Here are the primary stages in getting a migration project initiated:

Initiate Consulting Project. Meet with client and agree on the broad outline of the project and how it will be completed.

Define objective goals. These are visible, measurable goals. At the completion of these goals, the project will be complete.

Define where you are. Get a complete snapshot of the network as it exists.

Define where you want to be. Design the network as it will be when the project is complete.

Final project meeting. Get client sign-off on project to be performed. Agree on dates, times, and costs.

Begin the Migration Project. For details on this stage, we present the grand checklist you'll find in the appendices.

We'll come back to this in great detail. Believe us. Now let's look at project management generally.

SMB Consulting Project Management

As with any other technical undertaking, the three most important elements of designing a new Windows Server or Small Business Server network are planning, planning, and planning.

As any business matures, one of the things that falls into place is a reliance on SOPs—Standard Operating Procedures. Thus, you might fumble your way through your first installation of a new operating system. But after some time and experience, you begin to develop a procedure or protocol for this task.

If you're tackling a major project, such as a new domain controller, you are likely to have a checklist. This assures that you know all the steps, complete all the steps, and perform tasks in the correct order. It helps in documenting your work. Obviously, our Migration Checklist is a "macro" SOP.

A systematic approach to designing and implementing your new network will go a long way to making sure you're successful and your server will perform its duties "as advertised" for a long time to come. Whether you've installed just one Windows-based network, or several dozen, we're confident that the SOPs in this workbook will be very helpful to you and your business.

In this chapter we address one approach to project management. It is not the only approach, but merely one that has worked for us. If you're the "take it out of the box, plug it all in, and see what it does" type, this may be new for you. We will be using an extended example from a pretty standard Small Business Server network.

This chapter walks you through a high-level view of planning your server migration. First, we cover discovery and inventory of your existing systems. Where are your data? How are they backed up? That sort of thing.

Second, we address building a plan – architecting your new Small Business Server network. Here we discuss both the practical side of designing the new infrastructure and some of the philosophy behind setting goals and measuring performance.

Third, we address objections you are likely to come across. Aside from the obvious objections of cost and whether the technology is really needed, we address questions of product support and other less-obvious concerns. This section is good for a consultant who needs to justify a plan for a client.

Finally, we cover putting it all together. You'll need to address budgeting concerns, adjust the plan based on technical and non-technical feedback, and create the "final draft."

Most medium-size businesses have some sort of process in place for designing and approving major projects. Conversely, most small businesses do not. "The Process" consists of getting a little time with the owner and making your pitch. We hope you'll find that the pitch is better received if you follow this process.

As an SMB consultant, you will usually find that your clients do not have a pre-defined notion about how things will proceed. This is good for you. If you *do* have a standard operating procedure, and you go in with a plan, the client will be very likely to hand the project over to you with confidence. Just what you want.

Discovery and Inventory

The first thing you need to do before you go out and buy a bunch of hardware and software is to determine what you need. That sounds simple, but many projects don't start out that way. They start with someone saying "We need a Small Business Server." Then they get the boss to sign off on it, order the equipment, and proceed to cobble together a system that doesn't work very well.

That approach often leads to the boss having grave reservations about taking your advice in the future. It can also lead to a lot of lost time, energy, and money.

Introduction to the Project

If you are the regular consultant for this client, you probably don't need much introduction to your environment or the project ahead. But if you're an outside consultant or this is a new client, then you need to do some discovery of the business environment before you do discovery of the hardware, software, and network.

Whether the business discovery takes place by walking around with a key person or through a series of conference room meetings, your goal here is to understand the big picture. Later on you'll create some metrics to measure your success. That process begins way back here. We'll call this the "Interview Stage."

At the Interview Stage, you need to take lots of notes. But don't just focus on the technology. Who are the personalities involved? Who will be helping to define the goals for the system? Who will be paying for it (or approving payment)? Who will be involved in "using" the system?

For the most part, desktop users will not know that they are "using" a Small Business Server. Backup operators, database administrators, and IT folks will be the users of the Small Business Server. In most small businesses, all of these roles are played by you, the consultant.

Here are some questions to consider:

- Who will be "the lead" on this project? You must have a technical lead from your consulting practice and a project lead on the client's side.
- Who has final approval for funding?
- Who will be working on this project?
- What major software applications will be affected by the new server (e.g., CRM database)?
- What are the major challenges of the company that they hope to address with a new server?
- Whose idea was it to consider this specific server? This is important, especially if you are a consultant. See the callout on "Why Do You Want a Small Business Server?"
- What's the "big picture" of the proposed project?
- What known issues will be addressed by this project?
- Is the Small Business Server being proposed primarily to solve a current problem or to anticipate a future change?
- What is the budget for this project?
- What outside services do you need to coordinate? The most common examples are DNS, email, and the ISP.

Focus

Why Do You Want A Small Business Server?

It is extremely important to ask this question.

If you've been in tech support very long, you've had the experience of someone asking for something, but when you give them that something, they're unhappy because it doesn't fix their problem.

You might be tempted to say that this is the user's fault. But it's not the user's job to know and understand technology, it's yours. Too many times a client comes to us and says, "I want this solution," when they don't really know what the best solution is. Our job is to probe and discover what the core problem is and then recommend a solution that fixes that problem.

So, make sure you know why you need a Small Business Server. If they answer that it's the hot new technology, or they read about it in a magazine, or (worst of all) their golf buddy has one, you have to be say, "Let's schedule some time to discuss this."

More fundamental reasons for a Small Business Server will revolve around expected growth, need to consolidate data, and the need for a system that's easy to manage. Be sure to ask and probe about these topics.

Even if you want a Small Business Server because it's really cool technology, you must go through the process of defining your goals and metrics. You're going to need to be very clear about why you got into this, and what the advantages are, when it comes time to defend the budget.

And a year later, when the boss looks back and questions what she got for her money, you need to refer to those goals and metrics.

At the Interview stage, don't be too concerned with uncovering every tiny detail of the project. That's next. For now, you want to focus on the larger project, and make sure you have a real sense of why a Small Business Server might be right for this job.

As we'll see in a minute, we often stumble across some surprises when we begin the inventory of physical assets.

Case Study: Example Network

This is a quick introduction to our sample client. As you can see in the diagram below, the network is fairly simple, and something you're very likely to come across.

Notice that the client has no firewall. Either the ISP or their last consultant told them that the NAT feature in the ISP's DSL modem is all they need. And maybe that thing has a firewall built in. But you don't really know.

The server is old (six plus years) and is running out of disc space. The client says that sometimes it makes funny noises. A recent scare (blue screen) has made the boss want to verify that the backup system works.

The client is interested in having email in-house. And, more importantly, they want to share calendars, and to access their email from anywhere over the Internet.

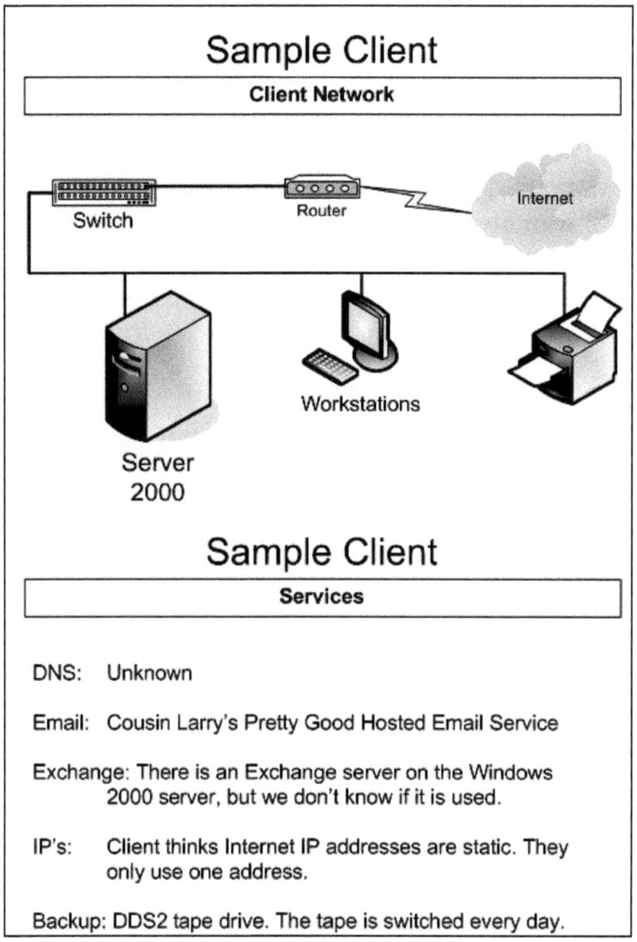

Inventory: Physical Assets

After you have an introduction to the project, the next step is to find out exactly *what you have* and begin to consider how you'll fit a Small Business Server into the picture.

We call this Discovery and Inventory. In this book and the checklists we provide, we refer to this as the Discovery Stage. Believe it or not, we also have a Pre-Discovery Stage to make sure we have a complete list of items for which discovery is needed.

Obviously, we want to know where your data are stored, how much disk space the data require, and what type of data you have. By "type of data," we mean, are you storing CAD files, graphic files, databases, etc.?

Perhaps the most helpful tool in this inventory process is Microsoft Visio. If you're on a serious budget at this stage of your planning, you could probably get by with a more entry-level product such as RF Flow (see Resources appendix). This discussion will be in terms of Visio. Substitute whatever product you're using.

Once you create a diagram of your network, you can begin to inventory resources. Keep in mind, for later in the process, both what you *do* with these resources and what you *want to do* with these resources.

When you start doing your inventory, pay attention to these six questions, for each body of data you come across:

1. What type of data is it (scanned documents, database, etc.)?
2. How is this body of data used?
3. If the files are not on the server, why not?
4. Who uses the data?
5. Is this collaborative data (several people or groups access it)?
6. Are there large file sets that are no longer used, or which could be moved to an "archive" area?

As you go through this process, you'll keep notes – lots and lots of notes. Remember, one of the keys to success with any project is that nothing gets dropped, lost, or forgotten. Even if you think something is outside the scope of the project (e.g., the archive project in #6 above), write it down. Acknowledge that this needs to be done, and plan to do it after the migration.

Also, be sure to listen very carefully to your client. If they keep mentioning the backup, or the desire for a SharePoint site, take note. If it's a natural part of the migration project, encourage them and tell them it's "all part of the package." If their key concern is not directly related to the migration project, acknowledge them, and explain that it needs to be kept separate.

One of the most important elements of troubleshooting is to change only one thing at a time. The client might lump all technical change into one category and say "do it all at once."

No, no, no, you'll say. You want to make sure that the "other" project (Line of Business upgrade, installation of CRM, etc.) is totally separate from the network migration. Each project must begin at a known state and end at a known state.

The Documentation Process

As you collect this information, it should be recorded on a form, such as you'll find in *The Network Documentation Workbook* by Karl W. Palachuk. For more information, see www.GreatLittleBook.com.

Here's a great tip for getting started with the documentation of a system you did not create:

Start at the wall.

A connection comes from your ISP. Fill out forms for each of the following:

- Internet Service Provider
- IP Range, contact information, account information
- ISP Router
- Password, configuration
- Firewall, if there is one
- Server
- Desktop machines
- Printers
- And so forth

You may wish to add additional information to this list. For example, if you have a server that's particularly slow, overburdened, or lacking in RAM, you should note that. It is particularly important to identify data that are being stored on a sub-optimal server or device.

If your primary storage system consists of the hard drives inside the servers, you should note how the drives are configured (stand alone, mirrored, RAID 5, etc.) and how much *used* and *free* space you have on each. If the client has a NAS or SAN, you also need to note how their storage is configured.

You should make sure you talk to all users about where they store things. Every once in a while we stumble across someone who copied an Access database to her local hard drive and just never remembered to copy it back to the server. As a result, it's not backed up!

The point is, this is a great opportunity to make sure you've "collected" all your data, and you know whether things are being stored where they should be. The most likely places you'll find data are on servers, storage devices, and desktops.

You also need to inventory all of your hardware resources. For example:

- How many servers do you have?
- How is each configured (operating system, memory, storage space, storage type, etc.)?
- What kind of storage arrays do you have?
- How is each configured (fibre channel, parallel SCSI, NAS)?
- How must storage space is on each, and how much is available?
- What kind of equipment do you have for connecting or managing storage (FC switches, cables, equipment rack, etc.)? What is the speed of the switches?
- If there's a firewall, do you have the password? Where is it?

The point of the hardware inventory, obviously, is to determine which pieces you can use on your new Small Business Server, and which parts you'll need to purchase. Do not begin with the assumption that you will re-use equipment just because it's there. You don't want to rely on an old switch just because you own it. Your inventory will also include notes about equipment that will be upgraded.

Finally, as part of the inventory process, you should summarize your backup strategy and how your backup-related resources are being used. If you do not have a written backup strategy or disaster recovery plan (DRP), you should at least write out a few paragraphs here.

Because a Small Business Server is so central to your data storage, and because it may introduce a fundamental change in how your networks are structured, your backups are extremely important. Today you need to know that you have backed up everything before you start making changes.

Once the Small Business Server is in place, you'll need to know how you will proceed with backups on the new infrastructure. This is particularly important if you are using this opportunity to increase your overall storage space.

Physical Inventory also includes software. In most SBS migrations, you won't be moving the old server license to a new server (either because you're replacing an old SBS Server or because you're replacing a non-SBS box with an SBS box). You also won't normally move other commercial software. In some cases you can't do so legally, but in almost all cases, you won't want to: it's too old. After all, you're replacing an old server. It probably has older versions of most software.

The programs most likely to move to the new server are the LOBs – Line of Business applications. Virtually all LOBs are licensed to the owner without regard to the hardware. As a result, they can be migrated without any problems. Make sure you have all the discs you need, and contact information for technical support. If you can, determine the hours for tech support and find out if they have a white paper on moving the LOB to a new machine.

Inventory: Services and Resources

Your inventory will also include filling out data sheets for the ISP and other "resources" that are needed. The most common resources you need to find are:

- DNS registrar
- Inbound email
- Outbound email (no, they're not always the same)
- ISP information
- Web hosting
- Anti-Spam or Anti-Virus hosted service

One of the keys to a smooth migration is to control the DNS registrar. We can't believe how often we come across someone who has a domain, but doesn't know where it's registered. Once we figure that out (via WHOIS database), then they don't have any logon info. Or, it's registered to their ISP, registered to a previous consultant, or registered with an email that no longer exists.

In a worst-case scenario, no one knows who is the official contact within the domain registry, and the registration is private. You know you're not the technical contact, but you don't know who is.

Wrestling control of a domain name can be a very long process. But you'll need to do it. The sweetest thing in the world is to set up the new Exchange server, flip the DNS, and email just flows into the new system. Zero downtime for email means having access to the DNS. You certainly don't have to serve DNS in-house (we don't recommend it), but you must have access to it.

In general, the Services and Resources Inventory will give you a complete list of everyone you need to call and a list of where the "outside" services are located.

Beware the Last Consultant

It is a very sad thing to say, but our business is filled with scoundrels and completely unqualified hacks who somehow manage to get work and hobble together systems that work only by miracle. All too often, we come across machines that are improperly configured, or loaded to the top with illegal software.

On more than one occasion we've acquired a new client with a very large directory called "Hacked Software" on their server. We've all seen it.

When these losers leave the scene, the client discovers that the server is registered in the consultant's name. The username for their ISP account? The consultant. They don't have legal licenses for some or all of their business critical software. That mission critical Line of Business application? He's been running a series of "demo mode" downloads for years.

It can be financially crippling for some companies to come up to speed on legal software.

Do not spend your time and energy badmouthing the old tech. He's gone now anyway. Focus on helping the client. Let them know that you're here to help, and we're going to make everything okay.

The good news, if there is any, is that you will be delivering a new server, with new operating system license, new anti-virus package, new file defragger, new backup package, etc. So most of their software issues will go away for the price of a basic install.

Checkpoint

At this point you have an organized list of all of your assets, where those data live, and how to contact all the outside resources. You also have an overview of the project, what your network "map" looks like, and a good idea of who's involved in the project.

Please note that one of the side benefits of going through this process is *project clarification*. As you go through the introduction and inventory (the last several pages), you learn some things that aren't on your list. You learn something about who favors this project, who's opposed to it, and who's paying for it.

You also learn about projects and planning you might not have otherwise known. We mentioned earlier that you need to talk to the users. If someone in the marketing department casually mentions that his new graphics management database will need extra disc space, that's important! It's not that people want to keep secrets from the IT folks. But if you don't ask, they might not have a reason to mention their plans.

Discovery: Future Plans

The final step in the "Discovery" process is also the first step in laying out your official proposal — planning for the future.

So now that you have an accurate view of what the world looks like today, it's time to draw a picture of what you want it to look like with a Small Business Server. Again, my first reaction is to open up the old Visio diagram and work from there.

It is probably best to begin with the logical connectivity and address the physical side later. Here's what we mean. We revised the Sample Client network map to add a Small Business Server and the firewall we recommend.

This is a pretty simple diagram, and your Small Business Server will probably be similar to this. If you are using ISA to protect desktops, you will have a second NIC on the server, and a switch between the server and the workstations, of course.

At this point, just make sure the configuration looks correct. Once you begin to start building a shopping list for parts, you'll want to look at the physical configuration. Do you have a rack for the equipment? If so, do you have room? If you're not buying rack equipment, do you have appropriate shelving?

The map for the proposed network is a great little tool for helping the client to visualize the project and see the benefits of the system you propose.

Building the Plan

Finally, you get to begin drafting your actual plan for a Small Business Server. Ideally, you will write a discovery narrative to explain the key features of your plan and justify why each is necessary.

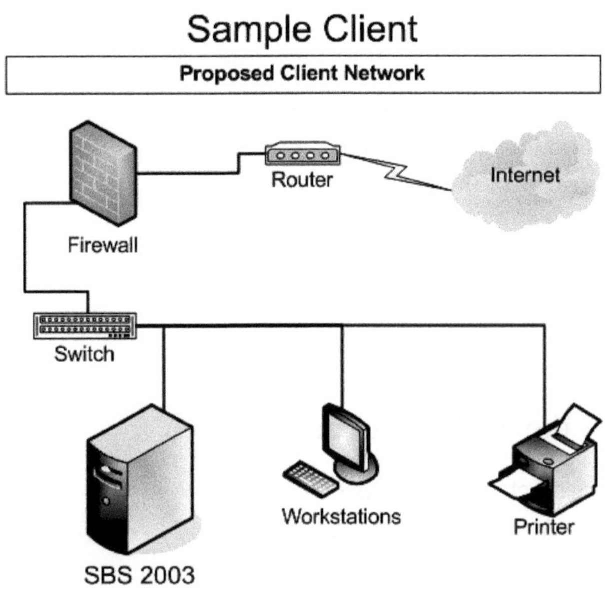

Start with a brief description of what you have. Then describe the system you want to move to. This would be the system in your second network diagram.

This is not the place to list every single item on the shopping list. All things in good time. For now, we want to list the big, visible items and the expensive items. Both the revised diagram and the narrative need to be descriptive without any "sales pitch." These are documents that may float around a while as you discuss and fine-tune the project. Details can cloud the discussion and sales pitches can sidetrack people quickly.

After you have this very brief overview, go back to your notes and determine who is supposed to be involved in this project. It's time to engage them. Take your pictures, your notes, and any brief descriptions you have. Sit down with a core group of people and begin the formal planning process.

The first thing you need to look at is your team (people from your company and from the client's company). Are you the only really technical person? Or is everyone pretty technical? Both of these extremes can introduce challenges.

If you're the only technical person, then you need give a quick overview and focus on *benefits* and *necessity*, not features. I've often heard the advice of focusing on benefits over features. But our experience in getting major projects approved has led us to also include discussions of necessity.

If you're the technical person, then it usually carries a lot of weight when you say "we need this because . . .." Try to be as non-technical as possible. But at some point, you're bound to lose people who just don't care how a network works as long as the network works.

If you're the only technical person, then your job will be to go away and come back with the best plan you can possibly put together. With luck you'll find one or more champions in this meeting. It might be the marketing director who is excited about Exchange, or it might be the owner who's tired of the network slowing to a crawl at 10:00 p.m. when the backup kicks off.

If you have a room full of nerds, then you have different challenges. First, you will probably need to find a subset to work with regularly. Second, Murphy tends to show up at these meetings and you may find that the most vocal person is someone who is technical but just doesn't understand *this* technology.

At some point, you should emerge from this meeting with a "team" of people who will develop the formal plan. You should also emerge with at least "big picture" approval of the concept. Be prepared to give some ballpark figure on cost. It doesn't matter how accurate you are, really, as long as the number you quote is big enough that they'll take it seriously.

Be careful on price estimates. You'd be shocked at how much technology, and your understanding, can change from this stage to the approval stage. If you think the price looks like $10,000, we recommend telling them that it's in the $10,000-$12,000 range.

And remember, you're not asking for approval. Tell them that. You just want permission to spec out the project and see if it makes sense. This will also give you a great opportunity to write down all their questions and tell them you don't know right now, but you'll make sure to address that in your research.

Writing the Plan

You will need to review the project several times to make sure you haven't left anything out. Your plan literally starts with what you've written so far:

- A description of the network today
- A diagram of the network today
- A one- or two-paragraph description of the proposed plan
- A diagram of the proposed plan

Will anyone really read this document? See the Focus on Goal Setting: Treating Your SBS Migration Like an Employee.

Focus

Goal Setting: Treating Your SBS Migration Like an Employee

Try this with your new Small Business Server migration project and you'll probably end up doing it for all your major systems in the future: Treat your SBS Project like an employee. How do we evaluate employees?

- Create criteria
- Define how you will measure performance
- Actually measure performance
- Review criteria as needed

As you work through the Network Migration Checklist, each section is a distinct, measurable event. Your commitment to performing each section perfectly will have a direct effect on your success. When you look back at a project that went awry, you'll be able to point to the exact spot.

For example, "We didn't complete the process of controlling DNS before we committed to the new server. Now we've got an SBS box in place, but we can't access it from the outside world, can't use it for Internet email, and can't set up Outlook Web Access." Lesson learned.

In fact, a painful lesson like this is exactly what you want to avoid. When you move ahead on a project out of sequence, you no longer control the outcome. In this example, you have a lot of work ahead of you, even though you've completed 98% of the project. And the client will want all that labor included.

You'll see later how we avoid this exact scenario.

Next, you will set goals for your Small Business Server. Remember again, "Why do we need a Small Business Server?" List those things in terms of measurable goals. Then discuss how you will actually measure them. Start with the big picture and add specifics as you go along.

The sad truth is that the final decision-maker is unlikely to read the document you create. But several people along the way are likely to read the parts they think are relevant. Just remember that the process of creating your written plan will allow you to answer all their questions (because that's what you promised).

We'll talk about addressing objections in the next section, but your written plan will go a long way toward addressing objections. No matter what question you're asked, you can flip to the right page and answer it. Don't simply answer it, use the report. Even if you know the information, this gives the impression that all the answers are in the report!

Include future plans in your report. By that we mean, make sure you address expandability. If your organization is growing and you need to adopt Small Business Server technology today, what happens when you need something else tomorrow?

Also include a revised backup strategy. If you add hard drive capacity, and move all the data off the desktops, how do you create a backup for all this? It may be that you're simply moving a small amount of data to the new server, in which case the effect on backups is minimal. But you need to say that!

If nothing else, you need to make sure you've addressed it to yourself. If you add a terabyte of data storage, you know it will begin to fill up. What will you do to provide for disaster recovery?

Once you've addressed all these topics, you're finished with the first draft of your project plan. That's right, the first draft. The next two steps are fairly easy but also critical. You need to present the plan to the decision-maker(s) and get money for the plan. At that point you'll take note of any final changes and finalize the budget and the plan.

It may feel like your plan could easily die in these final stages. But good preparation will prevent last-minute crises. The most important thing is to address all the objections that come up – technical, financial, and everything else.

Dealing with Objections

It's hard to believe, when the project is yours, but most objections to great plans are actually very reasonable concerns! As we prepared for this discussion, we asked people about the objections they've raised to proposals, as well as those they've heard. We got a huge list.

Luckily for you, we're going to spare you that list. But we will look at a variety of objections, broken into five categories:

- Price
- Preference
- Support and Quality of Product
- Complexity and Differentiation
- Security

Price

Price objections include purchase price as well as TCO—the Total Cost of Ownership. A simple discussion of price involves the sticker price or "bottom line." When someone asks about the cost of a project, he or she generally means the dollar amount at the bottom of the budget page.

TCO is another kind of discussion. TCO involves hard numbers today (price) as well as projections about the future. It includes maintenance costs as well as related costs, such as the need to upgrade other systems.

When discussing a project in terms of TCO, you need to address both "hard" costs and "soft" costs. Hard costs are the numbers you can point to in your budget, such as software, hardware, and signed maintenance agreements. Soft costs include things that are either "hidden" or are part of some other budget.

For example, if you need to redirect an employee three hours a week to make sure the Small Business Server is working properly, that's a soft cost because the salary dollars are already in some other part of the budget.

TCO discussions also include cost savings that might be realized from adopting this technology. Here you get to discuss ROI—Return On Investment. If there really are efficiencies in making the database go faster, you should be able to put a number on that and therefore a dollar sign. That's why, in the goal-setting session, we discussed measurable performance criteria.

Some bosses and owners will get stuck right away on the price of the project. More than once we've had a client look at the bottom line for a new server and say "No, not for that price." Sometimes they warm up to it, and sometimes they don't.

If a decision-maker is stuck on the bottom-line price, you need to make sure you've got a strong case on all the other criteria. Remember that "No. Too much money" is the default response for many people. But very often, after understanding the big picture, they say yes.

There is a definite correlation between company size and willingness to discuss total cost of ownership. Owners of small companies understand the concepts, but they can easily dismiss them. The willingness to engage in TCO and ROI discussions is also related to the company's ability to embrace technology.

Karl had a discussion with a client way back in 1995 about upgrading from CAT5 to fiber for parts of the network. The client understood that most traffic did not need the extra speed and would not benefit from the added expense. But he had one core measure of performance—programmer efficiency. He explained it this way:

He had about twenty highly-paid programmers. If they clicked the "compile" button and had to wait ten seconds, they took a sip of coffee and gave their eyes a rest. If they had to wait thirty seconds, they stood up and stretched. They might wander into the next cubicle. Or down the hall.

In other words, they stopped programming and did something else. That means that, once they sat down again, there was a little orientation time. This guy was no slave-driver, but he clearly understood the difference between taking a sip of coffee and coming to a full stop.

In this case, the intangible "lost productivity" was a key factor in discussing a faster network.

Before you discuss TCO and ROI, go back and review the discussion of advantages. Most of the advantages involve either direct or indirect savings.

Sometimes companies simply cannot afford a project. Remember, the boss has people pestering her all day with technologies that "pay for themselves." With luck, you'll have a nice long discussion about goals and strategies, TCO, and ROI.

Preference

The second category of objections is Preferences. Some people just prefer one thing over another. Sometimes they have rational reasons and sometimes not. Experience usually plays a role in preference.

The classic battle of the brands is Ford vs. Chevy. In our case, if Karl had to choose one of these, he'd choose the Chevy. Manuel would pick the Ford. Part of that's based on experience, part on irrational bias, and part on the fact that we've each just been on that side of the argument since we were kids and bought our first cars.

Perhaps the classic battle in the technical arena is Symantec vs. McAfee anti-virus. Our company has a preference, but it has mostly to do with consistency across clients, which gives us a predictable environment, installation path, and troubleshooting routine.

As you can see, preference can be irrational, or it can be directly related to productivity and profitability. There's a lot to be said for consistency.

In the category of Preference, we need to address several valid arguments. First, there is usually preference for what's already installed and working. Why switch to something else? You might think this is only true when the current system is working well. After all, if the current system is troublesome, you'd think people would want to try something else.

But people are slow to change, even if the current system is not great. After all, the current system is "the devil we know." We know what goes wrong. We know how long it takes to fix. We *don't* know these things about Small Business Server 2008.

Second, following immediately from the first, is that whatever you're proposing is *unknown*. As the immortal Garth says in *Wayne's World*, "We fear change."

If you get the objection that the client doesn't know enough about Small Business Servers, or doesn't know the track record of this technology, that's good for you. Rather than saying "no," the boss is saying that he's open to finding out more. As you know, Small Business Server technology is nothing new. So you can find lots of good information.

Support and Quality of Product

From the more technically-inclined stakeholders you are likely to get some objections related to the quality of the product and service after the sale. Depending on what they read, and what their personal experiences are, you might get questions about the vendor, the product itself, and the support community.

Questions regarding the hardware vendor tend to focus on reputation. Has the vendor been around long enough to have a reputation? If so, is it a good reputation? Do industry watchers such as the Gartner Group have good things to say? We only sell brand-name equipment with a three-year warranty, so these discussions are easy.

Technical folks are also likely to probe about support. In particular, "Can I get someone on the phone after the sale?" Does your company have a good tech support web site, or a Knowledge Base? Is there a peer support community?

It is probably good to prepare some information about support after the sale. Provide some client references. Invite the client to contact the references and ask about their support experiences. In particular, can SBS and your company deliver what you're claiming?

In general, you should be most comfortable dealing with the support and product quality objections. After all, it's your responsibility to do the research and make sure you're proposing the best system you can.

Complexity or Differentiation

The technical crowd will also have questions about the complexity of the product, and how to differentiate this product from similar products.

Some technologies are just very complex. For any given technology, there's more complexity when the technology is new than there is after it matures.

If you were one of the lucky people who got Windows 3.1 connected to the Internet before the World Wide Web was invented, then you know what we mean.

You had to start by installing a 32-bit emulator because you were working with 16-bit hardware (and software). Then you needed to replace some Windows "socket" DLLs. Of course TCP/IP didn't ship with Windows, so you needed to install it.

You get the idea.

Fifteen years ago, it was a major undertaking to get a corporation connected to the Internet. Now we do it with our cell phones!

Stable, mature products become easier to configure and administer over time. The underlying technology may be just as "complex," but the perception of complexity has changed.

At the same time, as experience grows, the perception of complexity shrinks. When I was at the University of Michigan, the instruction manuals for the mainframe system took up about three feet of shelf space. They were not simple to comprehend unless you already knew what you were doing. We had a name for this:

PCIPU:
Perfectly Clear If Previously Understood

So complexity is partly a matter of perception and experience. But there are also some subjective measures of complexity. If the various pieces of the project work well together, that's a sign that the solution is not overly complex. If the technology is stable and doesn't need a constant stream of updates, that's also a sign that the solution is not too complex.

The subject of complexity also looks to the future. For example, if we install this Small Business Server, what's involved in adding more storage or more servers? If we decide to add a stand-alone SQL server for our line-of-business application, how difficult will that be?

Security

The final category of objections is Security. With this one, you need to address some arguments from the business side and others from the technical side.

The good news is that Small Business Servers are very secure. Or, at least, there's no excuse for them to be any less secure than any other server. And there are many reasons for them to be even more secure. As you can see from the Proposed Client Network above, we favor putting the whole operation behind a hardware firewall with only a handful of "pinholes" to the SBS box. And those pinholes point to encrypted services!

The bottom line on security is that Small Business Servers are more secure than most other options, and certainly no less secure than your old servers.

Getting Approval For The Project

A project like the simple Small Business Server we proposed above may be a small line item for some companies, but for many in the SMB space, it is a major undertaking. That's why addressing these objections is so important.

The key to success is to take the objections seriously. As we said earlier, most concerns are legitimate. Treat them that way. But also make sure that you keep the big picture in mind. This has to be the right solution for *this* organization at *this* time.

Think of the "objection stage" as another fact-gathering stage. In addition to making your pitch, you are also gathering information you'll need to implement the project. It might be that you'll be asked to look at different configurations, or to increase or decrease the storage capacity. You may be asked to add a database to the project, or remove one.

Let's assume that you complete this stage and get general approval for the project.

Budgeting, Adjusting, and Final Draft

Now that you've jumped through all those hoops, you get to make one final re-write of your project plan. Note that it is no longer a proposal—it's a plan!

You need to work within the budget you've been given. If there are any changes (no matter how insignificant), they need to be reflected in the plan. After that you need to spend some time making a detailed parts list and checklist.

In Chapter Four we address Quoting The Migration Project. Below is a preview of the kind of quote we'll discuss. In this case, it's a sample quote for an SBS system we've been discussing. Note that it includes a firewall, new server, and all related software. These are all based on the discussions above.

Note, in particular, that we have broken down the labor into discreet sections. Each of these will become a "Service Ticket" once the quote is approved. Each part of the project stands alone, has discreet, measurable goals, and can be marked as "completed" when all tasks are successful.

See the Sample quote on the next page.

So, everything you need for this job is on the quote.

The final draft of your plan should include at least these sections:

- Diagram/Map
- Statement of Goals for the Small Business Server
- An Implementation Plan (the Network Migration Checklist)
- A Project Budget
- A Shopping List
- A Detailed Checklist
- A Timeline

At this final stage, most of the plan has already been written. All you're doing here is revising it according to the budget and objections discussions, and then adding the detail you need to make it "real."

This final draft will probably never go back up to the decision makers. At this point, it is really just your guide to finishing the project. Ideally, you should be able to file it away until you're ready to do that first "quarterly performance review" of your Small Business Server.

The next item you need to make your Small Business Server a reality is a checklist. We're huge fans of checklists. Karl's *Network Documentation Workbook* came out of our company's reliance on checklists. KPEnterprises thrives because all (All – not just major projects) include checklists.

Please note that the Network Migration Checklist, the focus of this book, is just one piece of the project. Once you get approval and actually begin implementing the project, it will be the *most important* element. But keep it in context. Every piece of your process has to be designed for success.

Speaking of documentation: Make sure you do it! As you actually work through your checklist, record every password, every configuration, and every "important thing to know" at every stage. It is always easier to document something while you're doing it than it is to come back later and figure it out.

Keep this in mind. You now have a major addition to your disaster recovery process. Your documentation should be good enough that you can re-create the Small Business Server network based on the documentation.

The last item on your checklist should be a review of the process. You might call it a post-project evaluation. Please don't use the term *post mortem*, since that has some negative connotations we'd rather avoid.

The review process should include a section on lessons you learned. In particular, make note of unexpected detours. If you were to do this all again, what would you add to the planning process?

Quote

	Client:	**Joe Blow Car Dealership**	**August 2009**	
			Quote expires	8/30/2009
	Project:	**Server Migration**		

Hardware and Software

Qty			
1	New Server. Includes: **Server - Proliant ML 350 Xeon 2.6 GHz, 4 GB RAM; 3x146 GB hard drives**; Drives configured in RAID 5 (290 GB total usable space); DVD+R/CDRW; Small Business Server 2008; Diskeeper defragmentation software.		$ 5,459.99
		Sales Tax	$ 423.15
		Total:	$ 5,883.14

Labor

-	Staff Training before installation: Introduction to the new system.		
-	Estimated Labor for Discovery process: documenting current system, shares, users, etc. Document New system.		
-	Estimated Labor for Server build: Set up server computer; configure SBS; create users, shares; Install and configure backup software, Anti-Virus; configure DHCP, DNS, other services; create shares, etc. Coordinate MAS 90 install and config. Document and test.		
-	Estimated Labor for Network Migration: Reconfigure firewalls, printers, routers, and additional equipment as needed. Restore data from tape or otherwise transfer to new system. Coordinate MAS 90 data transfer. Note: Extremely large data transfers may add additional time.		
-	Estimated Labor for Workstation Migration: Set up desktop PCs and connect to new server; configure; document everything. Estimate 5 desktops/laptops. NOTE: This is based on machines that are not "too" old and are in reasonable condition.		
-	Staff Training after installation: Becoming familiar with new features.		
		30 hours	$ 4,500.00
	Note: the first three hours of labor will be credited if the server is on a SuperStar I.T. Service Agreement.		

Summary

In this chapter we walked through the project planning process with a focus on Small Business Server technology. We used a Sample Small Business Server Network project as an example.

The first major stage is Discovery and Inventory, in which we get the ball rolling by defining what the project is, who's involved, and who has the authority to approve and fund the project. At this stage, we begin writing things down and documenting "the proposal."

We discussed setting goals for the Small Business Server, as well as defining how we will measure them. After that we did a thorough inventory of the hardware, software, services, and resources. We also looked ahead to plan how we might expand the Small Business Server network in the future.

The second major stage is to actually create the written proposal. The plan has enough detail to address concerns that might be raised, but doesn't need more detail than that.

The third major stage is to address all the objections to the proposal. We addressed objections in the categories of Price, Preference, Support and Quality of Product, Complexity and Differentiation, and Security.

Having successfully addressed all the concerns from the decision makers, you gain approval for the project. At this point, you integrate the budget and the proposal into a final, written plan, complete with diagrams, goals, a shopping list, a detailed checklist, and a timeline.

And so we've gone from the concept of a Small Business Server to the point of actually ordering the parts. In the next chapter we begin the process of introducing the Network Migration Checklist.

In fact, Chapter Three will give you an overview of everything else in the book or in your Network Migration Project.

The Network Migration Workbook

Overview and Flow

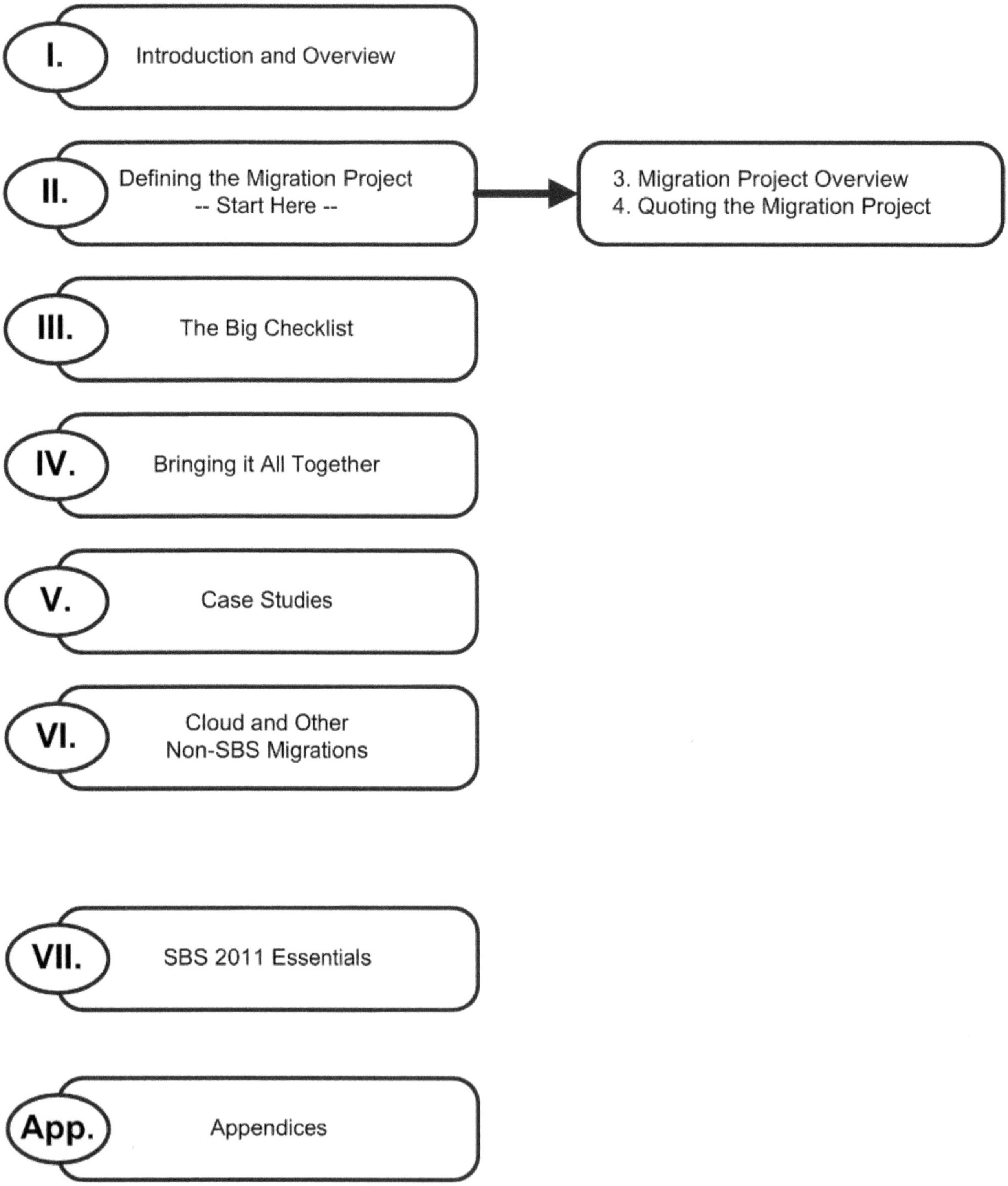

II. Defining the Migration Project – Start Here

Chapter 3

Migration Project Overview

Introduction

This chapter provides a quick introduction to the overall migration process from the ground up. In a sense, it's the Start Here section for the migration project.

Network migrations can be big and cumbersome. That's why we created the map: So you know where you are in the overall process. We start with a view of the migration process "from 30,000 feet."

This chapter will help you see how the pieces fit together. The goal here is to lay the foundation for quoting the project (Chapter Four) and give you a frame of reference for going through the big checklist (Section III).

Here, in four steps, is what you're doing to do with this workbook to manage your network migration project:

1 First, you're going to print out a checklist. We have provided sample checklists in this book and online. You will develop your own checklists eventually, customizing these for your firewall choice, your backup programs and procedures, your imaging tools, etc.

Note: Whether you're migrating to SBS 2003, 2008, or 2011, the Big Checklist covers them all. Why? Because many people are still managing older servers. That's the reality. You might only have access to 32-bit hardware. You might have to rebuild an existing network. You might find yourself with a client who bought the 2003 product near end of life and simply refuses to buy the newer product for several years.

It's also the case that you've probably done a number of SBS 2003 and 2008 migrations, so you are knowledgeable about how they're done. The Big Checklist will allow you to see "what you know" and make a smooth transition to the 2011 migration process.

The checklist is three-hole punched and placed into a binder with tabs. We've provided a set of tabs as we use them. Some sections are large. Many are just one page. The checklist and Network Migration Binder are now the "tool" you'll use to manage the migration project.

2 Second, you'll edit the checklist and fine-tune for the specific migration at hand. As you go through the discovery process, you'll fill in sections to define the old network, the new network, and how you'll get from here to there.

The Network Migration Binder provides instant access to every important piece of information in the migration process, no matter what stage you're at. If you're diligent at using this tool, it provides all the other information as well.

3 Third, once you have an overview of the project ahead, you'll decide how you'll accomplish the actual migration for each function being brought forth to the new server/domain. You'll record your decision in The Network Migration Binder so you and your team will have a record of what you're doing and how you'll get the job done.

You will refer to The Network Migration Binder every day of the project, with every decision and every task.

When the project is done, The Network Migration Binder will contain both the old network documentation and the new network documentation. You'll transfer the new network documentation to your PSA system and network documentation binder.

4 Finally, you'll complete all fine-tuning and evaluate the network migration project.

All of this is in the checklist. The sample checklist is about 275 pages. Of that, only three pages represent the actions you will take on-site over a two day period to execute the actual "migration." Everything else represents the work you'll do before and after the onsite migration.

Please note that there are instructions built into the checklist. These are, essentially, reminder-level instructions for a trained technician. They operate under the assumption that the user has gone through a migration and understands the big picture. They are not a substitute for the rest of the book. More on that in a minute.

That's the view from 30,000 feet.

A Few Caveats About the Checklist

Caveat One: The checklist are based 100% on what our company (KPEnterprises) does to migrate Windows networks. We have made things a little more "generic" in some places in order to be as applicable as possible to your environment. For example, it doesn't matter what your ticketing system is, so we don't call out one or the other.

In most cases, however, we have simply left the checklist "as is." For the most part, you will still find it very generic and easy to swap our preferred tools for your preferred tools.

But this list is necessarily biased. It represents how *we* migrate networks. The more your process matches ours, the higher confidence we have that you'll be able to achieve the results we call out.

Caveat Two: In some cases, you'll find the checklist incomplete. We talk here and there about SQL, SharePoint, ISA, Forefront, OneCare, and other tools. But this book is not about those programs. (In fact, Forefront and OneCare aren't even in SBS 2011). As with any other major project, we are trying to avoid scope creep. We have to draw some edges around the scope of work here.

This is not a SQL book. This is not an Exchange book. This is not a security book.

As a result, you may need to fill in some parts of the process for the tools you're using and the circumstances of the migration you're doing.

If you have a basic, fully functioning network and you're moving to SBS 2003, or SBS 2008, or SBS 2011, then the sample checklist includes everything you'll do to migrate your network. Other than actually printing out the checklist and executing it, no changes are needed.

But we live in a wonderfully complex world. So chances are very good that you'll have *some* changes to make.

Caveat Three: The process described in this chapter is a *Manual Migration* process. That means we are doing everything "by hand" rather than with scripts or other automated tools.

We do this for a reason. There's always a trade-off in hours spent doing a manual migration versus doing some sort of automated migration. Why? Because "automated" processes require a great deal of preparation. They might be just as labor-intensive, but the labor takes place at a different point in the process.

For example, let's say the Active Directory is a mess. The last consultant did all kinds of fancy stuff. Half of it never worked as expected and none of it is documented in any way.

In order to bring over that Active Directory, you need to spend some time cleaning up before you start.

At some point, it doesn't matter how good you are: It takes time to clean up a messy Active Directory.

If you place no value on your time, then you can spend an unlimited number of hours cleaning up A.D. But if you're paying someone, and their fully-burdened labor cost is $60 or $70 per hour, then there's a limit to how much time you'll spend on such a clean-up.

If the network is small (e.g., 5-10 users), then it is almost always better to create everything fresh from the start. After all, how much time does it take to create five user accounts and five computer accounts?

Clearly, with sixty users it's a different story. With sixty desktops, you will save a lot of time by using more automated tools and techniques.

So five users is an easy decision, and sixty users is an easy decision. But where do you draw the line in between? When does it make sense to automate some parts and do others manually?

We give you a totally manual process so that you can *know* and *control* every element of the migration process. Once you have that, you can decide when to use each approach.

Caveat Four: We are happy to answer your questions. But you have to read the whole book first.

We know we just gave you a "start here" section. Well, the checklist is in the Appendix for a reason. It comes after you have read everything and learned the whole process.

This book took quite awhile to write because we wanted to be as complete as possible within the defined scope. So, in our humble opinion, you've got quite a document here. The more you understand the explanations, the smoother your migrations will be.

The checklist is actually written to include the documentation needed to execute the checklist. So *after* you've read through all this and learned how to do a manual migration, you'll be able to simply print out a checklist and start working on a migration. But please don't do that with your first migration!

Running Successful Migration Projects

What are the big problems in project management? Ask anyone: The biggest problem in project management is *scope creep*. You start a project and the client says, "Oh yeah. This is going to include putting six people onto the new Office 2007 when you put in the new Small Business Server."

You agree. "Six people, Office 2007." But when you show up to do the work, you find six people's desktops, plus their six laptops, plus six other people that "we really didn't think they needed it, but it turns out they do."

In some cases, the client assumes that all of this will simply be inside the scope of the project and that they won't pay any extra for it. That happens all the time. And it happens because there isn't a *scope of project*. We skipped that step.

The scope of the project is your mutual understanding of what you're going to do. It helps you manage client expectations. You cannot assume that you understand the client's expectations. And this is not a slam on clients. There's nothing wrong with your clients. But we're all just human beings and we all communicate a little differently.

The most important phrases you need to learn are

Inside the scope of the project

and

Outside the scope of the project

Once you and your client agree on the *scope of the project*, your success is almost guaranteed.

Once you and your client agree on the *scope of the project*, you have a very powerful tool at your disposal. This is your agreement about what will be done. Everything else is outside the scope.

That doesn't mean that other tasks that come up will not get done. But those tasks need to be accounted for separately. Work outside the scope needs to be entered into service requests. It might be billable, or it might be covered by a managed service agreement. But it's outside the scope of the migration project.

Remember, clients don't tend to view the world in terms of technology projects. They worry about payroll, cash flow, and workload. In other words, they're thinking about *their* business, not your business. When they finally put their attention on technology, it's like opening a box.

Once the technology box is open, they think it's a great time to throw things into the box. For example, a client might say, "Oh this would be a great time to get a new firewall." You need to say: No. It wouldn't. We're going to separate these projects as much as possible. This is not the time to revamp everything.

You know the first rule of troubleshooting: You only change one thing at a time. If you change the firewall in the middle of a migration project, you might get yourself into a situation where one technician is looking for a problem in one room while other technicians are creating the problem in another room.

Do Not let the client muddy up the project. They think they're going to save money by combining projects. In fact, they're creating a troubleshooting nightmare. If you have a series of office upgrades, hardware refreshes, and a network refresh, you need to determine how you will complete each of them successfully.

If these chores really are included in the big migration project, you will create individual *stages* so that you can check them off in steps. You don't change two things at once; you change one thing at a time. If they are outside the scope of the migration project, then they might be individual service requests, or they might be separate projects.

It really doesn't matter how you organize all these things, except: 1) Everything needs to be written down and agreed upon; 2) Nothing gets lost, dropped, or forgotten; and 3) Nothing gets added without a change order or service request that makes it billable.

Closing the Loop

There's one thing *successful* managers have and others don't: A closed loop process. A closed loop process means that you have a system in which nothing ever gets dropped and nothing else gets added to your process.

If somebody wants to add something to the project, and it's inappropriate, you move it to another location (project or service request) so that it still never gets dropped. It simply gets completed outside the scope of the current project.

There are only three things that can happen with requests that are added in the middle of a project. Either 1) You determine that it is outside the scope of the project, and you create a service request; 2) You determine that it is so small you are just going to throw it in; or 3) You have made it irrelevant because you fixed something in the middle of the process. For instance, if someone was having an issue with the server, and you replaced the server during stage two of the project, then that request for service becomes irrelevant.

All of this may seem very hard-nose. But remember: the difference between *getting by* and *doing well* can be very small. When a client manages to open the technology box and add five or ten hours of non-billable labor to your project, that might be the difference between making money and breaking even. You make dollars by paying attention to the nickels!

Your client needs to understand that a major project does *not* mean that they have bought you for a day or two, and they can ask you to do anything they want while you're on site. If you let that happen, you will make the migration project messy and unprofitable.

Make sure your client understands the closed loop process. Assure them that you will create service requests for every little thing. Nothing will get dropped or forgotten. But it has to be outside the scope of the migration project.

Think about it this way:

Let's say you have a migration project that's estimated to take thirty hours. If you end up spending thirty-one hours on the project, you'll probably just give away that hour for free. But you don't want to ignore the time when the project gets to be thirty-five or forty hours. At forty hours, you're 33% over your estimate!

The really great thing about creating service requests for every little task is that you can discuss them all with the client. Print up the "out of scope" service requests. Then have a discussion with the client. Ask very plainly, "How many of them are you willing to pay for?" And, of course, you'll be happy to do whatever they want, because it's all outside the migration project and it's all billable.

The Migration Project Overview

In this section we'll briefly describe each step of the process. The goal here is to give you the big picture so you'll see how all the pieces fit together. We hope that, as we go through these, you'll see the logic and elegance of the process.

Remember that Rule #2 was "Do it our way first." In this chapter you'll get a real sense of what "our way" is. As a result, we hope you'll be a bit more eager to try our process without any changes, at least the first time.

If you have questions about any of this as you go along, write them down. After you've finished the chapter, if your questions remain, please email them to

migration@greatlittlebook.com

The Checklist

Chapter Five covers an explanation of *the checklist*. The checklist is the core list of tasks you will perform. It's not "everything" in the project. As we're already seen, a migration project involves a great deal of management and other non-technical activity.

But the checklist is still central to the process because, eventually, the planning stops and technicians start typing and clicking. These technical action steps are what's listed in the checklist.

Let's be honest. By now you've probably looked through the checklist to compare it to what your company is doing. Please don't tear out those pages and jump into a migration project without reading through the book first.

We know this is a lot of material. It's not difficult, but there's a lot of detail. If you go through the explanation, you'll see that the base "to do" checklist is not enough to give you the information you need to perform a true Zero Downtime Migration.

Outline of The Process

The following outline gives a quick "table of contents" view of the migration process. After that, we fill in more detail on each topic.

See the next page.

Note that items marked with two asterisks ** are the items you will complete onsite in a two-day period.

Notes:

Outline of The Migration Process

- Quote the project. Get approval.
  - Discovery. If it's a new client or a complicated network, do a complete discovery process.
  - Invoicing and payment. Once the project is approved, invoice for hardware, software, and labor according to your company policies. Once paid for, order hardware and software.
- Create the Service Requests (6 or 7)
- Print out the basic checklist (as presented in the appendix) to be used for markup.
- Define the major stages in the process and develop a timeline.
- Gather all the information you'll need. This includes everything from user names to contact information for third party support personnel.
- Finalize the checklist; customize for this client and this job.
- Checkpoint: Hardware and Software should be in hand at this point.
  - Build the physical server
  - Configure hardware as specified (e.g., build RAID arrays, install misc. hardware)
  - Install and configure server operating system
  - Install and configure server software
  - Create users, machine accounts, etc.
  - Move a copy of all core data from the old server (including Exchange and SQL databases)
- Perform onsite "Pre-Migration" training
- Place server at client office and begin synchronizing **
- Move core services to the new server (At this point, clients can access both systems.) **
- Migrate workstations **
  - Clean, fix, update
  - Move data to server
  - Migrate Profiles
  - When complete, end user is only accessing the new server
- When last end user is moved over, turn off the old server **
- Perform onsite "Post Migration" training **
- Review "spinoff" and fine-tuning service requests created during this process
- Proceed to work on fine-tuning service requests
- Report completion of all steps to client
- Evaluate all aspects of migration project, including accuracy of estimates and any unforeseen incidents.
- Update all processes and procedures for every aspect of the migration project that require refinement or clarification.

We understand that that looks like a long, drawn-out process, but it's not. In almost all cases, you will complete the starred ** tasks in a two-day time span. Before that, the server build can be done on a leisurely basis at your office. Data can be moved by backup tape, disc image, or by putting the servers side by side and using tools such as Sync Toy or Robocopy, two of the Microsoft tools available at www.microsoft.com/downloads

Now let's dig a little deeper.

A Little More Detail on the Process

Now let's look at each of the bullet points from the previous list. This will take us from 30,000 feet to 10,000 feet.

Quote the project. Get approval.

We don't know what you've done in the past, of course. So we're going to spell out how we quote the average migration project. And while every client is as unique as a snowflake, our experience is that 90% of our migrations look the same.

Before we begin, we know what we've got: a Small Business Server that handles email, file services, and maybe a small web site. Some use SQL. Some use SharePoint.

The new server will be Small Business Server on new hardware. In the transition we're going to be cleaning up a bunch of old data and moving it to archive storage. If we can, we'll do that on the new server.

Our primary goal will be to move all critical functions to the new system with zero downtime companywide and less than one hour of downtime per workstation.

With all that in mind, the process of quoting a migration is very straight forward. Labor to build a machine. Labor to move services and functions. Labor to migrate data and workstations.

In Chapter Four we'll go through the specifics of quoting a migration project.

You will do it differently than we do. Still, it's instructive to have a "standard" process for quoting a project.

Discovery.

There are basically two kinds of discovery for a network migration. One is for systems that we have been managing. The other is for systems that are new to us.

For systems we've been managing, there shouldn't be too many surprises. We know everything we want to know about the computers and the company.

Once in awhile we find a user who moved an Access database to her desktop some time ago and never put it back on the server. But that's pretty rare.

For the most part, we manage our clients from A to Z and we know everything we need to know.

Still, there's a process of moving information from the current documentation into the migration process and on to the new documentation.

For new clients, we have a standard process of documenting a network (big surprise, eh?). You'll see that we have both a "pre-discovery" and a discovery process.

First, we make sure we know all the things we need to know. Then we go in and make sure we know all the details.

Invoicing and payment.

We are rigorous about our cash flow process. That means that we get all hardware and software paid up front. Once we have the money, we order the equipment.

If you've been in business very long, you've experienced clients who change their minds. They fax over a purchase order on Friday and then change their minds on Monday.

If you ordered equipment in the meantime . . . ooops.

Create Service Requests

Technicians "Start Here."

Depending on your process, either the salesman or the service manager will create the Service Requests that will "be" this project inside your ticket tracking system.

As we mentioned earlier, these are the buckets that you put labor into and your client puts money into.

Define the major stages in the process and develop a timeline.

Again, 90% of your migrations will look the same. So we define a set of standard procedures that take you on a smooth trail from the old system to the new system.

You'll need to work harder at this stage than any other. This is the point where you need to define all the stages you'll take and the order in which you'll take them.

This is also the place where you'll identify the oddball things that can cause trouble. One of the rules Karl lives by is "Something's going to go wrong. We don't know what it is, but we'll overcome it when it shows up." This is the stage at which you try to figure out all the little things that could be the one you don't expect.

The outcome of this stage will be a written step-by-step plan of action. The more detail the better.

Gather all the information you'll need.

Here we continue the documentation process in excruciating detail. You'll gather every username, password, vendor, contact phone number, and every other detail you'll need.

The more experience you have, the better you'll be at listing all the information you need. We give you the most complete list we can. You'll supplement this with your experience on each job.

And, of course, your specialized knowledge within a vertical will help you at this stage.

Finalize the checklist; customize for this client and this job.

We give you a BIG checklist for each migration. But you have to believe us: That's not good enough.

At this point you need to rethink every item on the checklist and customize it for *this* client and *this* migration.

Checkpoint: Hardware and Software should be in hand at this point.

Build the physical server. Install and configure the operating system. Install and configure software.

We recommend that you perform the physical server build and software load at your office. Take your time. Go slow. Do it right. Document it thoroughly.

You will also begin the actual migration here. Remember, we're not migrating everything in one day in the middle of the night.

Create users, machine accounts, etc.

This is one of those "little things" that can come back to haunt you. You need to recreate all the users as they *should be* on the new system. This may not necessarily be how they are on the old system.

The safest way to do this is to ask the client for a complete list of users. If it does not seem complete, you can go back and ask for more information.

We provide a form for listing the users' real names, logons, and group membership. Make sure someone on the client's team signs off that the list is correct.

Small mistakes here can become larger rework headaches later. For example, if an old user "Sandy" was renamed to "Office Manager" and now the person using that logon is Lisa, you do NOT want to pull over their old username and profile.

Important safety tip: Lisa's profile name is Sandy if the same machine was used by all three incarnations of this user. If Office Manager got a new machine and the user was renamed, then Lisa's local profile is still Office Manager.

> Note on Profiles
>
> Please see the discussion of Profile Migrations in Chapter Six.
>
> Even though most of the attention in migrations is on the server, the truth is almost all of your labor is on the desktop side of the equation. We'll discuss this a bit in Chapter Four as it relates to quoting the project.
>
> Migrations are the perfect time to straighten out profiles, make sure they're named properly, keep what you need, discard the rest, and document the whole thing.

Move a copy of all core data from the old server (including Exchange and SQL databases)

There are several good tools for moving the data. We mentioned SyncToy (which we wish had a better name). Microsoft has pushed Robocopy for years, and now includes it in the operating system.

Microsoft also has a tool just for moving file shares. We'll talk about that later.

And of course you can use backup tapes, backup drives, and even copy the data from images.

There are at least two primary goals for this data move. First, 95% or more of the data won't change between now and project completion, so the onsite data management will be very easy.

Second, you will be able to install all software and test it using the stagnant data. Every function of every piece of software can be tested this way.

Perform onsite "Pre-Migration" training

Once you have things ready to move onsite, hold a company-wide meeting and go through the pre-launch PowerPoint presentation we've posted up on the web site (www.zerodowntimemigration.com).

Obviously, you'll fine-tune this for every client and put up screen shots as needed.

The point of this meeting is to get the entire staff "on board" with the move. There is much less resistance when people know what's coming. Plus, you can promise them smoother email management, faster performance, etc.

Most importantly, you can answer their questions and relieve some anxiety. We plan one hour for this presentation.

Place server at client office and begin synchronizing

In most cases, this is "Day One" of the onsite migration.

Once you place the server onsite, your clock starts ticking. Note that the time clock is a little different between SBS 2003 and SBS 2008/2011.

In either domain, you can have two SBS domain controllers on the same network for seven days.

That's more than enough time to complete the migration.

In the 2008/2011 universe, you have the option of actually joining the domain and "becoming" the domain controller for the existing domain. If you choose this option, you must be aware of the consequences (covered in detail later).

If you choose the 2008 domain control transfer, you have twenty-one days to complete the migration. In our scenario, that gives you nineteen days to spare!

If the client has a massive amount of data that changes, or you were not able to copy all the data before this point, then it's nice to have a weekend to synchronize the servers. But in 99% of all cases, overnight will do the trick.

The really good news is that you don't have to sit there and stare at the screen. All good copying tools have good reporting as well. So you'll know what didn't get moved.

Move core services to the new server (At this point, clients can access both systems.).

One by one, you'll move Exchange, anti-virus control, SQL, and other core services to the new server.

We will obviously go into great detail on this. For now, just understand that you'll be moving each of these separately. So there's a process for email, a process for the LOB, and so forth.

With very few exceptions, users can now access both systems. In some cases (e.g., financials or LOB apps), only one version can be live. Luckily, those systems tend not to be used by everyone in the office every minute of the day.

The one big function that *is* used by 99% of the office 99% of the time is Outlook/Exchange. So for that we have a special process that basically involves one system of access before the big cutover and one after.

Migrate workstations. Clean, fix, update; Move data to server. Migrate Profiles.

Workstation migration is a huge topic all by itself. But like everything else, you simply divide the chores into smaller tasks in order to make the larger job manageable.

Two key elements of the desktop migration process can be done weeks (or even months) before the actual server migration. The first is to completely clean each workstation.

This means removing viruses, spyware, excess programs, "ghost" profiles, etc. One of the most important things about modern Windows domains is that Domain Name Service (DNS) must be working properly.

Without DNS, you cannot see the server. Without good DNS, you cannot run the connection wizard.

And we know that many adware and spyware programs mess with DNS. So cleaning up the desktops as a routine sweep will dramatically improve you success with the larger migration picture.

The second key element of workstation migration that can be done in advance is to move data to where it belongs.

Our preferred policy is that 1) All important data belongs on the server, and 2) We would rather NOT have "My Documents" folders. Yes, you can redirect My Documents to the server, but you then have to manage the bloat of junk "data" that shows up.

Ideally, there's a central data directory on the server for each department. Ideally, everyone uses that directory to store their stuff. So, ideally, you won't have gigabytes of business-critical data on the desktops.

In the real world, the last several versions of Windows have made it increasingly difficult to keep track of where files actually exist. As a result, even diligent clients end up with data on their desktops – most likely never backed up in any way.

Anyway, part of the sweep to check viruses and spyware should also include moving all company data to *where it belongs* on the server.

Migrate workstations (continued). When complete, end user is only accessing the new server.

On the "day of" migration, the most important task will be to preserve the user's profile to the degree necessary (see the discussion of migration levels in Chapter Four).

Let's say that someone's desktop is cut over to the new system at lunchtime. In the morning, they are using resources on the old domain. Then you migrate their desktop to the new server or new domain. So, in the afternoon, they are accessing only resources on the new system.

The beauty of this process is that it is interruptible. You can do four desktops on Day One and twenty desktops on Day Two. If you need to, you can move ten desktops a day for five days.

When last end user is moved over, turn off the old server

We like to simply power down the old server and leave it where it is after a migration. This is what we call an "in place archive" of their system.

For a day or two it can be their fail-back option. More importantly, if some little piece of data didn't come across for any reason, you can simply fire up the old server, recover the data, and then shut it down again.

After a reasonable period of time – perhaps two weeks – you can recycle the old machine according to whatever standards or policies are in place.

Perform onsite "Post Migration" training.

This one varies based on client needs. But, basically, you should get the whole office together again to talk about the new features.

In some ways, this is pretty much the same material re-hashed from the preview training. But now it's "real" because the system is live and people are logging onto the new server.

Give everyone an opportunity to ask questions. And take this time to provide a handout on your technical support procedures. If you only perform work based on a service request (our recommendation), then show people how to do that.

They're going to have questions. Get some out of the way as a group and then make sure everyone knows how to contact you going forward.

Review "spinoff" service requests created during this process

We are very careful to avoid the phrase "fallout" when it comes to unexpected tasks in the migration project (see chapters 1-2).

Spinoff projects are normally outside the scope of the project, but not always. For example, if you discover that three different people have copied a certain access database to their desktops, and they all think theirs is "the" real version, that's a mess that you just need to keep outside the scope of the migration.

But let's say that half the people have usernames in the format *First Initial Last Name* and the other have are in the format *First Name Last Initial*. You should be able to standardize these on the new server/domain without adding any real billable labor.

In the diagrams of the closed loop process, this is the point where you gather up all the little "stuff" that came up during the project. Each of these items should be a service request. Remember, there are only three things you can do with each of these SRs:

1) The issue has been made irrelevant by the migration project or some stage of the project (e.g., "can't connect to server").

2) The issue is determined to be so minor that you simply include it in the big project. Remember, however, that lots of little things add up to big things.

3) The issue is truly separate from the migration project and is handled under separate billing (either hourly or under a managed service agreement).

> Note on Invoicing:
>
> It is critical that you and your team bill time against each of the appropriate Service Requests that you'll create in the next chapter.
>
> This helps you point out to the client that the total hours are in line with what you quoted.
>
> It also helps you keep track of the profitability of the project.
>
> And, it helps you track realistic numbers so that your quotes become more accurate over time.

Proceed to work on fine-tuning service requests

This step essentially consists of reviewing each stage in the project (each service request) and verifying that all work is done. If it's not done, assign someone to clean it up and check it off so you can mark it as complete.

Report completion of all steps to client

Once you've reviewed each stage (each service request) and marked each as complete, then the project as a whole is complete.

With luck you will have had great communication all along. So this step becomes simply a formality. But don't skip it! Clients rarely get to experience an official notice of completion in the SMB space. Give them this little bit of joy!

Evaluate all aspects of migration project, including accuracy of estimates and any unforeseen incidents.

Within your own team, take time to evaluate how well you did. Start with the quoting process, then move right on through the project.

How well did you do on the server build? On migrating workstations? On moving data? Etc.

And then ask the client. You don't have to perform an official survey. Take the client out to lunch and simply ask, "How did we do?"

Try to get honest feedback. That's the only kind that's really useful.

Notes:

So Where Does Zero Downtime Come In?

One of the promises we make is that we can migrate a network during business hours Monday through Friday with zero down time on the network and less than one hour of downtime for each user.

> Definitions are important. We define network as having no downtime for critical business applications during business critical hours. We define this as 8AM or 9AM until 5 PM. Thus, we can send in a tech at 7 AM or 5 PM to reboot a server. The hour before business starts and the hour at the end of the day are our "Golden Hours." In some cases, the lunch hour (12-1 PM) is also available as a Golden Hour.

The only time we have not done this in the last three years was with a client who just absolutely said "No, we are going to start at 5 pm Friday." We said okay, as long as you understand that after-hours support is twice as expensive.

He said "I don't care, we're not going to do it during business hours."

We practically begged him to save money. "But you won't be down during business hours, you won't know the difference, your employees won't know the difference."

He didn't care. He wanted to do it after hours. He has enough technical knowledge to know that's the way things *used to be done*, so that's the way he wanted it done.

We use three "golden hours" to reboot machines and do final data moves. We discuss those a bit more in a minute.

Other than that, we achieve ZDT by simply dissecting the big project and managing each piece of the project very carefully. We literally "divide and conquer." As you will see, there are many ways to achieve this.

The largest network that we have moved to a new server with zero downtime on the network and less than an hour per desktop was 70 users. This was a brand new client. When that client first came to us, we explained that we don't work weekends.

Why? Because the tech support that we may need (for hardware, Internet, firewalls, etc.) may not be available on weekends, or weekend support may be expensive. And because our labor would be more expensive. So, why should the client pay the overtime? Why should we pay the over-time? Why should everybody have a more expensive experience just because we worked weekends?

Ask the client! Most clients haven't even considered the possibility of a zero downtime migration because they're not in the business. It's not their job! But present it as an option.

Ask your client how much more they would pay to have a migration performed during normal business hours with zero downtime. Your additional labor will probably only be about five hours. If their answer is above that amount, then it's worth their money to take the ZDTM approach.

Methods for Achieving Zero Downtime

There are three fundamental strategies you'll use to achieve "Zero Downtime." There are also three golden hours that make your life easy.

The first ZDT strategy is to Intercept the Process. That means you set up the function you're working on so that it's functional on both servers at the same time. Then you move people over from the old server to the new server one at a time.

A great example of this is the migration of email. If you own Karl's *Super-Good Project Planner for Technical Consultants*, you've seen this process in detail. Basically, you install an outsourced email filter that caches the email (e.g., Reflexion, Exchange Defender, or Spam Soap). Then, when you're ready to make the switch, you report the email filter to the new server location.

The second ZDT strategy is to Run the Processes in Parallel. A great example of this is with files and folders. You simply synchronize the old and new folder sets. Some people are on the old system and some on the new. Both of them have total access to all data.

You'll see how we set up parallel systems and then have the "migrated" and "un-migrated" users.

The third ZDT strategy is to Flip the Big Switch. This is frequently done with LOBs (line of business applications).

Essentially, these are systems that cannot exist in two places at the same time. You will either update one database or the other. They can't both be the "live" database.

With some LOBs, the big switch is very simple. You start the new database, stop the old database, and then users just log into the new one. Others are more complicated because you need to remap data sources, overwrite configuration files, etc.

If the LOB that will go on the new server is a newer version, upgrade the old server first as a separate project to ensure compatibility.

Our general process here is to set up the new LOB with old data from a backup. That allows us to test all functionality and troubleshoot at the desktop level while leaving the old LOB in place and live.

Then, on the day of the migration, we set up a virtual machine or terminal server session that allows them to access one LOB (old or new) and their real desktop allows them to access the other LOB (new or old). Before the migration, they use the old LOB. After the migration they use the new LOB.

Several techniques for migrating functions (including the last one we described), require you to stop the old service, do a final data synch and start up the new service.

Zero downtime is accomplished by cheating a bit with the three Golden Hours. One golden hour is the lunch hour. If necessary, we tell the client that the network will not be available during lunch hour (12:00 PM – 1:00 PM). During that time, we can reboot one or both servers, move "live" services, access desktops for a quick re-point, etc.

The other golden hours are 7:00 AM – 8:00 AM and 5:00 PM – 6:00 PM. We generally don't work outside the normal business day (8:00 AM to 5:00 PM Monday through Friday). But on migration days, we might have a technician work 9:00 to 6:00 or 7:00 to 4:00. Once again, we tell the client that the network is going down at 5:00 PM. They send everyone home and we do our magic.

Zero downtime during business hours. Wink.

What's Next?

At this point, you've seen an overview of the project checklist. In the next chapter we'll go through quoting the project.

The quoting process is important – even for technicians – because it frames the whole project. When you're done with the quote, you will have outlined the seven primary steps that go into a network migration.

Once approved by the client, you will literally copy and paste the descriptions from your quote into six or seven service requests in your PSA system.

There are many more details involved in the migration project. Chapter Five explains the actual checklist in detail. In the Appendices you will find checklist for migrating to the three most recent versions for Small Business Server. The online content includes the old checklists for migrating to SBS 2003 only and SBS 2008 only.

Each checklist will be over 200 pages once you've completed it. But 197 of those pages will be documentation, planning, and strategy.

On the actual "Day Of" migration, you will only have a small handful of chores. They are, basically:

- ☑ Make any "day of" DNS changes that are required.
- ☑ Reconfigure the spam filtering device, if one exists.
- ☑ Test Email out bound and in bound.
- ☑ Reconfigure the Firewall if necessary.
- ☑ Reconfigure all Printers if necessary.
- ☑ Run through the Workstation Migration Checklist on a workstation that is not in use and modify the checklist as needed.
- ☑ Run the Workstation Migration Checklist on all remaining machines in the office.
- ☑ Contact remote users and step them through the Remote Users Checklist.

As you can see, the only really time-consuming activity on the Day Of the migration is to move the desktops over in an orderly fashion. And, because of the strategy of having "dual citizenship" on the old system and the new system, the desktop migrations do not all have to be completed on the same day.

There Are No Emergency Migrations

It is very important to note that every piece of this migration process can be stopped at any time and all systems will continue to work. Even the desktop migrations can be "half-done" and the overall process can be put on hold.

This results in a very low-stress migration! Think about it. You always have a road back. You can always stop with the "current" situation and all functions will be operational. Some functions will be on one server and some on the other. But all functions are "up."

For example, if you have a critical situation with the new LOB, or a third party vendor cannot be available at the last minute, you simply continue as you are and come back another day.

Zero Stress-Time Migration!

And when you're done, the old server is totally intact. You could, theoretically, stop all the functions on the new server, copy the data back, and crank up the old server.

The old-school migration method was to pick a weekend, shut everything down, and pray that you'll have everything moved over by sunrise on Monday. That's very stressful, especially if you hit a stopping point and need to come back another day.

This system is completely stress-free because you can move *functions* one at a time and no single function can create a critical stop point for the migration as a whole.

The Network Documentation Binder

From time to time, in the rest of this book, we will make reference to the Network Documentation Binder or NDB.

KPEnterprises uses a specific set of documentation worksheets, most of which have been published separately in *The Network Documentation Workbook* (see www.smbbooks.com).

You do not have to have this specific set of configuration pages, but you should have something in written form for your documentation. When we refer to the Network Documentation Binder or NDB, we mean your written documentation.

For example, at some point you will copy relevant pages from your NDB and past them into the Network Migration Binder. Later, when the migration is complete, you will update these forms and then move the new forms into your new NDB.

You will see that a great deal of the success of our system relies on solid documentation and consistent, repeatable processes. Both of those rely on good documentation.

Remember Rule Number Six from Chapter One:

Know What you Know

Part of knowing what you know is to have a system you can rely on. For example, "If it's in the NDB, it's true."

Knowing how all the printers are configured will save you time and money. Knowing how many switches you have in a two-suite office, and how they're configured, will save you time and money. And so forth.

Every migration is an opportunity to verify or create documentation for virtually every piece of hardware and software in the client's environment. Don't waste this opportunity. It would be shameful to complete a network migration and have no documentation about how the network is configured.

The Rest of This Book

The next Section is *Quoting and Defining the Migration Process.* It includes two chapters: Chapter Four covers quoting the migration and Chapter Five describes the "big" checklist in detail.

After that we'll cover The Time Line / Planning ZDTM, Gathering Information, and Filling Out The Checklist. After that we discuss *Working the Plan,* which includes Getting Started - Initiation Training, Building the Server, Network Migration, and Desktop Migration.

Finally, we conclude with *Details, Details.* That's the little but critical stuff such as ISPs, DNS, Routers, etc. and Finishing the Project.

After that we have a couple of case studies and some concluding thoughts.

We know you're eager to get going with the migration project, so let's jump in with the quoting process.

Chapter 4

Quoting the Migration Project

This section covers the most important aspects of packaging, estimating, and quoting the migration project. Note: This is not a sales primer, so we don't cover the fine points of getting the client to sign on the dotted line. For that, we refer you to the excellent sales books by Erick Simpson and Matt Makowicz. For more information, see www.smbbooks.com.

Our goal here is to cover the total management of the migration project. So this chapter will address the sales process only insomuch as it affects the management of the migration project as a whole.

Very frequently, project definition and delivery involve three roles within your company:

- Sales
- Sales engineer
- Engineer

The sales role focuses on pricing, packaging, and client agreement. The sales engineer role is responsible for making sure the right thing is sold—and making sure it can be delivered by your company. The engineer role will actually deliver the network migration project.

For most companies, these roles are played by at least two or three people. In many network migration projects, a team will deliver the engineering role. But it is also common for these roles to be combined. If you're a sole proprietor, you'll deliver all three.

It's very important that you *do* deliver all these roles. Do not skimp on any of these roles. Selling the right project is just as important as delivering the project that's sold.

Project Initiation

At some point you'll find yourself with the opportunity to propose a new server. For purposes of this chapter, we'll assume you've had an initial meeting, you've discussed the new system with the client, and you've been asked to put together a quote.

In a perfect world, you'll be able to charge for a complete audit of the client's systems. But, as we'll see in a minute, that's unlikely.

It is more likely that you'll need to leave this meeting with permission to poke around on the server and ask someone a few questions.

Since you need to generate a quote with minimal information, exactly what information do you need? Well, the most important information is the age of each computer and total number of desktops/laptops.

The amount of time you'll need to migrate machines depends in large part on their age and the age of the software they are running. For example, a three year old desktop with Office 2000 will take longer than a six month old laptop with Office 2007.

For newer machines, we use a base of 45 minutes (.75 hours) per PC. For machines older than two years, we use a base of 90 minutes (1.5 hours) per PC. Of course you'll round a bit.

So, you need to know as much as you can know about the machines being migrated. You don't have to touch every machine, but you should get an idea of the high and low end of the spectrum.

You should try to learn as much as you can about the server, particularly the amount of hard disc space in use, any databases that exist, and any LOBs – Line of Business applications.

If you're maintaining this site for a client, your job will be much easier. If not, try to get the basic information on our "68-point checklist" for examining client systems. You can get an electronic copy of this list by sending an email to checklist@greatlittlebook.com.

A Confident Approach

It is important, for your long-term success, that you take charge and control the entire project as early as possible. Here's what we mean by that: technology *users* and *owners* are rarely qualified to design or architect a modern computer network. They might know a great deal. And they might appear to know more than they actually do.

But, assuming you are a qualified technician, you need to take charge and run the show. The reasons for this are fairly obvious: You know how to architect an entire network; you know which hardware and software options are available; you know what's best for the job; and you know which alternatives are available while discussing options, expandability, etc.

In other words, you understand the technology. You can try to explain it to the client, but in the end they will never understand it as you do.

Let us put it this way: You're the consultant! It's your job to consult!

Your job is to help the client define the right network for their needs. Never simply give the client what they ask for. In the last twenty years, we have almost never seen a client request for a major network overhaul that turned out to be the right thing for the client. Sometimes they want to over-buy equipment, sometimes they want to under-buy software. They are rarely aware of the hardware or software vendors' latest packages or recommendations.

There are essentially three ways that network migration projects are initiated:

- By the client
- By the consultant
- By God (or "an act of God")

From time to time a client will simply come to you and say "That server's getting old." At other times, you need to go to them and remind them that the server's getting old, or that it's not fulfilling their needs. And finally, you have times when something fails and you find yourself patching things together long enough to get a replacement set up.

Luckily, that third option is rare these days.

No matter how the discussion starts, it's your job to move quickly to guide the conversation. In addition to technical knowledge, you will also rely on the client's needs, their plans for growth, their budget, etc.

You might be wondering why it's so important to take the project by the horns and lead the conversation from the start. The answer is pretty simple: you're planning your success. It's usually surprising how much you can control success when you control the conversation. Here's why.

There are two key factors that affect your relationship with business decision makers: their level of confidence in you, and their level of technical knowledge.

If their confidence in you is high, then you have no problems. But they can lose confidence if you're not a take-charge person. And, as you can imagine, their confidence will go way up as you assume control of the conversation.

Technical confidence is a little different. If their technical knowledge is low, they really need you to take charge. They actually need to be told what to do. If you come across as uncertain, you make it more difficult for them to agree to your proposal. If you give them two options, you'll need to state a preference for one over the other.

A high level of confidence on your part makes it easier for them to go along. In fact, you'll hear the client echoing your arguments as if they're facts. "Of course we need RAID 5 on the storage array."

If the client's technical knowledge is high, their tendency to challenge your recommendation is also high. You'll need good, clear explanations for your recommendations, but your sense of confidence will win the day.

Remember, also, that what appears as a challenge may simply be the client showing off a level of knowledge. If the client takes pride in knowing about technology, then they want to have a true discussion about the options available for their new network.

And best of all, once educated, the client is more likely to go along with your recommendations.

We have a client who owns two different companies. In discussing the benefits for a hardware-based RAID system for his new SBS 2008 installation, he really latched onto the idea of gaining speed with RAID five because the system was pulling data from more heads at the same time.

Literally one month later he asked us for a quote to fill up the one-year-old server at his old office with hard drives. We told him this was not necessary, but he was eager to spend the money. What can you do?

We tend to only make one set of recommendations for a prospect: the one we consider to be the best choice for the client. Unless the client really pushes, we don't give them choices. We'd much rather spend time learning about what the client needs than arguing with them about what they need. In fact, when we propose a new system for a client with a very high level of technical competence, we actually tell them "this is the only option we're quoting because it's the right system for you."

The bottom line is: Have confidence in what you propose – and propose it in a confident manner.

The Generic Two-Drawing Process

We like to give the client two basic Visio diagrams to work with. The first is a drawing of their current network—*what is*. The second is our proposed network—*what will be*.

See Illustrations *4-1: Existing Network* and *4-2: Proposed Network Map*.
(Note: These drawings are available online in electronic format. To access these, go to www.zerodowntimemigration.com and register the book. See Appendix D for details.)

Drawings are great because you can take the client on a tour from the firewall to the desktop, and everything in between. Is the firewall adequate? Do you need to add web filtering, VPN, etc.? Next are your switches. Do you have good gigabit switches that are still under warranty?

Move like this through the entire network. As a rule, you'll address one thing at a time. But when you make your proposal, the client will know that you really understand their environment.

As you can see, this entire approach is focused on what's best for the client. Yes, it requires a certain ego. But when you confidently propose only what's right and best for the client, the client will see that.

Illustration 4-1

Existing Network | **Schmoeville Autos**

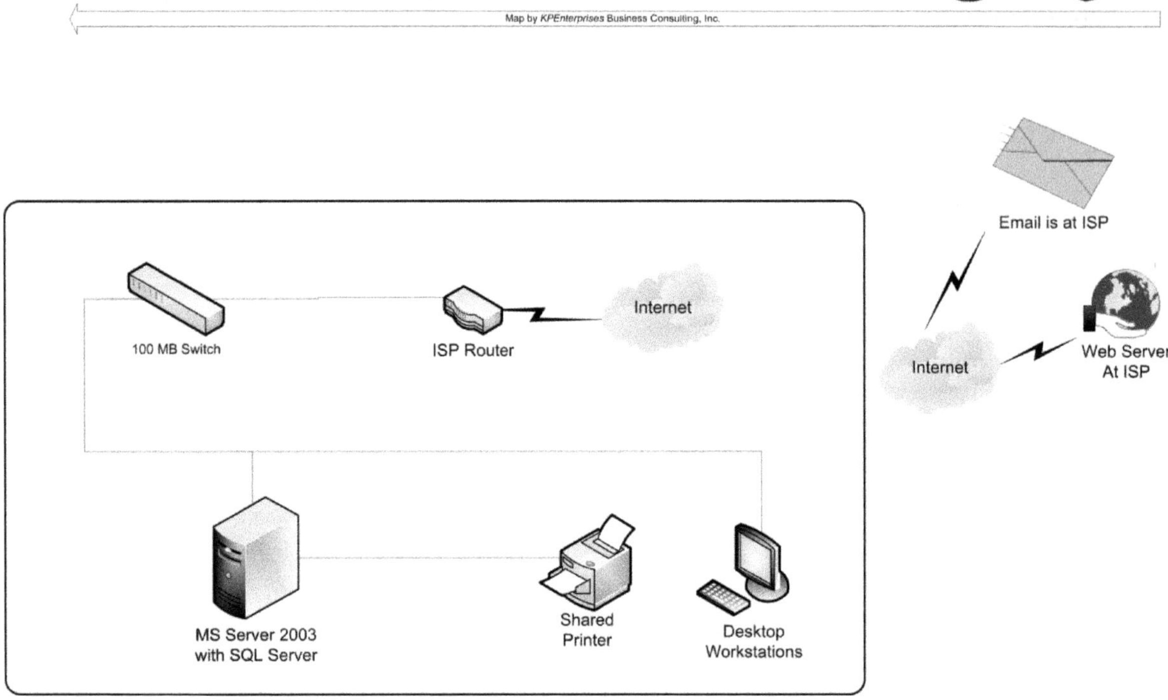

Illustration 4-2:

Proposed Network Map | **Schmoeville Autos**

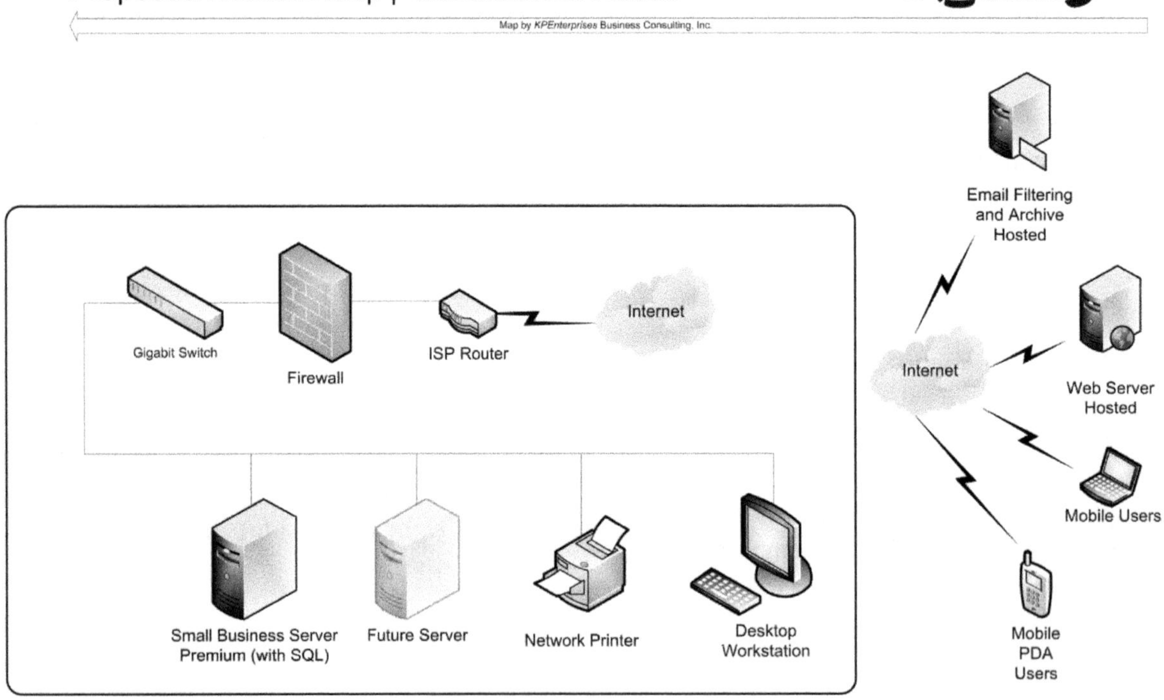

When you sit down with these maps, start by describing the first map strictly in terms of functionality. For example,

"Currently, your mail lives at the ISP. That means two important things for you. First, when you send a file to Jennifer, it has to leave your company and sit on the ISP's computer. Then, when she collects her email, she brings it back in-house. That's very inefficient.

Second, you don't currently have the ability to share calendars or use the other features of Microsoft Exchange Server. Let me show you how that works. . . ."

You should go through the entire "old" map first. We recommend that you do not flip back and forth between the two maps. That's a strong tendency for some technical people. Unless the client initiates this back-and-forth activity, you should avoid it because it can be very confusing. If the client initiates, they may be very visual and soak up the information more quickly that way.

Go through the entire map. The old system has no firewall. The old system has an old, slow (often full) switch. The old system has a standard server rather than Small Business Server 2008.

Once you get to the new map, it's like a shiny new toy. Suddenly they get a firewall, a gigabit switch, filtered email, SBS, etc.

And while every network is unique like a snowflake, the truth is that these network maps fit 90% of most small businesses for the "before and after" conversation.

We recommend that you go on their web site and snag their logo to paste into Visio. A small touch that they'll appreciate.

The Reality of Quoting in the SMB Space

In large companies, and with large projects, there is a standard process that companies go through. There's an official *Request For Quote* (RFQ), an official response (formal quote), a discovery process, and generally at least three bids are considered.

But that's not what the small/medium business world is like, at least most of the time. There is rarely an RFQ. And the discovery process can be very expensive, so it is usually cut. In reality, it's not cut: the discovery process is almost never considered as an element in the process.

But the good news is that small businesses don't normally ask three different companies to give them quotes on a project. In most cases, they ask their favorite consultant to give them a quote. If it's really just out of the ball park, they ask for some major fine tuning. But most of the time, they simply require a reasonable justification.

The very good news is that the focus is not on money, *per se*. In the SMB world, the most important elements in a relationship are communication, trust, and compatible values. So, on one hand, it would be nice to have an official RFQ process and get paid for every element of the process. But, on the other hand, it is nice to know that the focus will be on communication and trust rather than money alone.

It is important to note the fact that small businesses are *not* likely to pay the money needed to have a thorough discovery process. It means that you cannot estimate a job based on complete knowledge.

Stop. Highlight the previous sentence.

When you get rid of the discovery process and the project plan, then all you can do is to work the project on a "time and materials" basis. But without any sense of a budget, the client will end up being very unhappy with the cost of the project. Does this sound familiar?

All sales meetings involve a few key people. You get together the four personalities who will define the project:

- The business owner
- The client's technical advisor

- Your sales person
- Your technical advisor.

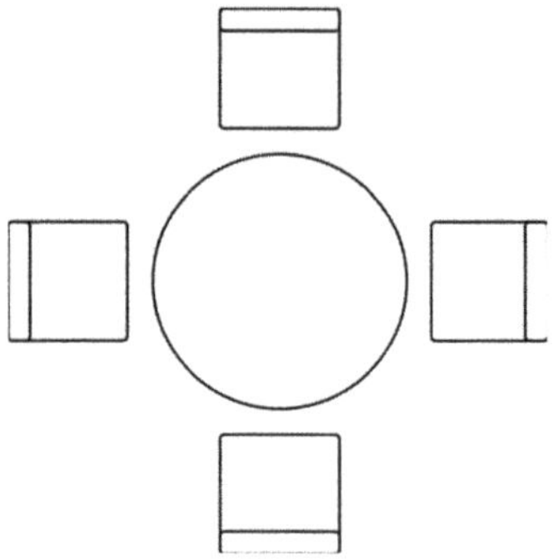

As we all know, these four personalities may be inside two people, or three people, or four people. But in all sales meetings, you will find these four personalities.

KPEnterprises used to do a lot of programming work. Here's a very common scenario from the world of defining a programming project:

- You put together a meeting to design what the project is going to look like. The client says, "Well, we cannot afford the mansion that you have presented. All we can afford is a two room shack. And we can't afford the discovery process. You want too much money just to define this project. So . . . just build a two room shack."
- You dutifully build the two room shack. Then the client says "Uh . . . yeah. There's no kitchen here." And you say "Well, you didn't ask for a kitchen; you asked for a two room shack."
- So you build the kitchen, and they say, "Well, we need a study. And we need a lobby. And we need a front porch. And I told you this was a two-story shack, didn't I?" Now the client starts to build what they wanted in the first place.
- But the project is now "time and materials," and they are adding labor and labor and labor. They are hobbling things together and it's not organized. It is not *designed.* It is merely clumped together.

What is that going to lead to? A huge expense, a kludgey project, and an unsatisfied customer.

Unfortunately, this is a very common scenario in small business. No money to plan things properly. So we waste money playing catch up.

Lesson Learned: The core problem in SMB is that we don't get to estimate costs the way big companies do because our clients are not willing to pay much for the estimation part of the process.

So one of the common things that grew up organically in our SMB space, is that we give away the network evaluation as a way to get our foot in the door. You have basically taken the thing the client needs most (an evaluation of how they should proceed) and you have given it away so that you can get the job.

The result of this is that we get accurate estimates only through experience.

Here's an example from Office 2007.

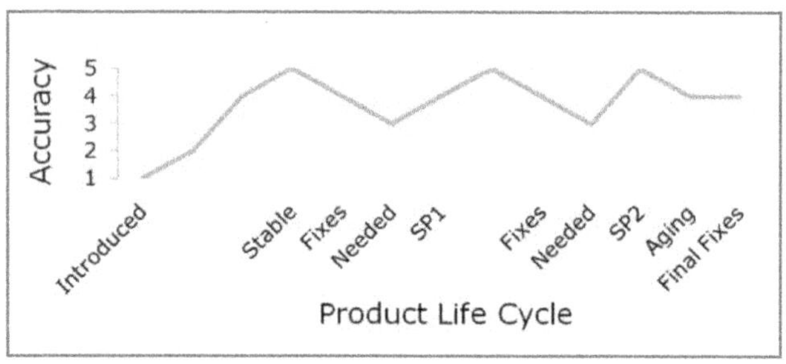

If you are selling Office 2007, you know about how long that takes on a brand new computer. So, if you have a new laptop and Office 2007, you can say, "I'm going to estimate a half hour per machine." In this scenario, you're safe. But in 2011, when that software is older and has a few service packs, fixes, updates, and patches, it's going to take longer to install. And there is a difference based on the age of the hardware. It might take half an hour, an hour, or even an hour and a half.

As you can see, the accuracy of your estimate changes over time. When a product is new, you have a very low level of accuracy. Think about Small Business Server 2008. When SBS 2008 was released, you started out with a very low level of accuracy about how long it would take to get that product installed and configured so that the client can sit down and use it.

And then, as your experience goes up, your accuracy goes up. As the years go by, there are patches, and fixes, and updates. Over time, you get used to the patches that need to be installed. And the accuracy of your estimates goes up. So, over time, the more stable that product is, and the more experience you have, the more accurate your estimates are.

But early on, when a product is new, you don't have a clue.

Software vendors are not always helpful. As you may recall, Microsoft promised that an OEM installation of SBS 2003 would take about 20 minutes! Did anyone actually have that experience? No. Most people planned on 5-10 hours of labor before the user was allowed near the server.

So, our experience is critically important to us. And, obviously, you only get experience by doing something again and again. You can get some server installation experience by reading a book, or by having somebody tell you that they think the install is six or eight hours.

But advice only goes so far. You have to use *your* procedures. And your procedures are different from our procedures. Your checklist is different from our checklist. Your technicians are different than our technicians. So, in the mix of things, you have to figure out how you can deliver that product and have good estimates for labor.

Over time, when your estimates are in that higher accuracy range, you are able to create cookie cutter projects. As you will see, we have a formula for estimating network migrations. We estimate so many hours for each desktop, so many hours for each laptop, so many hours for the server, so many hours for the data, etc.

We have good time estimates for SBS 2003 because it is very late in the lifespan of 2003. At the same time, our SBS 2008 experience is based almost entirely on installation of beta software. Other than that variable, we have a very good estimate of how long it's going to take us to migrate to a new server.

We've fine-tuned the server build portion of our checklist by having each of our technicians install the product and fine-tune the checklist. Then we have the next technician install the product and fine-tune the checklist. They each do this one at a time, so we can always build on the knowledge from the previous installation.

Back to the Maps:

Using the two-network-map process will give you a big step up in making sure that you don't forget anything. As you work your way through the office, you note that you need a new switch, a firewall, etc.

If you have separate people acting in the roles of sales engineer and sales person, then the sales person will rely on the sales engineer to make up the list of equipment needed and verify that nothing was missed when it's done.

Your Line Card

Whether you call it that or not, you have a standard "Line Card" for your business. That's a list of the standard products and services you sell. In reality, it's the stuff you sell most often. Chances are that you can sell almost anything you want.

But you sell a specific set of solutions. Your set is different from our set. For example:

In a nutshell, here's the vast majority of what we sell:

Hardware

- HP Servers
- HP Workstations
- HP Desktops / Laptops
- HP Monitors
- HP Thin Clients
- HP Tape Drives (various)
- HP Printers
- APC UPSs (various)
- Sonicwall Firewalls
- Sonicwall CDP
- Switches (a variety of brand names)

Software

- MS Windows Server
- MS Windows Small Business Server
- CALs as needed for all software
- MS SQL Server
- MS Exchange Server
- MS Windows
- MS Office (various)
- Trend Micro Anti-Virus
- Symantec Backup Exec
- Diskeeper defragmentation

Materials

- Brand-name Cat6 cables
- Brand-name tapes (various)

Your mileage will vary. You might sell Forefront security, Dell computers, Symantec Anti-Virus, and a whole host of other products.

The point is: You have a standard set of hardware and software that you offer.

The more you know about these things, the more likely you be able to sell the *right* solution for a given client.

At some level there's a bit of "When you sell hammers every problem looks like a nail."

But realistically, you have a standard map for your SMB clients and a standard solution set. The more you know what you sell, the more profitable you will be.

For example, we also like Watchguard firewalls and the BDR product from Zenith. These are good alternatives to what we have been selling.

But we don't attempt to know or carry every brand of computer hardware or software on earth. We don't change brands at the drop of a hat.

Keeping our Line Card consistent over time maximizes our relationship with the vendors we choose. It also increases our knowledge of those specific products, including our knowledge of their marketing promotions, rebates, etc.

Know what you know about what you sell.

Labor Estimates

One of the key values you'll need for your internal quoting process (next step) is the cost of delivering an hour of labor. Like everything else, this isn't as easy as it seems.

The most important thing about this calculation is that it includes a lot more than the employee in question. It takes your whole operation to deliver an hour of labor. So you need to look at the big picture rather than a single person.

You need to estimate the *fully burdened labor rate*. That means the true cost of labor, including taxes, time spent training, drive time, etc. Your fully burdened labor rate is essentially the entire cost of the employee per year divided by the number of hours you'll get.

Note: This is not the place where we figure in the effect of "billable" vs. "non-billable" hours. We take that into consideration when the create quotes. For example, if we thing it will take 12 hours of labor to produce 8 hours billable, we deal with that on a job-by-job basis. You must be careful not to do this calculation in both places or you'll really burden you yourself!

There are some calculators out in the world, but finding just the right one for your business is probably not worthwhile.

Here we present three ways to calculate your cost per hour of labor. There's Super-Fast, Quick, and Complete.

1. The Super-Fast Method is this:

Hourly Rate x 1.5

That's it.

Not perfect, but a darn safe place to start. So if the technicians working on this project make $20/hour, then your cost is $30/hour.

2. The Quick Method is almost as easy. First you need to know the total cost of running your company. Then back out costs of goods sold (COGS). This leaves you a total for labor plus all the expenses of running your operation.

Next you simply divide that by the hours worked by technicians. For example, let's say your cost of operations minus COGS is $200,000 and you have three fulltime technicians who have to produce all the labor to make that happen. They each work roughly 2080 hours per year. Times three = 6,240.

Now calculate the $200,000 cost of operations divided by 6,240 = $32 per hour.

3. The Complete Method. Finally, there's the Complete Method for calculating labor costs. This involves looking up several numbers.

You'll come up with a table that looks something like the table on the next page.

Note: Obviously these numbers are "made up" from some general calculations based on our industry.

When you choose to calculate the "Complete Method" you will need to go figure out *your* cost for rent, *your* cost for workers comp, etc.

Our experience has been that the more complete calculations of cost per employee or cost per hour of labor are lower numbers than the "quicker" methods. But, surprisingly, they're still in the ballpark.

The Final Labor Calculation has to do with your PSA (professional services administration) tool.

Here you need to figure out how much of the total labor available to you is actually billed out to clients. Consider, time spent

- Meetings
- Trainings
- Re-work
- Driving time
- Managing others
- Time spent in excess of estimates

Some companies get 1800 hours of billable labor from a technician in a year. Some get 1500. You need to know your number!

Note that lower-level technicians will have more billable hours than higher-level technicians. Our experience has been that lower-level technicians top out around 75-80% billable.

Managers might be only 10-15% billable. High-level technicians will tend to be in the 50-60% range.

Your PSA system should be able to generate a quick report that presents truly billable hours separated from all other hours.

Labor Cost Calculator

		Annual Cost
Base pay rate:	$20	
Hours worked per year:	2080	$ 41,600
Overtime hours worked per year:	100	$ 3,000
- Factor for overtime (e.g., 1.5 x base rate)	1.5	
Vacation		$ -
Holidays		$ -
Employer's Contributions:		$ -
FICA	6.20%	$ 2,765
Medicare	1.45%	$ 647
Federal Unemployment		$ 434
State Unemployment	1.00%	$ 446
Workmen's Compensation	7.00%	$ 3,122
Health Insurance		$ 2,000
Liability Insurance		$ 300
Uniforms		$ -
Tools and Supplies		$ 500
Training		$ 500
Fair Share of Office Supplies		$ 500
Computers and Equipment		$ 500
Fair Share of Operating Expenses		$ 500
Other		$ -
Total of All costs:		$ 56,814
Calculate Total Annual Cost÷ Total Hours worked:	=	$ 26.06

Warning #1: Make sure you check, verify, and trust the numbers coming from your PSA system. Some systems report billable, non-billable, managed service, and other labor in very convoluted ways. And then they round everything to even hours, so your average tech appears to work 5,000 hours year.

Make sure your tool is giving you accurate information before you make any major decisions based on it! Some systems are so bad at reporting numbers that there are third-party companies selling reporting tools so you can get accurate numbers from your PSA system.

Warning #2: Take this seriously and do not use casual calculations. At conferences we've heard people say that everyone on their team is 80% billable. That simply can't be true.

You need to calculate a real number that truly represents the bill-ability of your team. If you don't get this number right, then none of your profitability estimates will be right.

So what's the Final Calculation?

The final labor calculation is to multiply your labor estimate by the actual rate at which you can bill labor. Here's what we mean:

Let's say you have a technician who is 70% billable. And let's say that his true cost per hour is about $30, based on the Super-Fast Method above.

So you'll have to pay this technician for about 1.43 times as many hours as you can bill the client. In other words, ten hours of billable labor to the client will cost you 14.3 hours of labor to produce.

The true cost to provide an hour of labor from this technician is $30 x 1.43 = $42.90.

Now for the bad news.

Let's say you have a senior tech who is 50% billable and has a fully burdened labor rate of $50 per hour. For every hour you bill the client for this person, you have to pay her two hours.

The true cost to provide an hour of labor from this senior technician is $50 x 2.0 = $100.00.

You might have one round number for your team as a whole, knowing that some mix of hours will average a certain rate. Again, that knowledge comes from experience and documenting your experience.

Once again, let us remind you that your PSA system is an invaluable tool if you put the information into it in a manner that will allow you to get good reports out of it.

Check Point

Okay, here's where we are in the quoting process. You've defined the old network and the new network. From this you'll put together a list of things you need to sell the client.

You also have some vague idea of what it will cost. The labor estimate is based primarily on your experience.

The keys to making sure you can complete this job profitably are to *know as much as you can* and to make sure the client knows that your *labor estimates are estimates.*

If you get in the middle of a migration and the client comes up with a mission critical database that can't have downtime, you will have to make clear that all associated labor is outside the scope of the project.

Two Quotes

Now let's look at the actual quote. We've generated some Excel spreadsheets so you can play with them. These two Quotes are included as the last two pages of this chapter. Review them as we go through them.

One of the quotes is marked "internal use." The other is the actual quote that's given to the client.

(Note: The Excel spreadsheets for these quotes are on the web site for this book. See the Appendix for more information.)

As you can see, we divide the migration project into seven different categories and we create six or seven service requests in our ticketing system (two of the SRs are for training, so they can be combined). So they will literally say "Joe Blow Auto Sales Migration Project" and the first one is training. The second one will say "Joe Blow Auto Sales Server Build." And so forth. The first item and the sixth item are "training."

We have some pretty standard PowerPoint slide decks that we use. They're included on the web site as well. The first one covers an introduction to the process.

We get all the client's employees together and give them a heads up about what's going to happen. Knowledge reduces fear and resistance. It also introduces our team and our process to their team.

The second training is basically a "morning of" introduction to what exactly is going on as we move from the old server/system to the new server/system. At this point, the questions are pretty specific about how to collect email, how to connect remotely, etc. These may be accompanied by handouts describing the new network (e.g., collecting your email on the web).

The second item is an actual discovery process!

If this were not our client, and we are more or less coming in blind, we would probably put in three or four hours for the discovery process. But if we're managing the client's computers, we simply need to ask "is there anything I don't know that's not in the PSA system?"

The third item is the server build. This includes everything from opening the box to installing the RAID controller, installing the operating system, and everything needed to prep the machine for the client's use. We have a standard 10 hour build for an SBS server.

The fourth item is the network migration. This includes moving all the data, databases, etc. It normally includes getting old printers off the old server and onto a configuration we prefer. It includes reconfiguring the firewalls, network scanners, and anything else that touches the Ethernet.

If email is moving in-house, or to a spam filter, or moving out-of-house, it may also be included in this process. As a general rule, however, we like to separate such things so that they are two distinct projects and each has a definitive ending point.

The fifth item is the workstation migration. This includes all the work needed to get users and their data off the old system and onto the new. In this example, we have seven and a half hours for workstation migration. This is based on .75 hours per workstation. If they have a lot of old equipment it might go up.

And the seventh item? Did you spot it? It's the cleanup buffer. We add a buffer at the bottom just to make sure we're okay. Again, this is what we do internally. The client never sees this.

We all know how big projects are. Stuff happens. But we don't call it "stuff" and we don't call it "fallout." Think about it this way: You know something's going to go wrong. You don't know what it is right now, but something will go wrong. You also know that you'll find it, you'll fix it, and everything will be just fine. It might be your team's fault. Or it might be a piece of equipment that shipped with a broken part.

It doesn't matter.

Something will go wrong. You'll fix it.

You also know that there's a certain amount of overhead to running a project. In contracts with state agencies, they actually have a line of 10% or 15% for contract management. They recognize that that's the reality of running a project. We don't normally get to do that in the SMB space. So you need some buffer. We start with 10% and tweak it up or down to come up with a nice round number.

In our example here, we have a total of 26 hours with a buffer of three. That's 29 total and we'll quote 30 to the client.

Approval Process

Remember the discussion of the sales roles? The sales person is putting together this estimate. And then the sales person has to get approval of these estimates from the sales engineer.

You could, theoretically, set all these numbers to zero and make the sales engineer fill them in, but there's no real point to that. You should begin with estimates based on past jobs and let the sales engineer adjust the numbers based what the technical department knows about the clients, the operating system, the hardware, and the software.

Your process may vary. In fact, if you're not running *our company*, your process *will* vary. You might take the estimate to the service manager, the sales manager, or even the company president. Basically, you're hoping for an endorsement that it's a good estimate.

Note for growing companies: In the evolution of your company there will likely be a time when the one person who used to be the only person in the company is now primarily doing sales. The more you do sales, the less you deliver services. So, over time, your time estimates will be based less on experience and more on the advice of others.

Our internal rule is that we consider our estimate to be a cap on the number of hours we'll charge. We don't advertise that to the client, but it's what we do. So, we are never going to charge them more than that estimate, but we might charge them less. Why would we do that? As rarely as it happens, it really makes the clients think "Wow, they are good people." It is just not enough money to be worried about. If we are three hours underneath the estimate, we're going to be okay. In reality, we are never going to be ten hours underneath the estimate.

Note also that we put a major emphasis on staying inside the scope of the project. The result is that added work goes into separate service requests and is billed separately. So all the labor inside the Network Migration Project is really just what you'll find on the checklist in this kit. That makes estimation a lot easier, and it makes sticking to the estimate a lot easier.

Details

So, with good estimates and a 10% buffer, we come up with 29 hours for the project. Now move over to the quote that's given to the client. We round 29 to 30 and we remove the item-specific time estimates. We keep the detail about what's included. In fact, we keep the basis for our estimates on the workstations. This does three things.

First, we've given ourselves a pool of thirty hours in which to profitably migrate the network. This gives us a lot of flexibility. So, for example, if the network migration portion only takes two hours but the workstations take an extra three hours, we'll be okay and don't need a change order from the client.

Second, we eliminate nit-picking. We avoid having the client ask why it takes so long to configure a firewall, or migrate a workstation. If one category is too big, a client might ask to just do that piece themselves. We all know that never works out, and rarely saves any money. So we simply lump it all together.

That big number of hours looks pretty reasonable when you've got that those big blocks of text supporting it.

And third, we have left verbiage that gives you a basis for separating out work. For example (and this is the most common example), you find a workstation that's massively infested with viruses and spyware, loaded with data that should be on the server, AND it's five years old.

You're not going to migrate that machine for .75 hours labor. Since you've clearly laid out your criteria, you can go to the client and say that you'll create a service request to clean up that machine on a time and materials basis.

The second most common scenario is that you took the client's word about how many machines there are. And, on the day of migration, the number was way off. If you show up to migrate a 25-user network and face 35 machines, you can scurry over to the boss for either a change order or to create an SR for migrating those ten extra machines.

As you can see, we give the client two prices: One for the hardware and software, and one for the labor. Two dollar amounts. Even if they say, "let's look at that hardware a little more closely," they're not likely to engage in a discussion about specific hardware requires such as drive speed.

We give the client enough detail that they can make a decision, but not so much detail that we get embroiled in a lengthy discussion of the details. They need to trust that they are going to get a great server for a great price and that, three years from now, they are going to say you did the right thing for them. And they'll be ready to do it again!

A Little Focus on Workstation Profile Migrations

Let's look at larger networks for a mini

Please note that the rough estimate of .75, 1.0, or even 1.5 on the workstations should not be done without client feedback on larger networks.

Let's face it: The difference between .75 hours and 1.5 hours on a five-user network is a whopping 3.75 hours. In a 30-hours project, that's very near the margin of error we calculated.

You can be totally wrong about these estimates and still manage to make a profit.

But things are different with larger networks.

On larger networks, you need more information. After all, if you're off .75 hours for thirty desktops, that's more than 22 hours!

If the client is already on a maintenance agreement, you need to have a quick conversation about the three levels of workstation profile migration that can occur.

If the client has not been your client before, you need to spend time with someone who can give you a bit more information about the desktops and make decisions about the level of workstation profile migration for each.

See the form on the next page. You'll see this again as well. This is the "Workstation Profile Migration Level" form.

We don't want to make this too complicated, but you should also consider the age of the machines and the overall complexity of the network.

For example, we had a client one time that had a VERY complicated set of programs on each desktop. Most of the complication had to do with the client's choices and not the software itself. Be that as it may, it took four or five hours to set up a new computer. Migrating to a new network required making all that stuff work again.

Now, if you consider machines that are older, the time is extended considerably.

The point of this whole exercise, of course, is to get a realistic estimate of the time it will take to migrate all the machines to the new network.

In many ways, the time estimates for the server and network don't change much. Even with large data transfers, you'll see that the time required by your technicians doesn't vary much from client to client.

But desktops can kill you.

We have some clients who literally require that we take a screen shot and use it for the background so we can place icons exactly where they belong. And as long as we're making money doing it, that's fine with us!

Form

Workstation Profile Migration Level

Company: ______________________

Form Completed by: ______________________ Date: ______________________

Operating Systems in Use: W7 Vista XP 2000 NT4 98 Other

Office Systems in Use: 2010 2007 2003 XP 2000 97 95 Other

Please note if O.S. is anything other than Professional Edition.

Please note if Office is anything other than a version approved for commercial use.

Profile Migration Levels:

High: All settings, configurations, and "look and feel" will be preserved to the greatest extent possible.

Medium: In addition to the basic migration of the Low option, client will specify certain settings or data requirements.

Low: The machine will look factory-fresh when we are done. All settings will be the Windows or Office defaults. Company-wide drives and printers will be in place. Outlook will connect to the Exchange server. No customized settings will be moved.

Desktop / Machine	User	Operating System	Office Version	Data to Move	Migration Level

Estimated time for "High" Migrations: ______________ each x ______ = __________

Estimated time for "Medium" Migrations: ______________ each x ______ = __________

Estimated time for "Low" Migrations: ______________ each x ______ = __________

Total Hours estimated for desktop migrations: __________

Final Thoughts

This is obviously *our* process for quoting a network migration. Your process may be very different.

Our goals here are three-fold:

1) We want to create a quoting process that is easily replicated from client to client (and from operating system to operating system, for that matter).

2) We want to make sure we're making money on every job. This involves a couple of things. First, we need to know our cost for delivery. Second, we need to have accurate estimates. The dissection of the project into smaller parts helps us achieve both of these.

3) We want to start building a Scope of Project so that we can agree with the client on what's inside the scope of the project. Everything else, of course, is outside the scope.

As we've presented it here, you should be able to start plugging in your numbers and building similar quotes for your own migration projects. If you average 8 or 12 hours to build the server, just plug in those numbers.

Many people take a very different approach to project quotes: They produce a 20-30 page document that outlines why you chose this operating system, why you need RAID 5, etc. These tomes are not read by many clients and are primarily produced to create a thump factor when dropped on the client's desk.

Still, as one reviewer reminded us, analytical types (like CPAs and Engineers) really appreciate the details and want to understand as much as possible.

We prefer the shorter quote you see at the end of this chapter because the entire focus is on the project ahead. Everything fits on a page. Sign here, give us a check, and we're on our way.

As with all other business advice, integrate what works best for you and throw the rest away!

Final Steps / Approved Projects

Once you have a signed quote, your project begins.

In our case, we ask that all hardware and software be prepaid. So once we get a check for that, we create the service requests (six or seven) and order the equipment and software.

At this point, technicians can start working the discovery stage and gathering information.

It is also important that you begin the communication process with the client. When you've ordered the product and created the service requests, send the client an email that states what you've done and assures them that the project is moving along.

It is important to give the client an update at least once a week regarding the status of their project. Early on, they've given you a bunch of money and they don't see anything. You need to keep them confident that you're working on it.

If there are delays, make sure the client knows this. For example, if software hasn't arrived (especially the operating system), you can't really do much. Make sure the client knows that.

The next chapter digs into the big Network Migration Checklist. We'll describe each section and give tips about how to accomplish each task.

Note on PSA Project Management

We will discuss our process for managing the actual migration project in great detail.

If, at this point, you expect us to say that we created a project in the PSA system, you're probably 50% correct.

We create service requests rather than projects. This is a personal preference and you can certainly manage all of this within your PSA system. We will, however, be describing the project in extreme detail as if it were not in a PSA system. This should give you all the detail you need to create and manage your migration from inside your PSA system.

The ZeroDowntimeMigration.com web site associated with this book includes a section for readers to discuss the benefits of using PSA project modules, and a forum for sharing templates you've developed.

The Internal Quote:

	Quote	**Fax to 916-457-2924**		
Client:	**Internal Estimate**	**May 2009**		Notes
		Quote expires	6/30/2009	
Project:	**Server Migration -- 5 desktops**			Key info for pricing.
-- estimate Qty				
1	Staff Training before installation: Introduction to the new system.	$ 150.00	$ 150.00	PowerPoint presentation on what's coming.
1	Estimated Labor for Discovery process: documenting current system, shares, users, etc. Document New system.	$ 150.00	$ 150.00	Varies by network. Current clients, quote less. Larger shops (more pcs, more servers, quote more).
10	Estimated Labor for Server build: Set up server computer; configure SBS; create users, shares; Install and configure backup software, Anti-Virus; configure DHCP, DNS, other services; create shares, etc. Coordinate MAS 90 setup and data transfer. Document and test.	$ 150.00	$ 1,500.00	Always 10 hours per server. LOB transfer may be extra.
5	Estimated Labor for Network Migration: Reconfigure firewalls, printers, routers, and additional equipment as needed. Restore data from tape or otherwise transfer to new system. Note: Extremely large data transfers may add additional time.	$ 150.00	$ 750.00	A good starting place = 5 hours. If you believe (from engineers) that this will be more complicated, add some time.
7.5	Estimated Labor for Workstation Migration: Set up desktop PCs and connect to new server; configure; document everything. Note: this assumes there will only be minor cleanup needed on any machines, that machines are not "too" old, and that they are in reasonable condition.	$ 150.00	$ 1,125.00	Base is .75 hours per PC. For machines older than 24 months, figure 1.5 hours per PC. Round a bit.
1	Staff Training after installation: Becoming familiar with new features.	$ 150.00	$ 150.00	PowerPoint after installation.
26	Sub total	Subtotal	$3,825.00	
3.00	Add 10% buffer for hours for stuff they forgot to tell us.	$ 150.00	$ 450.00	
29	Grand Total	Total	$4,275.00	This number goes on the final quote.
				cost: $80 x hours
	Thank You for asking *KPEnterprises* to bid on this job!			$ 2,280.00

The Client Quote:

	Quote	**Fax to 916-457-2924**	
Client:	**Joe Blow Car Dealership**	**May 2009**	
		Quote expires	6/30/2009
Project:	**Server Migration**		
/are and Software			
Qty			
1	New Server. Includes: **Server - Proliant ML 350 Xeon 2.0 GHz, 4 GB RAM; 3x146 GB hard drives**; Drives configured in RAID 5 (290 GB total usable space); DVD+R/CDRW; Small Business Server 2008 Premium; Diskeeper defragmentation software.		$ 5,459.99
		Sales Tax	$ 423.15
		Total:	$ 5,883.14
	- Staff Training before installation: Introduction to the new system.		
	- Estimated Labor for Discovery process: documenting current system, shares, users, etc. Document New system.		
	- Estimated Labor for Server build: Set up server computer; configure SBS; create users, shares; Install and configure backup software, Anti-Virus; configure DHCP, DNS, other services; create shares, etc. Coordinate MAS 90 install and config. Document and test.		
	- Estimated Labor for Network Migration: Reconfigure firewalls, printers, routers, and additional equipment as needed. Restore data from tape or otherwise transfer to new system. Coordinate MAS 90 data transfer. Note: Extremely large data transfers may add additional time.		
	- Estimated Labor for Workstation Migration: Set up desktop PCs and connect to new server; configure; document everything. Estimate 5 desktops/laptops. NOTE: This is based on machines that are not "too" old and are in reasonable condition.		
	- Staff Training after installation: Becoming familiar with new features.		
		30 hours	$ 4,500.00
	Note: the first three hours of labor will be credited if the server is on a SuperStar I.T. Service Agreement.		
	Thank You for asking *KPEnterprises* to bid on this job!		

The Network Migration Workbook

Overview and Flow

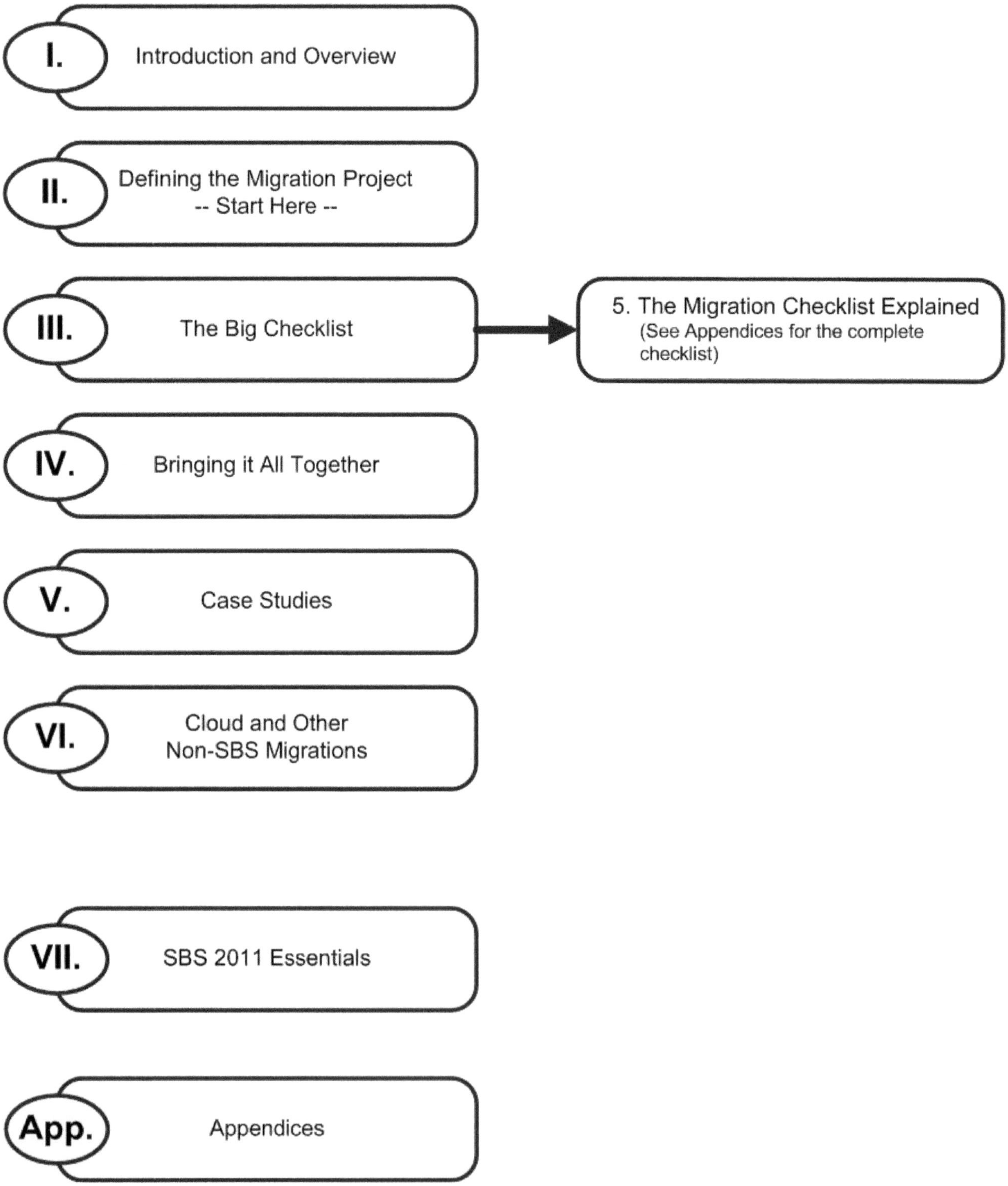

III. The Big Checklist

Chapter 5

The Network Migration Checklist Explained

At long last, we get to The Checklist!

Well, actually, we get to it in the appendices. There we simply present The Checklist. This chapter describes and explains each element of The Checklist.

Chapter Six will talk about strategies in using The Checklist. In the meantime, here's the description of the tool you'll use to execute your excellent Network Migration Project.

We refer here and elsewhere to "The" Checklist or "The Big Checklist." You will certainly customize your own checklist the first time you use it.

The Checklist As A Living Document

We literally consider The Checklist to be a living document. At several points in The Checklist you will find directives to update the documentation, including The Checklist itself.

We were long delayed in releasing this book because The Checklist kept changing. Once SBS 2008 was released, Microsoft released a series of white papers, blog posts, Knowledge Base articles, and other materials.

Then there were updates for various versions of Windows. And updates from third party vendors. And so forth and so on.

At some point we decided to just stop trying to update The Checklist. 99.9% of it remained the same anyway. Most of the documents from Microsoft were clarifying documents.

You should also be very clear about how we built this checklist: It is based on how KPEnterprises migrates networks. We have not made an attempt to include every configuration scenario or every third party vendor.

At the same time, the modular nature of The Checklist means that you can plug in a checklist for configuring your favorite firewall or your favorite anti-virus.

Before we go section by section through The Checklist, we want to cover some of the best practices and core philosophies that we believe make The Checklist useful and valuable. After that we give an overview of how The Checklist is used by the technicians who actually implement migration projects.

But first, let's look at the primary sections of The Checklist. We gave an initial overview in Chapter Three. Now let's go one level deeper.

The Checklist has twenty-seven sections, some of which are very long, and some of which are a single page. It is organized this way so that technicians can treat each section as a stage in the overall migration process. Some stages (such as moving profiles) are just more complicated than others (such as meeting with the client at the end.

Here are the sections for The Checklist:

1. Using This Document
2. Pre-Discovery
3. Project Description and Scope
4. Discovery
5. Planning / Timeline
6. Migration Strategies
7. Resources
8. Communications / Training
9. Old Network Documentation
10. System Build
11. Troubleshooting and Repair Log
12. Network Migration Preparation
13. Network Migration
14. Applications Migration
15. Sub-Systems Migration
16. Workstation Migration
17. Remote Migration
18. Migration Tracking Sheet
19. Shortages
20. Pack-Up / To-Do Checklist
21. Fine Tuning
22. Spin-Off Projects and Issues
23. Project Completion
24. Retrospective and Revision History
25. Project Notes
26. New Network Documentation
27. Index

Each of these sections represents one or more nested checklists.

What The Checklist Is and Isn't

We want to be very clear that this checklist is exactly as we use it within our company to achieve Zero Downtime Migrations. That means it relies on some assumptions about how we operate.

It also means:

- The Checklist is very detailed in some places and very sparse in others.
- Some parts of The Checklist are vendor specific. We left them that way in order to be as complete as possible. We explain how to switch out these sections for your own.
- The Checklist is very modular. If you don't need a section for a specific migration, cross it out. If you have a client with a different firewall, trade out one section for another.
- The 2003 Checklist is essentially "frozen in time" compared to the 2008 Checklist. When we revised processes for 2008, we did not go back and make all the changes to the 2003 Checklist.
- The Checklist does not contain a section for everything you can think of. It couldn't, of course. But it's modular construction allows for easy updates and changes.
- We believe the Pre-Discovery and Discovery processes are quite thorough, but they don't cover everything out there.

  NOTE: Your project success and fine tuning will both be directly proportional to the attention given to the Pre-Discovery and Discovery. If you already know and manage a client's network, the Discovery phases should be easy.
- The Checklist is designed to contain enough information for a trained technician to complete the tasks. Additional information on how to run a project is not included as it would only clutter up a large document.

So, The Checklist is not perfect. Nor is it necessarily complete unless you do migrations exactly as we do.

Best Practices And Core Philosophies

Just like you or any other consultant, we have developed some "best practices" that bring consistency, repeatability, reproducibility, and profit to our migration projects.

While we've scattered our best practices throughout the book, here are a few more key elements to making migrations successful. Please see the illustration entitled *Functional Map: KPE Migration Preferences*, below.

- We feel very strongly that we must control the client's Internet Domain registration, and DNS in particular. This gives us the ability to apply fully qualified domain names (FQDN) to machines on the network, including the SBS box, the Integrated Lights Out (ILO) card, and other machines and devices on the network. We don't want to be at the mercy of an ISP or other vendor.
- We maintain DNS at the domain registrar (Network Solutions or some other) because we don't want to maintain a DNS server, and we need absolute uptime for DNS.
- We insist that clients have Internet service with at least five usable IP addresses. That gives us the ability to connect remotely to the firewall, the server, the ILO, a web-enabled AC power switch, and a second server. We can reconfigure as needed, but we need a lot more functionality than you can get from a single IP.

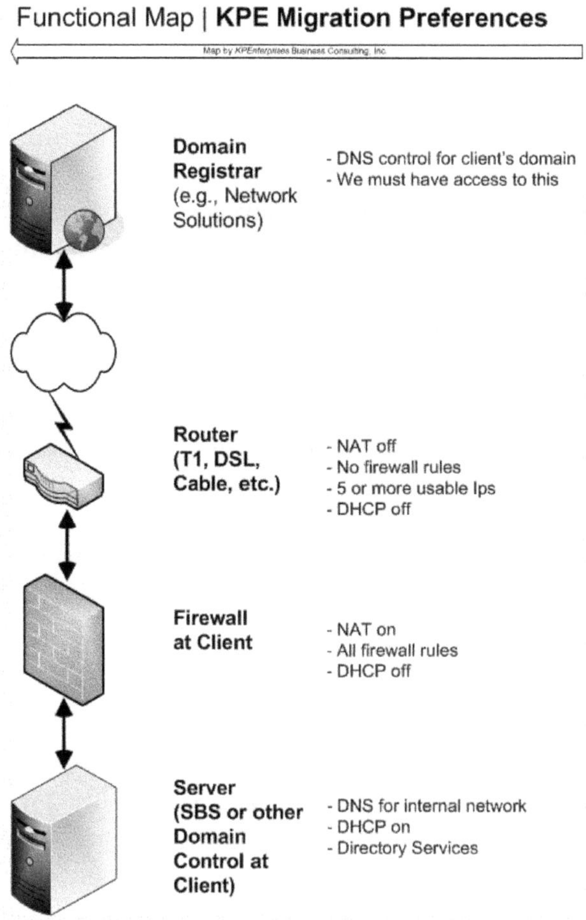

- We make sure the ISP has turned off Network Address Translation (NAT), firewall rules, and DHCP on their router. This allows them to push all the Internet traffic directly to our firewall.

  Again, this gives us complete control and we never have to wait for the ISP to make a change
- We have a standard set of configurations we use on the firewall. We also have a preferred brand, which makes management easier.
- We turn off DHCP on the firewall and turn it on at the server. This is true whether the network is SBS or plain Server 2008.

- We set up printers directly on the network and not in active directory. Today's laser printers have lots of memory and running print jobs through the server just doesn't make sense any more.

  Note: We do not have a checklist for migrating printers because we don't migrate them. Each user's machine is set to print to the closest printer. This is part of the New PC Checklist when we install the machine.
- We use standard, brand name battery backups (UPSs) with no special software. We configure them with the standard power management software that comes with the server operating system.
- And, finally: We use a Microsoft-Centric Approach.

Aside from being control freaks, this configuration allows us to have maximum flexibility during the switchover from one server to another in the migration.

For example, if we have OldServer and NewServer sitting side by side, we will want to access both of them through the Internet. The easiest way to do this is within our own firewall.

And when it's time to make the switch permanent for the rest of the world to see, we can simply make a change in DNS at the domain registrar and the new information will propagate very quickly. (Do this a 5:01 PM and all changes should be effective that night.)

Test Environments

Bench Testing is a Must

We cannot over emphasize the need to bench test all your migration solutions. It's how we got to where we are. It's how we wrote the book and it's how we learn what works best and what does not.

Every tech or engineer worth their salt has some place they test their strategies. We don't really care where it gets done, we just care that it does get done. You have to test these strategies for yourself for so many reasons.

At the very least, it's very common to simply steal a day or two on a new server before it gets built up for delivery. You load your OS and play with the new features and then burn it down and load the OS it's going to get delivered with. Other options are a junk box that has been beefed up and repurposed. For an entire network migration simulation it's a little more resource dependent but completely doable since this is the industry we're in and there are always resources available in one form or another.

The prime obstacle is that it is very hard to master something you've never seen work before. There is also simulating old migrations to see where things went wrong or to help develop tomorrow's strategies to ensure things go right. And we're not just talking about our Strategies for Zero Downtime Migration, although some may need to be *seen* to be clearly *understood* and mastered. One such strategy is the SQL DB migration. It's really not for the faint of heart if you've never so much as dismounted a database and copied it to a new server for remount.

What if you want to use your own revised version of one of our methods? How will you hammer it out without waiting for a live migration to experiment on? That's a practice we would never condone.

There are plenty of answers to this question and none are secret but many are not given the proper time, energy or effort required to become an integral part of your company's research and development practices.

Our Test Environments

We started with the environments we used in the writing of this book. What is detailed below is by no means the extent of our testing of the SBS products covered in this book. That would take an entire chapter or more with no problem.

Initial testing of the OS load and product features of Small Business Server 2011 was done by Manuel in late 2010 on his personal pc. Now his personal PC happens to be a Gigabyte motherboard with an i5 750 processor, 12GB memory and four 1TB SATA drives in a hardware RAID 5 configuration. Actually he loaded up four 250GB SATA drives so I would not have to alter his personal OS any. Then he just selected the desired system on boot. Since the work was being done from a remote location with no Internet connectivity (on his vacation) he used his Sprint Cube and his laptop to simulate an ISP environment. It was slow for downloading the SBS updates but it worked.

The next steps were to start building a physical environment for the migration testing not just playing with the server OS and its features. For this you need some resources whether physical or virtual. Karl focused primarily on the SBS Essentials in his West Coast office while Manuel focused on the SBS Standard product in the East Coast offices.

As the opportunity arose, we took advantage of new server installs to steal some time on brand new machines as described earlier. Manuel wrote the SBS OS load using the HP SmartStart CD section over the course of about six weeks using (among others) an HP Proliant DL 360 G7 with 12GB memory, Triple 300 GB SATA drives, Quad NIC's, and ILO capability.

We don't need new servers for all of our testing but we do need them for initial build testing and timing. We can't detail an HP OS load using SmartStart on a VM, Dell or older HP. We also need to verify the BIOS checklist and that is only available on the new servers. It should be noted that the HP SmartStart load checklist took over six weeks because on the first run (in February 2011) we found out that HP had not yet released their SmartStart CD to support a load up of SBS 2011. It finally showed up in March.

Manuel built out two complete test environments. One physical and one virtual and both environments with their distinct advantages. The physical environment is actually a hybrid in that the workstations are all virtual pc's running on a single beefy server.

The Physical Environment

The physical environment has the benefits of quick access to any CD or DVD for loading, its capable of an HP SmartStart, hands on to production brand Firewall (Sonicwall TZ180), Access to lots of hardware requiring testing such as tape drives, external drives, printers, Fax card, UPS, USB Key, RAID controllers, etc.

The physical environment was built using nothing but quality repurposed equipment. We say quality because we did not use no name PCs as servers. We already had most of the resources available (because this is what we do) and we spent some cash on parts and pieces to get the environment up to spec for the task. The harsh truth is that Manuel had to have one of his favorite servers shipped to Florida from California to build the environment. Then he had to scrounge up a new Fax modem that was supported by SBS 2011 and even memory to get the Destination server up to the Microsoft spec'ed 12GB for SBS 2011.

We settled for nothing less than what we needed which was a minimum requirement test environment for a modest budget of under $500 (including shipping).

Physical Environment:

Server 2008 - Virtual Workstation Server

- Hosting: 3 of each XP Pro, Vista and Windows 7. One each with Office 2003, 2007, 2010.
- XP Pro: 768mb RAM, 25GB HDD.
  Vista: 1GB RAM, 35GB HDD.
  Windows 7: 2GB RAM, 40GB HDD.
- Dell PowerEdge 1800, Dual 2.8 GHz Xeon Processors, 8GB Memory, 240GB SATA RAID 5 (5 x 80GB)
- 250GB internal SATA Drive for Backups

SBS 2003 and 2008 Source Server

- HP ML350 G4, Dual 3.0 GHz Xeon Processors, 8GB Memory, 291GB SCSI RAID 5+1 (6 x 72.8GB)
- 250GB internal SATA Drive for Backups
- HP DAT 72 Tape Drive with SCSI Controller
- US Robotics FAX modem

SBS 2011 Destination Server

- HP ML350 G4p, Dual 3.0 GHz Xeon Processors, 12GB Memory, 440GB SCSI RAID 5+1 (5 x 146.8GB)
- 250GB SATA Drive for Backups.
- HP DAT 160 Tape Drive with SCSI Controller
- US Robotics FAX modem

The Virtual Environments

The virtual environment has the advantage of unlimited machines, unlimited resources for each machine, fast spin up and cloning for testing different environment. The biggest benefits of having set up the virtual test environment is the ability present a complete migration test bed for any server combination to any other combination in very short order to anywhere in the world. And we can duplicate the entire environment. This environment is not limited to Small Business Server.

We selected Artisan Infrastructure (see www.artisaninfrastructure.com) to host our test environment for several reasons. For the first three reasons it is easiest to simply quote their own tag line:

Wholesale Only Infrastructure

for Cloud Solution Providers

Enterprise grade

On-Demand Platform ...

The key words here are Wholesale Only, Enterprise Grade, and On-Demand. Everything we want in a virtual infrastructure solution provider!

They are not going to try to sign up our clients for their reoccurring solution. It is the quality of product we believe any business intending to stay in business should seek out. It's infinitely scalable.

With minimal help from the back end support, we were able to spin up our software firewall and complete test environment for the re-write of the *Network Migration Workbook*. The best part about the virtual environment we were able to set up is that it takes up no space in our co-location facility, home office, east coast office, or west coast office. We downloaded the virtual hard drives (VHDs) for backup and it is available at a moment's notice, including spinning up almost any additional standard servers in just minutes.

Virtual Environment:

Virtual Workstations

- 3 of each XP Pro, Vista and Windows 7. One each with Office 2003, 2007, 2010.
- All machines are 2GB memory and 50GB HDD

SBS 2003 Source Server

- 2 processors, 4GB memory, 100GB IDE drives

SBS 2008 Source Server

- 2 processors, 8GB memory, 150GB SCSI drives

SBS 2011 Destination Server

- 4 processors, 16GB memory, 250GB SCSI drives

Your Test Environments

Many small companies have no resources to devote to a test bench let alone to simulate an entire network migration environment. They have no choice but to take their opportunities where they see them and do a quick SBS 2011 load on a new server before it goes out as something else. Otherwise they won't even touch the new product until shortly after their first sales.

But our industry is changing faster that most technicians and engineers can see. With the big push to the cloud, the truth is you may soon have more used hardware on your back loading dock that ever before. In some aspects processing time is getting cheaper but getting the right configuration to support your test environment as needed will still be a chore.

We say, do what you can where you can. Borrow a box or rent a box if you have to. Testing your strategies is absolutely critical to your ability to provide repeatable and reproducible solutions. Some technicians, engineers and companies have either participated in or hosted the good old install or load parties where someone brings in a suitable box and everyone gets to see the new "thing" in action and actually click here and there. Get with a partner company a client who has spare resources, or just get organized enough to use the free trial time on a cloud providers machines.

All we care is that you test everything!

Here's one more best practice:

A Good Rule

Use a Troubleshooting and Repair Log

One of the most valuable practices you can adopt is to use a TSR – Troubleshooting and Repair – log for specific procedures and for whenever you find yourself in "troubleshooting" mode on anything.

You'll find an example of a TSR Log in The Checklist. Basically, it is a lined piece of paper with a place for you to enter time stamps at fifteen minutes intervals, or as needed.

We always use a TSR Log when we are building a server. That way, if anything goes wrong, you'll be able to document exactly what happened and where it happened in the process. This is very handy if you find yourself rebuilding that server from scratch someday. You're going to hit the same snag and it will be very handy to have quick access to the solution.

A TSR Log helps you keep very accurate information about how long it actually takes to build a server. This number will change over time (see the discussion in Chapter Four) as you gain experience and Microsoft releases updates. But even though this is a bit of a moving target, the more accurate your information, the more profitable you can make your next migration!

The TSR Log evolved from our standard procedures for troubleshooting any problem that comes up. We keep very accurate records for several reasons.

First, we need to make sure that we're not continually performing the same "fixes" again and again. If you keep track of what you've tried, in a systematic manner, you can eliminate causes for whatever problem you're troubleshooting.

Second, when someone comes to help you (a team member, an outside consultant, or a vendor), you can relay exactly what you have and have not tried. Sometimes vendors insist on going over the same ground, but you can stop them from going over the same ground more than once!

Excellent records about what you've done can also help you get a problem escalated more quickly (sometimes).

Third, when you need to go over a problem with a client, you will have excellent records about what you did, what you didn't do, who was involved, and how long it took. This is all good information.

Whether it's a server build or some kind of troubleshooting, a TSR Log will serve you well. We ask our technicians to carry one printed out and ready to go at all times. We require them to use a TSR Log whenever they have been "stuck" on a problem for any amount of time.

For the server build, you will probably only have regular fifteen minute notes that say something like "setup continues" or "install complete." You don't need to detail when things are going right. But don't forget the details when things go wrong.

And finally: A TSR Log on the build and migration will help update your checklists for everything you need to change.

A Note About Microsoft-Centric Habits

As you will see in The Checklist, we have a bias for Microsoft-centric tools and techniques. That means we prefer to use a Microsoft tool or Microsoft procedure if it will do the job.

Notice that "if" qualifier. In our opinion, for example, Microsoft's NT Backup product has some excellent uses. But it not a product we would recommend system wide in a mission critical environment.

If we have choices of tools (e.g., Robocopy for synchronizing files and folders across servers), we'll choose the Microsoft product whenever it proves to be a good choice.

Why be Microsoft-Centric?

As a rule, the systems we support and sell are Windows server, loaded with Microsoft Office, Microsoft Exchange Server, Microsoft SQL Server, and other Microsoft products.

Even though Microsoft does not have support for their minor utilities, our experience is that they are very reliable.

Some of these utilities are shipped with various operating systems. They are in resource directories on the CD/DVD or distributed in the Resource Kits. Others are squirreled away on the Microsoft site.

Relying on Microsoft tools allows us to add a layer of consistency to our procedures over time. Many of the tools we've been using predate SBS 2003.

Consistency contributes to profitability.

So, what about Microsoft's procedure for migrating to SBS 2008 or 2011?

We have two responses. First, their procedure includes downtime and requires you to perform some critical work during that downtime. That means that you don't really have control over how long you'll be down. Second, their procedure does not give you a clean Active Directory.

In addition, the new profile tool built into SBS 2011 is intended to move profiles from a local or workgroup environment and not a domain environment. Huh? Yes. If you already have a domain, that tool is not intended for your use.

If you have a very large or complicated network and want to use a tool to clean the active directory and then migrate it without running around to each desktop, we recommend Jeff Middleton's Swing Migration. But don't forget: You still need a migration project binder and a plan. See www.sbsmigration.com.

Checklist Management

We started out this chapter referring to The Checklist as a living document. It lives because you feed it and take care of it.

To acquire your copy of the template printed in the Appendix of this book, you'll need to register this book and obtain credentials for the ZeroDowntimeMigration.com web site.

Place a copy of the template in a folder or on you SharePoint site so that everyone who needs access to it can get it.

Because The Checklist is based on the best practices of KPEnterprises, you might find some sections that you do not use. You will probably find some sections that refer to products by brand name and you'll want to create your own checklist for the brand you sell.

And, finally, you might find that you have a product or procedure that we have not addressed at all. You'll need to create your own procedure-specific checklist and figure out where it goes in the project.

You'll want to customize *our* checklist to create *your* "template" checklist. Don't customize too much or make the list universal. It is better to have too much in The Checklist and cross it out for a specific job than to have to go re-create it when the time comes.

When you begin a new migration project, you'll open this template and save it with a new name (and perhaps a client-specific location). Then you'll print out The Checklist for the new job. After doing the discovery, you'll customize The Checklist for this specific job and proceed from there.

Important safety tip: Do not edit your template for each job. Make a copy and edit the copy. At the end of each migration there's a call to update The Checklist template if necessary. That's the only time you should revamp your master template.

If you maintain a variety of brands (for example, two different firewalls), you may wish to separate out the vendor-specific portion of The Checklist and insert the appropriate pages into The Checklist for each client.

If you create these "plug-in checklists" make sure that they cover the relevant sections for Pre-Discovery, Discovery, Installation, Migration, etc. This can be a bit messy, however, as you'll need to insert each of these into the appropriate section of The Big Checklist.

You can see how you save money by standardizing your product offerings as much as possible.

Note: Please see the Focus Section in Chapter Six on *Building Custom Checklists*.

Now, let's put together your Big Checklist.

Build the Binder

We are no longer providing a preferred label template for the binder. Find a tabbing system that works for you. Use a series of tabs to build your binder. There is an old template for printing the Avery label tabs that we recommended in the first edition. See the zerodowntimemigration.com web site to access this template.

Note: Please don't get caught up worrying about the specific tabs we have a template for. There are lots of tab systems you can buy, some of which just stick over the edge of a regular page. If you need to, just use a label maker and cut up file folders to make your tabs. If you can find 5- or 10-tab file folders, that would be more convenient than 3-tab. Go to your office supply store and look at what they offer.

The tabs are very important for accessing the document once the migration begins. You will be able to re-use the tabs again and again.

For now, create the tabs, print The Checklist, and build the binder. We use a 3-ring "clear view" binder so we can print out a page with the client's name and put it on the front of the binder.

We recommend that you use a 1.5" or 2" binder. On rare occasions you'll need to move to a larger binder. Again, you'll re-use these binders. You should have one on the shelf and one for each current migration project. With luck, you'll need a lot of binders! Start with a minimum of three.

A Good Rule

Continuum (Zenith Infotech) is a "Best Practice"

You will note that we mention Continuum – formerly Zenith Infotech – from time to time in our procedures. See www.continuum.net.

Continuum is our outsourced "back office" network operations center. We call on them to perform key functions in the maintenance of client systems.

This comes into play during a network migration in several ways. First, there are certain "maintenance" functions that are key to a successful migration. For example, clean, virus-free desktops are essential.

Second, if we hit a snag in building the new systems, we can all on Continuum to assist in troubleshooting. This is particularly helpful if we find ourselves with a Blue Screen while building up a new server. It's obviously a driver, but which one? Continuum has a whole bunch of people who just examine memory dumps. They can usually find the culprit a lot faster than we can.

Third, in some cases Continuum will perform specific tasks after hours. When it's night over here, it's day over there.

If you use someone other than Continuum for your back office support, simply do a search for "Continuum" in the checklist document and replace with your preferred solution.

Note: This is not a paid ad or endorsement. We just love Continuum.

TIP: The cheapest good-quality binders we've found are from Sam's Club. They're about 30% of what you'll pay at the big office supply stores.

Specific instructions for building the binder are included in The Checklist.

Next we'll go through The Checklist section by section.

Note: We recommend that you go ahead and print out a copy of The Checklist to have on hand as you go through this.

The Big Checklist, Section by Section

Front Matter

Fill in the appropriate in formation and print out your cover sheet. This will go in the front of the "view binder" for your Network Documentation Binder or NDB.

When you're finished with the binder, you'll take all the pages out and staple them together with this on the front.

The Table of Contents goes in the front of the binder and serves an obvious purpose. Be sure to update the table after you make changes to The Checklist and before you print it out. To do this in Microsoft Word just right-click inside the table of contents and select Update Field.

Section 1: Using This Document

This section describes how The Checklist is used to manage the migration project. It also describes how you construct the binder with tabs.

Note that the binder tabs can be printed from Microsoft Word. The Word document for this is downloadable from the ZeroDowntimeMigration.com web site for registered owners.

Section 2: Pre-Discovery

Pre-Discovery is the collection of information you'll need to get the client a reasonably accurate quote for hardware, software and labor. See Chapter Four. The project manager will use this information to write the project description and scope.

Once the Pre-Discovery has been completed, the Project Manager and the sales person need to agree on what to recommend for the client.

This process can never be perfect, but the more complete and accurate it is, the more successful and profitable the project will be.

A client interview will be extremely handy at this stage. Even if you think you know the answer, you should ask the client how much downtime they can tolerate. In particular, which subsystems are critical and cannot have downtime?

One of the key things you'll need to learn from the client is the level of profile migration they want. See the *Focus on Profiles* section below for more details.

Section 3: Project Description and Scope

We have provided some very standard descriptions for the project description and project scope of work. Please do not accept these exactly as written unless you really defined your migrations that way.

Again, we refer you to Chapter Four. These descriptions here and in the quote to the client should either be identical, or very close.

We do not put a massive amount of detail in the quote, so any level of detail you need should be here. This is also the place to put notes about special requirements or companion projects.

Section 4: Discovery

It is assumed that most network and system information has been be recorded in a central location such as a Network Documentation Binder (NDB) of some sort. If there is no formal NDB, the forms found in the *New Network Documentation* section of this binder can be readily be copied and used to record information for the Discovery.

You will also get some information from the Pre-Discovery process and the Project Scope.

For example, what is the desired RAID configuration of the hard drives?

The Discovery process should always be done by a senior level technician. As you go through the process, keep notes about how you will approach the project. These will be useful when you get to the strategy section.

If for whatever reason you come across something that will change the Project Description or Project Scope, this should be discussed by the Project Manager and Sales Rep. If necessary, the client may need to be informed that there is a change, and you may end up changing the quote for the migration project.

Even minor changes to the Project Description or Project Scope should be initialed.

In most cases, changes will be minor and can be dealt with by explaining to the client that you're going to create a service request separate from the migration project. You'll obviously need to give an estimate of hours required.

You might notice that there are some things we *don't* ask about in the Discovery section. These tend to be areas that will be unique to the new system and therefore the configuration on the old system is not relevant.

For example, the configuration of the backup software is not covered. It is very common that the old backup software was never upgraded during the three year lifetime of the server and that the new server will be getting the latest version.

While these items should be documented in the Network Documentation Binder, there is no need to bring that information forward to the Migration Binder.

Note also that there are some great documentation forms built into the Discovery section. You may wish to copy these out to your regular NDB for all clients.

Section 5: Planning / Timeline

* This is a critical section.

The Planning and Timeline section contains the Master checklists for the entire project. There are only four subsections but each one is critical to the success of the entire project.

Pay close attention to the Timeline checklists as they contain all the checks for critical emails to the Client Technical Contact informing them of dates, upcoming changes and progress.

When you first review this section, you may get a headache. This is the part where entry level technicians become overwhelmed. Just remember that you're taking this one click at a time. Go slowly and carefully.

One the Project Manager had gone through section, he will have an excellent working knowledge of the details of this particular migration.

Note that the *Migration Strategy* subsection here includes day-by-day details of "the basic" migration project. You will also find a couple of different calendars here to help you organize each migration project.

Section 6: Migration Strategies

This section gives a summary of the time-tested strategies we use for moving specific components during network migrations.

The order of the subsections here closely follows the order of the Migration checklist.

If you haven't already worked through a network migration as described in this book, you will probably find this section to be very informative regarding the options available to you.

We do not list every possible way you could accomplish these tasks – just the ways that we believe work the best.

Section 7: Resources

This section is like the million dollar reference guide to Windows Migration Strategies.

We considered moving it to the appendices, but that would only save us a dozen pages (it would be printed once there instead of once in each checklist).

But the truth is that these million dollar resources should be inside your Network Migration Binder so they are instantly available to your technicians.

One of the most important resources is called My Favorite Whitepapers. You probably already have something similar to this for your company. We store the "live" version of this up on our internal technician SharePoint site.

My Favorite Whitepapers lists they key Knowledge Base articles and other information that we need in order to progress through a successful migration.

The version you download after registering this book has live links. We will also attempt to keep this updated on the secure web site for registered owners at www.ZeroDowntimeMigration.com.

The hard part with a resource like this is to keep it from getting bloated.

This subsection also includes scripts, batch files, and the important information you'll need for Robocopy, one of the important tools we use.

After that we give information and command switches for the Microsoft User State Migration Tool.

And there's a bunch more here.

This really is a valuable resource. Before the book was published, Karl was offered $200 for just this section of the checklist!

Section 8: Communications / Training

This section contains email templates for communicating with your client during the migration. These include specific milestones as well as regular weekly status reports.

We cannot emphasize enough the value of over-freakin' communicating! This piece of project management is often overlooked and leaves the client feeling lost. The client needs input about his project!

We have also created a "starter" FAQ for the migration process. You may wish to share this with your technicians and clients.

Section 9: Old Network Documentation

This is where you place the actual, physical copies of the documentation from the old Network Documentation Binder.

If you are using Karl's classic *Network Documentation Workbook* (available at www.smbbooks.com), we thank you for that. If not, use what you have or print configuration pages from your PSA system.

We have provided a list of the documents you'll need. The titles are from Karl's *Network Documentation Workbook*.

Section 10: System Build

Okay. *Finally* we get to the part that technicians think of when they start a migration: Building the actual server.

From this point forward all new documentation for any aspect of this system should be recorded on the forms found in the New Network Documentation section of the binder (see the last several pages of The Checklist).

All additional documentation acquired during the system build (e.g., information on access the ILO card) should also be inserted into the New Network Documentation section of the binder.

The goal is to end up with all documentation related to the new system up-to-date and in one place.

Section 11: Troubleshooting and Repair Log

This is the form for the TSR Log discussed earlier in this chapter.

You will need one TSR Log for the system build and one for ANY problem that takes more than thirty (30) minutes to troubleshoot. Once you hit the 30th minutes, you need to print out a TSR Log and be meticulous about keeping it up to date.

Section 12: Network Migration Preparation

This section covers the details you need to be aware of as you get ready to start flipping switches and moving functions.

We cover everything from the air conditioning to the physical location of the servers (old and new) during the transition process.

In addition to simply checking that things are ready, you will also make some changes to make sure the Internet domain registration, DNS, firewall, etc. are all configured according to the preferred methods discussed earlier in this chapter.

Section 13: Network Migration

* This is a critical section.

Although extensive planning is put into the migration strategy and the checklist order, the actual migration is a dynamic process of completing all required tasks in the most appropriate and efficient order possible based on all the elements presented on migration day.

If you need to run a utility such as Robocopy, we recommend running it on the new server because it will start out the day with essentially no load and it will certainly have more power and resources than the older server, even after the migration.

This is it.

Here you will actually start moving functions and live data to the new server. Exchange, SQL, everything. We give you all the details, click by click for more than 35 pages.

Section 14: Applications Migration

This section covers strategies for Line of Business (LOB) applications.

For basic SQL (or other database) migration, we refer you to the previous section. For details specific to a given LOB vendor, you will need to contact that vendor. At thing point you should have already gone through a migration to the new server with old data.

You documented that process and inserted it into this section of the Migration Binder. Now you need to use that documentation to do the final migration with live data.

This is also where you'll install SSL certificates, Blackberry servers, and any other applications that run on the server.

Section 15: Sub-Systems Migration

This section covers all the various systems that are not part of the server itself. These include the firewall, printers, routers, VPNs, network scanners, and so forth.

Some of these things will not be affected by your migration. If so, great. But if they are affected, you will document each procedure and configuration and insert them here.

Documentation goes into the new documentation section, of course.

Section 16: Workstation Migration

This section addresses what can be a very labor intensive chore of migrating user profiles and workstations.

It can also be easy if you do your homework and you have a checklist – and a plan!

In the average Network Migration, the majority of labor will be related to cleaning up and migrating user profiles. This is particularly true if you have not been managing the client since their last server was installed.

If you *have* been managing the client, then you should have a good idea of the policies, procedures, and data storage habits in the office. Otherwise, you'll need to do a very thorough discovery to make sure you understand what you've got on all those desktops.

Profiles get very messy for a number of reasons. One is that the users are human. A second is that the users are not technicians. So they figure out how to make something work, but they might be doing it in a manner that clogs up their workstation while keeping data in a location that's not part of the company backup plan.

Please see the section *Focus on Profiles* below.

Section 17: Remote Migration

This section covers the tasks involved in moving remote users to the new system. This includes Remove Web Workplace, Exchange access, VPN, and various devices such as phones.

Section 18: Migration Tracking Sheet

This is a simple form to keep track of what "Level" of migration each user is and where that user's workstation is in the migration process.

On levels of profile migration, please see the section *Focus on Profiles* below.

Section 19: Shortages

This is a place to keep track of any shortages that occur at any point in the migration process. These might be missing DVDs, software, or whatever.

List each shortage here, check back frequently, and make sure nothing is ever forgotten.

Section 20: Pack-Up / To-Do Checklist

This is your packing list for when you actually take everything on site to the client's office.

You may have some items drop shipped to the client and other items built up at your office. Whatever you'll need on site should be on this list.

Section 21: Fine Tuning

This section lists the items that are clearly within the scope of the migration project, but not quite perfect. You must have a place to list every single outstanding issue so that nothing is ever lost or forgotten. This is that place.

For example, in the course of your migration you might have three desktops that get an error with an LOB on the server. Write it down here and make sure to check back.

Section 22: Spin-Off Projects and Issues

This section is for new items that come up during the migration project but do not appear to be part of the migration project.

You must list every such item here. Eventually each of these items will have one of three resolutions:

1. It is extremely minor and was or will be included in the scope of the project.
2. It is made irrelevant by the migration project (fixed by something that was inside the scope of work).
3. It is determined to be outside the scope of work. A separate service request is created so work can be logged against it (outside the scope of the migration project).

As we discussed in earlier chapters, you will need to meet with the client to go over these issues and determine which ones the client is willing to pay for outside the scope of the migration project.

Section 23: Project Completion

The Project Completion is simply the official wrap up of the migration project itself, a double check of all checklists, and some tasks related to editing of the document to keep it up to date.

This section has a call-out to the next section. After all evaluations are complete, you come back here for instructions on finishing the paperwork, recycling the tabs and binder, and preparing for the next migration.

Section 24: Retrospective and Revision History

This section covers the basic steps in getting feedback on the project and the process. It is critically important that you evaluate these with each migration project so that the overall process can improve with each project.

Section 25: Project Notes

A place to keep notes on whatever you want.

Section 26: New Network Documentation

This section includes a sample network map and all the new Network Documentation forms. Some of these are newer versions of the forms used in *The Network Documentation Workbook* (mentioned earlier). There are also several new forms here that are specifically relevant to the migration process.

One of the most useful new forms is the Network Timing Diagram. You use this to keep track of when events are scheduled on the network. These include backups, virus scanning, batch jobs, etc.

Section 27: Index to the Network Migration Project

If you use the "live" version of the checklist, this index will be updated automatically. The "print ready" version has an orphaned index. In other words, it's just text and not linked to sections, so it won't be updated if you change things.

Profiles and Exchange

This chapter concludes with two special focus sections. Two of the most important pieces of a successful migration are User Profiles and Exchange mailboxes.

Focus on Profiles

One of the most important pieces of any migration project is the movement of profiles to the new systems. In addition to being very time-consuming, the user profiles are literally the domain users' window into their computing world.

Exactly what is a profile?

A Windows profile is the collection of settings and files that make up the user's entire experience on the network. It includes the desktop graphics, Internet favorites, connections to the Exchange server, and everything else that's customized for the user.

The user profile is created the first time a user logs on. For some programs (such as Outlook) a user must log on and have a profile built before the program properties can be edited. The following table lists the directories created when a new user logs on. (See Section Seven of The Checklist.)

Component	Location (XP / Vista & Windows 7) or (Office 2003 / Office 2007 & 2010)
Desktop	C:\Documents and Settings\username\Desktop C:\Users\username\Desktop
My Documents Documents	C:\Documents and Settings\username\My Documents C:\Users\username\Documents
My Favorites	C:\Documents and Settings\username\My Favorites C:\Users\username\Favorites
My Music Music	C:\Documents and Settings\username\My Documents\My Music C:\Users\username\Music
My Pictures Pictures	C:\Documents and Settings\username\My Documents\My Pictures C:\Users\username\Pictures
My Videos Videos	C:\Documents and Settings\username\My Documents\My Videos C:\Users\username\Videos
My Recent Documents Recent Items	C:\Documents and Settings\username\Recent C:\Users\username\AppData\Roaming\Microsoft\Windows\Recent
Quick Launch Toolbar	C:\Documents and Settings\username\Application Data\ Microsoft\Internet Explorer\Quick Launch C:\Users\username\AppData\Roaming\Microsoft\ Internet Explorer\Quick Launch
Windows Sidebar Settings (Does not apply to XP)	C:\Users\username\AppData\Local\Microsoft\Windows Sidebar
IE Cookies	C:\Documents and Settings\username\Cookies C:\Users\username\AppData\Roaming\Microsoft\Windows\Cookies
IE Links	C:\Documents and Settings\username\Favorites\Links
IE URL History List (Registry Entries)	Computer\HKEY_CURRENT_USER\Software\Microsoft\ Internet Explorer\TypedURLs

Component	Location (XP / Vista & Windows 7) or (Office 2003 / Office 2007 & 2010)
Office / Outlook Signatures	C:\Documents and Settings\username\Application Data\Microsoft\Signatures C:\Users\username\AppData\Roaming\Microsoft\Signatures
Office / Outlook Templates	C:\Documents and Settings\username\Application Data\Microsoft\Templates C:\Users\username\AppData\Roaming\Microsoft\Templates
Office / Outlook Stationary	C:\Documents and Settings\username\Application Data\Microsoft\Stationary C:\Users\username\AppData\Roaming\Microsoft\Stationery
Office Custom Dictionary	C:\Documents and Settings\username\Application Data\Microsoft\Proof C:\Users\username\AppData\Roaming\Microsoft\UProof
Office Recent Files	C:\Documents and Settings\username\Application Data\Microsoft\Office\Recent C:\Users\username\AppData\Roaming\Microsoft\Office\Recent
Outlook Data Files (.pst and .ost Files)	C:\Documents and Settings\username\Local Settings\Application Data\Microsoft\Outlook C:\Users\username\AppData\Local\Microsoft\Outlook
Outlook Address Cache (.NK2 file) (Office 2007 and earlier only)	C:\Documents and Settings\username\Application Data\Microsoft\Outlook C:\Users\username\AppData\Roaming\Microsoft\Outlook
Media Player Play Lists (Media Player 10 and up)	C:\Documents and Settings\username\Music\Playlists C:\Users\username\Music\Playlists
Media Player Database	C:\Documents and Settings\username\Local Settings\Application Data\Microsoft\Media Player C:\Users\username\AppData\Local\Microsoft\Media Player

Wow.

That's a lot more than background colors and My Favorites!

Now you might say that the users "get what they get," but a lot of users don't see it that way. And a lot of bosses don't either, because they know users whose desktops are different will waste an entire day changing colors and playing with settings.

After much trial and error, we have come up with three different levels of profile migration:

Basic Profile Migration means that we log the user on, let Windows create all the default settings, and copy over the user's My Documents after they've been cleaned a bit.

Before we leave the user's desktop, we make sure we can send/receive email via Outlook, browse the Internet with Internet Explorer, access company file shares, and print to the appropriate printers. Plain vanilla.

Full Profile Migration means that we perform all of the Basic items plus bring the following list of items from the old profile:

- Desktop Theme (background, etc.)
- Address Cache
- E-mail signatures
- Auto Archive settings
- Archive and other PST files open
- POP Connectors
- Junk Mail Filter lists
- Most Office and Outlook settings including the Outlook address cache (NK2), Quick Links

In our experience, the client will not know that they are on a new domain. The Full profile migration is our preferred default.

Custom Profile Migration means that we will bring forward all of the above, plus some customized settings for the client:

- Mailbox, Contacts and Calendars shares and permissions.
- Mailbox, Contacts and Calendars of other users to be opened.
- Contacts to be shown in address list and Address list order including which to check first when checking names.
- Out of Office Text
- Rules and Alerts
- Journal Settings

With a Custom profile migration, we will commonly be adding a specific shortcut to every desktop, removing certain programs from every PC, etc.

It is very important that you attempt to understand the level of user profile migration desired during the Pre-Discovery stage. That assures early on that the client understands the options available. It also allows you to create an accurate estimate for the sales cycle. You will literally ask the client whether each person gets a "high, medium, or low" amount of customization brought forward.

Generally, we find that most clients use the same level of migration for all desktops. Those who don't are larger companies and will have a few key people with very thorough profile migrations while everyone else gets the basic.

Understand Directories

Take another look at the table above and you'll see that almost all profile information is stored inside one directory:

C:\Documents and Settings\username for XP

C:\Users\username for Vista and Windows 7

That means, at some level, that you can use simple file copy and redirection to attach a directory to a profile name and magically reconnect the two.

Caution: The user's profile name and directory name may not be the user's logon name.

Let's say you're looking for the .nk2 cache file (this stores the addresses you've successfully emailed in Outlook) for SuzyQ. But there's no C:\Users\SuzyQ directory.

How is this possible?

It's pretty simple, really.

Let's say that a user was set up with the name Reception. In Windows XP, the directory C:\Documents and Settings\Reception is created. Later, the receptionist is hired fulltime and this user is renamed at the server to SuzyQ.

User SuzyQ's profile is still in the directory C:\Documents and Settings\Reception. Why? Because Windows really only cares about SIDs and not usernames.

The registry key

HKEY_LOCAL_MACHINE \ SOFTWARE \ Microsoft \ Windows NT \ CurrentVersion \ ProfileList

Will contain a SID for each user who ever logged on to that machine. A SID will be in the format

S-1-5-21-1240622783-1098249403-1302501037-1012

Within that registry is a key called ProfileImagePath with a value of C:\Documents and Settings\Reception.

Next, the machine is upgraded to Windows Vista. The registry still knows that SuzyQ = S-1-5-21-1240622783-1098249403-1302501037-1012, so it creates a profile home of C:\Users\Reception and copies all of SuzyQ's profile information there.

Why is this so important? Because you cannot assume that you know the profile associated with a user. There are techniques to point users to profiles. But you have to tread very lightly in this area.

What you can't do is to start cleaning up a machine by deleting every profile directory that's not called "SuzyQ." If SuzyQ every logged on as a local user, there will be a directory with her name on it, but all of her profile will still be under the C:\Users\Reception directory.

Note: You can get a lot of information about which directory is "live" for the current user with two commands:

ECHO %USERDOMAIN%\%USERNAME%

And

Whoami /all

Go slow. Know what you know.

Copying Profile Pieces

Unfortunately, there is a different tool for moving each generation of information from one profile to another. Each version of Windows has a different tool, and each brings forward a different collection of information. Each version of Office does the same.

So if you have an environment with different versions of Windows and different versions of Office, you will need a variety of tools to bring forward everything.

Consider how each of the following will be brought forward:

- Operating System / Desktop
    - Desktop background / Theme
    - Desktop data
    - Screen Saver
    - Language bar
    - Sound Scheme / Theme
    - Windows Sidebar
    - Startup Programs
    - Quick Launch (Contents and shown on taskbar)

- Internet Explorer
    - Web recent list
    - Links shown
    - Favorites
    - Cache size retained = ___________

- Office 200x
    - User Name and Initials
    - Save AutoRecovery frequency
    - Custom Dictionary
    - Recent Documents
    - Default File location
    - General Options

- Outlook
    - Outlook address cache .NK2 file
    - E-mail Signatures
    - Rules and Alerts
    - Out of office Assistant text and rule
    - Journal settings
    - Personal contact folders (contents and loaded)
    - Shared items and permissions (Inbox, Contacts, Calendar)
    - Auto Archive settings
    - Address Book
        - Address list shown first
        - Keep personal addresses in
        - Address list order when checking names
    - Pop Connectors
    - Archive or other.pst files loaded
    - Task links to other users
    - Inbox and other containers
        - Sort by category
        - Show in groups
    - Junk Mail Filter lists

We do not recommend simply re-pointing the registry and keeping the old, messed up profile the way it is. This is your opportunity to get rid of a lot of junk that has accumulated over the years. The user profile is a collecting place for all kinds of junk files and unused caches that never seem to get cleaned up unless someone logs on as the Administrator and deletes things by hand.

Instead, we recommend creating the new profile by logging on once as the new user (which creates the entire user structure) and then moving over just the things you want to bring forward.

The Good News

There are a couple of pieces of good news in all this. First, there are some great automated tools that do more than move a file or two. We prefer the Microsoft User State Migration Tool.

Second, if you are careful to always *copy* rather than *move* data, you will always have the old profile sitting and waiting to be accessed whenever you need it. In other words, you can always go back one way or another.

That means you can even disconnect from the new network, rejoin the old network, and your profile will work. Yes. Really.

The User State Migration Tool

The USMT gives you a great deal of power in moving profiles to new domains. It also gives you consistency across platforms (Windows/Office) and consistency across technicians.

USMT is the Microsoft standard of deploying and migrating workstations.

You should never have to do a completely manually profile migration. If you somehow break an Active Directory migration and a machine cannot log onto the new domain, the machine can still be logged in to any profile, even if you have to go back to the old domain.

It is also labor intensive and time consuming to move everything by hand. File copies may not capture all the hidden files and folder. Some items (for example Quick Launch items) will be moved over but won't show up because Quick Launch is not enabled by default.

If you copy profile pieces manually, you will a few extra reboots and logons. You'll have to log on as the new user to create the basic profile, then log on as the administrator to do the file copy.

The USMT is "best" in part because it is Microsoft's preferred method. It is the best even though you have some cleanup over all other options.

If you use the USMT you can clean the system completely of all old profiles and user files.

You will find extensive notes, instructions, and additional tool references in the profiles section of The Checklist. This section is intended to merely give you a little background on what you're getting into.

Focus on Exchange

The other major area that needs some focus is the Microsoft Exchange Migration. This is also a process that has evolved considerably over time. In the days of Exchange 6.x, you could only "migrate" an Exchange database to a server with the same name, same domain name, and samc directory structure. The SIDs didn't have to match up, but everything else did!

Now Exchange is a lot more flexible.

There are also many ways to migrate it. Unfortunately, the migration to SBS or Server 2008 also means the migration from Exchange 2003 to 2007 and from 32 bit to 64 bit. So you can't put in the DVD and click the "upgrade" button.

Again, Microsoft assumes that you will be experiencing downtime. We prefer zero downtime.

You have a few different tools available to you, including the Active Directory Migration Tool (ADMT). As a general rule, you only want to use the Exchange Migration tool if you used the ADMT to set up the domain, etc. For most networks, we call out a manual export and import of the contents of Exchange. This allows us to keep both databases "live" as we migration from one to the other. The most important overall migration question that affects the Exchange migration is the name of the domain. If you use ADMT, this is not an issue. With other processes, a different domain name is going to break some things in Outlook:

- Tasks
- Folder, Contacts, and Calendar permissions
- Some email rules pointing to mailboxes on the old server
- Address lists that are no longer shown

The basic rule about Exchange is that you're going to do some cleanup. You can choose to do most of it before the move or most of it after the move. You can't choose to not spend time cleaning up Exchange and Outlook. This is true with ADMT, with Jeff Middleton's Swing Migration, and with a totally manual migration.

There's just a bunch of things that need to be cleaned up. You will choose tools based on your familiarity with each, the number of users, the complexity of the client systems, and the level of downtime that can be tolerated by the client.

Outlook and Profiles

Exchange migration is closely tied to user profile migration because the user doesn't know or care about Exchange. The user sees Outlook. They see their contacts, their inbox, their calendar. The user doesn't see or care about Exchange databases, stores, or public and private databases.

No matter which tools you use, you will need a precise checklist to make sure that the user's *experience* is properly configured on the new system.

We once had a client whose migration we considered to be absolutely perfect, beautiful, and complete. They only had five users. The migration was very smooth. Absolutely zero downtime.

Then they called and wanted to know what the hell we did with their contacts. We connected remotely and looked. Contacts were in place. Everything looked fine.

Slow down. "What do you mean by contacts?" We had the client walk us through their Outlook click by click.

It turns out that this client – every user – had only ever stored "contacts" by simply typing a name in the "To" field and letting the Outlook cache save it. They had never right-clicked on an email address and added it to the contacts.

That was man years ago and that's when we discovered the .NK2 file that stores this information. We copied their old .NK2 files from the old profiles and everyone was back in business.

The better your checklist for user experience, the happier everyone will be – and the less rework you'll have to do.

To change the defaults for the Outlook migration, simply move items from one location to another in the Workstation Checklist and in the Pre-Discovery section. You will also need to adjust the list of items that define Basic, Full, and Custom profile migrations for *this* client.

Chapter Six includes a discussion of how we move users from the old Exchange Server to the new Exchange Server with zero downtime. In the meantime, here's a quick overview of the process.

Basically, we have users stand with one foot in each domain. In one they are access Exchange via Outlook and their new profile. In the other they are access Outlook via OWA (Outlook Web Access).

When we build the new server, and before we move it on site, we create all the user accounts and mailboxes. We use Exmerge to export data from the old Exchange database and Exmerge to import it to the new database.

This allows us to set up permissions, etc. as needed to make sure things work the way they're supposed to.

Thus, most of the client's data is on the new server, just not the most recent. Once we start pointing email to the new server, there's a small amount of data that arrived on the old server during the interim that is not on the new server.

Because no new data is moving to the old server, we can do a final export of just the newer data, and import this into the new server, making sure to not allow duplicates.

Once complete, the user simply stops using OWA on the old server.

There are many "gotchas" with Exchange and Outlook profiles. For example, if you just migrate the profile without using the Active Directory Migration Tool, nothing that had been shared from Outlook will be shared on the new system. Why? Because this sharing is not a function of the Outlook profile.

Note also that you have great flexibility to go back and peek into the old Exchange database. For any given user, you can simply change the name of the Exchange Server and connect *with Outlook* to the old server. (Be sure the clear the option to synchronize folders.)

From there you can check settings, permissions, shared folders, etc. When you're finished documenting the changes you need to make, just reconnect to the new server again.

That's not a tool available to you in the standard SBS Migration process. ☺

Back to the Skills Discussion

It is extremely important that the Project Manager have a good grasp of how Exchange works, where permissions take effect, and how all of this is related to the various profile migration options.

All too often, consultants will drag over a bunch of data from the old system, get things more or less working, and then have to come back and additional work to fine tune *this* or *that*.

The more you know about how all of this works, the more efficient and profitable you'll be. We have provided a great checklist for the process we use. Start there and customize it for your own needs.

Just remember that Outlook is one of the most important tools any client uses. Tolerance for rework is very low because, from the client's perspective, all time spent in Outlook is productive time.

The Network Migration Workbook

Overview and Flow

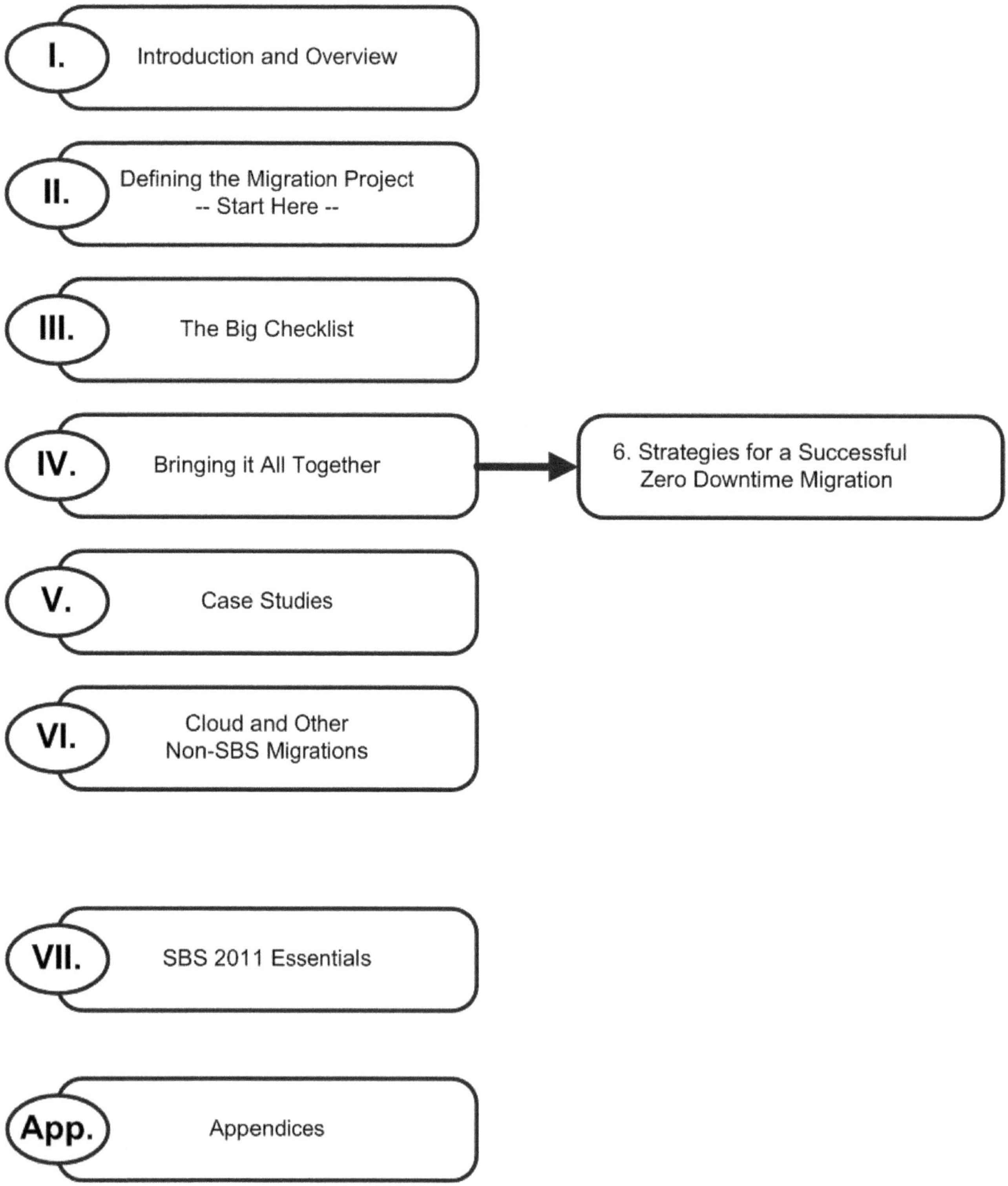

IV. Bringing It All Together

Chapter 6

Strategies for a Successful Zero Downtime Migration

At this point, you've seen the big checklist. Now you need to turn *pages in a book* into action in the real world. This chapter covers the planning of the migration project, including picking your strategies and a brief discussion of managing the timing as you work through the migration.

We're reluctant to agree that technicians shouldn't read about all aspects of the migration process, but we do admit that this chapter is focused primarily on the project manager or project lead. At the same time, a technician will gain a good understanding of how the migration process works.

Disclaimer

Everything changes all the time. This information is for advice only. We make no representation about its completeness or suitability for any specific project.

Please note, also, that software products change all the time, including those described in great detail in this book. This book is not intended to describe an exact process that will not change.

Quite the opposite: this book is intended to give you an approach to network migrations that will allow you to build and maintain a big, complicated collection of checklists that change after every successful migration project.

And finally: You're responsible for what you do.

To be successful with this material, you should read the book and the checklist, understand the process and the procedures, test your procedures on "bench" equipment, revise all checklists and procedures as needed, and then proceed with caution.

We cannot give extremely detailed descriptions of all the methods and processes in the checklist presented in the Appendix - there are simply too many details.

A Good Rule

All Work Requires A Service Request

One of the most profitable rules you can adopt for your business is: All work is performed inside a service request.

There are many reasons that this rule will make you more successful.

First, you should be tracking your time, and your employees' time, very accurately. If you don't do this, you will give away billable hours without knowing it.

Second, there are two ways you can collect money for your work: flat fee or hourly. If you charge a flat fee, you need to track hours to determine whether you're making money or losing it. If you charge by the hour, you need to track those hours for yourself and your clients.

Even if you charge a flat fee for some jobs, you need to track time to make sure you're not losing money. If an employee has an hour of time missing on a specific day, you don't know whether it was personal time, time billed to a "flat fee" job, or time given away to an hourly project because no one wrote it down.

Unless your employee agrees not to be paid for such hours, you're going to be out some money. So you have a right to know where the time went.

Buckets

Think of service requests as buckets into which time can be placed. These buckets are the only method you have for collecting money. When work is billed, these SRs represent the buckets into which the client will put payments.

Technicians live to solve problems. No matter what other personality traits they have, they all share this one: They love to solve problems.

So, when a call comes in, or someone asks them a question onsite, they are eager to help. They are easily distracted from the job at hand. But that tendency can cost you money!

Very often, these interruptions are for work that could be billable. So the technician is tempted to leave a "paying" job to go work for free on a job that could be paying, but isn't.

If a technician works on a job without a service request, the best you can hope for is that he creates one later that day and enters his time correctly.

And remember that keeping track of the "billability" of each technician requires keeping good track of each technician's time.

> The Truth About Time
>
> There are only three ways to keep track of all time worked:
>
> 1) Perfect Recall
> 2) Perfect Notes
> 3) Document all work in real time

Some technicians take perfect notes.

Most don't.

Encourage your technicians to be diligent about this. Make it this simple:

- If you go work a job without a service request, there may or may not be a bucket to put the money in.
- If you create a service request first, there will always be a bucket to put the money in.

Period.

So remember the rule: All work is performed against a service request.

Create Your SRs

Good. So we're all agreed!

As soon as you get approval for a migration project, you need to create the service requests that represent the buckets into which you will place *hours* and your client will place *dollars*.

See Chapter Four: Quoting the Migration Project. As you recall, we quoted the project with seven essential elements (see internal quote):

1. Staff Training Before
2. Discovery
3. Server Build
4. Network Migration
5. Workstation Migration
6. Staff Training After

7. Other and Misc. Labor

Note: If you combine the training items, you'll have six service requests. Otherwise, you'll have seven.

We recommend that you name the SRs with a clear and common format. For example:

1. Network Migration – Training
2. Network Migration – Discovery
3. Network Migration – Server Build
4. Network Migration – Network Migration
5. Network Migration – Workstation Migration
6. Network Migration – Fine Tuning

Allocate estimated time to each of these SRs according to your internal estimates during the quoting process.

Put any "fudge factor" into the fine-tuning stage.

There! You've done it. You now have buckets to put hours into. And the client has buckets to put dollars into! Everyone's happy. ☺

In our ticketing system, we have a status called "Schedule This." So, for example, if a ticket is Waiting on Parts and the parts arrive, the person who checks in the equipment and places it on the tech shelf changes the status to Schedule This.

Once you create SRs for the network migration project, you will put the status for each as Schedule This. That doesn't mean they're all ready to be worked right away, but it gives the Service Manager or scheduler a big heads up that you've got a major project coming down the road. It also gives them your best-guess estimate of the time needed to complete the project.

The Service Manager will take appropriate action for each SR.

Action Item: This is the point at which the service manager prints out the checklist and puts it in a binder.

The Strategy Begins

Once the Service Manager takes up the project, you must begin billing time against the SRs. You have some leeway about where you put "administrative overhead," but it has to be in one of the SRs.

As you recall from Chapter Four, we did not quote specific hours for each SR. We quoted a block of hours, based on our internal estimates of how long each stage of the process would take. Now we enter estimated time for each SRs into our ticketing system.

If the server build goes very fast, you might put administrative hours into that ten-hour block of time. Otherwise, fine-tuning is a fine place.

The Project Manager and the Project Lead

Notice right at the front of The Checklist we have a place for you to fill out the names for the Project Manager and the Project Lead. Elsewhere we mention Technicians. Who are these people?

The Project Manager is responsible for the high level planning and architecture. She will determine which tools to use, the order of the project, and so forth. She handles the "big picture" view of things.

The Project Lead is responsible for executing the project. In other words, the Project Lead *does* the project. In larger shops, the Project Manager may be designing and overseeing several unrelated projects at once. Each will have a Project Lead.

The Project Lead might be someone with particular skill or may just be a technician who is being given an opportunity to take on a little more responsibility.

The Project Manager will determine the overall timeline and planning. She will need to have regular (probably daily) contact with the Project Lead to make sure things are progressing as they should, and to make any mid-course corrections if needed.

The Project Lead is responsible for going down The Checklist and performing all tasks. Of course he may have assistance from other technicians.

Note that the client will probably recognize the Project Manager as the senior person on the project and address communications to her even though it might be more effective to communicate directly with the Project Lead.

Within your team, no matter how small, you must work to have excellent communication at all levels.

Skills Required

On one hand, there isn't really anything in any part of The Checklist that is beyond the skill level of a competent technician. On the other hand, taken as a whole the process is big, complicated, and overwhelming.

In fact, our experience has been that *every single* non-senior technician we've given a migration project to has called in sick the next day. Really. There's something about looking as a 200 page document with thousands of check boxes and feeling overwhelmed.

But it doesn't have to be that way! Remember how an ant eats an elephant: One bite at a time.

In every single section and sub-section of The Checklist there is more than one way to accomplish what you need to do. In fact, the biggest, messiest part of the whole operation is the migration of the desktop profiles.

Each version of Windows has some kind of profile migration tool. Each version of Office has some kinds of migration tool. Microsoft offers up the Active Directory Migration Tool (ADMT) as well as other migration tools.

So you have to choose the tools and techniques that are well matched with the expertise and experience of the technician.

As you choose which strategies you'll use for various pieces of the migration, be aware of the skill level and comfort level you have with each. If you give a technician a task he's not comfortable with, you might see very slow progress until you work with him to help him learn the skills required.

The Big Picture on Timing: From Sales Cycle to Project Completion

In our experience, a well-planned and well-executed server migration takes about fifty days. That's 50. It seems like a long time, but it's really not.

As you can tell, we believe that there is no such thing as an *emergency migration*. Other than a fire, flood, or some other emergency, you're not going to need to migrate a network on short notice. In such a case, you are really in disaster recovery mode. You would be forgiven if you simply recovered the old server configuration and left "migration" for another day.

Here's a common schedule for a small-ish network migration. You might add an additional week of planning to a large or complicated migration. We have allowed time for one department to inform another that work on a stage is complete and to have an orderly hand-off of information.

Note that these "days" are not just business days. Weekends will intervene. But the total operation can be completed from sales to sign-off in fifty calendar days. As you become more proficient, you will be able to squeeze this down to forty days.

But don't plan on shortening the process to less than thirty days unless you stock hardware and have a large staff. There are some realities you can't control.

Note: We understand that most consulting firms are 1-5 person shops. That means that some or all of the "departments" listed here are really one or two people in your business.

If that's the case with you, go get yourself a bunch of hats and switch department hats as needed.

Sales Cycle - Sales Dept.

Day 1: Client generally agrees to proceed.

Day 8: Pre-Discovery stages complete.

Day 10: Begin Quoting Process

Day 12: Quote Draft Complete

Day 13: Quote Draft reviewed by Sales and Technical team members.

Day 14: Quote to client.

Day 21: Project adjustments made, agreed to, and P.O. signed.

Day 22: Discuss financing with client. Get prepayment, arrange for financing, sign lease, etc.

Day 22: Sales - Create service requests and set appropriate statuses.

Acquisition and Discovery

Day 23: Sales - Verify money received. Determine sourcing for all hardware and software. Prep tracking documents.

Day 23: Tech Dept - Acknowledge service requests. Verify that hourly estimates are as expected. Schedule work.

Note: Hardware will begin showing up in a few days. You'll probably ship it to your own office. Software (MS licensing) will take 2-5 business days. If it gets shipped to the client, be sure to intercept. Clear email communications with client are important at this point.

Day 30: Tech Dept - Discovery and Project Description complete. Checklists customized for this job. Migration strategies finalized.

Migration - Tech Dept.

Day 37: Begin work on desktops and cleanup. Address any shortages. Schedule all remaining work with client. Review progress with client.

Day 38: Client training.

Day 44: Begin moving DNS, web, and other services. Move data and email to new server.

Days 45-46: Redirect email; Migrate server and network; Migrate misc. devices; Migrate users and workstations; Final sweep of data and email.

Day 47: Address any fine-tuning issues.

Day 48: All checklists completed and signed off.

Day 49: Client Training.

Day 50: Project retrospective meeting. Checklist revised and updated for next time.

Please also see the *Timeline and Project Calendar* in the relevant checklist.

You've heard the rules before, but let's review them in light of planning. We expect to do this during normal business hours. We're going to tip toe around the client's office while they work. So we don't have late nights (which bring reduced efficiency).

We expect excellent communications with clients and their LOB vendors. Anything else is outside the scope of the project!

We're going to schedule the cleaning of the desktops. We're going to move email without interrupting anyone. We're going to proceed in an orderly fashion.

From our perspective, there's no reason for such a project to take forty or fifty hours. If something goes wrong with hardware, that can cause a delay. But you stop work. So you only have a small amount of time to troubleshoot hardware. That hardware is brand new and under warranty. Pause the project and push the play button when you get new hardware.

All other side-tracks are related to client behavior, third parties (such as LOB vendors, copy machine people), or to inadequate discovery.

Client behavior should not affect the project because anything "else" they want you to do is, by definition, outside the scope of the project. So you might add some 10-hour detour, but you'll add it as a separate service request.

Poor communication with third parties is unexpected, but happens. You expect normal, good, professional communications. Anything else is outside the scope. Issues that come up with network scanners, time card machines, or other devices you don't control are outside the scope of work and become separate SRs.

That just leaves inadequate discovery. We believe we've outlined a very thorough discovery process. If you think you'll need more time for discovery in your first few migrations then you should add that to the estimate. But remember that we already added wiggle room in the quote (see Chapter Four).

The Realities of Time and Money

Karl has blogged about this topic on more than one occasion. Clients tend to have unrealistic views about time and money. To someone "outside" technology, things look simple. After all, you're good at what you do. So you make it look easy. But you don't help much when you use phrases like "we'll just move the SQL Server."

Just moving the server might be very complicated.

We know it sounds like we've beat the "Scope of Project" discussion into the ground, but constantly focusing on that language will do wonders for getting your client to go along with that view of technology projects.

Picking Your Strategies

Checkpoint: The Tech Department has created the service requests, printed out the checklist, and built a migration binder for the project.

If the client has been with you for some period of time, you probably already have a great idea about how you wish to proceed, where the stumbling blocks are, and so forth. If the client is new to you, then you'll need to pay special attention to the discovery process.

Sometimes you have to be fifty percent detective and fifty percent psychologist to get the information you need. You can poke and prod the machines to see what they tell you (disc usage, database sizes, number of users, etc.).

At other times, you need to rely on client interviews. Just be sure to keep asking "Is there anything else we need to know? Is there anything else?"

At this point you will build up the new server at your office. You'll do this so that you can verify every piece of the installation, and all components. Then you'll load it up with data from a recent backup.

There isn't much strategy to building the actual server. But once it comes time to create the SBS answer file and start installing software, you want to make sure you remember everything and operate as efficiently as possible.

So at this point you need to spend some time making sure you have all your software lined up, that you've downloaded all the updates you'll need, and have quick access to the white papers for special topics. For example, your virus scanner of choice probably has a white paper on how to exclude the Exchange directory structure from scanning.

For reference, the following Outline is repeated from Chapter Three:

Outline of The Migration Process

- Quote the project. Get approval.
  - Discovery. If it's a new client or a complicated network, do a complete discovery process.
  - Invoicing and payment. Once the project is approved, invoice for hardware, software, and labor according to your company policies. Once paid for, order hardware and software.
- Create the Service Requests (6 or 7)
- Print out the basic checklist (as presented in the appendix) to be used for markup.
- Define the major stages in the process and develop a timeline.
- Gather all the information you'll need. This includes everything from user names to contact information for third party support personnel.
- Finalize the checklist; customize for this client and this job.
- Checkpoint: Hardware and Software should be in hand at this point.
  - Build the physical server
  - Configure hardware as specified (e.g., build RAID arrays, install misc. hardware)
  - Install and configure server operating system
  - Install and configure server software
  - Create users, machine accounts, etc.
  - Move a copy of all core data from the old server (including Exchange and SQL databases)
- Perform onsite "Pre-Migration" training
- Place server at client office and begin synchronizing **
- Move core services to the new server (At this point, clients can access both systems.) **
- Migrate workstations **
  - Clean, fix, update
  - Move data to server
  - Migrate Profiles
  - When complete, end user is only accessing the new server
- When last end user is moved over, turn off the old server **
- Perform onsite "Post Migration" training **
- Review "spinoff" and fine-tuning service requests created during this process
- Proceed to work on fine-tuning service requests
- Report completion of all steps to client
- Evaluate all aspects of migration project, including accuracy of estimates and any unforeseen incidents.

The really important strategies involve migrating the major functions of the server. Remember the old line:

How does an ant eat an elephant?
One bite at a time.

That's how you're going to move to the new server. You will build the new server and then place it next to the old server.

It is very handy to have a spare firewall around for testing purposes. If possible, you want to isolate the new server so you can test everything including DHCP. But even without that, you can set up the machine at your office with the client's IP scheme.

You can use virtual machines on the same subnet to verify that you can successfully run the connection wizard, get DNS, etc.

Major Work Before The Server Move

There are a handful of things you need to do leading up to the day you deliver the server.

We've said it before, but the worst thing you can do is to show up at the client's site, run the SBS 2011 migration tool and expect to be successful. That tool (any migration) takes a great deal of preparation.

Here are some of the key actions we take to minimize downtime and stress on the day of the migration. These things can be done weeks before the migration takes place.

→ Make sure you have control of DNS. This means you need to either control it yourself of have quick access to whoever does control it.

The big gotcha here is the client who discovers that they have no idea who controls their DNS, their domain is registered to someone they've never heard of, and the whole domain registration is a time bomb waiting to go off. You need to fix all that before the migration can continue.

→ Manage your clients other vendors! More often than not, a server migration is associated with a Line of Business upgrade. This might be because the client didn't want to change, or the vendor didn't support specific configurations.

Whatever it might be, you need to have great communications with the LOB (line of business) vendor and make sure they know exactly what you're up to.

Ideally, you will install the newest, latest, greatest version of the LOB application on the new server and they will walk you through the process of importing the data. You'll run through the whole thing on the new server while it's at your office. That way, all the bugs get worked out while the client goes about their business.

You will document this entire process. This way, you have experience and documentation for the day you move the "live" data at the client's office.

As simple as this technique sounds, it will save you countless hours and stress as you repeat this successful practice again and again with client applications.

→ Clean up the workstations. This means getting rid of roaming profiles, or at least paring them down to a very small amount of data that needs to be moved. It also means doing thorough cleanup of all desktop and laptop computers.

Move important data to the server where it belongs. Check the profiles to make sure they're good to move to the new system.

If you have a lot of desktops to cover, this prep work can take a long time. That's okay. You included it in your quote. Just be sure to manage your time carefully.

If you use a service such as Continuum, you can assign most of the checking and cleanup activities to them. The price is very affordable and they can work on the job from 5 PM your time to 7 AM your time. Just be sure to give them a detailed checklist and manage them like an employee. We've had great success with this.

→ Document that old system! If you don't already have complete and excellent documentation, do it now. The more thorough your documentation, the more quickly you can get out of trouble if something goes wrong when you're onsite.

At the same time, you'll need to know how everything is configured on the old system so you can gradually turn things off as you migrate specific services to the new system.

→ If there are any other major moves taking place as part of the big project, try to separate them out and take care of them before the day of migration. The biggest example here is moving to a new Internet provider.

The primary rule of troubleshooting is that we only change one thing at a time. a) That's not possible with a server migration, and b) The client doesn't understand this. So when the client opens the coffers and starts spending money, you can't say no.

But that doesn't mean you have to mix up these two essentially-unrelated projects. Simply create a specific service request for moving to the new ISP and take care of that piece a week or two before the big move. Then you will know that all connection issues, DNS, DHCP, and firewall configurations are taken care of – and documented!

→ If major data moves need to take place, it's usually best to take care of these on the old server before you move. Again, the goal is to keep things as isolated as possible. Consolidate data and then move it.

→ Enable email archiving and web access through your hosted spam filter. Most spam filtering services will allow you to turn on this feature for a month or two. Enable it now so that a complete synchronization takes place before the migration.

This will give you a little extra peace of mind and creates an extra safety net in case there's a delay in the actual migration.

→ If anything is moving to a hosted or "cloud" environment, go ahead and make that move now. We take every opportunity to move client web sites off to a hosted site. For $200 a year, we get rid of a lot of headaches.

→ All the little stuff. If the client is buying new switches, firewalls, Office software, battery backups, monitors, or *whatever*, it is best to take care of all these things before the migration.

If you can't do that for whatever reason, then do them after the migration. Again, you want to isolate things and only change one thing at a time if possible.

Moving the Major Components

We like to remind people that there's no great mystery to a zero downtime migration. It uses "known" technical procedures and simply executes them in a specific sequence in order to avoid downtime.

In the previous section we addressed a large number of items that can simply be moved to a time before (or after) the major migration.

Now let's look at the functions you need to move when you put the new server in place. These are the things that need to be in place for everything to work from the client's perspective.

Items not on this list include integrated lights out access, RDP, or other functions that you use as a consultant but the client doesn't really need to have operational immediately.

A quick (incomplete) list includes:

- Email
- DNS
- DHCP
- User Accounts
- Computer Accounts
- Distribution Groups
- Security Groups
- Password Policies
- SMTP Email Addresses

- Exchange
- Disk Quota
- Backup / Backup Schedule
- Shares / Permissions
- Drive Mappings
- Printer Mappings
- SQL
- Terminal Services
- Web Sites and SharePoint
- Remote Web Workplace
- VPN
- Anti-Spam Software
- Anti-Virus Software
- Public Folders in Exchange
- FTP
- Fax Service
- OWA
- User Profiles
- Login Scripts
- Group Policies (at least the ones you want to keep)

Desktop to Desktop Procedures

For individual users, the process is very simple. Before they are migrated, they simply use the old system as always. The only exceptions to this are email and possibly a line of business application.

When it's time to migrate an individual desktop, the technician simply goes down the Workstation Migration Checklist to make sure that everything is completed, in order. When the technician is finished, that desktop user is completely moved to the new system.

See the *Focus on Exchange* sidebar.

Most Line of Business (LOB) applications use some kind of database. Clearly, you can't have people doing data entry on two different versions of the database.

We try to identify the people who really need access to the LOB application. It might be just the office manager, or just the doctors, etc. Ideally, we would like this to be as few people as possible. But sometimes everybody in the offices really has to be in the database all the time.

Remember, we're going to go around the office one desktop at a time and move people to the new system. So how do we handle this with everyone in the database? We cheat!

Generally, we will leave people pointed to the old database by either creating separate instance, or by setting up a virtual machine that accesses the old DB, or sometimes we use a terminal server session to access the old DB.

Then, during one of the Gold Hours (see below), we kick everyone out, shut down the database on the old server, and move it to the new server.

Then we scurry around and remove those temporary measures we'd put in earlier in the day. When people come back to their desks, everyone is on the new LOB on the new server.

See the *Focus on Databases* sidebar

The Golden Hours

If you review the Checklist in the Appendix you'll see the very brief description of what happens on the day of the actual onsite migration. It's really very simple because so much was done before "the day" arrived.

On the day of the migration, you are literally shutting down services on one machine and starting them up on the other. Most of this can be done "live," such as synchronizing file folders.

But for a handful of critical functions, we need to have exclusive access to the server. In addition, there are times when a server just has to be rebooted because a program setup requires it.

To handle these situations, we take advantage of three Golden Hours. The Golden Hours are 7-8

AM, 12-1 PM (lunch hour) and 5-6 PM. We reserve these hours for anything that requires our exclusive access to the server.

Even though many people work through lunch, they are willing to put up with a server reboot or even total lack of access.

The evening hour is golden because we simply have a technician come in an hour late that day, so we avoid the overtime. Client are normally leaving at 5:00 PM, so giving us the time from five to six is not a hardship.

And don't forget *outsourcing* and *flex time*. Because you have remote access to everything, you can do many chores remotely while the client is out of the office. That means you can assign them to Continuum or another outsourced help desk.

Or you can simply schedule a technician to work 10AM – 7PM. You'll avoid overtime and still get work done while the client is out of the office.

How To:
Focus on Exchange

One of the most common procedures you will perform is to move the Exchange database from one server to another. Moving Exchange is a great example of the techniques you can employ to move just about any function from one "live" server to another with zero downtime.

First, let's look at the architecture. In the average small office, your setup will look like this:

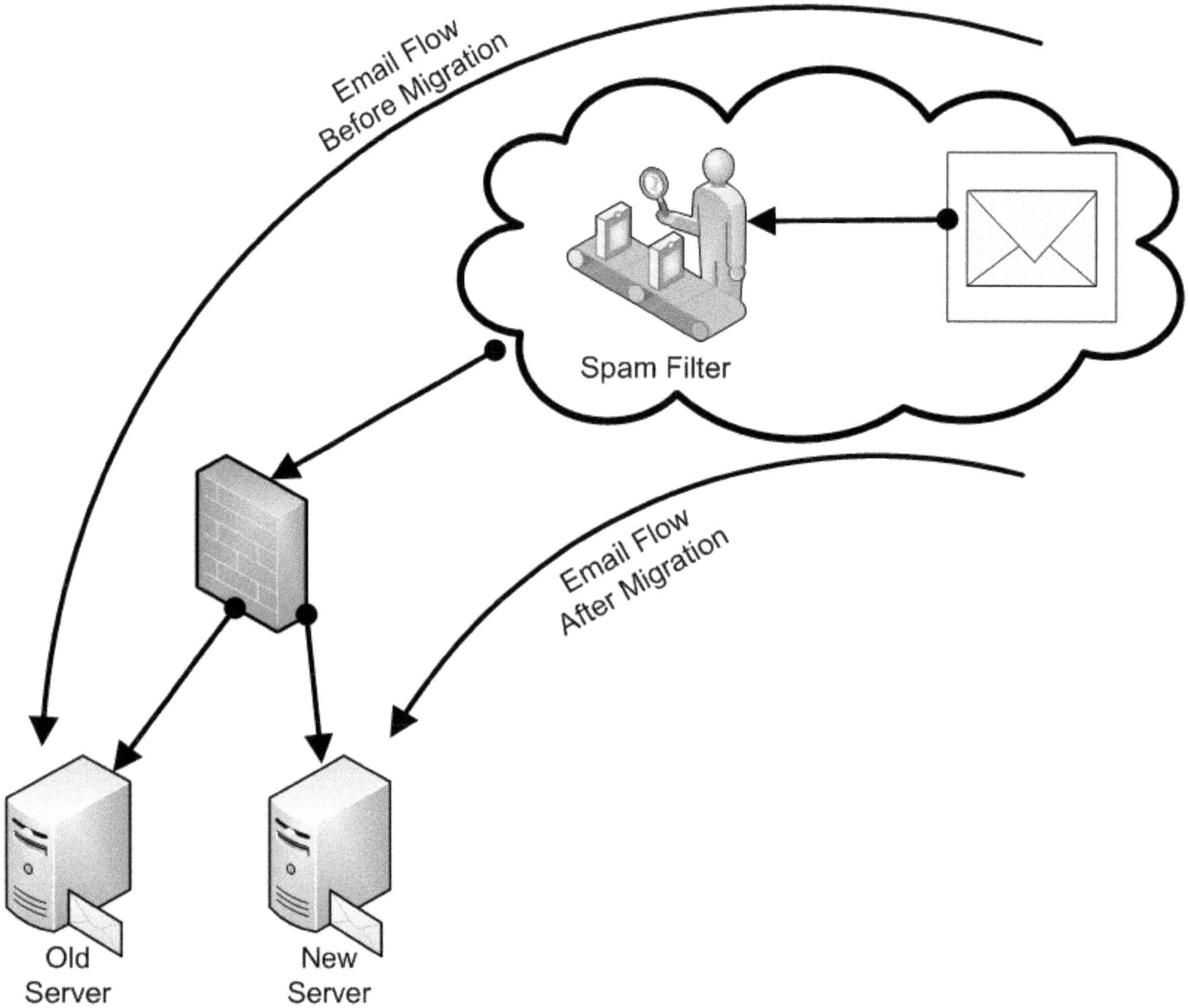

Old System	New System
SBS 2003	SBS 2008
32-bit	64-bit
Exchange 2003	Exchange 2007

In this scenario, you cannot simple stop the services and copy over the database. With a few caveats, you could do that in an "Exchange 2003 to Exchange 2003" migration. But whether it's SBS or not, here are the basic steps you'll need to do a ZDTM from Exchange 2003 to 2008.

Note, please, that we assume the use of a hosted spam filter in order to assist with this migration. A spam filter is not required, but you better make darn sure you have total control of the DNS and firewalls before you get started.

In any case, if all inbound SMTP traffic is only allowed from a single source (the spam filtering service) and all IP address translation is done on the firewall, then you can either reroute traffic at the firewall or at the spam filter.

We give the overview here. You can see all the click-by-click details inside the checklist.

Overview

System Build

- Verify that all email domains are defined within Exchange
- Setup and configure POP3 Connector if required
- Configure Exchange to not send non delivery replies
- Configure Exchange mailbox limits
- Create and configure all Exchange Public Content folders

Network Migration

- ExMerge all data out from the old server into .pst's on the new server after hours
- ExMerge all data into new server from pst's after hours
- Redirect email flow inbound to the new server. (Anytime)
- Users on old domain access email on new server using OWA until their workstation is migrated
    - Shortcut to the new OWA is placed on their desktops ahead of time
- Note:

  During the migration process, you now have "unmigrated" user connecting to the complete and up to date Exchange Database via OWA. You could set them up with a virtual machine or terminal service to connect with the regular Outlook client, but there really isn't a need for this.

  Once "migrated" to the new system, the users connect via the regular Outlook client.

  Eventually, everyone is migrated and therefore connecting via the regular Outlook client. The only data they could be missing is new email that snuck in, cached on the spam filter between which the ExMerge process had the systems offline. Nothing is lost, but it might be redirected. Therefore, we do the last step:
- Perform the "ExMerge out and ExMerge in" again to catch any data that may have changed. (If needed.)
- Of course, if the email database is very small, you can do all this during the Golden Hours.

How To:
Focus on Databases / Line of Business Applications

Another common procedure you will perform is to move databases from one server to another. These might be Microsoft SQL, line of business applications (LOBs), or some combination of databases. As with Exchange, moving databases is a great example of the techniques you can employ to move just about any function from one "live" server to another with zero downtime.

Earlier we made a big deal of trying to avoid "other" upgrades during the migration process. That's a good rule, if you can follow it. With LOBs, we are often stuck doing a data migration to a new version at the same time that we're moving everything else in the office to the new server.

Luckily, there's a pretty straight forward process for accomplishing this.

In a perfect world, we would like to move the data over to the new database while it's still on the old server. This allows us to separate the database upgrade from the migration. Our second choice would be to do the DB upgrade after the migration, but we're rather have no traces of the old version on the new server *just because.*

So, why do you need to do the upgrade during migration? Here are a few primary examples:

- The old server is SBS 2003, 32-bit, and an old version of the LOB application. Tech support won't help you install the old version on new hardware.
- The old version is not compatible with Server 2008. At the same time, the new version is incompatible with Server 2003.
- In any case, you are stuck exporting from the old system and running whatever data translation tool they have to import the data onto the new system

While it's a pain in the neck, this situation ends us giving you a high level of control, an opportunity to document the LOB application very thoroughly, and a migration in which *literally nothing* can go wrong.

If you've ever been stuck with an LOB migration tool or technician that wasn't up to the job, then you know how horrible it is to have a half-migrated database with the client out of business, and everyone breathing down your neck.

Let's look at a better way.

Here's the overview of the database migration process with upgrade at time of migration.

You can see all the click-by-click details inside the checklist.

Overview

System Build

Note: It is very likely that the LOB will need to be a newer version to work on the latest SBS release. This may require the existing version to be upgraded before data is exported or moved to the new server.

- Install the new version of the LOB and associated database (with assistance from tech support)
  - Take excellent notes. You will get help from tech support on this, but you might not get free assistance when you do it a second time.
- Export data from the old system and place on the new system (probably during a "Golden Hour")
- Alternatively, restore a copy of the old database from backup and place on new system
- Convert and Import the old data into the new system
- Test all functions on the new system. This may require assistance from the client.
- Once completely configured, document everything you can about this LOB setup

Network Migration

- This is the time to go slow and be clear. Map you migration or update process. Create a recipe you will follow to success.
- Stop all services on the old database. Export the latest data.
- You will now leave the service off on the old machine
- Convert and Import this data into the new system per the instructions you created previously (probably in an evening Golden Hour)
- Set up the key workstations only with temporary access to the new system via one of these methods:
  - Instance on their desktop connect to new DB
  - Instance in a virtual machine
  - Instance in a terminal server environment

  Note: At this point the only living version of the database is on the new version on the new server. Only a handful of people are using it.
- As you go around to each workstation and migrate it, you will bring them up on the new server
- Start with the people who use the LOB the least. Since the critical people already have access, there's no need to do them first.
- When you've migrated every workstation, everyone is on the new system

How To:
Focus on SharePoint / Companyweb

Ugh. SharePoint is the biggest "pain" with regard to a smooth migration. In particular, the SBS 2003 to SBS 2008 experience can be painful if you have a complicated or customized site.

Our experience is that an "upgrade" of the old system can render it unusable. At the same time, doing a wholesale move of the SQL database doesn't create a nice, usable Companyweb.

If you have a small, uncomplicated SharePoint site, you can do a pretty decent job of using the Windows Explorer view to copy content out of the old SharePoint and paste it into the new SharePoint. But for anything complex at all, Microsoft (and, apparently everyone else) recommends just running an instance of Version 2 side by side with Version 3. You'll simply call the old version OldCompanyweb.

We fully acknowledge that this is a very dissatisfying result. In fact, it is so dissatisfying that you might reconsider how much data you want to load into the new SharePoint site. After all, what will you be doing in the next version? And the next?

Our decision tree is very simple: If the old Companyweb has a large amount of data and you want to run the two systems in parallel, then follow the Microsoft process. If the old Companyweb is small OR you don't want to run the two in parallel, then do not install the old SharePoint on the new server. Just install the new SharePoint and move the data from the old server.

The process for that is pretty simple:

1) Open each section of the old Companyweb in Windows Explorer view and copy the data to a designated directory on the new server.

2) Clean up the data (remove duplicates, organize, delete old data, etc.).

3) Use Windows Explorer view to import the data into the new SharePoint site.

As you can see, our one great disappointment is the migration of SharePoint from one generation of Small Business Server to another. For example, moving from SBS 2003 to SBS 2008 is really a migration from Version 2 to Version 3, which Microsoft has made essentially impossible.

Several authoritative web sites address this issue. See

- The Official SBS Blog - http://blogs.technet.com/sbs/archive/2009/05/01/sbs-2003-to-sbs-2008-migration-to-a-different-domain-name.aspx
- Susan Bradley's Blog - http://msmvps.com/blogs/bradley/archive/2008/06/08/migratin-companyweb.aspx
- David Overton's Blog - http://uksbsguy.com/blogs/doverton/archive/2009/04/13/sbs-2008-installation-migration-and-configuration-chapter-7-migrating-the-companyweb-sharepoint-site.aspx
- Robert Crane's Blog - http://supportweb.ciaops.net.au/blog/archive/2008/06/09/sbs-2008-companyweb-migration-success.aspx

- Technet - http://technet.microsoft.com/en-us/library/cc527546(WS.10).aspx

Essentially, the advice is the same: Create a second SharePoint site on the new server that serves up the old data. But unless you really need to run the old Companyweb, this process is not necessary. If your goal is to eventually move the data to the new SharePoint (new Companyweb), then just do it.

Your two servers can live happily side by side for three weeks. Use DNS to point to the old site and let people access both at the same time. It doesn't matter whether they're on the same domain as long as they have valid logon credentials for the old site.

Why waste time and energy migrating the database when you're just going to copy all that data over anyway?

Again, we are extremely disappointed with the "process" here.

There are only a couple types of data: The entire site with different types of lists and the actual lists that populate a site. Neither can be exported and imported or copied via http access. All data has to be moved element by element.

You have to do an entry by entry rebuild of Calendars, announcements, links, and team discussions.

You can't really "move" the old Companyweb database unless you do an Active Directory migration. We do not recommend this as there are too many chances to mess up both the old Companyweb and the new Companyweb on the new server.

Fundamentally, we think it is bad policy to simply tell clients that they need to deal with two Companyweb sites. Even with very large sites, it may be worthwhile to hire a temporary employee to manually move all the data.

But we sure hope Microsoft comes up with a plan for the next migration, or people will stop putting critical information into SharePoint!

How To:
Focus on A Low-Stress Process That Can't Fail

Way back in Chapter Three we discussed the three methods of accomplishing Zero Downti

- Intercept the Process
  - Example: Email / Exchange
- Run the Processes in Parallel
  - Example: Files and Folders
- Flip the Big Switch
  - Example: Key Databases

Combined, these techniques allow you to craft a migration strategy that is very low stress and one that simply cannot fail. How is that? Think about the combinations.

With intercepting the process and flipping the big switch, you have people who are set up to use some functions on the old server and some functions on the new server.

This state of configuration is not optimal, but it can go on as long as needed. Days, weeks, months. It never does, but it can. In other words, the client is never out of business because you've given them the best of both worlds.

Again, when running the processes in parallel, you have people who access files on either the old or the new. If they're on the old system, it simply get mirrored to the new. Once they switch, they either wait 15 minutes for the next synch or you can go force it.

In either case, the entire office operation is up and running at full speed.

In many ways, the client will never understand the details of what you're doing here. And they don't need to. It's a little sad sometimes when you look at the technical miracles of balancing their entire office and keeping it live while the client just goes about his business. It would be nice if they understood enough to be really amazed at what you do. Oh well.

We point out the low-stress factor because you need to make sure you have a really great plan in place in order to achieve this low stress level.

If you take any shortcuts in planning, you will pay for them when the servers are running in parallel and you need to stop to go figure something out. It is critical that you figure things about before the migration!

And what about the "can't fail" piece? Well, you can't! At every single stage of this process, you have three things that keep you from failing:

1. You have the old server. It still works. You can go back if you need to.
2. You have the ability to completely build and test the new system – with data – before you migrate to the new server. Not only do you have the ability, you MUST do this! You can't fail if you've perfected the new system before you move people to it!
3. Because you can life with one foot in each world for an indefinite amount of time, you can stop the migration process at any time and come back to it. Normally, the worst thing that happens is that an ISP messes up something, or a third party vendor is totally unprepared despite your best efforts.

Will you feel stress anyway?

At first you will because you're used to it. But over time, you will find that ZDT migrations are pretty darn low stress events.

It helps a great deal if you really focus on good communications with the business owner (see Chapter One rules). Keep the client informed about where you are, how things are going, and what to expect next.

The client will be more nervous than you because they've had anyone attempt electronic organ transplant while the patient was up walking around!

Here's a key phrase to help you calm the client: "All the important functions of your network are up. You're in good shape."

Because of the meticulous documentation and planning, there really shouldn't be any surprises on your part. As preachy as it sounds, if something goes wrong that is the fault of your team, you need to focus very carefully on how that happened and make sure it doesn't happen next time.

All problems during the actual migration should consist of problems caused by third party tech support, suppliers, or the client. You can work to address each of these, but you need to make sure the client understands the big picture.

Here's a perfect example:

In early 2009 we moved a client off of an old server with an old Dynamics database. We made it very clear that we wanted the LOB vendor to build up the new database and migrate that data.

We would be in charge of the process and we would decide when and where. But we insisted that they build it up on the new server way before the day of migration arrived.

Well, it turns out that this guy was a completely incompetent technician. We could have "figured it out" a lot easier without his help. He had zero documentation and, apparently, no real knowledge of the product. His recollection was that you put in the CD and hit Next.

The result, of course, is that there were huge delays as he fumbled around trying different things and figuring out how to configure the system. We were in the unlucky position of needing to make sure the client knows why there's a delay, but not wanting to point fingers.

We simply gave a report each step of the way that Dude installed the database; Dude uninstalled the database; Dude reinstalled the database; Dude installed a toolset; Dude tried to convert data and ran into a problem; Dude installed the updated toolset; etc.

We've mentioned vendor management before, and this is a great place to mention it again. You need to be the one in charge of this project. You need to decide how things will proceed. You need to coordinate everyone who will be touching these systems (both servers, workstations, network attached equipment, ISPs, and so forth). Everyone.

Zero Downtime is not only possible, but it should be the norm in our business. With tools such as virtualization, remote access, and remote tech support, you should be able to move any system within the guidelines we've defined as Zero Downtime.

We believe clients will begin to expect it. We certainly hope they do!

Fine-Tuning, Spinoff Projects, and a Final Reminder About Closed Loop Processes

Way back in Chapters Two and Three we talked about the closed loop process. Basically, your project is designed so that no additional work is added until a service request is created.

So here you are, near the end of your project, and you've got some additional request for service that came up during the migration project.

Near the end of the project, two elements come into play. First, you have a stage in the migration called *Fine Tuning*. Some people are tempted to call this Fallout. But it's not fallout. It's not mistakes. It's not even cleanup.

When you do thirty or forty or fifty hours of labor on thousands of dollars worth of hardware and software, there are really thousands of tiny systems and subsystems. Ideally, all those individual pieces of hardware and software, on servers and desktops, just work together fine.

In reality, however, a little fine tuning has to take place. One wizard didn't complete here. A file didn't get copied there.

Stuff happens.

This stage is kind of the catch-all for tuning up all that little stuff so you can close up all the service requests and go home. After two days on site, the new system has had a small "burn-in" period and should be humming right along. But if anything isn't perfect, this is the place where you'll make it so.

The second element that comes into play is all the little requests that sprang up during the migration. For example:

- You found a cache of forgotten marketing photos that take up 80GB on someone's desktop and they need to be moved to an appropriate location and backed up or archived.
- One user reports a problem with her monitor. Another user's mouse goes out intermittently.
- Someone never got Access installed and needs it. Someone else just bought new software and needs it installed.

You know how it goes. Once you're on site, with your hands on the equipment, the service requests come out of the woodwork.

As you can see, you're likely to have a collection of service requests sitting and waiting for you at the "end" of the project. And, as we mentioned in Chapter Three, there are only three things that can happen to these requests:

1) The issue is fixed by, or made irrelevant by the migration project

2) The issue is determined to be so minor that you simply include it in the project

3) The issue is determined to be outside the scope of the project and is handled under a separate service request

For this final group of SRs, your project manager should meet with client and go through each SR. Just be sure to hold your ground regarding the scope of work.

It is very important, at every stage of the migration process, that out-of-scope requests be entered as new Service Requests so that you can sit down with the client at this point and go through them. The outcome of this meeting will be two-fold.

First, you will have a list of SRs for which you've been given permission to proceed (as billable labor). Second, you will have a very clear understanding of every single item remaining to be completed inside the scope of work. The result: The end is in sight! When you finish those last few items, the migration will be complete.

You may also come up with some "spin-off" projects. For example, the client may have decided, after the discussions about desktop configurations, to standardize on the latest version of Office software. So, there may be a new project to go around and upgrade all the systems. This is both a good idea and a completely separate project.

Note that there are forms at the end of the Big Checklist regarding both Fine Tuning and Spin-Off Projects.

Project Completion

The actual "completion" of the project involves the project manager going through the paperwork and meeting with the client.

First, you'll verify that all checklists have been completed and that every piece of the project is complete. Anything that's not complete for whatever reason should be moved to a new SR so that the project SRs can be closed and you have well defined end in sight.

Second, you'll meet with the client (or the client's technical contact) and get a review of the project. Be sure to write down the good, the bad, and the ugly. You want to take kudos back to your staff. At the same time, you want to make sure you know how to improve the process.

Depending on your client relationship, you may want to take the client to lunch and have a casual chat about how things went. Again, make sure you absorb the message they're sending. Don't be too eager to move to the next project until you'll fully evaluated the current one.

Project Retrospective

The Project Retrospective is your team's evaluation of the project. This will probably be very different from the client's perspective.

We've seen projects that the client thought was perfect but we saw as a never-ending series of blunders and turned out to be very unprofitable. We've also seen migrations that we considered flawless but which the client viewed as slow and disruptive.

Breaking News: You will never be perfect. ☺

Keep working on improving the process. At every stage, ask yourself and your team "How could we have made this better?"

You will never be able to foresee every strange thing that could go wrong in the world. But that doesn't mean you should ignore it. Ponder what you might do differently in the future.

How To:
Focus on Building Custom Checklists

We casually mentioned several times in this chapter and the last that you can build your checklists. We realize that such a task is not as easy as it sounds. We have literally built our consulting practice on checklists. We do it every day. But we also work with a lot of consultants who like to *use* checklists but don't like *create* them.

Here's a quick primer to get you started down the road to building your own checklists without wasting your time.

Tools: Ideally, you'll use a tool such as Snag-It or the screen snipping tool that ships with Windows Vista and Windows 7. You may also need an editing program that's a step up from the Paint program included in Windows. And, finally, you'll need Microsoft Word or WordPad.

When you start to build your own checklist, we hope you'll find good examples within The Big Checklists we've printed in the Appendix. The any given product or subsystem, you might one of the following five scenarios:

1. There is a complete checklist. Therefore, you just need to fine-tune for your purposes.
2. There is a reference to a whitepaper, Microsoft Knowledge Base article, or some other resource that gives a complete description of the process you're looking for.
3. There is a checklist that highlights the major steps but gives no granularity. For example, see the *Copier / Scanner* checklist within the Sub System migration (Section 15 of The Checklist).
4. There is a checklist *hybrid* that is specific about some aspects, much more generic about some aspects, and references whitepaper for other aspects.
5. No Checklist exists.

Obviously, if you can start with something to edit, your work will be a lot easier.

To create a checklist, you will simply need to sit down and go through the process you're documenting. But you'll go through it differently this time. You need to go very slowly and try to adopt a mindset that makes no assumption about the process. You need to write down literally every single click type keystroke.

You'll describe a bit about what you're doing. Then take screen shots as needed. Sometimes one screen shot can make all the difference. You may want to bring the screen shot into a paint program so you can circle an option or superimpose a comment or recommendation.

Go slow. Be careful.

And there's only one way to test your documentation: Give it to someone else and have that person execute the procedure using your documentation. You'll be amazed at how many times you assumed something that was not part of the documentation. It's the hardest problem to overcome.

But stick with it! The more you document procedures, the better you'll get. And the better your documentation, the better your business.

How To:
Focus on The Future of Computing and The Future of Migrations

The "Big Checklist" only changed a little from SBS 2003 to SBS 2008. It changed a bit more troduction of SBS 2011 and SBS 2011 Essentials.

In fact, this book was delayed a few months because of our attempt to make it as relevant to the future as possible. But change never stops. And in technology it doesn't even pretend to slow down.

So as we were writing, announcements came out about new checklists from Microsoft, the Windows 8 Consumer Preview, updates to Virtual Server, third party products for virtualization and hosting, release information dates for the next version of Office and Exchange.

At some point you have to give in to the inevitable and write a checklist that's as good as you can make it, as relevant as you can make it, and as forward-looking as you can make it.

The Checklist is a living work of technology. The processes will evolve over time. That's why we decided to create the companion online web site for book owners to exchange updates, specialty checklists, techniques, etc.

We see two major changes coming down the road with regard to Server Migrations in the SMB Space.

First, there will be a massive movement to hosted systems in the next four years. Note how much the world changed in the five year life of SBS 2003 and the three year life span of SBS 2008. It will change at least twice as much in the next few years.

We are proud to share a core belief with some key members of the SBS Development Team: We will all be more successful when we learn to place less burden on our SBS Servers. Line of Business Applications belong somewhere else. Whenever possible, Exchange and SQL belong somewhere else.

The move to "the cloud" will speed up this process. Soon, the most common SMB/SBS migration will be one that moves specific functions off the old server and onto the cloud – never to return. That's why, in the Second Edition, we have added entire chapters dedicated to migrating to the Cloud.

Many consultants have never let their clients house a web site in-house. So, the web site is hosted *somewhere* while SharePoint and Companyweb are in-house. Soon they will do the same with Exchange Server and SQL.

Microsoft is moving to make these hosted options integrate seamlessly with the on-premise server. It won't be long before your setup options will include the question

☐ Would you like to set up your Exchange Server . . .

- On this Server?
- At the Microsoft Hosting Service?
- At another Hosting Service?

And the same with SQL, www, etc.

In addition to Microsoft, you'll see all the major Line of Business applications making the same move. The database will be in the cloud, you'll connect to it remotely, and all you need to access it will be your browser.

In many ways, this first-of-its-kind migration book for the SMB space may also be the last version ever needed. After all, when you move your LOB and all the critical functions to a hosted (cloud) environment, what's left to move locally?

Keep that in mind as you begin moving people to hosted services. Create checklists. Keep them with the Big Checklist provided in Appendix B. Integrate them. Fine tune them with each migration. Soon your discovery process will include a checkbox for each function: Moving to the new server or off to the cloud?

But don't lose any sleep over the change. There will be a massive amount of work for consultants to do as we move clients onto their last server before things move off to the cloud.

We hope you will find this book very relevant for many years to come. We are confident that SBS 2011 will have a good five-year run. We are also confident that the world of SMB/SBS technology will change a great deal in that time.

We sincerely wish you the best of luck in all of your migrations. We encourage you to register your book in order to gain access to the online resources described in Appendix D. We encourage you to join us there to continue working on this "living" document of Small Business Migration Strategies.

www.zerodowntimemigration.com

The Network Migration Workbook

Overview and Flow

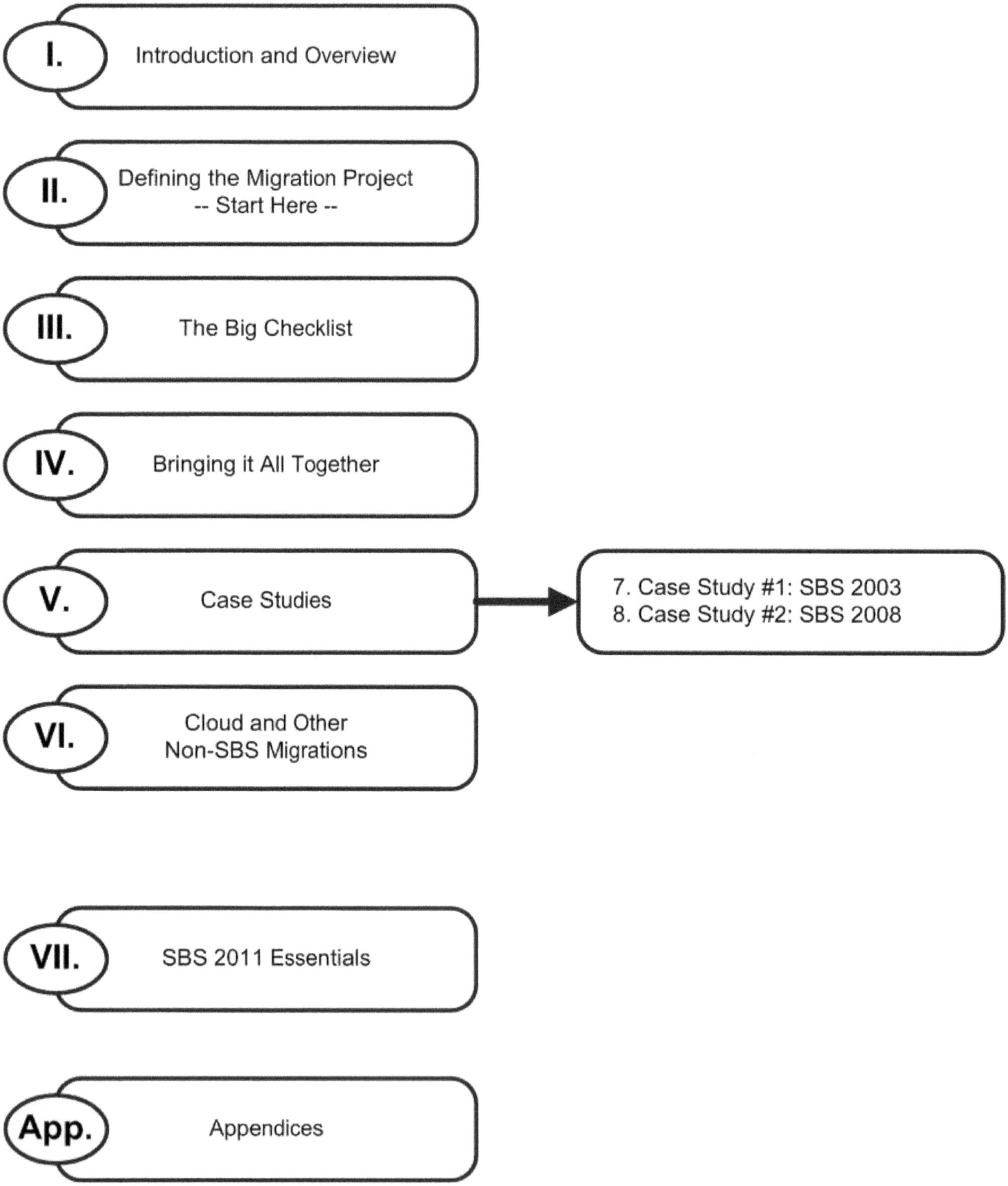

V. Case Studies

Chapter 7

Case Study #1: SBS 2003 – A Complicated Migration

Before we dive into this case study, please note that this is not an endorsement of putting every application you can on a Small Business Server. We neither endorse nor encourage such piling on of technology. There is already a tendency to over-burden the server with the components that ship with SBS.

Adding multiple mission critical applications on top of Exchange, SQL, and the entire security infrastructure of RWW, SharePoint, and VPN is asking for trouble. We're not saying it *can't* be done, just that we discourage it.

This case study is based on a real client of ours: A medical clinic with several doctors and multiple Line of Business applications (LOB's).

The equipment here is top of the line stuff. Their old server was a Dell, rack mounted. They took this opportunity to move to an HP-based multiple server environment. The first step in that process was to add an HP Storage Server into the mix.

All equipment is rack mounted in a 48" rack with isolated power. The client is totally dedicated to embracing technology as a means to differentiate his business from the competition.

The Older System

Over the years, through a variety of network consultants, the client has added one LOB after another onto the one SBS Box. The key components are as follows:

1. Centricity practice management software. Provides scheduling, billing, accounts receivable. Requires a component on the desktop and has a web based client.
2. Touch Charts software. Provides scanning and importation of data intro Centricity. A service monitors specific directories for forms and data, including cardio images from Kardia Health. Sends faxes to pharmacies via Touch Scrip add-in.
3. MIK – Milbrook Integration Kit gets scheduling and demographics information from Centricity to Touch Charts.
4. Kardia Health Systems software. Coordinates cardio data input from various machines designed to scan heart images. Delivers data to the monitored directory so Touch Charts can scoop it up.
5. Kardia Health Secure Web Delivery System. Operates on a very small, dedicated web server whose only job is to serve up video images of heart scans over a secure SSL connection. Not tied to active directory or any other elements of the primary server.

6. Imaging Workstations. These workstations access the Kardia Health Systems to view heart scans from inside the office. Can be shared over secure Internet connection with offsite imaging specialists in remote locations.

Please see the Functional Map at the end of this chapter. Don't forget that that primary server also contains the Exchange database. Fourteen total users were on this network, and a series of medical imaging equipment is attached to it.

The Challenge

In some sense this seems like an overwhelming task – especially the zero downtime part. But in reality, it is an excellent example of *why* you should be using this method for migration.

As you might expect, one of the major LOBs required a version upgrade because they would not assist with installation of an older version. Period. That required an updated connector because the shin-bone connected to the foot-bone.

And we ended up having to use a different tool for faxing because neither of the vendors involved in the fax solution could make it work consistently on the new setup.

Believe it or not, the zero downtime part was the least challenging.

The Migration Solution

The most important part of this migration was that we totally built up the new system at our office and tested every function before we went on site. Unfortunately that took a couple of months due to the coordination of outside vendors.

We added an HP Storage Server to the mix in order to move to completely manageable, flexible, expandable storage. The functional map remained unchanged.

Once we built up the new server and storage server, we tested every function – including the fax function. That's where we ran into a snag.

As the LOBs talked to each other, a "fix up" was needed to make the fax come out properly. That fix up was written by an individual who has since moved on to other things and was not interested in figuring out how to fix up the fix up for this project.

We implemented and tested the new solution. Once that was documented and added to the mix, we were ready to go.

Once we had the servers built and configured, we used data from backups to "fill" the databases so we could test their connectivity. We connected a virtual machine to the SBS network and then set up remote access to that machine (thus testing the RWW for SBS) so that the client's staff could poke around and verify that everything worked.

The process of creating a virtual machine did two things for us. First, it gave a VM to drop onto the desktops of key personnel on the day of migration. Second, it gave us the chance to build and document the process needed to successfully install the new client on each desktop.

We did all of this work on an isolated network behind a firewall so that it was completely separate and unaffected by our own network. This allowed us to use the IP address range of the client's office and configure all services exactly as they would need to be on Day One of the onsite work.

The only thing we could not test remotely was the ability of the scanning equipment to connect to the database. But we contacted the vendor involved and made sure this was not a problem.

And while it would be nice to have tested this before we were onsite, it did not really slow us down. We arranged for the equipment vendor to be onsite the first day we were there. So he could take one imaging system and get it connected to the new system while everything else kept working on the old system.

Once the scanning equipment was ready to go, we'd already synchronized data and completed several pieces of the big move.

Cool Tool Tip:

We were not involved in re-pointing the Kardia Health system (marked as 4/5 in the diagram) to the new server. So how did we test this connection?

First, we established a VPN with the client's office (remember, the new servers were at our office). Then we used a Golden Hour to simply re-point the connectors between the primary data server and the Kardia Health server. We had a doctor access a heartbeat video.

Documented. Done. Click.

We put the connector back the way they were on the Kardia Health system, but we now had the primary server configured so all we had to do was drop it in place.

Take another look at that diagram at the end of the chapter.

While it seems very complicated, it's really a matter of individual systems that connect to each other somehow. Those connectors allow us to move the functions one at a time.

Kardia Health Systems (and other systems) need to know where to drop files. So while they're on the old system, they simply drop the files where they used to. We synchronize that with the new system and all those files get scooped into the new database.

Once the transition is complete, we re-point the systems to the new location on the new server. We can do this one system (one device) at a time as everything is being copied to the new server.

Nothing ever gets dropped, lost, or forgotten.

Desktops were surprisingly straight forward. The key tool that people needed access to was Centricity. We set up virtual machines so that a handful of people were accessing the new database.

The VMs contained Centricity clients pointed to the new database. Users logged onto these machines in order to perform any tasks with Centricity. Access to the old Centricity database was disabled for everyone. So only a handful of users could access the database, and that was through the virtual machines.

These were the last people to be migrated. So as we gradually moved others to the new environment, we added more and more people to the new Centricity. Once everyone was moved, we simply turned off the virtual machines.

All other functions (Exchange, files, RWW, etc.) were moved according to the standard procedures described earlier, especially in Chapter Six.

Key Factors in Success

These are the "tools" in our tool belt that made this a successful migration:

- Building the Server off-site and testing completely. This was 90% of what we needed to achieve ZDT.
- A Thorough Pre-Discovery and Discovery process allowed us to stay within the allotted billable hours for the project (Although, see *What Went Wrong*).
- Complete management of the vendors allowed us to hammer out issues with the new versions, new connectors, and the fax side trip.
- Management of the vendors and building the entire system off site allowed us to create detailed documentation of how the connectors work and how to build up this system again, if required.

What Went Wrong

Three important things affected this project.

First, we had bad luck with two pieces of equipment. The new server showed up in a box with one of the big pieces of Styrofoam missing. It was basically beat to pieces.

We took pictures, refused delivery, and ordered another server.

The storage server showed up and had a boot error. A quick call to HP, a reload to factory specs, and we were good to go. This was literally a 20 minute delay, but it's worth noting.

Second, the vendor management part of this project was far more complicated than we had imagined. Because there were several LOBs that needed to interconnect, we needed to set client expectations better than we did.

Once we did complete discovery and determined the order in which we needed to proceed, we were frequently at the mercy of vendors. They had one- and two-day delays returning phone calls, scheduling a time to work together, taking days off, and so forth. In the end, this added weeks to the project. Luckily, it was not a live environment.

The client did not expect this, and neither did we. And while we saw the servers every day and tried to always move each piece forward every day, the client couldn't see that.

We believe more frequent communication would have been helpful. But at some point it just sounds like whining to call and say "We're still waiting on a vendor."

Third, we initially picked the wrong project manager for this project. This is a very important point to learn. As we've said in this book, nothing we do here is magic or requires specialized knowledge.

But just because someone can complete every single item on every single checklist does not mean that he can manage the project or move past the "planning" stage.

It takes a certain combination of skills to take on a really big project and not get bogged down in the details.

At some level, it's just another project. It's a server with this component, that component, and another component.

We ended up changing project managers and moving methodically through to a successful migration.

Unfortunately, we can't tell you how to pick those really good project managers. At some point, you have to stop training and hand over a project to your engineer. But you also have to be willing to take it back when it's not working out.

A Peek Into This Client's Future

This is one of our favorite clients. That's partly true because of their obvious dedication to using technology to differentiate themselves from their competition.

Their willingness to build up a system like this puts them in a class that few others are willing to attempt. It is no surprise that they are leaders in their profession and in their community.

They are also a favorite client because, as nerds, this is some very cool technology. In addition to what we've mentioned so far, this client uses a SonicWall CDP for onsite imaging, a series of tablet PCs for the doctors, and they have invested in good "computer room" facilities for all of their equipment.

As we look into the future, this is NOT one of those clients who has bought their last server. They have probably bought their last Small Business Server, although not necessarily.

When this server begins to age, we are hoping that at least one of their systems will move to a hosted model. The most likely candidate is the Kardia Health System because it is already nicely isolated, is totally web-based, and operates with a secure certificate.

The other major LOBs are top-notch brands and we trust they are developing web-based applications as well.

The biggest holdup in moving all of this to a series of cloud-based services is the latency in data transfer. At some level, you can buy as much bandwidth as you want. So, if the stability is there, and the bandwidth can be purchased, then moving everything to the cloud makes perfect sense.

Within the client's office, there will always be physical devices that create data (charts, x-rays, heart videos). Today each of these gets dropped into a folder and scooped into Touch Charts. Perhaps tomorrow, with enough bandwidth, Touch Charts will simply scoop that data off to a secure cloud.

In order to preserve the speed of the entire system for the users, their desktops will almost certainly need to exist in the cloud, right next to the server.

Access will be by thin client. So all data access and processing takes place on remote machines with all the computing capacity needed. Only video, keyboard, and mouse data need to be transmitted to the human user.

We're not sure how much of that transition will take place before the current server gets too old, but this is a very modular system. The modular nature will allow us to move applications off to hosted services one at a time. That, in turn, will leave more processing power for the other services.

Because the client bought a machine powerful enough to manage all these LOBs, plus SBS, we may actually be able to use this server for four or five years if we begin migrating individual modules off to the cloud.

At some point, the only elements the client will need on site are data storage, security, and backup. Normally, we would add "remote access" to that list. But once all the systems are hosted somewhere, remote access to the office will be irrelevant.

Come to think of it, maybe their next server *will* be a Small Business Server. It will be small-footprint SBS that doesn't run SQL and doesn't run Exchange. It simply provides the brains of the operation.

As you can imagine, we're very eager to see what's next for this client.

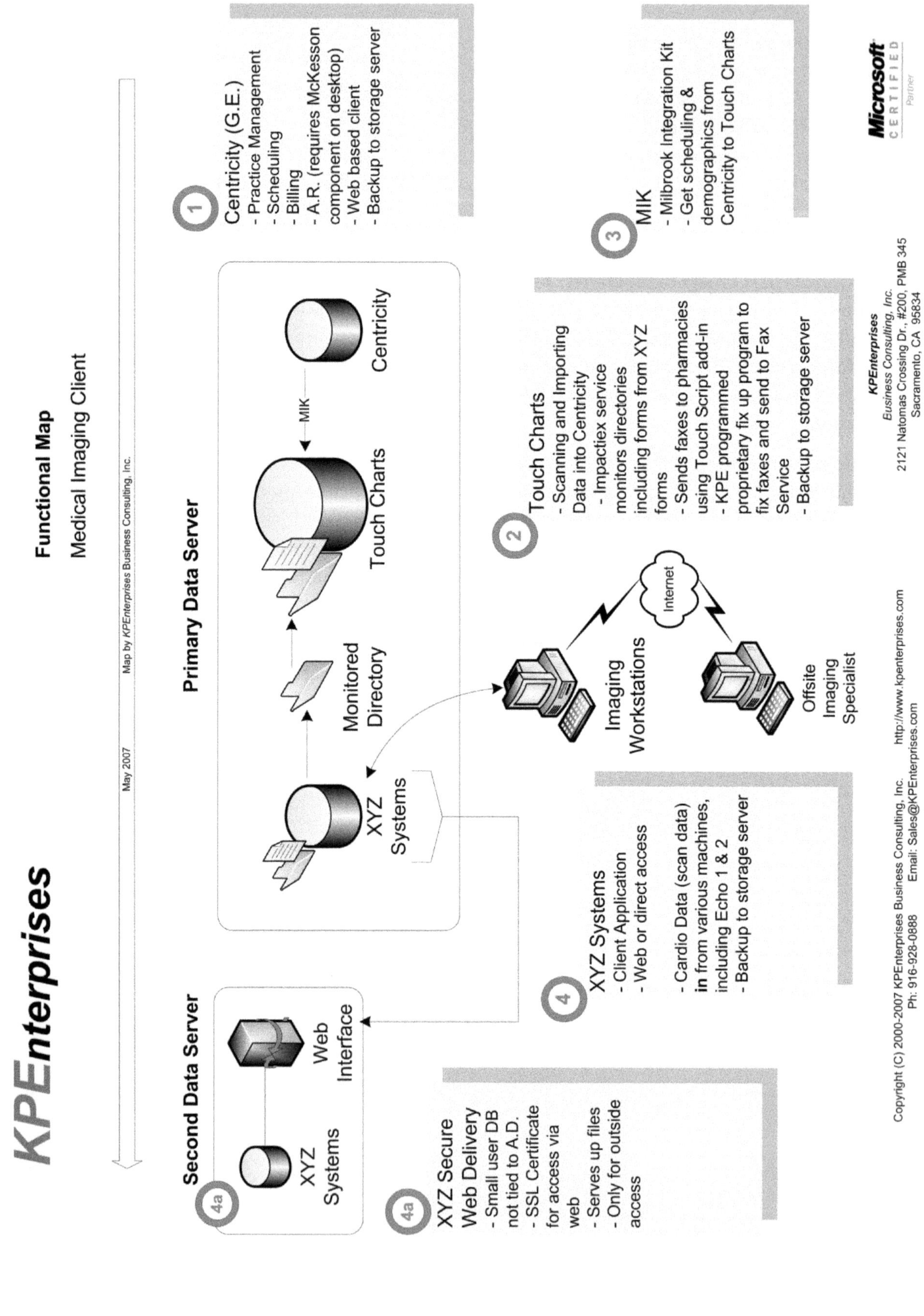
KPEnterprises
Functional Map
Medical Imaging Client
May 2007
Map by KPEnterprises Business Consulting, Inc.
Second Data Server
XYZ Systems
Web Interface
Primary Data Server
XYZ Systems
Monitored Directory
Touch Charts
MIK
Centricity
Imaging Workstations
Internet
Offsite Imaging Specialist
1
Centricity (G.E.)
- Practice Management
- Scheduling
- Billing
- A.R. (requires McKesson component on desktop)
- Web based client
- Backup to storage server
2
Touch Charts
- Scanning and Importing Data into Centricity
- Impactiex service monitors directories including forms from XYZ forms
- Sends faxes to pharmacies using Touch Script add-in
- KPE programmed proprietary fix up program to fix faxes and send to Fax Service
- Backup to storage server
3
MIK
- Milbrook Integration Kit
- Get scheduling & demographics from Centricity to Touch Charts
4
XYZ Systems
- Client Application
- Web or direct access
- Cardio Data (scan data) in from various machines, including Echo 1 & 2
- Backup to storage server
4a
4a
XYZ Secure Web Delivery
- Small user DB not tied to A.D.
- SSL Certificate for access via web
- Serves up files
- Only for outside access
Copyright (C) 2000-2007 KPEnterprises Business Consulting, Inc. http://www.kpenterprises.com
Ph: 916-928-0888 Email: Sales@KPEnterprises.com
KPEnterprises
Business Consulting, Inc.
2121 Natomas Crossing Dr., #200, PMB 345
Sacramento, CA 95834
Microsoft CERTIFIED Partner

Chapter 8

Case Study #2: SBS 2008 – A Simple Migration

This is a rather "plain vanilla" migration from SBS 2003 to SBS 2008. The old server was about four years old and was essentially on life support. It had experienced a catastrophic failure of the power supply and the vendor (Dell) could not get one delivered in less than several days. We rigged up a power supply from another server temporarily until the part arrived (see picture). But the client understood that it was time for a new server.

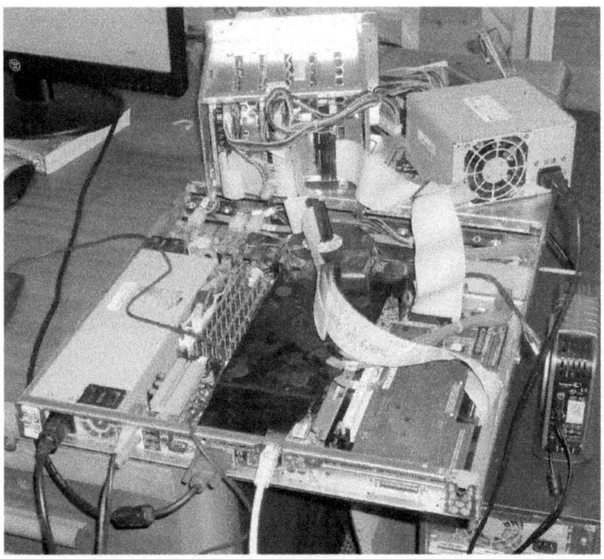

So after their system was back together the way it's supposed to be, we talked to them about getting a good server that would last them for another three years.

The Client

This client had been a casual break/fix client many years ago. They had an in-house I.T. person and called on KPEnterprises only for larger projects or for architecture advice on the network.

When KPEnterprises moved to all flat-fee monthly managed service agreements several years ago, this client did not sign up for one of the programs offered. They continued with their in-house I.T. and did reasonably well.

But we always kept them on our mailing list and sent them monthly newsletters, advertisements, and an occasional holiday card.

Then one day their in-house I.T. guy moved on and they called us. We met with them and explained our offerings. They signed a platinum managed service agreement and we proceeded to monitor their systems, document the network, and take care of things.

The Older System

The old server was a Dell. There were about fifty users connected to the network.

The operating system was SBS 2003. It was a fairly standard setup, although the in-house I.T. person had created a number of group policies that sometimes conflicted with one another. Because there was no good documentation when we got there, it was not always clear what he was trying to do with the GPs.

The client's web site was in-house and we recommended moving it to a hosted solution. The client's email was in-house on the SBS Exchange Server.

The client has one large home-made Line of Business application (LOB) that runs on a Linux system and is maintained by a relative. This was to remain in place and is not part of the migration scenario except that users must be able to access it when we are finished.

The Challenge

We chose this client for a case study because of the plain vanilla nature of the project. The only challenges were minor.

- Fifty desktops needed to be migrated. A few were on older, slower machines. A few had large amounts of data.
- We took this opportunity to move the client's web site to a hosting service.
- Because of the large number of people affected by downtime, keeping everyone working was important.
- We wanted to start over with a standard set of group policies and make sure everything was documented as it should be.

The Migration Solution

This was our standard SBS 2008 migration.

We built their new server at our office. We loaded data from backup. We configured, documented, and tested all functions.

Once it was time to place the server on site, we scheduled a two-day on site migration.

Here are the steps we took for this project:

- Acquired Hardware and Software (our office)
    - Built the physical server
    - Configured hardware (built RAID arrays, installed memory, etc.)
    - Installed and configured the server operating system
    - Installed and configured server software
    - Created users, machine accounts, etc.
    - From backup, moved a copy of all data from the old server (including Exchange database)
- Performed onsite "Pre-Migration" training
- Placed server at client office and begin synchronizing with old, live server
- Moved core services to the new server (DHCP, DNS, time service, etc.)
- Migrated workstations
    - Cleaned, fixed, updated as needed
    - Moved data to the server
    - Migrated Profiles
- When the last end user was moved over, we turned off the old server
- Performed onsite "Post Migration" training
- Reviewed "spinoff" and fine-tuning service requests created during this process
- Proceeded to work on fine-tuning service requests
- Reported completion of all steps to client
- Evaluated all aspects of migration project, including accuracy of estimates and any unforeseen incidents.

Turning Services On and Off

Because this was such a clean migration, we were able to simply enable services on the new machine and disable them on the old machine, leaving the old machine completely unchanged and operational.

The old machine was so "untouched" that we actually took it back to our office and used it to perform a series of practice migrations. As we worked through the various tools outlined in Appendix B, we ran the migration process again and again from the old, unchanged server.

This is a key point because it gives you a road back for most functions. If you've moved to Exchange 2007 from 2003, then the road back might be a bit bumpy, but not too bad.

An updated LOB with lots of new data will have no meaningful road back, of course. But pretty much everything else will work on the old system

And if someone somehow comes up with something that didn't get migrated, you can always fire up the old server and go get whatever it is.

Key Factors in Success

These are the "tools" in our tool belt that made this a successful migration:

- As an existing client, we had created good documentation of all systems.
- One mini-project (moving the web site) was separated from the migration project.
- One upgrade project (Office products) was delayed until after the migration was complete.
- We built and tested the entire system off site on an isolated network.
- As a "plain vanilla" installation, all members of our team understood the project and were able to operate with a high level of confidence.

What Went Wrong

There were no surprises, bumps, or delays in this migration project.

A Peek Into This Client's Future

As with most SMB clients, we are wondering whether this client has purchased their last server. In three years, we expect them to be using hosted Exchange Server.

As their LOB is a custom-build Linux application, it could just as easily move to the cloud as sit on their network.

So, what services do they need onsite? They need data storage, remote access, login security, and backup. These can all be provided by specialty server such as the mini-servers being developed by Microsoft.

Imagine a Small Business Server with no Exchange and no "premium" services. That would make migration even easier!

The Standard Diagram

Our standard diagram for a client system is on page five of this chapter. You probably have essentially the same diagram for many clients. You might add a network printer or scanner, but it's basically the same.

This client doesn't take advantage of remote access, so we haven't put any devices out on the Internet for them, such as hope PCs, Blackberries, or laptops.

Notice that we have turned off Network Address Translation (NAT) for the Internet router. We do this so that we can have complete control of NAT via the firewall.

We like to map things ourselves without the ISP being involved because we can change things very quickly as needed. We also know that we can back up a firewall configuration and put it back the way it was in an instant if it doesn't work the way we want.

Note, also, that we have an ILO port on the SBS server. That's HP's Integrated Lights Out feature. Dell has a less powerful version called Dell Remote Access Control or DRAC.

The ILO (or DRAC) card takes an IP address so we can connect to the machine console before any operating system is involved. So, for example, we can power down or power up the machine through this card.

ILO also allows you to totally manage the hardware, including flashing the motherboard or RAID controller. Basically, anything you can do while sitting in front of the machine, you can do remotely.

If you use an IP address on the private subnet, you'll need a way to get to it with a web browser. That might mean connecting to another server on the inside of the firewall, or from a desktop.

If you want to connect from the outside world, you'll need to either connect remotely to a desktop or server, or use NAT to assign a public IP address to the ILO card.

Just remember not to connect to it from the primary server itself, or via RWW unless you're just looking around. Many functions will break your connectivity and not let you back in if you are relying on the server you're going through to get to the ILO card.

Our preference is to use an SSL certificate and access the ILO card through a public IP address.

(As a complete side-note, this same technology is available for desktop systems with the Intel V-Pro chip.)

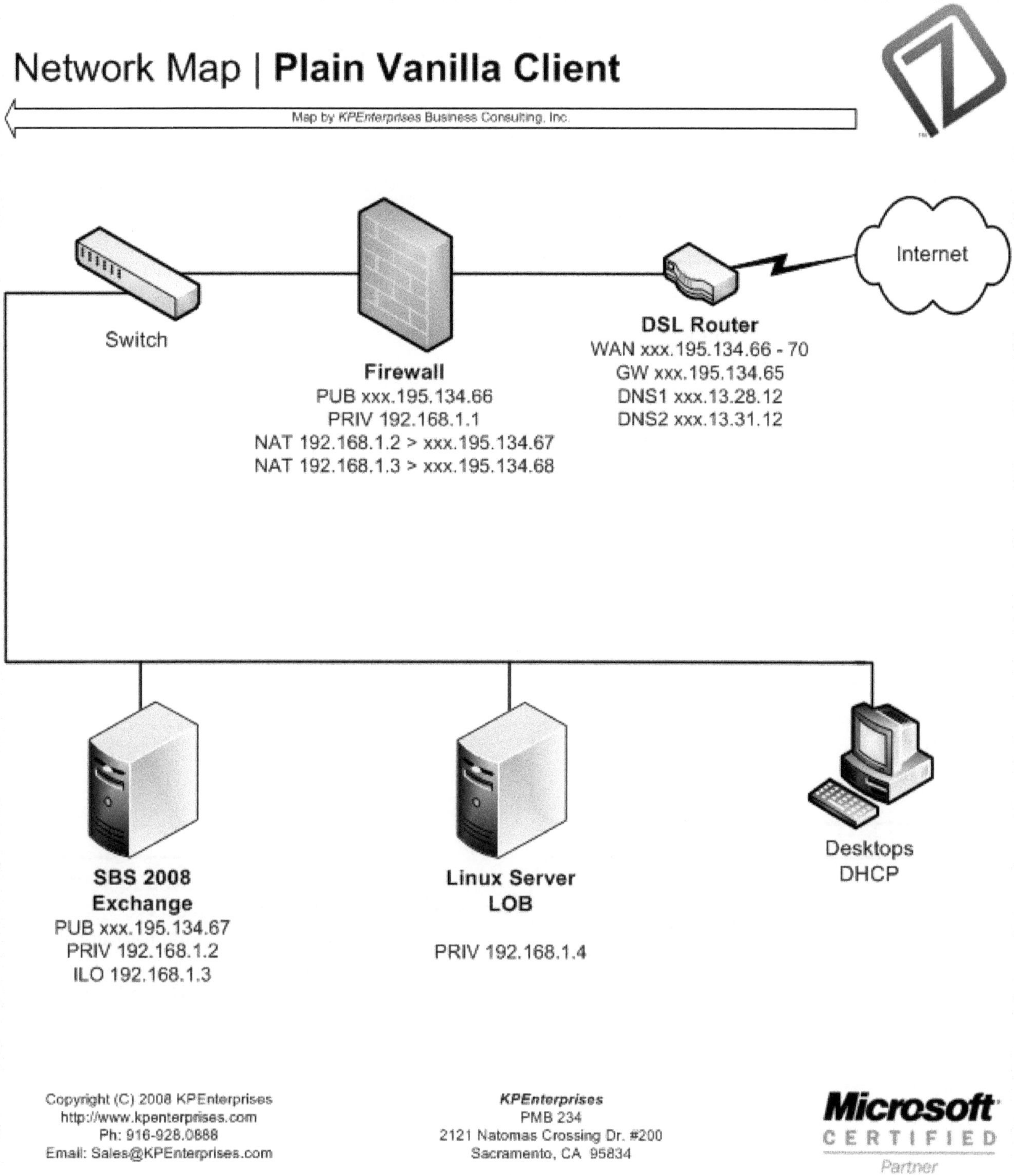
Network Map | Plain Vanilla Client
Map by KPEnterprises Business Consulting, Inc.
Internet
Switch
Firewall
PUB xxx.195.134.66
PRIV 192.168.1.1
NAT 192.168.1.2 > xxx.195.134.67
NAT 192.168.1.3 > xxx.195.134.68
DSL Router
WAN xxx.195.134.66 - 70
GW xxx.195.134.65
DNS1 xxx.13.28.12
DNS2 xxx.13.31.12
SBS 2008
Exchange
PUB xxx.195.134.67
PRIV 192.168.1.2
ILO 192.168.1.3
Linux Server
LOB
PRIV 192.168.1.4
Desktops
DHCP
Copyright (C) 2008 KPEnterprises
http://www.kpenterprises.com
Ph: 916-928.0888
Email: Sales@KPEnterprises.com
KPEnterprises
PMB 234
2121 Natomas Crossing Dr. #200
Sacramento, CA 95834
Microsoft
CERTIFIED
Partner

The Network Migration Workbook

Overview and Flow

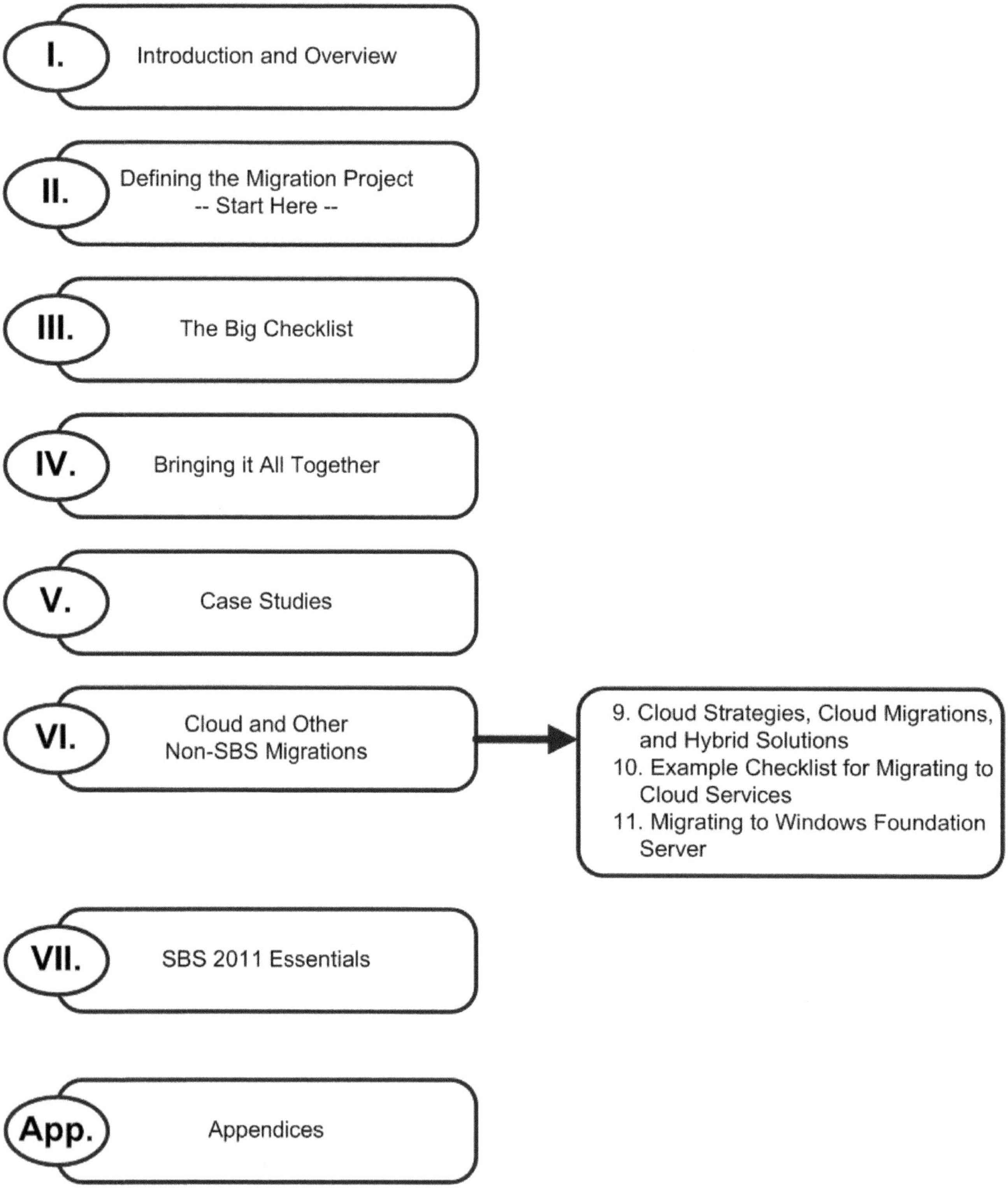

VI. Cloud and Other Non-SBS Migrations

Introduction to The Section

This book was originally a by-product of our company's rigorous *Zero Downtime Migration* (ZDTM) processes. We developed the processes over years of working with Microsoft's Small Business Server line. This included migrations to and from SBS versions 2000-2008.

It is amazing how much can change in just a few years. Since this book was released in 2009, KPEnterprises has moved heavily into Cloud Service offerings. In addition, some products have already been introduced to the "cloud market" and failed. This is a fast-moving environment, and it won't slow down any time soon.

Two interesting developments emerged at the same time in this market space. One is Cloud Services. These include hosted Exchange services, hosted SharePoint, and other products that directly affect clients who have been traditional users of SBS.

The other development is the emergence of appliance computers. Appliance computers include dedicated email machines, dedicated router/firewall products, and a series of small form factor hardware devices designed to accept specialty operating systems.

When we combine these developments, we see that it is very easy to migrate to a mix of cloud-based services and on-premise hardware and software. The most obvious first move to the cloud for many people is online backups. Or maybe it was web services. But hosted Exchange services aren't far behind.

Once you handle backups, web hosting, and Exchange in the cloud, the on-site piece becomes very straight forward. You need storage and Active Directory. You might need remote access (and you might not).

In this section, we'll address several alternatives to simply migrating to the next SBS Standard server. Chapter 9 addresses Cloud services and how you can migrate your clients to the cloud. There are many, many cloud options, of course, so we can't cover them all. But we provide a framework that addresses all of the core components.

Chapter 10 provides a sample checklist for a migration to the cloud. It is not as detailed as the "big" checklist for SBS 2011, but covers the basics of a small and simple office migration to the Cloud.

Chapter 11 takes a look at Microsoft's Foundation Server. We love this product and hope that it manages to stick around even though SBS Essentials is targeted to the same market. We present the most important things you need to consider when moving clients to Foundation Server from SBS or standard Windows Server.

In total, this section is intended to give an introduction to the various options available other than Small Business Server. It is not the case that you either choose to do or not do "Cloud Services." They are easily integrated into an overall strategy, and the choice of services depends in large part on the client's needs.

Chapter 9

Cloud Strategies, Cloud Migrations, and Hybrid Solutions

Introduction

Cloud services and *cloud computing* have come on very strong since about 2009. These two terms encompass a wide variety of services. Most of them are not "just right" for the small business space. But a few of them are perfect for SMB clients.

No matter which cloud service offerings you put together for your clients, there's a very clear shift in how you solve problems once you start including cloud services in the mix. Luckily, the most logical first services are easy and obvious to implement.

Before we get into the specifics of cloud services, let's look at the core functions that are needed for any small business to function in the modern world.

You may have more, but let's start with a list of 23 primary functions. Some of these are easily moved to the cloud. Others never will be. The primary functions are:

- Active Directory
- Backup (onsite) (online)
- Blackberry, etc.
- Desktop Environment
- DHCP
- DNS
- Domain Control
- Email / Exchange
- File Storage
- Firewall
- Internet Connection
- LAN/Network
- Line of Business (LOB)
- Printing
- Remote Access (desktop)
- SharePoint
- Spam Filter
- SQL Database(s)
- Telephone
- Terminal Server / Application
- Virus Protection
- VPN (if needed)
- WWW

Obviously, any given business might have additional functional requirements. Many businesses will not need everything on this list.

Whatever list of core functions you are addressing at a specific client office, you will need to make strategic decisions about the best technology for each function. We believe there are currently four types of cloud service offerings that are relevant to your decision-making.

And, truth be told, there are only three types of cloud service offerings that are relevant for most small businesses.

Four Types of Clouds

The most advanced type of cloud service offering is too young to be of practical use in the SMB space. It is the true cloud-based application totally separated from the server/software/product model we are all familiar with.

For example, Microsoft's Azure service is not a place where you can buy hosted Windows Servers and hosted Exchange services. Azure is a platform on which developers can create applications.

Those applications run within that environment. There are no servers, no server licenses. There is only "computing" power addressed to run tasks and made available to devices that are somehow connected to the environment.

This true cloud-based computing will evolve very quickly. Microsoft has literally bet their future on this technology.

But today there are three much more relevant types of cloud offerings for the SMB space: Internet-based clouds, partner clouds, and on-premise clouds.

Internet-based clouds are services that exist entirely in the Internet. These are true services in that you buy them on a month-to-month or yearly basis as needed. Perhaps the most successful example of such a service is Salesforce.com.

But there are plenty of other examples as well. Autotask provides a cloud-based line of business application within our own industry. IMIS provides one for managing membership-based organizations. And there are many more. Rent Manager provides one for managing rental properties.

Many clients who have on-premise line of business applications will be looking at cloud-based options in the years to come.

Partner Clouds or VAR Clouds are cloud services that your company has put together in your own data center or colocation facility.

The simplest of these is web hosting. Many consultants have housed web servers in their data centers for years. As our industry has moved clients away from in-house web servers, we have taken on those services ourselves.

Another great example is backup services. If you backup your clients' data to machines at your office or your colo, then you are offering a type of partner cloud solution for them.

As the technology advances, we expect more and more partners to develop their own partner cloud offerings, including hosted desktops and hosted servers based on virtual machine technology.

On-Premise Clouds are a little different in that they rely on virtualization technology but the hardware lives at the client's location (client's premises).

On-premise clouds are more than simple virtual machines. They include some management and licensing components that are housed offsite. And, most importantly, they are sold as a service and not as combination of hardware and software.

All of these cloud offerings have the service component in common: They involve selling technology as a service, on an on-going basis, and not as a "sale" of hardware and software.

The key selling points here are:

1) As a service, the cost of technology appears on the client's financial books as an operating expense and not a capital expenditure.
2) Generally speaking, these services are sold as needed, so the licenses increase and decrease automatically as service consumption changes.
3) The client has greater flexibility with regard to the services acquired. Clients do not necessarily expect a lower price if they get increased flexibility.
4) Increased reliability means lower maintenance costs and increased uptime.

So, realistically, you have three places where you can place each of the core functions we mentioned above:

- On an Internet-based service
- At your partner cloud
- On site at the client's office

One Step At A Time

Luckily, you can make this transition gradually over time. In fact, unlike most technology changes of the past, there is rarely any downtime or service interruption with a migration to cloud-based services.

In Karl's *Super Good Project Planner for Technical Consultants*, he gives an example of using cloud-base spam filtering to move a client from one email server to another with zero downtime. The checklists in this book detail a variety of other zero-downtime strategies. All of these are easier with cloud services.

When you consider the core functions outlined above, you can see how easy it is to plan a gradual move to the cloud for almost everything. For example, you might move these services in this order:

1) Web Servers
2) Spam Filtering
3) Virus Scanning (at least management)
4) Email / Exchange
5) Backup to Cloud

As you can see, each of these is pretty easy to move. The basic process is:

- Set up the new service
- Populate the new service (migrate data as needed)
- Repoint DNS, etc. so the new service is active
- Turn off the old service

Once you move these services to the cloud, the local network becomes MUCH easier to maintain, upgrade, and even migrate to new hardware.

Let's go through a little exercise. Let's begin dividing that list into categories and speculate about what goes where, and how to get it there.

What Has To Stay Onsite?

Some things clearly need to stay onsite. Printers, for example, would be pretty inconvenient outside your office! Here's a quick list of what you must leave onsite:

- Active Directory (unless you eliminate)
- Desktop Environment ☑
- DHCP ☑
- DNS ☑
- Domain Control
- Firewall ☑
- Internet Connection ☑
- LAN/Network ☑
- Printing ☑
- Telephone
- VPN (if needed)

Well, that's a small list. And the items with an checkboxes actually represent items that simply come into existence with the basic office setup of LAN and Internet connectivity.

Earlier we decided to move a few things to the cloud. They were:

- Web Servers
- Spam Filtering
- Virus Scanning (at least management)
- Email / Exchange – and Blackberry
- Backup to Cloud

So what's left?

- Backup (onsite)
- File Storage
- Line of Business (LOB)
- Remote Access (desktop)
- SharePoint
- SQL Database(s)
- Terminal Server / Application

Some of these are optional and could easily be moved to cloud services (SharePoint, some SQL databases, some LOBs). If people need terminal services, they probably need it on their server and not to a cloud server. If they need remote access to desktops, it's probably because of an old LOB that has to live on the server.

The only two universally-required critical functions left are onsite backup and file storage. Both of these can be eliminated if you have all file storage in the cloud. Backups will automatically be offsite.

But realistically, we're not there for many reasons. Even simple LOBs such as QuickBooks can have really terrible performance over a VPN or hosted virtual environment. In addition, big files and big databases require faster, onsite storage just to provide reasonable performance.

So today (2012), there are many reasons for having storage onsite, even if it's backed up to the cloud. For many people, the combination of onsite storage, onsite BDR (backup and disaster recovery) solution, and offsite backup of the BDR is ideal.

The "Server Lite" Concept

Way back in 2008, before SBS 2008 was released, Karl proposed a kind of server specifically geared to the 1-25 user market. And really, it's perfect for 1-10 and 1-15 markets.

As KPEnterprises began developing a set of cloud offerings, we brought this server into existence. Clients don't really care what their technology is, so we call it "Server Lite."

See blog posts

http://blog.smallbizthoughts.com/2007/10/new-server-family-revised.html

and

http://blog.smallbizthoughts.com/2008/02/karls-server-roadmap-for-microsoft.html

The core selling points of Server Lite are:

1. Activity Directory is onsite. That means fast logons and local security.
2. Storage is onsite and may be backed up locally or in the cloud.
3. Line of Business applications can be installed locally if needed.

That's it. Lite. Very lite. The thing to remember here is that you're asking the onsite server to do very little work. Logons and file serving take almost zero processing power or speed. Only a clunky LOB can slow you down.

We basically have two variations of the Server Lite. The first one assumes that the client only needs logon and file storage. Literally nothing else! With this version, we can provide a very inexpensive piece of hardware and not care if it fails. Because Active Directory is backed up, it can be restored to a new machine. Because the file store is backed up, it can be moved to anything . . . or the client can use the cloud storage in an emergency.

This is not a discussion of your business practices, but we generally provide an HP Microserver with Microsoft Foundation Server or Microsoft SBS Essentials. If the client gets more value from terminal services (now RDS) versus Remote Web Workplace, we go with Foundation Server over SBS. Other considerations are discussed below.

HP Microserver

If the client needs a little more beef, it's usually because they have an old LOB or they're using really large CAD files or graphics files. In such cases, we use the same operating systems but pump up the HP Microserver. On rare occasions we have put in a low-end tower machine such as an HP ML150.

For low-end servers, we own the server and provide it to the client for $100 a month as a *service*. This means we own it and the client is only using it. It depreciates on our asset list and not the client's.

For slightly beefier machines we spend more on RAM, processor, and maybe hard drives. As a result, we normally provide these Servers Lite at $200 per month. It's still a good deal for the client and for us.

Operating Systems

When we first started installing these systems, SBS Essentials did not exist. We put in a few Windows Home Servers. They were cheap, arrived in cute little cube-shaped boxes, and handled the storage. But they have no active directory. And after fifteen years with AD, we were reluctant to do without.

A much better server – and a perfect server in many ways – is the Microsoft Foundation Server. Active Directory. Simple licensing. Will take RDS licenses for "terminal service" access. This is, in fact, what we use in our own office. Our only server is a tiny little machine with Foundation server and QuickBooks, which we only access by RDS. In fact, QuickBooks is published as an application, so we can launch it without Remote Desktop. That's it. Everything else is stored directly on our cloud storage.

We could honestly see building an entire business on Microsoft Foundation Server and hosted email, storage, and Anti-Virus.

Then along came SBS 2011 Essentials. It's got many of the "nice to have" features of Small Business Server, but no Exchange Server, no SharePoint, and no SQL. Key features we use are active directory, storage, and RWA (Remote Web Access replaces Remote Web Workplace in 2011) if the client needs it. It also has super-easy licensing and handles more clients than Foundation Server

Assuming you don't go with Windows Home Server, let's take a quick look at the differences between Foundation Server and SBS Essentials.

NOTE: We have no idea who decides on naming conventions at Microsoft, but it is very difficult to find information on Foundation Server because Microsoft is putting a huge push on "Team Foundation Server," which is a complete un-related development system. To find information on Foundation Servers, Google

foundation server specifications -team

The official product name is Windows Server 2008 R2 Foundation. Obviously, searches for that will only get you a million links to Server 2008. So start here and poke around:

http://www.microsoft.com/en-us/server-cloud/windows-server/2008-r2-foundation.aspx

This product is an OEM-only product, which means that it must be sold as a new installation with hardware. If you are an OEM (original equipment manufacturer or system builder), you can order the OEM software for Foundation server, but you can only install it on a new server you are delivering to the client. There is no in-place upgrade to Foundation Server.

SBS Essentials is a little easier to find because it's simply a version of the SBS family. You can simply start at

http://www.microsoft.com/sbs

or Google *SBS Essentials*.

Both of these servers are available from HP, CDW, Dell, Amazon.com, Ingram, and Synnex. And other places, we're sure. As far as we've seen, you're only going to find these preinstalled from HP or Dell. That doesn't make it easy. Assuming you know what you want, we've found that you really have to scrounge around to find the right thing. Everyone carries some different combination.

It's worth the effort, though, so hang in there!

Now let's compare Foundation Server and SBS Essentials. Assuming you're using these in conjunction with some cloud services, both servers will have the following services onsite.

Onsite:

- Active Directory
- Desktop Environment
- DHCP
- DNS (in-house)
- Domain Control
- Firewall
- Internet Connection
- Line of Business (LOB)
- Printing
- RWA (on SBS Essentials) or Remote Desktop Services/Terminal Services (on Foundation)
- SQL Database(s)
- Storage (Files)
- Telephone
- Virus Protection

And both servers will have the following services in the cloud.

Offsite / Cloud / Hosted:

- Blackberry, etc.
- DNS (Internet)
- Email / Exchange
- Line of Business (LOB)
- Online Backup
- SharePoint
- Spam Filter
- WWW

Here are the limitations for each server.

Foundation Server Limits:

- 15 user licenses no more available
- One Physical Processor
- Max 8 GB RAM
- 50 Network Access Connections (RRAS)
- 10 Network Access Connections (NPS)
- Must be at the root of the forest
- OEM Licensing Only
- 64-bit only
- No Hyper-V host support

SBS Essentials Limits:

- 25 user licenses no more available
- Two Physical Processors
- Max 32 GB RAM
- 25 Computer Limit
- Must be the domain controller
- OEM Licensing Only
- 64 Bit Only
- No Hyper-V host support

SO all that boils down to four things, one of which is not obvious.

First, the license limits are 15 for Foundation and 25 for SBS Essentials. These are hard limits, so don't tempt fate. The really good news that most IT consultants are serving very small clients. See the discussion of opportunities below.

Second, there are serious limits on power – Memory and CPUs. Foundation Server, in particular, is limited to 8 GB of RAM. The 32 GB limit on SBS Essentials is quite generous. But that 8 GB limit can really hurt performance if you start overloading the server.

In addition, the ability to have a second physical process on SBS Essentials allows you to have a very powerful machines, if you need it.

Remember, both of these are intended to be "lite" servers, not workhorses with SQL, SharePoint, and a bunch of other stuff on top. If you need those servers, buy those servers!

Third, you have a choice between Remote Web Access and Remote Desktop Services. There is less and less reason for people to access their desktops remotely when you move services to the cloud. But still, people like it. Foundation Server offers a true Terminal Server environment while SBS Essentials gives you the new version of Remote Web Workplace.

The fourth, and less obvious difference between these servers is the fact that Foundation Server has a very simple, basic, straight-forward active directory. It doesn't know about SBS. It comes as a standard server. So if you want it to be a domain controller, you treat it just like Server 2008 Standard edition.

Foundation Server doesn't have to be a domain controller. It can be a backup domain controller, primary DC, or only DC. (Yeah, we know they don't call it that anymore, but since all the commands to promote/demote and deal with the status of the server use that terminology, we will.)

What does this mean? Simply:

Migrations to and from Foundation Server are *extremely* easy!

Chapter Eleven walks through the process of moving from an older server to Foundation Server. As you will see, the domain migration is very clean.

So how do we choose between these two? On rare occasions there's a preference for Remote Web Access. But most of the time, it comes down to the number of users and need for power.

If someone has ten users and really doesn't expect to grow, we're okay with Foundation Server. If they have 12 users and are growing, then we'll quote them SBS Essentials. The limit of our comfort with SBS Essentials is about 20 users. The last thing you want to do it sell a server and need to sell the client another one right away.

You can, and we have, put line of business applications on Foundation Server. But you need to be really sure that the LOB has a well-behaved database and doesn't suck up all the RAM. We never sell these machines with less than 8 GB RAM. If the client needs to have a beefier server, then we quote SBS Essentials.

Opportunity at the Small End of SMB

In preparing their market research for SBS Essentials, Microsoft estimated that there were 11 Million businesses worldwide with 1-4 PCs and another 25 Million businesses worldwide with 5-25 PCs. Of these, an estimated 75% do not have any server.

See the PDF entitled *Windows Server Small Business Solutions* at

https://partner.microsoft.com/download/HK/40166373

In other words, there are LOTS of clients out there who need exactly this solution. And why don't 27 million of them have servers? Probably because of the cost. If you sell a standard HP ML 350 with SBS Standard, a raid array, and enough memory to handle it all, you can easily quote the client $5,000 - $7,000 plus labor.

So a simple migration can quickly add up to $10,000 - $15,000. That's a lot of money for a very small business. As strange as it sounds, your clients with servers have been the top 25% who can actually come up with that kind of money all at once!

Cloud offerings – and a Server Lite solution – allow the client to buy their technology one month at a time, as needed. Even at $1,000 - $1,500 per month, they are still saving money over a new server, plus installation, plus maintenance.

Next: The Practical Side of Migrating to Small Servers

In the next chapter, we'll give a basic checklist for moving services to the cloud, leaving behind only the basics as discussed here. Chapter Eleven covers the step-by-step guide to migrating a client to Foundation Server.

Finally, Chapters Twelve and Thirteen cover the migration to SBS Essentials. As you can imagine, some pieces of that will be very similar to what we'll cover in chapters 10-11.

Chapter 10

Example Checklist for Migrating to Cloud Services

The Sample Project

This chapter builds on the previous. Let's assume you have a very standard small business environment. That means it looks very much like the picture on the bottom of this page. One server. Maybe ten users. Right now, that server is SBS 2008. It serves up files, handles logons (active directory), hosts Microsoft Exchange, and manages the backup.

You want to move the following services to the cloud:

- Email / Exchange
- Online Backup
- Spam Filter
- WWW

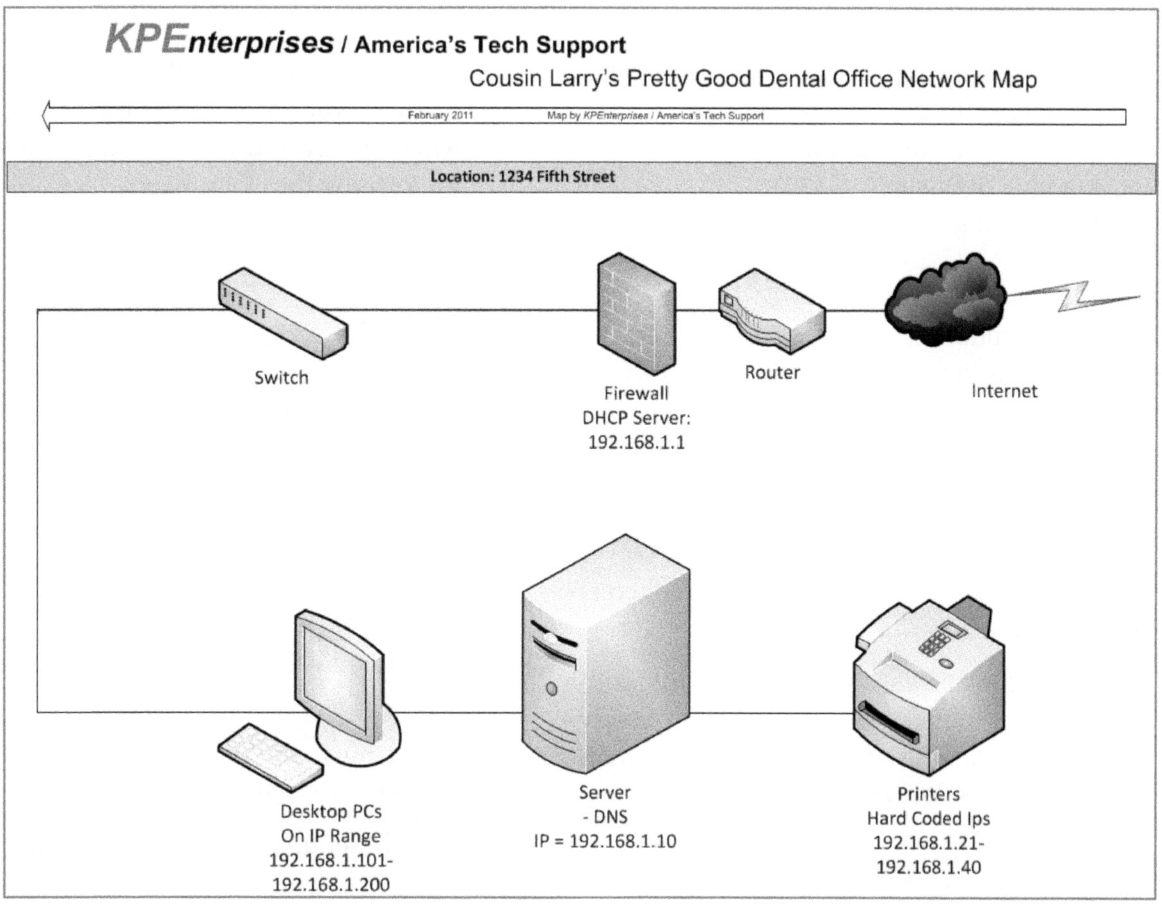

All of these – every one of them – is extremely easy to move to a hosted service. The basic process is the same as we described earlier in the discussion of Zero Downtime strategies (Chapter One and Chapter Nine).

It goes something like this:

1. Set up new service
2. Populate the new service (migrate data as needed)
3. Move the new service to "live" status (Repoint DNS, etc. so the new service is active)
4. Turn off the old service

This process is repeated for Web Services, Spam Filtering, Exchange, and Online Backup. Once completed, the following services will remain onsite:

- Active Directory
- Desktop Environment
- DHCP
- DNS (in-house)
- Domain Control
- Firewall
- Internet Connection
- Line of Business (LOB)
- Printing
- RWA
- Storage (Files)
- Telephone
- Virus Protection

Chapters 11-14 address migrations to Foundation Server and SBS Essentials. But let's take a minute and look at what remains on the server. From the list above, only a few items are actually on the server.

When you look at what's "left" after a migration to of services to the cloud, you see that the server onsite is much easier to migrate. That migration really boils down to active directory, file storage, anti-virus, and the line of business application.

Here's what's left onsite:

- Active Directory
- DNS (in-house)
- Domain Control
- Line of Business (LOB)
- RWA (on SBS Essentials) or Terminal Services (on Foundation)
- Storage (Files)
- Virus Protection

If nothing else, the move to cloud services for a few key components makes your onsite migration almost foolproof!

Note on Communications:

Just as with any migration, you need to Over Freakin' Communicate with the client. That means keeping them informed before you change something that could affect them (moving DNS, moving DHCP, etc.).

Use templates such as those in the Big Checklist or create your own. Occasional emails about where we are and what's next are very helpful for keeping the client happy.

The Cloud Migration Project

So you have your project: Migrate Exchange, Backup, Spam Filter, and Web Site to hosted services. First, we're going to re-order that list so that it has a nice progression. Now it looks like this:

First, migrate web site.

Second, migrate (or start using) hosted spam filter.

Third, move Exchange services and mailboxes to hosted Exchange.

Fourth, set up a cloud-based backup.

Just as with the "big" migration project, we're going to create separate service tickets for each of these four. There are two primary reasons for this. Separate tickets means that you can manage (and complete) each project separate from the others. After all, one project might get delayed or have problems. This should not affect the other projects.

In addition, separate tickets allow you to track time separately for each of these project. Most of them are very straight forward. Only the Exchange move has a lengthy process. But you never know how things will go. As a general policy, you want each project to be separated as much as possible.

So, you'll set up four Service Requests (SRs) and execute the four projects. Here are your checklists.

Note on Email Cleanup

One the biggest issues with email migration in general, and particularly to the cloud, is that big mailboxes take a long time. In addition, there's a 2 GB limit to PSTs before Outlook 2010, and very often there are severe limits on the size of hosted mailboxes.

Outlook 2010 has a 50 GB limit on PSTs, which is ridiculously large and we do not recommend taking advantage of this! Instead, we think it's a great idea to clean up the email as part of the migration project. That way you decrease the "junk" part of the Exchange database and reduce the time needed to upload the data to the hosted environment.

The cleanup process consists of exporting and then deleting certain files. You can save the exported PST files as "archive" files so clients always have them. But you'll remove them from the database. It is important to pick a cutoff date long enough in the past to keep "current" items in the database but get rid of really old stuff. In our example, we are keeping everything since January 1, 2011.

Here's basically what you'll find in the checklist regarding cleanup:

1. Export all Deleted Items to PST
2. Export all Sent Items before 12/31/2010 to PST
3. Delete all Sent Items before 12/31/2010
4. Empty the Delete Items folder
5. Export (archive) all items in the user mailbox older than 12/31/2010
6. Export the entire user mailbox, now much smaller than it was before

SR 1: Migrating Web Service to Hosted Web Site

Notes / Overview:

The client has decided to move the web site from in-house to a hosted service. This requires some prep work so that there is no downtime for visitors to the web site. The move to hosted web service makes this easy.

1. Gather Information

Collect the following information and record it here:

☐ Old Web Site is found on server: ______________________

☐ Domain of this web site: ______________________

☐ Directory / Physical Location: ______________________

☐ The Domain Registrar for this domain is: ______________________

- O Logon Address: ______________________
- O User Name: ______________________
- O Password: ______________________

☐ The DNS for this domain is maintained at: ______________________

- O Logon Address: ______________________
- O User Name: ______________________
- O Password: ______________________

☐ Will DNS be moved to the new hosting service? Yes No

☐ SQL Server Associated with this web site? Yes No

If so, describe: ______________________

____

____

☐ Additional notes on this web site (databases, security requirements, etc.) ______________________

____

____

____

☐ New Web Site will be at (FQDN or IP Address): ______________________

☐ Username on new hosting service: ______________________________

☐ Password on new hosting service: ______________________________

☐ Directory / Physical Location: ______________________________

☐ Web site-specific Username on new hosting service: ______________________________

☐ Web site-specific Username on new hosting service: ______________________________

☐ Will the new web site be a common hosted site or require a dedicated Virtual Private Server?

Hosted Site VPS

☐ The DNS for this domain is maintained at: ______________________________

- Logon Address: ______________________________
- User Name: ______________________________
- Password: ______________________________

☐ SQL Server Information: ______________________________

____

____

☐ Security Notes (private directories, etc.): ______________________________

____

____

☐ Additional notes on this web site: ______________________________

____

____

____

2. Prepare for Move

Even though the old web site is up and running, and will remain so for a short time after the new site is up, Do Not begin migrating this web site without a tested backup!

☐ Create a separate backup of the web site

☐ Note any special requirements

☐ Verify the backup by restoring the entire web site to a different directory. The preferred directory is C:\!Tech\del_www

3. Set Up New Web Site

Note: Specific steps for setting up new services and directories varies. But all are straight forward enough that details are not given here. If there are any "gotchas" be sure to note them.

☐ Log into the new hosting service

☐ Create a new web site instance or VPS, as required

☐ Verify directory location is correct

☐ Set up SQL Server instance if required

O SQL Security Information: ______________________________

____

____

☐ Verify directory location is correct

☐ Log into the new site with FTP using site-specific username and password noted above

☐ Log off of the FTP site

☐ Document all new web site functions, settings, usernames, and passwords in the PSA system

4. Move Data

☐ Log into the new site with FTP using site-specific username and password noted above

☐ Copy over files. The easiest place to do this from is the C:\!Tech\del_www directory you created earlier.

☐ If directory security is required, set up the directories and security settings as needed

☐ Test basic web site access

☐ Test directory security

☐ To the extent you can, test all functions of the web site

Note: Web site tests are only valid from outside the network where the web site is host OR maintained. You don't want your desktop environment to give you a "false positive" because you have something set up or installed. The most frustrating words a client can hear about their web site are "It work on my desk."

☐ Backup the new web site using the preferred tools of the new hosting service

☐ Log off of the FTP site

☐ Contact client. Give them all information needed to access and test the web site.

☐ Have client test the new web site

☐ Place this Service Request on HOLD until the client verifies that the new web site is working properly

5. Make the New Site Live

Once the client approves the functionality of the new web site/server, perform the following.

NOTE: It is a wise idea to request domain registry moves early in the day so you can track down problems as needed white tech support is available.

NOTE: It is wise to initiate DNS moves late in the day so that routers have all night to get the new DNS information. The best time is probably 4:30 PM on a Friday. That gives the routers on the Internet all weekend to find the new location.

☐ If DNS is to be moved to the new hosting site:

- O Log into the domain registry at the new hosting service
- O Initiate a domain name transfer request
- O Follow the process of the old domain registry to authorize the domain transfer
- O Log into the domain registry at the new hosting service
- O Following requirements of the new hosting service, point the domain to the new web site location

☐ If DNS is not being moved:

- O Log into the domain registry that houses the client domain
- O Following requirements of the new hosting service, point the domain to the new web site location

NOTE: At this point, some visitors will go to the new location and some will go to the old location. Gradually, as DNS records get updated, all users will be directed to the new web site location.

☐ Once you have given the DNS system time to propagate the new information, verify that requests are going to the new site

- O Ping the domain name (company.com)
- O Ping the fully qualified domain name of the web site (www.company.com)
- O If pings resolve to the old address, run a trace route to the web site (www.company.com). To do this, open a Command Prompt and type

  Tracert www.company.com

  A trace route sends ICMP packets to the first router that can resolve the route between your machine and the web site. Then it finds the next router on the path, then the next, etc. Sometimes ICMP packets take different routes. In each case, you are poking these routers and asking them to verify authoritative responses to DNS. This can speed up propagation of the new DNS information.

☐ Once you are consistently directed to the new web site location, have client test the new web site

☐ Place this Service Request on HOLD until the client verifies that the new web site is working properly

6. Turn Off Old Service

Once the client approves the functionality of the new web hosting service, perform the following.

☐ If there are other web sites running on the old server, remove the specific instance of this web site

(In a Small Business Server environment, there are going to be web services running for many functions. On other servers, you might have additional web sites running.)

☐ Verify that there is a good backup of the directories holding the old web site

☐ Delete the contents of the old web site from the old web site server

---

Hosted Spam Filters and Hosted Exchange Mailboxes

There are several options for connecting to email, and particularly to Microsoft Exchange. For those of us who have been supporting Small Business Server for some time, we're used to having Exchange on the primary server, the SBS box. See Illustration 10-1.

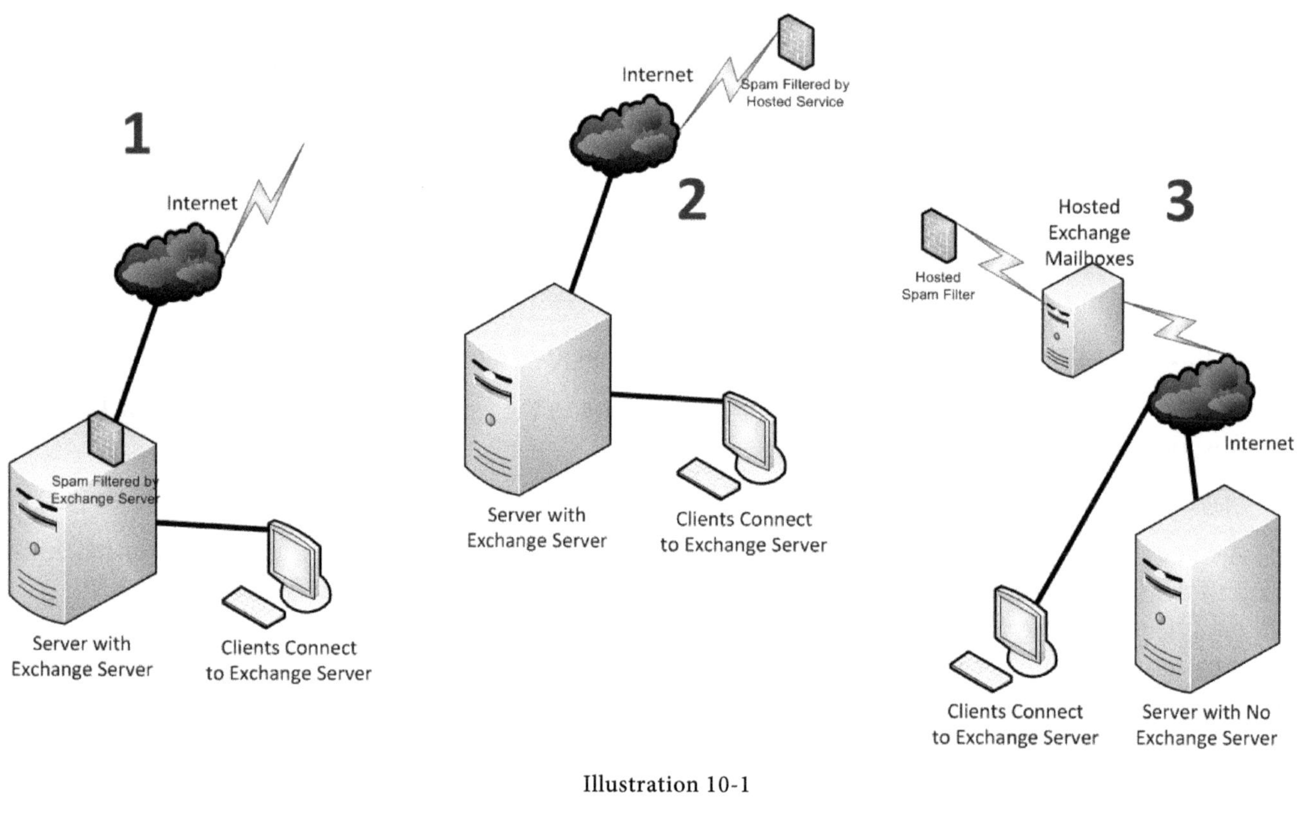

Illustration 10-1

In Scenario #1, spam filtering takes place on the in-house Exchange server. This means that all the traffic related to spam (95-99% of all email traffic) goes onto the client's network, slowing down all traffic on the LAN. It also means that the processing power to filter messages is all on the primary server, taking a significant amount of that server's process time.

In Scenario #2, spam filtering is done "in the cloud" by a hosted service. This dramatically reduces network traffic and server processor time. In both Scenarios #1 and #2, the client machines still connect to their local Exchange server to collect email.

In Scenario #3, spam filtering takes place in the cloud, and points to a hosted exchange server. This provides no additional traffic relief over Scenario #2, but does provide a significant reduction in resource demands on the server.

Our company has been putting in spam filtering devices and services for about ten years. Once we discovered hosted spam filtering, we have moved exclusively to that. 100% of our clients have hosted spam filtering. It is available at very low prices, so we simply include it in our managed service and cloud service offerings. It makes many headaches go away!

One of the reasons we are moving to a hosted spam filtering service request before the hosted exchange service request in our example is that hosted spam filtering makes any email migration significantly easier and faster. It also makes zero downtime very easy to achieve.

As a result, SR 2 show how to set up hosted spam filtering and SR 3 shows how to migrate to hosted Exchange services with a hosted spam filter in place.

SR 2: Setting Up Hosted Spam Filter

Notes / Overview:

While this procedure appears simple, knowledge of DNS and MX records are extremely useful in troubleshooting problems related to email.

1. Gather Information

☐ Exchange server (in-house) is: ______________________________

☐ Public IP Address for Exchange Server: ______________________________

☐ Domain to be moved to hosted spam filter: ______________________________

  O Aliases to point to that domain: ______________________________

  O Aliases to point to that domain: ______________________________

  O Aliases to point to that domain: ______________________________

☐ The Domain Registrar for this domain is: ______________________________

  O Logon Address: ______________________________

  O User Name: ______________________________

  O Password: ______________________________

☐ The DNS for this domain is maintained at: ______________________________

  O Logon Address: ______________________________

  O User Name: ______________________________

  O Password: ______________________________

☐ Generate a list of all mailboxes that will be moved to the new service (have this verified with client)

☐ Generate a list of aliases used by each mailbox (have this verified with client)

☐ From your spam filtering service, what are their preferred MX records?

  O MX 10: ______________________________

  O MX 20: ______________________________

  O MX 30: ______________________________

2. Set Up New Site

☐ Log into our company account at the hosted spam filtering service

☐ Create an account for each domain

  O Set up all required domain aliases

☐ Create mailboxes for each user/mailbox defined in the discovery phase

  O Create all required aliases for all users/mailboxes defined in the discovery phase

☐ Point all domains for the client to the Exchange server at the IP address defined in the discovery phase

NOTE: At this point, any email that comes into the spam filter for these domains will be forwarded to the Exchange server.

☐ Use Telnet to verify that email flows through the spam filter to the Exchange Server

  O On a machine with Telnet installed,

  O Enter the following commands

```
telnet mail.spamfilter.com 25
EHLO clientdomain.com (Enter)
MAIL FROM: mail@ourcompany.com (Enter)
RCPT TO: User@otherdomain.com notify=success,failure  (Enter)
DATA (Enter)
Subject: test message (Enter two times)
Type your test text  (Enter)
Type a period (.) at the next blank line, and then press ENTER
QUIT
```

Note: You must substitute the "place holder" domain names with real names. If you have problems, see the documentation of your spam filter service.

When everything checks out fine, proceed to Phase 3.

3. Make the New Site Live

☐ Log into the site that controls the DNS for the domain(s) you are moving

☐ Change the MX records for the domain(s) you are moving to match those designated by the spam filtering service

Note: At this point, some email will flow to the Exchange server directly. This will be unfiltered. Other mail will flow to the spam filter and then be forwarded to the Exchange server. Gradually over about three days all email should go directly to the spam filter.

Procedure for testing how email is flowing:

☐ Send a test message from your company account to the client's Administrator mailbox

☐ Log into the client's Administrator mailbox

☐ Retrieve the email you sent and look at its headers. This will tell you whether the email was received directly by the Exchange server or passed through the spam filter.

Wait at least three days before proceeding to the next phase.

4. Stop Email from Flowing Direct to the Exchange Server

☐ Log into the client's firewall

- O Backup the firewall configuration to `c:\!Tech\Hardware`
- O Disable the rule allowing incoming SMTP traffic (port 25)
  (You may choose to delete this rule.)
- O Create a rule allowing traffic to flow from the hosted spam filtering service to the Exchange server at port 25.
- O Save or commit the new firewall configuration
- O Backup the firewall configuration to `c:\!Tech\Hardware`

  At this point, all incoming email is allowed from the hosted spam filter and port 25 is closed off to all other machines on the Internet.
- O Reboot the firewall

☐ Send a test message from your company account to the client's Administrator mailbox

☐ Log into the client's Administrator mailbox

☐ Retrieve the email you sent. When this is successful, you know the configuration is correct.

SR 3: Migrating Exchange to Hosted Exchange

Notes / Overview:

In this service request, we'll move from the setup in Illustration 10-1 Scenario #2 to Scenario #3.

An Outlook 2010 installation file has been downloaded to the server and is on the "Migration Software" directory.

You will log on as the client, upgrade Outlook if they do not already have 2010, and use this process to migrate their email boxes to the new Outlook and to hosted Exchange.

1. Gather Information

☐ Exchange server (in-house) is: ______________________________

☐ Public IP Address for Exchange Server: ______________________________

☐ Name / FQDN of new hosted Exchange: ______________________________

☐ Public IP Address for hosted Exchange: ______________________________

☐ Domain to be moved to hosted Exchange: ______________________________

- O Aliases to point to that domain: ______________________________
- O Aliases to point to that domain: ______________________________
- O Aliases to point to that domain: ______________________________

☐ Generate a list of all mailboxes that will be moved to the new service (we should have this in documentation for the hosted spam filter)

☐ Generate a list of aliases used by each mailbox (we should have this in documentation for the hosted spam filter)

☐ Hosted spam filter logon address: ______________________________

☐ Hosted spam filter username: ______________________________

☐ Hosted spam filter password: ______________________________

Note that DNS and MX records will not change as email is still directed to the hosted spam filter. All we really need to do, once the hosted service is in place, is to repoint the spam filter so it delivers to the new Exchange server.

2. Set Up New Site

☐ Log into the hosted Exchange service

☐ Create an Exchange account for each domain

- O Set up all required domain aliases
- O Turn off spam filtering (Assumes you are using hosted spam filter)

☐ Create mailboxes for each user/mailbox defined in the discovery phase

- O Create all required aliases for all users/mailboxes defined in the discovery phase

☐ Set all user passwords for this process to be ______________________. These will be changed after the data migration.

☐ Setup Contacts

☐ Setup Public Folders

NOTE: At this point, any email that comes into the hosted Exchange server for these domains will be placed in appropriate user mailboxes.

3. Make the New Site Live

☐ Log into the hosted spam filter

☐ For each domain of this client, point the email to the new hosted Exchange service.

Note: At this point, all email sent to the relevant domains will go immediately to the new hosted Exchange server. This is essentially instant.

At this point, old email is at the old company server and works fine through the "old" Outlook.

New email may be accessed via web mail at:

Web Site: ______________________________

Username: ______________________ / Password: ______________________

At Each User's Desk

☐ Obtain the User's logon name and password: ______________ / ______________

If there are additional email accounts, you should have all usernames and passwords.

Account: ______________________

User / Password: ______________________ / ______________________

Account: ______________________

User / Password: ______________________ / ______________________

Account: ______________________

User / Password: ______________________ / ______________________

☐ Open Outlook

- O Note version: ______________________________
- O If not Outlook 2010, install Outlook 2010

Note on NK2 Cache. The NK2 file saves all the cached email addresses you've sent to. If users don't save contacts to a contacts folder, this may be the only list of email addresses they have. Outlook 2010 will take the NK2 file from previous versions of Outlook at add them to a "Suggested Contacts" folder.

☐ Export PSTs and Rules

Note: This subroutine should dramatically reduce mailbox sizes so they do not exceed the default limits of most hosted exchange providers. Ideally, all mailboxes with be less than the 2GB limit of Exmerge as well.

O Log into Outlook 2010

O Export the user's Deleted items

1) Click on File / Open / and Import

2) Select Export to a File and Click Next

3) Choose Outlook Data File (.pst) and click Next

4) Highlight Delete Items and check the Include Subfolders Box. Click Next

5) Save the file in the c:\!Tech\Email directory in the format

User-Deleted20120531.pst ← This number is a date in format YYYYMMDD

6) Select Finish. Do not enter a password. Click OK.

7) In the Deleted Items folder, select all items from December 31, 2010 backward. Hold down Shift and press Delete.

You will be asked to verify that you want to permanently delete these items. Say Yes.

O Export the user's Sent items

1) Using the same procedure, export all Sent items

2) Save the file in the c:\!Tech\Email directory in the format

User-Sent20110531.pst

3) In the Sent Items folder, select all items from December 31, 2010 backward. Hold down Shift and press Delete.

You will be asked to verify that you want to permanently delete these items. Say Yes.

O Empty the Delete Items Folder

We know it's scary. Just do it. You've got the PST files, which can be copied to the server and backed up forever.

O Archive <u>older emails</u>

1) Click on File / Cleanup Tools / and Archive
2) Select Archive this folder and subfolders: Inbox
3) In the field "Archive Items Older Than" enter 12/31/2010
4) Check the box labeled Archive Items with "Do Not Archive" checked
5) Save the file in the c:\!Tech\Email directory in the format

   User-Inbox-Archive2010.pst

6) Select OK.

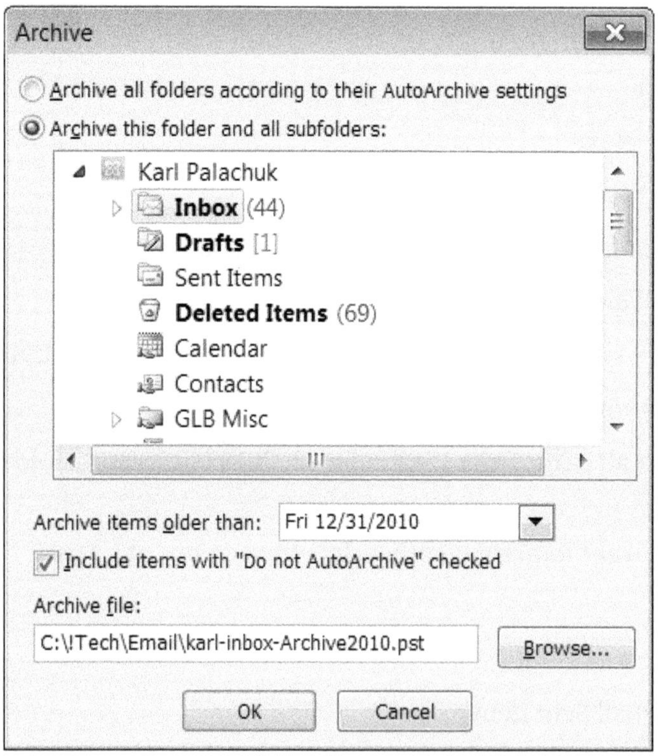

O Export entire (cleaned) mailbox

1) Click on File / Open / and Import
2) Select Export to a File and Click Next
3) Choose Outlook Data File (.pst) and click Next

4) Highlight The User's Name (top of mailbox) and check the Include Subfolders Box. Click Next

5) Save the file in the c:\!Tech\Email directory in the format

User-Exchange20110531.pst

6) Select Finish. Do not enter a password. Click OK.

○ Export Rules from Outlook

1) In Outlook 2010, select File / Info / and click on Manage Rules and Alerts

2) Click Options

3) Select Export Rules and save the rules to c:\!tech\email

Save Rules in c:\!Tech\Email directory in the format
User-Rules20110531.rwz

☐ Backup Exported Files

○ Copy all user pst and rwz files from the c:\!Tech\Email directory to the "Migration" share on the server

☐ Import PSTs and Rules

○ Connect to the hosted Exchange provider Server as the user you are migrating

○ Import the "Entire (cleaned) mailbox" PST to the hosted Exchange provider

1) Click on File / Open / and Import

2) Select Import from another Program or File and Click Next

3) Choose Outlook Data File (.pst) and click Next

4) Select the file you created in c:\!Tech\Email in the format

User-Exchange20110531.pst

5) Leave default settings and click Next.

6) The following settings should be selected:

Include Subfolders

Import items into the same subfolder in (user)

7) Click Finish

O Import the Rules

1) Click File and then Manage Rules and Alerts

2) Click the Options button and then select Import Rules

3) Select the file you created in c:\!Tech\Email directory in the format
User-Rules20110531.rwz

4) Click OK to accept.

5) To make the rules work, edit each rule and verify that it points to the appropriate resources (users, folders, etc.).

6) Click OK when finished.

☐ Test all connections

O For each email address, you should be able to send an email from an outside domain, receive that email, and reply to it.

1. Account tested: ______________________________
2. Account tested: ______________________________
3. Account tested: ______________________________
4. Account tested: ______________________________
5. Account tested: ______________________________
6. Account tested: ______________________________
7. Account tested: ______________________________
8. Account tested: ______________________________
9. Account tested: ______________________________
10. Account tested: ______________________________

Note: At this point, the migrated user's old and new email are both on the new hosted Exchange server and accessible through Outlook 2010.

Note: Outlook 2010 will copy contents of the NK2 cache file into a "Suggested Contacts" folder. Be sure the client is aware of this.

4. Disconnect Old Service

4.1. At each user's desktop

☐ Remove the old Outlook connection from in-house SBS/Exchange Server

O From the File menu, choose Account Settings and Account Settings

O Highlight the New Exchange Account you just set up

And click Set As Default

O Highlight the old Exchange Account from local SBS/Exchange Server
And Click Remove

O Close all dialogue boxes

☐ Test completely

O Close all programs

O Log off the computer

O Log onto the computer as the user

O Open Outlook

O Send an email to your company account

O Retrieve the email from your company account and reply

O Verify that email is received by the user

4.2. At the SBS/Exchange Server

Once all mailboxes have been migrated to the hosted Exchange server ...

☐ Log onto the server

☐ Disable all Exchange services

☐ Close off port 25 on the firewall

O Backup the firewall configuration to `c:\!Tech\Hardware`

O Disable the rule allowing incoming SMTP traffic (port 25)
(You may choose to delete this rule.)

O If there is a specific rule allowing traffic to flow from the hosted spam filtering service to the Exchange server at port 25, disable this rule
(You may choose to delete this rule.)

O Save or commit the new firewall configuration

O Backup the firewall configuration to `c:\!Tech\Hardware`

O Reboot the firewall

SR 4: Setting Up Hosted Backup Service

Notes / Overview:

We use a very specific hosted file storage system from Rackspace. These services vary significantly, so the specific steps here may not be right for you. But the overall flow of setting up a hosted backup is about the same. As always, you need to fine-tune procedures for what you do.

With Rackspace, there is a program called MySecureBackup (formerly Jungledisk) that allows you to map drive letters to hosted storage. Each partner has one account, in our case KPEnterprises. All client storage areas are created within that. Each client storage area has a unique name and password.

Note, also, that the initial seeding of the hosted backup will take a lot of CPU time, network bandwidth, and just plain time on the clock. In most cases, you're moving gigabytes worth of data through a small "UP" connection. Use resources at your disposal to minimize the impact on the client, such as bandwidth throttling and scheduling. I hosted backup is needed before some other piece of the project, be sure to start it early in the migration.

Now here's the checklist.

1. Gather Information

☐ Client Name: ______________________________

☐ Client's Username will be: ______________________________

☐ Client's Password will be: ______________________________

☐ Estimated initial storage area required: ______________________________

☐ Drive letter to be assigned to hosted storage: ______________________________

2. Set up New Service

☐ Log into the Storage Provider web site

☐ Create the Client account/username per the specification above

☐ From your desktop, create a new connection and connect to the new site. Copy a test file to it.

Prepare for Installation

☐ Determine how MySecureBackup program files will be distributed. Check one:

- O Server file share
- O SharePoint
- O USB key(s)
- O Direct from MySecureBackup web site
- O Shared from other source: ______________________________

☐ Download from MySecureBackup the following files and place in distribution area:

- O MySecureBackupXxx.msi ← 32 bit client program. Xxx represents version number.
- O MySecureBackup64-Xxx.msi ← 64 bit client program. Xxx represents version number.
- O MySecureBackupServer64-Xxxx.msi
- O MySecureBackupServerManagementXxxx.msi

Install on Each User's Computer

Note: Substitute "kpenterprises" for your company's data storage account.

☐ Download the appropriate client installation program for the machine you're at

- O MySecureBackupXxx.msi
- O MySecureBackup64-Xxx.msi

☐ Install MySecureBackup agent

- O Close all open programs
- O Double-Click the file you just downloaded
- O Choose "Next"
- O Check "License Agreement" and Choose "Next"
- O Leave installation directory as default and Choose "Next"
- O Choose "Install"
- O When installation is complete, Choose "Finish"
- O Choose "Yes" to reboot

☐ Configure MySecureBackup agent

Note: Once you restart you should see the "Welcome to My Secure Backup" screen.

- O Choose "Next"
- O Domain = kpenterprises
- O Username / Password = [As specified above]
- O Choose "Next"
- O Select GLB as the drive to backup to and Choose "Next"
- O Change "Day" to "Manual Only" and Choose "Next"
- O Enter the drive letter specified above
- O Leave the Cache size at default and Choose "Next"

  This option is totally up to you. The Synced folder is intended to allow several people to work on the exact same file at the same time and then merge changes.

- O Choose Next
- O Choose Finish
- O At this point, the agent will check in with the server and sync the settings
- O Close the My Secure Backup software. There should be an icon for it near the clock on your Windows Bar.

☐ Test installation and configuration

- O Close all programs and reboot the client computer
- O Log on as the user
- O Open Windows Explorer and verify that the drive is mapped
- O Copy a test file to the mapped drive

- O Delete the file you just placed on the mapped drive

Note: At this point, all client systems have the drive mapped but there is no data there.

If you will be setting up backups of local machines to the cloud storage area, you can set these up now.

3. Setup Server Backup

On the Server that holds client data,

☐ Log onto the Server

☐ Download the server software installation programs

- O MySecureBackupServer64-Xxxx.msi
- O MySecureBackupServerManagementXxxx.msi

☐ Install these programs on the server. This process is essentially identical to the client installation process.

☐ Setup a backup job to copy all data in the client data share every night

- O Open the MySecureBackup agent
- O At the top of the agent software, click Configure
- O On the left side of the screen, expand the KPE data disk
- O On the left side of the screen, select the item *Setup Automatic Backup*
- O Enter a job name such as "Daily Backup" and click Create

- O On the left side of the screen, select *Schedule*
  1. Backup is set to go off ______________________ (frequency)
  2. At ______________________ (time)
  3. When a scheduled backup is missed, select to *Backup at the next scheduled time*
  4. Check the box wake the computer in order to run the backup and click OK

- O On the left side of the screen, select *What to Backup*
  1. Click *Add or Change Backup Folders* button
  2. Select the client folders to be backed up and click OK

- O On the left side of the screen, select Backup Options
  1. Select *Backup In-Use Files*
  2. Select *Ignore Time Zone shifts . . .*
  3. Select *Expire previous versions and deleted files after* ______________________ days and click OK

- O Change the status of this service request to "Waiting on Results" until the backup job can be verified.

Chapter 11

Migrating to Microsoft Foundation Server

Introduction

One of Microsoft's hidden gems is the Windows Server 2008 R2 Foundation or "Foundation Server." This product is an OEM-only product, which means that it must be sold as a new installation with hardware. That saves you some money because it means the operating system is already installed when the server shows up. For a discussion of what the Foundation Server is and how we use it, see the Server Lite discussion in Chapter 9.

Chapter 11 takes a look at migrating to Microsoft's Foundation Server. Our assumption here is that you're migrating from an older operating system. Let up repeat what we said in Chapter 9: Migrating to Foundation Server is delightfully straight-forward, especially in comparison to Small Business Server.

With Foundation Server, you won't be bringing over Exchange or SharePoint. There are no options for virtualization (It cannot host Hyper-V servers and Microsoft says it cannot be virtualized. We won't argue here.)

The project here is very straight forward. We're going to talk about the migration process *to* Foundation Server. This could be *from* SBS or *from* Standard Server.

Because we generally move existing SBS clients to either SBS Standard or SBS Essentials, the example here will focus on moving from Windows Standard Edition to Foundation Server.

In the checklist that follows, you'll execute the following steps to move a client onto Foundation Server:

- Unpack the Foundation Server
- Prep it to go on the network
- Join it to the domain
- Make it the domain controller
- Move all data and services over
- Move FISMO roles to new server
- Demote the old server
- Remove the old server

What we won't cover here is all the delayed steps in the "Big Checklist" that are universal to all migrations. These include the discovery process, client communication, etc.

Where we do address these, we will just cover the basics. Believe us, if you can migrate SBS, you can fill in the details for foundation server.

The server we're migrating from looks like this:

- Server 2003 Standard Edition 32-bit
- Ten user licenses
- Company Files take up 34 GB of disc space
- There is a Line of Business application called Schmoozer. It has its own proprietary database that uses 12 GB of storage.
- There is one company-wide share for data and one for use by LOB
- Company Domain Name: CLPGSR (Cousin Larry's Pretty Good Stapler Repair)

- Backup is Symantec Backup Exec version 12
- Defragmentation software is Diskeeper
- Anti-Virus is Trend
- Continuum Remote Monitoring Agent is installed

It's also useful to note what the server is NOT:

- No SharePoint
- No Exchange
- No SQL
- Printers are mapped directly and not shared through the server

Our Checklist assumes that you've gone through the following procedures from the Big Checklist:

- Hardware Checklist
- Software Checklist
- Hardware Assembly
- Service Pack and Critical Update Install
- All drivers updated as needed
- General Settings
- Installation of RMM agent, anti-virus, and backup software, and Diskeeper

So, you have a basic Foundation Server that is up to date and has the basic software and tools installed. You can do all that offsite at your office.

Now let's boot up the new Foundation Server at the client office, plug it into the network and proceed with the migration checklist.

Why Migrating to Foundation Server is So Easy

One of the most important things about Foundation Server is that it's NOT Small Business Server. It has some limitations on users and hardware, but it is essentially Server 2008. That means (almost) everything you know about Server 2008 and migrations applies here.

The main restriction on Foundation server with regard to migrations is that it is not intended to be part of a large forest. It can only be installed at the root of the forest. If you install it anywhere else, it will reboot approximately every hour. Yikes.

But in the super-small environment (where it's intended to live), it's awesome! It can be part of a workgroup, a domain member server, or a domain controller.

And that's the juicy goodness we use: The ability to be a domain controller. Our basic migration process is to make the Foundation Server a domain controller, elevate it to be the "primary" domain controller, and then get rid of the old DC.

When you complete this process, all user accounts will be in place and completely unchanged. All computer accounts will be in place and completely unchanged.

In other words, there is no Desktop Migration component because all the desktop machines and their users will just work.

If you are familiar with the Windows Server Standard (non SBS) active directory, then this is very easy. If you're not, we give you the details you need to complete the job quickly and easily.

Checklist - Migrating to Foundation Server

Notes / Overview:

The client has decided to move the web site from in-house to a hosted service. This requires some prep work so that there is no downtime for visitors to the web site. The move to hosted web service makes this easy.

1. Prep For Migration

☐ Start a TSR Log !!!

☐ Log onto old server

☐ Verify that last night's backup was successful

☐ Log off old server

☐ Log onto Foundation Server

☐ Join the CLPGSR Domain

- O Run Windows Explorer
- O Right-click on "Computer" and select *Properties*
- O Under Computer Name, Domain, and Workgroup Settings, click *Change Settings*
- O In System Properties, on the Computer Name tab, click "Change . . ." to join a domain
- O Enter the domain name CLPGSR and okay the decision. Accept changes and reboot the Foundation Server

After the reboot, you will be able to log onto the Foundation Server as a member of the domain. Do not log on as the local administrator.

☐ Set Foundation Server's IP Address to a static address

- O In Control Panel, run the Network and Sharing Center applet
- O On the left side of the screen, click on *Change Adapter Settings*
- O Right-click on the Local Area Connection icon and select *Properties*
- O Configure the adapter to have a unique static IP address as documented in the Network Documentation Binder
- O Accept your changes and reboot the server if asked to

☐ Move DHCP to the firewall

> Note: In the discovery stage, you documented the DHCP scope and properties. This should also be in the Network Documentation Binder.

☐ Log onto the old server as domain administrator

  ○ Browse to Administrative Tools and open the Services applet

  ○ Locate the DHCP Server service and disable it

☐ Log on the new Foundation Server

☐ Log into the client's firewall

  ○ Backup the firewall configuration to `c:\!Tech\Hardware` (file location on new server)

  ○ Enable the DHCP function

  ○ Configure the DHCP range, exclusions, DNS, and any other settings documented above

    Note: DNS must point to the new Foundation Server

  ○ Save or commit the new firewall configuration

  ○ Backup the firewall configuration to `c:\!Tech\Hardware`

  ○ Reboot the firewall

2. Promote the New Foundation Server

Don't forget to update your TSR Log with each significant action, and at 15 minute intervals

☐ Log onto the Foundation Server as the Domain Administrator

☐ In Server Manager, click on *Roles* in the left-hand column

  ○ On the right side of the screen, click Add Roles and add the DNS Role

    Do not configure DNS service at this time

  ○ On the right side of the screen, click Add Roles and add the File Services Role

    1. Set up the company data share

    2 Set up the share for Schmoozer (LOB) program

  ○ On the right side of the screen, click Add Roles and add the Remote Desktop Services Role

    Note: at this point, each server should be able to connect remotely to the other server, so you don't have to go back and forth between different keyboards/monitors.

Note: Because the Active Directory schemas are different between Server 2003 and Server 2008, you will need to expand the schema. The ADprep tool (adprep.exe) is located on the installation DVD in the \support\adprep directory. Note that we have to use adprep32.exe because we are running it on a 32-bit server.

Run adprep on the OLD Server

☐ Log onto the old server (2003) as the domain administrator

☐ Copy the contents of the \support\adprep directory from the Foundation Server DVD to the C:\!Tech\Migration directory

☐ Open a command prompt and navigate to C:\!Tech\Migration\support\adprep

O Type the following command and press Enter:

```
Adprep32 /forestprep
```

This will display a readout telling you're the old schema version (e.g., 30) and the new schema version (e.g., 44)

O Type the following command and press Enter:

```
Adprep32 /domainprep
```

You should receive a message that you are successful.

O Type the following command and press Enter:

```
Adprep32 /forestprep /gpprep
```

You should receive a message that you are successful.

Promote the New Foundation Server

☐ Log onto the Foundation Server as the Domain Administrator

☐ In Server Manager, click on DNS Server to configure DNS services

Verify that DNS is set to look to self and forward to the ISP

☐ In Server Manager, click on *Roles* in the left-hand column

O On the right side of the screen, click Add Roles and add the Active Directory Domain Services

O Reboot the Server

☐ Click on the Start button and enter `dcpromo` in the command box, then press enter

This will start the Active Directory Domain Services Installation Wizard

O Follow the prompts

O When asked for operating system compatibility, select 2008

O When prompt to join a domain or create one, select to join an existing domain and add a domain controller to the domain

O Forest functional and domain functional levels should be 2008

Note: Unless you've setup a static IPv6 address, you will receive an error that the server has one or more dynamic IP Addresses. If there is no IPv6 on your network, ignore this warning.

O Accept the default directories for database, log files, and SYSVOL

O Enter the password for Directory Services Restore Mode Administrator and record it here:

____

The domain controller promotion may take some time. Be patient.

O When domain controller promotion is complete, reboot the server

☐ Transfer FSMO Roles to the Foundation Server

Note: FSMO stands for Flexible Single Master Operations. You will find an excellent description of the FSMO roles at in Microsoft Knowledge base article KB 255504.

There are several ways to transfer the FSMO roles. We have selected a method that gracefully transfers them.

O Log on to the Foundation Server as the Domain Administrator

O Click the Start button and type `ntdsutil` in the open box. Press enter.
This will open the NTDSUtil program in a command prompt box.

O Type `roles` and press enter
The prompt should now be

```
fsmo maintenance:
```

O Type `connections` and press enter

The prompt should now be

```
server connections:
```

O Type `connect to server YourServer` and press enter (Replace YourServer with the server name of the Foundation Server)

O Type `q` and press enter ← for Quit

O Type `transfer infrastructure master` and press enter. Proceed when this is complete.

O Type `transfer naming master` and press enter. Proceed when this is complete.

O Type `transfer pdc` and press enter. Proceed when this is complete.

O Type `transfer rid master` and press enter. Proceed when this is complete.

O Type `transfer schema master` and press enter. Proceed when this is complete.

O At the `fsmo maintenance` prompt, type `q` and press enter

O At the `ntdsutil` prompt, type `q` and press enter

O At the old server, verify that all programs are closed and reboot the server

O When the old server is finished rebooting,

At new Foundation Server, verify that all programs are closed and reboot the server

☐ Promote the Foundation Server to be the Global catalog server

O Log on to the Foundation Server as the Domain Administrator

O Click Start, point to Programs, click Administrative Tools, and then click Active Directory Sites and Services

O In the console tree, double-click Sites, double-click the name of the site, and then double-click Servers

O Double-click the target domain controller (the Foundation Server)

O In the details pane, right-click NTDS Settings, and then click Properties

O On the General tab, click to select the Global catalog check box

O Reboot the Server

Note: For additional information on Global Catalog Services, FSMO Roles, adprep, and related topics, see Microsoft Knowledge base article KB 255504. See http://support.microsoft.com/kb/255504.

3. Migrate Data to the New Foundation Server

Checkpoint: At this point, the new Foundation Server is the "primary" domain controller, is the Global Catalog Server, and has all of the FSMO roles. It is providing DNS to the network.

You will migrate the data use Robocopy with the same switches used in the Big Checklist (see the Resources section)

4. Fine Tuning

If you are using logon scripts or batch files, be sure and update these.

If the old server will be removed from the network, use dcpromo to demote it first.

Install the Line of Business application per its instructions and with the guidance of the Big Checklist.

Note: If you're using HP equipment, see the excellent document Implementing Microsoft Windows Server 2008 Foundation On HP Proliant Servers at

http://h20000.www2.hp.com/bc/docs/support/SupportManual/c01822381/c01822381.pdf

The Network Migration Workbook

Overview and Flow

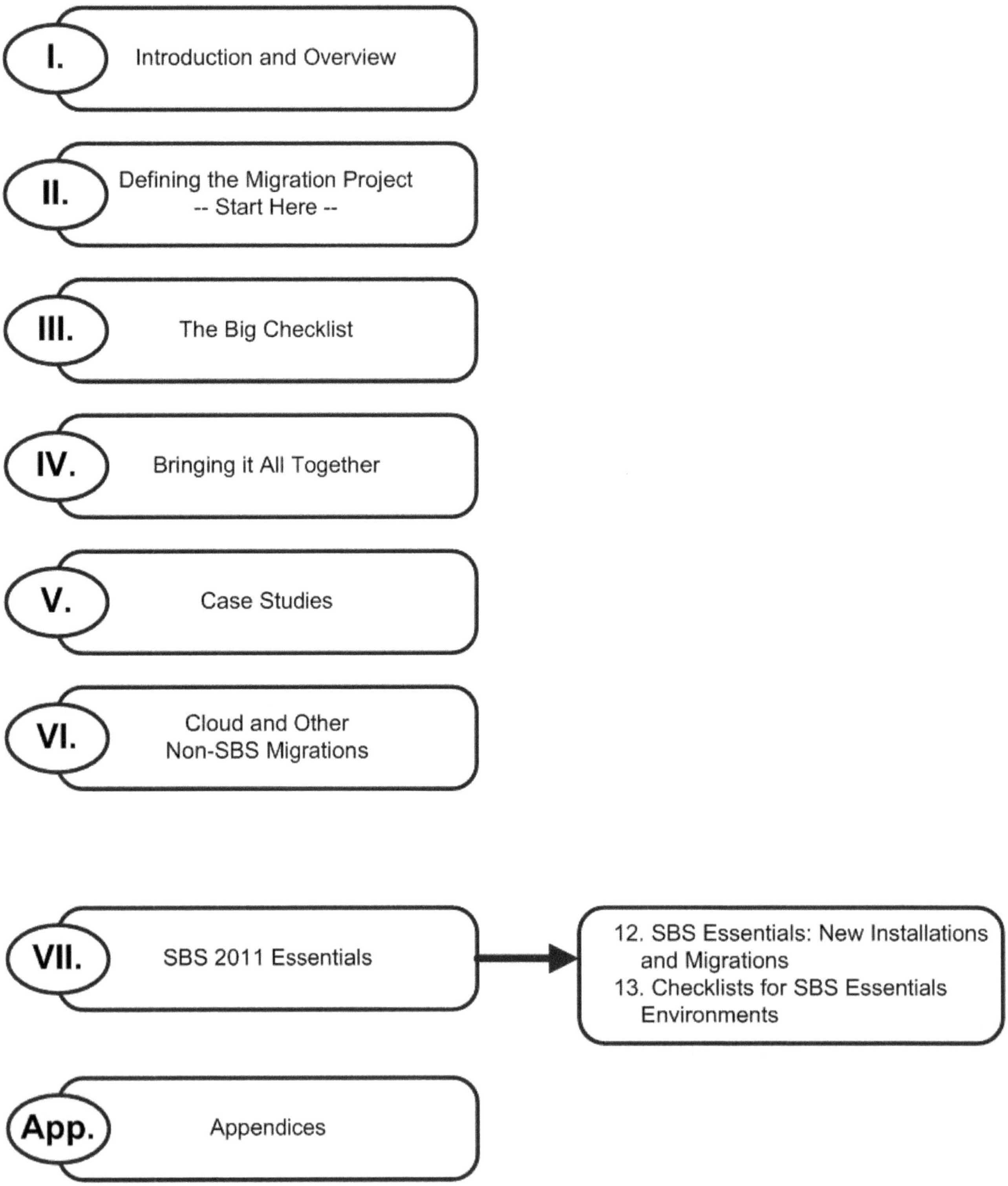

VII. SBS 2011 Essentials

Introduction to The Section

Karl had a seat on the Partner Advisory Council for the "Aurora" project that became SBS 2011 Essentials. As Microsoft prepared for the actual launch of SBS 2011 Essentials, KPEnterprises was involved in several of Microsoft's TAP migration projects, including "first server" installations and SBS 2003 migrations to SBS 2011 Essentials.

So we learned some interesting things. First on the list is that Microsoft is no closer to their dream of an "off the shelf" small business network than they were a dozen years ago. Yes, SBS Essentials is simple and straight forward and easy . . . if you're a computer technician who works with this stuff every day.

So if we assume that only technicians will install this product, is it so simple that you can just hand a machine to a technician and walk away, knowing the job will be done right? Of course not. One of the ways that any business stays profitable is that you adopt Standard Operating Procedures and processes. That means you need to establish a standard installation that you will use at all your clients.

The next two chapters cover some of the basic installations you'll used with SBS Essentials. These include moving from "no domain" to a domain and setting up a simple 1-10 user network.

Chapter 12 addresses many pieces of the migration to SBS 2011 Essentials, and the installation of a totally new Active Directory network on SBS Essentials. Migrating to this product is very easy. We talk about the business side of things and preparing for the SBS Essentials installation.

Chapter 13 provides some checklists for a new installation of SBS 2011 Essentials into a "first server" environment. Like Foundation Server, SBS Essentials is a great product that provides a great collection of services in the SMB space.

Chapter 12: SBS Essentials: New Installations and Migrations

Welcome a New Member to The Family!

There is literally a family of server products at Microsoft that are intended for the "micro" business environment. Strictly speaking, the network gets so micro that Windows Home Server is in this family. The most notable member of the family is Window Small Business Server, or SBS. The latest version is SBS 2011. SBS 2011 comes in three flavors:

- SBS 2011 Standard

- SBS 2011 Premium Add-on

- SBS 2011 Essentials

Microsoft describes SBS like this on their website:

> *Windows Small Business Server is an affordable, all-in-one solution to reduce complexity and increase manageability of server technology in a small business environment.*

Reduce complexity. Increase manageability.

Ironically, SBS Essentials evolved as a way to reduce the complexity that SBS had brought to many small businesses. SBS 2003 was an amazing and stable product. But it could be overloaded by the very features that made it so wonderful to use.

SBS can, and often does, run the following operations:

- Web site
- Remote access to desktops
- Backups
- Exchange Server
- SQL Server
- SharePoint Server
- File storage
- Domain control / security / logon
- Management console
- DNS, DHCP, and other network tasks

Add a line of business application to that and you need some serious computing power. In the SBS 2003 era, we frequently overloaded servers because we asked them to do all this with four gigabytes of RAM on a 32-bit processor.

Toward the end of life for SBS 2003 (that is, around 2007-2008), Microsoft started working on a simpler server concept that once again reduced complexity and increased manageability.

We gave a brief introduction to SBS Essentials in Chapter Nine. Read that if you haven't already. Basically, SBS Essentials is designed to do the basic things that really need doing, and not pretend to do the rest!

If you look at the needs of very small businesses (1-20 desktops), you'll see that about 90% of them absolutely have to have:

- Web site
- Backups
- Exchange Server (or other solution)
- File storage
- Domain control / security / logon

Let's ignore the management console and the basic elements of the network since all businesses with computers have those.

Most of these very small businesses do not need:

- Remote access to desktops
- SQL Server
- SharePoint Server

Move to the Cloud!

So, the SBS team looked at the way the world is spinning and came up with an interesting premise. If we move a handful of service out-of-house, we can have a server that's a lot less complex and easier to manage.

SBS Essential assumes that you have moved the following services to the cloud, or to another server:

- Web site
- Exchange Server (or some email)
- SharePoint Server

This makes perfect sense. Most of us have been moving our clients' web site to hosted services for ten years or more. Why have that attack surface on your network at all?

When we implement hosted spam filters and hosted Exchange services, everything gets easier on the server: network traffic, disc space, and CPU usage. Take SharePoint off site and it gets even easier.

And while backups could be onsite, moving them to a cloud-based model also decreases complexity on the server.

So think about what this server looks like now. It is 64-bit only, can take up to 32 GB of RAM, and cannot run Exchange or SharePoint. This machine could be beefy enough to run SQL if you wanted to, or to run a Line of Business application with plenty of power.

It is certainly capable of managing file storage, logons, and the basic tasks of running a network. We tend to sell the HP Proliant family of servers, and even a low-end Proliant would be a great SBS Essentials server.

The last bit of complexity is not really technical in nature: It's licensing. Ugh. Under NDA we discovered the percentage of tech support calls to the SBS team that had to do with licensing. We can't tell you what it is, but we assure you, it was ridiculously high!

So licensing is complicated. How can we address that? Having tested the model with Home Server, Microsoft decided to simply build in the licensing.

SBS Essentials comes with 25 licenses and you can't get any more. So there are no Server CALs or Device CALs. There are simply 25 users maximum.

Now if we think outside the United States for a minute, we see that there are very few business in the world that have more than 25 computer users. Globally, that means that almost every business in the world could buy this product and never have to worry about licensing!

Realistically, we're nervous selling this to anyone with more than twenty users. A little growth spurt and they'll be back to buy another server. No one wants that. Still, the 1-20 desktop market has been our bread and butter for seventeen years.

The killer combination of cloud services (for web, Exchange, SharePoint) and on-site services makes SBS Essentials an amazing product in the small business space. It also makes it possible to sell a much smaller server!

We just talked about the ability to have a beefier server. But if all you have is logons, domain control, and file storage, then you can get by with a much smaller server. Put in eight gigabytes of RAM and you will have all the power you need.

The Sales Process for SBS Essentials

Okay, SBS Essentials is awesome. Now how do you sell it? How do you configure it? How does an SBS Essentials network look different from an SBS Standard network?

In Chapter Thirteen, we'll present a number of checklists and processes for implementing SBS

Essentials. In preparation for that, this chapter will look at some basic configurations and considerations. The information-gathering process for SBS Essentials is a lot simpler than for a 25-user SBS Standard or Premium environment.

The target market for SBS Essentials is the very small market. At the low end of the market (under 25 desktops), Microsoft estimates that 75% of all business have no server.

Wow. It's 2012 and there are businesses with no server? You've seen them. In fact, you may have installed the first server for many clients. Microsoft has long had marketing campaigns geared toward "First Server, Right Server."

But that first server has been expensive for a very small business. Think about it. If you put together a good server with plenty of memory, RAID array, and all the goodness that allows the manufacturer to offer a 3-year warranty, that server probably specs out at $5,000 to $7,000 for hardware, software, operating system, and licenses.

Add migration labor to that and you've got a project in the range of $10,000 to $15,000. The businesses that can afford that are the cream of the crop of micro-businesses! So, even though you may have worked with small clients, they were not the smallest, most cash-poor clients.

SBS Essentials can be sold and delivered on a much less powerful machine. And if you have a cloud-based backup, it gets even cheaper. The machine on site can be truly "lite" in comparison to the machine you've been selling.

Even though the entire technology budget for three years might be the same for both systems, the hybrid system of combining on site server with cloud-bases services allows very small companies to afford this technology more easily because they are making monthly payments for most of it.

At the end of this chapter we've printed a sample "Technology Roadmap Interview" for SBS Essentials. This is an extremely simple and straight-forward interview. You might be reluctant to ask some of these questions, but don't be. Even the question about how much money they make is answered by most people without batting an eye. It's just a number. A few would rather not say, so you move on.

The Technology Roadmap Interview has two parts. One is for the business side of things, so you can get a sense of how the client operates and how they use technology. The second part is technical, so you have enough information to know what to sell them.

Note: If at any point you find yourself with a client that has a large network, a complicated domain, or severe requirements for bigger servers, then STOP thinking about SBS Essentials and move into a SBS Standard frame of mind.

When you stumble onto the following networks, they are ideal candidates for SBS Essentials:

A Workgroup environment. That is, a few machines with no real server. They might have all the files shared from the bookkeeper's desktop, or they might just have all the company data on a "NAS" they found for $100 at an office supply store.

A Simple Domain environment. Perhaps an old NT server that authenticates logons and stores files. It's basically the "big daddy" version of what you need to do with SBS Essentials.

A Small SBS environment with an owner who's willing to move some services to the Cloud. Again, remember that you need to avoid the 25-user limit. But if they're not using SharePoint, and they're willing to move Exchange to a hosted environment, they might be perfect.

Other than the fact that there are more users, and people might be used to the SBS features (such as Remote Web Workplace), a 6-20 user network will not be much different from a 1-5 user network when it comes to SBS Essentials. You just have more labor involved in moving them over.

For this number of users, we would not consider trying to move over active directory with a Swing Migration (see www.sbsmigration.com)

or anything like that. We would consider using a tool such as Profile Wizard to move the desktops very quickly without messing with Active Directory.

It is a bias of ours, especially with really old networks that we have not maintained, to avoid migrating AD because we don't want to clean it all up and get rid of the rat's nest we frequently find. This is particularly true of owner-managed systems where someone has downloaded a widget from the Internet, ran it against their AD, screwed up everything, and then uninstalled it.

If you find yourself looking at a complicated network, you need to look at the Discovery Section of the Big Checklist rather than the Technology Roadmap Questionnaire in this chapter. In this chapter and the next, we're looking at maximizing success with *very small* and *very simple* networks – exactly what SBS Essentials is designed to do.

Designing a Simple Network

After all that talk about how simple things are, you'd think you wouldn't need a section on designing your SBS Essentials network. Well, that's definitely not the case.

A few key planning steps will make everything go faster, smoother, and more profitable.

The basic document for setting up SBS Essentials is the first "checklist" in Chapter Thirteen: *Installing SBS Essentials on a Non-Domain Environment.* We promise that your first installation will go much more smoothly if you read that first, even if you don't run through the checklist. At least you'll know what the gotchas are.

Educating yourself on the core components of the client's network is critical. These are the services listed on the first page of this chapter, and "discovered" in the Technology Roadmap Questionnaire.

Outside the scope of the checklists in Chapter Thirteen is the move to the cloud. If you will be migrating Exchange to a hosted environment, for example, see Chapters Nine and Ten. Make that a separate project and begin *this* migration when that is complete.

Important: At this point we assume there is no Exchange Server, no SharePoint site, and no big SQL Server in the environment. After you set up the basic network, you can use the SQL-specific and Line of Business-specific sections of the Big Checklist to complete your migration.

With very small networks, you are likely to find yourself with a hodge-podge collection of desktops and laptops. You'll have Windows Home machines, Windows XP Pro, Windows 7 Ultimate. Whatever they bought and slapped into their network environment, you got.

The (somewhat) good news is that SBS Essentials does not require that desktop machines be part of the *domain* in order to be part of the *SBS network*. That means those Windows Home desktops are welcome to stay and you don't have to upgrade them to Professional edition.

Home machines cannot be accessed with RWA, and they can't connect to as a domain member. But they can have backups, they can have drives mapped, they can have logon scripts, and they can do the most important thing this network provides: Share files.

In addition, user profiles are not automatically moved over on Home editions. But, to be honest, that feature doesn't work much of the time on Professional edition machines either. Hence the final checklist in Chapter Thirteen.

Prepare the Network!

Because SBS Essentials is sold only as an OEM operating system, you will acquire it preinstalled on a server. As a result, you don't have to go through the setup process. That process is simple and fast. But, still, it's nice to have the machine just go straight to the client setup portion on its first boot.

Read through the "Installing SBS Essentials . . ." checklist in Chapter Thirteen and make sure you have the information you'll be asked for in setup. This includes the domain name, machine name, administrator's user name, hard drive configuration, etc.

You'll gather up the information in the "discovery" process with the Technology Roadmap Questionnaire, and then plan out the new network and domain.

Important Safety Tip:

The *worst thing you can do* with any migration is to show up and start running the migration project without 1) Knowing everything you can about the environment, and 2) Preparing the network in advance.

This is true of simple migrations as much as complicated migrations. When people call us and say they need the *Network Migration Book* right now because they have a migration project over the weekend, we cringe. We don't want to be responsible for your hurried, uniformed, unplanned attempt to migrate a network.

The "Installing SBS Essentials . . ." checklist in Chapter Thirteen outlines five keys to success that you need to address before you start an SBS Essentials installation. The checklist "Preparing the Network for the SBS Essentials Installation" walks you through these five items step by step.

It's not difficult or complicated. But here's why you need to do these things *before* the migration.

First, you never want to complicate one project with another. In addition to affecting each other, the client can easily confuse a project. You've seen it: One desktop takes four hours to update for some reason and the client thinks the problem is with the server migration not going smoothly.

Second, these item might be more complicated than they seem. Again, we've all seen situations where you think the fix will be really simple, but it takes two days to straighten out.

Third, you need the client to have reasonable expectations. If you estimate a migration will take one hour for the server, one hour for the network configurations, and two hours for desktop installations, you could be in for a BIG surprise.

A Cautionary Tale

Here's a quick (absolutely true) story of how bad a simple SBS Essentials migration can be. We've changed the client's name because we think our name is better. We'll call the client Cousin Larry's Pretty Good Yoga Studio. CLPGYS for short.

The scenario looks simple enough. Client has no server, four desktop computers, a slow but working Internet connection. One machine is new (Windows 7 Pro). Two machines are old (Windows XP Pro). One machine is a lost cause (Windows Vista Home).

The client has the new SBS Essentials Server onsite. It's still in the box. Of course it's brand new, fast, lots of hard drive space, etc.

The client wants us to show up one Friday and start installing their new network. We refuse. We insist on going through the discovery process. Here's what we discovered:

The Ugly Truth. What the client thought was a firewall was really just a small switch with a wire going through the wall. He explained that he was sharing the Internet connection with his neighbor. Um . . . okay.

That's not a show-stopper, but here's what was:

First, while discovering the network, we ran

```
ipconfig /all
```

and discovered a WINS server. Hmmm. How is that possible? Is the firewall on the other side of the wall handing out WINS? Probably not. We opened a web browser and went to the IP address. Up comes SBS 2003!

If we had installed a new SBS server into this environment, there would have been a server "election" within 30 days and we would win. That would leave the neighbor with a server that shuts itself down once a day. Oops.

Second, DHCP and DNS were being served by the SBS 2003 server on the other side of the wall. We absolutely must control DHCP and DNS.

So that's not okay.

Third, the desktops were horribly out of date. Over 100 updates needed on each. Service packs missing. Literally 15-20 hours of labor needed for four machines. The old XP machines were the worst. Old, slow, outdated. And updates needed to be pulled through that shared Internet connection.

Fourth, none of the machines (even Windows 7) had .Net 4.0 installed. This is critical to a smooth installation of SBS Essentials. This is a trivial installation, but it needs to be done.

We Informed The Client and decided on a plan of action. As you can imagine, the client's network is like this because it has been self-managed forever and he has not put money into it unless required. So we came up with a plan that involved two service requests.

<u>SR 1: Network Prep for CLPGYS</u>

1. Install a new firewall/router so that the network can be isolated from the office next door and the Internet.
2. Point firewall DNS to Google's public DNS servers (8.8.8.8 and 8.8.4.4).
3. Enable DHCP and note the address space being served up to devices on the LAN (for this discussion, we'll assume it's 192.168.1.x).
4. Verify that Universal Plug and Play (UPnP) is enabled.
5. Backup the firewall configuration.

That SR takes care of the network preparation. Since all this work is planned and you know what to do before you start, estimated time is one hour. That includes mounting the firewall on the wall or equipment rack.

<u>SR 2: Desktop Prep for CLPGYS</u>

1. Create a desktop checklist with these items for each desktop. Photocopy the checklist and place one at each desktop workplace.
2. Print out a Machine Documentation Spec Sheet for each machine and fill out any relevant information as you work though this SR.
3. Log onto computer with an administrator account
4. Change the local Administrator password to CLPGYSadmin and document.
5. Run Windows Updates and determine whether any Service Packs are needed. If machine is not on the latest service pack, install service pack and document. Repeat until machine is on the latest service pack.
6. Run Windows Updates and apply all updates. Repeat until machine is completely up to date.
7. Install .Net 4.0 on the desktop.

This SR guarantees that each desktop is ready to join the SBS Essentials domain. Because of the age of the machines, and their out-of-date status, this SR could easily take 15-20 hours.

Note: We actually had the client do all of the service packs and updates. In reality, we did items 1-4 and 7. This ended up taking about 30 minutes per machine.

At this point, we were able to start with a fresh project on a well-prepared network. We know where DHCP is served up, and it's exactly what we need. We will be moving DNS to the SBS Essentials server, but for now it's right where we want it – and we control it.

The Lesson is simple. If we had just walked in, plugged in that server, and started the installation, we would have lost control of our migration project almost immediately. We would be stuck on site for at least two days, doing work we had not planned on and the client had not budgeted.

There's an old Army saying that goes *"Proper prior planning prevents pitiful poor performance"* (or something like that). This is certainly the case with SBS Essentials installations.

Unfortunately, this scenario, or some variation of it, will be very common in the new world of installing "first servers" into very small businesses.

Because these networks are almost always managed by people who do something other than network management for a living, they are hobbled together enough to "work," but they're filled with traps and snares.

Know what you know!

A Standard Approach

It is obvious that a standardized approach is needed for SBS Essentials network. The basic process consists of

- Discovery

- Network Prep

- Desktop Prep

- Server Installation

If you are rigorous about doing a proper discovery, you will have much more accurate quotes for prospects. You will also have happier clients when they say "yes" and you finish the job exactly as you said you would.

And, happily, you will be more profitable because you won't find yourself working long hours on what should be a very simple and straight-forward migration project.

Up Next

The rest of this chapter consists of the 2-part *Technology Roadmap Questionnaire* for SBS Essentials networks. After that, Chapter Thirteen presents all the checklists we've discussed.

Sample Technology Roadmap Questionnaire

Technology Roadmap Questionnaire

For

(Prospect Name / Company)
___

Interview by Technician: ___

Prepared by
KPEnterprises
Sacramento, CA

Technology Roadmap Questionnaire

Part 1: Client Interview

Basic Business Information

Company Information

1. Legal Business Name ______________________
2. DBA Business Name ______________________
3. Primary Location: ______________________
4. Other Locations: ______________________
5. Years in Business: ______________________
6. Annual Sales: ______________________
7. Services/Products Provided: ______________________
8. Who are your clients? ______________________
9. Who does your company exchange information with regularly? (e.g., vendors, customers, partners, suppliers)

   ____

   ____

10. Cloud based services currently used (e.g., Google Apps, BPOS, hosted email):

    ____

    ____

    ____

    ____

11. Organizational Chart.
    Please provide a diagram of the key departments/functions and identify key roles and personnel.

    Sample:

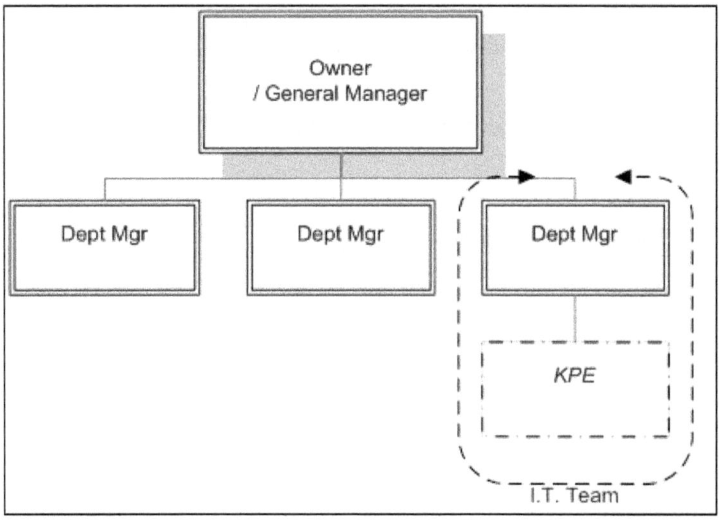

Organizational Chart:

Growth – Employees

1. How many employees do you have currently? ______________________________
2. How many desktop computers do you have currently? ______________________
3. How many laptop computers do you have currently? ______________________
4. How many servers do you have currently? ______________________________
5. How many "computer users" do you expect to have

   One year from now _____________

   Three years from now _____________

   Five years from now _____________

Technology Overview

1. Do you view technology as an
   - ______ asset, or
   - ______ expense, or
   - ______ necessary evil, or
   - ______ just plain evil?
2. How much downtime do you average per month . . .

   On your most important systems? ____________________

   Companywide? ________________________________
3. Does downtime cause enough of an impact on your business that you're willing to invest in preventing it? Yes / No
4. Who is responsible for technology support within your organization? ____________

   ____

Other

Is there anything else we should know? ____________________

Technology Roadmap Questionnaire

Part 2: Network Specs

Basic Technology Information

Note: This checklist is based on Karl's famous "68-Point Checklist" for evaluating client systems. You can get the whole checklist free. Just send an email to checklist@greatlittlebook.com and it will be echoed back to you.

Basic Information

1. Are there any known issues? ______________________________

____

____

2. How old is the server? ______________________________

3. If no server, where are important company files stored? ______________

4. How old are the PCs? ______________________________

5. What is the primary (proprietary?) line of business application? ______________

____

____

6. What are the major software applications used on the desktops? ______________

____

____

7. Does anyone need to access their desktops remotely? Yes or No (circle one)

8. If yes, how many? ______________________________

9. How do you connect remotely to your desktops? ______________________________

____

____

Network

10. Network Map

(Use Visio or draw by hand)

Describe how (whether) the following services are provided on the network:

11. Printing ____________________

12. Backup Strategy ____________________

13. Internet connection (type and speed) ____________________

14. Verify Virus Scanner brand and description: ____________________

____

____

Server Information, if there is a server:

15. Server Processor ____________________

16. Server CPU ____________________

17. Server RAM ____________________

18. Server Operating System: ____________________

19. Check Disc Space on Server C: Drive

Used / Free

C: = ______ / _____ out of ______ Gb Total

20. Check Disc Space on Server D: Drive

Used / Free

D: = ______ / _____ out of ______ Gb Total

Email

21. Is email in-house or out-of-house (circle one)

22. If out-of-house, how is email delivered to desktops?

Troubleshooting, Fixes, Notes, and Recommendations

Note any problems reported by client. If there are any recommendations for client based on this analysis, please list them here.

Chapter 13: Checklists for SBS Essentials Environments

Keeping SBS Essentials Easy

Remember that one of the goals of SBS is to make thing easier. SBS Essentials is a lot easier to install and migrate to than SBS Standard. But as we saw in Chapter Twelve, there are some pitfalls that can really ruin your day, especially if you have no real plan in place.

This chapter gives you the checklists you'll need for a few different scenarios. Checklist One covers the network preparation we discussed in the last chapter. Here we have a bit more click-by-click. Checklist Two covers the installation and configuration of SBS Essentials into a network with no existing domain. Checklist Three covers the setup of SBS Essentials in a very small domain. Checklist Four addresses the workstations and getting them connected once the SBS Essentials server is in place. And, finally, Checklist Five covers the workstation migration with the help for a tool called Profile Wizard.

If you haven't read the previous chapter, we really recommend that you do so. And we absolutely recommend that you read all the way through these checklists before you begin using one.

Remember a few key points. First, we assume that you have already moved to the cloud those services that will be in the cloud. This includes Exchange and SharePoint. Second, you will create a new domain, even if there is an existing domain. With a handful of desktops, it just doesn't make sense to do it any other way. Third, we assume you've done the network discovery outlined in the previous chapter.

Now let's dig in.

Introduction to Checklist One

There are five things that must be done on every network, no matter how small, in order for an SBS Essentials installation and migration to be as smooth as possible:

1. Verify there are no other servers. This is simple and seems obvious. But remember that you're probably working with someone who is not a network engineer and who got his network operating through trial and error, plus advice from friends who are also not network engineers. This simple thing can lead to big trouble. Of the first three installations we did for SBS Essentials, every one of them had another server in the environment, even if the client didn't know it.

2. DHCP must be working. Ideally, it will be on the firewall and not served up by the SBS Essentials server. In fact, DHCP is not installed by default on SBS Essentials. We prefer to have DHCP on the firewall so that the network can provide most services even when the server is rebooting or down for some other reason. In addition to handing out IP addresses, for example, the firewall can hand out the ISP's DNS server as a secondary DNS, so Internet browsing is not interrupted.

3. DNS should be on the Server. This one is a little bit of work because we need DNS on the firewall when we start out, and we put a static IP on the server. Once we start up the server and begin to configure it, we want DNS on the server so that there is no problem with desktops finding the server. We use the wizard in SBS Essentials to configure the firewall through Universal Plug and Play (UPnP).

4. Update desktops. Again, this seems simple. But it can be horribly time consuming, especially on older machines. You might want to bring with you, on USB drive, the Service Packs that you know you will need. Windows XP requires Service Pack Three or it won't even try to connect. For all others, it's just a great idea.

5. Install .Net 4.0 on all desktop and laptop computers. This is required to run the Connection Wizard. It is fast and easy 99% of the time. Theoretically, the Connection Wizard will get this and install it if not present, but that fails a lot. So just do it. After the workstations are all up to date, this will be pretty fast.

There's also one more thing you may need to do on the network. If you do not have a firewall with UPnP, you will need to configure the firewall manually to allow certain SBS services to work.

6. Create firewall rules for SBS Services – Only if the server is to be accessed remotely. Note: You should inform the client as early as possible that a Universal Plug and Play (UPnP) firewall is best for the new network. If you don't have this, additional labor is required.

Note: This checklist is like a set of "book ends" around the SBS Essentials server installation. You need to do the network prep before you install servers or connect workstations. And you could wait to update the desktops. But we prefer to take care of all of this before we take the server out of the box.

These final checklists rely heavily on your understanding of the Big Checklist and SBS Standard. We can be brief here because, if you've mastered the processes and procedures in the previous sections and learned SBS well, you will not run into anything you cannot handle here.

Here's the checklist. In many cases, details will vary based on your firewall and other equipment.

Checklist One: Preparing the Network for the SBS Essentials Installation

1. Verify There Are No Other Servers

Note: It is best to do this before you reconfigure the firewall because a server may be handing out IP addresses and you could cause problems on the network.

☐ Do a physical inventory. Ask to see every computer in the office. Check the operating system on each.

☐ Open a command prompt (DOS) window

- O At the prompt, type **`ipconfig /all`** and press enter
- O Examine the printout for clues.
    1. Is there a WINS server? If so, investigate.
    2. Is DHCP being served by the firewall or something else. If else, investigate.
    3. Is the DNS server on the local LAN but at an address other than the firewall? If so, investigate.
- O At the prompt, type **`arp -a`** and press enter
- O Examine the printout for clues.
    1. Look for static IP addresses. If there are any listed that are not printers or the firewall, investigate

2. Configure the Firewall

☐ From a machine on the network, log into the firewall

☐ Backup the firewall configuration to the local c:\!Tech\Migration directory

☐ Set DNS to point to Google's public DNS servers

- O Primary: 8.8.8.8
- O Secondary: 8.8.4.4

☐ Set Internal LAN IP address to 192.168.1.1

☐ Enable DHCP

- O Create DHCP scope in the range 192.168.1.201 – 192.168.1.250

☐ Verify that Universal Plug and Play (UPnP) is enabled

☐ Save or commit the new configuration

☐ Backup the firewall configuration to the local c:\!Tech\Migration directory

☐ Reboot the firewall

3. Update Desktop and Laptop Computers

☐ Create a desktop checklist with these items for each desktop. Photocopy the checklist and place one at each desktop workplace.

☐ Print out a Machine Spec Sheet for each machine

Perform the following on each desktop or laptop computer that will connect to the SBS Essentials network:

☐ Log onto computer with an administrator account

☐ Change the local Administrator password to ______________________________ and enter this on the Machine Spec Sheet

☐ Add the local user of this machine to the Local Administrators Group

(Yes, we know this is not optimal, but it is required by the SBS Essentials Connection Wizard.)

☐ Set the local user's password to ____________________________ and enter this on the Machine Spec Sheet

☐ Create a restore point for the computer

☐ Open Computer Properties and determine the machine operating system and service pack level

O.S.: __________________________ SP: ___________________________

- O If operating system is Windows XP 64-bit, it will not run the Connection Wizard. Document.
- O If O.S. is prior to Windows XP SP3, it will not run the Connection Wizard
    1. If O.S. is prior to Windows XP, it cannot run the Connection Wizard. Document.
    2. If O.S. is Windows XP, install all service packs

☐ Run Windows Updates and apply all updates. Repeat until machine is on the latest service pack and has all required updates.

- O Reboot as needed
- O Reboot after last set of installs, even if not required to

☐ Install .Net Framework 4.0

A redistributable installation package is on the Client Migration USB drive

- O Reboot client computer

4. Create Firewall Rules For SBS Services

This procedure is only needed if: 1) You will be using any of the remote access features of the SBS Essentials server, AND 2) The firewall is not UPnP capable.

Note: Microsoft has a really great document with click-by-click instructions and screen shots for many routers at
http://social.technet.microsoft.com/wiki/contents/articles/3038.sbs-2011-essentials-router-setup.aspx

☐ Determine the IP Addresses you'll need

O Public IP address that will be forwarded to server: ______________________________

O LAN IP address of the SBS Essentials server: ___________________________________

☐ From a machine on the network, log into the firewall

☐ Backup the firewall configuration to the local c:\!Tech\Migration directory

☐ Map the Public IP address above to the server LAN IP above. This process varies from one router to another.

☐ Forward the following traffic to the server LAN IP:

O HTTPS – Port 443

Note: On SBS Standard, you may open ports 25, 80, 987, 1723, and 3389. You do not need any of these on SBS Essentials because all services are provided through port 443.

☐ Save or commit the new configuration

☐ Backup the firewall configuration to the local c:\!Tech\Migration directory

☐ Reboot the firewall

Checklist Two: Installing SBS Essentials in a Non-Domain Environment

Introduction

Microsoft SBS 2011 Essentials is a very simple but powerful server operating system. It is designed to fit nicely in a small office environment that does not have or desire an in-house Exchange Server, but still needs local security, backup, and remote access.

Unlike previous versions of Small Business Server, SBS Essentials allows “home” class operating systems to exist on the network. These machines cannot take advantage of the remote desktop access feature or domain membership, but they can be backed up and centrally managed. Because a “home” class operating systems (e.g., Windows 7 Home edition) cannot join a domain, the user profile will not automatically move over when the Home machine is connected to the server.

This document is NOT intended to address moving active directory from an old network to the new SBS Essentials domain. In this document, we are not spending an extraordinary amount of time tweaking machines so they look the same on the new network as they did on the old.

Ideally, this document will be used to move a non-domain collection of machines to an SBS Essentials-based domain environment. The machines might be a collection of desktops, laptops, workgroup machines, Windows Ultimate, Windows Professional, or Windows Home operating systems.

Process Overview

1. Meet with client/onsite IT person and go through Technology Roadmap Interview
2. Document Network – Collect documentation
3. Document Network – Map it
4. Determine network changes that are required for success
5. Plan the server configuration, storage options, and backup strategy
6. Prep the network for SBS Essentials
7. Update all desktop/laptop machines so there will be no delays once you start
8. Install and set up the Server
9. Attach each desktop and laptop machine to the new domain
10. Configure and test remote access if needed

Note: You will document all settings and machines as you touch them throughout this process.

Gathering Information: Discovery Process

Schedule about an hour to do the Roadmap Interview. Some questions have more to do with building the client relationship than the network, but they're good to go through. You'll be amazed at what people leave out of a basic documentation because it just didn't pop into their head. Asking lots of questions and having a casual discussion will help those things pop into the client's head.

Forms You'll Need

The following forms are either in Chapters 12-13 or inside the Big Checklist. Find these forms and have them ready for the discovery, documentation, and installation of the new network.

- Technology Roadmap Questionnaire
- Network Documentation Forms
    - Network Map
    - Internet Domain Registration Information
    - Router Configuration Form
    - Firewall Configuration Form
    - IP Address Allocation Record
    - Hard Coded IP Address Record
    - Network Timing Diagram
    - Shared Resources Record
    - Shared Resources Permission Record
    - UPS Power Distribution Form
- Machine (desktop and laptop) Documentation
    - Machine Specification Sheet
      (One for every Server, Workstation, Laptop, Printer, Copier, NAS, SAN, CDP, Phone System, Time Clock, Surveillance System, etc.)
- User Documentation Forms
    - User Names, Logon ID and Passwords Records
    - Email Addresses Record
    - POP or MAPI Account and Credential Records
    - Security and Distribution Group Membership Record
    - Password Policy Form
- Procedures needed for this client's system (e.g., database maintenance on a line of business application)
- Products
    - Line of Business Application Record
    - License / Key / Code Documents for all LOB's, applications and software of any kind.
    - Service Agreements, Support Packs, Care Packs, etc.

Prep the Network

Run the previous checklist: Preparing the Network for the SBS Essentials Installation.

Remember the Big Five: DHCP, DNS, other servers on the network, desktop updates, and .Net 4.0.

Preparing to Install SBS Essentials

☐ Action Step: Map the Network

- O The first thing you need to do on the network is to create a network map. We use Visio, but any tool that gets the job done is fine.
- O Example:

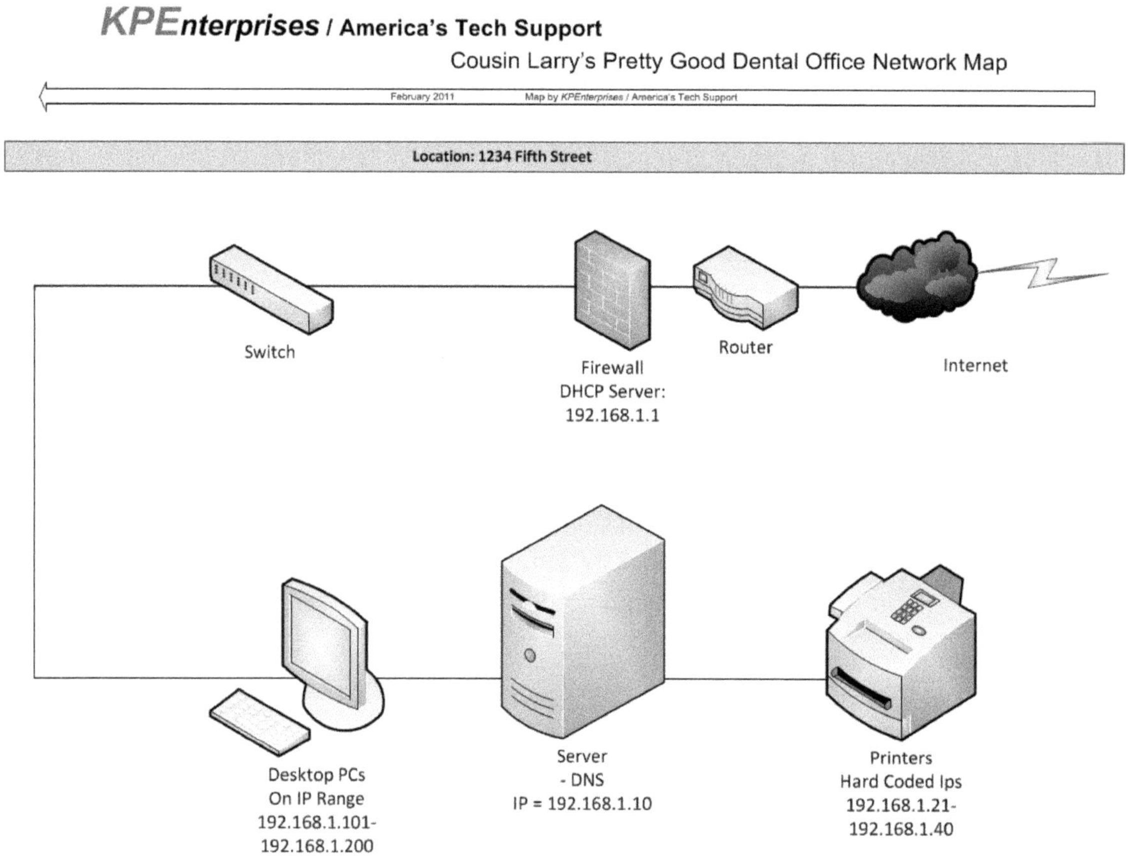

☐ Action Step: Document the router or firewall that will be handing out DHCP

- O Is this device "Plug and Play" capable? If so, the SBS Essentials Server will be able to configure it.
- O Do you have the username and password? If not, can your reconfigure the device by setting it to factory specifications and starting over?

Beware: If you have not done a complete discovery, you can be surprised to learn that some device on the network needs access through the firewall. For example, a security system or time clock device might stop working if you just drop in a standard firewall configuration.

☐ Action Step: Determine Network Settings

O What is the IP address range that will be used internally?

O Will you allocate a range of addresses for server, printers, and other hard-coded addresses? If so, what is it?

O Determine the DHCP range for desktops.

☐ Action Step: Agree on Machine and User Information

When you set up SBS Essentials you will need to give some information that can only be entered once and cannot be changed. Don't make this up on the spot. Determine beforehand what it will be.

You will also need to set up an Administrator and one non-admin user. Here's the information you should have available before setting up the SBS Essentials server:

- Domain Name ______________________________
- Machine Name ______________________________
- Administrative User Name ______________________________
- Admin User Password ______________________________
- Non Admin User Name ______________________________
- Non Admin User Password ______________________________

Note: You will choose a name for a domain administrator account. The domain administrator account "Administrator" already exists in Active Directory Users and Computers, so you cannot give your new administrator account the same name.

Strangely enough, the Non Admin user that you create during installation is not available to you when running the desktop Connection Wizard. So make sure not to use any names from the end user list.

☐ Action Step: Agree on Hard Drive Configuration and Storage Mapping

SBS Essentials will automatically pick a drive, format it, and install the operating system. But you might have additional drives on your system that you will use for storage.

You need to write up a plan for how these drives will be used (e.g., will you have two 1TB drives mirrored?).

SBS Essentials also wants to share "company data" through a share without a drive letter. That's fine as far as it goes. But 99.99% of all programs want to open a drive letter. So you should plan to map drive letters to the storage containers. As of this writing, SBS Essentials does not have a wizard for this.

Also: Since SBS Essentials setup automatically throws everything on the installation drive, you'll need to move those data stores after you configure additional hard drives and before connecting desktops or writing logon scripts. There IS a wizard for this.

For now, just make sure you've mapped out how you want storage to look on the server when you're done and on the desktops once they connect. Make the plan now and you can execute it later.

☐ Action Step: Collect User Names and Machine Names

The setup process is a great time to rename machines if needed. Many machines show up with generic names like "Dellx14" and the user might want something else.

Before the day of the installation, you should gather a list of users you will create on the SBS Essentials server. You also need to know whether they should be Administrators. In most small businesses, you only need three kinds of users:

- Basic

- Executive (have access to financial information and personnel data)

- Administrators

If you set up the data shares and users with this simple configuration in mind, it should be very easy to secure the network and have success with user and security configuration.

When you first set up users, we recommend a standard password for all, so you can jump around during the install process and not have to carry a list of passwords with you. Of course you'll need to make sure that users change the passwords after you're done.

See Checklist Three: *Setting Up a New SBS Essentials Server On a 1-10 Person, Simple Domain.*

When done with that, you'll move to desktops.

Desktop Configuration

The Desktop Very Short List

This applies to laptops as well. We'll just use the term desktop to mean both.

When moving desktops into a domain environment, there are just a few keys to success. Here are the two biggies. One will help you get the job done today. The other will make your life easier in the future when the network setup has been forgotten.

1. You need a local administrator password – And you need to know what it is!

   Someday this desktop machine might be removed from the domain. When that happens, you'll need to know the local administrator password. You might have a process to make sure the local admin password is changed before removing a machine from the network, but you might not be the person who does that job. So it's best to set the password now and document it in the Machine Spec Sheet.

Setting this password is part of the checklist to Connect a Computer To the SBS Essentials Network

2. The Desktop Must Have Good DNS

   That means you need to be able to ping the server by name. (e.g., "ping sbsserver" needs to respond with an IP address translation and packets.)

   To accomplish this, you need to make sure that the desktop does not have static IP addressing AND that it does not have static DNS entries.

   If for any reason DHCP doesn't work, or can't be used, you will need to use static IPs and make sure they are exactly what you want. This is not preferred, but it will work.

   In the worst case scenario, you will need to configure the local hosts file (c:\windows\system32\drivers\etc\hosts) to address the server.

   The ultimate measure of success here is the ability to ping the server by machine name and get a response. Once you do that, you should be able to successfully run the Connection Wizard.

There are other minor details, especially regarding profiles. But since Exchange/Outlook are not part of the migration process, Microsoft has done a great job with bringing over profiles to the new SBS Essentials network. You will need to be careful about profile names and directories, but these are normally minor issues on a machine that has been operating stand-alone.

See Checklist Four: *Connecting a Computer To The SBS Essentials Network.*

Note on tools: In the final checklist, we use a tool called Profile Wizard. It is one of the rare non-Microsoft tools we use. We selected this tool because it is powerful, lightweight, and works well. And, in the SBS Essentials environment, it is much easier to use than Microsoft's User State Migration Tool.

Notes:

Checklist Three: Setting Up SBS Essentials On a 1-10 Person, Simple Domain

This checklist is intended for setting up a simple SBS Essentials domain for the first time. In other words, we are not going to go out of our way to migrate anything from an earlier domain. We will move a few things if we can, but we won't fret over it.

We assume at this point that you have prepared the network and documented what you will need for the SBS Essentials setup. Many of the answers here come from the checklists you just completed.

Basic SBS Essentials Setup

☐ Create a Machine Spec Sheet for the SBS Essentials Server. You'll find this in the Big Checklist.

- O Fill out the information you can immediately and then fill out additional information as it is configured

☐ Start a TSR (Trouble Shooting and Repair) Log. You'll find this in the Big Checklist.

- O Follow the instructions. Write down something at least every 15 minutes. Write down significant events, decisions

☐ Boot the Server

☐ Go through the basic mini-setup process of an OEM server

- O Enter regional settings, time, and date
- O Enter product key

☐ Personalize your server:

Company Name: ______________________________

Internal Domain Name: __________________________

Server Name: __________________________________

☐ Create Initial Users

Administrative User: ______________________ / Password: __________________

1st Non-Admin User: ______________________/ Password: __________________

☐ If you will not be installing a remote monitoring and management agent, you should enable automatic updates

Note: There will be several reboots. Note any anomalies in the TSR Log.

Post Installation Tasks

Once you can log on, perform the following tasks:

☐ Create Users with the user names and passwords specified in the User documentation

☐ Set the SBS Essentials Server IP address to be Static within the appropriate range defined in the Network Documentation

☐ Configure DNS on the SBS Essentials Server

- O DNS should automatically be setup to point to itself for DNS (127.0.0.1) and forwarders should point to 8.8.8.8 (Google DNS)

☐ Configure Hard Drives the way you want them

- O In the Storage Manager, verify that all discs are configured as they should be and document that configuration on the Machine Spec Sheet for the Server

☐ Configure Backup and document the backup process

Backups will run:

Time: ____________________ Days: ____________________

Time: ____________________ Days: ____________________

Time: ____________________ Days: ____________________

☐ Run the initial backup job

☐ Turn off Enhanced Internet Security so the IE is usable

☐ Configure the firewall DHCP so that it sends client machines to the SBS Essentials server for DNS

- O From a machine on the network, log into the firewall
- O Backup the firewall configuration to the local c:\!Tech\Migration directory
- O Change the DHCP scope so that it points to the SBS Essentials server for DNS
- O Save or commit the new configuration
- O Backup the firewall configuration to the local c:\!Tech\Migration directory
- O Reboot the firewall

☐ Shut down the server completely

- O Note the time in the TSR Log
- O Power down and then restart from a cold start
- O Note any errors upon bootup
- O Check server logs for errors. Note them in the TSR Log

☐ Run Windows Updates and apply all appropriate patches, fixes, updates.

- O Reboot as needed. Note anomalies in the TSR Log

☐ Install Monitoring / Patch Management Agent from your Remote Monitoring and Management service

☐ Configure company shares and note how they will be mapped on individual PCs

Physical Share: ________________________________ Mapped as: ______

Physical Share: ________________________________ Mapped as: ______

Physical Share: ________________________________ Mapped as: ______

Physical Share: ________________________________ Mapped as: ______

Physical Share: ________________________________ Mapped as: ______

☐ Configure UPS and document settings in the UPS documentation.

☐ Configure Dynamic DNS and record all settings so that users can connect remotely.

O Run the Dynamic DNS Wizard

O Note that this process will install a third party secure certificate.

O Public FQDN for this server: ______________________________

O Connect to a remote session on one of the machines at your office and use it to test connecting back into this SBS Essentials Server.

O Note: Do not be concerned if this public domain name does not work for 30-60 minutes.

☐ Configure Desktops

See Checklist Four: *Connecting a Computer To The SBS Essentials Network.*

☐ Additional Configuration Tasks:

____

____

____

____

____

____

____

____

____

Checklist Four: Connecting a Computer to an SBS Essentials Server Network

Machine: ____________________

User: ____________________

Password: ____________________

1. Preparing the Machine

☐ Note Server Configuration here:

SBS Essentials Server Name (e.g., SBSCompany): ____________________

SBS Essentials Server IP Address: ____________________

☐ Create a Machine Spec Sheet for the Desktop / Laptop PC.

Fill out the information you can immediately and then fill out additional information as it is configured.

☐ Log on as a local administrator

O If the local Administrator account is disabled, enable it

O Set the local Administrator password to ____________________

O Verify that the local user is a member of the local administrator's group

☐ Create the directory c:\!Tech\Migration

☐ Apply all updates

In order for the installation to be successful, you should apply all Service Packs, patches, fixes, and updates to the machine before you attempt to connect to the Server. If the machine is not up to date, the installation will fail.

☐ Set the desktop PC to use DHCP

- O Test this by opening a CMD window and typing
  `IPCONFIG / ALL`
- O DNS should be pointing to the SBS Essentials IP address noted above
- O DHCP should be coming from the same IP as the gateway (router/firewall)
- O `PING` the server by NAME –
  E.g., `PING sbscompany`

☐ Fix issues with DHCP and DNS as needed.

If you cannot contact the server by its machine name, you will not be able to connect via the Connection Wizard!

If all else fails, edit the hosts file at c:\windows\system32\drivers\etc and enter the server's host name and IP address.

☐ Reboot the Desktop

☐ Set up local user

- O Determine which local user/profile will be connected to the server:

  User: ________________________ Password: ________________________

- O If you are not sure who the local user is and what the profile directory is, open a CMD and enter the command
  `WHOAMI`
- O This will display the user's name and the directory will be their user profile directory
- O Record User / Profile info:

  Username: ______________________________________

  Password: ______________________________________

  Profile Directory: ______________________________________

  Default Printer: ______________________________________

Mapped Drives: ______________________________

____

____

PST's Open in Outlook: ______________________________

____

____

Note: Do not get confused. You must run the Connection Wizard as a local administrator. For best results, log on as "the" local machine administrator.

When asked for network credentials by the Connection Wizard, you must give the credentials of the person whose profile you hope to migrate.

On newer operating systems with good DNS, the Connection Wizard is pretty good at pulling over profiles. On older machines with older operating systems, you might not get anything. In such cases, you'll need to migrate profiles manually.

2. Connect Desktop / Laptop to SBS Essentials Network

☐ Log on to the client desktop as the local administrator

☐ Open a web browser and go to http://Servername/Connect

On this network, that is ______________________________/Connect

○ Download the installation file to c:\!Tech\Software
- If this directory does not exist, create it now

○ Fill out machine description

○ Choose OK to Wake Up this machine for backups

○ Choose YES to participate in Customer Experience program

☐ Configure drive mappings

○ From Server Configuration documentation, map the following drives:

Physical Share: ______________________________ Mapped as: ______

Physical Share: ______________________________ Mapped as: ______

Physical Share: ______________________________ Mapped as: ______

☐ Install Monitoring / Patch Management Agent from your Remote Monitoring and Management service

3. Additional Configuration Tasks

☐ Additional Configuration Tasks:

Checklist Five: Connecting a Computer to SBS Essentials Using Profwiz

In some environments, profile migration just isn't successful. One of the tools we really like for attaching the old profile to the new user is called Profile Wizard or Profwiz. For more information on Profile Wizard, see http://www.forensit.com/products.html.

Machine: ____________________

User: ____________________

Password: ____________________

Note the following changes to *Checklist Four: Connecting a Computer to an SBS Essentials Network.*

2. Connect Desktop / Laptop to SBS Essentials Network

☐ Log on to the client desktop as the local user whose profile you wish to migrate

☐ Run the profile wizard

This joins the domain without having to leave the current domain or workgroup and mess up the profile.

O Run ProfWiz.exe

O Choose `Yes` to close any popup windows, then select `Next`

O Choose `Local Computer` and click `Next`

O Use these settings:

- Enter domain: ____________________
- Make sure `Join Domain` is checked
- Account Name: Username that is being migrated
- Make sure that `Set as Default Logon` is checked and click `Next`
- In the Select a User Profile Window, choose the profile directory recorded earlier and choose `Next`

O If it asks for a username and password, use a domain administrator account – NOT the user

- Admin Username: ____________________
- Password: ____________________

O Reboot the desktop machine

☐ Open a web browser and go to http://Servername/Connect

On this network, that is ______________________________/Connect

○ Download the installation file to c:\!Tech\Software
- If this directory does not exist, create it now

Note: When you run the Connection Wizard at this point, the User already has a profile on the new SBS Essentials domain, so it just works.

Of course, the username must be identical to the old username. If not, you'll have to run Profile Wizard again and connect the older profile to the new domain user.

○ Fill out machine description

○ Choose OK to Wake Up this machine for backups

○ Choose YES to participate in Customer Experience program

☐ Verify the profile migration

○ Log on as the user on the domain

○ Browse to files/folders (mapped drives)

○ Browse the Internet

○ Verify that Outlook works properly

- Open Outlook
- Send/receive email
- Verify NK2 cache by open a new email and start typing a name
- Verify that all PSTs you recorded earlier are present

○ Verify that the default printer is still connected and prints

☐ Log off

☐ Have user test everything if possible

If there are problems, create a service request or add them to the network migration "tune up" service request.

Continue with "Configure drive mappings" section in previous checklist.

Additional Configuration Tasks

☐ Additional Configuration Tasks:

Final Thoughts on SBS Essentials

As you can tell from the last two chapters, plus Chapter Nine, we think SBS Essentials is a great product and a great addition to the Small Business Server family. But we can't forget that it's still a complicated product. And while we respect Microsoft's goal to create network that's easy to install, we're not there yet.

As with any migration project, SBS Essentials requires planning and forethought. Granted: It's a whole lot easier than a full SBS Standard migration, but it still has some serious gotchas. Primarily, you need a very clean network and you need to tune up those desktops!

Having said that, SBS Essentials has proven to be a very robust product. As an experienced technician, you won't find any real "stoppers" here. The problems you'll run into are very familiar. They'll be things like incomplete profiles, missing mapped drives, and poking around for an NK2 cache file. Between the Big Checklist and this chapter, we think you have all the information you need to solve these problems.

In the big, big picture, here are the things you need to keep in mind to have successful, profitable migrations to SBS Essentials:

1) Know what you know. Document the network and do a complete discovery.
2) Prep the network. Set it up exactly as you want it before you open the server box.
3) Prep those desktops!
4) Separate network prep and desktop prep from the server installation.
5) Plan your installation. Don't think of a domain name while you're running the setup.
6) Document, document, document. That means document what you found, what you did, and the decisions you made. Write everything down and build the client's Network Documentation Binder.

We believe that there is so much opportunity as the Small end of the Small and Medium Business market that you could make a business doing only SBS Essentials installations combined with a few cloud services (e.g., Exchange, hosted backup, hosted spam filtering).

On the downside, you will have to deal with clients who have historically been "cheap" with their networks. And you'll see a lot more of the do-it-yourself business owners. But even there, you can focus your business on the micro businesses that are now ready to make an investment in technology.

Microsoft has made a big commitment to this very business model. They want you to sell their server into this market and combine it with hosted services. This hybrid model of on site and hosted services works great for them.

As a result, the Technet web site and SBS blog are filled with lots of great information in support of SBS Essentials. Google almost anything that begins with the phrase "SBS Essentials" or "SBS 2011 Essentials" and you will get good, useful hits on the Microsoft sites.

As a couple of Microsoft-centric geeks who have been supporting networks from 1-2 users to Fortune 100 companies for more than twenty years, we are very happy to see that companies like Microsoft are still creating niche products that fit perfectly in the small business market.

The Network Migration Workbook

Overview and Flow

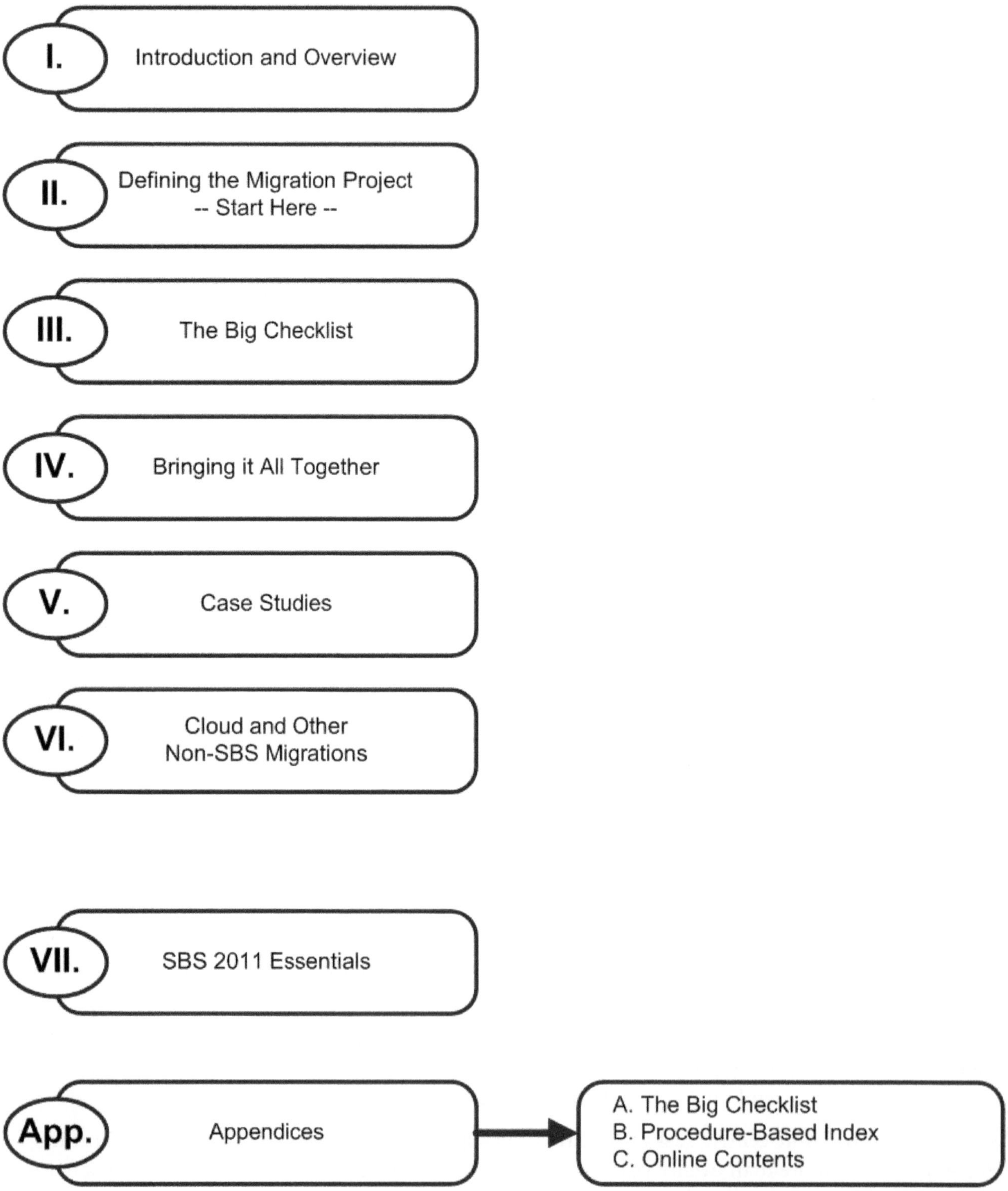

Appendices

Appendix A: The Big Checklist for SBS Migrations (2003-2011)

Note: The checklist is number separately from the remainder of the book.

Great Little Book
7485 Rush River Dr. #710 ♦ PMB 267 ♦ Sacramento, CA 95831 ♦ Phone 916-248-4301

Revision 2011.09.01.01

ZDTM

Client Company Logo Goes Here

Client Name
Network Migration Project

Project Manager: ______________________________

Project Lead: ______________________________

Primary Client Contact: ______________________________

Secondary Client Contact: ______________________________

Other Contact: ______________________________

Other Contact: ______________________________

Target Migration Date: ______________________

Migration Duration: ______________________

Refer to the Planning Section of this binder for complete detailed contact information for everyone listed above.

Table of Contents

1. Using This Document

General

This document is a proprietary tool of KPEnterprises and is copy written. It, like other KPEnterprises products are proprietary and are not for distribution or use outside of the company for any reason.

This document (SBS 2011 Network Migration Project Template 20xx.xx.xx.xx.docx) is a template for system migration projects and therefore must be tailored to each individual project before being put to use. It is a living document that will most likely change after every use.

Note: The correct nomenclature for the document name is the name of the document "SBS 2011 Network Migration Project Template" followed by the full Revision Number of the document. The revision number is simply the year month day nn, Where nn starts at 01 and increments with each intraday revision. Example: SBS 2011 Network Migration Project Template 2011.07.04.01.docx.

The current revision number of this document can be found in the upper right hand corner of the first page of this document and should always be up to date.

Do not edit or change the original document to fit each new project. Instead, save a copy of the original document as *Client Company Name* Network Migration Project 20xx.docx. Post the new document on the KPEnterprises SharePoint site in the Tech Documents\KPEnterprises Procedures\Current Projects directory. Make all edit specific to the current migration project in the posted copy.

Most sections in this binder are self-explanatory but many have some instructional text. It is assumed that the Project Manager understands how this system works and is familiar with the layout and content of each section.

When the project is completed you will strip out the pages from the binder that are unique to the project for archiving. Most other non-checklists sections will not likely change and can remain in the binder for the next project. The Project Review and Retrospective sections will cover any required changes to the original template.

All Revisions to the original document should be summarized in the Retrospective and Revision History section. Refer to the Retrospective section of this document for the procedure on revising this document.

Putting Together the Project Binder

After printing out the document, three hole punch the pages and insert tabs for each section. (See below) Having tabs for each section is key to being able to navigate the sections fast and to being able to view the project as a simple series of checklists to complete.

Label the spine and front cover of the binder "*Company Name* Network Migration Project. Alternatively the first page of the document can be inserted into any binder that has a clear front sleeve.

The Network Migration Project binder has many tabs and although some sections are scant, the tabs make it easy to maneuver through the binder and project fast. The binder is best laid out using an 8 tab system. Some section names can be abbreviations so that they can easily fit on a standard Avery label using two printed lines per label. Subsections of the New (and Old) Network Documentation should have tabs at the top of the page for easiest reference. Below are the primary section tab names and sub section tab names.

If Avery products are not readily available an alternative to the 8 tab divider system is to purchase any standard 10, 8, or 5 tab divider packs then use a standard label machine to print all tab labels. If a label machine will be used for printing labels it may be best to use a 5 tab system to allow more room for the label names. An alternative to the top labels is to simply cut the tabs (and a little extra) off of 5 tab dividers and glue or otherwise affix them across the top of another divider page. You will need to also remove the side tab of the dividers as it will not be used. The end result is that you will be using two side tab dividers to get one top tab divider.

Recommended binder products:

- 2" Three ring binder (minimum width)
- 5 Pack of 8 Tabs dividers including labels.
  Avery Product: Avery Clear Label Index Marker Presentation Dividers. #11437
- Tabs at top of the Old Network Documentation and New Network Documentation sections.
  Avery Product: Avery Printable Self-Adhesive Tabs 1¼" x 1" White. #16280

Note: 8 cut tab labels can be purchased in bulk if necessary.
Avery Product: Clear Label Dividers. #612798 - 80 per sheet multipack

Tab Names: (Top edge Tab Names are indented)

Table Of Contents
Using This Document
Pre Discovery
Project Description and Scope
Discovery
Planning / Timeline ✳
Migration Strategies
Resources
Communications / Training
Old Network Documentation
  - Procedures
  - Net Specs
  - Machines Specs
  - Users & Passwords
  - Products

System Build
TSR Log
Network Migration Prep
Network Migration ✳
Applications Migration
Sub-Systems Migration
Workstation Migration
Remote Migration
Migration Tracking Sheet
Shortages
Pack-Up / To-Do
Fine Tuning
Spin-Off Projects
Project Completion
Retrospective / Revision History
Project Notes
New Network Documentation
  - Procedures
  - Net Specs
  - Machines Specs
  - Users & Passwords
  - Products

Index to the Network Migration Project

Running the Project

The Project Manager is ultimately responsible for the projects timely and successful completion. It is up to the Project Manager to coordinate, control and synthesize the time, resources and strategies of the project.
The Project Lead is responsible for timely and successful completion of the various objectives, activities and tasks of the project. The Project Lead is typically s Senior Engineer. A project lead may also perform technician tasks.
The technician is the primary resource of the project. The technician is the workhorse of the project who performs that many tasks and activities required to meet the objectives that make up the project.

Running the project is simply defining the resources for the project, reviewing the Network Migration Project binder, selecting strategies, planning the migration and then working through the project page by page from the beginning. Use the Timeline and Communications sections to help communicate the progress to the client and to schedule resources and events.

Migration Checklists

The checklists are designed to be very complete based on the currently accepted methods used for migration. Be certain technicians following the procedure as laid out in the order shown. There is a specific reason for every entry in the checklist and for the order laid out. When specific strategies are added or integrated this becomes even more critical.

All additional items to be performed on the workstations outside the scope of a typical migration should be defined in one of the last section of the Workstation Migration Checklist called Other. All work that is outside the project scope must also be documented and fully approved as it will be billable.

Checking the Boxes

When it comes to actually completing the checklists be certain to check each box or bullet only after it is in fact done. If the step cannot be performed or is no longer applicable, check the box only after you have actually read the step(s) and completely understand why they cannot be performed or are no longer applicable.

- If a checklist item cannot be performed, circle the checkbox and write a note to explain why it cannot be performed.

  For example: There are no available public IP addresses to assign to the Lights Out interface.
- If a checklist item is no longer applicable or does not apply put an X in the box and if necessary write a note to explain. For example: The service pack is no longer applicable as it has been slipstreamed in to the latest full product release.
- If an item needs to be updated, deleted, etc. put the edit notes in the left page border and an arrow to the item.

2. Pre-Discovery

General

The Pre-Discovery is the collection of the minimum required information to get the client a reasonably accurate quote for hardware, software and labor. The Project Lead or Senior Engineer will need this information to begin writing the Project Description and Scope. The Sales Team will need the information to know what hardware and software to recommend and to estimate the number of hours the project will take.

The Pre-Discovery and the Discovery sections are both interspersed with Grey highlighting. The intention is that the Project Lead or Senior Engineer can have a Technician perform as much of the Pre-Discovery and Discovery as possible and very clearly know what questions and entries are for the Project Lead or Senior Engineer and what are for the Technician.

Note: The Project Lead or Senior Engineer are still responsible for the verification of the data collected by a Technician.

The Pre-Discovery must be performed on site. Start with the server. Then sit at a workstation or two. Finally, interview with the Client Technical Contact.

Note: The interview with the Client Technical Contact.is Greyed out as it is for the Project Lead or Senior Engineer, not a Technician.

When exporting lists or collecting information in digital format all files should be save to the c:\!tech\migration directory on the old server. This will ensure that all related migration files are readily available for transport to the new system.

- ☐ This Discovery is being initially performed: (Circle one)
    - o By the Project Lead or Senior Engineer
    - o By a Technician

Note: For Technicians: Unless specifically directed, do not make any entries or otherwise make decisions for any Greyed out section of this Discovery. All of the Greyed out sections are for the Project Lead or Senior Engineer to fill in and make decisions for.

- ☐ Log on to the old server as Administrator and create the directory c:\!tech\migration if it does not already exist.

Client Contacts

- ☐ Request the name of the proposed Primary Client Contact and Secondary Client Contact who will be managing and championing the client side of this project.
    - o Primary Client Contact: ______________________________
    - o Secondary Client Contact: ______________________________

Hardware and Environment

- ☐ Take pictures of the entire server room, rack or closet.

  Note: It may be required that this be done remotely by client or a trusted contractor.

    - o Front and back of servers and from as many angles as possible including close ups as needed.

- Net cable landings and punch down racks or blocks.
- Network devices such as Firewalls, Routers, Switches from as many angles as possible including close ups as needed.
- UPS's

☐ If the Server is not new or was not purchased from KPEnterprises, research and verify that the machine is capable of running the proposed operating system and applications before committing to the installation. ____________________

☐ What are the physical limitations for equipment at the proposed installation location? e.g. Is there space in the rack, on the shelf, etc.? ____________________

____

☐ Is there sufficient air flow or air conditioning at the proposed installation location? __________

☐ Is there a proper dedicated AC outlet for the proposed new equipment? __________

☐ Is there an existing primary UPS in place that might be eligible to be used for the new server? Y / N

- How old is the existing UPS? __________
- Does the existing UPS have the power output capable of keeping the new server up long enough for a clean shutdown? __________
- Does the existing UPS have a data port? __________
- If the UPS has a data port, is there a data cable? USB / Serial / Other:__________
- If there is a data port but no compatible cable, identify the exact UPS brand and model.

  ____

☐ If Faxing is in use on the existing system:

- Is a specific or proprietary modem or modem system being used? e.g. Digi 4 port serial controller or Brooktrout dual line device. __________
- Is the existing faxing hardware compatible with the new system (Bus, drivers, etc.)? __________
- If the existing faxing hardware is compatible are there specific hardware requirements? (ports, Controllers, etc.) ____________________
- Is SBS faxing utilized for Inbound, Outbound, Both or Neither? __________

☐ Is there an existing tape drive and controller system in place that is eligible to be used for the new server? __________

- How old is the existing tape drive and controller system? __________
- Is the existing tape drive controller bus compatible with the new system? __________
- Is the existing tape drive capacity sufficient to hold all and data on one tape? __________

☐ ____________________

☐ ____________________

Users / Machines / Remote Access

☐ How many servers, other than the SBS Server or DC, are in Active Directory? __________

☐ User Profiles:

- How many valid users are in Active Directory? __________

- How many users hand held devices will need to be re-synced or migrated? __________
- How many users log on to multiple machines? (Multiple profile migration required) __________

☐ Workstation Machine List:

- How many functioning and in use workstations are in Active Directory? __________
- How many of these are Laptops? __________
- Discuss user profile migration levels with the Client Technical Contact.
  - Verify the User Profile use as discovered in the previous steps.
  - Discuss specifically the Basic, Full (default) and Custom. Use a copy of the Workstation Migration Checklist for reference and notes.
    - Basic: Joined to the domain, Test of Outlook, Internet access, File access, Printing. My Documents moved. As if you logged onto a machine for the first time.
    - Full: All items listed in Basic plus desktop theme, background, desktop icons, favorites, Office settings, basic Outlook settings such as Outlook address cache, Email Signature, Out of office text, Auto Archive settings, POP connectors, Junk Mail filter lists.
    - Custom: All items listed in Basic, all items listed in Full and other items as needed such as Outlook content being shared and used (Folder, Contacts, Calendars) or specific shortcuts to be put on desktop, certain items to be deleted from all workstations, etc.
- Copy the entire Workstation Migration Checklist from the Workstation Migration section or print out the Workstation Migration section of the SBS 2011 Network Migration Project Template 20xx.xx.xx.xx.docx.
  - Mark the new copy as Reference Copy for use during the planning phase of the project.
  - Annotate the Reference Copy of the Workstation Migration Checklist with any useful notes including all client requested Custom Migration criteria.
  - Insert the Reference Copy of the Workstation Migration Checklist into the Planning and Timeline section of this binder.
- Export the list of Client Computers from Server Manager to the c:\!tech\migration directory of the old server.
- Print out the list and perform a physical inventory of the computers on the network including discovery of the users of each computer.
- Update the exported version of the computer list and then email it to the Client Technical Contact.
  - Be certain the outgoing email has been correctly formatted with a proper subject, the correct client company name, reply to address and technician name. Also verify every variable piece of data in the email body. e.g. dates, times, passwords, etc.
  - Instruct the Client Technical Contact to mark up and the list based on the expected migration level for each user or machine and ask them to forward the completed list to migration@kpenterprises.com.

☐ ______________________________

☐ ______________________________

Premium Content

Microsoft SQL Server

- ☐ List all SQL Servers and their Version that are installed and in use on the Server that will be migrated over. e.g. Pervasive Ver. 8, My SQL Ver. 5, MS SQL 2005, MS SQL 2008, etc.
- ☐ Verify that each of these SQL servers listed is compatible with and will run on the proposed new Small Business Server version.

  SQL Server Version Runs on SBS 2003 / 2008 / 2011

  - ____________________
  - ____________________
  - ____________________
  - Verify that each of these SQL servers listed is compatible with and will run on the proposed new Small Business Server version.
- ☐ What is the total size of all SQL and non SQL databases to be migrated? __________ GB

Microsoft Internet Security and Acceleration Server

- ☐ Is Microsoft ISA Server installed and in use? ____________________

  Note: If Microsoft ISA Server is currently used, be certain to inform the sales team as soon as possible so they may accommodate a timely hardware replacement well in advance of the Network migration date.

Active Directory / Group Policies

- ☐ Is Active Directory used extensively to manage users and Machines? ____________________
- ☐ How extensive or intricate is the Group Policy use beyond the defaults? ____________________

  ____
- ☐ ____________________
- ☐ ____________________

File and Data Storage

- ☐ What is the total uncompressed size of all data that will be migrated to the new system?
  - Company or Public Data? __________ GB – Excluding SQL and non SQL databases
  - Users Shared Folders? __________ GB
  - Users redirected My Documents? __________ GB
- ☐ What is the expected file transfer speed over the network? __________ MB / minute

  Note: Test the transfer speed by timing the copy of 500 MB of data from one server to another server or from a fast workstation to a server.
- ☐ What is the expected data restore speed to drive or over the network? __________ MB / minute

  Note: Review backup logs for actual backup speeds attained or perform a restore test of 1 GB of data to the server.

Email / Outlook / Exchange

- ☐ Is email hosted in Microsoft Exchange on this system? __________
- ☐ If not, how is email delivered to the desktops / users ? ____________________

- ☐ What is the total size of the Private Store database (.edb and .stm) ? __________ GB
- ☐ What is the total size of the Public Store database (.edb and .stm) ? __________ GB
- ☐ How many domains is this system receiving email for? __________
- ☐ Are SMTP addresses maintained for some, most, or all of these domains? __________
- ☐ To what extent are Public Folders, Calendars and Contacts used? __________
- ☐ To what extent do users share Folders Calendars and Contacts? __________
- ☐ __________
- ☐ __________

Line of Business Applications

- ☐ List all Line of Business Applications and their Version on the Server or System that will be migrated over. Accounting Package, Practice Management, CRM, etc.
- ☐ Verify that each of the Line of Business Applications listed is compatible with and will run on the proposed new Small Business Server version.

  LOB Application Version Runs on SBS 2003 / 2008 / 2011

  - __________
  - __________
  - __________
  - __________
  - Verify that each of the application listed is compatible with and will run on the proposed new Small Business Server version.

System Applications

- ☐ BlackBerry Server installed? __________ No. of users?__________
  - Is this application compatible with and will it run on the proposed new Small Business Server version? SBS 2003 / 2008 / 2011 __________
- ☐ Encrypted / Keyed Security access used for logon? __________
  - Is this application compatible with and will it run on the proposed new Small Business Server version? SBS 2003 / 2008 / 2011 __________
- ☐ Antivirus Application? __________ Centrally managed? Y / N
  - Is this application compatible with and will it run on the proposed new Small Business Server version? SBS 2003 / 2008 / 2011 __________
- ☐ Drive Maintenance Solution? __________
  - Is this application compatible with and will it run on the proposed new Small Business Server version? SBS 2003 / 2008 / 2011 __________
- ☐ Drive Imaging Solution? __________

- Is this application compatible with and will it run on the proposed new Small Business Server version? SBS 2003 / 2008 / 2011 ______________________

☐ ____

- Is this application compatible with and will it run on the proposed new Small Business Server version? SBS 2003 / 2008 / 2011 ______________________

☐ ____

- Is this application compatible with and will it run on the proposed new Small Business Server version? SBS 2003 / 2008 / 2011 ______________________

Sub-Systems

List all sub-systems that may be effected by the migration. Verify if and where the sub-systems management application is installed.

☐ Phone System – VOIP, Digital, Analog, Voice Mail (Management Application?) ____________

- Is the Management Application compatible with and will it run on the proposed new Small Business Server version? SBS 2003 / 2008 / 2011 ______________________

☐ Number of Printers (Networked or Shared) ______________________

☐ If printers are shared from the server are the permissions intricate? ____________

☐ If printers will be shared from the new server, what hardware requirements are there? (ports, controllers, etc.) ______________________

☐ Copier / Scanner (Management Application?) ______________________

☐ ____

☐ ____

☐ ____

☐ ____

Backup Software, Devices and Methods

☐ Primary Backup Application and Version: ______________________

- Is this application compatible with and will it run on the proposed new Small Business Server version? SBS 2003 / 2008 / 2011 ______________________

☐ Describe all data backup methods that are used or available for recovery of the existing system or migration to the new system. Verify how frequently any backup is run for each method.

- ____
- ____
- ____
- ____

IIS / Web Sites / FTP Sites

- ☐ If the Company's primary public facing Website (or any other) is housed on this system:
  - Is the content static or dynamic? ________
  - Is it tied to any LOB? ________
  - Is it tied to a database? ________
  - Is it managed in-house or by another company? ________
  - What are the email requirements? ________
  - What are the uptime requirements? ________
- ☐ Are there other websites or ftp sites setup and in use on this system? ________
  - ________
  - ________
  - ________
- ☐ ________
- ☐ ________

Companyweb / SharePoint

Note: Just because there is data in Companyweb or SharePoint, it does not mean the client is actively using it or that it will need to be migrated. Verify whether SharePoint or Companyweb is actually in use with the Client Technical Contact.

- ☐ If Companyweb is actively used, how many sites or workspaces are set up? ________
- ☐ If SharePoint is actively used, how many sites or workspaces are set up? ________
- ☐ How many of the SharePoint sites or workspaces are available to the internet? ________

  How intricate is the security for either Companyweb or SharePoint? ________

  ____

  ____
- ☐ How many internal or external users actively use Companyweb or SharePoint? ________
- ☐ Evaluate the overall use of Companyweb and SharePoint and briefly describe how it is used so a reasonable estimate of time required to migrate can be determined.

  ____

  ____
- ☐ ________
- ☐ ________

Miscellaneous Items

- ☐ ________
- ☐ ________
- ☐ ________
- ☐ ________

- ☐ ____________________
- ☐ ____________________

Downtime and Availability

Research and document the tolerance for downtime for each item listed below. Interview the Client Technical Contact and if necessary each department head.

Ask questions like:

> *"If we need to have the Server / Email / Copier / etc. offline for a short time, what is the longest downtime you can accept?"*
>
> *"When would be the best time to have any of these systems off line?"*
>
> *"Is downtime during the lunch hour acceptable?"*
>
> *"On the day of the migration (April 32nd), we may need to have unrestricted access to reboot systems, take the network down, etc. between 7:00 AM and 8:00 AM or between 5:00 PM and 6:00 PM. Would there be any problems with this?*

Note: There is also an email template with these questions in the Communications / Training section of this binder. Be certain it is formatted correctly, critical systems and applications are listed and the correct migration dates are added before sending the email to the Client Technical Contact.

- ☐ Server(s) ____________________
- ☐ Internet Connectivity ____________________
- ☐ Email ____________________
- ☐ CRM System ____________________
- ☐ Accounting System ____________________
- ☐ Copier / Scanner ____________________
- ☐ Phone System ____________________
- ☐ Time clock ____________________
- ☐ ____________________
- ☐ ____________________
- ☐ ____________________
- ☐ ____________________

Project Managers Review

Note: The entire Project Manager Review section is for the Project Manager or Senior Engineer to complete. Not the Technician.

- ☐ Review the Pre-Discovery completely and then meet with the sales team if necessary to discuss possible solutions to present to the client for each of the items listed below.
  - If the Server is not new or was not purchased from KPEnterprises and the machine is not capable of running the proposed operating system and applications.
  - If there are physical limitations for equipment at the proposed installation location.
  - If there is insufficient air flow or air conditioning at the proposed installation location.

- If there is no proper AC outlet or a dedicated outlet is required but does not exist for the proposed new equipment.
- If the existing primary UPS is not eligible to be used with the new server. (Too old, does not have a data port, does not have a data cable or does not have the power output capable of keeping the new server up long enough for a clean shutdown)
- If a specific or proprietary fax modem or fax modem system is being used and the existing hardware is not compatible with the new system. (Bus, drivers, etc.)
- If there is an existing tape drive and controller system in place but it is not eligible to be used for the new server, is too old, the drive controller bus is incompatible with the new system or the existing tape drive capacity is insufficient to hold all and data on one tape.
- If Microsoft ISA Server is installed and in use on the existing network.
- IF any SQL servers listed is not compatible with and will not run on the proposed new Small Business Server version.
- If any of the Line of Business Applications listed is not compatible with and will not run on the proposed new Small Business Server version.
- If any of the System Applications listed is not compatible with and will not run on the proposed new Small Business Server version.
- If any of the Sub-System Applications or hardware listed are not compatible with and / or will not run on the proposed new Small Business Server version.

  Note: This includes shared printers and their drivers. e.g. Proposed OS is SBS 2011 and the shared printer does not have 64-bit drivers available and the 32-bit drivers will not work.
- If the Primary Backup Application is not compatible with and will not run on the proposed new Small Business Server version.
- If the Companyweb or SharePoint sites are extensive in their content and will require assistance in their migration.

☐ Create Service Tickets for all approved work that is required to resolve any of the items discussed.

☐ List all projects related to these issue in the Spin-Off Projects and Issues section of this binder and note each of these projects as being a prerequisite to the Network Migration.

☐ Meet with the Sales and Engineering teams to discuss and formulate:

- The estimate of labor required for the migration
- The Project Description and Scope
- The strategy for a Zero Downtime Migration

☐ Create all Service Tickets related to the Network Migration in anticipation of the quote being accepted and the project being approved.

  - Server Migration – Training
  - Server Migration – Discovery
  - Server Migration – Server Build
  - Server Migration – Network Migration
  - Server Migration – Workstation Migration
  - Server Migration – Fine Tuning
  - Server Migration – Retrospective

3. Project Description and Scope

Project Description

The project description is a narrative of the common understanding between KPEnterprises and the Client of the goals and objectives to be reached. It may include a brief narrative of any relevant background including specific problems being addresses, history of the systems or sub-systems or anything else that will help in the planning of a successful project.

- ☐ ______
- ☐ ______
- ☐ Staff Training before installation: Introduction to the new system including SharePoint, Remote Web Workplace and Outlook Web Access.
- ☐ Discovery process: Documenting current system, subsystems, users, machines, shares and network.
- ☐ Server build: Set up server computer; configure SBS; create users, shares; install and configure backup software, Antivirus; configure DHCP, DNS, create shares. Document and test of all hardware and software.
- ☐ Network Migration: Migrate all company data and Line Of Business applications to the new server. Reconfigure firewalls, printers, routers, and SBS reliant subsystems as needed.
- ☐ Workstation Migration: Connect all documented workstations to the new server, migrate user profiles as agreed in the Discovery section of this binder and configure workstations for access to the resources in the new server. Configure all documented remote workstations to access resources on the new server as needed.
- ☐ Document everything about the new network.
- ☐ Staff Training after installation: Becoming familiar with new system including SharePoint, Remote Web Workplace and Outlook Web Access.
- ☐ Fine tuning as needed for any system, subsystem, application or workstation installed or migrated during this project.
- ☐ ______
- ☐ ______
- ☐ ______
- ☐ ______

Project Scope

The Project Scope should clearly define the deliverables and the project constraints. To keep it simple the deliverables should be defined in terms of physical and functional. Functional includes the expected completeness of user profile migration. The constraints should include target install dates and times, expected downtime for Web, Internet and local data access, the level of workstation migration, etc. Carefully detail any items that are not within the scope of the project and discuss them with the client.

☐ ______________________________

☐ ______________________________

☐ The project scope includes:

☐ The complete build of the new server as purchased including all software and hardware purchased with and for that server.

☐ The complete migration of all existing client data from the old server to the new server. Extremely large data transfers may add additional billable time to the project.

☐ The complete migration of all applications currently running on the old system provided that the application intended to run on the new system (server or workstations);

1) Can legally be installed on another machine.

2) Can logically run on the new system. e.g. Can run on a 64 bit machine or this server version, etc.

3) All applications to be migrated to the new system must have clear documentation on how to install or migrate the application including the server and workstation components.

4) There is a technical support plan in place or at a minimum technical support available. The client will bear all expenses for technical support if required for installation or migration.

☐ The migration of all documented workstations and their user profiles as documented in the Discovery section of this binder. Workstation migration assumes there will only be minor cleanup needed on any workstation and that the machine(s) are not "too old" and that they are in reasonable condition.

☐ Migration dates will be as indicated on the first page of this project document. Migration duration will be kept as closely as possible to what is planned but cannot be guaranteed due to the many possibilities of issues related to system, subsystem, application and workstation migrations.

- ☐ Due to the nature of user profiles and the possible complexity of any workstation configuration users profiles are not guaranteed to be completely migrated under any circumstance. Every effort will be made to have the workstation transition as smooth as complete as possible but it is already know that when migrating workstation profiles to a workstation on a new domain many Outlook related settings and configurations cannot be maintained. These include but are not limited to: Multiple contact lists in the address book, RSS feeds, Address search order, Mailbox permissions, Task links and more. Additionally shortcuts to network content will in almost all instances be broken as the server name will be changed.
- ☐
- ☐
- ☐
- ☐
- ☐
- ☐
- ☐
- ☐
- ☐
- ☐
- ☐
- ☐
- ☐
- ☐
- ☐
- ☐
- ☐
- ☐

4. Discovery

General

This section and the Old Network Documentation section is where all data used for the Migration Planning and Migration will culminate. Each section must be carefully detailed for there to be the minimum amount of delay and rework on the project.

The Discovery section is interspersed with Grey highlighting. The intention is that the Project Lead or Senior Engineer can have a Technician perform as much of the Discovery as possible and very clearly know what questions and entries are for the Project Lead or Senior Engineer and what are for the Technician.

Note: The Project Lead or Senior Engineer are still responsible for the verification of the data collected by a Technician.

When filing in the information in this section for the new server / system do not arbitrarily enter data. All new server and system specifications must be based on the research done during the discovery. If you are not sure what to enter, leave it blank. The Project Manager will verify all information before the server build begins.

When filling out this section be certain to integrate any relevant items from the Project Description and Project Scope sections. e.g. configuration changes such as drive layout, New Group policy decisions, etc.

When exporting lists or collecting information in digital format all files should be save to the c:\!tech\migration directory on the old server. This will ensure that all related migration files are readily available for transport to the new system.

Note: Do not duplicate work. Many places in the Discovery require documentation be generated and even refer to forms that are available for use in the New Network Documentation section. However, if the information already exists somewhere such as a preexisting Network Documentation Binder or File System, simply verify and update the existing documentation rather than create duplicate data.

- ☐ This Pre-Discovery is being initially performed: (Circle one)
  - By the Project Lead or Senior Engineer
  - By a Technician

Note: For Technicians: Unless specifically directed, do not make any entries or otherwise make decisions for any Greyed out section of this Pre-Discovery. All of the Greyed out sections are for the Project Lead or Senior Engineer to fill in and make decisions for.

- ☐ Log on to the old server as Administrator and create the directory c:\!tech\migration if it does not already exist.

Client Contacts

- ☐ Locate the Contact Details subsection of the Planning Section of this binder as it is where all contact information for all persons or companies who will be involved in the migration is to be recorded.
- ☐ Verify and document the names and complete contact information of the KPEnterprises Project Manager and Project Lead.
- ☐ Verify and document the names and complete contact information for the Primary Client Contact and Secondary Client Contact who will be managing and championing the client side of this project.

☐ Document the names and complete contact information for all Other Contacts or Companies who will be involved in the migration in any way. e.g. IT Pro's, LOB support, Vendors, etc.

Hardware and Environment

☐ What machines will be recycled when the migration is complete? ____________________

____

☐ Are there any physical drive configuration requirements for the new system? e.g. LOB requires a separate OS and Data partition. ____________________

☐ Drive RAID configuration plan for the new system.

Note: The RAID configuration must match what was quoted to the client.

- First two drives mirrored for the OS partition? Y / N
- Hardware level mirror or Operating System level mirror? __________
- The first _____ drives will be RAID ____ for the OS partition. - Hot spare? Y / N
- The next _____ drives will be RAID ____ for the 1st data partition. - Hot spare? Y / N
- The next _____ drives will be RAID ____ for the 2nd data partition. - Hot spare? Y / N
- If there will be separate OS and Data drives or partitions how large will each partition be?
  - OS Partition: __________ GB (Typical is 100% of the drive or Array)
  - Data Partition 1: ________ GB (Typical is 100% of the drive or Array)
  - Data Partition 2: ________ GB

Domain Names, IP's, DNS and DHCP

☐ Company / Organization Complete Name: ____________________

☐ City: ________________ State: ______________ Country: ______________

☐ Company / Organization Short Name or Acronym: ____________________

☐ What FQDN name will the RWW Certificate have? ____________________

Example: sbs.company.com or remote.company.com (remote. Is the default for SBS 2008 and 2011)

☐ Is there an existing trusted certificate from a Certificate Service Provider for the above mentioned site or any other site on this system that is eligible to be migrated? Y / N

- List the Certificate FQDN for each certificate that will be migrated to the new system:
  - ____________________
  - ____________________
  - ____________________

☐ Will any new Trusted Certificates from a Certificate Service Provider be required for the new system? Y / N

	Old	New
☐ DNS Internal domain name:	____________.Local	____________.Local
☐ NETBIOS domain name:	____________	____________

- ☐ SBS Server Names: ______________________ ______________________
- ☐ Server Private IP Address: ______________________ ______________________
- ☐ Server Public IP Address: ______________________ ______________________
- ☐ Lights Out Priv IP Address: ______________________ ______________________
- ☐ Lights Out Pub IP Address: ______________________ ______________________
- ☐ Are special DNS changes required for the migration such as new DNS entry for the Lights Out interface or the Web server friendly name like sbs.company.com or remote.company.com? Y / N
  - Domain Name: ______________________ IP: ______________________
  - Domain Name: ______________________ IP: ______________________
  - Domain Name: ______________________ IP: ______________________
  - Domain Name: ______________________ IP: ______________________
- ☐ Acquire, verify and document all DNS hosting information required to access the clients DNS records.
  - Username, Password, Site Access URL e.g. networksolutions.com.
  - Insert the completed list into the Old Network Documentation section – Net Specs subsection of this binder.
- ☐ DHCP Usable Range: __________ to __________ __________ to __________
- ☐ DHCP exclusion Range: __________ to __________ __________ to __________
- ☐ Will the DHCP scope on the old server need to be narrowed to allow the new servers to have its own range for the migration? Y / N What range will allow for no overlap?: ________ to __________
- ☐ Firewall Private IP Address: ______________________ ______________________
- ☐ ISP's primary DNS servers: ______________________ ______________________
- ☐ ISP's secondary DNS servers: ______________________ ______________________

Small Business Server and Related

- ☐ What Exact Version and Platform of SBS has been purchased and is being installed?

  Small Business Server 20___ Standard Premium 32 Bit 64 Bit
- ☐ Which Small Business Server Web site services are currently utilized and require access from the internet?
  - Outlook Web Access? __________
  - Remote Web Workplace? __________
  - Server Performance and usage reports? __________
  - Outlook Mobile Access? __________
  - Outlook via the Internet? (RPC over HTTP) __________
  - Windows SharePoint Services intranet site? (Companyweb) __________
  - Business Web site? (wwwroot) __________
- ☐ Is VPN currently configured and utilized? __________ DHCP Range:____________________
- ☐ If faxing is installed on the old server and will be installed on the new server which modems are configured for:

	Old System	New System
○ Inbound:	______________________	______________________
○ Outbound:	______________________	______________________

- ○ Detail here the Fax routing settings on the old server so they may be may be recreated on the new server. (Public folder, printer, etc.)

  ____

  ____

☐ Is Server Performance and Monitoring configured and in use? ______________________

- ○ Who will receive notifications? ______________________

☐ If the Domain Controller is configured to synchronize time with a specific source, and the new SBS server will also need to synchronize with that source, record the specifics here.

- ○ ____

☐ Detail here any Scheduled Tasks that will need to be migrated to the new system.

- ○ ____
- ○ ____
- ○ ____

Note: There is a forms in the New Network Documentation section that can help record and manage all timed network events. It is the Network Timing Diagram. It will be useful to copy it and use it for many of the applications listed below.

Service Pack and Critical Updates

☐ Is there any reason the following should NOT be on the latest service pack or be fully updated?

- ○ Server Operating system ______________________
- ○ Exchange Server ______________________
- ○ SharePoint ______________________
- ○ Microsoft SQL ______________________
- ○ Workstation Operating Systems ______________________
- ○ Line Of Business Applications ______________________

Premium Content

Microsoft SQL Server

☐ If Microsoft SQL Server is installed on the old server as part of the SBS Premium Content and will be required on the new server:

Note: Do not fill out this section if any non SBS Premium Content SQL will be installed as part of a Line of Business Application installation. That will be covered for each individual LOB.

- ○ What version and SP will be installed? ______________________
- ○ What is the Instance name? ______________________
- ○ What account and password are the SQL service running under? ______________________

- What is the Security Mode? Windows Authentication Mixed mode
- What is the SA Password? ________________
- What SQL components are required? Integration Services Reporting Services

  ____
- Note here any other specifics about the SQL installation such as Collation selections, etc.:

  ____
- If the application is currently installed on a server or somewhere in the system, verify that the application license allows for transfer of the application to a new server or system. Y / N
- Identify and secure the SQL application media (Including software keys, codes and passwords) that will be required for the new system.
- List all Databases that will require migration to the new server.

  ____

  ____

Microsoft Internet Security and Acceleration Server

☐ If Microsoft ISA Server is installed and in use verify that the sales team has in fact been informed so a timely hardware replacement can be scheduled and implemented well in advance of the Network migration date.

Active Directory / Group Policies

☐ Acquire a complete list of System Critical Passwords in written form only. e.g. Administrator, SA, etc.

Note: There is a form in the New Network Documentation section that can help manage this information. It is the User & Password Record. Copy the form, do not use the original.

- Insert the printed list or completed forms into the Old Network Documentation section – Users and Passwords subsection of this binder.

☐ User naming convention. e.g. First initial Last name or just first name etc.:

Note: It is always strongly recommended to keep the existing convention especially for users.

Old	New
____________________	____________________

☐ Workstation naming convention. e.g. Workstation01, Laptop01:

Old	New
____________________	____________________

Note: For the next several items there are two options for acquiring the information easily into digital form.

First, a digital list can be exported as follows: In Server Manager in the appropriate section such as Distribution Groups, select the Action menu and then Export list. Some simple editing will result in a clean list for printing.

Second, the LDIFDE command can be used to export all the information in one digital list. Again, some simple editing will result in a clean list for printing. The command line to use is detailed in the Resource section of this binder in the Scripts and Batch Files section.

☐ Acquire the complete list of users, logon ID's and primary email address in printed and digital form.

Note: There are two forms in the New Network Documentation section that can help manage this information. They are the User & Password Record and the Email Address Record. Copy the forms, do not use the originals.

- Insert the printed list or completed forms into the Old Network Documentation section – Users and Passwords subsection of this binder.
- Save the digital version to the c:\!tech\migration directory on the old server.

☐ Acquire the complete list of Security and Distribution Groups in printed and digital form.

Note: There is a form in the New Network Documentation section that can help manage this information. It is the Security and Distribution Group Membership Record. Copy the form, do not use the original.

- Insert the printed list or completed forms into the Old Network Documentation section – Users and Passwords subsection of this binder.
- Save the digital version to the c:\!tech\migration directory on the old server.

☐ Acquire the complete list of Client Computers in printed and digital form.

- Insert the printed list or completed forms into the Old Network Documentation section – Net Specs subsection of this binder.
- Save the digital version to the c:\!tech\migration directory on the old server.

☐ Is a Password Policy and/or an Account Lockout Policy configured on the old system? Y / N

- Document the existing Policy settings directly from the Group Policy that is enforcing it.

Note: There is a form in the New Network Documentation section specifically for the Password Policy and Account Lockout Policy. It is the Password Policy form. Copy the form, do not use the original.

- Insert the completed forms into the Old Network Documentation section – Users and Passwords subsection of this binder.

☐ Acquire the complete list of the Group Policies that will be migrated to the new system. Exclude default policies unless specific unique configuration information needs to be recorded.

Note: There is a form in the New Network Documentation section that can help manage this information. It is the Group Policy Object Record. Copy the form, do not use the original.

- Insert the printed list or completed forms into the Old Network Documentation section – Net Specs subsection of this binder.

☐ Acquire the SBS logon scripts and batch files that are in use, in printed and digital form.

- Insert the printed versions into the Old Network Documentation section – Net Specs subsection of this binder.
- Save the digital versions to the c:\!tech\migration directory on the old server.

☐ Detail here the current connections (Net Use's) on workstations, as some may not controlled by the logon script. Logging on to multiple workstations and comparing the mapped drives to the known maps from all scripts to discover what additional drive maps are in use.

- ____
- ____
- ____

File and Data Storage

- ☐ Will Disk Quota Management be enabled on the new system? Y / N
  - Deny disk space to users exceeding quota limit? Y / N
  - Limit disk space to: __________ MB / GB
  - Set warning level to: __________ MB / GB
  - Log events when users exceed their quota limit? Y / N
  - Log events when users exceed their warning level? Y / N
- ☐ Will Shadow Copies be utilized on the new system? Y / N
  - Drive: _____ - Maximum size limit: _____ MB / GB - Frequency: ____________________
  - Drive: _____ - Maximum size limit: _____ MB / GB - Frequency: ____________________
  - Drive: _____ - Maximum size limit: _____ MB / GB - Frequency: ____________________
  - Drive: _____ - Maximum size limit: _____ MB / GB - Frequency: ____________________
- ☐ Are Users My Documents redirected by Group Policy on Old Server? Y / N
  - Redirect to: ____
  - Exclusions: ____

    ____
- ☐ Will Users My Documents be redirected on New Server? Y / N
  - Redirect to: ____
  - Exclusions: ____

    ____
- ☐ Will storage quotas be used to limit the size of users data being stored on the server? Y / N

  If so, max size: _______ GB
- ☐ Users' Desktop will be redirected on New Server? Y / N
- ☐ Users Start menu will be redirected on New Server? Y / N
- ☐ Location of the Users Redirected Documents Data on the new server will be on drive: ______ (C: = default)

  Note: This is where the users My Documents, Desktop and Start Menu data is stored on an SBS 2011 server.
- ☐ Location of the Users Shared Data (Users Shared Folders) on the new server will be on drive: _____ (C: = default)
- ☐ Will storage quotas be used to limit the size of users shared data on the server? Y / N

  If so, max size: _______ GB
- ☐ Acquire the complete list of shared data resources (shares) and their permissions.

  Note: There are two forms in the New Network Documentation section that can help manage this information. They are the Shared Resources form and the Share Permissions Record. Copy the forms, do not use the originals.
  - Insert the completed list into the Old Network Documentation section – Net Specs subsection of this binder.

☐ Will there be a change in the way data is accessed or used? e.g. old share method is to share out five directories and map five drives to those shares. New method is to have a single share and map drives to the share\subdirectory. ______________________________

____

☐ During the Workstation Migration, will all company data found locally on the workstation be moved to the server? Y / N

Move to: x:\ (users mapped share) or *servername\companydatashare\username* or other

____

☐ During the Workstation Migration, will all Archive and Personal Folders files (.pst's). found locally on the workstation be moved to the server? Y / N

Move to: x:\ (users mapped share) or *servername\companydatashare\username* or other

____

Email / Outlook / Exchange

☐ Email the Client Technical Contact with the How Users Use Outlook email to distribute to the users, requesting their input as to how each of them use Outlook. The email template can be found in the Communications / Training section of this binder.

- Be certain the outgoing email has been correctly formatted with a proper subject, the correct client company name, reply to address and technician name. Also verify every variable piece of data in the email body. e.g. dates, times, passwords, etc.

☐ List all domains this system will be receiving email for. Note the Primary Domain first.

Primary Domain: ____________________ ____________________

____________________ ____________________

____________________ ____________________

☐ Will Exchange Mailbox Store limits be implemented? Y / N

- Issue warnings at: __________ KB
- Prohibit send at: __________ KB
- Prohibit send and receive at: __________ KB

☐ Will Exchange Public Folder Store limits be implemented? Y / N

- Issue warnings at: __________ KB
- Prohibit send at: __________ KB
- Prohibit send and receive at: __________ KB

☐ If POP3 connector accounts are configured in Exchange and will be migrated, document them including passwords.

Note: There is a form in the New Network Documentation section that can help manage this information. It is the POP and MAPI Account Record. Copy the form, do not use the original.

- Insert the printed list or completed forms into the Old Network Documentation section – Net Specs subsection of this binder.

☐ Document all additional user SMTP addresses for each domain the system receives email for.

Note: There is a form in the New Network Documentation section that can help manage this information. It is the Email Address Record. Copy the form, do not use the original.

- Insert the printed list or completed forms into the Old Network Documentation section – Users and Passwords subsection - of this binder.

☐ Is a third party email filter system implemented? Y / N

- What is the address all email is forwarded to? ______________________
- What is the address(s) all email is received from? ______________________
- ______________________

☐ How do users get to and use Exchange Public content?

- Public Folders? ______________________
- Public Calendars? ______________________
- Public Contacts? ______________________

  ____

  - Which ones are used? (No guessing) ______________________
  - Which ones are Email enabled? ______________________

Line of Business Applications

☐ List all Line of Business Applications on the old server that require migration to the new server.

	Line of Business Application	OK to Transfer*	Media and Keys*
o	______________________	__________	__________
o	______________________	__________	__________
o	______________________	__________	__________
o	______________________	__________	__________
o	______________________	__________	__________

- For each application listed above, if it is currently installed on a server or somewhere in the system, verify that the application license allows for transfer of the application to a new server or system. Note it in the list above.
- For each application listed above, identify and secure the LOB application media (Including software keys, codes and passwords) that will be required on the new system, for each application listed. Note it in the list above.
- Document each Line of Business Application on separate pages, detailing all of the following information for each application:
  - What platforms will this application run on?
  - The current and most recent version of this application.
  - The current and most recent service pack for this application.
  - The most critical server requirements for this application. (SQL for example)
  - The most critical workstation requirements for this application.
  - Support contract for the applications expiration date.
  - Support contract is from the Publisher / Third Party or Other.
  - Support method is Open / Per incident / Per hour or Other.
  - Complete Support Provider contact information.

  - Installation / Configuration / Migration Notes.

  Note: There is a form in the New Network Documentation section that can help manage this information. It is the Line of Business Applications Record. Copy the form, do not use the original.

Note: Be certain all information requested is verified as it can significantly impact the migration timeline and downtime for business critical applications.

- Insert the printed list or completed forms into the Old Network Documentation section – Products subsection of this binder.

System Applications

☐ BlackBerry Server requiring migration to the new system? Y / N

- Is this application certified by the publisher / manufacturer to run on the proposed operating system of the new server? Y / N
- Document the schema, access rights, settings, users, passwords and any other pertinent information for the existing system on separate pages so it may be recreated on the new server.
- All exported configuration information should be directed to the c:\!tech\Migration directory on the old server.
- Insert any printed or written documentation of the Blackberry server into the Old Network Documentation section – Products subsection of this binder.
- Identify and secure the BlackBerry Server application media (Including software keys, codes and passwords) that will be required for the new system.

☐ Encrypted / Keyed Security Access System requiring migration to the new system? Y / N

- Is this application certified by the publisher / manufacturer to run on the proposed operating system of the new server? Y / N
- Document the schema, access rights, settings, passwords and any other pertinent information for the existing system on separate pages so it may be recreated on the new server.
- Insert any printed or written documentation into the Old Network Documentation section – Products subsection of this binder.
- If the application is currently installed on a server or somewhere in the system, verify that the application license allows for transfer of the application to a new server or system. Y / N
- Identify and secure the Encrypted/Keyed Security application media (Including software keys, codes and passwords) that will be required for the new system.

☐ Antivirus Solution requiring migration to the new system? Y / N

- Is this application certified by the publisher / manufacturer to run on the proposed operating system of the new server? Y / N
- Is the solution centrally managed? Y / N
- Document the schema, access rights, settings, passwords and any other pertinent information for the existing system on separate pages so it may be recreated on the new server.
- If there are passwords required for the clients to unload or uninstall the application record those passwords here: Unload: ________________ Uninstall: ________________
- Record all scheduled scans and updates (server and workstations) on the Network Timing Diagram in the Old Network Documentation section – Net Specs subsection of this binder.

- Insert any printed or written documentation into the Old Network Documentation section – Products subsection of this binder.
- If the application is currently installed on a server or somewhere in the system, verify that the application license allows for transfer of the application to a new server or system. Y / N
- Identify and secure the Antivirus application media (Including software keys, codes and passwords) that will be required for the new system.

☐ Drive Maintenance Solution requiring migration to the new system? Y / N

- Is this application certified by the publisher / manufacturer to run on the proposed operating system of the new server? Y / N
- Record all scheduled routines and updates on the Network Timing Diagram in the Old Network Documentation section – Net Specs subsection of this binder.
- If the application is currently installed on a server or somewhere in the system, verify that the application license allows for transfer of the application to a new server or system. Y / N
- Identify and secure the drive maintenance or management application media (Including software keys, codes and passwords) that will be required for the new system.

☐ Drive Imaging Solution requiring migration to the new system? Y / N

- Is this application certified by the publisher / manufacturer to run on the proposed operating system of the new server? Y / N
- Record all scheduled images including delta's on the Network Timing Diagram in the Old Network Documentation section – Net Specs subsection of this binder.
- If the application is currently installed on a server or somewhere in the system, verify that the application license allows for transfer of the application to a new server or system. Y / N
- Identify and secure the Drive Imaging application media (Including software keys / codes) that will be required for the new system.

Sub-Systems

☐ Router

- Document the network Router configuration completely.

Note: There is a form in the New Network Documentation section that can help manage this information. It is the Router Configuration form. Copy the form, do not use the original.

- Verify the complete Public IP range available for use on this network including available IP's.
- Verify that the documented Logon ID and Password work.
- Insert any printouts, lists or other information into the Old Network Documentation section – Net Specs subsection of this binder.

☐ Firewall

- Document the network Firewall configuration completely.

Note: There is a form in the New Network Documentation section that can help manage this information. It is the Firewall Configuration form. Copy the form, do not use the original.

- Verify that the documented Logon ID and Password work.
- Insert any printouts, lists or other information into the Old Network Documentation section – Net Specs subsection of this binder.

☐ Phone System

- Document the Phone System, Voice Messaging System and related devices fully including IP address, access methods, passwords, applications and directories protected, etc.

Note: There is a form in the New Network Documentation section that can help manage this information. It is the Machine Specifications form. Copy the form, do not use the original.

- Is there a Phone or Voice Messaging System management application installed on the old system that will require migration to the new system? Y / N
  - ______________________________
- Is this application certified by the publisher / manufacturer to run on the proposed operating system of the new server? Y / N
- Does any part of the Phone or Voice Messaging Systems use hard coded IP addresses? Y / N
  - Range or IP's: ______________________________
- Does the Phone or Voice Messaging Systems tie into the Network, Server or Email? Y / N

  e.g. VOIP system notifies users of vmail via email or Unified Messaging agent on desktops.
  - ______________________________
  - ______________________________
- Will anything about the Phone System configuration be effected by the migration? Y / N
  - ______________________________
  - ______________________________
- Insert the document or completed forms into the Old Network Documentation section – Products subsection of this binder.
- Identify and secure the Phone System application media (Including software keys / codes) that will be required for the new system.

☐ Printers

- Identify and document all printers shared from the old server that will be migrated to the new server including permissions.

Note: There are three forms in the New Network Documentation section that can help manage this information. They are the Machine Specifications form, Shared Resources form and the Share Permissions Record. Copy the forms, do not use the originals.

- List her only the printer names and note the drivers that will be required by various operating systems on the network.

	Drivers required for:					
○ ______________	2003	2008	2011	XP	Vista	Windows 7
○ ______________	2003	2008	2011	XP	Vista	Windows 7
○ ______________	2003	2008	2011	XP	Vista	Windows 7
○ ______________	2003	2008	2011	XP	Vista	Windows 7

- Insert the printed list or completed forms into the appropriate subsection of the Old Network Documentation section of this binder. (Net Specs or Machine Specs)
- Secure all required drivers for all printers listed here.

Note: Complete drivers may be copied to the c:\!tech\migration directory on the old server to ensure they are transferred to the new server or the complete driver disk may be collected.

☐ Copier / Scanner

- Identify and document all copiers and scanners that are networked.

Note: There are three forms in the New Network Documentation section that can help manage this information. They are the Machine Specifications form, Shared Resources form and the Share Permissions Record. Copy the forms, do not use the originals.

- List her only the copier names and note the drivers that will be required by various operating systems on the network.

	Drivers required for:					
______________________	2003	2008	2011	XP	Vista	Windows 7
______________________	2003	2008	2011	XP	Vista	Windows 7
______________________	2003	2008	2011	XP	Vista	Windows 7

- Using a Machine Specifications form, Document how scanning is configured: Scan to file, Scan to email, using SMB?, server name, IP, access link, logon ID and password, etc.
- ____
- ____
- Insert the printed list or completed forms into the appropriate subsection of the Old Network Documentation section of this binder. (Net Specs or Machine Specs)
- Secure all required drivers for all printers listed here.

Note: Complete driver sets may be copied to the c:\!tech\migration directory on the old server to ensure they are transferred to the new server or the complete driver disk may be collected.

☐ Update / Patch Management Solution requiring migration to the new system? Y / N

- What application, program other solution is used for System updates on the server and the workstations? ______________________________
- Is this application certified by the publisher / manufacturer to run on the proposed operating system of the new server? Y / N
- Document the schema, access rights, settings, passwords and any other pertinent information for the existing system on separate pages so it may be recreated on the new server.
- Record all scheduled scans and updates (server and workstations) on the Network Timing Diagram in the Old Network Documentation section – Net Specs subsection of this binder.
- Insert any printed or written documentation into the Old Network Documentation section – Products subsection of this binder.
- If the application is currently installed on a server or somewhere in the system, verify that the application license allows for transfer of the application to a new server or system. Y / N
- Identify and secure the Update / Patch Management application media (Including software keys, codes and passwords) that will be required for the new system.

Backup Software, Devices and Methods

☐ Tape Backup Solution employed on the old system that will be migrated to the new system? Y / N

- Will the tape device be migrated to the new system? Y / N
- Will the controller be migrated to the new system? Y / N
- Is this hardware and any associated application certified by the publisher / manufacturer to run on the proposed operating system of the new server? Y / N

- If the application is currently installed on a server or somewhere in the system, verify that the application license allows for transfer of the application to a new server or system. Y / N
- Identify and secure the Backup application (Including software keys / codes) that will be required for the new system.

☐ Continuous Data Protection System employed on the old system that will be migrated to the new system? Y / N

- Is this application certified by the publisher / manufacturer to run on the proposed operating system of the new server? Y / N
- Document the device or software fully including IP address, access methods, passwords, applications and directories protected, etc.

Note: There is a form in the New Network Documentation section that can help manage this information. It is the Machine Specifications form. Copy the form, do not use the original.

- Insert the document or completed forms into the Old Network Documentation section – Product subsection of this binder.
- Identify and secure the CDP application (Including software keys / codes) that will be required for the new system.

☐ Offsite Backup System employed on the old system that will be migrated to the new system? Y / N

- Is this application certified by the publisher / manufacturer to run on the proposed operating system of the new server? Y / N
- Document the device or software fully including IP address, access methods, passwords, applications and directories protected, etc.

Note: There is a form in the New Network Documentation section that can help manage this information. It is the Machine Specifications form. Copy the form, do not use the original.

- Insert the document or completed forms into the Old Network Documentation section – Product subsection of this binder.
- Identify and secure any Offsite Backup software (Including software keys / codes) that will be required for the new system.

☐ Backup Strategy - Detail here all current backup strategy for the entire system (regardless of method). Selection, Frequency, Start Timing, Full, Incremental, etc.

Note: All Backup schedule must be recorded on the Network Timing Diagram form in the Old Network Documentation section – Net Specs subsection of this binder.

- ______________________________
- ______________________________
- ______________________________
- ______________________________

☐ SQL Server Maintenance Routine - Detail here any current SQL Server backup or Maintenance Routines.

Note: All Backup schedule must be recorded on the Network Timing Diagram form in the Old Network Documentation section – Net Specs subsection of this binder.

- ______________________________
- ______________________________

IIS / Web Sites / FTP Sites

☐ If FrontPage Server Extensions is installed on the old system and actively used, and will be installed on the new system, which users will need access?

____

____

☐ List all in house Web sites that will need to be migrated to the new system.

- Detail any links to databases or other active content or applications.
- Insert any printed list or information into the Old Network Documentation section – Net Specs subsection of this binder.
- Save any digital information or versions to the c:\!tech\migration directory on the old server.
- ____
- ____
- ____
- ____
- ____
- ____

☐ If FTP service is installed on the old system and actively used, and will be installed on the new system, which users will need access?

- ____
- ____

Note: Do not attempt to export, backup or otherwise copy the data from these sites at this time. It will be done during the migration.

Companyweb / SharePoint

☐ List all Companyweb and SharePoint sites or workspaces that require migration to the new system. Include the public address for each public facing workspace. e.g. https://workzone.com/team1

- ____
- ____
- ____
- ____
- For each site listed here, detail the configuration, settings and permissions on separate pages so it may be recreated on the new server. There is no form for this.
- Insert any printouts, lists or other information into the Old Network Documentation section – Net Specs subsection of this binder.

Note: Do not export, backup or otherwise copy the data from these workplaces at this time. It will be done during the migration.

Miscellaneous Items

- ☐ Collect and copy all existing Procedure notes and documents pertaining to Software, Hardware, System installation, configuration or migration and place it into the Old Network Documentation section – Procedures subsection.

  Note: If there is an existing Network Documentation Binder, most of this information should already be collected in the Procedures section of that binder.

- ☐ Remote into or sit at least two workstations to verify how the system is used. Net maps, LOB's, Outlook components, etc. ____________________

  ____
- ☐ ____________________
- ☐ ____________________
- ☐ Acquire an accurate copy of the clients stationary complete with company logo, fax number and primary mailing address.
  - If digital version of the logo are available, save a copy to the c:\!tech\migration directory on the old server.
  - Insert any printouts, lists or other information into the Old Network Documentation section – Net Specs subsection of this binder.
- ☐ Email a digital copy of all User Names and their Email Addresses to the Client Technical Contact for verification. Request a return date no later than the expected server build start date.
  - Be certain the outgoing email has been correctly formatted with a proper subject, the correct client company name, reply to address and technician name. Also verify every variable piece of data in the email body. e.g. dates, times, passwords, etc.
  - Instruct the Client Technical Contact to verify the spelling of each users name, their email address and if they are authorized and will need remote access to their workstation.
  - Instruct the Client Technical Contact to note expected migration level for each user or machine.
  - Ask them to forward the completed list to migration@kpenterprises.com.
- ☐ Compile all TCP/IP address data:
  - Make a copy of the IP Address Allocation record, Hard Coded IP Address record and the Network Map from the New Network Documentation section of this binder to use for this data.
  - Review all Discovery data collected and complete these three forms as accurately as possible.

    Note: Do not enter IP information for the new system or server. Only document the old data for now.
  - Include IP information for all printers, phones, storage systems, hard coded workstations etc.
  - Insert the completed documents into the Old Network Documentation section – Net Specs subsection of this binder.
- ☐ Document below in the Notes section all things not covered in the Discovery including items that may have been missed, overlooked or under documented.
- ☐ Compile all Discovery data from the old system c:\!tech\migration directory to CD, DVD or USB for transfer to the new system.
- ☐ Compile the software and drivers for all LOB's, Sub Systems, Applications, etc. collected during the Discovery and place them in expandable manila folders. Label the folder appropriately with the Company name and Product. (if separate folders are used for each product)

- ☐ Return all compiled Discovery data and media to the KPEnterprises main office to begin the system build.

Downtime and Availability

- ☐ Review the previously documented tolerance for downtime for the critical systems including network, servers, applications and systems in the Pre-Discovery.
- ☐ Note here anything that will change the perceived requirements.
- ☐ ______
- ☐ ______
- ☐ ______
- ☐ ______

Notes

- ☐ ______
- ☐ ______
- ☐ ______
- ☐ ______
- ☐ ______
- ☐ ______
- ☐ ______
- ☐ ______
- ☐ ______
- ☐ ______
- ☐ ______
- ☐ ______
- ☐ ______
- ☐ ______
- ☐ ______

5. Planning / Timeline ✳

General

✳ This is one of two critical sections that the Project Manager must keep close tabs on. The other section is the Network Migration section.

The Planning and Timeline section contains the Master checklists for the entire project. There are only four subsections but each one is critical to the success of the entire project.

Pay close attention to the Timeline checklists as they contain all the checks for critical emails to the Client Technical Contact informing them of dates, upcoming changes and progress.

Contact Details

- Project Manager: ______________________________
  - Company: ______________________________
  - Email Address: ______________________________
  - Cell Phone: ____________________ Office + Ext.:____________________
- Project Lead: ______________________________
  - Company: ______________________________
  - Email Address: ______________________________
  - Cell Phone: ____________________ Office + Ext.:____________________
- Primary Client Contact: ______________________________
  - Company: ______________________________
  - Email Address: ______________________________
  - Cell Phone: ____________________ Office + Ext.:____________________
- Secondary Client Contact: ______________________________
  - Company: ______________________________
  - Email Address: ______________________________
  - Cell Phone: ____________________ Office + Ext.:____________________
- Other Contact: ______________________________
  - Company: ______________________________
  - Email Address: ______________________________
  - Cell Phone: ____________________ Office + Ext.:____________________
- Other Contact: ______________________________
  - Company: ______________________________
  - Email Address: ______________________________
  - Cell Phone: ____________________ Office + Ext.:____________________

Project Lead and Project Manager Review of Discovery

This subsection is for the Project Managers review of all the Discovery section data and planning for the migration. Certain subsections of the Discovery require not only verification but also approval due to the content.

When reviewing and completing the Discovery and other sections be certain to integrate any relevant items from the Project Description and Project Scope sections. e.g. Workstation migration levels, New Group policy decisions, etc.

Refer to the quote for the new server when setting parameters based on the new systems expected resources. For example, the number of IP's required is based on presence of an ILO controller or 2nd NIC. The size of the Shadow Copies is related to the total size of drives. Etc.

- ☐ Scrutinize each section of the Discovery for completeness and accuracy before proceeding. Annotate sections and needed.
- ☐ Hardware and Environment check.
  - Verify and approve each item in this section paying close attention to Drive RAID configuration and any required or suggested separate OS and Data partitioning.
- ☐ Domain Names, IP's, DNS and DHCP check.
  - Verify and approve each item in this section paying close attention to all names and IP addresses.
  - Will the exiting Trusted Certificates be migrated to the new server? Note which ones will be migrated in the Discovery section.
  - Will a new Trusted Certificate be generated for the new SBS server site? Y / N

    e.g. remote.*company.com*
- ☐ Small Business Server and Related check.
  - Verify an approve each item in this section paying close attention to the OS platform (32 or 64 bit).
- ☐ Service Pack and Critical Updates check.
  - Verify and approve each item in this section.
- ☐ Premium Content check.
  - Verify and approve each item in this section paying close attention to any intention of using SQL in only Windows Authentication mode.
- ☐ Active Directory / Group Policies check.
  - Verify and approve each item in this section paying close attention to the proposed User and Workstation naming conventions.
- ☐ File and Data Storage check.
  - Verify and approve each item in this section paying close attention to
    - Proposed disk quotas.
    - Proposed redirection of users profiles or shared documents.
    - Proposed plan to move company data found on the desktop to the server.
    - Proposed plan to move archived email (.pst's) found on the workstation to the server.
- ☐ Email / Outlook / Exchange check.

- Verify and approve each item in this section paying close attention to proposed mailbox store limits and the list of email domains.

☐ Line of Business Applications check.

- Verify and approve each item in this section paying close attention to applications that are not eligible to be moved to a new server and application that will not run on the proposed operating system version or platform.
- Will third party resources be required during the migration? Y / N

☐ System Applications check.

- Verify and approve each item in this section paying close attention to applications that are not eligible to be moved to a new server and application that will not run on the proposed operating system version or platform.

☐ Sub-Systems check.

Verify and approve each item in this section paying close attention to applications and hardware that are not eligible to be moved to a new server or application and hardware that will not run on the proposed operating system version or platform.

Note: This includes shared printers and their drivers. e.g. Proposed OS is SBS 2011 and the shared printer does not have 64-bit drivers available and the 32-bit drivers will not work.

- Will third party resources be required during the migration? Y / N

☐ Backup Software, Devices and Methods check.

- Verify and approve each item in this section paying close attention to applications that are not eligible to be moved to a new server and application that will not run on the proposed operating system version or platform.

☐ IIS / Web Sites / FTP Sites and check.

- Verify and approve each item in this section.

☐ Companyweb / SharePoint check.

- Verify and approve each item in this section.
- Will third party resources be required during the migration? Y / N

☐ Miscellaneous Items check.

- Verify and approve each item in this section.

☐ Downtime and Availability check.

- Verify and approve each item in this section.

Resources and Training

☐ Begin scheduling resources as needed for each item listed below. Have a paper trail and keep a notes in the Notes section of this binder.

- Third party technical support for the migration of applications, sub-systems, SharePoint, Companyweb etc.

  ____

  ____

- Training for users on Small business Server features

  ____

____

- Training for technicians on proposed Migration Strategies.

  ____

  ____

Migration Strategy

The Migration Strategy is the overall plan for the actual migration of data, applications, systems, user and machines. It is the heart and focus of this entire document.

The Migration Strategy layout below is the generic layout of the standard Zero Down Time Migration. The Migration Strategy should certainly be used for simple progress tracking of the project to ensure nothing major gets overlooked.

Listed below are all the Migration Preparation and Migration subsections in the same order they appear in the checklist. This list can be re-arranged according to the desired Migration Strategy including adding or removing sections as needed. e.g. adding a specific LOB migration checklist or Sub-System checklist.

If this Migration Strategy is re-ordered or sections are added or removed, the actual checklist subsection can also be rearranged to match the new strategy order. Alternatively the actual execution of the checklists must be closely monitored by the project manager to ensure the desired order is followed.

☐ Modify the Migration Strategy below to represent the current network migration project according to the requirements outlined in the Pre-Discovery and Discovery sections.

Server Installation Day Minus 3

☐ Review and Prerequisite Projects

☐ Preparing the Old Network

☐ Preparation for Server Installation

Server Installation Day *(Friday – Noon)*

☐ Server Installation
- Old Server Move
- New Server Installation
- Backup Secured
- DNS and Firewall Changes
- DNS and DHCP Setup

☐ Company Data Synchronization – Initiating

☐ Users Shared Data (Users Shared Folders) Synchronization – Initiating

Migration Day Minus 2 *(Monday – End of Day)*

☐ IIS / Web Sites / FTP Sites Migration

☐ Drive Map Redirection

☐ Email Migration – Initial Export from Old Server
- Exchange Permissions Setup – Old Server

- Email Export – Old Server

☐ SQL Server Data Synchronization – Initiating

Migration Day Minus 1 ***(Tuesday - End of Day)***

☐ Email Redirected to New Server

☐ Email Migration – Initial Import to New Server
  - Exchange Permissions Setup – New Server
  - Email Import – New Server

☐ Exchange Public Folder Migration

☐ Email Migration – Final Export from Old Server
  - Email Export (Recent only) – Old Server

Migration Day 1 and 2 ***(Wednesday and Thursday)***

☐ Email Migration – Final Import to New Server
  - Email Import – New Server

☐ Fax System Migration

☐ Companyweb and SharePoint Migration

☐ SQL Server Data Synchronization – Finalizing

☐ Line Of Business Application Migration

☐ System Application Migration
  - Antivirus Migration

☐ Sub-System Migration
  - Router
  - Firewall
  - Phone System
  - Printers
  - Copier / Scanner
  - Update / Patch Management

☐ Company Data Synchronization – Finalizing

☐ Users Shared Data (Users Shared Folders) Synchronization – Finalizing

☐ Workstation Migration

☐ Remote User Migration

☐ Server Fine Tuning

☐ Documentation

☐ Post Migration

Timeline

These Timelines are a generic layout of the standard Zero Down Time Migration and can be used as is or change to suite the new project or used as is. These Timelines should certainly be used for simple progress tracking of the project to ensure nothing major gets overlooked especially emails to the Client Technical Contact informing them of upcoming changes and progress.

Three Weeks Prior

- ☐ Service Tickets to track hours for the project are created
- ☐ A Project Manager and Project Lead are assigned
- ☐ Consultation with the Client Technical Contact to answer basic discovery questions, clarify project description and scope
- ☐ Project Description and Scope are drafted
- ☐ Define target migration dates
- ☐ Full Discovery begins
- ☐ Migration Strategies planning begins
- ☐ System Build Checklists revision begins
- ☐ Network Migration Checklist revision begins
- ☐ Workstation Migration Checklist revision begins
- ☐ Sub-System and Other Migration Checklists revision begins
- ☐ Email the Client Technical Contact with the Where we are and What's Next email

Two Weeks Prior

- ☐ Monday review of project overview
- ☐ Email the Client Technical Contact with the How Users Use Outlook email to distribute to users
- ☐ Discovery complete
- ☐ Project Description and Scope are finalized and shared with Client Technical Contact and migration team
- ☐ Migration dates are finalized and verified with Client.
- ☐ All Migration Checklist revisions completed
- ☐ System Build begins
- ☐ Define any Tech Training that will be required by the Migration team and initiate it
- ☐ Schedule any third party resources required – Have an Email trail!
- ☐ Schedule Pre Migration Training with Client Technical Contact
- ☐ Migration Strategies planning completed
- ☐ Email the Migration FAQ to the Client Technical Contact to distribute to users

One Week Prior

- ☐ Monday review of progress status
- ☐ Email the Client Technical Contact with the Workstation cleanup email to distribute to users
- ☐ Schedule the server installation for noon on the Friday before migration and send the Client Technical Contact the Server Install reminder email
- ☐ Review the Shortages Checklist
- ☐ Schedule technicians for the migration
- ☐ Email the Client Technical Contact with the What to expect email to distribute to users
- ☐ Create complete user list with email addresses and Email it to the Client Technical Contact to be verified.
- ☐ Present Pre Migration Training for client
- ☐ Update the Pack-Up and To-Do checklist for the server and check all documentation for completeness
- ☐ Review progress with Client Technical Contact
- ☐ Install New Server in its destination location
- ☐ Begin data synchronization to the new server as required

The Week Of

- ☐ Email the Client Technical Contact with the Outlook shortcut email to distribute to users.
- ☐ Schedule post Migration Training for client
- ☐ Migrate email to the new server as required and redirect Outlook or set up OWA links
- ☐ Migrate any web sites to new server / location if planned
- ☐ DNS housing or entry changes initiated
- ☐ Schedule LOB Application and Sub-System migrations – Inform third parties as needed
- ☐ Fix up Server data share redirection to new server using logon batch file
- ☐ Final sweep of data and email migration to new server as required

The Day(s) Of

- ☐ Acquire a sufficient supply of donuts for the client users and deliver
- ☐ Re-point remaining email, web and other services to new server as required
- ☐ Email the Client Technical Contact with the RWW and VPN Change email to distribute to users
- ☐ Network Migration (General Items)
- ☐ System Migration
    - ☐ LOB Application Migration
    - ☐ Sub-Systems Migration
    - ☐ Workstations Migration
    - ☐ Remote Users Migration
- ☐ Down old server and recycle if required
- ☐ Double check all Checklists in the project
- ☐ Review progress with Client Technical Contact

The Week(s) After

- ☐ Email the Client Technical Contact with the Password Change Policy email to distribute to users
- ☐ Email the Client Technical Contact informing them of all Fine Tuning and Spin Off Projects
- ☐ Follow up and Fine Tuning
- ☐ Project Completion Checklist completed
- ☐ Client Post Migration Meeting scheduled and attended
- ☐ Present Post Migration Training for client
- ☐ Retrospective meeting planned and attended
- ☐ All Migration Project documents updated and ready for next project
- ☐ Verify all Service Tickets have correct time and details entered and their status' are correct
- ☐ Project Complete!
- ☐ Send Migration Complete emails to the Client Technical Contact

Notes

- ☐ ______________________________
- ☐ ______________________________
- ☐ ______________________________
- ☐ ______________________________
- ☐ ______________________________

Planning Calendar

Sunday	Monday	Tuesday	Wednesday	Thursday	Friday	Saturday
☐	☐	☐	☐	☐	☐	☐
☐	☐	☐	☐	☐	☐	☐
☐	☐	☐	☐	☐	☐	☐
☐	☐	☐	☐	☐	☐	☐
☐	☐	☐	☐	☐	☐	☐
☐	☐	☐	☐	☐	☐	☐

Notes

- ☐ ______
- ☐ ______
- ☐ ______
- ☐ ______
- ☐ ______
- ☐ ______

6. Migration Strategies

General

This section is a collection of the strategies that have been time proven and are eligible for use in a migration and those being fleshed out or tested. In the list of possible strategies for each item the strategies are listed according to preference. The order of the subsections here closely follows the order of the Migration checklist.

All strategies "In test" should be clearly noted as such so they are carefully considered before being used in an migration of an in production system.

Note: Active Directory Migration Tool (ADMT) as a Strategy requires in depth knowledge of AD and is beyond the scope of this document. It is listed as a Strategy because it is a valid option for those who command the knowledge to use it.

Strategies

Active Director / Group Policies

Domain

1) Build new Domain (with same Domain name if desired). Recreate Users, Machines, Groups, etc.
2) ADMT Migration.

Users

1) Document and Recreate.
2) ADMT Migration.

Groups

1) Document and Recreate.
2) ADMT Migration.

Machines

1) Document and Recreate.
2) ADMT Migration.

Group Policies

1) Document and Recreate.
2) Migration Table Editor and Export/Import.

Hardware and Environment

Fax modem

1) Physically move the device during off hours.

UPS

1) Physically move the device during off hours.

Company Data Including Users Shared Data (Users Shared Folders)

1) RoboCopy to synchronized data from the old server to the new server.

   Run multiple instances if required.

2) Sync Toy.
3) Xcopy.
4) Microsoft File Server Migration Wizard – Only if ADMT was used.

Drive Map Redirection

1) Use batch file manipulation to redirect workstations to new server until their workstation is joined to new domain.
    a. Consolidate all logon batch files or scripts into one batch file or script on the old server.
    b. Point all existing drive maps to the new server so that users will only be accessing data from the new server where it has been synchronized to.
    c. Use the users credentials if possible to access the shares on the new server.

       Use a power user or admin account if not.
    d. Once workstations are joined to the new domain the new logon batch or script will take over.

IIS / Web Sites / FTP Sites

1) Archive Web site from old server then Restore to new server then redirect DNS.
    a. Use MSDeploy to archive sites from the old server and to restore them to the new server.
    b. Re-create FTP sites on new server and migrate data from old server to populate sites. (Robocopy, xcopy, etc.)
    c. Redirect Web and FTP via DNS or Firewall to new server after new site is verified as running.

Exchange

1) Email Export out of old server and Email Import into new server. Redirect email flow when ready.
    a. Export all user mailbox data out from the old server into .pst's on the new server after hours.
    b. Import all user mailbox data into new server from .pst's after hours.
    c. Redirect email flow inbound to the new server. (Anytime)

       Note: This may be done before first Export out only if the entire Export out and in will be completed in a short amount of time. e.g., Small data stores allow for single pass migration with minimal or zero downtime for users.
    d. Users on old domain can access email on new server using OWA until their workstations are migrated.
    e. Shortcut to the new OWA is placed on their desktops ahead of time.
    f. Perform the Export out and Import in again to catch any data that may have changed. (Anytime)

       Only required if data stores are very large and initial Export out will take too long and cause downtime for users.
2) Migrate all user Exchange data using a product such as Reflexion RADAR.
    a. Set up Reflexion RADAR to sync email with old server.
    b. Redirect email flow to new server.

c. Users on old domain can access email on Reflexion RADAR web based interface or OWA until their workstations are migrated.

d. A Shortcut to the RADAR web interface or for the new OWA is placed on their desktops ahead of time.

e. Set up Reflexion RADAR to sync email with new server.

3) Export out and Import in all users Outlook data using Outlook at the desktops.

4) Combination of ExMerge, Mailbox Export, or Outlook for Export and Import.

5) Migrate using Exchange Move-Mailbox – Only if ADMT was used. (Not available for SBS as the internal domain will not be the same)

Exchange Public Folder

1) Folders and their contents are Exported from the old server and Imported into the new server using an Outlook client and a .pst file.

SQL Server and Data

Note: Always upgrade old server to new DB server software as a separate project long before the migration.

1) Migrate using passive Backup and Restore after hours. Redirect applications when ready.

   a. Schedule backup of SQL databases from old server to a local folder once a day early in the AM.

   b. Synchronize the SQL backups to the new server using a RoboCopy routine.

   c. Schedule restore of SQL databases to new server from a local folder once a day early in the AM

   d. After applications that utilize the databases have been migrated, disable the SQL and RoboCopy routines.

2) Migrate using simple Dismount, Move to new server and Mount.

3) Migrate by copying DB's.

   a. Stop SQL services.

   b. Copy DB.

   c. Create new DB on new server.

   d. Stop services.

   e. Put files in place.

   f. Restart SQL services.

Note: Use virtual workstations on either the old network when critical applications and database migration lag behind the workstation migration or on the new network when critical applications and database precede the workstation migration.

Fax System

1) Move any fax stored to same location on new server. e.g. Directories, public folder or SharePoint container.

Companyweb and SharePoint

1) Build out new Companyweb using data from old Companyweb.

a. Redirect public access to the new Companyweb via DNS when it is ready.

b. Record basic web component settings and permissions from the old Companyweb.

c. Apply basic web component settings and permissions to the new Companyweb.

d. Replicate data item by item to the new Companyweb.

Line of Business Applications

1) Install applications on new server and re-point workstations or server when ready.

   a. Install the new applications on the new server.

   b. Verify old version is updated or upgraded to match new server.

   c. Perform a dry run migration of the data and map the steps required.

   d. Move the data (SQL DB, flat files, etc.) after hours or on off hours.

   e. Redirect workstations using Group Policies, scripts, logon batch files etc.

Note: Use virtual workstations on either the old network when the LOB migration lags behind the workstation migration or on the new network when the LOB precedes the workstation migration.

Notes: New server or workstations can point to data on the old system until ready.
Old server and workstations can also point to data on new server if it is moved fist (See SQL migration).

System Applications

BlackBerry Server

1) If there is no paid support plan – Use Knife Edge Migration – Whitepaper is on Blackberry site.

2) With support contract you can get a temporary SPF and SEF.

   a. If upgrading and migrating to Version 5 or higher – get an Upgrade Key for the new software from Customer Care and then you can have BlackBerry running on both server at the same time.

   b. There is a whitepaper for migrating the DB.

Encrypted / Keyed Security Access System

See LOB and SQL migration.

Security logistics must be planned very well.

Antivirus Solution

There should be no special migration required. Simply install program on new server(s) and redirect workstations or push client out.

Most AV solutions have a simple whitepaper to redirect client to the new server but it requires logging on to each workstation. Usually it is much easier to just push the new client.

Sub-Systems

Router

1) There should be almost nothing to do on migration. If there is, a configuration should be set up, tested and saved to disk. On migration day it would simply be loaded over existing config and the device rebooted.

Firewall

1) There should be almost nothing to do on migration. If there is, a configuration should be set up, tested and saved to disk. On migration day it would simply be loaded over existing config and the device rebooted.

Phone System

See LOB and SQL migration.

Printers

1) First choice should be to get users to print directly to the printers not through a server.

   This would be a Pre-migration project.

2) Re-Share printers from the new server then move them on off hours.
   a. Add all printers to the new server that are networked (have an IP address) or are already physically connected to the new server (Serial, LPT, USB).
   b. Share new printers from the new server as required.
   c. Attach to (use) printers that are physically connected to the old server and share them out from the new server.
   d. At the appropriate time, disconnect physically connected printers from the old server and connect them to the new server.
   e. Rebuild printer shares. e.g. Stop re-sharing the printer from the old server and share directly from new server.
   f. Workstations on the old domain will still be able to print to all printers and as they are migrated to the new server.

Copier /Scanner

See Printer migration.

Workstation Migration

1) Connect to new domain and Migrate users profiles.
   a. Record certain critical information about the users profile including many Outlook settings.
   b. Clean up the users profile so it is a small reasonable size that will save fast.
   c. Use the Microsoft USMT tool to save the users profile.
   d. Migrate to the new domain.
   e. Use the Microsoft USMT tool to restore the users profile.
   f. Re-set all previously recorded settings for the user and test critical functions like printing, email, file and Internet access.
2) ADMT Migration. (Not available for SBS)

Note: Use virtual workstations on either the old network when critical applications and database migration lag behind the workstation migration or on the new network when critical applications and database precede the workstation migration.

Backup Software, Devices and Methods

Tape Backup Solution

1) Physically move the device during off hours.

Continuous Data Protection

There should be no special migration required. Simply install agent on new server(s) and configure backups.

Offsite Backup System

There should be no special migration required. Simply install agent on new server(s) and configure backups.

7. Resources

General

This section is a collection of resources that are used on a regular basis or have particular use during a migration. Sample scripts, batch files and command syntax are documented to reduce the research time before use or deployment and to allow for consistency in use.

This section should be maintained carefully as it could grow unnecessarily large.

Building Installation and Migration Checklists

An installation checklist can be built by first documenting a clean installation on either a test server or the new server while still on the bench. Documenting a clean install on a production server is least desirable as there are always many things that are no longer as they were out of the box.

Note: An excellent tool for recording installations (among other things) is the Problem Steps Recorder that is built into Windows 7 or later. To run it simply click Start then type psr in the search window and then hit the Enter key. The tool is pretty straight forward and will give you notes and screen caps of each step taken.

A Migration checklist can be built by comparing an existing installation with a new or clean installation and documenting all aspects of what will need to get configured, changed, copied, moved, etc.

When building a checklist for the first time, it can be very short and does not necessarily need to be granular right from the start to get put into the process. It can be fleshed out as needed or you can rely on the repetitive installation of the product to lend itself to continuous improvement by adding steps every time it is installed.

The new checklist will need to be sectional in nature to allow for insertion into the Network Migration Project Template. Checklist sections will need to be inserted into their corresponding section in the Network Migration Project Template. Review the layout and flow of this entire Project Template to help determine what all must be modified.

In the Network Migration Project Template the basic flow for checklist building is as follows: Pre-Discovery – Discovery – Planning – Build –Server Migration – Network Migration – System Migration – Sub-Systems Migration – Workstation Migration.
An emphasis must be made on the Discovery and Documentation. This combined with timing will ensure success.

My Favorite Whitepapers

Active Directory

- ☐ **ADMT Guide: Migrating and Restructuring Active Directory Domains**
  - Most recent link: http://technet.microsoft.com/en-us/library/cc974332(WS.10).aspx
- ☐ **How to Audit Active Directory Objects in Windows Server 2003**
  - Document ID: 814595
  - Most recent link: http://support.microsoft.com/kb/814595/en-us
- ☐ **Using Repadmin.exe to troubleshoot Active Directory replication**
  - Article ID: 229896
  - Most recent link: http://support.microsoft.com/kb/229896

- ☐ **LDIFDE - Export / Import data from Active Directory - LDIFDE commands**
  - Article ID: 555636
  - Most recent link: http://support.microsoft.com/kb/555636

Active Sync

- ☐ **Exchange ActiveSync Client Comparison Table**
  - Most recent link: http://social.technet.microsoft.com/wiki/contents/articles/exchange-activesync-client-comparison-table.aspx
- ☐ **Deploying Windows Mobile 6 with Windows Small Business Server 2008**
  - Most recent link: http://technet.microsoft.com/en-us/library/dd252611(WS.10).aspx
- ☐ **Managing Exchange ActiveSync Devices**
  - Most recent link: http://technet.microsoft.com/en-us/library/aa998933.aspx
- ☐ **How to Configure Mobile Devices to Synchronize with Exchange Server**
  - Most recent link: http://technet.microsoft.com/en-us/library/bb123704.aspx
- ☐ **How to Install Root Certification Authority Certificates on a Windows Mobile-based Device**
  - Most recent link: http://technet.microsoft.com/en-us/library/aa997575.aspx
- ☐ **How to Install Client Certificates for Authentication on a Windows Mobile Powered Device**
  - Most recent link: http://technet.microsoft.com/en-us/library/bb738128.aspx
- ☐ **Exchange ActiveSync: Frequently Asked Questions**
  - Most recent link: http://technet.microsoft.com/en-us/library/aa995986(EXCHG.65).aspx
- ☐ **Microsoft Exchange Server ActiveSync Web Administration Tool**
  - Most recent link: http://www.microsoft.com/downloads/details.aspx?familyid=e6851d23-d145-4dbf-a2cc-e0b4c6301453&displaylang=en

Antivirus

- ☐ **Migrating Worry-Free Business Security (WFBS) clients to another server**
  - Most recent link: http://esupport.trendmicro.com/solution/en-us/1037744.aspx
- ☐ **Using the Move tool to migrate Worry-Free Business Security (WFBS) clients to a new server**
  - Most recent link: http://esupport.trendmicro.com/solution/en-us/1037742.aspx
- ☐ **Hot issues for Worry-Free Business Security (WFBS) Standard / Advanced 5.0**
  - Most recent link: http://esupport.trendmicro.com/Pages/Hot-issues-for-Worry-Free-Business-Security-WFBS-Standard-Advanced-50.aspx
- ☐ **Migrating Worry-Free Business Security (WFBS) Standard / Advanced 5.0 / 5.1 clients to another server**
  - Most recent link: http://esupport.trendmicro.com/Pages/Migrating-Worry-Free-Business-Security-WFBS-Standard-Advanced-50-51-cl.aspx
- ☐ **Preventing Symantec AntiVirus 10.x from scanning the Microsoft Exchange directory structure**
  - Document ID: 2005040513412648
  - Most recent link: http://service1.symantec.com/SUPPORT/ent-security.nsf/docid/2005040513412648
- ☐ **Moving Symantec Client Security 3.x or Symantec AntiVirus Corporate Edition 10.x clients from one parent server to another**

- Most recent link: http://service1.symantec.com/support/ent-security.nsf/854fa02b4f5013678825731a007d06af/bc47595cfe90098288256fe000671146?OpenDocument

Backup

- ☐ **Backing Up and Restoring Data on Windows Small Business Server 2008**
  - Most recent link: http://technet.microsoft.com/en-us/library/cc527505(WS.10).aspx
- ☐ **Backing Up and Restoring Windows Small Business Server 2003**
  - Most recent link: http://www.microsoft.com/technet/security/smallbusiness/prodtech/SBS/backup_restore_sbs2003.mspx
- ☐ **How to change the default port used by the Backup Exec Remote Agent for Windows Servers (RAWS)**
  - Document ID: 255174
  - Most recent link: http://seer.entsupport.symantec.com/docs/255174.htm
- ☐ **Backup Exec for Windows Servers TCP/UDP port listing**
  - Document ID: 278758
  - Most recent link: http://seer.entsupport.symantec.com/docs/278758.htm

BlackBerry

- ☐ **How to migrate from Microsoft Exchange Server 2003 or 2007 to Microsoft Exchange Server 2010 in a BlackBerry Enterprise Server 5.0 environment**
  - Most recent link: http://btsc.webapps.blackberry.com/btsc/microsites/search.do?cmd=displayKC&docType=kc&externalId=KB22601&sliceId=1&docTypeID=DT_SUPPORTISSUE_1_1&dialogID=1522872168&stateId=0 0 1522868156
- ☐ **BlackBerry Enterprise Server Installation Tool Kit**
  - Most recent link: http://www.blackberry.com/select/toolkit/02.shtml
- ☐ **Assigning permissions for a BlackBerry Enterprise Server service account**
  - Document ID: 02276
  - Most recent link: http://www.blackberry.com/btsc/search.do?cmd=displayKC&docType=kc&externalId=KB02276
- ☐ **How to perform a knife-edge cutover for BlackBerry Enterprise Server software versions 4.0 and 4.1**
  - Document ID: 10278
  - Most recent link: http://www.blackberry.com/btsc/search.do?cmd=displayKC&docType=kc&externalId=KB10278
- ☐ **Locate and change the SRP ID and SRP Authentication Key**
  - Document ID : KB04744
  - Most recent link: http://www.blackberry.com/btsc/search.do?cmd=displayKC&docType=kc&externalId=KB04744&sliceId=SAL_Public&dialogID=132546217&stateId=1%200%20132544293
- ☐ **Locate the SRP ID and SRP Authentication Key in Microsoft Exchange**
  - Document ID : KB02632
  - Most recent link: http://www.blackberry.com/btsc/search.do?cmd=displayKC&docType=kc&externalId=KB02632&sliceId=SAL_Public&dialogID=49298877&stateId=0%200%2024314564

Exchange

- ☐ **How to Import and Export Mailboxes using PST Files in SBS 2011 Standard**
  - Most recent link: http://blogs.technet.com/b/sbs/archive/2011/05/09/how-to-import-and-export-mailboxes-using-pst-files-in-sbs-2011-standard.aspx
- ☐ **Understanding Mailbox Import and Export Requests**
  - Most recent link: http://technet.microsoft.com/en-us/library/ee633455.aspx
- ☐ **Filterable Properties for the -ContentFilter Parameter (Exchange 2010 MailboxExportRequest)**
  - Most recent link: http://technet.microsoft.com/en-us/library/ff601762.aspx
- ☐ **Cannot Reply To Old Emails Or Modify Old Calendar Items After PST Mail Migration**
  - Most recent link: http://blogs.technet.com/b/sbs/archive/2009/05/21/cannot-reply-to-old-emails-or-modify-old-calendar-items-after-pst-mail-migration.aspx
- ☐ **How to Export Mailbox Data (Exchange 2007)**
  - Most recent link: http://technet.microsoft.com/en-us/library/bb266964(EXCHG.80).aspx
- ☐ **How to Export and Import Mailboxes To PST files in Exchange 2007 SP1**
  - Most recent link: http://msexchangeteam.com/archive/2007/04/13/437745.aspx
- ☐ **Microsoft Exchange Server 2007 Management Tools (32-Bit)**
  - Most recent link: http://www.microsoft.com/downloads/details.aspx?FamilyID=6be38633-7248-4532-929b-76e9c677e802&displaylang=en
- ☐ **How to Install the Exchange 2007 Management Tools**
  - Most recent link: http://technet.microsoft.com/en-us/library/bb232090.aspx
- ☐ **Exchange Server Intelligent Message Filter**
  - Most recent link: http://www.microsoft.com/downloads/en/details.aspx?familyid=B1218D8C-E8B3-48FB-9208-6F75707870C2&displaylang=en
- ☐ **Exchange Remote Connectivity Analyzer**
  - Most recent link: https://www.testexchangeconnectivity.com/
- ☐ **How to Configure Message Format Settings for a Remote Domain (NDR's)**
  - Most recent link: http://technet.microsoft.com/en-us/library/bb125174.aspx
- ☐ **How to control non-delivery reports when you use Exchange 2000 or Exchange 2003**
  - Article ID: 294757
  - Most recent link: http://support.microsoft.com/default.aspx?scid=kb;en-us;294757
- ☐ **How to block open SMTP relaying and clean up Exchange Server SMTP queues in Windows Small Business Server**
  - Article ID: 324958
  - Most recent link: http://support.microsoft.com/kb/324958
- ☐ **Testing SMTP using telnet to Port 25**
  - Article ID: 153119
  - Most recent link: http://support.microsoft.com/default.aspx?scid=kb;en-us;153119
- ☐ **Microsoft Exchange Server Mailbox Merge Wizard (ExMerge)**
  - Most recent link: http://www.microsoft.com/downloads/details.aspx?familyid=429163ec-dcdf-47dc-96da-1c12d67327d5&displaylang=en
- ☐ **Microsoft Exchange Mailbox Merge program (Exmerge.exe) information**
  - Article ID: Q174197
  - Most recent link: http://support.microsoft.com/kb/174197

- ☐ **Windows Server 2003 Administration Tools Pack**
  - Most recent link: http://www.microsoft.com/downloads/details.aspx?FamilyID=c16ae515-c8f4-47ef-a1e4-a8dcbacff8e3&displaylang=en

- ☐ **How to configure an account to use the ExMerge utility in Exchange 2000 Server and in Exchange Server 2003**
  - Article ID: 292509
  - Most recent link: http://support.microsoft.com/kb/292509

  Note: I have never been able to make this work on 2003! - Manuel Palachuk

- ☐ **How to increase the Exchange Server 2003 Service Pack 2 18-gigabyte database size limit**
  - Article ID: 912375
  - Most recent link: http://support.microsoft.com/kb/912375

- ☐ **Users cannot send e-mail messages from a mobile device or from a shared mailbox in Exchange 2000 Server and in Exchange Server 2003**
  - Article ID: 886208
  - Most recent link: http://support.microsoft.com/kb/912918

- ☐ **Exchange queues fill with many non-delivery reports from the postmaster account in Small Business Server 2003**
  - Article ID: 886208
  - Most recent link: http://support.microsoft.com/?kbid=886208

- ☐ **How to configure RPC over HTTP on a single server in Exchange Server 2003**
  - Article ID: 833401
  - Most recent link: http://support.microsoft.com/default.aspx?scid=kb;en-us;833401

  Note: This is the premier paper on setting up and troubleshooting RPC over HTTP

- ☐ **How to troubleshoot client RPC over HTTP connection issues in Offices Outlook 2003**
  - Article ID: 827330
  - Most recent link: http://support.microsoft.com/kb/827330

- ☐ **How to defragment with the Eseutil utility (Eseutil.exe)**
  - Article ID: 192185
  - Most recent link: http://support.microsoft.com/kb/192185

- ☐ **Exchange Best Practices Analyzer 2.8**
  - Article ID: 107393
  - Most recent link: http://go.microsoft.com/fwlink/?LinkID=107393

Group Policies

- ☐ **How fix GPO's on a domain controller (backup or restore from another clean machine)**
  - Most recent link: http://blogs.technet.com/sbs/archive/2007/09/17/restoring-the-sbs-gpos-from-a-different-server.aspx

- ☐ **How to Configure Windows Firewall in a Small Business Environment Using Group Policy**
  - Most recent link: http://www.microsoft.com/technet/security/smallbusiness/prodtech/windowsxp/fwgrppol.mspx

- ☐ **Using Group Policies to Control Printers in Active Directory**
  - Article ID: 234270
  - Most recent link: http://support.microsoft.com/kb/234270

- ☐ **Group Policy Settings Reference**
  - Most recent link: http://www.microsoft.com/downloads/details.aspx?familyid=7821C32F-DA15-438D-8E48-45915CD2BC14&displaylang=en

- ☐ **Implementing Common Desktop Management Scenarios with the Group Policy Management Console**
  - Most recent link: http://technet.microsoft.com/en-us/library/cc758350.aspx

Internet Information Services (IIS)

- ☐ **Editing Internet Information Services (IIS) 7.0 configuration files**
  - Most recent link: http://windowshelp.microsoft.com/Windows/en-GB/help/e5b36e97-d424-4ef9-9a52-7ed14f9d79af1033.mspx
- ☐ **How to backup/restore IIS7 configuration**
  - Most recent link: http://blogs.iis.net/bills/archive/2008/03/24/how-to-backup-restore-iis7-configuration.aspx
- ☐ **Web Deployment Tool**
  - Most recent link: http://technet.microsoft.com/en-us/mscomops/cc424869.aspx
  - Documentation Link: http://technet.microsoft.com/en-us/library/dd569088(WS.10).aspx
- ☐ **Migrate from IIS 6.0 to IIS 7.0** (The best whitepaper on a simple move)
  - Most recent link: http://learn.iis.net/page.aspx/427/migrate-from-iis-60-to-iis-70/
- ☐ **Backing Up and Restoring Internet Information Manager (IIS) Metabase 6.0**
  - Most recent link: http://www.microsoft.com/technet/prodtechnol/WindowsServer2003/Library/IIS/d40b56ee-90d4-45e1-9b82-4aaea90eb02e.mspx

Migration

- ☐ **Migrating to Windows Small Business Server 2011 Standard**
  - Most recent link: http://technet.microsoft.com/en-us/library/gg490796.aspx
- ☐ **Microsoft Assessment and Planning Toolkit**
  - Most recent link: http://www.microsoft.com/download/en/details.aspx?displaylang=en&id=7826
- ☐ **Windows Small Business Server Migration Portal**
  - Most recent link: http://blogs.technet.com/b/sbs/archive/2011/06/24/announcing-the-windows-small-business-server-migration-portal.aspx
- ☐ **Migrate to Windows Small Business Server 2008 from Windows Small Business Server 2003**
  - Most recent link: http://technet.microsoft.com/en-us/library/cc546034(WS.10).aspx
- ☐ **Windows Small Business Server 2008 Migration Help**
  - Most recent link: http://www.microsoft.com/downloads/details.aspx?FamilyId=95E4863E-BB59-4A66-9FEE-9874E8903888&displaylang=en
- ☐ **SBS 2008 Migrations from SBS 2003 – Keys to Success**
  - Most recent link: http://blogs.technet.com/sbs/archive/2009/02/19/sbs-2008-migrations-from-sbs-2003-keys-to-success.aspx
- ☐ **Software Update to Support "Join Domain" Migration of Windows Small Business Server 2003 Data and Settings to New Hardware**

  (Extends the time allowed for two SBS servers to be on the same network)
  - Most recent link: http://support.microsoft.com/default.aspx?scid=kb;EN-US;943494
- ☐ **Migrating from Small Business Server 2000 or Windows 2000 Server to Windows Small Business Server 2003**

- Most recent link: http://www.microsoft.com/downloads/details.aspx?FamilyID=fa187d1e-8218-4501-9729-222bd8ebb64c&DisplayLang=en

☐ **The Windows Automated Installation Kit (AIK) for Windows 7**
- Most recent link: http://www.microsoft.com/downloads/en/details.aspx?FamilyID=696dd665-9f76-4177-a811-39c26d3b3b34&displaylang=en

☐ **Software Update to Support "Join Domain" Migration of Windows Small Business Server 2003 Data and Settings to New Hardware**
- Article ID: 943494
- Most recent link: http://www.microsoft.com/downloads/details.aspx?FamilyId=64903D3C-3264-418D-9199-2963A599E268

Miscellaneous

☐ **Windows Mobile 6 Localized Emulator Images**
- Most recent link: http://www.microsoft.com/download/en/details.aspx?id=7974

☐ **Deploying Printers by Using Group Policy (Server 2008)**
- Most recent link: http://technet.microsoft.com/en-us/library/cc754699.aspx

☐ **Deploying Printers by Using Group Policy (Server 2003)**
- Most recent link: http://technet.microsoft.com/en-us/library/cc722179(WS.10).aspx

☐ **How to Add a Default Printer Using a Visual Basic Script**
- Most recent link: http://support.microsoft.com/?id=263226

☐ **Recognized Environment Variables**
- Most recent link: http://technet.microsoft.com/en-us/library/dd560744(WS.10).aspx

☐ **Windows PowerShell 1.0 Installation Package for Windows Vista (KB928439)**
- Most recent link: http://www.microsoft.com/downloads/details.aspx?displaylang=en&FamilyID=c6ef4735-c7de-46a2-997a-ea58fdfcba63

☐ **How To Determine Which Program Uses or Blocks Specific Transmission Control Protocol Ports in Windows Server 2003**
- Article ID: 23352
- Most recent link: http://support.microsoft.com/?kbid=323352

☐ **Reveal hidden devices or devices that were previously attached but are not connected to the computer at the present time**
- Article ID: 241257
- Most recent link: http://support.microsoft.com/kb/241257

☐ **Sysinternals Suite**
- Most recent link: http://technet.microsoft.com/en-us/sysinternals/bb842062.aspx

☐ **How to back up and then restore printers when you upgrade from Windows Server 2003 to Windows Server 2008**
- Most recent link: http://support.microsoft.com/?id=938923

Registry

☐ **How to add, modify, or delete registry subkeys and values by using a registration entries (.reg) file**
- Article ID: Q310516
- Most recent link: http://support.microsoft.com/default.aspx/kb/310516

SharePoint

- ☐ **Move the internal website for Windows SBS 2011 Standard migration**
  - Most recent link: http://technet.microsoft.com/en-us/library/gg563792.aspx#BKMK_ConfigureSearch
- ☐ **How to move a Windows SharePoint Services Web site from one server to another by using FrontPage 2003**
  - Article ID: 825536
  - Most recent link: http://support.microsoft.com/kb/825536
- ☐ **How to back up and restore http://companyweb data in Windows Small Business Server 2003**
  - Article ID: 829112
  - Most recent link: http://support.microsoft.com/kb/829112/en-us
- ☐ **How to remove and how to install the Windows Small Business Server 2003 SharePoint Services companyweb Web site**
  - Article ID: 829114
  - Most recent link: http://support.microsoft.com/kb/829114

Small Business Server 2003

- ☐ **Error message when you access the http://companyweb Web site in Windows Small Business Server 2003: "HTTP 401.1 - Unauthorized"**
  - Article ID:
  - Most recent link: http://support.microsoft.com/kb/961143/en-us
- ☐ **How to install the Windows Recovery Console**
  - Article ID: 216417
  - Most recent link: http://support.microsoft.com/kb/q216417/
- ☐ **How to configure an authoritative time server in windows server 2003**
  - Article ID: 816042
  - Most recent link: http://support.microsoft.com/kb/816042
- ☐ **Using ifmember.exe for logon scripts**
  - Most recent link: http://www.microsoft.com/downloads/details.aspx?FamilyID=07C2F6D7-815E-4FA0-9043-4E4635CCD417&displaylang=en
- ☐ **How to create a self-signed SSL server certificate**
  - Article ID: 955933
  - Most recent link: http://support.microsoft.com/kb/955933
- ☐ **How to reset "Internet Protocol (TCP/IP)" in Windows Server 2003**
  - Article ID: 317518
  - Most recent link: http://support.microsoft.com/?id=317518
- ☐ **Windows Server 2003 Resource Kit Tools**
  - Most recent link: http://www.microsoft.com/downloads/details.aspx?familyid=9D467A69-57FF-4AE7-96EE-B18C4790CFFD&displaylang=en
- ☐ **Windows Small Business Server 2003 Best Practices Analyzer**
  - Most recent link: http://go.microsoft.com/fwlink/?LinkID=113752

Small Business Server 2008

- ☐ **Windows Small Business Server 2008 Installation Guide**
  - Most recent link: http://technet.microsoft.com/en-us/library/cc527604(WS.10).aspx

- ☐ **Windows Small Business Server 2008 Technical FAQ**
  - Most recent link: http://technet.microsoft.com/en-us/sbs/cc817589.aspx
- ☐ **Key Small Business Server 2008 Log Files**
  - Most recent link: http://blogs.technet.com/sbs/archive/2008/10/01/key-small-business-server-2008-log-files.aspx
- ☐ **Catalog of Windows Small Business Server 2008 Installation Error Messages**
  - Most recent link: http://technet.microsoft.com/en-us/library/cc546065.aspx
- ☐ **Windows Small Business Server 2008 Repair Guide**
  - Most recent link: http://technet.microsoft.com/en-us/library/dd430085.aspx
- ☐ **How to Configure Windows SharePoint Services and Windows File Share Integration for Outlook Web Access**
  - Most recent link: http://technet.microsoft.com/en-us/library/aa998576.aspx
- ☐ **How Do I Distribute the SBS 2008 Self-Signed SSL Certificate to My Users?**
  - Most recent link: http://blogs.technet.com/sbs/archive/2008/09/30/how-do-i-distribute-the-sbs-2008-self-signed-ssl-certificate-to-my-users.aspx
- ☐ **Internet test fails when running the Connect to the Internet Wizard in Windows Small Business Server 2008**
  - Article ID: 957715
  - Most recent link: http://support.microsoft.com/kb/957715
- ☐ **Unable to Install SBS 2008 with a Public IP Address**
  - Article ID: 957717
  - Most recent link: http://support.microsoft.com/kb/957717

Small Business Server 2011

- ☐ **Windows Small Business Server 2011 Standard Editions Overview**
  - Most recent link: http://www.microsoft.com/sbs/en/us/editions-overview.aspx
- ☐ **Windows Small Business Server 2011 Standard Installation Guide**
  - Most recent link: http://technet.microsoft.com/en-us/library/gg697164.aspx
- ☐ **Using the Microsoft Windows Small Business Server 2011 Standard Best Practices Analyzer**
  - Most recent link: **Error! Hyperlink reference not valid.**http://technet.microsoft.com/en-us/library/gg508357.aspx
- ☐ **Windows Small Business Server 2011 Standard Repair Guide**
  - Most recent link: http://technet.microsoft.com/en-us/library/gg697169.aspx

SQL Server

- ☐ **Using SQL Server in Windows Small Business Server 2008 Premium Edition**
  - Most recent link: http://technet.microsoft.com/en-us/library/cc794697(WS.10).aspx
- ☐ **Microsoft SQL Server Management Studio Express**
  - Most recent link: http://www.microsoft.com/downloads/details.aspx?FamilyID=c243a5ae-4bd1-4e3d-94b8-5a0f62bf7796&displaylang=en

Terminal Services

- ☐ **How to lock down a Windows Server 2003 or Windows 2000 Terminal Server session**
  - Most recent link: http://support.microsoft.com/kb/278295

- ☐ **Locking Down Windows Server 2003 Terminal Server Sessions**
  - Most recent link: http://www.microsoft.com/windowsserver2003/techinfo/overview/lockdown.mspx

User State

- ☐ **User State Migration Tool 4.0 User's Guide**
  - Most recent link: http://technet.microsoft.com/en-us/library/dd560801(WS.10).aspx
- ☐ **Information about the User State Migration Tool (USMT) 4.0 update**
  - Most recent link: http://support.microsoft.com/kb/2023591
- ☐ **Exploring the User State Migration Toolkit (USMT) 4.0 (Video)**
  - Most recent link: http://technet.microsoft.com/en-us/edge/exploring-the-user-state-migration-toolkit-usmt-4.0.aspx?query=1
- ☐ **Windows User State Migration Tool (USMT) Version 3.0.1**
  - Most recent link: http://www.microsoft.com/downloads/details.aspx?FamilyID=799ab28c-691b-4b36-b7ad-6c604be4c595&displaylang=en
- ☐ **Configuring User State Management Features (Version 3.x)**
  - Most recent link: http://technet.microsoft.com/en-us/library/cc778656.aspx
- ☐ **Moving Data Folders for Windows Small Business Server 2003**
  - Most recent link: http://technet.microsoft.com/en-us/library/cc708031.aspx
- ☐ **Implementing Folder Redirection**
  - Most recent link: http://technet.microsoft.com/en-us/library/cc737434.aspx
- ☐ **Implementing Offline Files and Synchronization**
  - Most recent link: http://technet.microsoft.com/en-us/library/cc782388.aspx

Workstation Operating System

- ☐ **How To Disable Automatic Search for Network Printers and Folders in Windows XP**
  - Article ID: 320138
  - Most recent link: http://support.microsoft.com/kb/320138

Blogs Blogs Blogs

(In no particular order)

- ☐ **Microsoft Connect**
  - Most recent link: https://connect.microsoft.com/default.aspx
- ☐ **Microsoft Discussions Groups**
  - Most recent link: http://www.microsoft.com/communities/newsgroups/en-us
- ☐ **The official SBS Blog**
  - Most recent link: http://blogs.technet.com/sbs
- ☐ **The Microsoft SMB Channel Community Blog**
  - Most recent link: http://blogs.msdn.com/mssmallbiz
- ☐ **The USMT Team Blog**
  - Most recent link: http://blogs.technet.com/usmt/archive/2008/08/06/next-usmt-release.aspx
- ☐ **Official Microsoft IIS Site**

  - Most recent link: http://blogs.iis.net

- ☐ **Microsoft Exchange Team Blog**
  - Most recent link: http://msexchangeteam.com
- ☐ **Microsoft SharePoint Team Blog**
  - Most recent link: http://blogs.msdn.com/sharepoint
- ☐ **Windows Server Division WebLog**
  - Most recent link: http://blogs.technet.com/windowsserver
- ☐ **Windows Live OneCare Team Blog**
  - Most recent link: http://windowsonecare.spaces.live.com
- ☐ **Forefront Server Security Support Blog**
  - Most recent link: http://blogs.technet.com/fssnerds
- ☐ **Windows Server Update Services Product Team Blog**
  - Most recent link: http://blogs.technet.com/wsus
- ☐ **Microsoft Update Team Blog**
  - Most recent link: http://blogs.technet.com/mu

Scripts and Batch Files

LDIFDE Command Line

This command line has been formulated to dump out all domain user names, their SMTP addresses and their group memberships. The output is somewhat raw and could benefit from being further filtered or sorted with additional command line parameters. Refer to the LDIFDE command reference for more detail on each parameter listed here. Only change the *servername* and *domainname*.

ldifde -f C:\!tech\migration\userinfodump.txt -s *servername* -d "dc=*domainname*,dc=local" -p subtree -r "(&(objectCategory=person)(objectClass=User)(givenname=*))" -l "cn,proxyaddresses,memberof,givenName"

Logon.bat File Sample

Note: Run the command ifmember.exe /l /v to verify a group will be recognized by the ifmember program. Typically only certain built in groups and new security groups created using the SBS Add a Security Group wizard will be recognized.

```
echo off
rem Last edited by ManuelP KPEnterprises 2011.07.16


rem Clear old persistent net uses.
rem These can be deleted after the migration is complete.
rem ------------------------------------------------------------------
Net use p: /d
Net use s: /d
Net use u: /d

Rem Map users to their own folder
Rem --- SBS 2011 users share -------------------------------
Net use u: \\zdtmsbs\users\%username%
```

```
Rem --- SBS 2011 users share --------------------------------
Net use u: \\zdtmsbs\usershares\%username%

rem Repeat each ifmember routine for each security group requiring a specific drive mapping.
rem ifmember checks to see if a user is a member of a group and returns errorlevel 1 if true.
rem -----------------------------------------------------------------------------------------------------
\\zdtmsbs\netlogon\ifmember "ZDTM Users"
   if errorlevel 1 net use p: "\\zdtmsbs\public data"

\\zdtmsbs\netlogon\ifmember Sales
   if errorlevel 1 net use s: \\zdtmsbs\sales
:end
```

RoboCopy Command

The RoboCopy command syntax as documented below allows for the most universal, cleanest and least interactive copy of all data on one share to another share. Only the switches used are documented. Changes to the command syntax is not recommended unless a complete understanding of the command line switches and the full impact on the copy are understood.

It is recommended that a batch file be created to allow for easy editing and repeated running of the RoboCopy. Multiple instances of RoboCopy can be run simultaneously.

robocopy *oldservernameoldsharename* *newservername**newsharename* *.* /e /purge /mon:1 /mot:30 /rh:1800-0700 /xo /r:10 /w:2 /v /fp /tee /log:*newservername*\\tech\\migration*sharename*-robocopy.log**

Explanation of Switches used:

Source directory = A UNC is used so that the path is universal and can be run from either server.
Destination directory = A UNC is used so that the path is universal. And can be run from either server.
File specification is *.* = Used to be certain all files regardless of extension are copied.
Options:

/E = Copies all subdirectories (including empty ones)

/PURGE = Deletes destination files and directories that no longer exist in the source

/MON:*n* = Monitors the source directory for changes, and runs again when n changes have been detected, and the minimum time interval specified by /MOT has elapsed.

/MOT:*n* = Monitors the source directory for changes, and runs again when a further n minutes have elapsed, and the minimum number of changes specified by /MON have been detected.

/RH:*hhmm-hhmm* = Defines the time slot during which starting new copies is allowed. Useful for restricting copies to certain times of the day. Both values must be 24-hour times in the range 0000 to 2359.

/XO = Excludes files tagged as "Older".

/R:*n* = Specifies the number of retries on failed copies. (The default is 1 million.)

/W:*n* = Specifies the wait time between retries. (The default is 30 seconds.)

/V = Produces verbose output (including skipped files).

/FP = Displays full pathnames of files in the output log.

/LOG: = Redirects output to the specified file, overwriting the file if it already exists.

/TEE = Displays output in the console window, in addition to directing it to the log file specified by /LOG or /LOG+.

USMT 3.x (User State Migration Tool 3.x) – Only for use with Windows XP machines

The User State Migration Tool 3.x syntax as documented below allows for the most universal, cleanest and least interactive migration of a user's profile on Windows XP and Vista machines. Only the switches used are documented. Changes to the command syntax is not recommended unless a complete understanding of the command line switches and the full impact on the user state migration are understood.

It is recommended that a batch file be created to allow for easy editing and repeated running of the scanstate or loadstate on multiple machines and in varied environments. The recommended USMT batch files are detailed below the command syntax details.

Note: USMT 3.x will not work on Windows 7 machines. You must use USMT 4.x on Windows 7 machines. The next subsections covers the command line syntax for USMT 4.x.

Note: The USMT batch files subsection found further down in this section are designed to call the USMT 3.x for Windows XP machines and USMT 4.x for Vista and Windows 7 machines.

Note: The USMT 3.x commands here and in the batch files rely on the user names being the same on the old and the new domains. If the user names will not be the same, the USMT 3.x commands and the batch file will need to be edited to accommodate the method used.

Example of complete Scanstate and Loadstate command as used:

scanstate c:\!tech*username* /nocompress /i:miguser.xml /i:migapp.xml /i:migsys.xml /localonly /c /v:5 /o /ue: /ue:* /ui: *olddomainname\username /l:c:\!tech\username-scanstate.log /progress:c:\!tech\username-scanprogress.log***

loadstate c:\!tech*username* /nocompress /i:miguser.xml /i:migapp.xml /i:migsys.xml /c /v:5 /ue: /ue:* /ui:*olddomainname\username* /md:*olddomainname:newdomainname /l:c:\!tech\username-loadstate.log /progress:c:\!tech\username-loadprogress.log***

Explanation of Switches used:

StorePath = Local directory relative to the c:\ directory so that the path is universal across all machines in case a batch file is used.
/nocompress - Disables compression of data. Migration files will not be compressed into a single usmt file.
/i: - Specifies the .xml files that contains rules that define what state to migrate. All three .xml files used are the default files supplied with USMT 3.x and must be listed on the command line.
/localonly - Migrates only files that are stored on the local computer. Only used for scanstate.
/c: - ScanState will continue to run even if there are nonfatal errors. Only used for scanstate.
/v:n - Enables verbose output in the ScanState or LoadState log. n=5 Enables verbose and status output.
/ue: - Excludes the specified user(s) from the migration.
Full syntax: /ue:*DomainName\"User Name"* or /ue:*LocalUserName*
Therefore: /ue:** - Excludes all users in any domain.
And: /ue:* - Excludes all local users.
/ui: - Includes the specified user(s) in the migration.
/md:*olddomainname:newdomainname* - This option changes the domain from old domain to new domain for the user(s) on a computer.
/l:*drive:path\filename*.log - Sets the location and name of the ScanState or LoadState log file.
/progress: :*drive:path\filename*.log - Sets the location and name of the ScanState or LoadState progress log file.
/o – Overwrites an existing store.

USMT 4.x (User State Migration Tool 4.x) – Only for use with Windows Vista and Windows 7 machines

The User State Migration Tool 4.x syntax as documented below allows for the most universal, cleanest and least interactive migration of a user's profile on Windows Vista and Windows 7 machines. Only the switches used are documented. Changes to the command syntax is not recommended unless a complete understanding of the command line switches and the full impact on the user state migration are understood.

Note: USMT 4.x will not work on Windows XP machines for restoring the System State back to an XP machine. It is designed only to move the State to a newer OS such as Vista or Windows 7. You must use USMT 3.x on Windows XP machines. The previous subsections covers the command line syntax for USMT 3.x.

Note: The USMT batch files subsection found further down in this section are designed to call the USMT 3.x for Windows XP machines and USMT 4.x for Vista and Windows 7 machines.

It is recommended that a batch file be created to allow for easy editing and repeated running of the scanstate or loadstate on multiple machines and in varied environments. The recommended USMT batch files are detailed below the command syntax details.

Note: The USMT 4.x commands here and in the batch files rely on the user names being the same on the old and the new domains. If the user names will not be the same, the USMT 4.x commands and the batch file will need to be edited to accommodate the method used.

Example of complete Scanstate and Loadstate command as used:

scanstate c:\!tech*username* /nocompress /i:miguser.xml /i:migapp.xml /localonly /c /v:5 /o /ue: /ue:* /ui: *olddomainname\username /l:c:\!tech\username-scanstate.log /progress:c:\!tech\username-scanprogress.log***

loadstate c:\!tech*username* /nocompress /i:miguser.xml /i:migapp.xml /c /v:5 /ue: /ue:* /ui:*olddomainname\username* /md:*olddomainname:newdomainname /l:c:\!tech\username-loadstate.log /progress:c:\!tech\username-loadprogress.log***

Explanation of Switches used:

StorePath = Local directory relative to the c:\ directory so that the path is universal across all machines in case a batch file is used.
/nocompress - Disables compression of data. Migration files will not be compressed into a single usmt file.
/i: - Specifies the .xml files that contains rules that define what state to migrate. Both .xml files used are the default files supplied with USMT 4.x and must be listed on the command line.
/localonly - Migrates only files that are stored on the local computer. Only used for scanstate.
/c: - ScanState will continue to run even if there are nonfatal errors. Only used for scanstate.
/v:n - Enables verbose output in the ScanState or LoadState log. n=5 Enables verbose and status output.
/vsc – This option enables the volume shadow-copy service to migrate locked files if possible.
/ue: - Excludes the specified user(s) from the migration.
Full syntax: /ue:*DomainName\"User Name"* or /ue:*LocalUserName*
Therefore: /ue:** - Excludes all users in any domain.
And: /ue:* - Excludes all local users.
/ui: - Includes the specified user(s) in the migration.
/md:*olddomainname:newdomainname* - This option changes the domain from old domain to new domain for the user(s) on a computer.
/l:*drive:path\filename*.log - Sets the location and name of the ScanState or LoadState log file.
/progress: :*drive:path\filename*.log - Sets the location and name of the ScanState or LoadState progress log file.
/o – Overwrites an existing store.

USMT Batch Files

Note: There are only two batch files. One for ScanState and one for Loadstate. All decisions are performed inside the batch file.

The batch file tests and acts accordingly on the following:

- First the current OS version is tested to determine if it is Windows XP. (True or False only)
- Second the OS is tested to determine if it is 32-bit or 64-bit.
- USMT ver. 3.x for the correct OS bit version is called for all Windows XP machines.
- USMT 4.x for the correct OS bit version is called for all Windows Vista and Windows 7 machines.

The batch files detailed here assume the following:

- The user profiles being migrated will be saved locally to the c:\!tech*username* directory.
- The log files will all be saved locally to the c:\!tech directory and will contain the user name in the filename.
- The batch files will be created in the new server *newservername*\tech\usmt directory.

The batch files detailed here require the following changes before use:

- The old domain name and new domain names are embedded into the batch files and must be edited when the batch files are created to reflect the correct old and new domain names.
- The server name is embedded into the batch files at the begging of the usmt command line and must be edited when the batch files are created to reflect the correct server name.

Both batch files utilize only one command line variable. It is the users logon ID.

Example 1: *newservername*\tech\usmt\usmtscan.bat *username*

Example 2: *newservername*\tech\usmt\usmtload.bat *username*

Note: Pay close attention to the full command line when creating the batch file. Due to words wrapping in this document it may appear that the single command is actually three lines. It may be best to copy the exact command line from the Workstation Migration Project Template document into notepad for verification and to build the batch files.

Note: You must change all occurrences of each of the following variables in the batch files or the results will be random at best:
newservername
oldservername
newservername

- USMTScan.bat -

```
@echo off
cls
rem USMT 3.x and 4.x Scan State batch file

rem Make a unique place for the users profile backup.
md c:\!tech >nul
md c:\!tech\%1 >nul
```

rem Find out if it's XP and if so jump to the XP version otherwise run the Vista Win7 version now.

ver | find "XP" > nul

if %errorlevel% == 0 goto XP

rem Here is the Vista and Win7 version (USMT 4) command.

newservername\tech\usmt\usmt4\%processor_architecture%\scanstate c:\!tech\%1 /nocompress /i:*newservername*\tech\usmt\usmt4\%processor_architecture%\miguser.xml /i:*newservername*\tech\usmt\usmt4\%processor_architecture%\migapp.xml /localonly /c /v:5 /vsc /ue:** /ue:* /ui:*olddomainname*\%1 /l:c:\!tech\%1-scanstate.log /progress:c:\!tech\%1-scanprogress.log

goto end

rem Here is the XP version (USMT 3) command.

:XP

newservername\tech\usmt\usmt3\%processor_architecture%\scanstate c:\!tech\%1 /nocompress /i:*newservername*\tech\usmt\usmt3\%processor_architecture%\miguser.xml /i:*newservername*\tech\usmt\usmt3\%processor_architecture%\migapp.xml /i:*newservername*\tech\usmt\usmt3\%processor_architecture%\migsys.xml /localonly /c /v:5 /ue:** /ue:* /ui:*olddomainname*\%1 /l:c:\!tech\%1-scanstate.log /progress:c:\!tech\%1-scanprogress.log

:end

Pause

- USMTLoad.bat -

@echo off

cls

rem USMT 3.x and 4.x Load State batch file

rem Find out if it's XP and if so jump to the XP version otherwise run the Vista Win7 version now.

ver | find "XP" > nul

if %errorlevel% == 0 goto XP

rem Here is the Vista and Win7 version (USMT 4) command.

newservername\tech\usmt\usmt4\%processor_architecture%\loadstate c:\!tech\%1 /nocompress /i:*newservername*\tech\usmt\usmt4\%processor_architecture%\miguser.xml /i:*newservername*\tech\usmt\usmt4\%processor_architecture%\migapp.xml /c /v:5 /ue:** /ue:* /ui:*olddomainname*\%1 /md:*olddomainname*:*newdomainname* /l:c:\!tech\%1-loadstate.log /progress:c:\!tech\%1-loadprogress.log

Goto end

rem Here is the XP version (USMT 3) command.

:XP

newservername\tech\usmt\usmt3\%processor_architecture%\loadstate c:\!tech\%1 /nocompress /i:*newservername*\tech\usmt\usmt3\%processor_architecture%\miguser.xml /i:*newservername*\tech\usmt\usmt3\%processor_architecture%\migapp.xml

/i:*newservername*\tech\usmt\usmt3\%processor_architecture%\migsys.xml /c /v:5 /ue:** /ue:* /ui:*olddomainname*\%1 /md:*olddomainname*:*newdomainname* /l:c:\!tech\%1-loadstate.log /progress:c:\!tech\%1-loadprogress.log

:end
Pause

Port Reference

Note: When creating custom services in a firewall use the friendly name where possible for clarity.

Common ports we usually open on the firewall			
Service	**Friendly Name**	**Port Number**	**Notes**
SMTP	Email	25	Simple Mail Transfer Protocol
HTTP	Web or WWW	80	Hypertext Transfer Protocol
HTTPS	Secure Web	443	Hypertext Transfer Protocol Secure
Custom	SharePoint 03	444	SharePoint (Not required by 208 or 2011)
Custom	SharePoint 08	987	New SharePoint port for 2008 and 2011
Terminal Services	RDP	3389	Terminal Services / Remote Desktop Protocol
Custom	RWW	4125	Remote Web Workplace (Not required by 2011)
Custom	HP ILO	17899	Integrated Lights Out

Common ports we usually DO NOT open on the firewall			
Service	**Friendly Name**	**Port Number**	**Notes**
Ping		*	When you ping another computer the ICMP (Internet Control Message Protocol) is used, no actual ports are used.
FTP		20	File Transfer Protocol – In
FTP		21	File Transfer Protocol - Out
Telnet		23	Telnet
GRE		47	The Generic Route Encapsulation (Used in conjunction with Point-to-Point Tunneling)
DNS		53	Domain Name Service
POP3		110	Post Office Protocol
NNTP		119	Network News Transfer Protocol
NTP		123	Network Time Protocol
L2TP		1701	Level 2 Tunneling Protocol
PPTP		1723	Point to Point Tunneling Protocol

User Profile Component General Reference

Note: On any current Windows operating system the variable %userprofile% can be substituted for c:\Documents and Settings*username* (XP Pro) or c:\Users*username* (Vista and Windows 7).
e.g. to get to a path listed below without having to type the exact users logon ID simply use:
%userprofile%\\AppData\Roaming\Microsoft\Internet Explorer\Quick Launch.

Note: In both Vista and Windows 7 the operating system manipulates the true path presented to the users in any GUI. This is apparent when attempting to browse to locations such as My Documents or Recent Items.
For example, the path for the users documents is:
C:\Users*username*\Documents
but will always show as:
C:\Users*username*\My Documents in the GUI.
Similarly the path to Recent Items is:
C:\Users\ *username*\AppData\Roaming\Microsoft\Windows\Recent
but will be presented as:
C:\Users\ *username* \AppData\Roaming\Microsoft\Windows\Recent Items in the GUI.

Component	Location (XP / Vista & Windows 7) or (Office 2003 / Office 2007 & 2010)
Desktop	C:\Documents and Settings*username*\Desktop C:\Users*username*\Desktop
My Documents Documents	C:\Documents and Settings*username*\My Documents C:\Users*username*\Documents
My Favorites	C:\Documents and Settings*username*\My Favorites C:\Users*username*\Favorites
My Music Music	C:\Documents and Settings*username*\My Documents\My Music C:\Users*username*\Music
My Pictures Pictures	C:\Documents and Settings*username*\My Documents\My Pictures C:\Users*username*\Pictures
My Videos Videos	C:\Documents and Settings*username*\My Documents\My Videos C:\Users*username*\Videos
My Recent Documents Recent Items	C:\Documents and Settings*username*\Recent C:\Users*username*\AppData\Roaming\Microsoft\Windows\Recent
Quick Launch Toolbar	C:\Documents and Settings*username*\Application Data\Microsoft\Internet Explorer\Quick Launch C:\Users*username*\AppData\Roaming\Microsoft\Internet Explorer\Quick Launch
Windows Sidebar Settings *(Does not apply to XP)*	C:\Users*username*\AppData\Local\Microsoft\Windows Sidebar
IE Cookies	C:\Documents and Settings*username*\Cookies C:\Users*username*\AppData\Roaming\Microsoft\Windows\Cookies
IE Links	C:\Documents and Settings*username*\Favorites\Links

IE URL History List *(Registry Entries)*	Computer\HKEY_CURRENT_USER\Software\Microsoft\Internet Explorer\TypedURLs
Office / Outlook Signatures	C:\Documents and Settings*username*\Application Data\Microsoft\Signatures C:\Users*username*\AppData\Roaming\Microsoft\Signatures
Office / Outlook Templates	C:\Documents and Settings*username*\Application Data\Microsoft\Templates C:\Users*username*\AppData\Roaming\Microsoft\Templates
Office / Outlook Stationary	C:\Documents and Settings*username*\Application Data\Microsoft\Stationary C:\Users*username*\AppData\Roaming\Microsoft\Stationery
Office Custom Dictionary	C:\Documents and Settings*username*\Application Data\Microsoft\Proof C:\Users*username*\AppData\Roaming\Microsoft\UProof
Office Recent Files	C:\Documents and Settings*username*\Application Data\Microsoft\Office\Recent C:\Users*username*\AppData\Roaming\Microsoft\Office\Recent
Outlook Data Files *(.pst and .ost Files)*	C:\Documents and Settings*username*\Local Settings\Application Data\Microsoft\Outlook C:\Users*username*\AppData\Local\Microsoft\Outlook
Outlook Address Cache (.NK2 file) *(Office 2007 and earlier only)*	C:\Documents and Settings*username*\Application Data\Microsoft\Outlook C:\Users*username*\AppData\Roaming\Microsoft\Outlook
Media Player Play Lists *(Media Player 10 and up)*	C:\Documents and Settings*username*\Music\Playlists C:\Users*username*\Music\Playlists
Media Player Database	C:\Documents and Settings*username*\Local Settings\Application Data\Microsoft\Media Player C:\Users*username*\AppData\Local\Microsoft\Media Player

8. Communications / Training

Informing the Client

Use Email Templates from this section to generate emails or printouts as needed to communicate with the client as the project moves forward. Edit, format and update as needed.

You will find templates for pre training, what to expect before, during and after their migration, post training and more.

As new questions are generated add them to the Migration FAQ section and include a clear short answer.

Note: Always be certain the outgoing email has been correctly formatted with a proper subject, the correct client company name, reply to address and technician name. Also verify every variable piece of data in the email body. e.g. dates, times, passwords, etc.

Email Templates

Migration Downtime Tolerability

Hello *ClientTechnicalContact*,

We need to collect some information regarding the upcoming migration.

If we must have any of the systems listed below off line or unavailable for any reason during the migration, what is the longest period of time during the work day they can be down or offline and when would be the best time to have any of these systems off line?

We do understand that some system or programs cannot be offline at all during business hours. Please note those system or programs.

Internet access (ability to surf the internet)
Server file access (files on the server or a network drive)
Email
Companyweb or SharePoint site
Main Copier
Accounting Program
CRM System
Time Clock
Phone System

Is downtime of some of the more critical systems or programs during the lunch hour acceptable?

“On the day of the migration (*April 32nd*), we may need to have unrestricted access to reboot systems, take the network down, etc. between 7:00 AM and 8:00 AM or between 5:00 PM and 6:00 PM.
Would there be any problems with this?

If you have any other questions please feel free to give us a call anytime.

Thank you.

The KPEnterprises Network Migration Team

Pre Migration and Post Migration Training

Hello *ClientTechnicalContact*,

We would like to schedule a brief Pre Migration / Post Migration training for you users. It will take less than an hour.
It is preferred to have the training presented right before the lunch hour as it usually results in the highest turnout rate. Of course any time of day is fine with us.

We would like to have the training toward the end of the week just before the migration.

Please let us know what date and time you would like us to come in and present the training and we will accommodate.

If you have any problems or questions please feel free to give us a call anytime.

Thank you.

The KPEnterprises Network Migration Team

Where we are and What's Next – Server Has Been Received

Hello *ClientTechnicalContact*,

We wanted to let you know where we are with your server migration:

- A series of service tickets have been created in our system. You will see that they each begin with "Server Migration"
- We have received the server. If you want a picture, let me know and we'll email one when we unbox it.
- We have received most of the other hardware and software.

What's next?

- Assuming there are no delays in getting any remaining hardware or software our project manager will schedule work on our end and proceed to "build" the server
- The project manager will also arrange an estimated delivery date. We normally expect to be onsite for only two days.

General notes:

- Our expectation is that we will build the server, move the data and databases, and test almost everything before we "bother" you or any other users for anything. This may involve working with any third party vendors or support teams.
- Once the server is ready, we'll move it onsite and make final data migration.
- We expect to perform all work during normal business hours (8:00 AM – 6:00 PM Monday-Friday).
- We do not expect any companywide downtime during this migration process. You can expect about an hour of downtime on each workstation as it is moved to the new system.

If there is anything we have failed to cover please email us or give us a call.
We want this to be an easy and simple transition for you so let us know if there is anything we can do.

Thank you once again for putting your faith in KPEnterprises. We trust you will have a very successful network migration.

Thank you.

The KPEnterprises Network Migration Team

How Users Use Outlook (Full Migration) – The week Before Migration if Necessary

Hello *ClientTechnicalContact*,

**Please strip off these first few lines and forward this email on to users as soon as possible. Thank you.

From the KPEnterprises Network Migration Team

Hello *ClientCompany* network users,

Next week we will be migrating your network to a new server. To help make the migration go smoothly we need a little help from you.
We would like you to make some simple notes about how you use your email program (Microsoft Outlook).
It is the only way we can help ensure you have access to all the same Outlook items after the migrating of your workstation is complete.

Please simply forward this email to Migration@KPEnterprises.com and answer the following questions:

- If you frequently open the Inbox, Calendar or Contacts of other users please make a list of those users and the Outlook item that you use.

- If you have set up your Outlook to allow other users to see your Inbox, Calendar or Contacts please make a list of those users and which of you Outlook item they use.

- What Public Folders, Calendars or Contacts do you use in Outlook?
  If you are not sure about which Public Folders you use please contact your companies Technical Contact for help.

If you have any problems or questions please feel free to give us a call anytime.

Thank you.

The KPEnterprises Network Migration Team

How Users Use Outlook (Custom Migration) – The week Before Migration if Necessary

Hello *ClientTechnicalContact*,

**Please strip off these first few lines and forward this email on to users as soon as possible. Thank you.

From the KPEnterprises Network Migration Team

Hello *ClientCompany* network users,

Next week we will be migrating your network to a new server. To help make the migration go smoothly we need a little help from you.
We would like you to make some simple notes about how you use your email program (Microsoft Outlook).
It is the only way we can help ensure you have access to all the same Outlook items when the migrating of your workstation is complete.

Please simply forward this email to Migration@KPEnterprises.com and answer the following questions:

- If you frequently open the Inbox, Calendar or Contacts of other users please make a list of those users and the Outlook item that you use.

- If you have set up your Outlook to allow other users to see your Inbox, Calendar or Contacts please make a list of those users and which of you Outlook item they use.

- What Public Folders, Calendars or Contacts do you use in Outlook?
  If you are not sure about which Public Folders you use please contact your companies Technical Contact for help.

If you have any problems or questions please feel free to give us a call anytime.

Thank you.

The KPEnterprises Network Migration Team

Workstation Cleanup – The week Before Migration

Hello *ClientTechnicalContact*,

**Please strip off these first few lines and forward this email on to users as soon as possible.
Thank you.

From the KPEnterprises Network Migration Team

Hello *ClientCompany* network users,

Next week we will be migrating your network to a new server. To help make the migration go smoothly we would like you to perform a little workstation clean up if possible.

Please go through your email and delete anything you don't absolutely need. Start with the large emails first as one 5mb attachment can take up more space than 1000 singe emails with no attachment. Do not bother exporting email as it will still be taking up space somewhere in the system, it's just not in the Exchange server anymore.

Move (not copy) any company data that may be on your desktop to one of the server shares. If you're not sure where it should go please consult you companies technical contact.

Remove any large collections of music or pictures from your workstation.
Do NOT move or copy them to the server or any other network location.
Most music and pictures can be burnt to CD or DVD before deleting from the workstation.

Note: This does not apply to a personal laptop or a home workstation, only company owned machines.

If you have any problems or questions please feel free to give us a call anytime.

Thank you.

The KPEnterprises Network Migration Team

What to Expect - Monday the Week Before Migration

Hello *ClientTechnicalContact*,

Here is a brief overview of what to expect this week and next week when we are installing your new server and migrating your network.

While the actual network migration is scheduled for Wednesday and Thursday of next week we will deliver the server this coming Friday just before noon to set it up for final testing.
We may need to shut down the old server for about 15 minutes during the lunch hour to relocate it or to swap out certain hardware.

We will be there on Wednesday morning to get started on the actual migration of workstations to the new server. We will do a final review of the workstations migration order when we meet up. Provided each workstation is in good health the migration should be virtually seamless and should take no more than 30 minutes to an hour per machine.

Users can expect that sometime Wednesday morning they will stop seeing new email in Outlook program they usually use for email. They will have to use the web based Outlook to access new email until their machine is migrated. We will send a separate email next week explaining how to do this.

Thursday we will finish any incomplete workstation migrations and decommission your old servers.

Remote users will have no file connectivity (VPN) until we step them through creating a new connection on their home or laptop workstation.
They should arrange a time early on Wednesday to either have their laptop in the office or to be available over the phone. We should be able to remote into their system and step them through pretty much anything.

If there is anything we have failed to cover please email us or give us a call.
We want this to be an easy and simple transition for you so let us know if there is anything we can do.

Thank you.

The KPEnterprises Network Migration Team

Frequently Asked Questions - Monday the Week Before Migration

Hello *ClientTechnicalContact*,

**Please strip off these first few lines and forward this email on to users as soon as possible.
Thank you.

From the KPEnterprises Network Migration Team

Hello *ClientCompany* network users,

Below is a list of Frequently Asked Questions regarding network Migrations.
We believe they will answer many questions you may have.

If there is anything we have failed to cover please email us or give us a call.
We want this to be an easy and simple transition for you so let us know if there is anything we can do.

Thank you.

The KPEnterprises Network Migration Team

- *Attach all relevant FAQ questions here* -

Server Install - Friday the Week Before the Migration

Hello *ClientTechnicalContact*,

**Please strip off these first few lines and forward this email on to users as soon as possible.
Thank you.

From the KPEnterprises Network Migration Team

Hello *ClientCompany* network users,

We will be moving all server data to the new server starting Monday evening at 5pm. To avoid any data loss, please inform all users that they should not be accessing any data on the server until Tuesday morning after 8am.
On Tuesday morning all users will be accessing company data via the new server but they should not know the difference.

If there is anything we have failed to cover please email us or give us a call.
We want this to be an easy and simple transition for you so let us know if there is anything we can do.

Thank you.

The KPEnterprises Network Migration Team

Outlook Shortcut - Monday the Week of Migration

Hello *ClientTechnicalContact*,

**Please strip off these first few lines and forward this email on to users as soon as possible.
Thank you.

Note: The default user password for all users on the new server is *xxx20xx!*

From the KPEnterprises Network Migration Team

Hello *ClientCompany* network users,

We will be migrating you network on Wednesday and Thursday of this week and there are a few very important things you must know.

- Starting Wednesday morning you will need to access all of your email by using the Web based Outlook through Internet Explorer using the address noted below.
- Although you may be able to open Outlook as you have before, no new email will be coming in and anything you send may not get to whom you have sent it.
- Please write down the address below as you may not be able to get to this email on Wednesday morning. Alternatively you may open the link now and then add the page to your favorites.
- The address is: https://*newservername*.local/owa
- Please do not start actively using the Web based Outlook until Wednesday.

If you have any problems or questions please feel free to give us a call anytime.

Thank you.

The KPEnterprises Network Migration Team

RWW and VPN Change - The Day of Migration

Hello *ClientTechnicalContact*,

**Please strip off these first few lines and forward this email on to users as soon as possible. Thank you.

From the KPEnterprises Network Migration Team

Hello *ClientCompany* network users,

The web link used to get to your companies Remote Web Workplace has changed.
So has the web link to company email.

The new web link for Remote Web Workplace is http://*remote.clientdomain.com*

The new web link for email is http://*remote.clientdomain.com*/owa

If your logon ID and or password was changed during the network migration, be sure to use the new logon ID and password. If you're not sue contact your company technical contact.

If you have any problems or questions please feel free to give us a call anytime.

Thank you.

The KPEnterprises Network Migration Team

Password Policy Change - The Monday After Migration

Hello *ClientTechnicalContact*,

**Please strip off these first few lines and forward this email on to users as soon as possible. Thank you.

From the KPEnterprises Network Migration Team

Hello *ClientCompany* network users,

Your company has a password policy for their network. It is detailed below.
Now that the network migration is complete the policy will be enacted.
It is schedule to be activated on Wednesday of this week.

What this means to you as a user is pretty simple. On Wednesday morning when you come in to work and log on to your computer the system will require you to create a new password.

Your new password must meet the requirements listed below or the system will not accept it.
As a general rule it is easier to remember pass phrases rather than a single password.

Do not write down your password and do not share it with anyone else.

Password Policy:

Your passwords will expire every ***X*** days. The system will notify you several days in advance.
X Passwords will be remembered. e.g. you cannot reuse a password until the system forgets it.
Once you enter a new password it cannot be changed again for ***X*** days.
Your new password must be at least ***X*** characters long.

Please Note: If you incorrectly enter your password ***X*** times in a row your account will be locked out.
If your account is locked out you will need wait ***XX*** minutes before attempting to log on again or contact your companies technical contact to get the account unlocked.

If you have any problems or questions please feel free to give us a call anytime.

Thank you.

The KPEnterprises Network Migration Team

Post Migration Questionnaire - The Friday After Migration

Hello *ClientTechnicalContact*,

Your network Migration is complete and now we would like some feedback on how we did.
Please take a few minutes to answer as many of the questions below as possible.

In addition to the questions we've come up with please feel free to tell us anything you feel important to note.

Thank you once again for putting your faith in KPEnterprises for your network migration.

The KPEnterprises Network Migration Team

Remember, feel free to add any notes to any answer you feel needs comments.

Q: How would you rate the migration of the critical Line Of Business applications on a scale of 1-10 ?
e.g. Was it smooth, event free with minimal downtime?
A:

Q: How would you rate the migration of the Workstations and Users on a scale of 1-10 ?
e.g. Was it smooth, event free with minimal downtime?
A:

Q: How would you rate the migration team on a scale of 1-10 ?
e.g. Professional, knowledgeable.
A:

Q: How would you rate the migration of the critical Line Of Business applications on a scale of 1-10 ?
e.g. Was it smooth, event free with minimal downtime?
A:

Q: How would you rate our communications during the project on a scale of 1-10 ?
e.g. Emails, calls, planning updates, etc.
A:

Q: How would you rate any training you may have received on the new Small Business Server features or other technologies on a scale of 1-10 ?
A:

Q: How would you rate the migration project overall on a scale of 1-10 ?
e.g. Time line met, cost met, downtime expectations met, etc.
A:

Q: How would you rate the migration project overall on a scale of 1-10 ?
A:

Q: How can we improve on any aspects of our migration process?
e.g. Communications, timing, training, technical skills, etc.
A:

Fine Tuning and Spin Off - The Tuesday After Migration

Hello *ClientTechnicalContact*,

Your network Migration is complete! / *Almost complete!*
Thank you for your patience during the migration.

We have a few fine tuning things to complete. They are:

- *Item 1*
- *Item 2*
- *Item n*

We have a few spin off projects that have come up. They are:

- *Item 1*
- *Item 2*
- *Item n*

If there is anything we have failed to cover please email us or give us a call.

Thank you once again for putting your faith in KPEnterprises for your network migration.

The KPEnterprises Network Migration Team

Migration FAQ (Frequently Asked Questions)

Q: What is a Small Business Server?

A: A Small Business Server is a computer specifically designed to provide many business critical functions such as secure storage and sharing of company data, Email services, Application sharing, Fax services and much more.

Q: What operating system will the new server be running?

A: The new server operating system will be Small Business Server 2011.

Q: Why do we need to migrate to a new server?

A: There are many reasons but the most typical is that as more programs, data and users are added to the server it causes excessive load on the older server. Sometimes it is simply because the hardware in the server is failing.

Q: What's so special about the new server?

A: The new server will represent the latest technology in hardware and the Small Business Server operating system. It will have more memory, more storage space and it will run faster.

Q: How long will migration take?

A: A typical network migration is completed in two days.

Q: Will we be able to continue working and have access to all network programs and documents while the migration is taking place?

A: The migration has been planned out so that there will be minimal downtime to any business critical applications or services during normal business hours.

Q: Will we have internet access while the migration is taking place?

A: You should have uninterrupted internet access during the migration.

Q: Will we still be receiving our email in a normal timely manner during the migration?

A: Yes. Email flow to and from your network should be uninterrupted.

Q: How will I get to my email while the migration is going on?

A: You will use either the full version of Outlook most of the time but for a short period while email is being migrated you will use the very robust web based version of Outlook.

Q: Will all my printers run with the new server?

A: Most all existing printers should continue to work just fine. Some older printers may not have drivers that work on the new server.

Q: Will workstations automatically connect to the new server?

A: For a standard network migration the answer is no. We must run a program on your computer to get it joined to the new network.

Q: If migration to the new server fails, will the old server still be fully available?

A: Our process for migration ensures the old server will be available and should be fully functional for just this reason.

Q: Will our files be backed up while the system migration is taking place?

A: Data backups will continue as scheduled during the migration.

Q: How will I know if my computer is done being migrated?

A: We will leave a form at your keyboard indicating your computer migration is complete.

Q: What will happen to my password? Can I change it later?

A: Your password will be changed on the new system and it will be

Q: Will any of my data be lost?

A: No data stored on the server will be lost. If you have any questions about where your critical data actually stored please consult your companies technical contact.

Q: What will happen to all my addresses in Outlook?

A: All cached email addresses and contact lists will be migrated to the new profile. If you cannot find something when you look around for the first time, let us know as soon as possible.

Q: If we have employees who remote in to work, how will the migration affect them? Will they continue to have access to the system during the migration?

A: All remote users will be informed of how the migration is expected to affect them specifically but it is expected that the typical remote user will have only limited interruptions.

Q: If we are hosting a website on our server, how does the migration affect that? Will the outside world still be able to access our website during the migration?

A: We expect there to be no interruption in availability to your public website.

Q: Will KPEnterprises remain onsite until migration is complete?

A: They may not. With the technology available today many of the migration steps can be performed remotely. We will however always be available as several technicians will be assigned full time to the migration.

9. Old Network Documentation

General

Insert an up-to-date copy of the listed Network Documentation Binder sections here for reference.
If there is no formal Network Documentation Binder or existing network documentation, the forms found in the New Network Documentation section of this binder can be readily be copied and used to record information for this section.

Below is a list of the sections and the respective documents one would expect to find in a well-organized Network Documentation Binder.

Procedures

Documentation of all procedures relevant to the system. The more critical the component the more extensive the documentation of the procedure should be.
Procedures found here may be simply marked up whitepapers specific to common network tasks.

Net Specs

- Network Map
- Internet Domain Registration Information
- Router Configuration Form
- Firewall Configuration Form
- IP Address Allocation Record
- Hard Coded IP Address Record
- Network Timing Diagram
- Shared Resources Record
- Shared Resources Permission Record
- UPS Power Distribution Form
- Group Policy Object Record

Machines Specs

- Machine Specification Sheet
  For every Server, Workstation, Laptop, Printers, Copiers, NAS, SAN, CDP, Phone System, Time Clock, Surveillance System, etc.

Users & Passwords

- User Names, Logon ID and Passwords Records
- Email Addresses Record
- POP or MAPI Account and Credential Records
- Security and Distribution Group Membership Record
- Password Policy Form

Products

- Line of Business Application Record
- *License / Key / Code Documents for all LOB's, applications and software of any kind.*
- *Service Agreements, Support Packs, Care Packs, etc.*

10. System Build

General

From this point forward all new documentation for any aspect of this system should now be recorded on the forms found in the New Network Documentation section of this binder. If forms do not exist for what needs to be documented they will need to be improvised. All documentation acquired during this build and migration should also be inserted into the New Network Documentation section of this binder.

The goal is to end up with all documentation related to the new system up-to-date and in one place. The New Network Documentation section.

The technician should become familiar with the pre-defined forms available in the New Network Documentation section before continuing.

Note: During the build and Migration, references are made to specific sections of the Discovery for data required for the installation or migration. Much of the actual reference data is contained in the Old Network Documentation section of this binder. It is inferred here that if the Discovery section does not contain the actual data, it will be found somewhere in the Old Network Documentation section.

Documentation Checklist

☐ Copy of the Up-To-Date critical sections of the Old Network Documentation Binder inserted into the Old Network Documentation section of this binder.

- Procedures
- Net Specs
- Machine Specifications
- Users and Passwords
- Products

☐ Discovery section of this binder completed.

☐ Equipment pick list from sales team.

☐ Support Pack(s) or hardware warranty documentation for the new server(s).

☐ The complete, verified list of user names and email addresses returned from the Client Technical Contact. This file should be saved to c:\!tech\migration directory on the new server once it exists.

☐ The complete, verified list of machine that will be migrated, returned from the Client Technical Contact or the sales team. If this is returned in digital form the file should be saved to c:\!tech\migration directory on the new server once it exists.

☐ ____

☐ ____

☐ ____

Hardware Checklist

☐ Create a hardware checklist here based on the quote the client has approved and the pick list from the sales team and the required equipment for the system build.

☐ Test Bench Firewall configured to simulate the client's subnet. e.g. The private side of the firewall exactly emulates the existing client network.

- ☐ Additional Memory
- ☐ Additional NIC's
- ☐ DVD R/W Drive (Verify capacity of the device if a Double Layer DVD is required for the OS)
- ☐ Tape Drive
- ☐ Hard Disk Drive(s)
- ☐ SCSI or SAS controller(s)
- ☐ SCSI or SAS cables
- ☐ Fax Modem
- ☐ UPS

Note: A new UPS may not have been purchased with the system.

- ☐ ______________________________
- ☐ ______________________________
- ☐ ______________________________

Software Checklist

Create a software checklist here that includes all LOB's, Sub-System and System Applications that will be installed on the new server or system. Review the Discovery section to ensure this list is complete.

Note: Pre-existing records of software Keys, Codes, CAL's etc. should be kept in the Old Network Documentation section.
New records of software Keys, Codes, CAL's etc. should be kept in the New Network Documentation section.
All other Network Documentation will be merged into the New Network Documentation section at the appropriate time in the project.

- ☐ HP Proliant Foundation Essentials Pack
- ☐ Small Business Server 20___ R2 Standard Premium Essentials 64Bit
  - All media including Outlook and Premium Content if applicable
  - Software Keys (Volume license keys registered with eOpen?)
  - SBS CAL's (Volume license registered with eOpen?)
- ☐ RAID or Drive Controller drivers required for setup. (On 3.5" floppy)
- ☐ Drivers for all network attached printers, scanners and copiers, Scanners, USB and other devices.
- ☐ Antivirus Solution and Software Keys. Including any add-ons such as Exchange component.
- ☐ Backup Solution and Software Keys. Include any add-ons such as Database, SharePoint or Exchange component.
- ☐ Disk Management Solution and Software Keys.
- ☐ Fax modem, drivers, application and management software.
- ☐ UPS management solution.
- ☐ ______________________________
- ☐ ______________________________

☐ ____________________
☐ ____________________
☐ ____________________
☐ ____________________
☐ ____________________
☐ ____________________
☐ ____________________
☐ ____________________

Hardware Inventory and Assembly

☐ Remove the Pack-Up / To-Do Checklist from the Pack-Up / To-Do section of this binder and tape it to the monitor or to the new server.

☐ Copy and fill out a Machine Specification Sheet for the new server. Leave the completed sheet in the Machine Spec subsection of New Network Documentation section of this binder.

☐ Set up a folder for all the New Server documentation such as the SmartStart CD or DVD set, Server documentation book, CD or DVD, controller manuals, etc. Label the folder with the servers name. Use expandable manila folders. More than one may be required.

☐ Begin recording all progress on the system build in the Troubleshooting and Repair Log section so there is a record of issues and for reference by anyone who works on this system.

☐ Unpack all server hardware and components, inspect and inventory. Check items off from the Hardware Checklist created earlier in this section as they are inspected.

Note: Do not discard any packages or packing materials.

☐ Record any damage or shortages in the Shortages section of this binder and then immediately inform the Sales Team of these damages or shortages.

☐ Place a dated KPEnterprises product label on each major component. Tape drive, Memory, Controller, Server, Monitor, etc.

☐ Remove the server door / bezel keys, unlock the door or bezel and then attach keys to the back of the machine.

☐ Open the server chassis and check all equipment for good seat as parts may have slipped during shipment.

☐ Connect Monitor, keyboard and mouse or KVM.

Note: The next step must be performed BEFORE any additional hardware including memory is installed. It is a test of the unit as shipped to verify it will post and all existing hardware is recognized.
DO NOT continue setup until you complete this next step.

☐ Power up the system, enter the BIOS configuration and review settings.

☐ Verify that any Automatic Power-On option is set to "Enabled" or "On" so that the server will power up when AC is returned to the system after power outages.

☐ Verify that the boot order does not have USB as the first, second or third device.

☐ Power down and re-cable drives if necessary for the desired hardware RAID levels as documented in the Discovery section – Hardware and Environment subsection.

☐ Physically label and Install each Hard Disk Drive. Label the drive not the cages or rails.

☐ Install any additional hardware required including Memory, Tape drive, Controllers, etc.

- ☐ Double check all connections and settings.
- ☐ If a new UPS was purchased with the system plug the server power into the UPS.

Note: Do not plug the data cable from the UPS into the server at this time.

- ☐ If there is an HP Support Pack, register it at HP.com
  - Associate the Support Pack in HP's system with the new server it was purchased for.

  Note: Be certain the email addresses entered for registration is the client companies administrators email address.

  - Print out all registration records, keys, codes etc. from the registration sites and insert them into the New Network Documentation section.
- ☐ If a new tape drive was installed, run a cleaning tape through the tape drive before ever putting in a data cartridge. (3 times) Be certain to mark three uses on the cleaning cartridge.
- ☐ If an Integrated Lights Out (ILO) controller is present, configure it now.
  - Record the Logon ID and Password for the ILO controller on the server Machine Specification Sheet and on the User Name, Logon ID and Password Record in the New Network Documentation section of this binder. Leave the ILO tag on the back of the machine.
  - Power up the system and when the Integrated Light Out BIOS posts, press the F8 key.

  Note: There is an HP Lights-Out Configuration available from the Maintenance menu once the HP SmartStart is loaded but it is significantly slower than configuring the ROM BIOS directly. Therefore configuring the ILO controller through the HP SmartStart is not currently covered in this checklist.

  Note: On newer HP servers all Option ROM messages and prompts are suppressed unless you have actually pressed a key when prompted during the initial Post. There will be a message indicating "Press any key to view Option ROM messages".

  Note: Do not change the ILO Logon ID or password.

  - Select DNS/DHCP from the Network Menu.
    - Set DHCP Enabled to Off.
    - Press F10 to save.
  - Select NIC and TCP/IP from the Network Menu.
    - Configure the IP settings as documented in the Discovery section - Domain Names, IP's, DNS and DHCP subsection.
    - Press F10 to save.
  - Document the ILO IP on the server Machine Specification Sheet.
  - Exit the ILO utility.
- ☐ If RAID Array(s) require configuration and the HP SmartStart will not be used to deploy the server or the controller is not recognized by the HP SmartStart, configure the RAID Array(s) now.
  - Reboot the server and when the RAID controller BIOS posts, press the appropriate key to enter the controller configuration utility.

  Note: Most controller BIOS use the F8 key.

  Note: On newer HP servers all Option ROM messages and prompts are suppressed unless you have actually pressed a key when prompted during the initial Post. There will be a message indicating "Press any key to view Option ROM messages".

  - From the Main Menu select View Logical Drive and review any existing configuration.

    - If there are existing Logical Drives, verify they are configured as documented in the Discovery section - Hardware and Environment subsection.
- If the listed drives are correct, exit the Array BIOS and move to the next section.
- If they are not correct, delete the existing Logical Drives and proceed to create new Logical Drives as follows:
    - Press Esc to return to the Main Menu.
    - From the Main menu, select Delete Logical Drive.
        - Select the drive to be deleted and press F8.
        - At the Warning prompt press F3 to confirm the logical drive deletion.
        - At the Configuration Saved prompt press Enter to return to the Main Menu.
        - Follow the above steps to delete any other logical drives as necessary.
    - From the Main menu, select Create Logical Drives.
        - Configure the drives into RAID Array(s) as documented in the Discovery section - Hardware and Environment subsection, by selecting the drive(s) to be included in the first Logical Drive, the RAID Configuration and if appropriate select to utilize a Spare.

          Example Steps: For a RAID 5 Array using all available drives:
            - Select each Physical Drive to be included in the Array by pressing the Space Bar.
            - Navigate to the RAID Configurations section by pressing the Tab key.
            - Select RAID 5 from the list by pressing the Space Bar.
            - Verify that the Use one drive as a spare setting is not selected in the Spare selection.
            - Verify that the Disable (4GB maximum) setting is enabled in the Maximum Boot partition section.
            - Verify that there is nothing selected in the Parity Group Count section.
            - Press Enter to create the logical drive (Array).
            - At the next prompt indicating your selections press F8 to save the configuration.
            - At the Configuration Saved prompt press Enter to return to the Main Menu.
        - Repeat the process outlined above until all Logical Drives have been created as documented in the Discovery section.
        - Exit the RAID controller utility.

      Note: The underlying RAID Array(s) are created automatically as Logical Drives are created. For more control of the Array and Logical Drive creation, use the HP Array Configuration and Diagnostics utility available in the HP SmartStart Maintenance menu if possible.
- Reboot the server if it does not do so automatically.

Server Installation

Note: During the OS and other software setup or installations, If prompted for a name to personalize the software (Not the Organization name) always use the companies short name for the client as documented in the Discovery section – Domain Names subsection. e.g., ZDTM Inc. Not Joe Power user or Administrator.

☐ Setup and Check Network Connectivity.

Note: This checklist assumed that a Test Bench Firewall is being used to isolate this server and provide the optimal environment for installation. It should be preconfigured so that the private side of the firewall exactly emulates the existing client network.

Note: The process outlined in this checklist assumes that the SBS installation has a live Internet connection available through the Test Bench Firewall. If it does not several additional steps will be required to complete the installation that are not detailed here.

Note: There can be no active DHCP server on the local network (private side) this server is being set up on or the SBS Setup may not continue.

- Plug in the Test Bench Firewall to the AC outlet of any functioning UPS and power it on.
- Verify there is a trusted network connection via CAT5 or CAT6 cable, with access to the internet, plugged into the Test Bench Firewall public side port. Usually labeled (WAN).
- Select a laptop or desktop pc to use for verifying the internet connectivity through the Test Bench Firewall.
    - Connect a CAT5 or CAT6 cable from any private side port of the Test Bench Firewall (Usually labeled LAN) to the test machines wired NIC port.
    - Power up the test machine and log on to the OS with any account that has administrative level permission.
    - Configure the TCP/IP setting for the primary wired NIC of the test machine to exactly match the selected IP configuration for the new server.
    - Verify all NIC devices on the test machine are disabled except for the primary wired NIC.
- Verify internet connectivity through the Test Bench Firewall from the test machine by surfing to any website that is not cached in the browser.

Note: It is sometimes best to simply search for an abstract set of words on either google.com or yahoo.com to be certain.

Note: Do not proceed until internet connectivity has been verified through the Test Bench Firewall.

- Disconnect the network cable for the test machine used for verifying the firewall internet connectivity. Be certain to reset all TCP/IP configurations for the test machine.
- Connect a CAT5 or CAT6 cable from any private side port of the Test Bench Firewall (Usually labeled LAN) to the new server ILO NIC port.
- Connect a CAT5 or CAT6 cable from any private side port of the Test Bench Firewall (Usually labeled LAN) to the new server primary NIC. (Usually labeled NIC 1)

☐ Select the appropriate Server Installation Subsection to follow.

- If the Server is an HP Server and the exact target Small Business Server version is listed in the SmartStart Operating System Selection page, proceed to the subsection immediately below tilted "Server Installation First Phase using the HP SmartStart Deployment".
- If the Server is not HP Server or the target Small Business Server version is not listed in the SmartStart Operating System Selection page, skip the subsection immediately below and proceed to subsection tilted "Server Installation First Phase using the SBS 2011 DVD".

Server Installation First Phase using the HP SmartStart Deployment

☐ HP SmartStart Reminder! For the proper installation of this product it is assumed and expected that the default selection will be made for everything not specifically noted here including language selections, agreements, licenses, etc.

☐ Read all HP SmartStart related installation and configuration documentation and verify that this system meets all system requirements before proceeding.

Note: The following checklist is valid only for HP SmartStart 8.70 64-bit. If a newer version is being installed, take notes where there are discrepancies so that this checklist can be updated.

- ☐ Microsoft Small Business Server Reminder! For the proper installation of this product it is assumed and expected that the default selection will be made for everything not specifically noted here including language selections, agreements, licenses, etc.
- ☐ Read all Microsoft Small Business Server related installation and configuration documentation and verify that this system meets all system requirements before proceeding.

Note: The following checklist is valid only for Microsoft Small business Server 2011 Standard. If a newer version is being installed, take notes where there are discrepancies so this checklist can be updated.

- ☐ Remove, disconnect or unplug all USB devices other than the keyboard or mouse before beginning the Small business Server installation. Do not plug them back in until the installation is complete.
- ☐ Insert the 64-bit HP SmartStart DVD that came with the server into the DVD drive and reboot or repower the server.
- ☐ If RAID Array(s) require configuration select Maintenance from the Media Options section then Launch the HP Array Configuration and Diagnostics Utility.

  Note: If software mirroring for the C: drive will be will implemented do not attempt to set it up until the server is fully built. There is a specific checkpoint for this.

  - Select the desired device from the drop down window on the Configuration in the Array Configuration Utility (ACU).
  - If there are existing Logical Drives, verify they are as documented in the Discovery section – Hardware and Environment subsection as follows:
    - In the Systems and Device tree in the left pane navigate to the desired Logical Drive then select More Information from the Available Tasks list in the right pane.
    - If all settings are correct, exit the ACU and return to the SmartStart Home page.
    - If the settings are not correct, delete the existing Logical Drive(s).
      - In the Systems and Device tree in the left pane navigate to the desired Logical Drive then select Delete from the Available Tasks list in the right pane.
      - In the warning window indicating that all data on the logical drive will be lost click OK.
  - To create a new Logical Drive, in the Systems and Device tree in the left pane navigate to the desired Array Controller then select Create Array from the Available Tasks list in the right pane.
    - Configure the drives into RAID Array(s) as documented in the Discovery section - Hardware and Environment subsection, by selecting the drive(s) to be included in the first Logical Drive, the RAID Configuration and if appropriate select to utilize a Spare.

      Example Steps: For a RAID 5 Array using all available drives:

      - Select the appropriate Drive Type from the dropdown in the Drive Type section.
      - Select all drives to be included in the Array from the list presented in the Select Physical Drives fort the New Array section then click OK.
      - Select the new Logical Drive from the Systems and Device tree in the left pane then select Create Logical Drive from the Available Tasks list in the right pane.
      - Select RAID5 from the Fault Tolerance section.
      - In the Size section verify the selected size matches the maximum size available.
      - Accept the defaults for Stripe Size, Size and all other options.
      - Click Save.

        - If the Array configuration will utilize a spare physical drive they can be configured by selecting the Logical Drive from the Systems and Device tree in the left pane then select Spare Management from the Available Tasks list in the right pane.
            - Select the drive(s) to be utilized from the list of drives in the Add/Remove Spare Drives panel on the right then click Save.
    - Repeat the process outlined above until all Logical Drives have been created as documented in the Discovery section - Hardware and Environment subsection.
    - Exit the ACU and return to the SmartStart Home page.

- ☐ From the SmartStart Home page select Install from the Media Options section.
- ☐ Select the logical drive that the server will be installed to and click Next.

  Note: If the selected target drive does not meet all HP requirements for installation you will not be allowed to proceed until the discrepancies are corrected.
- ☐ On the Operating System Selection page select and verify the Windows Small Business Server version that matches the SBS product that was purchased for this system or delivered with the system then click Next.
- ☐ Select the appropriate Operating System Media Source and Format then click Next.

  Note: The default is DVD-ROM Media and Standard folder/directory format.
- ☐ Select Boot Partition Size for the primary partition based the specifications in Discovery section – Hardware and Environment subsection and click Next.

  Note: If there is no previously determined and documented requirement for the size select Maximum.
- ☐ On the Product Set Up Information page:
    - For the Computer Name enter the new Server name as documented in the Discovery section - Domain Names subsection.
    - For the Administrator password enter the same password this account uses on the old domain as documented on the User Name, Logon ID and Password Record in the Old Network Documentation section.
    - For the Organization Name enter the Complete Company Name as documented in the Discovery section - Domain Names subsection.
    - For the Owner Name enter the accepted abbreviation or acronym of the Complete Company Name as documented in the Discovery section - Domain Names subsection.
    - Select the appropriate Time Zone.
    - Click Next.
- ☐ On the WBEM/SNMP Configuration page leave the defaults selected and click Next.

  Note: Defaults are: Install SNMP? = Yes, Install WBEM? = No.

  Note: Low level HP events will not be able to communicate with the OS if SNMP is not installed.
- ☐ On the SNMP Configuration page leave the defaults selected and click Next.

  Note: Defaults are: Monitor String = public, Control String = private, Trap Server IP = 127.0.0.1, Allow Trap Server to access management information from this system. = Checked.
- ☐ On the Proliant Support Pack page leave the defaults selected and click Next.

  Note: Defaults are: PSP Installation Mode = Express.
- ☐ On the Installation Information page verify all warnings and if the only warning is regarding the drives being reset to a freshly installed state, click Next.

Note: All other warnings must be reconciled or the installation may fail.

☐ When prompted insert the Small Business Server Installation disc as requested by the Server Deployment application.

☐ When the Installation Wizard presents the License terms page check the box I accept the license terms and then click Next.

☐ SmartStart deployment will prep the partitions and drive, expand files and perform the core OS installation including HP software and management components. The server will be rebooted automatically as needed.

☐ When the First Phase of the installation is complete and the Installation Wizard presents the Continue Installation page select Clean Install then click Next.

☐ Now skip the subsection immediately below and proceed down to the section titled "Server Installation Phase Two".

Server Installation Phase One using the SBS 2011 DVD

☐ Microsoft Small Business Server Reminder! For the proper installation of this product it is assumed and expected that the default selection will be made for everything not specifically noted here including language selections, agreements, licenses, etc.

☐ Read all Microsoft Small Business Server related installation and configuration documentation and verify that this system meets all system requirements before proceeding.

Note: The following checklist is valid only for Microsoft Small business Server 2011 Standard. If a newer version is being installed, take notes where there are discrepancies so that this checklist can be updated.

☐ Remove, disconnect or unplug all USB devices other than the keyboard or mouse before beginning the Small business Server installation. Do not plug them back in until the installation is complete.

☐ Insert the Microsoft Small Business Server installation disc into the DVD drive, reboot or repower the server and boot from the DVD.

☐ On the first page of the Windows Small business Server 2011 Installation Wizard click next to accept the defaults for Language, Time and currency and Keyboard input method.

☐ On the SBS Installation Wizard menu select Install now.

☐ On the license terms page check the box I accept the license terms and then click next.

☐ On the installation selection page click on the Custom (advanced) selection.

☐ On the Where do you want to install Windows? page:

- If third party SCSI or RAID driver are required to see the desired primary hard disk drive click the Load Driver button.
  - Insert the driver disk for the device to be loaded then click Browse.
  - Navigate to the drive and or directory that contain the drivers then click OK.
  - Select the appropriate driver from the list then click Next.
- Select the desired operating system partition as documented in the Discovery section - Hardware and Environment subsection then click Next.

☐ The Install Wizard will prep the partitions and drive, expand files and perform the core OS installation. The server will be rebooted as needed.

☐ When the First Phase of the installation is complete the Install Wizard Continue installation page is presented prompting to Choose a setup mode of Clean Install or Server Migration. Select Clean Install then click Next.

Server Installation Phase Two

- ☐ On the Verify clock and time zone settings page click the Open Date and Time to verify the clock and time zone settings link.
  - On the Date and Time tab verify the correct Date, Time and Time zone.
  - Change each settings as required then click OK to close the Date and Time settings window.
  - On the Verify clock and time zone settings page click Next.
- ☐ On the Server network configuration page select Manually choose the network settings as follows:
  - Enter the Default Gateway and IP Address for the new server as documented in the Discovery section - Domain Names subsection then click Next.
- ☐ On the Get important updates page click the Go online and get the most recent installation updates (recommended) link.

  Note: This process may cause the installation to take several minutes to an hour longer depending on the available internet speed.
- ☐ On the Company Information page enter the Complete Business Name and Address information as documented in the Discovery section – Domain Names subsection and Miscellaneous Items subsection then click Next.
- ☐ On the Personalize your server and your network page enter the new Server name and Internal domain name as documented in the Discovery section - Domain Names subsection then click Next.
- ☐ On the Add a network administrator account page enter the generic administrative account name used for all KPEnterprises clients as follows:
  - For the first name enter KPE
  - For the Last name enter Admin
  - For the Administrator user name enter KPEAdmin
  - For the Administrator password enter the same password this account uses on the old domain as documented on the User Name, Logon ID and Password Record in the Old Network Documentation section.
  - Enter the password again in the Confirm administrator password field then click Next.

  Note: The password cannot contain the first name, last name or user account name.

  Note: The password must be at least 8 characters long and must contain at least three of the following 4 types of characters: A-Z, a-z, 0-9 and a symbol.

  Note: If the old password does not meet these requirements, create a password that does meet these requirements (even if only for temporary use) then document it on the User Name, Logon ID and Password Record in the New Network Documentation section.

  Note: If the password being used is only for temporary use, indicate this on the Password Record.
- ☐ On the That is all the information needed page verify each name before continuing.
  - If all names are in fact correct click Next.
- ☐ The Install Wizard will copy, expand and install files to the drive and reboot as needed.
- ☐ When the Second Phase of the installation is complete the Installation Wizard should present one of two screens.
  - If the Windows Successful installation page is presented, click the Start using the server button.
  - If the Installation finished page is presented prompting, The installation finished, but some non-critical issues were encountered, click the view installation issues button.

- As recommended, review and address all issues before continuing.

Small Business Server Configuration

Note: It is assumed that whenever prompted by the User Access Control (UAC) that Windows needs your permission to continue the request will be acknowledged with Continue.

Note: Now that the operating system installation is complete, as updates, service packs or small software packages, printer drivers, etc. are installed, first copy them to the appropriate folders in c:\!tech\software or c:\!tech\hardware on the new server so that they are readily available to the entire network.

General Tasks

☐ When the Second Phase of the SBS install is completed or at logon the Windows Small Business Server 2011 Standard Console will be open and on the Home page. If it is not, run the program now.

☐ Review and reconcile all alerts indicated in Network Essentials Summary section of the SBS Console Home page.

Note: Do not proceed until all critical issues have been resolved.

Note: Some minor issues may self-resolve after completing the SBS Getting Started Tasks.

☐ Open Device Manager and verify that all hardware has been correctly detected and drivers loaded.

- If there are devices missing that are required for setup such as a modem, NIC, etc. do not proceed until the correct drivers are installed and the devices are recognized.

Note: Do not load any tape device drivers (unless the tape device utilizes a USB interface) if Symantec or Veritas Backup Exec will be the Backup solution as the Symantec / Veritas drives will be loaded during installation of that application.

☐ Enable the Administrator account as follows:

- Open Active Directory Users and Computers from the Administrative Tools menu and navigate to the *domainname*.local\Users container.
- Right-click on the Administrator account and select Reset Password from the menu.
  - On the Reset Password page:
    - Clear the checkbox User must change password at next logon.
    - Check the checkbox to Unlock the user's account.
    - For the New password enter the same password uses for the administrator on the old domain as documented on the User Name, Logon ID and Password Record in the Old Network Documentation section.
    - Enter the password again in the Confirm password field then click OK.

    Note: The password cannot contain the first name, last name or user account name.

    Note: The password must be at least 8 characters long and must contain at least three of the following 4 types of characters: A-Z, a-z, 0-9 and a symbol.

    Note: If the old password does not meet these requirements, create a password that does meet these requirements (even if only for temporary use) then document it on the User Name, Logon ID and Password Record in the New Network Documentation section.

    Note: If the password being used is only for temporary use, indicate this on the Password Record.
  - Click OK on the Activate confirmation pop-up then close the Active Directory Users and Computers window.

Note: If the old password does not meet these requirements, create a temporary administrator password that does meet these requirements then document it on the User Name, Logon ID and Password Record in the New Network Documentation section.

Note: Be certain to note it as the Temporary Administrator password.

- ☐ Log off of the server as KPEAdmin and then log back on as Administrator.
- ☐ Verify that the only network adapter in the server that is enabled is the adapters that has been designated as the primary and active network adapter.
  - Click Start then right click on the Network menu item and select properties from the menu.
  - Select Change Adapter Settings from the list on the left side of the window.

  Note: There should be only one Local Area Connection indicating it has connectivity. If more than one are indicating connectivity a mistake was made during the Test Bench Firewall setup. Reconcile the discrepancy in connections before continuing.

  Note: If no adapters indicate connectivity reconcile the issue before continuing. One adapter was and should have connectivity or the server installation would not have made it to this point.

  - For each Local Area Connection that is not designated as the primary and active connection right click on the device and select Disable from the menu.
  - Close the Network Connections window.
- ☐ Set the screen resolution to 800x600 or 1024x768 or whatever is appropriate for the monitor and for remote access of the system.
- ☐ Set up the !tech directory and share it out as follows:
  - Create the directory !tech in the root of the c:drive.
  - Share the c:\!tech directory as "tech" and set the share permissions to Everyone - Full Control.

  Note: Full details of setting up a share including setting permissions can be found later in this section in the File and Data Storage\Data Shares subsection.

  - Create the following five subfolders in the c:\!tech directory
    - c:\!tech\hardware
    - c:\!tech\software
    - c:\!tech\software\microsoft
    - c:\!tech\migration
    - c:\!tech\sslcertificates
  - Migrate all data compiled during the Discovery from the CD, DVD or USB device into the c:\!tech\migration directory on the new server now.
- ☐ Set System Properties configuration – Advanced System Settings
  - Click Start then right click on the Computer menu item and select Properties from the menu.
  - Select Advanced System Settings from the list on the left side of the window.
  - In the System Properties window select the Advanced tab then click on the Settings button in the Startup and Recovery section.
    - Set Time to display list of Operating Systems to 5 seconds.
    - Verify the Write debug information option is set to Kernel memory dump then click OK.
  - In the System Properties window on the Advanced tab click the settings button in the Performance section.

  - In the Performance Options window select the Advanced tab.
  - Verify the Processor scheduling is set to Background Services.
  - In the System Properties window select the Data Execution Prevention tab.
  - Select the option Turn on DEP for essential Windows programs and services only then click OK.
  - On the System Properties popup indicating that the changes made require you to restart your computer click OK.
  - Click OK to close the System Properties window.
- Restart the server to allow all changes to take effect and log on as the Administrator now.

☐ Configure the little things to make an installation less annoying:

- In Display Settings – Screen Saver Settings turn off On resume, display logon screen.
- In the Customize Start Menu turn off Highlight newly installed programs.

Note: These items will also have to be performed for each user that logs onto the server for the first time.

Windows SBS Console - Getting Started Tasks

Note: As Getting Started Tasks are performed be sure to check them off on that checklist and here to record the progress and for verification that each item was in fact performed.

☐ View installation issues.

☐ Review the Using the Windows SBS Console article.

☐ Run the Connect to the Internet wizard.

- On the Before you begin page click Next.
- On the Detecting the router and configuring your network page:
  - Verify the Router IP Address was correctly detected. If it was not enter the correct IP address for the router.
  - In the Server IP Address field enter the IP address as documented in the Discovery section - Domain Names subsection then click Next.
- Click Finish when the wizard has completed.

☐ Run the Customer feedback options wizard, select I don't want to join the program at this time and then click OK.

☐ Run the Set up your Internet address wizard.

- On the Before you begin page click Next.
- On the Do you want to register a new domain name page select I already have a domain name that I want to use then click Next.
- On the How do you want to manage your domain name page select I want to manage the domain name myself then click Next.
- On the Store your domain name information page enter the FQDN domain name as documented in the Discovery section - Domain Names subsection then click Next.

Note: Do not enter a domain prefix in this field. e.g. remote.

- If a prefix other than the default of remote. is required as documented in the Discovery section - Domain Names subsection click the Advanced Settings link below the Domain name extension field, enter the correct prefix then click OK.

Note: When the Internet Address Manager wizard completes there may be a warning icon to the left of the Internet router feature. This is most likely due to the fact that most business class routers cannot be programmed by Windows. If so, it may be safely ignored as router programming will be performed in a later section of this Checklist.

- Verify that the Remote Web Access site name is the correct and desired name as indicated in the Discovery section - Domain Names subsection.
- If there are any Warnings for any feature, click the View Warning Details link.
- Review all information presented and do not proceed until all items have been reconciled.
- Click Finish to completed the wizard.

☐ Run the Configure a Smart host for Internet e-mail wizard only if a third party email filtering system will be used.

- On the Before you begin page click Next.
- On the Specify settings for outbound Internet mail page select I need to configure a Smart Host server for Internet e-mail.
  - In the Smart Host Server information field enter the server address or name that email will be forwarded to as documented in the Discovery section - Email / Outlook / Exchange subsection.
  - If the Smart Host service provider requires credentials check the box My Internet Service Provider requires authentication.
    - Enter the User name and password as documented in the Discovery section - Email / Outlook / Exchange subsection.
- Click Next and then click Finish when the wizard has completed.

☐ Run the Add a trusted Certificate wizard only if a new or existing trusted certificate will be installed as documented in the Discovery section - Domain Names subsection.

Note: There are two processes outlined below. Typically it will only be required to perform one or the other depending on weather a new certificate will be installed or an existing certificate migrated.

Note: If performing the New Certificate process pay close attention to what steps have been completed as it is a two phase process. Request and Install.

- Open Windows Explorer, navigate to the c:\!tech directory and create a subfolder named SSLCertificates if it does not already exist.

New Certificate Process (The importing an existing Certificate process is below)

- Run the Add a trusted Certificate wizard from the Getting Started Tasks in Windows Console.
  - On the Before you begin page click Next.
  - On the Get Certificate page select I want to buy a certificate from a certificate provider and then click Next.
  - Populate all fields with the correct, verified information from the Discovery section - Domain Names subsection then click Next.

  Note: Be certain that the Issued To: field reflects the exact name remote users will access.

  Example: https://remote.zdtminc.net

  - On the Generate a certificate request page click save to File then navigate to the c:\!tech\sslcertificates directory, accept the default name of SBSCertRequest then click Save.
  - On the Generate a certificate page click Next.

    - On the A request is in progress page select My certificate provider needs more time to process the request then click Next.
    - Click Finish when the wizard has completed.
- Perform the steps required by the Certificate Service Provider to formally request the new certificate.
    - When entering the request be certain to use the administrator@*company.xxx* account for all communications.

  Note: It is beyond the scope of this checklist to detail all the steps required to actually purchase and generate a certificate from any Certificate Service Providers.
- When the certificate or the link to the certificate has been delivered to the administrators e-mail:
    - Log on to the new server as the domain administrator.
    - Log in to the domain administrator email account of the old server using OWA.
    - Open the email from the certificate provider.
        - If the certificate is attached save the attached certificate(s) to the c:\!tech\sslcertificates directory on the new server.
        - If a link to the certificate is provided follow all directions outlined in the email to access the certificate and save the certificate(s) to the c:\!tech\sslcertificates directory on the new server.
        - If the certificates are in a zip file, open the zip file and copy all of the contents to the c:\!tech\sslcertificates directory.
    - Re-run the Add a Trusted Certificate Wizard from the Windows SBS Console - Getting Started Tasks.
    - On the Before you begin page click Next.
    - On the A request is in progress page select I have a certificate from my certificate provider then click Next.
    - On the Import the trusted certificate page click the Browse button, navigate to the c:\!tech\sslcertificates directory, select the newly generated certificate and click Open then click Next.
    - Click Finish when the wizard has completed.

Import an Existing Certificate

- Export all trusted certificates from the old server as follows:
    - Log on to the old server as the administrator.
    - Click Start, click Run, type mmc.exe then press Enter on the keyboard.
    - On the console, click File, and then click Add/Remove Snap-in.
    - On the Add/Remove Snap-in page click Add, choose Certificates from the list and click Add.
    - On the Certificate Snap-in page select Computer account, click Next then click Finish.
    - Close the Add Standalone Snap-in window (If open) and the Add/Remove Snap-in window.
    - Navigate to the Certificates (local computer) – Personal – Certificates container.

      Note: If the certificate that you want to export is not listed, you can search for it as follows:
        - Right-click on the Personal container and select Find Certificates from the menu.

- Right-click the certificate that is issued to your Remote Web Workplace site e.g. remote.*company.xxx*, select All Tasks – Export from the menu.

  Note: There may be multiple certificates with the same name. Refer to the Discovery Section - Domain Names, IP's, DNS and DHCP subsection.

  - Verify that the certificate you are exporting has a valid expiration date and was issued by a trusted authority.

  Note: Do not export any self signed certificates. These will not be usable on the new server.

  - In the Certificate Export Wizard, click Next.
  - Select Yes, export the private key then click Next.
  - If the option is presented to Include all certificates in the certificate path if possible select it.
  - If the option is presented to Export all extended properties select it.
  - Verify that the checkbox is cleared for Delete the private key if the export is successful then click Next.
  - Enter the domain administrators password in the password field then click Next.
    - On the File to Export page click the browse button and navigate to the c:\!tech\sslcertificates directory. (create it now if it does not already exist).
    - In the file name field enter the full public name of the RWW site. e.g. remote.*company.xxx* then click Save.
  - Click Next then Finish to allow the wizard to complete.
- Close all open windows.

- Import the trusted certificate to the new server as follows:
  - Log on to the new server as the administrator.
  - Open Windows Explorer and copy the exported certificate .pfx file from \\oldserver\tech\sslcertificates directory on the old server to the new server c:\!tech\sslcertificates directory.
  - Click Start, type mmc.exe then press Enter on the keyboard.
  - On the console, click File, and then click Add/Remove Snap-in.
  - On the Add or Remove Snap-ins page select Certificates from the list on the left then click Add.
  - On the Certificate Snap-in page select Computer Account, click Next then click Finish.
  - Close the Add or Remove Snap-ins window.
  - Navigate to the Certificates (local computer) – Personal – Certificates container.
  - Right-click on the Certificates container and select All Tasks – Import from the menu.
    - On the Certificate Import Wizard Welcome page click Next.
    - Click Browse and in the Browse window click the dropdown box to the right of the filename field. Select Personal Information Exchange (*.pfx;*.p12) from the list.
    - Navigate to the c:\!tech\sslcertificates directory and select the newly exported certificate .pfx file then click Open.
    - On the Certificate Import Wizard click Next, enter the password as used in the export procedure above.

        - Check the box to Mark this key as exportable and Include all extended properties are selected then click Next.
        - Select Place all certificates in the following store and verify that the Personal Certificate store is selected then click Next.
        - Click Finish to allow the wizard to complete.
    - Close all open windows.
  - Run the Add a trusted Certificate wizard from the Getting Started Tasks in Windows Console.
    - On the Before you begin page click Next.
    - On the Get Certificate page select I want to use a certificate that is already installed on the server, and then click Next.
    - On the Choose an installed certificate page select the newly imported certificate from the list then click Next.
    - Click Finish when the wizard has completed.

☐ Configure Server Backup only if the Windows Backup program will be implemented as documented in the Discovery section and the Planning section.

  - Physically connect any external devices designated as backup destinations and verify their driver correctly load and the device is recognized by the operating system before continuing.
  - Run the Configure Server backup wizard and on the Specify the backup destination page check the box to Show all valid internal and external backup destinations.
  - Select the Disk Drive that will be used as the backup destination and click Next.
  - On the Label the destination drives page enter the disk Label as outlined in the Discovery section then click Next.

    If no labeling scheme currently exists use the following:

        Internal Drives: Internal Backup 1 (2, 3, etc.)

        External Drives: External Backup 1 (2, 3, etc.)

        * Treat removable and swappable drives as external.

  - On the Select the drive to backup page select any additional drives or locations as documented in the Discovery section then click Next.
  - On the Specify the backup schedule page configure the frequency and times as documented in the discovery section then click Next.
  - On the Confirm backup details page verify all information is correct, click Configure then on the Format warning pop-up click Yes.
    - Click Finish when the wizard has completed.

☐ Open the link How can users access computers on the network and read the information presented.

☐ Do not run the Add a new user account wizard. Users will be added in mass later in this section. Also User Roles have not been properly configured yet.

☐ Run the Connect computers to your network wizard.

  - Read the information presented on the welcome page then click Next.
  - On the Run the connect computer program select Copy the program to portable media.
  - On the Specify a location page click Browse and navigate to the C:\Windows\sysvol\sysvol*domainname*.local\SCRIPTS directory, click Make New Folder and enter the folder name Connect then click OK.

   - On the Specify a location page click Next and click Finish when the wizard has completed.
- ☐ Open the link How can I add a shared printer to the network and read the information presented.

Other Tasks

- ☐ Configure VPN (Routing and Remote Access) only if it is designated as being required as documented in the Discovery section - Small Business Server and Related subsection.
   - Run Windows SBS 2011 Console and select Network from the Navigation bar then select the Connectivity tab.
   - Run the Configure a virtual private network wizard from the Tasks list on the right.
      - Select Allow users to connect to the server by using a VPN.

   Note: When the Virtual Private Networking wizard completes there may be a warning icon to the left of the Internet router feature. This is most likely due to the fact that most business class routers cannot be programmed by Windows. If so, it may be safely ignored as router programming will be performed in a later section of this Checklist.

   - If there are any Warnings for any feature, click the View Warning Details link.
   - Review all information presented and do not proceed until all items have been reconciled.
   - Click Finish to completed the wizard.
- ☐ Configure the Fax Server only if it is designated as being required as documented in the Discovery section - Small Business Server and Related subsection.

   Note: If the Fax device will not be installed until later or is being moved from the old server do not attempt to configure the Fax Server now. Skip this subsection. There will be another opportunity to configure the Fax Server during the Pre-Migration.

   - Run Windows SBS 2011 Console and select Network from the Navigation bar then select the Devices tab.
   - Run the Start Fax Service wizard from the Tasks list on the right.
      - When prompted Do you want to install the Fax service click Yes.
      - When prompted that the Fax Service has been started successfully click OK.
   - In the Start the Fax services window, when prompted that The Fax service is started, but it is currently not configured click Yes.

      Note: If Routing to a printer (or to users who have not yet been created) is required the wizard will have to be run again once a printer is installed or once users have been added to the domain. There is a later subsection that covers this scenario.

      - On the first page of the Configure Fax Service wizard enter the fax cover page information as documented in the Discovery section – Miscellaneous Items subsection then click Next.
      - On the Configure Fax Service wizard Type the fax header text page enter the fax header text as documented in the Discovery section – Miscellaneous Items subsection then click Next.
      - On all remaining Configure Fax Service wizard pages refer to the Discovery section - Small Business Server and Related subsection for all configuration information.
      - Click Next only after each page has been verified and on the last page click Configure Fax.
      - When the wizard has completed click Finish.
   - Set up and test the Fax client on the server as follows:

      Note: If there is no analog line available to test the fax it will have to be tested when the server is on site.

- Run the Windows Fax and Scan application from the Start All Programs menu and click the New Fax button on the navigation bars.
- On the Fax Setup wizard Choose a fax modem or server page select Connect to a fax modem.
- On the Choose a modem name page accept the default name of Fax Modem then click Next.
- On the Choose how to receive faxes page select Answer automatically (recommended).
- The Fax Setup wizard will complete and the New Fax window will be presented.
- Create a test fax requesting a reply via Fax and send it out.
- Verify both inbound and outbound faxing as well as all routing options configured are working.
- Close the Windows Fax and Scan application.

☐ Configure the Server Network Reports that are required as documented in the Discovery section - Small Business Server and Related subsection.

- Run Windows SBS 2011 Console and select Reports from the Navigation bar.
- Modify existing reports or create new reports as required.

☐ If the SBS Server is required to synchronize time with a specific source as documented in the Discovery section – Small Business Server and Related subsection, refer to the Resources section of this binder for the appropriate whitepaper: How to configure an authoritative time server in windows server 2003 (Most of this document is also relevant to SBS 2011)

☐ Verify all activated SBS Web site services before continuing. If one is found to be broken, valuable time will be saved if it is discovered now.

Note: You can test all the public facing sites by setting up a hosts file on a workstation. You will need to set up at least two names. First, the FQDN the server certificate was configured with earlier (e.g. remote.*company.xxx*) and second www.*company*.xxx . Both should point to the new servers IP address. This will work from either side of the Test Bench Firewall with two exceptions. The http://companyweb will only work on the inside and VPN will only work from outside unless VPN was specifically configured to use an alternate IP subnet range from the default.

SBS Web Site	Address	
Companyweb	http://companyweb	From the Server and local network only
RWW	https://*ServerFQDN*	Example: https://remote.zdtminc.net
SharePoint	https://*ServerFQDN*:987	
RDP	*ServerFQDN*	
OWA	https://*ServerFQDN*/owa	
Public Website	http://www.*ServerFQDN*	Example: http://www.zdtminc.net
VPN	*ServerFQDN*	

☐ Configure the DHCP Scope as documented in the Discovery section - Domain Names, IP's, DNS and DHCP subsection as follows:

- Run the DHCP applet and navigate to IPv4 - Scope [*xxx.xxx.xxx*.0]
    - Right click on the Scope and select Properties form the menu.
    - On the General tab modify the existing scope as required then click OK to close the Scope.
- Select the Address Pool container below the Scope and create or delete exclusions as required.

- Select the Scope Options container below the Scope, right-click on the DNS Servers scope option in the middle pane and select Properties from the Menu.
  - Add the ISP's primary DNS as the second DNS server being passed out to clients. The ISP's DNS servers are documented in the Discovery section - Domain Names, IP's, DNS and DHCP subsection.
- Close all open windows.

☐ Open the HP System Management Home Page, Logon and verify all systems are functioning OK.

Note: The HP System Management Home Page logon require the full *domain*\administrator name.

☐ Briefly review the Setup, System and Application event logs for errors. Address all issues found.

Service Pack and Critical Update Installation

☐ Verify that there is no reason the Server should NOT be on the latest service pack or be fully updated as documented in the Discovery section – Service Pack and Critical Update Installation subsection.

Note: All updates and service packs are most readily available from the Microsoft.com/download site.

☐ Install the Latest applicable Server 2011 Service Pack.

☐ Install the Latest applicable Exchange Server Service Pack.

☐ Install the Latest applicable SharePoint Service Pack.

☐ Install the Latest applicable SBS 2011 Server Service Pack.

☐ Install the latest applicable Internet Explorer version.

☐ Open Control Panel System and Security Windows Update and check for additional Microsoft updates.

- Apply all critical and required updates. Reboot as required.
- Repeat this Update process until there are no more updates available.

☐ Re-Verify all activated SBS Web site services before continuing. If one is found to be broken, valuable time will be saved if it is discovered now.

SBS Web Site	Address	
Companyweb	http://companyweb	From the Server and local network only
RWW	https://*ServerFQDN*	Example: https://remote.zdtminc.net
SharePoint	https://*ServerFQDN*:987	
RDP	*ServerFQDN*	
OWA	https://*ServerFQDN*/owa	
Public Website	http://www.*ServerFQDN*	Example: http://www.zdtminc.net
VPN	*ServerFQDN*	

General Settings and Configuration

☐ If software mirroring for the C: drive will be will implemented as documented in the Discovery section - Hardware and Environment subsection, establish the mirror now as follows:

- Run Server Manager and navigate to Storage – Disk Manager.
- Right-click on the Primary Partition and select Add Mirror from the menu.
- Select the appropriate drive from the list and click Add Mirror.

- o If Disk Management presents a pop-up warning regarding conversion of the selected disks from basic to dynamic, read the information presented and if the correct drives have been selected for the mirror click Yes.

Note: Do not reboot or shutdown the server until the mirror is reported as Healthy in disk manger.

☐ If this server is a Managed services machine install the Continuum server agent for the company this system is being built for as follows:

- o Open internet Explorer and surf to https://control.itsupport247.net
- o Add the site itsupport247.net to the trusted site list as follows:
  - o Select Internet Options from the Tools menu.
  - o Select the Security tab, highlight the trusted Sites zone then click the Sites button.
  - o Clear the checkbox Require server verification (https:) for all sites in this zone.
  - o In the Add this website to the zone filed enter *.itsupport247.net then click Add.
  - o Click Close to close the Trusted sites list, close the Internet option window then close Internet Explorer.
- o Open internet Explorer and surf to https://control.itsupport247.net and log into the site with the appropriate credentials.
  - o Select the Configuration Tab from the top most menu then select Site Management from the Base Configuration menu.
  - o Select the Download Setups icon to the right of the clients Site Name.
- o In the Download setups window select the Server Agents tab.
- o If the desired setup package is available click the Download button for the appropriate agent then select Run from the download window.

  Note: If the agent Download is not currently available click on the Request Setup button for the appropriate agent and then wait for the agent package to be processed and made available.
- o When the agent finishes downloading and begins running select all defaults if prompted.
- o Monitor the progress of the installation and verify the new server properly checks in with the Continuum's Control Portal and that the Continuum LogMeIn agent loads and is functional.
- o After the server has successfully checked in with the Continuum Control Panel update the site notes to reflect its current status and disposition as follows:
  - o In the Continuum Control Panel select the Quick Access tab from the tab set in the upper right corner of the window then click on the Notes icon to the left of the new site (server).
  - o Select the Device Notes tab, select the Add Note tab then select the new server from the Machine Name dropdown list.
  - o Enter the following notes (edit as needed):

    Please note this is a new server for this site. It is under construction.

    Please disregard all alerts for this server until (*migration complete date*) as it may be off line or rebooted at any time.

    Thank you.
  - o Click Submit to complete the Note entry, click OK on the Success pop-up, close the Note window then close the Continuum Control Panel.

☐ In Active Directory Users and Computers set the Terminal Services account preferences for the Administrator and the KPEAdmin users as follows:

- Open Active Directory Users and Computers and navigate to the *domain*.local Users folder.
- Right click on the Administrator account and select properties from the menu.
  - On the Environment tab, clear the checkboxes for:
    - Connect client drives at logon
    - Connect client printers at logon
    - Default to main client printer
  - Close the Administrator Properties window.
- In Active Directory Users and Computers navigate to the *domain*.local MyBusiness Users SBSUsers folder.
- Right click on the KPEAdmin account and select properties from the menu.
  - On the Environment tab, clear the checkboxes for:
    - Connect client drives at logon
    - Connect client printers at logon
    - Default to main client printer
  - Close the KPEAdmin Properties window.

☐ Hide the KPEAdmin account from the Global Address list in Exchange as follows:

- Open Exchange Management Console and navigate to the Microsoft Exchange On-Premises - Recipient Configuration - Mailbox container.
- Right click on the KPEAdmin user and select Properties from the menu.
- On the General tab check the box Hide from Exchange address list.
- Click OK to close the KPEAdmin users properties then close the Exchange Management Console.

☐ Download and then install each of the following applications from the manufacturers site:

Note: If required, save the download to the appropriate subdirectory in the c:\!tech\software directory.

- Adobe Acrobat Reader.
- Microsoft Word and Excel viewers.
- Microsoft Office Compatibility Pack for Word, Excel, and PowerPoint 2007 File Formats.

☐ Download the IfMember.exe Resource Kit Web Package from the Microsoft.com/downloads site to the c:\!tech\software\microsoft directory.

- Run the executable and install the files to the c:\windows\sysvol\sysvol*domainname*.local\scripts directory.

☐ Prepare the User State Migration Tool 3.x (USMT) for use by x86 and x64 Windows XP workstations as follows:

Note: If there are no Windows XP machines to be migrated the USMT 3.x download and installation subsection can be skipped as USMT will work for Windows Vista and newer OS's.

Note: If there are no Windows XP 64-bit workstations to be migrated the USMT 3.x 64-bit version does not need to be downloaded or installed.

Note: USMT 3.x will not work on Windows 7 machines. You must use USMT 4.x on Windows 7 machines. The next subsections covers the download and installation of USMT 4.x.

- Open Windows Explorer and navigate to the c:\!tech directory.

- Create a subdirectory called usmt. i.e. c:\!tech\usmt
- Open the c:\!tech\usmt directory and create two directories named usmt3 and usmt4.
- Open the c:\!tech\usmt\usmt3 directory and create two directories named x86 and amd64.

  Note: There is no need to create x86 and amd64 directories in the usmt4 subdirectory.
- The final structure should be as follows

  C:\!tech\usmt\usmt3\x86

  C:\!tech\usmt\usmt3\amd64

  C:\!tech\usmt\usmt4

- Download both the 32-bit and 64-bit versions of the User State Migration Tool 3.x from Microsoft.com/downloads.com to the c:\!tech\softwate\microsoft directory on the new server.

  Note: Do not attempt to run either installation program on the new or old server. They will not install correctly.
- Run the 32-bit installation on any 32 bit Windows XP or Vista workstation to expand the files.
  - After installation copy the entire contents of the c:\program files\usmt301 directory of the workstation to the new server *servername*\tech\usmt\usmt3\x86 directory.
- Run the 64-bit installation on any 64 bit Windows XP or Vista workstation to expand the files.
  - After installation copy the entire contents of the c:\program files\usmt301 directory of the workstation to the new server *servername*\tech\usmt\usmt3\amd64 directory.

  Note: Do not copy the usmt301 directories. Only the contents.

☐ Prepare the User State Migration Tool 4.x (USMT) for use by x86 and x64 Windows Vista and Windows 7 workstations as follows:

Note: USMT 4.x or higher is required for proper workstation profile migration on Windows 7 and will also work for Windows Vista.

Note: USMT 4.x will not work on Windows XP machines for restoring the System State back to an XP machine. It is designed only to move the State to a newer OS such as Vista or Windows 7. You must use USMT 3.x on Windows XP machines. The previous subsections covers the download and installation of the USMT 3.x.

Note: It is not required to download or install any Service Pack for the AIK. There are no required tools in the Service Pack.

Note: The only reason for installing the AIK is to gain access to and copy the USMT folder. An alternative to installing the AIK on the new Server is to select any machine that meets the AIK system requirements. The machine does not need to be connected to either of the new or old domain and can be a laptop or virtual machine.

- Download the Windows Automated Installation Kit (AIK) for Windows 7 from the Microsoft.com/downloads site and burn the ISO to DVD.
- Insert the DVD in to the new server DVD drive and run StartCD.exe when prompted by AutoPlay or browse to the root of the DVD and run StartCD.exe from there.
  - When the Welcome to Windows Automated Installation Kit window is presented select Windows AIK Setup from the menu on the left.
  - When the Welcome to Windows Automated Installation Kit Setup Wizard is presented click Next.
  - On the License Terms page select I agree then click Next.
  - On the Select Installation Folder page accept the defaults and click Next.

- On the Confirm Installation page click Next.
- When the installation completes close all open windows.

- Open Windows Explorer and navigate to C:\Program Files\Windows AIK\Tools\usmt folder and copy the x86 and amd64 folders to the c:\!tech\usmt\usmt4 subdirectory.
- Uninstall the AIK by navigating to Control Panel, Programs, Uninstall a program, and selecting the Windows Automated Installation Kit from the list.
  - Right click on the name and select Uninstall form the menu.
  - On the uninstall Warning popup click Continue.
  - On the Programs and Features window prompting Are you sure click Yes.
  - When the uninstallation wizard completes close all open windows.

☐ Update USMT4.0 for use with Office 2010

- Open Internet Explorer and enter the following link: http://support.microsoft.com/kb/2023591
- In the upper left hand corner of the site click the link to View and request hotfix downloads.
  - On the Terms and Conditions page click I Accept.
  - On the Hotfix Request page in the Step 1 section click on the link above the Product list that says Show hotfixes for all platforms and languages.
  - Check the box to select both the x86 and x64 products.
  - In the Step 2 section enter the email address for the domain administrator of the client network and confirm it in the second field.
  - Enter the security characters then click Request hotfix.
- Log in to the Administrators email account via OWA and retrieve the Hotfix download link you requested email from Microsoft.
  - In the email click each of the Location links for the requested hotfixes and save them both to the c:\!tech\software\microsoft directory.
- Open Windows Explorer and navigate to the c:\!tech\software\microsoft directory then run each of the newly downloaded hotfix .zip files and extract the .cab content files into the c:\!tech\software\microsoft directory.
- Open the x86 .cab file, select all files in the cab and copy them to the c:\!tech\usmt\usmt4\x86 directory.
  - When prompted by the Copy File wizard check the box Do this for the next *x* conflicts then click Copy and Replace.
- Open the x64 .cab file, select all files in the cab and copy them to the c:\!tech\usmt\usmt4\amd64 directory.
  - When prompted by the Copy File wizard check the box Do this for the next *x* conflicts then click Copy and Replace.

☐ Restart the server to have a clean boot before continuing with additional software Installations.

☐ Briefly review the Setup, System and Application event logs for errors. Address all issues found before continuing.

Hardware and Environment

UPS Power Management Configuration

Note: If a new UPS was not purchased with this system and the UPS that this server is currently plugged into is not the UPS that will remain with this server, skip this subsection.

Note: Do not install any manufacturer supplied UPS management software unless specifically required for this system as documented in the Discovery section – Hardware and Environment subsection.

☐ Plug the data cable for the UPS into the UPS then into the Server. The device should be automatically recognized and drivers loaded.

Note: Only install UPS device drivers if the device is not automatically recognized by the operating system and they are certified to be compatible with SBS 2011.

☐ Configure the Power Options as follows:

- Open the Control panel, System and Security, Power options applet.
- On the Select a power plan page select High performance then click the change plan settings link for the High performance plan.
- On the Change settings for the plan page click the Change advanced power settings link.
- In the Power Options window on the Advanced settings tab select High performance from the dropdown list.
- Navigate to and expand the Battery settings.
- Expand the Low battery level setting and verify that the On Battery (%) setting is 25%.
- Expand the Critical battery level setting and verify that the On Battery (%) setting is 10%.
- Expand the Low battery notification setting and verify that the On Battery setting is On.
- Expand the Critical battery action, select the On Battery setting and change it to Shut down.
- Expand the Low battery action, select the On Battery setting and change it to Shut down.
- Click Apply then close all open windows.

☐ Test the UPS as follows:

Note: Do not perform this test remotely. It must be performed while standing at the console.

- Close all running applications.
- Pull the AC plug for the UPS out of the wall.
- Watch the computer screen for a notification about a low battery level.
- Monitor the server an UPS until the battery reaches the 25% Low Battery threshold and initiates a server shutdown.

Note: If the UPS / Battery status icon in the system tray does not update with the current power source and other status information it means the UPS data cable is not plugged in or not recognized by the system. Correct any issues and do not proceed until the status icon correctly reflects the system state.

- After shutdown repower the server, log in as the administrator and verify that the system did shut down clean. One major indicator is the absence of the Unexpected Shutdown prompt at logon.
- If the UPS does not have sufficient battery remaining at the 25% level to keep the server up long enough for a clean shut down, adjust the Low and Critical battery levels up as required.

Premium Content Installation

Microsoft SQL Server – SQL Server 2008 R2 Standard

- ☐ SQL Setup Reminder! For the proper installation of this product it is assumed and expected that the default selection will be made for everything not specifically noted here.

Warning!: Microsoft has very specific requirements for SQL servers and SQL instances on Small Business Server. Failure to read and understand the documentation available for SQL server installation on a SBS 2011 server or failure to follow the procedure outlined below exactly may result in irreparable damage to the SBS 2011 server.

Warning!: Microsoft officially does not recommend installing SQL Server 2008 R2 on a domain controller however it is widely supported.. The Windows Small Business Server 2011 Premium Add-On package contains a full version of Windows Server 2008 Standard intended for deployment of additional servers in the Small Business Server environment including SQL Server.

Note: The following checklist is valid only for Microsoft SQL Server 2008 R2 Standard 64-bit. If a newer version is being installed, take notes where there are discrepancies so this checklist can be updated.

Note: If any other SQL version than SQL 2008 R2 will be installed this checklist may not be accurate. Any discrepancies must be resolved by the project manager before completing the installation.

Note: If specific Account Names for SQL Services will be required as detailed in the Discovery section - Premium Content subsection they will need to be created in Active Directory first. If there are specific Account Names required skip to the Active Directory / Group Policies section directly below to create all accounts required. Return to this section when that section is complete.

- ☐ Read all Microsoft SQL Server 2008 R2 related installation and configuration documentation and verify that this system meets all system requirements before proceeding.
- ☐ Log on to the new Small Business Server as administrator and run setup.exe from the SBS 2011 Premium Add-On DVD to install SQL Server 2008 R2.
  - On the SQL Server Installation Center page select Installation from the menu on the left then select New installation or add features to an existing installation from the list of actions.
  - On the Setup Support Rules page, if any operations are indicated to have Failed or have issued Warnings, click the Show details button.
    - Reconcile all Errors and Warnings before attempting to continue.
    - Click OK to continue.
  - On the Setup Support Files page click Install.
  - Once again, On the Setup Support Rules page, if any operations are indicated to have Failed or have issued Warnings, click the Show details button.
    - Reconcile all Errors and Warnings before attempting to continue.
    - Click Next to continue.
  - On the Installation Type page accept the default of New Installation or add shared features and click Next.
  - On the Product Key page select Enter the product key, enter the correct product key for the purchased product then click Next.
  - On the License Terms page check only the box I accept the license terms then click Next.
  - On the Setup Role page select SQL Server Feature Installation then click Next.
  - On the Feature Selection page select all of the following Features:
    - Database Engine Services and all sub components.
    - Client Tools Connectivity
    - SQL Server Books Online

- Management Tools - Complete

Note: Management Tools – Complete will be greyed out and can only be installed by method of upgrade if SQL Server 2008 R2 is being installed on a Small Business Server 2011 server or any server which has SQL Express previously installed.
The steps to perform the shared feature upgrade and Management Tools –Complete Install are detailed below.

- Select all other features that are required for the installation as documented in the Discovery section - Premium Content subsection. e.g. Reporting Services, Analysis Services, or Integration Services.
- Click Next.

- On the Installation Rules page, if any operations are indicated to have Failed or have issued Warnings, click the Show details button.
  - Reconcile all Errors and Warnings before attempting to continue.
  - Click Next.
- On the Instance Configuration page select Default instance unless another Instance Name is specifically documented in the Discovery section - Premium Content subsection then click Next.

Note: Do not select any existing Installed instances.

- On the Disk Space Requirements page review the disk space summary and if there are no issues click Next.
- On the Server Configuration page enter the Account Names and Passwords for each Service as follows:
  - For all Account Names and Passwords documented in the Discovery section - Premium Content subsection enter those credentials for the corresponding Service.
  - For each Service that is not documented select the drop down arrow to the right of the Account Name and select NT AUTHORITY\SYSTEM.

  Note: All Services must have an Account Name or the Setup will not continue.

  - Click Next.
- On the Database Engine Configuration page Account Provisioning tab select Mixed Mode unless Windows Mode is specified in the Discovery section - Premium Content subsection.
  - If Mixed mode is selected:
    - Enter the SA password as: sqlsa20xx! (all lower case – replace the x with the current year), unless a specific SA password has been documented in the Discovery section - Premium Content subsection.
    - If a new SA password is created document the new SA password on the User Name, Logon ID and Password Record in the New Network Documentation section.
  - In the Specify SQL Server administrators section of the Account Provisioning tab enter all SQL Server administrator account names as follows:
    - If specific SQL Server administrator account names are indicated in the Discovery section - Premium Content subsection click the Add button at the bottom of the section and enter each SQL Server administrator account name to be added.
    - If no specific SQL Server administrator account names are indicated in the Discovery section - Premium Content subsection click the Add Current User button

    Note: It is assumed this Setup is being run as the domain administrator.

  - Click Next.

- If Analysis Services was selected for installation, on the Analysis Services Configuration page Account Provisioning tab enter all Analysis Services administrator account names as follows:
  - If specific Analysis Services administrator account names are indicated in the Discovery section - Premium Content subsection click the Add button at the bottom of the section and enter each Analysis Services administrator account name to be added.
  - If no specific Analysis Services administrator account names are indicated in the Discovery section - Premium Content subsection click the Add Current User button

  Note: It is assumed this Setup is being run as the domain administrator.

  - Click Next.
- If Reporting Services was selected for installation, on the Reporting Services Configuration page accept the default of Install the native mode default configuration then click Next.
- On the Error Reporting page accept the default then click Next.
- On the Installation Configuration Rules page, if any operations are indicated to have Failed or have issued Warnings, click the Show details button.
  - Reconcile all Errors and Warnings before attempting to continue.
  - Click Next.
- On the Ready to Install page review the entire summary. Reconcile all discrepancies before attempting to continue. Click Install to continue.
- When Setup has finished the Complete page will present directions to the Summary log, information about the Setup and Supplemental Information. Review all presented information and then click Close.

☐ Run the SQL Server Installation Center application to perform an Edition Upgrade to the SQL shared features installed for SQL Express.

Note: The Edition Upgrade steps are only required if SQL Server 2008 R2 was installed on the Small Business Server 2011 server. If this is not the case skip to the Install the latest applicable SQL Server Service Packs steps below.

- On the SQL Server Installation Center page select Maintenance from the menu on the left then select Edition Upgrade from the list of actions.
- On the Setup Support Rules page review the details for any Status Errors or Warnings. Reconcile all Errors and warnings before attempting to continue. Click OK to continue.

Note: For each subsequent Setup Support Rules page encountered, perform the same function of reviewing the details for any Status Errors or Warnings. Reconcile all Errors and warnings before attempting to continue then click the appropriate button to continue.

- On the Product Key page enter the appropriate product key then click Next.
- On the License Terms page check the box I accept the license terms then click Next.
- On the Select Instance page click the dropdown box to the right of the Specify the instance of SQL Server field and select <<Upgrade shared features only>> then click Next.
- On the Edition Upgrade Rules page, if any operations are indicated to have Failed or have issued Warnings, click the Show details button.
  - Reconcile all Errors and Warnings before attempting to continue.
  - Click Next.
- On the Ready to Upgrade edition page review the entire summary. Reconcile all discrepancies before attempting to continue. Click Upgrade to continue.

- When Upgrade has finished the Complete page will present directions to the Summary log and information about the Setup. Review all presented information and then click Close.

☐ Run the SQL Server Installation Center application to install the Management Tools – Complete feature.

Note: The Management Tools steps are only required if SQL Server 2008 R2 was installed on the Small Business Server 2011 server. If this is not the case skip to the Install the latest applicable SQL Server Service Packs steps below.

- On the SQL Server Installation Center page select Installation from the menu on the left then select New installation or add features to an existing installation from the list of actions.
- On the Setup Support Rules page, if any operations are indicated to have Failed or have issued Warnings, click the Show details button.
  - Reconcile all Errors and Warnings before attempting to continue.
  - Click Next.

Note: For each subsequent Setup Support Rules page encountered, perform the same function of reviewing the details for any Status Errors or Warnings. Reconcile all Errors and warnings before attempting to continue then click the appropriate button to continue.

- On the Installation Type page accept the default of New Installation or add shared features and click Next.
- On the Product Key page accept the default entered product key and click Next.
- On the License Terms page check the box I accept the license terms then click Next.
- On the Setup Role page select SQL Server Feature Installation then click Next.
- On the Feature Selection page check only the box Management Tools – Complete then click Next.
- On the Installation Rules page, if any operations are indicated to have Failed or have issued Warnings, click the Show details button.
  - Reconcile all Errors and Warnings before attempting to continue.
  - Click Next.
- On the Disk Space Requirements page review the disk space summary and if there are no issues click Next.
- On the Error Reporting page accept the default then click Next.
- On the Installation Configuration Rules page review the details for any Status Errors or Warnings. Reconcile all Errors and warnings before attempting to continue. Click Next to continue.
- On the Ready to Install page review the entire summary. Reconcile all discrepancies before attempting to continue. Click Install to continue.
- When Setup has finished the Complete page will present directions to the Summary log, information about the Setup and Supplemental Information. Review all presented information and then click Close.

☐ Install the latest applicable SQL Server Service Packs unless there is a reason not to do so documented in the Discovery section – Service Pack and Critical Updates.

- SQL Server 2008 R2 SP1 (if released) can be found on the Microsoft.com/download site.

Active Directory / Group Policies

User Roles

☐ Run Windows SBS 2011 Console and on the navigation bar select Users and Groups then select the User Roles tab.

- Right-click on the Standard User role and select Edit user role properties.
  - Select E-mail from the navigation pane on the left then clear the checkbox Enforce the mailbox quotas.

  Note: Any required mailbox quotas will be managed system wide in the Exchange Management Console.

  - Select Folders from the navigation pane on the left.
  - If no Shared folder quota will be enforced clear the checkbox to Enforce shared folder quota, otherwise configure the Enforce shared folder quota as documented in the Discovery section - File and Data Storage subsection.
  - If no Folder redirection will be enabled clear the checkbox for Enable folder redirection to server, otherwise configure the Enable folder redirection to the server as documented in the Discovery section - File and Data Storage subsection.
  - Review and if necessary modify other Standard User role settings based on:
    - The information generated during the planning of the migration.
    - The desired settings based on the information collected in the Discovery.
  - When all settings have been configured click Apply then click Yes on the Apply user roles changes warning.
  - Click OK to acknowledge the user changes have been applied then close the Standard User Properties window.

Note: For all settings not specifically detailed here always leave settings as they are unless it has been specifically determined that management of these settings is best attained using User Roles.

Password Policy - Account Lockout Policy

Note: The Password Policy and the Account Lockout Policy are both configured and active by default in SBS 2011. Also, the Password Policy is integrated into the default domain policy and cannot simply be disabled. All Policy settings will have to be turned off to disable it.

Note: Regardless of the desired Password Policy for the new domain all Password (not Account Lockout) settings will be disabled until after the migration as the migration relies heavily on all users having a known password.

☐ Run the Group Policy Management application from the Administrative Tools group.

- Navigate to the Domains*domainname*.local\Group Policy Objects\Default Domain Policy, right-click on the object and select Edit from the menu.
- Navigate to Computer Configuration\Policies\Windows Settings\Security Settings\Account Policies/Password Policy.
- Disable each settings by clearing the checkbox to Define this policy setting on the Security Policy Setting tab of each policy.

☐ If the Account Lockout Policy is to be defined for this domain as documented in the Discovery section– Active Directory / Group Policy subsection proceed as follows:

- In the Default Domain Policy navigate to the Computer Configuration\Policies\Windows Settings\Security Settings\Account Policies/Account Lockout Policy

- Configure each Account Lockout Policy as documented in the Discovery section– Active Directory / Group Policy subsection by right clicking on the policy and selecting Properties from the menu.
  - Disable any settings not specifically designated to be configure as documented in the Discovery section by clearing the checkbox to Define this policy setting on the Security Policy Setting tab of each policy.

☐ Close the Group Policy Management Editor then close the Group Policy Manager.

Users

☐ Re-Set the Administrator account password to match the old server as follows:

- Open Active Directory Users and Computers from the Administrative Tools menu and navigate to the *domainname*.local\Users container.
- Right-click on the Administrator account and select Reset Password from the menu.
  - On the Reset Password page:
    - Clear the checkbox User must change password at next logon.
    - Verify the checkbox to Unlock the user's account is cleared.
    - In the New password field enter the same password uses for the administrator on the old domain as documented on the User Name, Logon ID and Password Record in the Old Network Documentation section.
    - Enter the password again in the Confirm password field then click OK.
  - Click OK on the Activate confirmation pop-up then close the Active Directory Users and Computers window.

☐ Record the Default User Password on the User Name, Logon ID and Password Record in the New Network Documentation section. It should follow the convention: *company acronym Year*! e.g. zdtm2011!

☐ Run Windows SBS 2011 Console and on the navigation bar select Users and Groups then select the User tab.

☐ Run the Add multiple user accounts wizard from the User Tasks list.

- Click the Add button on the bottom of the Add Multiple New User Account page.
- When adding user accounts, cut and paste the names from the electronic list returned from the Client Technical Contact. Avoid typing them in by hand. It will lead to errors.

Note: The user list should be found in the c:\!tech\migration directory on the new server.

- Follow the "User naming" convention as documented in the Discovery section– Active Directory / Group Policy subsection.
- Be certain to set the password for each account to previously recorded default user password.
- When all user accounts have been entered click Add user accounts and when all accounts have been created click Finish.

☐ Record the Default Local Administrator password that will be used during workstation migration on the User Name, Logon ID and Password Record in the New Network Documentation section. It should follow the convention: *IT Management Company acronym Year*! e.g. kpe2011!

Distribution and Security Groups

☐ Run Windows SBS 2011 Console and on the navigation bar select Users and Groups then select the Groups tab.

☐ Run the Add a new group wizard from the User Tasks list.

- Enter the Group Name, Description, select the group type and enable e-mail for the group as documented in the Discovery section– Active Directory / Group Policy subsection.

Note: Do not enable any group to receive e-mails from outside the company unless it is specifically documented in the Discovery section to do so.

Note: Do not enable Archive of E-mail messages sent to any group unless it is specifically documented in the Discovery section to do so.

- Add Users and Groups to the new Security Group as documented in the Discovery section– Active Directory / Group Policy subsection.
- Repeat this process for each Security and Distribution Group as documented in the Discovery section– Active Directory / Group Policy subsection.

Group Policies

☐ Run the Group Policy Manager from the Administrative Tools group and create the IT Management policy.

- Navigate to the Domains*domainname*.local\Group Policy Objects container, right-click on the container and select New from the menu.
- Enter the New GPO name as "*ManagementCompany* IT Management Policy" then click OK. e.g. KPEnterprises IT Management Policy.
- Link the new group policy to the *domainname*.local domain as follows:
    - Right click on the *domainname*.local domain and select Link an existing GPO.
    - In the Select GPO window select the newly created *ManagementCompany* IT Management Policy then click OK.

☐ Navigate to the new Group Policy Object, right-click on the object and select Edit from the menu.

- Navigate to each of the Policies noted below and configure them as indicated.
    - Offline Files:
        - Computer Configuration\ Policies\Administrative Template\Network\Offline Files
            - Allow or Disallow use of the Offline Files feature – Disable
            - Prohibit user configuration of Offline Files – Disabled
            - Remove "Make Available Offline" - Enabled
    - Remote Registry:
        - Computer Configuration\Policies\Windows Settings\Security Settings\System Services
            - Remote Registry - Automatic
    - Printer Publishing:
        - Computer Configuration\ Policies\Administrative Templates\Printers
            - Allow Printers to be published - Disabled
            - Automatically publish new printers in the Active Directory - Disabled
- Close the Group Policy Object Editor and the Group Policy Manger.

Logon Script / batch file

Note: Do not allow a drive to be conditionally mapped to multiple shares. e.g. s: drive is mapped to \server\sales for the Sales group but to \\server\accounting for the Accounting group. It is bad practice with the exception of the %username% mapping to a user drive such as u: for user or p: for personal etc.

- ☐ Open Windows Explorer and navigate to the c:\windows\sysvol\sysvol*domain*.local\scripts directory.
- ☐ Create a logon.bat file in this directory.
  - Copy and Paste the contents of the Logon.bat File Sample as found at the end of the Resources section of the Network Migration Project Template document or enter each line by hand from that section of this binder.
  - Update the Last edited by line to reflect the technician and date the batch file was last edited.
  - Enter the correct server name everywhere it appears in the file.
  - Update the Clear old persistent net uses section to include all old mapped drives from workstations so that persistent connections from the workstations are cleared.

    For a complete list of previously used maps, refer to the Discovery section - Active Directory / Group Policies subsection.
  - Update (or delete) the line that maps the user (%username%) directory to a drive. Refer to the Discovery section -File and Data Storage subsection for which drive to map to.
  - Update the ifmember routine section to include all required drive mappings based on:
    - The Security Groups as documented in the Discovery section - Active Directory / Group Policies subsection.
    - The Shared Resources as documented in the Discovery section -File and Data Storage subsection.

    Note: Run the command ifmember.exe /l /v to verify a group will be recognized by the ifmember program. Typically only certain built in groups and new security groups created using the wizard will be recognized.
  - Add any unconditional net map lines as required as documented in the Discovery section -File and Data Storage subsection.
  - Test and troubleshoot the new logon.bat file from any workstation on the old domain before continuing.
- ☐ Configure the Logon.bat to run under the Small Business Server Client Computer Group Policy.
  - Run the Group Policy Manager from the Administrative Tools group.
  - Navigate to the Domains*domainname*.local\Group Policy Objects\Windows SBS Client Policy, right-click on the object and select Edit from the menu.
    - Navigate to the User Configuration\Policies\Windows Settings\Scripts (Logon/Logoff) policy
    - Edit the Logon properties and add the UNC path of the new logon.bat file.
      - The full path must be a UNC as follows: *servername*\netlogon\logon.bat.
    - Click OK to close the Add a script window, click OK to close the Logon Properties.
  - Close the Group Policy Object Editor and the Group Policy Manger.

File and Data Storage

Disk Quotas

- ☐ Run Windows Explorer and on the Local Disk Properties - Quota tab, configure Disk Quota as documented in the Discovery section - File and Data Storage subsection.
  - Perform this configuration on each drive in the system.

Note: Be certain to utilize the new Quota Entries option where it is appropriate for restricting user data usage.

Shadow Copies

☐ Run Windows Explorer and on the Local Disk Properties – Shadow Copies tab, configure Shadow Copies for each volume as documented in the Discovery section - File and Data Storage subsection.

Users Shared Data (Users Shared Folders) Move

☐ If the Users Shared Data Folders is to reside on a drive other than C: as documented in the Discovery section - File and Data Storage subsection, move it now.

Note: There must be another hard drive (not USB) in the system with sufficient space to hold all the users shared data.

- Run Windows SBS 2011 Console and on the navigation bar select Backup and Server Storage then select the Server Storage tab.
- Run the Move Users' Shared Data wizard from the Storage Tasks list.
- On the getting Started page click next.
- When the Move Users' Shared Data window pops-up prompting do you want to back up the data now? Click No.
- Select the new location for the users shared data as documented in the Discovery section - File and Data Storage subsection then click Move.
- Click Finish when the wizard has completed.

Users Redirected Documents Data Move

☐ If the Users Redirected Documents are to reside on a drive other than C: as documented in the Discovery section - File and Data Storage subsection, move it now.

Note: If the Users Shared Data has been redirected it is most likely that Users Redirected Documents Data will also be redirected to the same location.

Note: There must be another hard drive (not USB) in the system with sufficient space to hold all the users redirected documents data.

- Run Windows SBS 2011 Console and on the navigation bar select Backup and Server Storage then select the Server Storage tab.
- Run the Move Users' Redirected Documents Data wizard from the Storage Tasks list.
- On the getting Started page click next.
- When the Move Users' Redirected Documents Data window pops-up prompting do you want to back up the data now? Click No.
- Select the new location for the users shared data as documented in the Discovery section - File and Data Storage subsection then click Move.
- Click Finish when the wizard has completed.

My Documents, Desktop and Start Menu Redirect

☐ If the user My Documents, Desktop or Start Menu location is to be redirected as documented in the Discovery section - File and Data Storage subsection, configure it now.

- Run Windows SBS 2011 Console and on the navigation bar select Users and Groups then select the Users tab.
- Run the Redirect folders for users accounts to the server wizard from the Users Tasks list.

- On the Folder Redirection properties page select Folder names from the pane on the left of the window then check the box for each component that will be redirected for users to the server.
- Select User Accounts from the pane on the left of the window and click on the Select all users button.
- Click OK to apply the new settings and then click Close on the Folder Redirection properties pop-up indicating Success.

Note: All new users will inherit the same redirection settings. There should be no need to run this wizard again unless there is a policy change.

Data Shares

Note: When creating data shares always set the Share Permissions to Everyone - Full Control. Access will be restricted using NTFS permissions.

☐ Create Shared Folders as documented in the Discovery section - File and Data Storage subsection as follows:

- Run Windows SBS 2011 Console and on the navigation bar select Shared Folders and Web Sites then select the Shared Folders tab.
- Run the Add a new shared folder wizard from the Shared Folder Tasks list.
    - On the Shared Folder Location page click Browse and navigate to the drive and directory where the data folders will reside.
    - Click the Make new Folder button if the folder does not already exist and enter the name for the new folder as documented in the Discovery section - File and Data Storage subsection.
    - Click OK to accept the folder name and location then click Next on the Share Folder Location page.
    - On the NTFS Permissions page select yes, change NTFS permissions then click the Edit Permissions button.
        - In the Permissions for *sharename* window on the Security tab add or Remove Groups and set Permissions as documented in the Discovery section - File and Data Storage subsection.

    Note: Removing a Group (Object) from the list that is inheriting it's permissions from its parent will require turning off the option for inheriting permissions. When turning off the option you will be prompted to either Copy or Remove the existing permissions already inherited. Always select Copy.

        - Click OK to close the Permissions window then click Next on the NTFS Permissions page.
    - On the Share Protocol page accept the defaults and click Next.
    - On the SMB Settings page accept the defaults and click Next.
    - On the SMB Permissions page select Users and groups have custom share permissions then click the Permissions button.
        - In the Permissions for *sharename* window select Everyone from the Group or user names list then check the box for Allow Full Control.
        - Click OK to close the Permissions window then click Next on the SMB Permissions page.
    - Click next for all remaining pages and on the Confirmation page click Close.
- Repeat this process for all Shared Folders as documented in the Discovery section - File and Data Storage subsection.

Email / Outlook / Exchange

Add all additional Email Domains to Exchange if required

☐ Create Accepted Domains as follows:

- Run Exchange Management Console and navigate to the Microsoft Exchange On-Premises – Organization Configuration – Hub Transport container.
- Select New Accepted Domain from the Actions menu on the right side of the window.
  - In the name field enter a descriptive name for the domain. e.g. ZDTM Inc.
  - In the Accepted Domain field enter only the domain name this server will be receiving email for as documented in the Discovery section - Email / Outlook / Exchange subsection. e.g. zdtminc.net

  Note: Do not enter the primary domain name as it should already be in the list and active.

  - Verify the Authoritative Domain option is selected then click New.
  - Click Finish when the wizard has completed.
- Repeat this process for each domain name listed in the Discovery section - Email / Outlook / Exchange subsection.

☐ Create E-mail Address Policies as follows:

- Run Exchange Management Console and navigate to the Organization Configuration – Hub Transport container.
- Select New E-mail Address Policy from the Actions menu on the right side of the window.
  - On the introduction page enter a descriptive name for the domain. e.g. ZDTM Inc.
    - Verify the All recipients types option is selected then click Next.
  - On the Conditions page accept the defaults and click Next.
  - On the E-Mail Address Policy page click the Add button and in the SMTP E-mail Address window select the option to Select accepted domain for e-mail addresses then click Browse.
    - Select the corresponding Accepted Domain for the Address Policy being created then click OK.
    - Click OK to close the SMTP E-mail Address window then click Next on the E-Mail Addresses page.
  - On the remaining pages accept the defaults and click Next.
  - Click Finish when the wizard has completed.
- Repeat this process for each Accepted Domain created in the previous subsection.

☐ If this server is accepting email for multiple domains, verify each users default email address (Reply address) is correct as documented in the Discovery section– Active Directory / Group Policy subsection.

Note: These steps are only required in a user has a different default SMTP address than the domain default.

- Run Exchange Management Console and navigate to the Recipient Configuration – Mailbox container.
  - Edit the User Properties and select the E-mail Addresses tab.

    - Clear the checkbox at the bottom of the window to Automatically update e-mail addresses based on recipient policy.
    - Highlight the E-mail Address that should be the default address as documented in the Discovery section– Active Directory / Group Policy subsection and click the Set As Reply.
    - Click Apply, then click OK to close the User Properties window.
  - Repeat this process for each user who's default e-mail address (reply Address) must be changed.

Setup and configure POP3 Connector if required

- ☐ Run Windows SBS 2011 Console and on the navigation bar select Network then select the Connectivity tab.
  - Select POP3 Connector from the list, right-click and select View POP3 Connector properties from the menu.
    - In the Windows SBS POP3 Connector window Click Add.
      - On the POP3 mailbox account page enter all required information for the POP connector as documented in the Discovery section - Email / Outlook / Exchange subsection then click OK.
    - Repeat this process for each POP Connector listed in the Discovery section - Email / Outlook / Exchange subsection.
  - When all POP Connectors have been added click on Apply then select Scheduling from the pane on the left.
  - Click the Retrieve now button. Verify all connectors are properly configured and connecting.
  - Click OK to close the Windows SBS POP3 Connector window.

Configure Exchange to Not send NDR's

- ☐ Run Exchange Management Console, navigate to the Microsoft Exchange On-Premises – Organization Configuration - Hub Transport container then select the Remote Domains tab.
  - Right click the Default domain, select Properties from the menu then select the Format of original message... tab.
    - Clear the checkbox for Allow non-delivery reports.
  - Click OK to close the Default Properties window then close the Exchange Management Console.

Configure Exchange Mailbox Limits

- ☐ To configure Exchange Mailbox Database Limits as documented in the Discovery section - Email / Outlook / Exchange subsection proceed as follows:
  - Log on to the new server as the administrator.
  - Run Exchange Management Console and navigate to the Microsoft Exchange On-Premises – Organization Configuration – Mailbox container.
  - Select the Database Management tab, right-click on the Mailbox Database and select Properties from the menu.
    - In the Mailbox Database Properties window select the Limits tab.
    - Configure Database Limits as documented in the Discovery section - Email / Outlook / Exchange subsection.
    - Click OK to close the Mailbox Database properties.
  - Close the Exchange Management Console.

Create Exchange Public Folders and Configure User Permissions

Note: Use OWA (Outlook Web App) to create all public folders, not the Exchange Management Console as the Exchange Management Console only allow for creation of Message folders.

- ☐ Create all Public Folder as documented in the Discovery section - Email / Outlook / Exchange subsection proceed as follows:
    - Log on to the new server as the administrator.
    - Open Internet Explorer and enter the address public address for OWA.

      e.g. remote.*company.xxx*\owa

      Example: remote.zdtminc.net/owa
    - Log in to Outlook as the administrator.
    - Select the Public Folder container from the navigation pane on the left.
    - Right click on the Public Folder container select Create New Folder from the menu.
        - Select the appropriate folder type from the drop down menu as documented in the Discovery section - Email / Outlook / Exchange subsection.
        - Enter the name for the new Public Folder in the current field as documented in the Discovery section - Email / Outlook / Exchange subsection.
    - Repeat this process for all Public Folder to be created as documented in the Discovery section - Email / Outlook / Exchange subsection.
    - Close Internet Explorer.
- ☐ To configure all Public Folder User Permissions as documented in the Discovery section - Email / Outlook / Exchange subsection proceed as follows:
    - Log on to the new server as the administrator.
    - Run Exchange Management Console, navigate to the Microsoft Exchange On-Premises – Toolbox in the left pane then double-click the Public Folder Management Console tool.
    - In the Public Folder Management Console select the Default Public Folders container from the navigation pane on the left.
    - Select the desired Public Folder from the list in the middle pane, right click on the folder and select Properties from the menu.
        - In the public folder Properties window select the Permissions tab.
        - To add specific Users or Groups click the Add button then select Users or Groups from the Entire Forest list and click OK.
        - To remove specific Users or Groups select the name and click the Remove button.
        - Set permissions for each User or Group as documented in the Discovery section - Email / Outlook / Exchange subsection as follows:
            - Selecting the User or Group name then selecting a Permission Level from the dropdown list or set individual Permissions by checking or clearing Permissions checkboxes.
        - Click Apply to save all changes then click OK to close the Folder Properties window.
    - Repeat this process for all Public Folder requiring User Permission changes as documented in the Discovery section - Email / Outlook / Exchange subsection.
    - Close the Public Folder Management Console then close the Exchange Management Console.

Mail Enable Public Folders

- ☐ To configure Mail Enabled Public Folders as documented in the Discovery section - Email / Outlook / Exchange subsection proceed as follows:
  - Log on to the new server as the administrator.
  - Run Exchange Management Console, navigate to the Microsoft Exchange On-Premises – Toolbox in the left pane then double-click the Public Folder Management Console tool.
  - In the Public Folder Management Console select the Default Public Folders container from the navigation pane on the left then select the desired Public Folder from the list in the middle pane.
  - Right-click on the folder to be Mail Enabled and select Mail Enable from the menu.
  - To change send as permissions for the newly Mail Enabled folder right-click on the folder again and select Manage Send As permissions from the menu.
    - In the Manage Send As Permission window click the Add button, select all users who should be allowed to Send As then click OK.
    - When all names have been added to the Security Principal window click Manage.
    - Click Finish when the wizard has completed.
  - Repeat this process for all Public Folder to be mail Enabled as documented in the Discovery section - Email / Outlook / Exchange subsection.
  - Close the Public Folder Management Console then close the Exchange Management Console.
- ☐ To change additional settings related to Public Folders as documented in the Discovery section - Email / Outlook / Exchange subsection proceed as follows:
  - Log on to the new server as the administrator.
  - Run Exchange Management Console, navigate to the Microsoft Exchange On-Premises – Toolbox in the left pane then double-click the Public Folder Management Console tool.
  - In the Public Folder Management Console select the Default Public Folders container from the navigation pane on the left then select the desired Public Folder from the list in the middle pane.
  - Right-click on the folder requiring changes to additional settings and select Properties from the menu.
    - If this folder should not be allowed to receive email from users on the domain or from the internet, select the Exchange General tab and check the box Hide from Exchange address list.
    - If additional E-Mail addresses are required for the folder or the existing addresses need to be modified select the E-Mail Addresses tab.
      - To add an SMTP address click the Add button, enter the desired E-mail address then click OK.
      - To Edit an address select it from the list and click the Edit button, enter the desired E-mail address and click OK.
      - If any address was added, removed or changed, clear the checkbox for Automatically update e-mail addresses based on recipient policy.

      Note: If any address was added, removed or changed and the checkbox for Automatically update e-mail addresses based on recipient policy is not cleared, the changes will not be retained.
    - Click Apply to save all changes then click OK to close the Folder Properties window.
  - Repeat this process for all Public Folder requiring changes to additional settings as documented in the Discovery section - Email / Outlook / Exchange subsection.

- Close the Public Folder Management Console then close the Exchange Management Console.

Configure Exchange Public Folder Limits and Quotas

☐ To configure Exchange Public Folder Database Limits as documented in the Discovery section - Email / Outlook / Exchange subsection proceed as follows:

- Log on to the new server as the administrator.
- Run Exchange Management Console and navigate to the Microsoft Exchange On-Premises – Organization Configuration – Mailbox container.
- Select the Database Management tab, right-click on the Public Folder Database and select Properties from the menu.
    - In the Public Folder Database Properties window select the Limits tab.
    - Configure Database Limits as documented in the Discovery section - Email / Outlook / Exchange subsection.
- Click OK to close the Public Folder Database properties.

☐ Configure individual Public Folders Quotas as documented in the Discovery section - Email / Outlook / Exchange subsection proceed as follows:

Note: If specific quotas for individual Public Folders are not specifically indicated in the Discovery section - Email / Outlook / Exchange subsection they will (and should be allowed to) take on the limits indicated in the Public Folder Database Properties.

- In Exchange Management Console navigate to the Microsoft Exchange On-Premises – Toolbox in the left pan then double-click the Public Folder Management Console tool link.
- In the Public Folder Management Console select the Default Public Folders container then select the desired folder from the list in the middle pane of the window.
    - Right-click on the folder requiring quota changes, select Properties from the menu then select the Limits tab.
        - Configure Quotas as documented in the Discovery section - Email / Outlook / Exchange subsection.
    - Click OK to close the folder Properties
- Repeat this process for all Public Folder requiring changes to additional settings.
- Close the Public Folder Management Console.

Configure Windows Mobile 6 on the New Server

Note: Configure Windows Mobile 6 only if it has been determined that it should be utilized.
Refer to the Discovery section - Email / Outlook / Exchange subsection.

Note: By default all new users are granted OWA permissions. This step is to verify the users who will be using Mobile Devices have sufficient access. OWA is not required for users to access their Exchange mailbox but it will help with troubleshooting issues, if there are issues, during device configuration.

☐ Configure Outlook Web Access for the correct users as documented in the Discovery section - Email / Outlook / Exchange subsection proceed as follows:

- Log on to the new server as the administrator.
- Run the Windows SBS Console and select Users and Groups.
- For each user who should have Outlook Web Access, right click on the account and select Properties from the menu.

    - Select Web Sites from navigation pane on the left and verify the box for Outlook Web Access is checked.
    - Click OK to close the users properties page.
  - Repeat this process for each user who will be accessing their Exchange mailbox using a Windows Mobile 6 device as documented in the Discovery section - Email / Outlook / Exchange subsection.
  - Close the Windows SBS Console.

☐ Verify Exchange ActiveSync is enabled for the correct users as documented in the Discovery section - Email / Outlook / Exchange subsection proceed as follows:

Note: By default all new users are granted Exchange Active Sync permissions. This step is to verify the users who will be using Mobile Devices have sufficient access.

  - Log on to the new server as the administrator.
  - Run the Exchange Management Console and navigate to the Microsoft Exchange On-Premises – Recipient Configuration – Mailbox container.
    - For each user who should have Exchange Active Sync permissions, right click on the account and select Properties from the menu.
    - Select the Mailbox Features tab, select Exchange Active Sync feature and if it is not Enabled click the Enable button above the feature list window.
    - Click OK to close the users properties page.
  - Repeat this process for each user who will be accessing their Exchange mailbox using a Windows Mobile 6 device as documented in the Discovery section - Email / Outlook / Exchange subsection.
  - Close the Exchange Management Console.

Line of Business Applications Installation

Line of Business Application name goes here – Repeat as needed

Note: Insert here the checklist for any Line of Business Application installation. If one does not exist, please refer to the Resources section of this binder for details on how to create installation and migration checklists for this product.

System Applications Installation

BlackBerry Professional

Note: Insert here the checklist for BlackBerry Professional installation. If one does not exist, please refer to the Resources section of this binder for details on how to create installation and migration checklists for this product.

Encrypted / Keyed Security Access System

Note: Insert here the checklist for any Encrypted / Keyed Security Access System installation. If one does not exist, please refer to the Resources section of this binder for details on how to create installation and migration checklists for this product.

Antivirus Solution - Trend Micro Worry Free Business Security 7.0

Note: The following checklist is valid only for Trend Micro Worry Free Business Security 7.0. If a newer version is being installed, take notes where there are discrepancies so this checklist can be updated.

Note: The following application installation checklist section assumes that Trend Micro is either the existing Antivirus solution being migrated, was purchased with the new system or is being installed as part of KPEnterprises Platinum Managed Services protection plan.

If another Antivirus solution will be installed or migrated as documented in the Discovery section - System Applications subsection, this checklist should be replace with the checklist for the product being installed.

- ☐ Trend Micro Setup Reminder! For the proper installation of this product it is assumed and expected that the default selection will be made for everything not specifically noted here.
- ☐ Read all Trend Micro Worry Free Business Security related installation and configuration documentation and verify that this system meets all system requirements before proceeding.
- ☐ Copy the Line of Business Application page from the New Network Documentation section and fill out all useful information for Trend Micro Worry Free Business Security on the new page.
- ☐ Insert the Trend Micro Worry Free Business Security CD or run the Setup.exe from the source directory.
    - On the Welcome screen click Next.
    - On the License Agreement pages select I accept ... then click Next.
    - On the Setup Type page select Custom Installation then click Next.
    - On the Product Activation page enter the Activation Code then click Next.
        - If the Registration Key has not yet been registered do it now by clicking on the Register Online button.

          Note: Be certain the email addresses entered for software registration is the client companies administrators email address.
        - Print out all registration records, keys, codes etc. from the registration sites and insert them into the New Network Documentation section.
    - On the Worry-Free Business Security Advanced Components page click Next.
    - On the Choose Installation Location page accept the default and click Next.
    - On the Select Components page accept the default of all components selected and click Next.
    - On the Configure Security Server page click Next.
    - On the Computer Prescan page select Prescan my computer for threats then click Next.
    - On the first Web Server (host selection) page select Use IIS to host the Security Server (Virtual website) then click Next.
    - **Note:** If you select the Use IIS to host the Security Server (default website) you will break Small Business Server.
    - On the second Web Server (configuration) page:
        - Verify that FQDN is selected and the full local name of the new SBS server is correct. e.g. *server.domain*.local

          Example: zdtmsbs.zdtminc.local
        - Accept all the default port settings for HTTP and HTTPS.
        - Record the HTTP and HTTPS ports used on the Trend Micro Worry Free Business Security Line of Business Application page started earlier.

- Click Next to continue.
- On the Administrator Account Password page:
    - Generate two unique passwords for the Web console and the Client Agent and enter them in the corresponding fields.
    - Document both passwords now on the User and Password record in the New Network Documentation section.
    - Click Next to continue.
- On the SMTP Server and Notification Recipient(s) page:
    - Verify the SMTP server name is correct. E.g. *server.domain*.local.
    - Accept the default Port of 25.
    - Enter the client companies administrator email address as the only recipient then click Next.
- On the Trend Micro Smart Protection Network page accept the defaults then click Next.
- On the General Proxy Settings page do not configure a proxy server unless there is a proxy device protecting the network. Click Next.
- On the Configure Security Agent page click Next.
- On the Security Agent Installation Path page:
    - Record the Security Agent Listening Port on the Trend Micro Worry Free Business Security Line of Business Application page started earlier.
    - Accept all the defaults then click Next.
- On the Security Agent Settings page:
    - Clear the checkboxes for Web Reputation and Behavior Monitoring in both the Server and Workstation sections.
    - Accept all other defaults then click Next.
- On the Proxy Settings for Additional Services page accept the default then click Next.
- On the Configuring Messaging Security Agent page click Next.
- On the Install Messaging Security Agent page:
    - Select Yes, I would like to install Messaging protection to the following server.
    - Enter administrator in the Account field and enter the administrator password in the Password filed then click Next.
- On the Messaging Security Agent Settings page accept the defaults then click Next.
- On the Start Copying Files page click Next to begin the installation.
- On the Installing Third Party Components page click Next to continue.
- If prompted by a Warning indicating to Please refer to Microsoft Knowledge Base article 2493361 regarding the improvement of network performance click OK.

  Note: This KB article should be reviewed after the Trend Micro Installation is complete but do not apply the hotfix unless the exact symptoms indicated in the KB article are effecting this server exactly as described in the KB article.
- On the Installing Trend Micro Worry-Free Business Security Agent page monitor the progress until the Setup Complete page is presented then Click Finish.

Note: During the Trend Micro installation a Restart notice may be presented if a previously existing Antivirus solution was removed during the Trend Micro installation.

- ☐ If during the Trend Micro installation a prompts for restart of the server is presented select Restart Later.
- ☐ Configure Preferences and Settings as follows:
  - Navigate to the Trend Micro Worry-Free Business Security Advanced folder in All Programs and select Worry-Free Business Security from the list to run the application.
  - When Internet Explorer opens and presents the security certificate warning page open Internet Options by clicking the Tools icon from the Toolbar and selecting Internet Options.
    - Select the Security tab, select the Trusted Sites zone then click the Sites button.
    - In the Trusted sites window click Add to add the https link to the local server then click Close.
    - Click OK to close the Internet Options window.
  - On the security certificate warning page click Continue to this website.
  - Click the Security report icon to the right of the address bar at the top of the Internet Explorer window then click View certificate.
    - In the Certificate window click Install Certificate.
    - On the Certificate Install Wizard welcome page click Next.
    - On the Certificate Store page select Place all certificates in the following store then click the Browse button.
      - Browse to the Trusted Root Certification Authorities then click OK.
      - Click Next then click Finish.
      - On the Security Warning that pops up indicating You are about to install a certificate click Yes.
      - Close the Certificate Import Wizard success popup and then click OK in the Certificate Information window to close it.
    - Close Internet Explorer.
  - Re-Run the Trend Micro Worry-Free Business Security management console.
    - Verify that the Trend Micro Worry-Free Business Security management console Logon page loads without any security warning.
    - Frequent prompts by internet Explorer will be presented that this website wants to install add-on or other components including Active-X, allow them to be installed.
    - Follow any on screen instruction for these installations to allow them to complete.
  - Log into the console using the previously recorded credentials.
  - From the Main Menu across the top of the page select Security Settings then select the Servers group then click the Configure tool.
    - Select Antivirus/Anti-spyware from the sidebar menu then select the Action tab.
      - In the For Malware Detections section ActiveAction.
      - In the Advanced Settings section check the box to Display an alert message on the desktop or server when a virus/spyware is detected.
      - Click Save to save the new configuration then Click the Back button.
  - From the Main Menu across the top of the page select Security Settings then select Desktop group and click the Configure tool.
    - Select Antivirus/Anti-spyware from the sidebar menu then select the Action tab.

        - In the For Malware Detections section ActiveAction.
        - In the Advanced Settings section check the box to Display an alert message on the desktop or server when a virus/spyware is detected.
        - Click Save to save the new configuration then Click the Back button.
    - Select Client Privileges from the sidebar menu.
        - In the Antivirus/Anti-spyware section check the box to Enable Skip Scheduled Scan.
        - Click Save to save the new configuration then Click the Back button.
- From the Main Menu navigate to Scan – Scheduled Scans.
    - On the Settings tab check the box for both Server and Desktops.
    - Select the Schedule tab and in the Server section, select Daily and set the time as documented in the Discovery Section.
    - On the Schedule tab in the Desktop section, select Daily and set the time as documented in the Discovery Section.
    - Click Save to save the new then Click the Back button.
- From the Main Menu navigate to Preferences - Notification page and select the Settings tab.
    - Verify Email Notifications are going to Administrator@*company.xxx*
    - Click Save to save the new configuration then Click the Back button.
- From the Main Menu navigate to Preferences - Global Settings page and select the System tab.
    - In the Inactive Security Agent Remove section check the box for Enable automatic removal of inactive Client/Server Security. Leave the setting at 30 days.
    - In the Quarantine Maintenance section:
        - Set the Quarantine folder capacity to 10 MB (The minimum)
        - Set the maximum size for a single file to 1 MB (The minimum)
    - Click Save to save the new configuration then Click the Back button.
- Close Trend Micro Dashboard.

☐ Add the Trend micro Client installation program autopcc.exe to the logon.bat file.

- Open Windows Explorer and navigate to the c:\windows\sysvol\sysvol*domain*.local\scripts directory.
    - Edit the logon.bat file and as the first command after the Last updated line enter the following command:

      rem *servername*\ofcscan\autopcc.exe

  Note: The command is rem'ed out to keep the installation of a new or newer version of the antivirus solution from interfering with the workstation migration.
  The rem statement will be removed during the Migration - Server Fine Tuning.

    - Update any "last edited by" or version information for the logon.bat file.
    - Close and save the logon.bat file.

☐ If during the installation a Warning indicating to Please refer to Microsoft Knowledge Base article 2493361 was presented open Internet Explorer and surf to the site: http://support.microsoft.com/kb/2493361/

- Read all presented material and evaluate the need for the Hotfix.

- If the Hotfix is necessary follow all outlined steps to complete the installation.

☐ If the server has not been rebooted since before the beginning of the Trend Micro install reboot it now.

Drive Maintenance Solution

> **Note:** Insert here the checklist for any Drive Maintenance Solution installation. If one does not exist, please refer to the Resources section of this binder for details on how to create installation and migration checklists for this product.

Drive Imaging Solution

> **Note:** Insert here the checklist for any Drive Imaging Solution installation. If one does not exist, please refer to the Resources section of this binder for details on how to create installation and migration checklists for this product.

Sub Systems

Update / Patch Management Solution

> **Note:** Insert here the checklist for any Update / Patch Management Solution installation. If one does not exist, please refer to the Resources section of this binder for details on how to create installation and migration checklists for this product.

Phone System

> **Note:** Insert here the checklist for any Phone System installation. If one does not exist, please refer to the Resources section of this binder for details on how to create installation and migration checklists for this product.

Backup Software, Devices and Methods

Tape Backup Solution - Backup Exec 2010 R3

Note: The following checklist is valid only for Backup Exec 2010 R3. If a newer version is being installed, take notes where there are discrepancies so this checklist can be updated.

Note: The following application installation checklist section assumes that Symantec Backup Exec is either the existing Backup application being migrated or was purchased with the new system.

If another Backup application will be installed or migrated as documented in the Discovery section, this checklist should be replace with the checklist for the product being installed.

☐ Backup Exec Setup Reminder! For the proper installation of this product it is assumed and expected that the default selection will be made for everything not specifically noted here.

☐ Read all Backup Exec related installation and configuration documentation and verify that this system meets all system requirements before proceeding.

- Insert the Backup Exec software DVD or run the Browser.exe from the source directory, select English from the Select Language window then click OK.
- From the Symantec Backup Exec Welcome screen select Install Products.
- From the Symantec Backup Installation page select Backup Exec.
- On the Welcome page in the License Agreement section select I accept the terms of the license agreement then click Next.

- On the Installation page select Custom installation then click Next.
- From the Menu page select Local Installation – Install .Backup Exec software and options then click Next.
- When the Environment Check page is presented, review and correct all critical items listed before continuing.
    - When all critical items have been reconciled click Next to continue.
- On the License Keys page enter the License Key(s) for the product that was purchased for this server then click Next.
    - If the License Key(s) has not yet been acquired and the serial number registered do that now at the https://licensing.symantec.com.
- On the Configuration Options page select all Features or Options that Licenses were purchased for, otherwise accept the defaults then click Next.
- On the Destination page accept the default locations then click Next.
- On the Service Account page accept the default name of administrator and enter the same administrator password that is used on the old server / domain as documented in the Discovery section then click Next.
    - A popup window indicating that the account has been granted the following rights is presented click OK.
- On the Choose SQL Server page select Create a local Backup Exec SQL Express instance... then click Next.
- On the Tape Device Drivers page accept the default of Use Symantec device drivers for all tape devices then click Next.
- On the Installation Review page reconcile all warnings then click Install.

Note: If at any time during the installation a Windows Security pop-up indicating that Windows can't verify the publisher of this driver software, select install this driver software anyway.

- When the Install Wizard is finished clear the check boxes for Participate in the product improvement program, View ReadMe, and Create desktop Icon.
    - Leave only the Run LiveUpdate box checked then click Next. LiveUpdate will run.
    - On the LiveUpdate wizard options page click Next to detect available updates.
    - Click Next to allow LiveUpdate to download and install the detected updates.
    - When all updates have been successfully downloaded and installed click Finish.
- Exit the Symantec Backup Exec 2010 DVD Browser.

☐ Configure Symantec Backup Exec 2010 by following the Getting Started steps.

- Navigate to the Symantec Backup Exec folder in All Programs and select Backup Exec 2010 from the list to run the application.

Note: Step 1) Create Logon Accounts in the Getting Started section of the Home tab can be skipped as the only required Logon Account was created during the initial setup.

- Select the Devices tab from the Toolbar at the top of the window.
    - Navigate to and expand the Device Pools All Devices container.
    - Verify that any tape device that is physically installed or attached to the server are correctly listed here and are enabled.

    - If there are tape devices physically installed or attached that are not listed here drivers may need to be installed and / or they must be configured as outlined in the next steps.

Note: If the only installed or attached tape device(s) utilizes a USB interface and are not listed in the All Device container as outlined above, do not run the wizards indicated in the next steps.

Symantec does not Supply tape device drivers for USB tape devices therefore the drives must be supplied by the manufacturer and must be installed before attempting to continue with the Symantec Backup Exec configuration.

- If tape devices (other than USB tape devices) require driver installation or configuration click on the Home tab and select step 2 Configure Devices from the Getting Started section to run the Configure Devices Assistant.
    - In the Configure Devices Assistant select Tape Devices from the Tape Storage Section.
        - On the Tape Device Configuration Wizard welcome page click Next.
        - On the Create and Configure Tape Devices page select Install tape device drivers then click Next.
            - On the Welcome to the Symantec Device Driver Installation page click Next.
            - On the Symantec Tape driver Information page indicating that Symantec does not supply tape device drivers for USB tape devices click Next.
            - On the Symantec Tape Driver Options page accept the default of Use Symantec tape drivers for all supported tape devices and Use Plug and Play drivers for Windows 2000 or later then click Next.
            - On the Scanning Hardware page click Next when the scan has completed.
            - If a Windows Security window pops up indicating that Windows can't verify the publisher of this driver software select Install this driver software anyway.
            - On the Installing Symantec Drivers page click Next when the installation is complete then click Finish.
        - On the Completing the Tape Device Configuration Wizard page click Finish.

    Note: Some drivers may require a reboot before they can complete their registration and correctly load. If a reboot is required, Reboot the server now.

    - Verify the tape devices as follows:
        - Select the Devices tab from the Toolbar at the top of the window.
            - Navigate to and expand the Device Pools All Devices container.
            - Verify that any tape device that is physically installed or attached to the server are correctly listed here and are enabled.
            - If all tape devices physically installed or attached are not listed here troubleshoot the issue with the drivers or hardware before proceeding.
- Select step 3 Create Media Sets from the Getting Started section of the Home tab to run the Media Set Wizard.
    - On the Welcome to the Media Set Wizard page click Next.
    - On the Create or Edit a media Set page select Edit an existing media set then click Next.
    - On the Select a Media Set to Edit page select the media set Keep Data for 4 Weeks and click Next.
    - On the Name the Media Set page change the name of the media set to be the company short name or acronym as documented in the Discovery section then click Next. e.g. ZDTM

- On the Set the Overwrite Protection Period page change the overwrite protection period to be 0 hours unless there is a library or carousel installed then click Next.

  For a library or carousel set the overwrite protection to 72 hours.
- On the Set the Append Period page set the period to be Infinite – Allow Append then click Next.
- On the Media Set summary page click Next and when the wizard has completed click Finish .

☐ Configure the Application Defaults by Selecting Options from the Tools menu.

Note: Change only the settings listed below.

- Job Defaults section
  - Device and Media page:
    - Device = *Primary installed or attached tape device* (Do not leave as All Devices)
  - Backup page:
    - Media Overwrite Protection = Overwrite Media
    - Compression Type = Hardware [if available, otherwise software]
    - Verify after backup = Checkbox cleared

      Note: A warning will pop up regarding Symantec recommendations. Click OK
    - Enable single instance backup for NTFS = Checked
  - Advanced Open File Option page:
    - Use Advanced Open File Option = Checked
  - Schedule page:
    - Edit Schedule Details
      - Set Recurring Week Days = All Mon. – Fri. boxes selected. Then click OK.
- Settings section
  - Media Management page:
    - Set media type to match the correct tape type. e.g. 4mm or DLT etc.
- Click OK to complete the changes and close the Options window.

☐ Run the Alert Autoresponse Wizard from the Tools \ Wizards menu.

- On the Welcome to the Alert Autoresponse Wizard page click Next.
- For each page in the wizard follow the on screen prompts and configure all alerts as follows:
  - Select Automatically clear after 1 minute.
  - If a Response with is available select Yes.
  - Click next on each page and click Finish when the wizard has completed.

☐ Configure a Full Backup Job as follows:

- Click on the File menu, select the New submenu then select Backup Job from that menu.
  - If this is the first backup job to be set up, and this server is a Small Business Server or has Microsoft SharePoint installed an Important Message from Backup Exec will be presented indicating a server farm node has been added … Check the box Do not display this message again then click OK to close the message.

- In the Backup Job Properties window on the Selections page type in a new Selection list name of Full Backup.
  - Enter the same name for the Selection list description.
- Select the View by Resource tab and check the box to the left of the SBS Server name.
  - If this is the first backup job to be set up an Important Message from Backup Exec indicating there may be some resources displayed below … Check the box Do not display this message again then click OK to close the message.
  - Verify all resources on the SBS Server are now selected.
  - In the Resource Selection tree navigate to the root of the C: drive and de-select the pagefile.sys file.
- Select Device and Media from the Destination section of the menu on the left of the Backup Job Properties window.
  - Verify that Overwrite media is selected in the When this job begins section.
  - Check the box to Eject media after job completes.
- Select General from the Destination section of the menu on the left of the Backup Job Properties window.
  - On the General page type in Full Backup for the job name.
  - Enter the same name for the Backup set description.
- Select Schedule from the Frequency section of the menu on the left of the Backup Job Properties window.
  - Select Run according to schedule.
  - Close the Advanced Schedule Options window when it pops up by clicking OK.
- Click on the Submit button to submit the new backup job.
- Review the Job Summary then click OK.
- In the pop up window indicating that the job has been scheduled check the box Do not display this message again then click OK to close the message.

☐ Run the Full backup now by selecting the Job Monitor tab, right clicking on the Full Backup job and selecting Run now from the menu.

- Monitor the backup, change tapes if required and verify it completes as expected.
- When the backup completes remove the Full Backup tape, label it as New System Full Backup, write protect it and place it into one of the Server Documentation Folders.

☐ Close Backup Exec.

Continuous Data Protection System

> **Note:** Insert here the checklist for any Continuous Data Protection System installation. If one does not exist, please refer to the Resources section of this binder for details on how to create installation and migration checklists for this product.

Offsite Backup System

> **Note:** Insert here the checklist for any Offsite Backup System installation. If one does not exist, please refer to the Resources section of this binder for details on how to create installation and migration checklists for this product.

IIS / Web Sites / FTP Sites

Web Site Creation

Note: Only create new Web Sites that are required and do not exist on the old system. The migration process for existing Web Sites will cover creating those sites.

Note: For all site specific settings refer to the documentation in the Discovery section - IIS / Web Sites / FTP Sites subsection.

☐ If the Web Site source files for new sites already exist, copy them to the server now.

Note: The default location for Web Site files is the c:\inetpub\wwwroot directory.
Do not put site files directly into the c:\inetpub\wwwroot directory. Create a folder specifically for the new site in the c:\inetpub\wwwroot directory as each site should have its own folder.

☐ Create all required new Web Sites as follows:

- Run the Internet Information Services (IIS) Manager and navigate to the Sites container in the Connections pane on the left side of the window.
- Click on the Add Web Site link in the Action pane on the right side of the window.
  - For all settings, stating with the Site name, refer to the documentation for this site in the Discovery section - IIS / Web Sites / FTP Sites subsection.
  - Enter the full path to, or browse to the location where the website files will reside.
  - Accept default settings for anything not specifically noted here or in the Discovery section documentation.
  - When all information has been entered click OK to create the site and have it start up immediately.
- Repeat this process for all required new Web Sites.

☐ Configure additional features and settings for the new Web Site follows:

- Navigate to the Sites container and then to the site to be configured in the Connection pane on the left side of the window.
- Open and configure each feature as needed.

  Note: Features are represented by the individual icons in groups in the center pane of the IIS Application window.

  Note: If you are unfamiliar with IIS 7 a good way to become familiar and to complete the configuration of the new Web Site is to systematically select, review and configure each feature page.
  - For all settings refer to the documentation in the Discovery section - IIS / Web Sites / FTP Sites subsection.
  - Do not change any setting not specifically noted here or in the Discovery section documentation.
- Repeat this process as required for all new Web Sites.

☐ Test each Web Site completely. e.g. connectivity, content and security.

Note: You will not be able to simply test the Web Site by entering the public or private IP into a browser from another machine. The header for the new site must match the FQDN entered into the address bar of the browser. To test the Web Site create a host file on any workstation inside or outside the test network that points the FQDN to the temporary public IP of the server.

Example host file entry:

207.123.123.100 www.zdtminc.net

- ☐ Close the Internet Information Services (IIS) Manager.

FTP Site Creation

Note: Configure the File Transfer Protocol (FTP) Role only if it is required. If it is not, skip this subsection.

Note: For all site specific settings refer to the documentation in the Discovery section - IIS / Web Sites / FTP Sites subsection.

- ☐ Add the FTP Role Service as follows:
  - Launch the Server Manager application from the Administrative Tools folder.
  - Navigate to the Roles container in the panel on the left side of the window, expand it then select the Web Server (IIS) sub container.
  - In the center panel scroll to the Role Services section and click on the Add Role Services icon to run the Add Role Services wizard.
    - Scroll to the bottom of the Role services list and check the box for FTP Server.
      - If FTP files will not be published to any web site hosted on this server as specifically outlined in the Discovery section - IIS / Web Sites / FTP Sites subsection clear the checkbox for FTP Service.
      - If FTP Extensibility features will not be utilized as specifically outlined in the Discovery section - IIS / Web Sites / FTP Sites subsection clear the checkbox for FTP Extensibility.
      - Click Next to continue and on the Confirm Installation Selection page click Install.
      - On the Installation Results page click Close Server Manager.
- ☐ Create all required FTP Sites as follows:

  Note: There is no Default FTP Site. Only create new FTP Sites that are required but that do not exist on the old system. The migration process for existing FTP Sites will cover creating those sites.

  Note: For all site specific settings refer to the documentation in the Discovery section - IIS / Web Sites / FTP Sites subsection.

  - Run the Internet Information Services (IIS) Manager and navigate to the Sites container in the Connections pane on the left side of the window.
  - Click on the Add FTP Site link in the Action pane on the right side of the window.
    - On the Site Information page enter the FTP site name.
    - Enter the physical path to, or browse to the location where the FTP files will reside then click Next.

      Note: There is no default location for FTP Site files. Choose a location carefully to ensure security of the files.
    - On the Bindings page accept the default settings for anything not specifically noted in the documentation for this site in the Discovery section - IIS / Web Sites / FTP Sites subsection then click Next.

      Note: If the IP address and the port are both the same as any other FTP site the site will not start after it is completed.
    - On the Authentication and Authorization Information page configure the access as indicated in the Discovery section - IIS / Web Sites / FTP Sites subsection then click Finish.
  - Repeat this process for all required new FTP Sites.
- ☐ Configure additional features and settings for the new FTP Site follows:

- Navigate to the Sites container and then to the site to be configured in the Connection pane on the left side of the window.
- Open and configure each feature as needed.

  Note: Features are represented by the individual icons in groups in the center pane of the IIS Application window.

  - For all settings refer to the documentation in the Discovery section - IIS / Web Sites / FTP Sites subsection.
  - Do not change any setting not specifically noted here or in the Discovery section documentation.
- Repeat this process as required for all new FTP Sites.

☐ Test each FTP Site completely. e.g. connectivity, content and security.

Note: You will not be able to simply test the FTP Site by entering the public or private IP into a browser from another machine. The header for the new site must match the FQDN entered into the address bar of the browser. To test the FTP Site create a host file on any workstation inside or outside the test network that points the FQDN to the temporary public IP of the server.

Example host file entry:

207.123.123.100 ftp.zdtminc.net

☐ Close the Internet Information Services (IIS) Manager.

11. Troubleshooting and Repair Log

Client: ______________________ **Date:** ______________________

Contact: ______________________ **Technician:** ______________________

Phone: ______________________ **Log #:** ______________________

Description of Issue: ____

____

____

____

____

Support Service: ______________________ **Required Numbers or Codes:**

SR(X): ______________________ **MS Partner ID:** ______________________

Phone Number: ______________________ **MS MCP ID:** ______________________

Extensions: ______________________ **Service Contract:** ______________________

Date and Time Initiated: ______________ ______________________

Log Use and Instructions:

- Begin by copying the actual log entry page several times. Do not write on the original.
- Use this form for logging Troubleshooting and Repair of any issue that has reached the 30 minute mark or for projects that just needs to be well documented.
- If you are tracking a System build, It is typical to remove the TSR Log from this binder, staple the pages together and keep it on the tech bench while the system is being built.
- The Log # should be created as follows: Year.month.day.issue # e.g. 2011.04.13.01 For each subsequent issue in a given day increment the issue number on the end.
- Fill in **all** available information before making a call to an escalated or paid support provider.
- Always log SRX, call tracking numbers and contacts as you get the information.
- Make log entries for any significant or notable item or every 15 minutes depending on how intricate the issue is.
- For more intricate issues DO NOT skip the ¼ hour entries! They will keep you aware or time on the issue and actual progress.
- Once this document is created, try to keep all related notes for the issue on (or attached to) these pages. It will make references much easier and will help keep duplicate work to a minimum.
- Remember to request a copy of all tech notes from whoever you work with on this issue. Microsoft, Symantec, etc. Attach a copy of those notes to this document.
- When the issue is resolved, three hole punch this document and place it in the Tech Notes section of the Network Documentation Binder.
- Annotate any related Service Tickets with a brief description of the problem and final resolution. Then simply refer to this TSR log by number for full details on the issue.
- Be certain to copy this document for internal service records or for the post mortem or the issue.

__:__

__:__

__:__

__:__

__:__

__:__

__:__

__:__

__:__

__:__

__:__

__:__

__ : __

__ : __

__ : __

__ : __

__ : __

__ : __

__ : __

__ : __

__ : __

__ : __

__ : __

__ : __

12. Network Migration Preparation

Review and Prerequisite Projects

- ☐ Review the status of the system build with the Project Manager in preparation for Installation.
- ☐ Verify that all Prerequisite Projects listed in the Spin-Off Projects and Issues section have been completed.
  - Server room cooling system installed
  - Dedicated AC outlet installed
  - Server rack installed
  - Equipment moved to make room for new server
  - New ISP connection installed
  - ______________________________
  - ______________________________
  - ______________________________

Preparing the Old Network

- ☐ Schedule an installation of .NET Framework 4.0 for all workstations as soon as possible using Continuum for managed machines or by whatever means available including script, emailed link, etc. for non-managed machines.
  - Coordinate any downtime with the Client Technical Contact.
  - Check on the deployment status frequently.
  - Create a Service Ticket for any machine that has not successfully been updated.
  - Mark the tickets as high priority so they get completed well in advance of the migration.
- ☐ Review all workstation Antivirus scan histories and statuses.
  - Verify each workstation has recently been completely scanned and cleaned.
  - Create a Service Ticket for any machine that has not recently been scanned or has un-cleaned viruses or malware.
  - Mark the Ticket as high priority and schedule it to be completed before the migration date.
- ☐ Create a group policy on the old system to disable Offline File Synchronization.
  - On the old server run the Group Policy Manager from the Administrative Tools group.
  - Navigate to the Domains*domainname*.local\Group Policy Objects container.
  - If an "*IT Management Company* Management Policy" does not already exist right-click on the container and select New from the menu.
    - Enter the New GPO name as "*IT Management Company* Management Policy". e.g. KPEnterprises Management Policy. Click OK.
  - Navigate to the "*IT Management Company* Management Policy" Policy Object, right-click on the object and select Edit from the menu.
    - If the old server is SBS 2003: Navigate to the Computer Configuration\Administrative Template\Network\Offline Files policy folder.

        - If the old server is SBS 2008 or 2011: Navigate to the Computer Configuration\Policies\Administrative Template\Network\Offline Files policy folder.
        - Adjust Offline File policy settings as follows:
            - Allow or Disallow use of the Offline Files feature – Disable
            - Prohibit user configuration of Offline Files – Disabled
            - Remove "Make Available Offline" - Enabled
    - Close the Group Policy Object Editor and the Group Policy Manger.

- ☐ Verify the DHCP scope on the old server has been narrowed so that it does not conflict with the new server when it is brought on line as follows:
    - Log on to the old server as the administrator and run the DHCP applet from Administrative Tools folder.
    - Navigate to the current Activated Scope, right click on it then select Properties from the menu.
    - Enter the new Start IP address and the End IP address as documented in the Discovery section - Domain Names, IP's, DNS and DHCP subsection.
    - Click OK to close the DHCP Scope properties window then close the DHCP applet.
- ☐ Schedule a reboot of all workstations as soon as possible using Continuum for managed machines or by emailing the Client Technical Contact requesting all users reboot their workstations as soon as possible.

Preparation for Server Installation

- ☐ If the old server will have to be moved from its location to allow for the new server to be placed there, Email the Client Technical Contact notifying them that the old server will be shut down temporarily during the lunch hour on the proposed move date. Be certain the email is cc'ed to the project manager.
- ☐ Verify that the DHCP service has been disabled on the new server before it is shut down so that it does not conflict with the old server when it is brought on line as follows:
    - Log on to the new server as the administrator and run the Services applet from Administrative Tools folder.
    - Location the DHCP Server service, right-click on the service and select Properties from the menu.
    - Click the Stop button to stop the service then change the Startup type to Disabled.
    - Click OK to close the DHCP Service Properties and then close all open windows.
- ☐ Verify that all the To-Do items on the Pack-Up / To-Do Checklist have in fact been done before power down the system.
- ☐ Shut Down the new server and begin pack up for move.
- ☐ Check off all Pack-Up items from the Pack-Up / To-Do Checklist only after they have in fact been packed up.
- ☐ Put the Pack-Up / To-Do Checklist back into the Network Migration Project binder in the Pack-Up / To-Do section.

Server Installation

Old Server Move

- ☐ If the location for the new server is the same as the location of the existing server, the old server will have to be shut down and moved.
  - Notify users the server is going to be shut down and then shut down the old server at the designated time.

Note: The client should already have been notified about downtime and the equipment change should have been scheduled ahead of time. If it was not, contact the Project Manager before proceeding.

- ☐ Remove any hardware from the old server that is to be migrated into the new server at this time as designated in the Discovery section of this binder. e.g. Tape drive and controller, DVD Burner, etc.
- ☐ Set up the old server in its designated location and verify all connections. Keyboard, Mouse, Monitor, Network cables, ILO connection, etc.

Note: If there is only one UPS the new server should be plugged into that UPS. If there is a concern over power failure before the old server is retired, a loaner or temporary UPS must be provided. At a minimum the old server must be plugged into a surge protector power strip.

- ☐ If the old UPS is being used by the new server and the old server simultaneously (even temporarily) verify all of the following:
  - Maximum load capability of the UPS.
  - Total maximum load for both servers during initial power up. (This is when any server will draw the most power)
  - Total load of all additional devise that must be plugged into the UPS in addition to the servers.
  - Verify that there is no possibility of overload with both servers powering up simultaneously before continuing.
- ☐ Power up the old server, logon and verify it can connect to the internet.
- ☐ Verify users can:
  - Print
  - Send and receive email
  - Connect to the internet
  - Connect to server resources such as mapped drives

New Server Installation

- ☐ Remove any equipment that may be located where the new server and UPS are to be installed.
- ☐ Take a few minutes to clean up the area where the server and UPS will be placed. Sweep or vacuum, straighten cables and label critical connections.
- ☐ Unpack and install the new UPS (if purchased) in its designated location and plug it into the wall outlet.
- ☐ Unpack and install the new server in its designated location and verify all connections. Keyboard, Mouse, Monitor, Network cables, ILO connection, Etc.
- ☐ Install any hardware that is being migrated from the old server at this time. e.g. Tape drive and controller, DVD Burner, etc.
- ☐ If a parallel or serial connected printer are being migrated from the old server plug them into the new server now.

Note: Do not move any printer from the old server to the new server at this time if it is being shared out by the old server. These printers will be migrated later.

- ☐ If a KVM will be used be sure to label all cables and the KVM display accordingly.
- ☐ Plug the server power chord into the UPS. Plug the data cable from the UPS into the server and power up the server.
- ☐ If the new UPS is being used by the new server and the old server simultaneously (even temporarily) verify all of the following:
  - Maximum load capability of the UPS.
  - Total maximum load for both servers during initial power up. (This is when any server will draw the most power)
  - Total load of all additional devise that must be plugged into the UPS in addition to the servers.
  - Verify that there is no possibility of overload with both servers powering up simultaneously before continuing.
- ☐ Power up the new server, log on to the administrator account and verify it can connect to the internet.
- ☐ Send a test Email to an account outside the local area network from the administrator account using OWA and verify it is received in that accounts email box.
- ☐ If the current UPS was not available during the server build and the server has not been configured for this UPS device, perform all steps in the System Build section - Hardware and Environment - UPS Power Management Configuration subsection.
- ☐ Label all new server connections and cables. Both ends. Power, UPS data, Net, etc.
- ☐ Open Windows explorer and connect to the old server !tech directory (*oldservername*\tech) to copy the entire !tech directory contents from the old server to the new server.

  Note: Only copy data and files that are relevant to the new system.
- ☐ Add and / or configure the default printer on the new server if possible. Typically the closest LaserJet.

  Note: Only set up a single default printer for the new server if it is a networked printer with an IP address or is physically connected via parallel or serial port. Do not connect to a shared printer on the old server at this time.

  Note: Only basic local or networked printer configurations are detailed here as there are too many possibilities for connections, drivers and configurations. These two procedures will cover most printers on most systems.
  - Open the Control Panel and navigate to the Devices and Printers container.
  - If the default printer uses a parallel, serial or USB interface to the server look at the list of printers to see if it was automatically detected and the drivers already loaded.
  - If the printer is present:
    - Right-click on the printer and select Set as Default printer from the menu.
    - Right-click on the printer again and select Printer Properties from the menu.
      - Click the Print Test Page button.
      - When the Print Test Page confirmation pop-up is presented click Close.
      - On the Printer Properties page click OK.
    - Close all open windows and skip to the next subsection.
  - If the desired printer is not present run the Add a printer Wizard and install the drivers as follows:

- Clicking the Add a printer button on the menu at the top of the Devices and Printers container.
- On the Choose a local or network printer window select the appropriate type of printer being installed.
- For a Local printer select Add a local printer on the Add Printer page.
  - Select the correct port from the Use an existing port dropdown list then click Next.
  - Now skip down past the For a Network printer... section to install the printer drivers.
- For a Network printer select Add a network, wireless or Bluetooth printer on the Add Printer page.
  - If the desired printer was automatically detected select it from the list of printers then click Next.
  - If it was not detected click the button indicating The printer that I want isn't listed.
    - On the Find a printer by name or TCP/IP address page click Add a printer using TCP/IP address or hostname then click Next.

  Note: Do not select Find a printer or Select a shared printer as this will result in a printer connection that will not likely be available after the migration.

    - On the Type a printer hostname or IP address page enter the IP address of the printer to be added in the hostname or IP field then click Next.
    - If the Additional Port Information Required page is presented select the correct device type from the dropdown list then click Next.

  Note: The default device type of Generic network Card will work for most printers. Only change the device type if the exact device type is known.

- On the Install the Printer driver page select the Manufacturer and Printer model from the list then click Next.
  - If the printer Manufacturer or Model are not listed click the Windows Update button to allow Windows to download additional older and newer drivers. Otherwise skip down to the step to type a printer name.
  - When the list has been updated select the Manufacturer and Printer model from the list then click Next.
  - If the printer Manufacturer or Model are still not listed click the Have Disk button to browse for the drivers. . Otherwise skip down to the step to type a printer name.
    - Navigate to the c:\!tech\hardware\printers directory and then on to the specific subdirectory for the model of printer being installed and the target operating system then click OK.

      Note: This assumes the !tech directory is on the C: driver and that the drivers have already been copied to the !tech directory. If not, they should be copied before continuing.

    - Select the correct printer from the presented list and click Next.
- On the type a printer name page accept the defaults then click Next.
- On the Printer Sharing page select Do not share this printer then click Next.

  Note: If at any time during the installation a Hardware Installation warning pops up indicating The software you are installing for this hardware: device name has not passed Windows Logo testing... Select Continue Anyway.

  - On the Success page click the Print a test page button.

- On the test page pop-up click Close then on the Success page click Finish.
- Edit the properties for the newly added printer and set the default resolution and color for this printer to the lowest resolution and B/W.
- Close all open windows.

Backup Secured

☐ Locate the two most recent, known good, Full Backup sets of the old system. Isolate them and if they can be write protected do so now.

Note: Many BDR and Offsite backup systems do not lend themselves to the easy isolation or duplication of landmark or historic backups. It is beyond the scope of this document to explain all the pitfalls of today's backup methods but in most cases they can easily be remedied by simply attaching a high speed (USB 2.0+) drive to the system and performing a Windows backup. Any time after hours.

DNS and Firewall Changes

☐ Review the Firewall Sub-System Migration checklist and perform any tasks possible. Refer to the Discovery section - Small Business Server subsection and the Domain Names, IP's, DNS subsection.

Note: At this time it is only required that the NAT Policy, Port Polices and Access Rules for the new server be created and configured for the new server.

Note: Unless otherwise explicitly detailed do not change or redirect any existing public IP entries

☐ Make or change any Public DNS entries required at this time. Refer to the Discovery section - Small Business Server subsection and the Domain Names, IP's, DNS subsections.

Note: Unless explicitly detailed otherwise this will likely only be a new DNS entry or a change for the HP Lights Out controller address. (*ilo.company.xxx*)

- If access to Public DNS records is directly available (NetworkSolution.com, GoDaddy.com, etc.) follow all directions applicable to the interface used to make edits to the DNS records for the client domain.
- If access to DNS is through the ISP or other third party initiate the changes according to the outlined methods of that entity.

Informing the Client

☐ Email the Client Technical Contact with the Server Install email to distribute to the users, informing them of the upcoming data migration. The email template can be found in the Communications / Training section of this binder.

- Be certain the outgoing email has been correctly formatted with a proper subject, the correct client company name, reply to address and technician name. Also verify every variable piece of data in the email body. e.g. dates, times, passwords, etc.

13. Network Migration ✳

General

✳ This is one of two critical sections that the Project Manager must keep close tabs on. The other section is the Planning / Timeline section.

Although extensive planning is put into the Migration Strategy and the checklist order, the actual migration is a dynamic process of completing all required tasks in the most appropriate and efficient order possible based on all the elements presented on migration day. Read Synergy.

During the entire life of the network migration process, data directory and file permissions may need to be set or reset more than once to accommodate subsequent tape restores or file synchronization operations.

As a general rule, always lock down critical company data but leave public data open until all data has been migrated. Then assign the required group and user level permissions.

Note: Whenever possible run migration processes such as RoboCopy on the new server as it has more resources.

Review

- ☐ Review all Checklists in this section to become familiar with the content and the order before proceeding.
- ☐ Review the entire Planning / Timeline section to become familiar with the planned migration Strategies and Methods proposed.

DNS and DHCP Setup

- ☐ Set up a DNS forwarder on the old server as follows:
  - Log on to the old server as the administrator.
  - Run the DNS applet from Administrative Tools folder.
  - Right-click on the SBS server name and select properties from the menu.
  - If the old server is SBS 2003:
    - Select the Forwarders tab and in the DNS domain section click new.
    - Enter the name of the new SBS server (Server name only, no suffix as in *servername*.local) in the New Forwarder field then click OK.
    - In the Selected domain's forwarder IP address list enter the new servers internal IP address then click the Add button.
    - Click OK to close the DNS Properties window. Close all open windows.
  - If the old server is SBS 2008 or 2011:
    - Select the Forwarders tab and click the Edit button.
    - Enter the name of the old SBS server (Server name only, no suffix as in *servername*.local) in the field at the top of the window then click OK.
    - Verify that the old server IPv4 entry shows OK in the Validated column.

    Note: Unless IPv6 was configured on the old server an entry for IPv6 will show up but will say no IPv6 address was found for the DNS name entered in the Validated column.

    - If IPv6 is not implemented on this network delete the IPv6 entry by selecting it, (The field will change to a data entry line with the old server name listed) then clicking the Delete button.

- Click OK to close the Edit Forwarders window then click OK to close the DNS Properties window.

☐ Set up a DNS forwarder on the new server as follows:

- Log on to the new server as the administrator.
- Run the DNS applet from Administrative Tools folder.
- Right-click on the SBS server name and select properties from the menu.
  - Select the Forwarders tab and click the Edit button.
  - Enter the name of the old SBS server (Server name only, no suffix as in *servername*.local) in the field at the top of the window then click OK.
  - Verify that the old server IPv4 entry shows OK in the Validated column.

  Note: Unless IPv6 was configured on the old server an entry for IPv6 will show up but will say no IPv6 address was found for the DNS name entered in the Validated column.

  - If IPv6 is not implemented on this network delete the IPv6 entry by selecting it, (The field will change to a data entry line with the old server name listed) then clicking the Delete button.
  - Click OK to close the Edit Forwarders window then click OK to close the DNS Properties window.

☐ Repoint Companyweb DNS resolution on the new server to indicate the old server as follows:

Note: In the next subsection the DHCP services will be changed from the old server to the new server and all machines will then be receiving DNS from the new server.

This means that DNS on the new server must be configured to point workstations to the old server when they attempt to surf to Companyweb, until the Companyweb is actually migrated to the new server.

- Log on to the new server as the administrator.
- Run the DNS applet from Administrative Tools folder.
- Navigate to the *servername* – Forward lookup Zones container, right-click on the container and select New Zone from the menu.
  - On the Welcome page of the wizard click Next.
  - On the Zone Type page select Primary zone, verify the box is checked for Store the zone in Active Directory then click Next.
  - On the Active Directory Zone Replication Scope page accept the defaults then click Next.
  - On the Zone Name page enter the internal domain name of the old domain then click Next. e.g. zdtminc.local.
  - On the Dynamic update page select Do not allow dynamic updates then click Next.
  - On the Complete the New Zone Wizard page click Finish.
- Expand the Forward Lookup Zones container and right-click on the newly created zone then select New Host A record from the menu.
  - On the New Host window enter the name of the old server in the Name field.
  - Enter the IP address of the old server in the IP address field.
  - Verify the box is checked to Create associated pointer (PTR) record then click Add host.
  - Click OK on the DNS success pop-up then click Done on the New Host window.

- In the Forward Lookup Zone navigate to the new domain that all workstations and users are being migrated to. (Not the newly created domain that points to the old server)

  e.g. DNS – *newservername* – Forward Lookup Zones – *newdomain*.local.

  - If the Companyweb entry is a Host A Record:
    - Right-click on the Companyweb Host (A) record and select Properties from the menu.
    - On the Host (A) tab in the IP address field enter the IP address of the old server then click OK.
  - If the Companyweb entry is a CNAME Record:
    - Right-click on the companyweb Alias (CNAME) record and select Properties from the menu.
    - On the Alias (CNAME) tab click Browse.
      - Navigate to the newly created A record for the old server by double-clicking on the new server name. It will present the Forward Lookup Zones container.
      - Double-click on the Forward Lookup Zones container and it will present the list of forward lookup zones.
      - Double click on the *olddomain*.local record and it will list the newly created A record for the old server.

        e.g. *olddomain*.local
      - Select the Host A record of the old server then click OK in the Browse window.
    - Click OK to close the Companyweb properties.
- In DNS manger right-click on the new server name in the folder tree on the left side of the window, select All Tasks – Restart from the menu.
- Close the DNS Manager.

☐ Change the server that is performing DHCP services from the old server to the new server now as follows:

Note: The DHCP cutover should be performed during off hours so as not to interrupt workstation access when IP information is renewed by workstations.

- Log on to the old server as the administrator and run the Services applet from Administrative Tools folder.
  - Location the DHCP Server service, right-click on the service and select Properties from the menu.
  - Click Stop to stop the service then change the Startup type to Disabled.
  - Click OK to close the DHCP Service Properties and then close all open windows.
- Log on to the new server as the administrator and run the Services applet from Administrative Tools folder.
  - Location the DHCP Server service, right-click on the service and select Properties from the menu.
  - Change the Startup type to Automatics, click Apply and then click Start to start the service.
  - Click OK to close the DHCP Service Properties then close all open windows.

☐ Test the new DHCP and DNS settings on a workstation as follows:

- Select a workstation to test and reboot that workstation.

- Log on to the workstation and from the Command Prompt run the command ipconfig /all to verify the DHCP server is pointing to the new server.
- Open Explorer, Internet Explorer, and Outlook to verify the workstation can see all local drives, access the internet, the old companyweb, and access email.

☐ Schedule a reboot of all workstations as soon as possible using Continuum for managed machines or by emailing the Client Technical Contact requesting all users reboot their workstations as soon as possible.

Note: Although most healthy workstations may not need to be rebooted to successfully change DHCP configuration it is highly recommended to avoid issues during production hours for critical workstations that must access critical applications.

Company Data Synchronization – Initiating

General

The Company Data Synchronization Strategy is as follows:

1) Use RoboCopy to synchronized data from the old server to the new server.
2) Run multiple instances if required.
3) After all drives are re-mapped at all workstation the RoboCopy session(s) are stopped.

Note: This section relies on the latest version of the program RoboCopy having already been downloaded and the executable being copied to the c:\windows directory of the new server. If it has not, do so now.

Synchronization Setup

☐ Verify there are no special instructions in the Discovery section - File and Data Storage subsection regarding data restore or redirection such as changing the Company Data directory name etc.

- Log on to the new server as administrator.
- Verify or establish authentication from the old server as follows:
- Open a Command Prompt window and enter the command net use *oldservername*\ipc$ and then press enter on the keyboard.
- If the response is The command completed successfully, authentication has been established, proceed to the next checkbox.
- If the response is The password or user name is invalid for *oldservername*\ipc$:
  - Enter *olddomainname*\administrator for the user name and press enter on the keyboard.
  - Enter the password for the old domain administrator and press enter on the keyboard.
  - The response should be The command completed successfully and authentication has been established. Do not proceed until this connection has been made.

☐ Create and run a batch file to synchronize all company data from the old server to the new server using the RoboCopy command as follows:

Note: This RoboCopy process assumes that both domain administrators have the default full access to all files and directories in the file structure being copied on their respective servers. If there are access problems during the copy, force full control permissions for the domain administrator on the entire directory structure at the root of the shared folder on either server as necessary.

- Create the batch files in the c:\!tech\migration directory and name them with the share name being synchronized. e.g. companydata.bat or publicdata.bat

- Copy and Paste the complete contents of the RoboCopy command line as found at the end of the Resources section of the Network Migration Project Template document or copy each line by hand from that section of this binder.
- Edit the command line to reflect the correct source and destination server names, share names and log file name.
- Run the batch file now. The command line should look like the entry below.
    - Verify the Source and Destination directories carefully.

Note: It is assumed the batch file(s) are being set up during normal business hours. If the test of the batch file is after hours the files will immediately begin copying and the program configuration output will scroll off the screen.

To prevent this and to verify the batch file command line is formatted correctly, temporarily change the run hours command line switch /R to exclude the current hour. After verifying the output is as indicated below, reset the /R switch and re-run the batch file allowing the files to begin copying.

> Log File : *newservername*\tech\migration\companydata.log
>
> ---
>
> ROBOCOPY :: Robust File Copy for Windows
>
> ---
>
> Started : Mon June 1 1423:18:02 2011
> Source : *oldeservername*\companydata\
> Dest : *newservername*\companydata\
> Files : *.*
> Options : *.* /V /FP /TEE /S /E /COPY:DAT /PURGE /B /XO /MON:1 /MOT:30 /RH:0000-0700 /R:1000 /W:2
>
> ---
>
> Hours : Paused at 14:23 until 18:00...

- Repeat the above process of creating and verifying batch files as required for each share being migrated to the new server as documented in the Discovery section – File and Data Storage subsection.
- Notify everyone on the Migration team that the batch file(s) have been created and launched and are to be left running on the server.
- Monitor the running batch file(s) regularly including shortly after the specified run time to verify the RoboCopy is running and copying as expected and that there are no issues.

Users Shared Data / Users Shared Folders Synchronization – Initiating

General

The Users Shared Data Synchronization Strategy is as follows:

1) Use RoboCopy to synchronized data from the old server to the new server.
2) Run multiple instances if required.
3) After all drives are re-mapped at all workstation the RoboCopy session(s) are stopped.

Synchronization Setup

- ☐ Verify there are no special instructions in the Discovery section - File and Data Storage subsection regarding data restore or redirection such as changing the Users Shared Data location.
- ☐ Log on to the new server as the administrator.

- ☐ Verify or establish authentication from the old server using the same method outlined in the previous subsection Company Data Synchronization – Initiating.
- ☐ Create and run a batch file to synchronize all Users Shared Data from the old server to the new server using the RoboCopy command as follows:

  Note: This RoboCopy process assumes that both domain administrators have the default full access to all files and directories in the file structure being copied on their respective servers. If there are access problems during the copy, force full control permissions for the domain administrator on the entire directory structure at the root of the shared folder on either server as necessary.

  - Create the batch file in the c:\!tech\migration directory and name it usersshared.bat
  - Copy and Paste the complete contents of the RoboCopy command line as found at the end of the Resources section of the Network Migration Project Template document or copy each line by hand from that section of this binder.
  - Edit the command line to reflect the correct source and destination server names, share names and log file name.

  Note: The default User data located is not the same on SBS 2003, SBS 2008, and SBS 2011.

      - If the old server is SBS 2003:
        - Stores user's data in a share called Users
        - Location is referred to as Users Shared Folders
        - Physical location is C:\Users Shared Folders
      - If the old server is SBS 2008 or 2011
        - Stores user's shared data in a share called UserShares
        - Location is referred to as Users Shared Data
        - Physical location is C:\Users Shares

  - Run the batch file now. The command line should look like similar the entry described in the previous subsection Company Data Synchronization – Initiating.
    - Verify the Source and Destination directories carefully.
  - Notify everyone on the Migration team that the batch file has been created and launched and is to be left running on the server.
  - Monitor the running batch file(s) regularly including shortly after the specified run time to verify the RoboCopy is running and copying as expected and that there are no issues.

IIS / Web Sites / FTP Sites Migration

General

The IIS / Web Sites / FTP Sites Migration Strategy is as follows:

Web Sites

1) Use MSDeploy to archive sites from the old server and to restore them to the new server.
   a. Redirect Web and FTP via DNS or Firewall to new server after new site is verified as running.

FTP Sites

1) Create FTP sites on new server.
   a. Copy FTP date from the old server to new server.

Attempting to move any other type of site may result in loss of data or connectivity issues.

Site Archive

☐ Log on to the old server as the administrator.

☐ Create a location for the Web Sites to be archived for migration as follows:

- If it does not already exist, create the directory c:\!tech\migration
- Create the directory c:\!tech\migration\sites

☐ Run the Internet Information Services (IIS) Manager, navigate to and select the Web Sites (or FTP Sites) container.

- Locate the site to be moved in the list in the right pane of the IIS Manger window (IIS6) or middle pane (IIS7).
  - Record here the site name and the Identifier.

Note: The Identifier must be exact or the archive process will fail.

Site Name: ________________________ Identifier:___________________________

Site Name: ________________________ Identifier:___________________________

Site Name: ________________________ Identifier:___________________________

☐ Download the appropriate Web Deploy v2.0 application (32-bit or 64-bit) from the Microsoft.com/downloads site to the c:\!tech\software\microsoft directory.

- Run the setup executable and follow the prompts of the Setup Wizard to complete the installation.
  - Accept all defaults including Typical installation.

☐ Run the Web Deploy Command console from the All Programs IIS 7.0 Extension folder.

- If a Run As window is presented select Current user, clear the checkbox to Run this program with restricted access then click OK.

☐ Run the following command from inside the Web Deploy Command console to archive a single site from IIS:

msdeploy -verb:sync -source:metakey=lm/w3svc/*siteidentifier* -dest:archivedir=c:\!tech\migration\sites*sitename*,encryptPassword=*administratorpassword* > c:\!tech\migration\sites*sitename*.log

Replace the following words in the command:

Siteidentifier with the site identity number recorded earlier

sitename (two locations in the command) with the actual name of the site

administratorpassword with the new administrator password

Note: This is one complete command. The line wraps because of the page width. Please pay attention to all spaces, comas and dashes. If there is any question use the msdeploy -help command for clarification.

Note: If a web site name contains a space the entire path (two locations) to the site in the command must be trapped by quotes.

e.g. -dest:archivedir="c:\!tech\migration\sites*website name*"

and

e.g. > "c:\!tech\migration\sites*website name.log*"

- Repeat this process until all Web Sites to be migrated have been archived.

Site Restore

- ☐ Log on to the new server as the administrator.
- ☐ Backup the existing IIS Web Sites now as follows:
  - Click Start, All Programs, Accessories, then click Command Prompt.
  - At the Command Prompt, type cd c:\windows\system32\inetsrv then press the Enter key.
  - At the Command Prompt type: appcmd add backup "BeforeNewSites" then press the Enter key.

  Note: To list all existing backups including the most recent by using appcmd.exe use the command: appcmd list backup

  Note: To restore a backup using appcmd.exe use the command:

  appcmd.exe restore backup "*backupname*"
- ☐ Download the appropriate Web Deploy application (32-bit or 64-bit) from the Microsoft.com/downloads site to the c:\!tech\software\microsoft directory.
  - Run the executable and when prompted install the complete version. Accept all defaults for location etc.
- ☐ Run the Web Deploy Command console from the IIS 7.0 Extension folder.
  - If a Run As window is presented select Current user, clear the checkbox to Run this program with restricted access then click OK.
- ☐ Run the following command from inside the MSDeploy Command console to restore a single site from IIS:

  msdeploy -verb:sync -source:archivedir=*oldservername*\tech\migration\sites*sitename*,encryptPassword=*administratorpassword* -dest:metakey=lm/w3svc/*siteidentifier* > c:\!tech\migration\sites*sitename*.log

  Replace the following words in the command:

  oldservername with the name of the old server

  sitename (two locations in the command) with the actual name of the site

  administratorpassword with the new administrator password

  siteidentifier with the site identity number recorded earlier

  Note: This is not two commands. The line wraps because of the page. Please pay attention to all spaces, comas and dashes. If there is any question use the msdeploy -help command for clarification.

  Note: If a web site name contains a space the entire path (two locations) to the site in the command must be trapped by quotes. e.g. -dest:archivedir="c:\!tech\migration\sites*website name*",

  e.g. -dest:archivedir="c:\!tech\migration\sites*website name*"

  and

  e.g. > "c:\!tech\migration\sites*website name.log*"

  - Repeat this process until all Web Sites to be migrated have been restored.
- ☐ Verify all site settings for each site that was restored as follows:
  - Refer to the site documentation in the Discovery section - IIS / Web Sites / FTP Sites subsection.
  - Run the Internet Information Services (IIS) Manager and navigate to the Web Sites container in Connections pane on the left.
  - Select the site to be verified from the Connections pane.

- Select Bindings from the Actions pane on the right.
- Modify Bindings as required. Most will incorrectly show the IP from the old server.
- Close the Internet Information Services (IIS) Manager.

IIS Backup

☐ Backup the new and existing IIS Web Sites now as follows:

- Open a Command Prompt, run as Administrator (Right-click on the program and select Run as from the menu)
  - At the Command Prompt type: appcmd add backup "AfterNewSites"

  Then press Enter on the keyboard.

Note: To list all existing backups by using appcmd.exe use the command: appcmd list backup

Note: To restore a backup using appcmd.exe use the command:

appcmd.exe restore backup "backupname"

FTP Sites

☐ Create FTP sites by following the directions outlined in the System Build section - IIS / Web Sites / FTP Sites subsection. Refer to the Discovery section - IIS / Web Sites / FTP Sites subsection for settings information about the old site(s).

☐ Copy FTP date from the old server to the new server using the procedure outlined earlier in this section called Company Data Synchronization.

DNS and Firewall Changes

☐ Review the Firewall Sub-System Migration checklist and perform any tasks that may be required to allow access to the new Web and FTP sites. Refer to the Discovery section - Small Business Server subsection and the Domain Names, IP's, DNS subsection.

Note: Unless otherwise explicitly detailed, there should be no additional changes required.

☐ Make or change any Public DNS records required at this time. Refer to the Discovery section - Small Business Server subsection and the Domain Names, IP's, DNS subsections.

Note: Unless explicitly detailed otherwise this will likely only be the Public Web and FTP sites that have just been migrated.

- If access to Public DNS records is directly available (NetworkSolution.com, GoDaddy.com, etc.) follow all directions applicable to the interface used to make edits to the DNS records for the client domain.
- If access to DNS is through the ISP or other third party initiate the changes according to the outlined methods of that entity.

☐ Test each Web or FTP site completely once the DNS changes have taken effect. e.g. connectivity, content and security. Test from the local network if required.

Drive Map Redirection

General

The Drive Map Redirection Strategy is as follows:

1) Consolidate all logon batch files or scripts into one batch file or script on the old server.

2) Point all existing drive maps to the new server so that users will only be accessing data from the new server where it has been synchronized to.
3) Use the users credentials if possible to access the shares on the new server. Use a power user or admin account if not.
4) Once workstations are joined to the new domain the new logon batch or script on the new server will take over.

Note: The overall goal of the steps outlined below is to redirect all drive mappings to the new server from the old server logon.bat file while using each users own logon ID for access. (Assuming it is the same for both the old and new servers or domains).

Note: Another credential (Including a temporary credential) that has sufficient permission to allow all users to access the migrated data without interruption may also be used.

Redirection Setup

☐ Log on to the old server as the administrator.

☐ Disable all existing logon scripts, batch files and group policies that map drives for workstations including the current SBS_LOGIN_SCRIPT.bat

Refer to the Discovery section - Active Directory / Group Policies subsection.

Note: Do not cripple or delete batch files, scripts or policies. Rename batch files and scripts (including those called by group policies) but leave the files and policies in place.

☐ Open Windows Explorer and navigate to the c:\windows\sysvol*domain*\scripts directory.

☐ Copy the file *newservername*\netlogon\logon.bat to the c:\windows\sysvol*domain*\scripts directory on the old server.

☐ Edit the logon.bat file that was just copied from the new server as follows:

Note: During editing remember that in SBS 2003 the users share name is Users and in SBS 2008 and 2011 it is UserShares.

- Replace all conditional drive mappings (except the net use for the %username%) with unconditional net uses so that all drives are mapped for all users regardless of group membership.

  e.g. Delete the ifmember line and remove the if errorlevel etc. so that each line is just a net use x: *server**sharename*

Note: This step is required because group membership may not be complete or correct at this time but all users will see all drives.

Note: If there are security concerns, they can be easily managed at the file and folder level.

- Add the following line as the first line of the batch file:
  - Net use *newservername*\ipc$ /user:%username% *defaultuserpassword*
  - Change the *newservername* name to be the name of the new server and change the *defaultuserpassword* to be the documented Default User Password.
  - Further modifications to this command line may be required as follows:
    - If the user naming convention used on the new server does not match the user naming convention used on the old server replace the %username% and *defaultuserpassword* with either the user name administrator and the administrators password or the username and password of any power user who will have access to all the shares being mapped.

      e.g. Net use *newservername*\ipc$ /user:*administrator administratorpassword*

        - If certain users accounts on the new server do not use the Default User Password enter an additional net use line for each of those users.

          e.g. Net use *newservername*\ipc$ /user:*JUser JUserPassword*

    - Test and troubleshoot the new logon.bat file from any workstation on the old domain before continuing.

    Note: The end result should be that all drives previously mapped to the old server now are mapped to the new server.

- ☐ Configure the Logon.bat to run under the Small Business Server Client Computer Group Policy on the old server.
    - Run the Group Policy Manager from the Administrative Tools group.
    - If the old server is SBS 2003:
        - Navigate to the Domains*domainname*.local\Group Policy Objects\Small Business Server Client Computer policy, right-click on the object and select Edit from the menu.
        - Navigate to the User Configuration\Windows Settings\Scripts (Logon/Logoff) policy.
    - If the old server is SBS 2008 or 2011:
        - Navigate to the Domains*domainname*.local\Group Policy Objects\Windows SBS Client policy, right-click on the object and select Edit from the menu.
        - Navigate to the User Configuration\Policies\Windows Settings\Scripts (Logon/Logoff) policy.
    - Edit the Logon item as follows:
        - Highlight the Logon Scripts item, right click then select Properties from the menu.
            - In the Script Name field click the Browse button then navigate to the location of the new logon.bat file.
            - Highlight the new logon.bat file and click Open.
            - The full path must be a UNC as follows: *oldservername*\netlogon\logon.bat.
            - Click OK to close the Edit Script window.
        - Click Apply in the Logon Properties window then click OK.
    - Close the Group Policy Object Editor and the Group Policy Manger.

Email Migration – Preparation

General

The Email Migration Strategy is as follows:

1) Export all user mailbox data from the old server into .pst's on the new server after hours.
2) Import all user mailbox data into new server from pst's after hours.
3) Redirect email flow inbound to the new server. (Anytime)
    a. This may be done before first Export only if the entire Export and Import will be completed in a short amount of time. e.g. Small data stores allow for single pass migration with minimal or zero downtime for users.
4) Users on old domain can access email on new server using OWA until their workstation is migrated.
    a. Shortcut to the new OWA is placed on their desktops ahead of time.

5) Perform the Export and Import again to catch any data that may have changed. (Anytime)
   a. Only required if data stores are very large and initial Export will take too long as to cause downtime for users.

Note: If it has been planned that email will be migrated in one sweep (Export then Import with no final sweep) the steps required to redirect email flow to the new server must be performed before continuing with any Email Migration – Initial Mailbox Export subsection.

Those steps are detailed in the Email Redirected to New Server subsection below.

Refer to the Discovery and Planning sections regarding the planned Migration Strategy.

Refer to the Email Redirected to New Server subsection later in this section for the checklist on redirecting email flow.

Specifics

The exact method used to export email from the migration Source System (old system) is determined by the Exchange Server version in place on the migration Source System (old system).

It must be clearly understood that each export method has its limitations and it is assumed that the Project Manager and Project Lead understand the implications related to each method.

The title of each Email Migration Export subsection clearly indicates the Exchange version the detailed steps are intended for.

The subsections titles are:

- Email Migration – Initial Mailbox Export from Old Server – Exchange 2003
- Email Migration – Initial Mailbox Export from Old Server – Exchange 2007
- Email Migration – Initial Mailbox Export from Old Server – Exchange 2010

Note: There is only one method used to import email into the new system.

☐ Log on to the new server as the administrator and create the directory named email in the c:\!tech\migration directory.

  - If a directory other than c:\!tech\migration\email will be used for storing exported email data note the exact location here:

    ____

Email Migration – Initial Mailbox Export from Old Server – Exchange 2003

Note: This subsection is intended only for a Source Migration System running Exchange 2003 (Small Business Server 2003). If the migration Source System is running a newer version of Exchange proceed to the Email Migration Export subsection indicating the correct Exchange version.

ExMerge Setup – Old Server

☐ Log on to the old server as the administrator.

☐ Download the Microsoft Exchange Server Mailbox Merge Wizard (ExMerge) from the Microsoft.com/downloads site to the c:\!tech\software\microsoft directory on the old server.

☐ Run the executable and when prompted for the extraction directory browse to or enter c:\!tech\software\microsoft then click OK. Click OK when the extraction is complete.

☐ Open Windows Explorer and navigate to the c:\!tech\software\Microsoft\exmerge directory.

☐ Copy the contents of the exmerge directory to the c:\program files\exchsrvr\bin directory.

☐ Create a shortcut to the ExMerge application on the server desktop.

Exchange Mailbox Store Permissions Setup – Old Server

Note: The changes that are about to be made to the Mailbox Store permissions must be done correctly or Exchange may be rendered unusable! If you are not clear on each step do not continue!

☐ Log on to the old server as the administrator.

☐ Run Microsoft Exchange System Manager and navigate to *DomainName*\Servers*Servername*\First Storage Group\Mailbox Store (*Servername*).

Note: If Display administrative groups is turned on the path will be *DomainName*\Administrative Groups\first administrative group\Servers*Servername*\....

- Right-click on the Mailbox Store (*Servername*) container and select Properties from the menu.
- Select the Security tab then click on the Advanced button.
- On the Permissions tab clear the checkbox Allow inheritable permissions from the parent to propagate to this object and all child objects.
- A Security warning window will prompt that Selecting this option means that the parent permission entries that apply to child objects will no longer be applied to this object... Click Copy.
- In the Permission entries list, delete all of the following entries:
  - Deny Administrator (*Domainname*\Administrator) Receive As
  - Deny Administrator (*Domainname*\Administrator) Send As
  - Deny Domain Admins (*Domainname*\Domain Admins) Receive As
  - Deny Domain Admins (*Domainname*\Domain Admins) Send As
  - Deny Enterprise Admins (*Domainname*\Enterprise Admins) Receive As
  - Deny Enterprise Admins (*Domainname*\Enterprise Admins) Send As
- Click OK on the Advanced Security Settings Window to close it.
- A Security warning window will prompt that You are setting a deny permission entry... Do you want to continue? Click Yes.
- A Permission warning window will prompt that The changes you are about to make will result in permissions being added to the access control list... Do you want to continue making this change? Click Yes.
- Click OK to close the Mailbox Store Properties window and then close Microsoft Exchange System Manager.

ExMerge Step 1 – Extract From Old Server

Note: The target location for the Extracted PST files is on the new server in the !tech\migration\email directory.

If the drive that the !tech resides does not have sufficient space to hold all the extracted PST files from the old server a new location and share must be set up before continuing.

The expected size of the Public and Private Stores can be found in the Pre-Discovery section - Email / Outlook / Exchange subsection.

☐ Log on to the old server as the administrator.

☐ Run the ExMerge application and at the Welcome screen click Next.

- Select Extract or Import (Two Step Procedure) and click Next.
- Select Step 1: Extract data from an Exchange Server Mailbox and click Next.

- Enter the old server name in the Microsoft Exchange Server Name filed then click the Options button.
  - On the Data tab check the boxes for User messages and folders, Associated folder messages and Items from Dumpster.
  - Click OK to close the Data Selection Criteria window then click Next.
- Select the mailbox for each user who will be migrated to the new system as documented in the Pre-Discovery Section - Users / Machines / Remote Access subsection. Always include the Administrator mailbox. Click Next.
- In the Locale Selection window accept the defaults and click Next.
- In the Target Directory window click Change Folder and navigate to the *newservername*\tech\migration\email directory ad click Next.

  Note: If a directory other than *newservername*\tech\migration\email will be used for storing exported email data refer to the Email Migration – Preparation section - Specifics subsection for that exact path.
- On the Save Settings window click the Save Settings button then click OK when the Program settings successfully saved window pops up.
- Click next to begin the Extract process.
- When all Processes are complete verify there are no failures. If there are failures you must review the ExMerge log files in the c:\program files\exchsrvr\bin directory.
- Click the Finish button to close the ExMerge application.

Email Migration – Initial Mailbox Export from Old Server – Exchange 2007

Note: This subsection is intended only for a migration Source System running Exchange 2007 (Small Business Server 2008). If the migration Source System is running a newer version of Exchange proceed to the Email Migration Export subsection indicating the correct Exchange version.

Note: Do not assume that Exchange Management Shell commands are interchangeable between Exchange 2007 to 2010. All commands in this subsection are tested and intended only for Exchange 2007.

Note: It will be necessary to perform these procedures from a workstation and not from the old server due to limitations in Exchange 2007.

☐ Select and designate a workstation as the Transfer Workstation for performing these procedures.
  - The machine should preferably a newer workstation. The faster the better.
  - The machine can be a technicians Laptop or even a virtual machine.
  - It must be joined to the old Domain.

Exchange Management Tools Setup – Transfer Workstation

☐ Log on to the Transfer Workstation as the administrator.

☐ Create a !tech directory in the root of the local drive on the Transfer Workstation.

☐ Download the Microsoft Exchange Server 2007 Management Tools SP3 (32-Bit) from the Microsoft.com/downloads site to the c:\!tech directory on the old server.

☐ Run the executable and if prompted by the UAC or any other security warning, select to allow the program to run.
  - When prompted for the extraction directory enter c:\!tech\ExchangeTools then click OK.

- ☐ Run the C:\!Tech\ExchangeTools\setup application.
  - On the Exchange Server 2007 setup welcome page select Step 5: Install Microsoft Exchange Server 2007 SP3.
  - On the Introduction page click Next.
  - On the License Agreement page select I accept the terms in the license agreement then click Next.
  - On the Error Reporting page select No then click Next.
  - On the Installation Type page select Custom Exchange Server Installation then click Next.
    - On the Server Role Selection page check only the box for Management Tools then click Next.
    - On Exchange Organization page accept the default of First Organization then click Next.
  - On the Readiness Checks page:
    - If the Readiness Check indicates no Failed Components click Install.
    - If the Readiness Check indicates an Failed Components review any Failed Management Tools Prerequisites.
      - For each component indicating as Failed, review the Error and perform the Recommended Action so that the Exchange Management Tolls installation can continue.

    Note: Most Failed components require only that certain built in Windows Features be installed, turned on, or configured or that specific updates have been applied to the workstation.

      - When all Failed components have been addressed return to the Exchange Server 2007 SP3 Setup Readiness Check page and click Retry.

    Note: If the setup program was closed for any reason re-run the setup and follow all steps above to return to the Readiness Checks page.
  - On the Completion page review any errors that may have prevented a successful installation.
    - Correct any errors and re-run the Setup wizard if required.
    - If there are no errors click Finish then close the Exchange Server 2007 setup wizard.
  - The Microsoft Exchange Management Console will be run automatically. Close it.

Exchange Server Permissions Setup – Old Server

- ☐ Log on to the old server as the administrator.
- ☐ Run the Exchange Management Shell from the Microsoft Exchange Server 2007 program group.
  - Run the following command to set permissions for the network administrator account to allow export to pst files.

    get-mailbox -server *oldservername* | add-mailboxpermission -user administrator -accessrights FullAccess
  - Verify the resulting output indicates no errors.

Mailbox Export from the Old Server

- ☐ Log on to the Transfer Workstation as the administrator.
- ☐ Run the Exchange Management Shell from the Microsoft Exchange Server 2007 program group.
- ☐ To export a single mailbox use the following Exchange Shell command:

  Export-Mailbox –Identity *username* –PSTFolderPath *newservername*\tech\migration\email

Note: This is one complete command. The line wraps because of the page width. Please pay attention to all spaces, comas and dashes.

Note: This command exports all data in the source mailbox to a new pst file with a name matching the mailbox alias in the location indicated by the PSTFolderPath.

Note: If a directory other than *newservername*\tech\migration\email will be used for storing exported email data refer to the Email Migration – Preparation section - Specifics subsection for that exact path.

- When prompted by the command to confirm Are you sure you want to perform this action, press enter on the keyboard to accept the default of Yes.

☐ To export multiple mailboxes based on a list:

- Create a text file called users.txt in the *newservername*\tech\migration\email directory.
- Populate the text file with only the aliases of the email users who's mailbox is to be exported.
  - The file should be a simple list of user alaises, one per line, no header or other data, as follows:

    JoeG

    Tom

    Bob

    SuzieS

    Administrator
- Run the following Exchange Shell command:

  Get-content *newservername*\tech\migration\email\users.txt | Export-Mailbox -PSTFolderPath \\newservername\tech\migration\email

  Note: This is one complete command. The line wraps because of the page width. Please pay attention to all spaces, comas and dashes.

  Note: This command exports all data in the source mailbox to a new pst file with a name matching the mailbox alias in the location indicated by the PSTFolderPath.

  Note: If a directory other than *newservername*\tech\migration\email will be used for storing exported email data refer to the Email Migration – Preparation section - Specifics subsection for that exact path.
- For each mailbox, when prompted by the command to confirm Are you sure you want to perform this action, press enter on the keyboard to accept the default of Yes.

☐ Monitor all Export processes carefully. For exports that have errors or have failed the solution often is simply to re-run the export for that particular mailbox.

Email Migration – Initial Mailbox Export from Old Server – Exchange 2010

Note: This subsection is intended only for a migration Source System running Exchange 2010 (Small Business Server 2011). If the migration Source System is running a newer version of Exchange proceed to the Email Migration Export subsection indicating the correct Exchange version.

Note: Do not assume that Exchange Management Shell commands are interchangeable between Exchange 2007 to 2010. All commands in this subsection are tested and intended only for Exchange 2010.

Exchange Server Permissions Setup – Old Server

- ☐ Log on to the old server as the administrator.
- ☐ Run the Exchange Management Shell from the Microsoft Exchange Server 2010 program group.
  - Run the following command to set permissions for the network administrator account to allow export to pst files.

    New-ManagementRoleAssignment –Role "mailbox import export" –User "administrator"
  - Verify the resulting output indicates no errors.

Mailbox Export from the Old Server

- ☐ Log on to the old server as the administrator.
- ☐ Run the Exchange Management Shell from the Microsoft Exchange Server 2010 program group.
- ☐ To export a single mailbox use the following Exchange Shell command:

  New-MailboxExportRequest –Mailbox *username* –FilePath *newservername*\tech\migration\email*username*.pst

  Note: This is one complete command. The line wraps because of the page width. Please pay attention to all spaces, comas and dashes.

  Note: If a directory other than *newservername*\tech\migration\email will be used for storing exported email data refer to the Email Migration – Preparation section - Specifics subsection for that exact path.
- ☐ To export multiple mailboxes based on a list:
  - Create a text file called users.txt in the *newservername*\tech\migration\email directory.
  - Populate the text file with only the aliases of the email users who's mailbox is to be exported.
  - The first line of the file must be only the word alias.
    - The file should be a simple list of user aliases, one per line, the header of alias, as follows:

      Alias

      JoeG

      Tom

      Bob

      SuzieS

      Administrator
  - Run the following Exchange Shell command:

    foreach ($i in (Import-Csv *newservername*\tech\migration\email\users.txt)) { New-MailboxExportRequest -Mailbox $i.Alias -FilePath "*newservername*\tech\migration\email\$($i.Alias).pst"}

    Note: This is one complete command. The line wraps because of the page width. Please pay attention to all spaces, comas and dashes.

    Note: This command exports all data in the source mailbox to a new pst file with a name matching the mailbox alias in the location indicated by the PSTFolderPath.

    Note: If a directory other than *newservername*\tech\migration\email will be used for storing exported email data refer to the Email Migration – Preparation section - Specifics subsection for that exact path.
- ☐ To export all mailboxes regardless of the username use the following Exchange Shell command:

$Export = get-mailbox; $Export|%{$_|New-MailboxExportRequest -FilePath "*newservername*\tech\migration\email\$($_.alias).pst"}

Note: This is one complete command. The line wraps because of the page width. Please pay attention to all spaces, comas and dashes.

Note: This command looks systematically at each mailbox on the old Exchange Store then attempts to export all data to a new pst file with a name matching the mailbox alias.

Note: If a directory other than *newservername*\tech\migration\email will be used for storing exported email data refer to the Email Migration – Preparation section - Specifics subsection for that exact path.

☐ The following Exchange Shell commands can be run at any time during the Mailbox Export to review the status and progress of the export.

- Single user Export Request:
  Get-MailboxExportRequest -Identity *username*\MailboxExport
- All recent Export Requests:
  Get-MailboxExportRequest

☐ Monitor all Export processes carefully. For exports that have errors or have failed the solution often is simply to re-run the export for that particular mailbox.

SQL Server Data Synchronization – Initiating

General

SQL Server Data Synchronization Strategy is as follows:

1) Schedule backup of SQL databases from old server to a local folder once a day early in the AM.
2) Synchronize the SQL backups to the new server using a RoboCopy routine.
3) Schedule restore of SQL databases to new server from a local folder once a day early in the AM
4) After all applications that utilize the databases have been migrated, disable the SQL and RoboCopy routines.

Note: All SQL procedures outlined in this checklist are for general use and assume that the compatibility of any database and eligibility for migration from or between any two versions of SQL has been previously verified by an appropriately qualified engineer.

Note: Two methods of backing up and restoring a SQL database are outlined in this section.

For Backup and Restore in a full versions of SQL (not Express, Workgroup, or MSDE) the preferred method is to create a database job using SQL Server Management Studio (not Express).

For Backup and Restore in a less robust version of SQL (Express, Workgroup, or MSDE) the preferred method is using NT task scheduler to run a SQL script created using SQL Server Management Studio Express.

Note: The methods outlined for SQL Express, Workgroup, and MSDE may not be readily be used on a server running a full version of SQL as the script file and command line do not specify an SQL Instance and therefore will likely fail.

Note: If SQL Server Workgroup Edition or higher is installed on the server it must have its corresponding full version of Management Studio installed as well.

Note: The steps and procedures detailed here are focused on Microsoft SQL Server Management Studio and Studio Express. Although no consideration is made for SQL Server Enterprise Manager the steps detailed for SQL Server Management Studio (not Express) should work with few exceptions for SQL Server Enterprise Manger.

Note: The Backup procedures are written for SQL Server 2005. The restore procedures are written for SQL Server 2008. Although some steps may differ slightly, the overall processes should be valid for SQL 2000 through SQL 2008.

Preparation – Old Server (SQL Server Management Studio Method Only)

☐ Logon to the old server as the administrator.

☐ Set the SQL Server Agent to run automatically as follows:

Note: These steps are only for a server that is running Microsoft SQL Server Management Studio. Do not perform these steps if the installed product is Microsoft SQL Server Management Studio Express (SSMSE).

- Run the Services applet from the Administrator Tool folder and Locate the SQL Server Agent (MSSQLSERVER) in the services list.
- Right-click on the service and select Properties from the menu.
- Set the startup type to Automatic, click apply then click the Start button if the service is not already running.
- When the service is started click OK to close the SQ Server Agent service properties window and then close the Services applet.

☐ Enable the 'Agent XPs' component as follows:

Note: These steps are only for a server that is running Microsoft SQL Server Management Studio. Do not perform these steps if the installed product is Microsoft SQL Server Management Studio Express (SSMSE).

- Run Microsoft SQL Server Management Studio and in the Connect to Server page (Object Explorer) in the Server name field enter the name of the old server then click Connect.
- In Microsoft SQL Server Management Studio click New Query on the Standard menu bar.
- Enter each line below one at a time exactly as shown

```
sp_configure 'show advanced options', 1;
go
reconfigure;
go
sp_configure 'Agent xps', 1;
go
reconfigure
go
```

- Click Execute on the SQL Editor Toolbar.
  - The SQL query results should be similar to the following:

    Configuration option 'show advanced options' changed from 0 to 1. Run the RECONFIGURE statement to install.

    Configuration option 'Agent XPs' changed from 1 to 1. Run the RECONFIGURE statement to install.
  - Review any entries in the messages window below the query window and address errors and correct issues as needed.
- Close Microsoft SQL Server Management Studio and if prompted to save changes to the query click No.

Preparation – New Server (SQL Server Management Studio Method Only)

☐ Log on to the new server as the administrator.

- ☐ Set the SQL Server Agent to run automatically as follows:

  Note: These steps are only for a server that is running Microsoft SQL Server Management Studio. Do not perform these steps if the installed product is Microsoft SQL Server Management Studio Express (SSMSE).

  - Run the Services applet from the Administrator Tool folder and Locate the SQL Server Agent (MSSQLSERVER) in the services list.
  - Right-click on the service and select Properties from the menu.
  - Set the startup type to Automatic, click apply then click the Start button if the service is not already running.
  - When the service is started click OK to close the SQ Server Agent service properties window and then close the Services applet.

- ☐ Enable the 'Agent XPs' component as follows:

  Note: These steps are only for a server that is running Microsoft SQL Server Management Studio. Do not perform these steps if the installed product is Microsoft SQL Server Management Studio Express (SSMSE).

  - Run Microsoft SQL Server Management Studio and in the Connect to Server page (Object Explorer) in the Server name field enter the name of the new server then click Connect.
  - In Microsoft SQL Server Management Studio click New Query on the Standard Toolbar.sbs2011
  - Enter each line below one at a time exactly as shown

    ```
    sp_configure 'show advanced options', 1;
    go
    reconfigure;
    go
    sp_configure 'Agent xps', 1;
    go
    reconfigure
    go
    ```

  - Click Execute on the SQL Editor Toolbar.
    - The SQL query results should be similar to the following:

      Configuration option 'show advanced options' changed from 0 to 1. Run the RECONFIGURE statement to install.

      Configuration option 'Agent XPs' changed from 1 to 1. Run the RECONFIGURE statement to install.

    - Review any entries in the messages window below the query window and address errors and correct issues as needed.
  - Close Microsoft SQL Server Management Studio and if prompted to save changes to the query click No.

Database Backup Job Setup – Old Server (SQL Server Management Studio Method Only)

Note: If SQL Server Management Studio is not installed (only the Express version or no version installed) skip this subsection and move on to the SQL Server Management Studio Express Method subsection below.

Note: During the setup of the backup job it is assumed and expected that the default selection will be made for everything not specifically noted here.

- ☐ Log on to the old server as the administrator.

- ☐ Create the directory named dbmigration in the primary public data folder so that it will be included in the previously configured RoboCopy synchronization. e.g. c:*companydata*\\dbmigration.
    - If a directory other than c:*companydata*\\dbmigration.is used note the exact location here:

      ____

Note: If an alternate location for the dbmigration folder or the database backup files is specified all steps outlined regarding SSQL database backup and restore must be modified accordingly.

Note: The location of the dbmigration folder must be included in an active synchronization routine or the files will not be copied to the new server automatically. Later procedures rely on this occurring.

- ☐ Run Microsoft SQL Server Management Studio and in the Connect to Server page (Object Explorer) click the dropdown arrow to the right of the Server name field, select the SQL server instance that contains the database to be migrated then click Connect.
    - Refer to the Discovery section – Premium Content subsection for which database(s) are being migrated.
    - If the instance is not listed select Browse for more, expand the Database Engine container select the SQL server instance that contains the database to be migrated, click OK to close the browse window then click Connect.

  Note: Sometimes the desired instance may not be listed no matter what. Any instance including the default SQL Server instance for any server can be connected to by simply typing just the name of the server (or server name*instance if known*) into the server field. e.g. zdtmsbs or zdtmsbs\\mydbases.

- ☐ In Object Explorer open the Databases container and select the database to be backed up (migrated) as documented in the Discovery section - Premium Content subsection.
- ☐ Create the database backup job as follows:
    - Right-click on the database and select Tasks – Back Up from the menu.
    - Select the General page and in the Backup set section enter *databasename*-migration for both the Name field and the Description field.
    - In the Destination section highlight each pre-existing backup destination listed and click the Remove button. Repeat this process until the list is empty.
    - In the Destination section select the Disk radio button then click the Add button.
        - On the Select Backup Destination page click the browse button to the right of the File name field.
        - In the Locate Database Files – *Servername\\sqlinstancename* window, navigate to the *c:\\companydata*\\dbmigration directory and then enter *databasename*-migration.bak for the filename.
        - Click OK to close the Locate Database Files window, click OK to close the Select Backup Destination window.
    - Select the Options page and in the Overwrite media section select Overwrite all existing backup sets.
    - Click the dropdown arrow to the right of the Script menu at the top of the window and select Script Action to Job from the menu.
        - In the New Job window on the General page enter *databasename*-migration for both the Name field and the Description field.
        - Select the Schedule page and click New.
            - Enter *databasename*-migration for the Name field.

        - In the Frequency section click the dropdown arrow to the right of the Occurs field and select Daily.
        - In the Daily frequency section change the Occurs once at field to 05:00:00 AM.
        - In the Duration section select End date and enter a date two weeks after the expected migration completion date then click OK to close the New Job Schedule window.
    - Select the Notifications page and check the box for Write to the Windows Application event log and verify the option is When the job fails.
    - Click OK to close the New Job window.
- Click OK to close the Back Up Database – *databasename*. The backup will run immediately.
- Click OK on the job completion notification window If the completion status is anything other than completed successfully address errors and correct issues as needed.
- Close SQL Server Management Studio.

☐ Repeat the above process as required for each database being migrated from the old server.

Database Backup Job Setup – Old Server (SQL Server Management Studio Express Method Only)

Note: If all Backup Jobs were successfully created using the SQL Server Management Studio Method outlined in the previous subsection skip this subsection and move on to the Database Synchronization subsection below.

Note: During the setup of the backup job it is assumed and expected that the default selection will be made for everything not specifically noted here.

☐ Log on to the old server as the administrator.

☐ Create the directory named dbmigration in the primary public data folder so that it will be included in the previously configured RoboCopy synchronization. e.g. c:\companydata\dbmigration.

- If a directory other than c:*companydata*\dbmigration.is used note the exact location here:

  ____

Note: The location of the dbmigration folder must be included in an active synchronization routine or the files will not be copied to the new server automatically. Later procedures rely on this occurring.

☐ If Microsoft SQL Server Management Studio Express (SSMSE) is not currently installed on the server download it from the Microsoft.com/downloads site to the c:\!tech\software\microsoft directory.

- Run the executable and accept all defaults.

☐ Run Microsoft SQL Server Management Studio Express and in the Connect to Server page (Object Explorer) click the dropdown arrow to the right of the Server name field, select the SQL server instance that contains the database to be migrated then click Connect.

- Refer to the Discovery section – Premium Content subsection for which database(s) are being migrated.
- If the instance is not listed select Browse for more, expand the Database Engine container select the SQL server instance that contains the database to be migrated, click OK to close the browse window then click Connect.

  Note: Sometimes the desired instance may not be listed no matter what. Any instance including the default SQL Server instance for any server can be connected to by simply typing just the name of the server (or server name\instance if known) into the server field. e.g. zdtmsbs or zdtmsbs\mydbases.

☐ In Object Explorer open the Databases container and select the database to be backed up (migrated) as documented in the Discovery section - Premium Content subsection.

☐ Create the database backup job as follows:

- Right-click on the database and select Tasks – Back Up from the menu.
- Select the General page and in the Backup set section enter *databasename*-migration for both the Name field and the Description field.
- In the Destination section highlight each pre-existing backup destination listed and click the Remove button. Repeat this process until the list is empty.
- In the Destination section click the Add button.
  - On the Select Backup Destination page click the browse button to the right of the File name field.
  - In the Locate Database – *Servername* window navigate to the *c:\companydata*\dbmigration directory and then enter *databasename*-migration.bak for the filename.
  - Click OK to close the Locate Database window.
- Select the Options page and in the Overwrite media section select Overwrite all existing backup sets.
- Click the dropdown arrow to the right of the Script menu at the top of the window and select Script Action to File from the menu.
  - In the Save As window navigate to the *c:\companydata*\dbmigration directory, enter *databasename*-migration for the filename then click Save.
- Click OK to close the Back Up Database – *databasename*. The backup will run immediately.
- Click OK on the job completion notification window If the completion status is anything other than completed successfully address errors and correct issues as needed.
- Close SQL Server Management Studio Express.

☐ Schedule the database backup as follows:

- In Control Panel open the Scheduled Tasks folder and select Add Scheduled Task.
- On the Scheduled Task Wizard initial page click Next then click the Browse button.
- Navigate to c:\program files\microsoft sql Server\90\tools\binn directory, select the sqlcmd.exe file then click Open.
- In the Task name field enter *databasename*-migration, select Daily in the perform this task section then click Next.
- On the schedule page set the Start time to 05:00 AM then click Next.
- On the credentials page enter the password for the Administrator account then click Next.
- On the final page of the Scheduled Task Wizard check the box Open advanced properties for this task when I click Finish then click Finish.
- In the Advanced Properties page on the Task tab add the SQL command switch –i followed by the complete path and name of the newly created SQL script line to the Run command:

  -i *c:\companydata\dbmigration\databasename*-migration.sql

  - The complete command should look as follows: "c:\program files\microsoft sql server\90\tools\binn\sqlcmd.exe" -i *c:\companydata\dbmigration\databasename*-migration.sql

  Note: This is one complete command. The line wraps because of the page width. Please pay attention to all spaces, comas and dashes.
- In the Advanced Properties page select the Schedule tab then click on the Advanced button.
  - Check the box for End Date and enter a date two weeks after the expected migration completion date.

- Click OK to close the Advanced Schedule Option window then click OK to close the Advanced Task Properties window.
- If prompted with a Set Account Information page enter the password for the Administrator account again then click OK.

☐ Test the scheduled task by navigating to the Control Panel – Scheduled Tasks, right-clicking on the new database backup task and selecting Run from the menu.

- Verify the backup ran successfully by first verifying the file was created as expected and then reviewing the Application event log. Address any errors and correct issues as needed.

☐ Repeat the above process as required for each database being migrated from the old server.

Database Directory Synchronization (All Methods)

☐ If there is no RoboCopy routine already configured and running that will migrate the dbmigration directory to the new server follow the steps outline in the previous subsection entitled Company Data Synchronization – Initiating to create and deploy a synchronization routine that will copy the directory to the new server.

☐ Monitor the RoboCopy routines running on the new server. Verify that the dbmigration directory is in fact being copied to the new server. Address any errors and correct issues as needed.

Database Restore Job Setup – New Server (SQL Server Management Studio Method Only)

Note: If Server Management Studio is not installed (only the Express version or no version installed) skip this subsection and move on to the Server Management Studio Express Method subsection below.

Note: During the setup of the backup job it is assumed and expected that the default selection will be made for everything not specifically noted here.

☐ Log on to the new server as the administrator.

☐ Run Microsoft SQL Server Management Studio and in the Connect to Server page (Object Explorer) click the dropdown arrow to the right of the Server name field, select the SQL server instance that either does contain or is to contain the new database that is being migrated then click Connect.

Note: The SQL Server 2008 default instance is the best location for new databases on a Small Business Server. The default instance will usually have the exact same name as the server.

- Refer to the Discovery section – Premium Content subsection for which database(s) are being migrated.
- If the target instance is not listed select Browse for more, expand the Database Engine container select the SQL server instance that contains the database to be migrated, click OK to close the browse window then click Connect.

Note: Sometimes the desired instance may not be listed no matter what. Any instance including the default SQL Server instance for any server can be connected to by simply typing just the name of the server (or server name*instance if known*) into the server field. e.g. zdtmsbs or zdtmsbs\mydbases.

☐ Create the new database if required as follows:

- Refer to the Discovery section – Premium Content subsection for all information required in creating the new database(s).
- In Object Explorer open the Database container, right-click on the container and select New Database from the menu.
  - Select the General page, enter the Database name and then enter the Owner name as documented.

    Note: If there is no previously designated owner leave the default entry of <default>.

  - In the Database files section change the Logical Names for each file listed to be exactly as documented for the database being imported.

    Note: If the database file names are not exactly correct the restore may not complete.

  - Click OK to close the New Database window and the new database will be created.

☐ Create the database restore job as follows:

- Right-click on the newly created database and select Tasks – Restore – Database from the menu.
- Select the General page and in the Source for restore section select From device then click on the browse button to the right of the From device field.
  - In the Specify Backup window select File from the Backup media dropdown then click the Add button.
  - In the Locate Backup File window click the dropdown arrow to the right of the Files of type field and select All files.
  - Navigate to the c:*companydata*\dbmigration directory and select the exact database backup file to restore from.
  - Click OK to close the Select the file window then click OK to close the Specify Backup window.
- In the Select the backup set to restore section check the box in the Restore column for all components listed.
- Select the Options page and check the box Overwrite the existing database.
- Click the dropdown arrow to the right of the Script menu at the top of the window and select Script Action to Job from the menu.
  - In the New Job window on the General page enter *databasename*-migration for both the Name field and the Description field.
  - Select the Schedule page and click New.
    - Enter *databasename*-migration for the Name field.
    - In the Frequency section click the dropdown arrow to the right of the Occurs field and select Daily.
    - In the Daily frequency section change the Occurs once at field to 06:00:00 AM.
    - In the Duration section select End date and enter the date that represents day one of the migration then click OK to close the New Job Schedule window.
  - Select the Notifications page and check the box for Write to the Windows Application event log and verify the option is When the job fails.
  - Click OK to close the New Job window.
- Click OK to close the Restore Database – *databasename*. The restore will run immediately.
- If the completion status is anything other than completed successfully address errors and correct issues as needed. Click OK on the job completion notification window to close it.
- Close SQL Server Management Studio.

☐ Repeat the above process as required for each database being migrated from the old server.

Database Restore Job Setup – New Server (SQL Server Management Studio Express Method Only)

Note: If the Restore Job was successfully created using the SQL Server Management Studio Method outlined in the previous subsection skip this subsection and move on to the next appropriate migration section.

Note: During the setup of the backup job it is assumed and expected that the default selection will be made for everything not specifically noted here.

- ☐ Log on to the new server as the administrator.
- ☐ If Microsoft SQL Server Management Studio Express (SSMSE) is not currently installed on the server download it from the Microsoft.com/downloads site to the c:\!tech\software\microsoft directory.
  - Run the executable and accept all defaults.
- ☐ Run Microsoft SQL Server Management Studio Express and in the Connect to Server page (Object Explorer) click the dropdown arrow to the right of the Server name field, select the SQL server instance that will contain the new database that is being migrated then click Connect.

  Note: The SQL Server 2008 default instance is the best location for new databases on a Small Business Server. The default instance will usually have the exact same name as the server.
  - Refer to the Discovery section – Premium Content subsection for which database(s) are being migrated.
  - If the target instance is not listed select Browse for more, expand the Database Engine container select the SQL server instance that contains the database to be migrated, click OK to close the browse window then click Connect.

  Note: Sometimes the desired instance may not be listed no matter what. Any instance including the default SQL Server instance for any server can be connected to by simply typing just the name of the server (or server name\instance if known) into the server field. e.g. zdtmsbs or zdtmsbs\mydbases.
- ☐ Create the new database as follows:
  - Refer to the Discovery section – Premium Content subsection for all information required in creating the new database(s).
  - In Object Explorer open the Database container, right-click on the container and select New Database from the menu.
    - Select the General page, enter the Database name and then enter the Owner name as documented.

      Note: If there is no previously designated owner leave the default entry of <default>.
    - In the Database files section change the Logical Names for each file listed to be exactly as documented for the database being imported.

      Note: If the database file names are not exactly correct the restore may not complete.
    - Click OK to close the New Database window and the new database will be created.
- ☐ Create the database restore job as follows:
  - Right-click on the newly created database and select Tasks – Restore – Database from the menu.
  - Select the General page and in the Source for restore section select From device then click on the browse button to the right of the From device field.
  - In the Specify Backup window click the Add button.
  - Navigate to the c:*companydata*\dbmigration directory and select the exact database backup file to restore from.
  - Click OK to close the Select the file window then click OK to close the Specify Backup window.

- In the Select the backup set to restore section check the box in the Restore column for all components listed.
- Select the Options page and check the box Overwrite the existing database.
- Click the dropdown arrow to the right of the Script menu at the top of the window and select Script Action to File from the menu.
- In the Save As window navigate to the *c:\companydata*\dbmigration directory, enter *databasename*-migration for the filename then click Save.
- Click OK to close the Restore Database – *databasename*. The restore will run immediately.
- If the completion status is anything other than completed successfully address errors and correct issues as needed. Click OK on the job completion notification window to close it.
- Close SQL Server Management Studio Express.

☐ Schedule the database backup as follows:

- Open the Task Scheduler from the Administrative Tools folder.
- Navigate to the Task Scheduler Library container then click Create Task from the Action pane on the right side of the window.
    - On the General tab in the Name field and the Description field enter *databasename*-migration.
    - Select the Triggers tab then click the New button.
        - In the New Trigger window in the Settings section select Daily, change the Start time to 06:00 AM.
        - In the Advanced section check the box Expire and change the date to represents day one of the migration.
        - Click OK to close the Edit Trigger window.
    - Select the Action tab then click the New button.
        - In the new Action window in the Settings section click the Browse button.
        - Navigate to c:\program files\microsoft SQL Server\100\tools\binn directory, select the sqlcmd.exe file then click Open.
        - In the Add arguments field enter:
          -i *c:\companydata\dbmigration\databasename*-migration.sql

          Note: Be certain there is a space at the beginning of the argument.
        - Click OK to close the new Action window.
    - Click OK to close the Create Task window.
- Test the scheduled task by right-clicking on the task and selecting Run from the menu.

☐ Verify the backup ran successfully by first verifying the file was created as expected and then reviewing the Application event log. Address any errors and correct issues as needed.

☐ Repeat the above process as required for each database being migrated from the old server.

Email Redirected to New Server

☐ Call the Client Technical Contact and follow up with an email informing them that new email has now been redirected to the new server and that until otherwise notified users should only use the Outlook shortcut on their desktop to get to their email.

- ☐ Redirect email to the new server as follows, referring to the Discovery section - Small Business Server subsection and the Domain Names, IP's, DNS subsections:
  - For changes related to DNS, gain access to the DNS zone records for this domain.
    - If access to Public DNS zone records is directly available (NetworkSolution.com, GoDaddy.com, etc.) follow all directions applicable to the interface used to make edits to the DNS zone records for the client domain.
    - If access to Public DNS is through the ISP or other third party, initiate the changes according to the outlined methods of that entity.
  - If there is no third party email filter being used such as Reflexion or Postini, change all MX records and email related A and CName records to point to the new server public IP address for each domain this Exchange server receives email for.
  - If a third party email filter service or system is used, change the delivery address the service uses so that it points to the new server public IP address.
  - Verify that the Exchange Autodiscover SRV record (Service record) exists and is correctly configured to point to the new server.
    - The format for the Service Record is indicated below.
      - The Target must indicate the new SBS server FQDN.
      - The Port must be the correct SSL port used for that public facing https site.
    - Service= _autodiscover, Protocol= _tcp, Name= @, Priority= 0, Weight= 0, Port= 443, Target= *remote.company.xxx*, TTL= ½ Hour

  Note: For Small Business Servers the Target name must match the Certificate issued to the Small Business Server. If it does no Autodiscover will pop up a security warning indicating a mismatched certificate name during Outlook configuration for clients outside the local network.

- ☐ Test email flow inbound by composing a new message to the administrator from an outside email account. Do not proceed until the email is successfully received by the administrator account.

  Note: If a third part email filter service is utilized by the new server do not send the test email from any account on any system that utilizes the same email filter service.

- ☐ Test email flow outbound by composing a new message to an email recipient on a mail system outside the local network. Do not proceed until the email is successfully received by the outside users account.

  Note: If a third part email filter service is utilized by the new server do not send the test email from any account on any system that utilizes the same email filter service as it will never leave that service and the test will be a false indicator of email flow outside the actual mail system.

Email Migration – Initial Import to New Server

General

Email Import will be performed on the new server using the Exchange Management Shell.

Note: By default, the import checks for duplication of items and doesn't copy the data from the .pst file into the mailbox or archive if a matching item exists in the target mailbox or target archive.

Exchange Server Permissions Setup – New Server

- ☐ Log on to the new server as the administrator.
- ☐ Run the Exchange Management Shell from the Microsoft Exchange Server 2010.

- Run the following command to set permissions for the network administrator account to allow import of pst files.

  New-ManagementRoleAssignment –Role "mailbox import export" –User "administrator"

- Verify the resulting output indicates no errors.

☐ Close the Exchange Management Shell now as new role assigned in the previous step do not take effect until EMS has been re-started.

Mailbox Import to New Server

Note: If Mailbox Quotas have been set they will directly affect the ability to import all email for some users.

Note: If any PST file is larger than the value set for the Mailbox Quota the limit must be raised, the PST must be filtered during import or email deleted from the PST before import.

☐ Log on to the new server as the administrator.

☐ Open Windows Explorer and navigate to the c:\!tech\migration\email directory.

Note: If the PST's were exported to an alternate directory refer to the ExMerge Step 1 – Extract From Old Server section for that exact location.

- Fix-up each PST name to exactly match the logon ID of the user mailbox the PST will be imported into. Refer to the electronic list returned from the Client Technical Contact.

  Note: If the PST name does not exactly match the user account name the import for that users PST will fail.

☐ Run the Exchange Management Shell from the Microsoft Exchange Server 2010.

☐ To import a single mailbox use the following Exchange Shell command:

New-MailboxImportRequest –Mailbox *username* –FilePath *newservername*\tech\migration\email*username*.pst

Note: This is one complete command. The line wraps because of the page width. Please pay attention to all spaces, comas and dashes.

☐ To import multiple mailboxes use the following Exchange Shell command:

$Import = get-mailbox; $Import|%{$_|New-MailboxImportRequest -FilePath "*newservername*\tech\migration\email\$($_.alias).pst"}

Note: This is one complete command. The line wraps because of the page width. Please pay attention to all spaces, comas and dashes.

Note: This command looks systematically at each mailbox on the new Exchange Store then attempts to import the corresponding pst by matching the mailbox alias with the name of the pst.

☐ The following Exchange Shell commands can be run at any time during the Mailbox Import to review the status and progress of the Import.

- Single user Import Request:
  Get-MailboxImportRequest -Identity *username*\MailboxImport
- All recent Import Requests:
  Get-MailboxImportRequest

Exchange Public Folder Migration

General

Exchange Public Folder Migration Strategy is as follows:

1) Folders and their contents are Exported from the old server and Imported into the new server using an Outlook client and a .pst file.
2) Set Permissions from Microsoft Outlook.

Public Folder Export

- ☐ Log on to any workstation as the domain administrator.
  - Preferably a newer workstation. The faster the better.
  - Can be a technicians Laptop or even a virtual machine.
  - It does not matter which Domain the workstation is on.
- ☐ Configure a new Outlook profile named Administrator for the old domain administrator and connect to the old Exchange server then Run Microsoft Outlook.

Note: The following steps are for Outlook 2010.

- ☐ Run the Import and Export wizard to export the Public Folders data as follows:
  - If exporting from Outlook 2010, click on the File menu and select Options then Advanced then click the Export button.
  - If exporting from Outlook 2007 or 2003, click on the File menu and select Import and Export from the menu.
  - On the Choose an action to perform page select Export to a file then click Next.
  - On the Create a file of type page select Personal Folder File (.pst) then click Next.
  - On the Select the folder to export from page navigate to and select All Public Folders that is inside the Public Folders container.
  - Check the box to Include subfolders then click Next.
  - On the Save exported file as page click browse and then navigate to the *newservername*\tech\miration\email directory, enter PublicFolders.pst as the file name then click OK.
  - Select the option Do not export duplicate items then click Finish to begin the export.
  - In the Create Microsoft Personal Folders pop-up window do not enter a password, just click OK.
  - Monitor the export until it has completed. Full control of Outlook will be returned when it is complete. When the export has completed click OK to close the Outlook Options window then close Outlook.
- ☐ Reconfigure the Administrator Outlook profile for use as the new domain administrator and connect to the new Exchange server, then run the Microsoft Outlook.
  - Click on the File menu and select Open then select Open Outlook Data File.
  - Navigate to the *newservername*\tech\miration\email directory and select the PublicFolders.pst as the file name then click OK.
  - In the Navigation pane on the left side of the window select the Folder List view then navigate to the newly opened folder.
    - For Office 2007 and 2003 this should be named Personal Folders.
    - For Outlook 2010 this will should be named Public Folders.

  Note: If the folder you have identified does not contain the IPM_SUBTREE subfolder you have not navigated to the correct folder.

- Navigate to the subfolder named IPM_SUBTREE.

☐ Review the folder contents and verify all public folder content has been correctly exported.

Public Folder Import

☐ Clean up the exported folders in the Public Folders.pst as follows: Refer to the Discovery section Email / Outlook / Exchange subsection.

- Delete any Public Folder that will not be imported into the new server. e.g. Internet Newsgroups.
- Rename any Public Folder who's name does not exactly match the existing target Public Folder so it will import directly into the existing folder instead of creating a new folder.

  Example: Rename the ZDTM Holdings Archive Public Folder to be the exact name of the target Public Folder ZDTM Inc Archive.

☐ Import the old Public Folder data into the new Public Folders as follows:

- From the subfolder named IPM_SUBTREE, right-click on the first Public Folder to move to the new Public Folders store and select Move "*publicfoldername*" from the menu.
- In the Move Folder window navigate down to and select the Public Folders – All Public Folders container then click OK.
- Repeat this process for each folder to be moved from the Personal Folder (PublicFolders.pst) into the new Public Folders store.
- Right-click on the Personal Folders container and select Close "Personal Folders" from the menu.

Public Folder Permissions

Note: Public Folder permissions can also be configured from Exchange Management Console by following the steps outlined in the Server Build section Email / Outlook / Exchange subsection

☐ Set the permissions for all Public Folders as follows:

- In Outlook navigate to the Public Folders – All Public Folders container, right-click on the first newly imported Public Folder to set permissions for and select Properties from the menu.
- Select the Permissions tab.
- Add or remove users and adjust the Default, Administrator and Anonymous users permissions as needed. Refer to the Discovery section Email / Outlook / Exchange subsection.
- Click OK to close the folder properties window.

☐ Close Microsoft Outlook and if necessary remove the Administrator Outlook profile.

☐ If the new Public Folders require storage limits to be set based on the Discovery section Email / Outlook / Exchange subsection configure them according to the procedure outlined in the System Build section - Email / Outlook / Exchange - Configure Exchange Public Folder Limits subsection.

Email Migration – Final Export from Old Server – Exchange 2003

Note: If it has been planned that email will be migrated in one sweep (Import then Export with no final sweep) the steps in this section will not be required and should not be performed.

Refer to the Discovery and Planning sections regarding the planned Migration Strategy.

ExMerge Step 1 – Extract From Old Server

Note: Extract of Mailbox data will be restricted to only the most recent data. Therefore the steps below are not exactly the same as the first Extract.

Note: The target location for the Extracted PST files is in the same location as the Initial Extract.

☐ Log on to the old server as the administrator.

☐ Run the ExMerge application and at the Welcome screen click Next.

- Select Extract or Import (Two Step Procedure) and click Next.
- Select Step 1: Extract data from an Exchange Server Mailbox and click Next.
- Enter the old server name in the Microsoft Exchange Server Name filed then click the Options button.
  - Select the Data tab and check the boxes for User messages and folders, Associated folder messages and Items from Dumpster.
  - Select the Dates tab then select Dates button.
    - In the From field enter the day before the migration began.

    Note: This will allow a small overlap for safety but as the import does not import duplicate items it will cause no issues.

    - Leave the To field as default.
    - Verify the Delivery Time button is selected in the Which message date/time attribute section.
  - Click OK to close the Data Selection Criteria window then click Next.
- Select the mailbox for each user who will be migrated to the new system as documented in the Pre-Discovery Section - Users / Machines / Remote Access subsection. Always include the Administrator mailbox. Click Next.
- In the Locale Selection window accept the defaults and click Next.
- In the Target Directory window click Change Folder and navigate to the *newservername*\tech\migration\email directory ad click Next.
- On the Save Settings window click the Save Settings button then click OK when the Program settings successfully saved window pops up.
- Click next to begin the Extract process.
- When all Processes are complete verify there are no failures. If there are failures you must review the ExMerge log files in the c:\program files\exchsrvr\bin directory.
- Click the Finish button to close the application.

Email Migration – Final Export from Old Server – Exchange 2007

Note: If it has been planned that email will be migrated in one sweep (Import then Export with no final sweep) the steps in this section will not be required and should not be performed.

Refer to the Discovery and Planning sections regarding the planned Migration Strategy.

Note: Exporting email based on the Sent or Received date is not recommended as it has been proven to miss critical data. This is simply because the criteria of Sent and Received date does not apply to all desired mail items. To properly perform a filtered export requires a very detailed and custom script which is beyond the scope of this document.

Because there is no reliable method to perform a Mailbox Export of only the most recent mailbox items refer to the Email Migration – Initial Mailbox Export from Old Server – Exchange 2007 section - Mailbox Export from the Old Server subsection and perform all steps outlined there to re-export all mailboxes required.

The import process default is to not import duplicate items.

Email Migration – Final Export from Old Server – Exchange 2010

Note: If it has been planned that email will be migrated in one sweep (Import then Export with no final sweep) the steps in this section will not be required and should not be performed.

Refer to the Discovery and Planning sections regarding the planned Migration Strategy.

Note: Exporting email based on the Sent or Received date is not recommended as it has been proven to miss critical data. This is simply because the criteria of Sent and Received date does not apply to all desired mail items. To properly perform a filtered export requires a very detailed and custom script which is beyond the scope of this document.

Because there is no reliable method to perform a Mailbox Export of only the most recent mailbox items refer to the Email Migration – Initial Mailbox Export from Old Server – Exchange 2007 section - Mailbox Export from the Old Server subsection and perform all steps outlined there to re-export all mailboxes required.

The import process default is to not import duplicate items.

Email Migration – Final Import to New Server

Note: If it has been planned that email will be migrated in one sweep (Import then Export with no final sweep) the steps in this section will not be required and should not be performed at the risk of data loss.

Refer to the Discovery and Planning sections regarding the planned Migration Strategy.

Mailbox Import to New Server

Note: If Mailbox Quotas have been set they will directly affect the ability to import all email for some users.

Note: If any PST file is larger than the value set for the Mailbox Quota the limit must be raised, the PST must be filtered during import or email deleted from the PST before import.

- ☐ Log on to the new server as the administrator.
- ☐ Open Windows Explorer and navigate to the c:\!tech\migration\email directory or wherever the PST files have been Extracted to.
    - Fix-up each PST name to exactly match the logon ID of the user mailbox the PST will be imported into. Refer to the electronic list returned from the Client Technical Contact.

  Note: If the PST name does not exactly match the user account name the import for that users PST will fail.
- ☐ Run the Exchange Management Shell from the Microsoft Exchange Server 2010.
- ☐ To import a single mailbox use the following Exchange Shell command:
    - New-MailboxImportRequest –Mailbox *username* –FilePath *newservername*\tech\migration\email*username*.pst

  Note: This is one complete command. The line wraps because of the page width. Please pay attention to all spaces, comas and dashes.
- ☐ To import multiple mailboxes use the following Exchange Shell command:
    - $Import = get-mailbox; $Import|%{$_|New-MailboxImportRequest -FilePath "*newservername*\tech\migration\email\$($_.alias).pst"}

Note: This is one complete command. The line wraps because of the page width. Please pay attention to all spaces, comas and dashes.

Note: This command looks systematically at each mailbox on the new Exchange Store then attempts to import the corresponding pst by matching the mailbox alias with the name of the pst.

☐ The following Exchange Shell commands can be run at any time during the Mailbox Import to review the status and progress of the Import.

- Single user:
  Get-MailboxImportRequest -Identity *username*\MailboxImport
- All recent Import Requests:
  Get-MailboxImportRequest

Fax System Migration

General

Fax System Migration Strategy is as follows:

1) If the existing Fax device must be moved from the old server to the new server:
   a. At noon the previously arranged time down the old server and remove the specific faxing hardware. Re-start the old server.
   b. Down the new server and install the specific faxing hardware. Re-start the new server.
2) Configure the faxing service and test.

Note: Some of the tasks in this section only apply if the Fax device is being migrated from the old server into the new server. Refer to the Discovery section - Small Business Server and Related subsection.

Note: The client should already have been notified about downtime and the equipment change should have been scheduled ahead of time. If it was not, contact the Project Manager before proceeding.

☐ Notify users early in the day that the server is going to be shutdown at noon (or other previously arranged time) for approximately 30 minutes.

☐ At noon (or other previously arranged time) shutdown both the old server and the new server.

☐ Remove the specified Fax modem or controller from the old server and install it into the new server. Refer to the Discovery section - Small Business Server and Related subsection.

☐ Start up the new server, log on as the Administrator.

☐ Configure the Fax System by following the procedure outlined in the System Build section – small Business Server – Other tasks subsection.

☐ If the fax modem or controller was migrated from the old server to the new server inform the Client Technical Contact that faxing services from the old server will no longer be available and that as soon as workstations are joined to the new server users will again be able to fax from their workstation applications.

Companyweb and SharePoint Migration

General

Companyweb and SharePoint Migration Strategy is as follows:

1) Redirect public access to the new Companyweb via DNS when it is ready for use.
2) Record basic web component settings and permissions from the old Companyweb.
3) Apply basic web component settings and permissions to the new Companyweb.

4) Replicate data item by item to the new Companyweb.

Note: Due to the innumerous possibilities of configuration for SharePoint sites including Companyweb the successful timely migration of these sites may rely heavily on resources outside of the Migration team.

For intricate SharePoint or Companyweb sites it is assumed that the project manager has arranged for the same resources who built or maintain these sites to be closely involved in the migration of those sites.

Note: The procedure outlined below is focused on a basic (and mostly standard) Companyweb site. These methods will likely work well for other sites with some modifications and or expansion.

Note: It will be necessary to perform these procedures from a workstation and not from the new server due to security setting in Internet Explorer on the new server.

☐ Select and designate a workstation as the Transfer Workstation for performing these procedures.

- The machine should preferably a newer workstation. The faster the better.
- The machine can be a technicians Laptop or even a virtual machine.
- It does not matter which Domain the workstation is on.

Redirecting Access to Companyweb

☐ At the appropriate time during the network migration notify the Client Contact that the Companyweb migration is going to take place.

Ask them to inform all users that:

- There will be a brief interruption in the availability of Companyweb.
- Users may have to reboot their computer before they can access the new company web.

Note: Access to the Companyweb from either domain relies on the default method of user name and passwords matching during migration. If they do not the user may need to enter credentials for the appropriate domain to access Companyweb.

Note: Any users who attempts to access the new Companyweb will see the new Companyweb content being migrated in and content becoming available as it happens.

DNS and Firewall Changes

☐ Review the Firewall Sub-System Migration checklist and perform any tasks that may be required to allow access to the new Companyweb and SharePoint sites. Refer to the Discovery section - Small Business Server subsection and the Domain Names, IP's, DNS subsection.

Note: Unless otherwise explicitly detailed, there should be no additional changes required.

☐ Make or change any Public DNS records required at this time. Refer to the Discovery section - Small Business Server subsection and the Domain Names, IP's, DNS subsections.

Note: Unless explicitly detailed otherwise this will likely only be the Public DNS record for the specific Companyweb and SharePoint sites that are about to be migrated.

- For changes related to Public DNS, gain access to the Public DNS zone records for this domain.
  - If access to Public DNS records is directly available (NetworkSolution.com, GoDaddy.com, etc.) follow all directions applicable to the interface used to make edits to the DNS records for the client domain.
  - If access to Public DNS is through the ISP or other third party initiate the changes according to the outlined methods of that entity.

☐ Restore the Original Companyweb internal DNS entry on the new server as follows:

- Log on to the new server as the administrator and run the DNS applet from Administrative Tools folder.

- Navigate to the new domain Forward Lookup Zone.

  e.g. DNS – *newservername* – Forward Lookup Zones – *newdomain*.local.

  - If the Companyweb entry is a Host A Record:
    - Right-click on the Companyweb Host (A) record and select Properties from the menu.
    - On the Host (A) tab in the IP address field enter the IP address of the new server then click OK.
  - If the Companyweb entry is a CNAME Record:
    - Right-click on the companyweb Alias (CNAME) record and select Properties from the menu.
    - On the Alias (CNAME) tab click Browse.
      - Navigate to the A record for the new server by double-clicking on the new server name. It will present the Forward Lookup Zones container.
      - Double-click on the Forward Lookup Zones container and it will present the list of forward lookup zones.
      - Double click on the *newdomain*.local record and it will list all A record for the new domain.
      - Select the *newservername* Host (A) record then click OK.
    - Click OK to close the Companyweb properties.
- In DNS manger right-click on the new server name in the folder tree on the left side of the window, select All Tasks – Restart from the menu.
- Close the DNS Manager.

☐ Test the Companyweb and SharePoint sites completely once the Internal and Public DNS changes have taken effect.

e.g. Connectivity, Content and Security.

Restricting Access to the Old Companyweb – SBS 2003 Only

☐ Log on to the old server as the administrator and run the Internet Information Services (IIS) Manager.

☐ Navigate to the Web Sites\Companyweb container.

- Right-click on the companyweb Site and select Properties from the menu.
- Select the Directory Security tab and in the IP address and domain name restriction section click on the Edit button.
- In the IP address and domain name restriction window select the option Denied access and then click the Add button.
- In the Grant Access window select Singe computer as the type and enter the IP address of the old server and click OK.
- Click OK to close the IP address and domain name restriction window, click OK to close the Companyweb Properties window and then close IIS Manager.

Restricting Access to the Old Companyweb – SBS 2008 or 2011 Only

☐ Log on to the old server as the administrator and run the Internet Information Services (IIS) Manager.

☐ Navigate to the Sites\SBS SharePoint container.

- Double Click on the IPv4 Address and Domain Restrictions feature icon in center pane of IIS Manager.
- Select Edit Feature Settings from the Actions pane on the right side of the IIS Manager.
  - In the Edit IP and Domain Restrictions Settings window change the Access for unspecified clients to Deny then click OK.
- Select Add Allow Entry from the Actions pane on the right side of the IIS Manager.
  - In the Add Allow Restriction Rule window enter the IP address of the new server in the Specific IPv4 address field then click OK.
- Close IIS Manager.

Export Content From Old Server - Preparation

Note: Only perform the steps outlined in this subsection if the Companyweb site is to be migrated as documented in the Discovery section - Companyweb / SharePoint subsection.

☐ Log on to the designated Transfer Workstation as the domain administrator.

☐ Edit the hosts file on the Transfer Workstation to allow access to the old companyweb site from Internet Explorer as follows:

- Open Windows Explorer and navigate to the c:\windows\system32\drivers\etc directory, right click on the hosts file and select Edit from the menu.
- At the bottom of the file enter a new line that reads:
  - *ipaddressofoldserver* companyweb

  Example: 192.168.16.1 companyweb
- Close notepad and when prompted to save the file select Save.

  Note: If prompted that the file cannot be saved in the current directory due to permissions it may be required that the file be saved in an alternate directory then moved into the c:\windows\system32\drivers\etc after permissions to edit files in that directory are set and the original hosts file renamed to hosts.bak.

  Note: If the host file is saved to an alternate location it will likely be named hosts.txt. When moved to the c:\windows\system32\drivers\etc directory it must have the file name extension removed or it will not be recognized.

  Note: If at any time the UAC requires verification to perform any operations related to editing the hosts file on the workstation permissions, select to allow those actions.

☐ Open Windows Explorer, navigate to the *newservername*\tech\migration directory and create a new directory called companyweb.

☐ Open Internet Explorer and navigate to http://companyweb.

- If prompted to connect as a user, enter the credentials for that domains administrator.

  Note: If the companyweb that is presented is not the old companyweb site, review the steps outlined above involving the edit of the hosts file.
- Do not proceed until the old companyweb site is presented as expected.

Export Content From Old Server – SBS 2003 Only

☐ Record the critical settings information for the Companyweb top level site as follows:

- On the Companyweb Home page select Site Settings from the main menu at the top of the page.

- Document in detail the critical settings for each of the links in the Administrator, Customization, and Information sections.

  Note: Print Screens and Print outs are sometimes the easiest.

  - Administration
    - Manage users
    - Manage sites and workspaces
    - Configure Site and Workspace Creation
  - Customization
    - Change site title and description
    - Apply theme to site
  - Manage My Information
    - My alerts on this site

☐ Record the critical settings and data for the Companyweb home page as follows:

- On the Companyweb site select Home from the main menu at the top of the page.
- On the Internet Explorer menu bar select Page – Save As from the menu.

  Note: On IE 9 the Command bar must be visible to use the Page menu items.

  - In the Save Webpage window Navigate to the *newservername*\tech\migration\companyweb directory.
  - Enter Companyweb-Home in the File name field.
  - Select the file type of Web Archive, single file (*.mht) then click Save.
- On the Companyweb Home page in the upper right corner click on the dropdown arrow to the right of the Modify Shared Page link, select Modify Shared Web Parts - Announcements from the menu.
  - Document in detail the critical settings for the List Views, Appearance, Layout, and Advanced sections.
- On the Companyweb Home page in the upper right corner click on the dropdown arrow to the right of the Modify Shared Page link, select Modify Shared Web Parts – Site Image from the menu.
  - Document in detail the critical settings for the List Views, Appearance, Layout, and Advanced sections.
  - Locate the site image, right-click on the image and select Save Picture As.

    Note: The default location is Companyweb > Pictures > Photos

    - In the Save Picture window navigate to the *newservername*\tech\migration\companyweb directory.
    - Accept the default name for the image and click Save.
- On the Companyweb Home page in the upper right corner click on the dropdown arrow to the right of the Modify Shared Page link, select Modify Shared Web Parts – Links from the menu.
  - Document in detail the critical settings for the List Views, Appearance, Layout, and Advanced sections.
- Repeat the above processes as required for any additional Web Parts on the Home page not listed here.

- ☐ Record the critical settings and data for Companyweb Documents and Lists as follows:
    - o On the Companyweb Home page select Documents and Lists from the main menu at the top of the page.
    - o Select the first Documents and Lists component that critical settings will be documented for and that page will open.
        - o Select modify settings and columns from the Select A view menu on the left.
        - o Document in detail the critical settings for the component.
    - o Repeat the above processes as required for all utilized Documents and Lists.

      Projects, Presentations, Archived Documents, Incoming Faxes, General Documents,

      Company Photos, Help Desk, Vacation Calendar, General Discussion
- ☐ Download data for Documents and Lists components as follows:
    - o Open Windows Explorer and navigate to the *newservername*\tech\migration\companyweb directory.
    - o On the Companyweb Home page select Documents and Lists from the main menu at the top of the page.
    - o Select the Documents and Lists component that contains the data to be migrated and that page will open.
        - o Select Explorer View from the Select A view menu on the left.
        - o Select all documents and folders in the library, right-click on the selection and select Copy from the menu.
        - o Switch to the previously opened Windows Explorer, right-click in the*newservername*\tech\migration\companyweb folder and select New\Folder, enter the name of the Documents and Lists component for the new folder name.
        - o Open the newly created folder, right-click and select Paste from the menu.
    - o Repeat the above process as required for each Documents and Lists component to be migrated.

Export Content From Old Server – SBS 2008 Only

- ☐ Record the critical settings information for the Companyweb top level site as follows:
    - o On the Companyweb Home page select Site Settings from the Site Actions menu at the top of the page.
    - o Document in detail the critical settings for each of the links in the Users and Permissions, Look and Feel, and Site Administrator sections.

      Note: Print Screens and Print outs are sometimes the easiest.
        - o Users and Permissions
            - o People and groups
            - o Advanced permissions
        - o Look and Feel
            - o Title, description, and icon
            - o Site theme
            - o Quick Launch
        - o Site Administrator

- Site libraries and lists
- User alerts
- Sites and workspaces

☐ Record the critical settings and data for the Companyweb home page as follows:

- On the Companyweb site select Home from the main menu at the top of the page.
- On the Internet Explorer menu bar select Page – Save As from the menu.

  Note: On IE 9 the Command bar must be visible to use the Page menu items.

  - In the Save Webpage window Navigate to the *newservername*\tech\migration\companyweb directory.
  - Enter Companyweb-Home in the File name field.
  - Select the file type of Web Archive, single file (*.mht) then click Save.
- On the Companyweb Home page in the upper right corner click on the Site Actions menu dropdown and select Edit Page.
  - In the Announcement Web Part click the Edit menu dropdown and select Modify Shared Web Part from the menu.
    - Document in detail the critical settings for the List Views, Appearance, Layout, and Advanced sections.
    - Close the Modify Shared Web Part window by selecting Cancel at the bottom of the window.
  - In the Calendar Web Part click the Edit menu dropdown and select Modify Shared Web Part from the menu.
    - Document in detail the critical settings for the List Views, Appearance, Layout, and Advanced sections.
    - Close the Modify Shared Web Part window by selecting Cancel at the bottom of the window.
  - In the Links Web Part click the Edit menu dropdown and select Modify Shared Web Part from the menu.
    - Document in detail the critical settings for the List Views, Appearance, Layout, and Advanced sections.
    - Close the Modify Shared Web Part window by selecting Cancel at the bottom of the window.
  - In the Site Image Web Part click the Edit menu dropdown and select Modify Shared Web Part from the menu.
    - Document in detail the critical settings for the List Views, Appearance, Layout, and Advanced sections.
    - Close the Modify Shared Web Part window by selecting Cancel at the bottom of the window.
  - Locate the site image, right-click on the image and select Save Picture As.

    Note: The default location is Companyweb > Pictures > Photos

    - In the Save Picture window navigate to the *newservername*\tech\migration\companyweb directory.
    - Accept the default name for the image and click Save.

- Repeat the above processes as required for any additional Web Parts on the Home page not listed here.

☐ Record the critical settings and data for Companyweb Site Libraries and Lists as follows:

- On the Companyweb Home page in the upper right corner click on the Site Actions menu dropdown, select Site settings then select Site Libraries and Lists from the Site Administration section.
- Select the first Site Libraries and Lists component that critical settings will be documented for and that page will open.
    - Document in detail the critical settings for the component.
- Repeat the above processes as required for all utilized Site Libraries and Lists.

  Announcements, Calendar, Fax Center, Links, Pictures, Shared Documents, Tasks, Team Discussion.

☐ Download data for Site Libraries and Lists components as follows:

- Open Windows Explorer and navigate to the *newservername*\tech\migration\companyweb directory.
- On the Companyweb Home page select Documents from the View All Site Content menu on the left side of the window.
- Select the Site Libraries and Lists component that contains the data to be migrated and that page will open.
    - Select Explorer View from the View dropdown menu on the upper right.
    - Select all documents and folders in the library, right-click on the selection and select Copy from the menu.
    - Switch to the previously opened Windows Explorer, right-click in the*newservername*\tech\migration\companyweb folder and select New\Folder, enter the name of the Site Libraries and Lists component for the new folder name.
    - Open the newly created folder, right-click and select Paste from the menu.
- Repeat the above process as required for each Site Libraries and Lists component to be migrated.

Export Content From Old Server – SBS 2011 Only

☐ Record the critical settings information for the Companyweb top level site as follows:

- On the Companyweb Home page select Site Settings from the Site Actions menu at the top left of the page.
- Document in detail the critical settings for each of the links in the Users and Permissions, Look and Feel, and Site Administrator sections.

  Note: Print Screens and Print outs are sometimes the easiest.
    - Users and Permissions
        - People and groups
        - Site permissions
    - Site Administrator
        - Site libraries and lists
        - User alerts

    - Sites and workspaces
  - Look and Feel
    - Title, description, and icon
    - Site theme
    - Quick Launch

- ☐ Record the critical settings and data for the Companyweb home page as follows:
  - On the Companyweb site select Home from the main menu at the top of the page.
  - On the Internet Explorer menu bar select Page – Save As from the menu.

    Note: On IE 9 the Command bar must be visible to use the Page menu items.

    - In the Save Webpage window Navigate to the *newservername*\tech\migration\companyweb directory.
    - Enter Companyweb-Home in the File name field.
    - Select the file type of Web Archive, single file (*.mht) then click Save.
  - On the Companyweb Home page in the upper left corner click on the Site Actions menu dropdown and select Edit Page.
    - In the Announcement Web Part, hover the mouse over the title bar of the Web Part then click the menu dropdown and select Edit Web Part.
      - Document in detail the critical settings for the List Views, Appearance, Layout, Advanced, AJAX Options, and Miscellaneous sections.
      - Close the Modify Shared Web Part window by selecting Cancel at the bottom of the window.
    - In the Calendar Web Part, hover the mouse over the title bar of the Web Part then click the menu dropdown and select Edit Web Part.
      - Document in detail the critical settings for the List Views, Appearance, Layout, Advanced, AJAX Options, and Miscellaneous sections.
      - Close the Modify Shared Web Part window by selecting Cancel at the bottom of the window.
    - In the Links Web Part, hover the mouse over the title bar of the Web Part then click the menu dropdown and select Edit Web Part.
      - Document in detail the critical settings for the List Views, Appearance, Layout, Advanced, AJAX Options, and Miscellaneous sections.
      - Close the Modify Shared Web Part window by selecting Cancel at the bottom of the window.
    - In the Site Image Web Part, hover the mouse over the title bar of the Web Part then click the menu dropdown and select Edit Web Part.
      - Document in detail the critical settings for the List Views, Appearance, Layout, Advanced, AJAX Options, and Miscellaneous sections.
      - Close the Modify Shared Web Part window by selecting Cancel at the bottom of the window.
    - Locate the site image, right-click on the image and select Save Picture As.

      Note: The default location is Companyweb > Pictures > Pictures

  - In the Save Picture window navigate to the *newservername*\tech\migration\companyweb directory.
  - Accept the default name for the image and click Save.
- Repeat the above processes as required for any additional Web Parts on the Home page not listed here.

☐ Record the critical settings and data for Companyweb Site Libraries and Lists as follows:

- On the Companyweb Home page in the upper left corner click on the Site Actions menu dropdown, select Site Settings then select Site Libraries and Lists from the Site Administration section.
- Select the first Site Libraries and Lists component that critical settings will be documented for and that page will open.
  - Document in detail the critical settings for the component.
- Repeat the above processes as required for all utilized Site Libraries and Lists.

  Announcements, Calendar, Fax Center, Links, Pictures, Shared Documents, Site assets, Site Pages, Style Library, Tasks, Team Discussion.

☐ Download data for Site Libraries and Lists components as follows:

- Open Windows Explorer and navigate to the *newservername*\tech\migration\companyweb directory.
- On the Companyweb Home page select Libraries from the Quick Launch menu on the left side of the window.
- Select the Document Library component that contains the data to be migrated and that page will open.
  - On the Companyweb Library Tools bar select the Library tab then select Open with Explorer.
  - Select all documents and folders in the library, right-click on the selection and select Copy from the menu.
  - Switch to the previously opened Windows Explorer, right-click in the*newservername*\tech\migration\companyweb folder and select New\Folder, enter the name of the Site Libraries and Lists component for the new folder name.
  - Open the newly created folder, right-click and select Paste from the menu.
- Repeat the above process as required for each Site Libraries and Lists component to be migrated.

Import Content to New Server

Note: It will be necessary to perform these procedures from a workstation and not from the new server due to security setting in Internet Explorer on the new server.

☐ Edit the hosts file on the Transfer Workstation to restore access to the new companyweb site in Internet explorer as follows:

- Open Windows Explorer and navigate to the c:\windows\system32\drivers\etc directory, right click on the hosts file and select Edit from the menu.
- At the bottom of the file remove the line that reads:
  - *ipaddressofoldserver* companyweb

  Example: 192.168.16.1 companyweb
- Close notepad and when prompted to save the file select Save.

- ☐ Open Internet Explorer and navigate to http://companyweb.
    - If prompted to connect as a user, enter the credentials for that domains administrator.

    Note: If the companyweb that is presented is not the new companyweb site, review the steps outlined above involving the edit of the hosts file.

    - Do not proceed until the new companyweb site is presented as expected.
- ☐ Restore the critical settings information for the Companyweb top level site as follows:
    - On the Companyweb Home page in the upper left corner click on the dropdown arrow to the right of Site Actions and select Site Settings from the menu.
    - Restore all previously documented critical settings as required.

    Note: When migrating from an older SharePoint system to a newer, most settings found on the old server have been disseminated into different (and sometime also multiple) alternate locations.

        - Administration
            - Manage users
            - Manage sites and workspaces
            - Configure Site and Workspace Creation
        - Customization
            - Change site title and description
            - Apply theme to site
        - Manage My Information
            - My alerts on this site
- ☐ Restore the critical settings and data for the Companyweb home page as follows:
    - On the Companyweb home page navigate to the Pictures – Photos container and select Upload Picture from the Upload dropdown menu.
        - On the Select Picture page click Browse, navigate to *newservername*\tech\migration\companyweb, select the site image then click open then on the Select Picture page click OK.
        - On the Picture page indicating the document was uploaded successfully page click Save.
    - On the Companyweb Home page in the upper left corner click on the dropdown arrow to the right of Site Actions and select Edit Page from the menu.
        - Restore all previously documented critical settings for the Site Image, Links, Announcements and other web parts.

    Note: The Site image is now in the Companyweb Pictures Photos All Pictures directory.
- ☐ Upload data for Documents and Lists that will allow it, as follows:
    - On the Companyweb Home page select All Site Content from the link list on the left side of the page.
        - Create new Sites, Web Parts, Pages, and Items as required for the incoming content. Configure all settings and permissions to match the component they are being migrated from on the old site.
    - Open Windows Explorer and navigate to the *newservername*\tech\migration\companyweb directory.

  - Open the director containing the files to migrate into the Documents and Lists component, highlight all the documents and folders in the directory, right-click on the selection(s) then select Copy from the menu.
- On the All Site Content page select the Documents and Lists component that the files will be migrated into and it will open.
  - Select the Library tab from the menu at the top of the page.
  - Select Open with Explorer from the Connect and Export section of the tool ribbon.
  - Right-click in the file area of the new Explorer window and select Paste from the menu.
- Repeat the above process as required for each Documents and Lists component requiring files to be migrated in.

☐ Compare the completed Company web Home page to the *newservername*\tech\migration\companyweb\Companyweb-Home.mht page to verify everything appears to be in the right place.

SQL Server Data Synchronization – Finalizing

Note: It is assumed that the tasks required to migrate an application that utilizes one of the SQL database being migrated are synchronized with the steps outlined here for finalizing the SQL Server Data Synchronization.

e.g. If the next major step in the Migration Strategy is to migrate an LOB that uses one of the databases that is scheduled for synchronization, then the synchronization of the database must be finalized before moving the application or data loss may occur.

Database Final Synchronization and Restore

☐ Log on to the old server as the administrator.

☐ Verify that each scheduled database backup has run as scheduled by reviewing the Application event log for MSSQLSQL entries near the schedule run times of the database backup jobs.

☐ If the most recent schedule backup has failed start the backup job as follows:

- If the backup job is scheduled to run in SQL, run Microsoft SQL Server Management Studio:
  - In the Connect to Server page (Object Explorer) click the dropdown arrow to the right of the Server name field, select the SQL server instance that contains the database that is being migrated.
  - Navigate to the SQL Server Agent\Jobs folder, right-click on the SQL backup job to run and then select Start from the menu.
  - If the completion status's are anything other than success address errors and correct issues as needed. Click Close on the Start jobs *–sqlinstancename* window to close it.
  - Close SQL Server Management Studio.
- If the backup job is scheduled to run as a scheduled task navigate to the Control Panel\Scheduled Tasks container, right-click on the desired migration task and select Run from the menu.
  - If the completion status is anything other than success address errors and correct issues as needed. It may be necessary to check the Application event log for useful output.

Note: Do not proceed until all scheduled database backups have been verified to have successfully run.

☐ Log on to the new server as the administrator.

- ☐ Verify that each scheduled database restore has run as scheduled by reviewing the Application event log for MSSQLSQL entries near the schedule run times of the database restore jobs.
- ☐ If the most recent schedule restore has failed (or if the backup it relies on had failed but has since succeeded) log on to the new server and start the restore backup job as follows:
  - Wait for and verify the synchronization of the company data RoboCopy (or other RoboCopy plan). Alternately the database files required can be copied from the old server to the new server manually. Be certain the location is correct or the restore will not complete as desired.
  - If the restore job is scheduled to run in SQL run Microsoft SQL Server Management Studio.
    - In the Connect to Server page (Object Explorer) click the dropdown arrow to the right of the Server name field, select the SQL server instance that contains the new database that is being migrated.
    - Navigate to the SQL Server Agent\Jobs folder, right-click on the SQL restore job to run and then select Start from the menu.
    - If the completion status's are anything other than success address errors and correct issues as needed. Click Close on the Start jobs *–sqlinstancename* window to close it.
    - Close SQL Server Management Studio.
  - If the restore job is scheduled to run as a scheduled task:
    - Open the Task Scheduler from the Administrative Tools folder.
    - Navigate to the Task Scheduler Library container.
    - Right-click on the desired migration task and select Run from the menu.
    - If the completion status is anything other than success address errors and correct issues as needed. It may be necessary to check the Application event log for useful output.

  Note: Do not proceed until all scheduled database restores have been verified to have successfully run.
- ☐ Repeat the above processes as required during the migration for each database being migrated to the new server.

Database Maintenance Routine Configuration

Note: The procedure outlined below only applies to systems that have Microsoft SQL Server Management Studio (not Express) installed.

Note: During the setup of the Maintenance Routine it is assumed and expected that the default selection will be made for everything not specifically noted here.

- ☐ Log on to the new server as the administrator.
- ☐ Run Microsoft SQL Server Management Studio and in the Connect to Server page (Object Explorer) click the dropdown arrow to the right of the Server name field, select the SQL server instance that the Maintenance Routine will be configured for then click Connect.
  - Refer to the Discovery section – Backup Software, Devices and Methods for which database(s) will have Maintenance Routine created.
  - If the target instance is not listed select Browse for more, expand the Database Engine container select the SQL server instance that contains the database the Maintenance Routine will be created for, click OK to close the browse window then click Connect.
- ☐ Create the Maintenance Routine as follows:

  Note: Refer to the Discovery section – Backup Software, Devices and Methods subsection for all information required in creating the Maintenance Routine.

- In Object Explorer navigate to the Management\Maintenance Plans container, right-click on the container and select Maintenance Plan Wizard from the menu.
  - Maintenance Plan Wizard welcome page click Next.
  - On the Select Plan Properties page:
    - Enter the appropriate name for the Maintenance Plan in the Name field and in the Description field.
    - Click the change button to the right of the Schedule field.
      - Complete the Job Schedule Properties page accepting the defaults for anything not specifically documented.
      - Click OK to close the Job Schedule Properties page then click Next on the Select Plan Properties page.
  - On the Select Maintenance Tasks page select all required tasks then click Next.
  - On the Select Maintenance Task Order arrange the tasks as required then click Next.
  - Depending on the Maintenance Tasks selected several Define Task pages will be presented.
    - The task definition pages will be presented in the same order the tasks are set to follow.
    - For each task definition page enter the appropriate information accepting the defaults for anything not specifically documented.
    - Click Next when each page is completely configured.

    Note: If the Back Up Database Task was selected pay close attention to the backup type and destination.
  - If prompted Select the appropriate Authentication method: Windows Authentication or SQL Server Authentication and enter the correct user name and passwords.
  - On the Select Report Options page select and configure all options as required then click Next.
  - On the Complete the Wizard page review the entire Maintenance Plan then click Finish.
- On the Maintenance Plan Wizard Progress window review status for each action and If the status is anything other than completed, address errors and correct issues as needed. Click Close on the Maintenance Plan Wizard Progress window to close it.

Line of Business Applications Migration

☐ Review the Migration Strategy and coordinate with the project manager before initiating any Line of Business Applications Migration checklist.

☐ Run through each checklist in the Line of Business Applications Migration section of this binder at the appropriate time.

☐ Track the completion of each checklist that is utilized for this migration here.

  - Accounting Package
  - Business Contact Management Package
  - Other Package ______________________
  - Other Package ______________________
  - Other Package ______________________

System Application Migration

- ☐ Review the Migration Strategy and coordinate with the project manager before initiating any System Application Migration checklist.
- ☐ Run through each checklist in the System Application Migration section of this binder at the appropriate time.
- ☐ Track the completion of each checklist that is utilized for this migration here.
  - BlackBerry Server
  - Encrypted / Keyed Security Access System
  - Antivirus Solution
  - Drive Maintenance Solution
  - Drive Imaging Solution
  - Other Package ______________________
  - Other Package ______________________

Sub-Systems Migration

- ☐ Review the Migration Strategy and coordinate with the project manager before initiating any Sub-System Migration checklist.
- ☐ Run through each checklist in the Sub-System Migration section of this binder at the appropriate time.
- ☐ Track the completion of each checklist that is utilized for this migration here.
  - Router
  - Firewall
  - Phone System
  - Printers
  - Copier / Scanner
  - Update/ Patch Management
  - Other Package ______________________
  - Other Package ______________________

Company Data Synchronization – Finalizing

- ☐ Review the current status of all RoboCopy batch files running on the new server to synchronize Company Data. The Command Prompt should have an output similar the entry below.
  - Verify there are no mismatched or failed files.
  - There should be zero changes pending for the RoboCopy.
  - Troubleshoot any copy issues found.

Note: If for some reason the batch file(s) are not running as expected refer to the log file or simply modify the allowed run time in the batch file(s) and run them to get the synchronization status.

```
------------------------------------------------------------------------------
              Total    Copied   Skipped   Mismatch    FAILED    Extras
    Dirs :       94         2        92          0         0         0
```

```
Files :        110         3       107          0          0        0
Bytes :   35.10 m     1.7 k   35.10 m          0          0        0
Times :   0:00:03   0:00:00                          0:00:00  0:00:02

Speed :           5465 Bytes/sec.
Speed :          0.312 MegaBytes/min.

Ended : Mon  June 1 19:25:04 2011

Monitor : Waiting for 30 minutes and 1 changes...
  0 mins : 0 changes.
```

☐ Review permissions on the new server data shares as follows:

- Verify files in the lowest directories of the company shared data structure are inheriting permissions as expected. e.g. Users have full control of public files etc.
- Verify files in company sensitive directories are inheriting explicit deny permissions as expected. e.g. Human Resources directory is accessible only by members of the Management group etc.

Note: Do not perform this next set of steps unless the drive map redirection for the share has been completed and all applications have been migrated. If the drive map has not been redirected or an application is still attempting to access data on the share users or applications will no longer be able to access data and data loss may occur.

☐ Stop sharing each shared directory on the old server that has been successfully synchronized.

- Open Server Manager on the old server and navigate to Advanced Management\Computer Management (Local)\System Tools\Shared Folders\Open Files container.
  - Verify there are no open files in the directory that is about to have its share stopped.
  - If there are open files verify they are not being actively accessed by users, processes or applications.
  - Close all open files for the directory that is about to have its share stopped by right-clicking on the file(s) and selecting Close Open Files from the menu.
- In Server Manager navigate to the Shared Folders\Shares container.
- Select the share that is to be stopped, right-click on it and select Stop Sharing from the menu.
  - If prompted that There are *x* file(s) open by *x* user(s) connected to *sharename*. ... Do you want to continue? Click No.
    - Recheck what user, process or application is actively opening files on the share before continuing.
    - Do not proceed with this step unless it can be verified there will be no data loss.
  - If prompted with only the short message Are you sure you wish to stop sharing *sharename*? Click Yes
- Repeat the above process as required for each share that has been synchronized and its drive remapped.

Users Shared Data / Users Shared Folders Synchronization - Finalizing

☐ Review the current status of all RoboCopy batch files running on the new server to synchronize Users Shared Data. The Command Prompt should have an output similar the entry in the previous subsection Company Data Synchronization – Finalizing.

- Verify there are no mismatched or failed files.

- There should be zero changes pending for the RoboCopy.
- Troubleshoot any copy issues found.

Note: If for some reason the batch file(s) are not running as expected refer to the log file or simply modify the allowed run time in the batch file(s) and run them to get the synchronization status.

☐ Review permissions on the new server Users Shared Data by selecting two or three users directories and verifying that files in the lowest directories of the structure are inheriting permissions as expected. e.g. Joe User has full control.

Note: Do not perform this next set of steps unless the drive map redirection for Users Shared Data has been completed. (If applicable) e.g. drive u: is mapped to %username% on the new server now and all applications have been migrated. If the drive map has not been redirected or an application is still attempting to access data on the share users or applications will no longer be able to access data and data loss may occur.

☐ Stop sharing the Users Shared Folders share on the old server.

- Open Server Manager on the old server and navigate to the Advanced Management\Computer Management (Local)\System Tools\Shared Folders\Open Files container.
  - Verify there are no open files in the directory that is about to have its share stopped.
  - If there are open files verify they are not being actively accessed by users, processes or applications.
  - Close all open files for the directory that is about to have its share stopped by right-clicking on the file(s) and selecting Close Open Files from the menu.
- In Server Manager navigate to the Shared Folders\Shares container.
- Select the Users share, right-click on it and select Stop Sharing from the menu.
  - If prompted that There are *x* file(s) open by *x* user(s) connected to *sharename*. ... Do you want to continue? Click No.
    - Recheck what user, process or application is actively opening files on the share before continuing.
    - Do not proceed with this step unless it can be verified there will be no data loss.
  - If prompted with only the short message Are you sure you wish to stop sharing *sharename*? Click Yes

Workstation Migration

General

Workstation Migration Strategy is as follows:

1) Record certain critical information about the users profile including some Outlook settings.
2) Clean up the users profile so it is a small reasonable size that will save fast.
3) Use the Microsoft USMT tool to save the users profile.
4) Migrate to the new domain.
5) Use the Microsoft USMT tool to restore the users profile.
6) Re-set all previously recorded settings for the user and test critical functions like printing, email, file and Internet access.

Migration

☐ Create the User State Migration Batch files in the new server *newservername*\tech\usmt directory.

- The USMT command line syntax and batch file command lines are detailed in the Resources section – Scripts and Batch Files subsection.
- Be certain to edit the domain names, server name and other variables in the batch file example when building the batch files.
- Do not change the command line syntax as documented without consulting the project manager.

Note: The USMT commands and the batch files rely on the user names being the same on the old and the new domains. If they are not the USMT commands and the batch file will need to be edited to accommodate the method used.

☐ Create a Master Workstation Migration checklist as follows:

- Retrieve the Reference copy of the Workstation Migration checklist that was marked up during Pre-Discovery and placed in the Planning and Timeline section of this binder.
- If any User Profiles will be migrated using a Custom Migration, review the Discovery section - File and Data Storage subsection for exactly how to handle company data and archived email found locally on the workstation.
  - Us the above information to fill in the header section of the Reference Copy of the Workstation Migration checklist.
- Select the first workstation to migrate. It should be a workstation that first represents the typical workstation for the system and is least used or will cause the least impact on the system if it is off line for an hour or more.
- Step through the Reference Copy of the Workstation Migration checklist, performing each of the required tasks on the first workstation.
  - Annotate additions, omissions and changes required to critical sections of the Workstation Migration checklist. These annotations should be based on the actual workstation migration and the migration strategies and plans for this project as documented in the Discovery section and the Planning /Timeline section.
- Create a Master Workstation Migration checklist for this project by incorporating the revisions from the previous steps into a clean digital copy of the Workstation Migration section of the SBS 2011 Network Migration Project Template 20xx.xx.xx.xx.docx.
  - Delete out anything from the checklist that will not be used or implemented to keep the checklist as small and clean as possible. e.g. If there will be no Custom level migrations of user profiles strip those sections out. This alone will save three pages per checklist.

  Note: For simple revisions just mark up a clean copy of the original Workstation Migration section using a pen and / or whiteout.
- Print out (or copy) the new Master Workstation Checklist and write across the first page MASTER using a yellow highlighter. Three hole punch the master so it can be put back into the binder.

☐ Migrate all workstations on the network as follows:

- Copy the Master Workstation Migration checklist (one per workstation) and fill in the header information on the first page.
- Perform all steps required in the Workstation Migration checklist for each workstation listed on the Migration Tracking Sheet.

☐ Configure Users access to workstations as follows:

- Run Windows SBS 2011 Console and on the navigation bar select Network then select the Computers tab.

- Select the workstation to assign a user access to from the list, right-click on the name and select View computer properties from the menu.
  - Select User Access from the pane on the left side of the window.
  - For each user who should have access to this workstation select their name from the user list then set the Access level using the dropdown list below the user list.
    - Refer to the verified list of user names and email addresses returned from the Client Technical Contact and the Discovery section for access requirements.

  Note: Do not grant access for any user to any workstation unless it is explicitly indicated they should have access by the Client Technical Contact.

  - When all users access permissions have been set click OK to close the computer properties window.
- Repeat this process for each workstation any users require access to.

Remote User Migration

☐ Migrate all remote users or workstations as follows:

- Copy the original Remote Migration checklist from this binder (one per user or workstation) and fill in the header information on the first page.
- Perform all steps required in the Remote Migration checklist for each remote user or workstation listed on the Migration Tracking Sheet.

Note: Any remote user who is using a laptop machine that is joined to the domain must bring their machine into the office and have both the Workstation Migration and the Remote Migration checklists run against that machine.

Server Fine Tuning

General

☐ Configure any additional Scheduled Tasks in control panel (or wherever appropriate) as documented in the Discovery section – Small Business Server and Related subsection.

☐ Check and if required reconfigure backups to accommodate all the data on the new system.

DNS Cleanup Old Server

☐ Log on to the old server as the administrator.

☐ Remove the DNS forwarder to the old server from the new server as follows:

- Run the DNS Applet from Administrative Tools folder.
  - Right-click on the SBS server name in the navigation pane and select properties from the menu.
  - In the Properties window select the Forwarders tab.
  - Select the old server name from the DNS Domain list and click Remove.
  - Click OK to close the DNS Properties window.

☐ In DNS manger right-click on the server name in the folder tree on the left side of the window, select All Tasks – Restart from the menu.

☐ Close the DNS Manager.

DNS Cleanup New Server

- ☐ Log on to the new server as the administrator.
- ☐ Remove the DNS forwarder to the old server from the new server as follows:
  - o Run the DNS Applet from Administrative Tools folder.
    - o Right-click on the SBS server name in the navigation pane and select properties from the menu.
    - o In the Properties window select the Forwarders tab and click the Edit button.
    - o Select the old server name from the Server FQDN list and click Delete.
    - o Click OK to close the Edit Forwarders window. then click OK to close the DNS Properties window.
- ☐ Remove the Forward Lookup Zone for the old server as follows:

  Note: Pay very close attention to the exact domain being removed from the Forward Lookup Zones container.

  Removal of the new domain will result in system wide communications failures.
  - o In the DNS Applet navigate to the *servername* – Forward lookup Zones container.
  - o Right-click on the *olddomainname*.local zone and select Delete from the Menu.
    - o On the DNS delete confirmation pop-up click Yes.
    - o On the DNS Active Directory warning pop-up click Yes.
- ☐ In DNS manger right-click on the server name in the folder tree on the left side of the window, select All Tasks – Restart from the menu.
- ☐ Close the DNS Manager.

Password Policy Implementation

Note: If no policy is to be defined or active, all settings should already have been disabled during the system Build. There should be nothing to disable and therefore nothing in this subsection to do.

- ☐ If a Password Policy and/or an Account Lockout Policy were previously configured, email the Client Technical Contact with the Password Policy Change email to distribute to the users informing them that the policy will be activated on Wednesday of the week following the migration. (Or other previously arranged date) The email template can be found in the Communications / Training section of this binder.
  - o Be certain the outgoing email has been correctly formatted with a proper subject, the correct client company name, reply to address and technician name. Also verify every variable piece of data in the email body. e.g. dates, times, passwords, etc.
- ☐ If a Password Policy is to be configured now, Configure it on the date specified in the Planning / Timeline section. Typically this is the Wednesday of the week following the migration.
- ☐ Log on to the new server as the administrator.
- ☐ Run the Group Policy Management application from the Administrative Tools group.
- ☐ Configure the Password Policy as defined for this domain as documented in the Discovery section–Active Directory / Group Policy subsection as follows:
  - o Navigate to the Domains*domainname*.local\Group Policy Objects\Default Domain Policy, right-click on the object and select Edit from the menu.
  - o Navigate to Computer Configuration\Policies\Windows Settings\Security Settings\Account Policies/Password Policy.

- Configure each Password Policy as documented in the Discovery section– Active Directory / Group Policy subsection by right clicking on the policy and selecting Properties from the menu.
  - Disable any settings not specifically designated to be configure as documented in the Discovery section by clearing the checkbox to Define this policy setting on the Security Policy Setting tab of each policy.
- Close the Group Policy Management Editor then close the Group Policy Manager.

Database Synchronization, Backup and Restore Decommission

- ☐ Verify that the migration of any application that utilized the SQL backup and restore method for transfer of data to the new server, have been successfully completed.
- ☐ Log on to the new server as the administrator.
- ☐ Remove restore jobs scheduled in SQL Server Management Studio as follows:

  Note: These steps only apply if SQL Server Management Studio full version is installed.

  - Run Microsoft SQL Server Management Studio and in the Connect to Server page (Object Explorer) click the dropdown arrow to the right of the Server name field, select the SQL server instance that will contain the new database that is being migrated as documented then click Connect.
    - If the target instance is not listed select Browse for more, expand the Database Engine container select the SQL server instance that contains the database that were migrated, click OK to close the browse window then click Connect.
  - In Object Explorer navigate to the SQL Server Agent\Jobs container.
  - For each job that has been verified as no longer required and OK to remove, right-click on the restore job and select Delete from the menu and then in the Delete Object window click OK.

    Note: All restore jobs related to the network migration should have similar names such as *databasename*-migration. Do not delete any job that is not specifically related to the network migration.
  - Close SQL Server Management Studio.
- ☐ Remove restore jobs scheduled as a Task as follows:
  - Open the Task Scheduler from the Administrative Tools folder.
  - Navigate to the Task Scheduler Library container.
  - For each job that has been verified as no longer required and OK to remove, right-click on the restore job task in the list, right-click on the task and select Delete from the menu.
    - On the Task Scheduler delete confirmation window click Yes.
  - Close the Task Scheduler.

  Note: All restore tasks related to the network migration should have similar names such as *databasename*-migration. Do not delete any task that is not specifically related to the network migration.

Logon.bat cleanup

- ☐ Log on to the new server as the administrator.
- ☐ Open Windows Explorer and navigate to the c:\windows\sysvol*domain*\scripts directory.
- ☐ Edit the logon.bat file.
  - Remove the rem statement from the beginning of the antivirus client installation line.

Note: The new antivirus solution will now be loaded onto any workstation that logs onto the new domain and does not have it installed.

- Update the Last edited by line to reflect the technician and date the batch file was last edited.
- Remove the entire Clear old persistent net uses section.
- Close and save the batch file and close Windows Explorer.

Documentation

Note: Follow the steps outlined below to migrate all usable and useful data from the Old and New) Network Documentation sections of this binder into the clients Existing Network Documentation binder.

Do not just pile all documents found into one binder and close it.

- ☐ If a Network Documentation Binder of any type does not exist for this system, create a new one now.
  - Label the front and Spine Network Documentation Binder.
  - Create tab dividers for all major sections:

    Procedures, Net Specs, Machine Specs, Users, Products
- ☐ Migrate all data in the New Network Documentation subsections of this binder into the same subsections in the clients Network Documentation Binder (NDB) as follows:
  - Section by section review each page and place it into the appropriate section of the client NDB.
  - For any pages of the client NDB being replaced or retired, archive them in place by simply write a big X across the page and put them in the back of the section they belong in.

    e.g. When the IP Address Allocation Record is inserted into the client NDB the old record is moved to the back of that section and a n X drawn across the whole page.
- ☐ Update and or Edit any other existing Procedures and migrate them to the clients Network Documentation Binder.
- ☐ Update all third party service providers configuration documentation in the client NDB to reflect changes made during the Network Migration. e.g. LOB Record, ISP Record, Router Configuration, etc.
- ☐ Insert all new product certifications, registrations and related documentation acquired during this build and migration into the Product section of the clients Network Documentation Binder.
- ☐ Migrate all data in the Old Network Documentation subsections of this binder into the same subsections in the clients Network Documentation Binder as follows:

  Note: Much of what is in the Old NDB subsections of this binder is redundant and should not be moved into the client NDB. Only migrate what is now relevant or adds to the existing data.
  - Section by section review each page and place it into the appropriate section of the client NDB.
  - For any pages of the client NDB being replaced or retired, archive them in place by simply write a big X across the page and put them in the back of the section they belong in.
- ☐ Verify all of the most critical content of the client NDB has been updated to reflect changes since the migration. e.g. All IP changes recorded on the appropriate pages, passwords updated, etc.

  * Use new clean forms or records wherever possible.
  - Procedures
  - Network Specs section
    - Network Map

        - Internet Domain Registration Information
        - Router Configuration Form
        - Firewall Configuration Form
        - IP Address Allocation Record
        - Hard Coded IP Address Record
        - Network Timing Diagram
        - Shared Resources Record
        - Shared Resources Permission Record
        - UPS Power Distribution Form
        - Group Policy Object Record
    - Machines Specs
    - Users & Passwords
    - Products

☐ Make a photocopy of the Network Map after it is annotated so it can be re-built in Visio. Add this task to the Fine Tuning page in the Fine Tuning section of this binder.

Post Migration Tasks

☐ Update the Machine Migration Checklist to indicate the Server Migration is complete.

☐ Permanently delete all PST files exported from the old server during the migration to the new server. The default location is *newservername*\tech\migration\email directory.

Note: Before deleting any files or directives verify this is the correct location that was configured to hold the databases migration files as outlined in the Email Migration – Initial Export from Old Server section.

☐ Permanently delete all SQL database files backed up from the old server during the migration to the new server. The default location is *newservername\companydatashare*\dbmigration directory

Note: Before deleting any files or directives verify this is the correct location that was configured to hold the databases migration files as outlined in the SQL Server Data Synchronization – Initiating section.

☐ Check all data backup strategies and adjust as needed and as documented in the Discovery section - Backup Software subsection.

☐ Check all SQL Server backup or Maintenance Routines adjust as needed and as documented in the Discovery section - Backup Software subsection.

☐ Return the previously isolated, known good, Full Backup sets to rotation after removing the write protection.

☐ Briefly review the Server Event Logs for any new issues and address as needed.

☐ Remove the Continuum SaaZ server agent from the old server and update notes for the new server.

- Open internet Explorer and surf to https://control.itsupport247.net and log in.
- Select Uninstall Server Agents from the House Keeping menu, select the correct site from the Select Site dropdown list then click on the magnifying glass icon to the right of the list.
    - Find the old server name in the System list
    - Check the box in the Select column to the right of the server

    - Enter the words Retired Server in the reason field then click Remove.
    - On the uninstall Server page verify the correct server is being uninstalled then click Remove again. Click OK on the Success pop-up.
  - In the Continuum Control Panel select the Quick Access tab from the tab set in the upper right corner of the window then click on the Notes icon to the left of the new site (server).
    - Select the Device Notes tab, click on the Edit icon on the left side of the window to edit each note related to the migration.
    - Delete or update the notes as appropriate.
    - Follow the on screen prompts to complete the notes deletion or update then close all open windows.

- ☐ Shut down and remove any old server(s) and other abandoned equipment.
- ☐ Recycling all equipment as documented in the Discovery section – Hardware and Environment subsection. Create Recycle Verification Forms for all equipment.
- ☐ ____
- ☐ ____

14. Applications Migration

Line Of Business Applications

> **Note:** Insert here in the appropriate subsection all migration checklists for Line of Business Applications.
>
> Please refer to the Resources section of this binder for details on how to create installation and migration checklists.
>
> As useful content related to commonly used Line of Business Applications are either developed or submitted to the ZDTM website, they will be made available.

Accounting or Finance Package

> **Note:** Insert here the checklist for any Accounting or Finance Package migration. If one does not exist, please refer to the Resources section of this binder for details on how to create installation and migration checklists for this product.

Business Contact Management Package

> **Note:** Insert here the checklist for any Business Contact Management Package migration. If one does not exist, please refer to the Resources section of this binder for details on how to create installation and migration checklists for this product.

Other Package or Application – Copy and change heading as required

> **Note:** Insert here the checklist for any Other Package or Application migration. If one does not exist, please refer to the Resources section of this binder for details on how to create installation and migration checklists for this product.

System Applications

> **Note:** Insert here in the appropriate subsection all System Applications Migration checklists.
>
> Please refer to the Resources section of this binder for details on how to create installation and migration checklists.
>
> As useful content related to commonly used System Applications are either developed or submitted to the ZDTM website, they will be made available.

BlackBerry Server

> **Note:** Insert here the checklist for BlackBerry Server migration. If one does not exist, please refer to the Resources section of this binder for details on how to create installation and migration checklists for this product.

Encrypted / Keyed Security Access System

> **Note:** Insert here the checklist for the Encrypted / Keyed Security Access System migration. If one does not exist, please refer to the Resources section of this binder for details on how to create installation and migration checklists for this product.

Antivirus Solution – Trend Micro Worry Free Business 7.0

- ☐ Log on to the old server as Administrator.
- ☐ Verify the HTTP port used by the new server as follows:
  - Open Windows Explorer and browse to the *newservername*\ofcscan directory and open the file ofcscan.ini.
  - Find the value of Master_Domainport and note it here: ______________

  Note: The default port is 8059.
- ☐ On the old server open Trend Worry Free Business Security Console and log in.
- ☐ Select the Security Settings tab and on the Security tab select the group that contains the desktop machines to be migrated. Typically this is the Desktop (default) group.
- ☐ Select all the client computers from the list that are to be moved to the new server then click Move.
  - On the Move Desktop/Server page type the name of the new server in the Server Name field.
  - Type the port number of the new Security Server in the HTTP Port field then click Move.

  Note: Trend Security Server will automatically apply the target group's settings to the new member.
- ☐ Log on to the new server as Administrator.
- ☐ Open the Trend Worry Free Business Security Console and log in.
- ☐ Select the Security Settings tab and on the Security tab select the Desktop (default) group.

  Note: If the machines moved from the old server have shown up in a group other than the Desktop group move them to the desired group on the same Security Server by dragging-and-dropping them to the correct group
- ☐ Verify all machines that were moved from the old server have correctly checked in with the new server.

☐ For any computer that has not checked in with the new server within a reasonable amount of time list that machine name and the issue "Not communicating with AV server after migration" on the Fine Tuning page in the Fine Tuning section of this binder.

Note: Machines that are offline or are in Roaming mode cannot be Moved using this method.

Unless there is a large number of remote users in roaming mode and the current configuration of the firewall and new server allow for roaming mode it will be easiest and most efficient to simply pull the Trend client to these machines during the Remote Machine migration.

Drive Maintenance Solution

Note: Insert here the checklist for the Drive Maintenance Solution migration. If one does not exist, please refer to the Resources section of this binder for details on how to create installation and migration checklists for this product.

Drive Imaging Solution

Note: Insert here the checklist for the Drive Imaging Solution migration. If one does not exist, please refer to the Resources section of this binder for details on how to create installation and migration checklists for this product.

15. Sub-Systems Migration

Note: Insert here in the appropriate subsection all Sub-System Migration checklists.

Please refer to the Resources section of this binder for details on how to create installation and migration checklists.

As useful content related to commonly used Sub Systems Migrations are either developed or submitted to the ZDTM website, they will be made available.

Router

Note: Insert here the checklist for the Router migration. If one does not exist, please refer to the Resources section of this binder for details on how to create installation and migration checklists for this product.

Note: The Router migration should look quite like the Firewall migration in that they both should be backed up before and after changes, documentation should be updated and the device access information should be labeled on the device itself.

Firewall

Note: Due to the extensive possibilities of firewalls available this checklist can only be a general checklist of steps to be performed. However, documenting the steps for commonly used firewalls should be done when possible.

☐ Backup the old Firewall configuration to the new Server c:\!tech\hardware\firewall directory before changing anything.

☐ Create any required Firewall NAT Policies for the server primary IP address and the HP Lights Out Controller.

Note: An NAT policy can only be created if there is an unused public IP available as documented in the Discovery section – Sub-Systems \ Router subsection.

☐ Create all required Firewall Port Policies or Custom Services required for the new server if they do not exist. e.g. RWW = Port 987, etc. Refer to the Resource section of this binder - Port Reference subsection.

☐ Create all required Firewall Access Rules using the new Port Policies as documented in the Discovery section - Small Business Server and Related subsection. Refer also to the Domain Names, IP's, DNS and DHCP subsection.

☐ Verify all activated SBS Web site services before continuing. If one is found to be broken, valuable time will be saved if it is discovered now.

- RWW https://*ServerFQDN* Example: https://remote.zdtminc.net
- SharePoint https://*ServerFQDN*:987
- RDP *ServerFQDN*
- OWA https://*ServerFQDN*/owa
- Public Website http://www.*ServerFQDN* Example: http://www.zdtminc.net
- VPN *ServerFQDN*
- FTP (Only if required) ftp://*ServerFQDN* (or custom port e.g. FTP://serverFQDN:66)

☐ Review and clean up NAT Policies, Port Policies, Custom Services and Access Rules once the old server is no longer in user or is off line.

☐ ____

☐ ____

☐ Backup the new Firewall configuration to the new Server c:\!tech\hardware\firewall directory after changes have been verified.

☐ Update the Firewall Configuration page in the Old Network Documentation section and move it to the New Network Documentation section. If there is no preexisting Firewall Configuration page, there is a form in the New Network Documentation section – Net Specs subsection of this binder.

☐ Verify the Firewall has the correct Internal IP, Logon ID and Password labeled on the bottom of the device.

Phone System

Note: Insert here the checklist for the Phone System migration. If one does not exist, please refer to the Resources section of this binder for details on how to create installation and migration checklists for this product.

Printers

General

The Printers Migration Strategy is as follows:

1) Add all printers to the new server that are networked (have an IP address) or are already physically connected to the new server (Serial, LPT, USB).
   a. Share new printers from the new server as required.
   b. Attach to (use) printers that are physically connected to the old server and share them out from the new server.
   c. At the appropriate time, disconnect physically connected printers from the old server and connect them to the new server.
   d. Rebuild printer shares. e.g. Stop re-sharing the printer from the old server and share directly from new server.
   e. Workstations on the old domain will still be able to print to all printers and as they are migrated to the new server.

Note: During the setup and configuration of printers it is assumed and expected that the default selection will be made for everything not specifically noted here.

For all settings related to printers and their shares Refer to the Discovery section - Sub-Systems subsection.

Be sure drivers are copied to the c:\!tech\harware\printers directory for access by workstation if needed.

Add Printers

☐ Log on to the new server as the administrator.

☐ Install or load any printer manufacturer applications or drivers that are required.

Note: Do not install or load any application that is not absolutely required for the proper use or maintenance of the printer being set up.

- ☐ Open Control Panel – View Devices and Printers container and double click on the Add a Printer button.
    - On the What type of printer do you want to install select the appropriate type of printer being installed.
    - For a Local printer select Add a local printer.
        - Select the correct port from the Use an existing port dropdown list then click Next.
        - Now skip down past the For a Network printer… section.
    - For a Network printer select Add a network, wireless or Bluetooth printer.
        - If the desired printer was automatically detected select it from the list of printers then click Next.
        - If it was not detected click The printer that I want isn't listed.
            - On the Find a printer by name or TCP/IP address page click Add a printer using TCP/IP address or hostname then click Next.

          Note: Do not select Find a printer or Select a shared printer as this will result in a printer connection that will not likely be available after the migration.

            - On the Type a printer hostname or IP address page enter the IP address of the printer to be added in the hostname or IP field then click Next.
            - If the Additional Port Information Required page is presented select the correct device type from the dropdown list then click Next.

          Note: The default device type of Generic network Card will work for most printers. Only change the device type if the exact device type is known.

    - On the Install the Printer driver page select the Manufacturer and Printer model from the list then click Next.
        - If the printer Manufacturer or Model are not listed click the Windows Update button to allow Windows to download additional older and newer drivers. Otherwise skip down to the step to type a printer name.
        - When the list has been updated select the Manufacturer and Printer model from the list then click Next.
        - If the printer Manufacturer or Model are still not listed click the Have Disk button to browse for the drivers. . Otherwise skip down to the step to type a printer name.
            - Navigate to the c:\!tech\hardware\printers directory and then on to the specific subdirectory for the model of printer being installed and the target operating system then click OK.

              Note: This assumes the !tech directory is on the C: driver and that the drivers have already been copied to the !tech directory. If not, they should be copied before continuing.

            - Select the correct printer from the presented list and click Next.
    - On the type a printer name page accept the defaults then click Next.
    - On the Printer Sharing page select Do not share this printer then click Next.

      Note: If at any time during the installation a Hardware Installation warning pops up indicating The software you are installing for this hardware: device name has not passed Windows Logo testing… Select Continue Anyway.

        - On the Success page click the Print a test page button.

  - On the test page pop-up click Close then on the Success page click Finish.
  - Edit the properties for the newly added printer and set the default resolution and color for this printer to the lowest resolution and B/W.
    - Configure all other settings as documented.
  - Repeat the above process as required for each printer being added.

Share New Printers

- ☐ Log on to the new server as the administrator.
- ☐ Open the Control Panel – View Devices and Printers container.
- ☐ Select the printer to be shared, right-click on the printer and select Printer Properties.
  - In the Printer Properties window select the Sharing tab and check the box Share this printer.
  - Enter the Share name as documented.
  - Select the Security tab and configure group and user security as documented.
  - Configure all other settings as documented for the new share.
  - Click OK to close the Properties page.
  - Repeat the above process as required for each printer being shared.

Attach to Printers shared from Old Server (and share)

- ☐ Log on to the new server as the administrator.
- ☐ Attach to printers on the old server as follows:
  - Open Control Panel – View Devices and printers container and double click on the Add a Printer button.
  - On the Add Printer page select Add a network, wireless or Bluetooth printer.
    - If the desired printer was automatically detected select it from the list of printers then click Next.
    - If it was not detected click The printer that I want isn't listed.
    - On the Find a printer by name or TCP/IP address page select, Select a shared printer by name then enter the full UNC for the printer on the old server and click Next.

      e.g. *\\oldserver\hplaserjet4p*

    Note: Do not select Find a printer or Select a shared printer as this will result in a printer connection that will not likely be available after the migration.
  - On the You've successfully added… page click Next.
  - On the next You've successfully added… page click Finish.
  - Click Finish to close the Add printer wizard.
  - Right click on the newly created printer and select Printer Properties from the menu.
    - On the General tab click the Print a test page button. When the Test page has been sent pop-up is presented click Close.
- ☐ Share the printer out as follows:
  - Select the printer to be shared, right-click on the printer and select Printer properties.
  - In the Printer Properties window select the Sharing tab and check the box to Share this printer.

- Enter the Share name as documented.
- Select the Security tab and configure group and user security as documented.
- Configure all other settings as documented for the new share.
- Click OK to close the properties page.

☐ Repeat the above process as required for each printer on the old server being re-shared.

Physically Connect Printers to New Server

☐ Log on to the new server as the administrator.

☐ Verify that all workstations have either been migrated to the new server or do not regularly use the printer to be physically moved to the new server.

☐ At the appropriate time before hours, after hours or at noon disconnect the printer to be physically moved to the new server and connect it to the new server.

☐ Follow all the steps outlined in the Add Printers subsection above.

Rebuild Shares for Newly Attached Printers

☐ Delete the network printer share on the new server for the printer that was just moved to the new server as follows:

Note: Only delete a printer shares that is a re-share from the old server.

- Open Control Panel – View Devices and printers container.
- Right-click on the shared printer to be deleted and select Remove Device from the menu.
- On the Remove device verification pop-up click Yes.

☐ Follow all the steps outlined in the Add Printers subsection above to add and if required share the new printer.

Copier / Scanner

Note: Perform all steps required based on the copier / scanner configuration. Take notes during the configuration so this section may be updated later to be more generically accurate.

☐ If the server will be printing to this device or will be sharing this device as a resource, load the printer drivers on the server and perform a print test now.

☐ If this device will be shared from the server, establish the share and set the permissions for the resource as documented in the Discovery section – Sub System subsection.

☐ Log in to the Copier web based interface using the admin account.

☐ If Scan to Email is configured, change the SMTP server address to point to the new server.

☐ If Scan to File is configured, change the SMB server connection information to point to the new server.

☐ Test Scan to Email and Scan to File to verify all settings are correct.

☐ ____

☐ ____

☐ Update the Machine Specification page for the Copier /Scanner in the Old Network Documentation section and move it to the New Network Documentation section.

If there is no preexisting Machine Specification page for the Copier /Scanner, there is a form in the New Network Documentation section – Machine Spec subsection of this binder.

Update / Patch Management Solution

- ☐ If this server is managed by Continuum verify the Patch Management configuration as follows:
    - Log on to the new server as the administrator.
    - Open internet Explorer and surf to https://control.itsupport247.net and log in.
        - Select Site Management from the Base Configuration menu then click on the Edit Site icon to the right of the clients Site Name.
        - On the Site management window select the Patch Management Microsoft Updates page.
        - Review and adjust settings according to the settings documented in the Discovery section – Sub System subsection.
        - Close all open windows.
- ☐ If this server is managed by Continuum and Patch Management is configured, disable Microsoft SUS as follows:
    - Log on to the new server as the administrator.
    - Run the Microsoft Windows Server Update Services application from the Administrative Tools folder.
        - In the Update Services window navigate to the *Servername*\Options container.
        - In the Options pane in the middle of the window select Synchronization Schedule from the list.
            - On the Synchronization Schedule tab select Synchronize manually then click OK to close the Synchronization Schedule window.
        - In the Options pane in the middle of the window select Automatic Approvals from the list.
            - On the Update Rules tab check the box for the Default Automatic Approval Rule and then click Delete.
            - Select the Advanced tab and in the WSUS Updates section clear the checkbox for Automatically approve new revisions of updates that are already approved.
            - Click OK to close the Automatic Approvals window then close the Update Services window.

16. Workstation Migration

Company:____________________________ **Date:** ______________________________

Full User Name: _______________________ **Technician:** _________________________

Logon ID: ___________________________ **Old Machine Name:** ___________________

Password: ___________________________ **New Machine Name:** __________________

Start Time: _________ **Per the Client Technical Contact,**

Finish Time: _______ **this Users Profile Migration level is: Basic – Full – Custom**

☐ All Company Data found on the workstation will be moved to the Server? Y / N

x:\ (users mapped share) or *servername**companydata**username* or other

____

☐ All Archive and Personal Folders files (.pst's). found locally will be moved to the Server? Y / N

x:\ (users mapped share) or *servername**companydata**username* or other

____

Note: All tasks outlined here are user specific and must be performed while logged on as the user who's profile is being migrated. Failure to do so may result in the loss of data.

Note: Anytime during the migration whenever prompted for the user's name do not simply accept the default of blank or fist initial last name. Always enter the full correctly spelled name and proper initials. e.g. Phil McCracken - PM

Note: Anytime during the migration it is assumed that whenever prompted by the User Access Control (UAC) that Windows needs your permission to continue, the request will be acknowledged with Continue.

Workstation Migration Preparation

General Tasks

☐ Remove the Workstation Migration notice from the back of this checklist.

- Fold the notice in half and fill out the lower half with the users logon ID and password.
- Prop the notice up near the keyboard on the desk with the Workstation Migration in Progress! side showing.

☐ Log on to the machine with the current users logon ID and password.

☐ Close all running programs including instant messaging applications.

☐ Set the local administrator password to kpe20xx. (Where xx is the current year).

Note: If the current user does not have sufficient permission to change the local administrator password you must log on with an account that does have sufficient privileges and complete this step. Once the local administrator password has been set, log back on as the current user of the machine.

☐ Run the Command Prompt or Windows Explorer and create the directory c:\\!tech*username.*

☐ To verify the exact user profile directory run the Command Prompt and type: echo %userprofile% then press enter on the keyboard.

Record the users profile directory here: ____________________________________

☐ Record the current users default printer here: ____________________________________

☐ At the Command Prompt run the command ipconfig /all to verify the workstation IP address and the DNS and WINS server addresses are being obtained automatically from the new Small Business Server. i.e. The new SBS server is the DHCP server.

- If the IP address or DNS and WINS server addresses are being acquired automatically but not from the new SBS server, run the Command Prompt and then run the following command: ipconfig /release && ipconfig /renew.

  Note: For Vista and Windows 7 machines you must have elevated privileges to run this command.

  - To run the Command Prompt with elevated privileges right-click on the Command Prompt application and select Run as administrator from the menu.
- Verify the DHCP server is now the new SBS server.
- Watch for indication the WINS server may be hard coded even if all other data is from the new DHCP server.
- If the workstation IP address or DNS and WINS server addresses are not being acquired automatically change the default network controller properties as follows:
  - Open Control Panel and navigate to the Network Connections folder, right-click on the default (current) Local Area Connection and select Properties from the menu.
  - In the list of components select the Internet Protocol (TCP/IP) or Internet Protocol (TCP/IPv4) item and then click Properties.
  - In the properties window select Obtain an IP address automatically and Obtain DNS Server address automatically.
  - Click the Advanced button and in the advanced window select the WINS tab and remove all entries from the WINS address list.
  - Click OK or Close to close all open windows then close the Network Connections window.
  - In the Command Prompt window re-run the ipconfig /all command and verify the DHCP server is now the new SBS server.

☐ If the Users Profile Migration level indicated at the top of this checklist is Basic, proceed directly to the Migrating To the New Domain section below.

Full Migration Tasks

☐ Log on to the machine with the user logon ID and password for the user who's profile is being migrated.

☐ Clean up Internet Explorer temporary files as follows:

- Run Internet explorer and from the Toolbar select Tools -Internet Options then click the Settings button in the Browsing history section.
- Set the Disk space to use to 50 MB then click OK to close the Temporary Internet Files and history Settings window.
- In the Browsing history section click the Delete button.
  - In the Delete Browsing History window check the boxes to delete Temporary Internet files then click the Delete button.
- Close all settings windows and close Internet Explorer.

☐ Record the Microsoft Outlook Address List configuration as follows:

- Open Microsoft Outlook and from the Tools menu select E-mail Accounts (Office 2003) or Account Settings (Office 2007 and 2010).
  - Office 2003 only: In the E-Mail Accounts window select View or change existing directories or address books and click Next.
  - Outlook 2007 and 2010 only: In the E-Mail Accounts window select the Address Books tab, highlight the Outlook Address Book then click Change.
    - Record the names and locations of the Contact Folders here: ____________________

      ____
  - Close the Address Book and the Account settings window.
- In Outlook, Select Address Book from the Tools menu then select Options from the Address Book Tools menu.
  - Record the Show this address list first setting: ____________________
  - Record the Keep personal addresses in setting: ____________________
  - Record the When sending mail address list order: ____________________
- Close the Addressing window and the Address Book.

☐ Document and then Move all Archive and Personal Folders that are open in Microsoft Outlook as follows:

- Open Microsoft Outlook and select Data File Management from the File menu.
- For each Archive Folder or Personal Folder listed record the filename and original path here:
  - ____
  - ____
- Close Outlook, open Windows Explorer and navigate to the directory where the Archive or Personal Folders are located. All .pst's are typically stored in the same location.

Note: These files are either hidden, in a hidden folder or both. It is not required to change the Windows Explorer view to be able to get to or see these files. Simply enter the file location or directory on the address line of Windows Explorer and the location will be exposed for access.

Note: If the file name extension is not visible verify the file is of type Microsoft Office Outlook Personal Folder and not Microsoft Office Outlook Offline Folder.

- If all Archive and Personal Folders files found locally will be moved to the Server as indicated at the top of this checklist, move each of the files listed above to the location noted at the top of this checklist.
- If the there is no indication that the Archive and Personal Folders are to be moved to a specific location, move each of the files listed above to the c:\!tech*username* directory.

☐ Disable Cached Exchange Mode and Delete all Offline Folder files (.ost's) as follows:

- Open Microsoft Outlook and navigate to the Account Settings as follows:
- Outlook 2010: Select File menu, Info tab, then select Account Settings button, then select Account Settings from the dropdown.
- Outlook 2007: From the Tools menu select Account Settings.
- Outlook 2003: From the Tools menu select E-mail Accounts.
  - In the E-Mail Accounts window select View or change existing e-mail accounts and click Next.
- Select the Exchange account and click Change.

    - Clear the checkbox to Use Cached Exchange Mode then click Next then click Finish.
  - Close any open windows and then close Microsoft Outlook.
  - Delete all Offline Folder files (.ost's) from the directory listed below. The file name is not relevant since we are simply cleaning up potentially large files that are no longer needed. Delete all .ost's.

    Note: If the file name extension is not visible verify the file is of type Microsoft Office Outlook Offline Folder and not Microsoft Office Outlook Personal Folder.
    - XP Pro file location: C:\Documents and Settings*username*\Local Settings\Application Data\Microsoft\Outlook
    - Vista and Windows 7 file location: C:\Users*username*\AppData\Local\Microsoft\Outlook

☐ If the Users Profile Migration level indicated at the top of this checklist is Basic or Full (Not Custom), proceed directly to the Backing up the User Profile subsection below.

Custom Migration Tasks

Note: Do not perform the steps outlined in this subsection unless the Client Technical Contact has authorized a Custom User Profile Migration and the extra time required for these steps.

☐ Log on to the machine with the user logon ID and password for the user who's profile is being migrated.

☐ If all Company Data found on the workstation is to be moved to the Server as indicated at the top of this checklist, open Windows Explorer and navigate to the users Documents directory to get started.
  - Identify and move any large collections of company data to the location noted at the top of this checklist.
  - Look for data on the Desktop, in My Documents and in the root of the c: drive.
    - Move all data in an organized manner. Do not merge dissimilar directories.
    - Verify the location the data is being moved to is appropriately secured for the user and the content.

☐ Record Sharing Permissions for Outlook folders such as Inbox, Calendar or Contacts as follows:
  - Open Microsoft Outlook and navigate to the Folder List in the Navigation Pane on the left.
  - Right-click on the folder being shared (Inbox, Calendar, Contacts, etc.) and select Sharing (Outlook 2003) or Change Sharing Permissions (Outlook 2007 and 2010) from the menu.
  - List permissions here: Use the back of this page for extensive permission lists.

Folder name	Name(s)	Permission Level

☐ Record all Outlook Mailboxes belonging to other users that are open and listed in the Folder List here:

____

☐ Record all Public Folders\Favorites as follows:
  - Open Microsoft Outlook and navigate to the Public Folders\Favorites folder in the folder list.
  - For each item in the folder, right-click on the item, select Properties from the menu and record the Type and Location of the folder here:

____

____

- ☐ Additional tasks to perform on this workstation as outline by the Client technical Contact:
  - ____
  - ____
  - ____

Backing up the User Profile

- ☐ Log on to the machine with the user logon ID and password for the user who's profile is being migrated.
- ☐ Record the size of the users profiles that will be migrated as follows:
  - Open the Computer Properties and select the Advanced tab (XP Pro) or Advanced System Settings page (Vista or Windows 7) then in the User Profiles section click the Settings button.
  - Record the size of the users profiles that will be migrated here: ________ MB
- ☐ For any user profile over 200 MB clear out or move all unnecessary files from the profile as follows until it is below 200 MB in size:
  - Open Windows Explorer and navigate to the users Documents directory to get started.
  - Identify and move any large collections of company data to the server. Look on the desktop, in My Documents and in the root of the c: drive.
    - Verify the location the data is being moved to is appropriately secured for the user and the content.
    - Record here files were moved and where they were moved to: ________________________

      ____
  - Identify and move any large collections of Music, Picture or Video's from the users Documents directory or the desktop to the c:\!tech*username* directory for temporary storage.
    - Do not move the actual Music, Pictures or Video directory as they will still be seen by the system as part of the users profile. Create new directories and subdirectories as needed and Move the content into new directories created for the content. e.g. c:\!tech*username*\Music, c:\!tech*username*\Pictures, etc.
    - Record here files were moved and where they were moved to: ________________________

      ____
  - If the profile size has not been reduced to below 200 MB consult with the project manager as to how to proceed. If it is reasonably close (300 MB) it may be faster to proceed knowing the profile will take a little longer to backup and restore rather than searching for another 100 MB.
- ☐ Run the User State Migration Tool batch file to Save the users Profile as follows:
  - Run the Command Prompt with elevated privileges by right-clicking on the Command Prompt application and selecting Run as (XP Pro) or Run as administrator (Vista and Windows 7) from the menu. If prompted for Which user account to use, enter the current domain administrator username and password.
  - Run the usmtscan.bat file from the command line with the users name as the input to the batch file.. e.g. *newservername*\tech\usmt\usmtscan.bat *username.*

    Example: C:> \\zdtmsbs\tech\usmt\usmtscan.bat philm

- Monitor the progress of the USMT until it completes successfully. If it does not complete successfully review the progress.log and scanstate.log files that can be found in the c:\!tech directory.

Migrating the Workstation to the New Domain

Note: The two most common reason for Connect Computer application to fail are:

1) The .net Framework version installed is too low of a version number or it is damaged. The Connect Computer error may not be explicit enough to indicate that .net is the problem.
2) There is still a connection of some sort to the “new” server. Use the Net Use command to close them.

☐ Drop any connections to the new server (Net Use’s) that may have been set up previously as follows:

- At the Command Prompt run the net use command to list all connection to the new server.
- For each connection to the new server issue one of the following commands:
  - Net use *drive*: /d where *drive* is the drive letter in use for the connection.
  - Net use *servername**resourcename* /d (for connections that were used without a drive)

☐ Connect to the new domain as follows:

- Open Internet Explorer (XP Pro) or (for Vista and Windows 7) Right-click on the Internet Explorer application and select Run as administrator from the menu.
- Type in the URL http://connect on the address line and press enter on the keyboard.
- On the Welcome to Windows Small Business Server page click the Start Connect Computer Program link.
  - If prompted Do you want to run or save Launcher.exe from connect? Select Run.
  - If prompted by the UAC that A program needs your permissions to continue Click Continue.
  - On the Choose how to set up this computer page select Set up this computer for myself.
  - On the Computer requirements are verified page click Next.
  - On the Type your user name and password page enter the exact user name and the default new domain password then click Next.

    Note: Some users may not be using the default domain password for security reasons. If this user is not using the default domain password enter the appropriate password for the user.
  - On the Verify computer description page enter the correct complete computer name for this workstation then click Next.

    Note: Unless otherwise documented the name for the workstation should not be change.
  - On the Move existing users data and settings page verify the default name of none is selected then click Next.

    Note: Do not select any name from the dropdown list as these users are all local users only, not domain users, and should not be moved to the new domain.
  - On the Confirm your user data and settings selection page review the settings then click Next.

    Note: If all steps above have been followed as written the should be no settings to review as no local users are being moved to the new domain.
  - On the Restart the computer page check the box to automatically log the new user on to the workstation when the program is finished then click Restart.

Note: If the Connect Computer wizard fails and review of the error details indicate that there are Multiple connections to a server or shared resource by the same user, open the Command prompt and use the Net use command to close (delete) any connections to the new server then begin the steps in this section again from the top.

- Monitor the workstation through the migration process. The workstation may reboot several times before the Wizard is complete. When the Connect Computer complete page is presented click Finish.

☐ Add the Domain Users group to the Local Administrators group as follows:

- For Windows XP machines only, log on to the workstation as the domain administrator.
- Click Start then right-click on My Computer (XP Pro) or Computer (Vista and Windows 7) and select Manage from the menu.
- Navigate to the Local Users and Groups – Groups container and open the Administrators group.
- Highlight and delete each broken entries in the group.

  Note: Broken entries have an icon that is a head with a question mark and the name of the entry is the SID of the broken entry.
- Click the Add button and in the Select User, Computer, or Group window enter all the names of the Domain User who's profiles are being migrated to this machine then click OK to close the Selection window.
- When prompted for credentials by the Windows Security window enter the new domain administrator user name and password then click OK.
- Click OK to close the Administrators Properties window and then close the Computer Management window.
- For Windows XP machines only, log off of the workstation as the domain administrator.

☐ If the Users Profile Migration level indicated at the top of this checklist is Basic, proceed directly to the Final Check section below.

Migrating the User Profile

Restoring the User Profile

☐ Log on to the machine with the user logon ID and password for the user who's profile is being migrated.

☐ Run the User State Migration Tool batch file to Restore the users Profile as follows:

- Run the Command Prompt with elevated privileges by right-clicking on the Command Prompt application and selecting Run as (XP Pro) or Run as administrator (Vista and Windows 7) from the menu. If prompted for Which user account to use, enter the current domain administrator username and password.
- Run the usmtload.bat file from the command line with the users name as the input to the batch file.. e.g. *newservername*\tech\usmt\usmtload.bat *username.*

  Example: C:> \\zdtmsbs\tech\usmt\usmtload.bat philm
- Monitor the progress of the USMT until it completes successfully. If it does not complete successfully review the progress.log and scanstate.log files that can be found in the c:\!tech directory.
- Log off of the workstation and then log back on as the user to allow the new profile to load completely.

Full Migration Completion

☐ For Outlook 2010 configure Outlook for the current user as follows:

- Run Outlook and when prompted with the Microsoft Outlook popup indicating that The Microsoft Exchange administrator has made a change that requires you to quit and restart Outlook click OK.
- Re-run Outlook and do not close it until the Exchange cache is fully synchronized.

The message "All Folders are up to date" will be displayed in the status bar in the lower right corner of the Outlook window.

☐ For Outlook 2007 configure Outlook for the current user as follows:

- Run Outlook and on the Outlook 2007 Startup Welcome page click Next.
  - On the E-mail Accounts page accept the default of Yes and click Next.
  - On the Auto Account Setup page verify the email address for the current user is correctly detected and populated in the E-mail Address field then click Next.
  - On the Add new E-mail Account page verify all configurations where completed then click Finish.
  - When prompted for the User Name enter the full, correctly spelled, first and last name, and capitalized initials, for the current user then click OK.
  - When the Welcome to the 2007 Microsoft Office system window is presented, accept the defaults and click OK.
  - When the prompt to save RSS Feeds is presented click No.
- Do not close Outlook until the Exchange cache is fully synchronized.

The message "All Folders are up to date" will be displayed in the status bar in the lower right corner of the Outlook window.

☐ For Outlook 2003 configure Outlook for the current user as follows:

Note: The Outlook Profile applet (Mail icon) in Control Panel will not be available in control panel until Outlook Installer is run. Proceed as follows:

- Run Microsoft Outlook and then immediately close it again.
- Change the Exchange account server name in the Outlook profile as follows:
  - Open the Microsoft Office Outlook Profiles applet (Mail icon) from Control Panel \ User Accounts.
    - In the Mail Setup window click on the E-mail Accounts button.
    - In the E-Mail Accounts Wizard select View or change existing e-mail accounts and click Next.
    - Highlight the Microsoft Exchange Server account and click Change.
    - Enter the new server name in the Microsoft Exchange Server field and check the box to Use Cached Exchange Mode.
    - Click the Check Name button to the right of the User Name field and once the name is verified click Next then click Finish to close the E-mail Accounts window
  - Close all other open windows.
- Run Microsoft Outlook and do not close it until the Exchange cache is fully synchronized.

  The message "All Folders are up to date" will be displayed in lower right corner of the Outlook window.

☐ If custom Microsoft Outlook Address List configurations were recorded earlier re-configure the Microsoft Outlook Address Lists as follows:

Note: For all settings in this subsection refer to the Address List configuration recorded earlier in the Full Migration Tasks subsection.

- Open Microsoft Outlook and navigate to Address Book settings as follows:
  - Outlook 2010: Select File menu, Info tab, then select Account Settings button, then select Account Settings from the dropdown.
    - In the E-Mail Accounts window select the Address Books tab.
  - Outlook 2007: From the Tools menu select Account Settings.
    - In the E-Mail Accounts window select the Address Books tab.
  - Outlook 2003: From the Tools menu select E-mail Accounts.
    - In the E-Mail Accounts window select View or change existing directories or address books then click Next.
- Highlight the Outlook Address Book, click Change and then remove all Address books listed.
  - Close the Address Book and the Account settings window.
- Open Microsoft Outlook and navigate to the Folder List in the Navigation Pane on the left.
  - Right-click on the desired contact folder in the users Mailbox or the Public Folders and select properties from the menu then select the Outlook Address Tab.
    - Check the box to Show this folder as an e-mail Address Book, change the Name of the address book if required and then click OK.
  - Repeat this process for each Contact Folder to be used as an Outlook Address List.
- In Outlook, Select Address Book from the Tools menu (Outlook 2003 and 2007) or from the Home menu bar (Outlook 2010).
  - Select Options from the Address Book Tools menu.
    - Click on the dropdown arrow to the right of the Show this address list first field and select the correct address list.
    - Click on the dropdown arrow to the right of the Keep personal addresses in field and select the correct address list.
    - Reorder the address lists as required by highlighting any list and clicking either the up or down arrow to the right of the list to move it up or down in the list.
  - Close the Addressing window and the Address Book.

☐ If opened Archive or Personal Folders were recorded earlier re-Open the Archive and Personal Folders in Outlook as follows:

Note: For all settings in this subsection refer to the Archive and Personal Folders list recorded earlier in the Full Migration Tasks subsection.

Note: All .pst's should be in either the previously designated server location or c:\!tech\migration*username*.

- Outlook 2003 or 2007:
  - Open Microsoft Outlook and select Data File Management from the File menu.
    - Click Add and then select the appropriate .pst type from the list and click OK.
    - In the Create or Open Outlook Data File window navigate to the directory where the .pst file to be loaded exists, select the file and click OK.

- In the Personal Folders window change the Name of the folder if required and then click OK.
- Repeat this process for each .pst to be loaded, then close the Account Settings window.
- Outlook 2010:
  - Open Microsoft Outlook and from the File menu, Open tab select Open Outlook Data File.
    - In the open Outlook Data File window navigate to the directory where the .pst file to be loaded exists, select the file and click OK.

☐ If the Users Profile Migration level indicated at the top of this checklist is Basic or Full (Not Custom), proceed directly to the Final Check section below.

Custom Migration Finalization

Note: Do not perform the steps outlined in this subsection unless the Client Technical Contact has authorized a Custom User Profile Migration and the extra time required for these steps.

☐ If Sharing Permissions for Outlook folders were recorded earlier set the Sharing Permissions for Outlook folders as follows:

Note: For all settings in this subsection refer to the Sharing Permissions for Outlook folder list recorded earlier in the Full Migration Tasks subsection.

- Open Microsoft Outlook and navigate to the Folder List in the Navigation Pane on the left.
  - Right-click on the folder to be shared (Inbox, Calendar, Contacts, Public Contacts, etc.) and select Sharing (Outlook 2003) or Properties (Outlook 2007 and 2010) from the menu.
  - On the Permissions tab click Add and in the Add Users window select all the names requiring permissions of any kind.
  - Click the Add button and then click OK. The names should now be in the Permissions list.
    - Select a user name (or Default, or Anonymous) and then set the appropriate permissions for that Name by either selecting a pre-defined Permission Level from the dropdown list or checking radio buttons and checkboxes in the Read, Write, Deleted items and Other sections of the window as required.
    - Repeat this process for all users requiring permissions to this folder and then click OK to close the folder Properties window.
  - Repeat this process for each folder in either the users Mailbox or Public Folders as required.

☐ If Outlook Mailboxes belonging to other users were recorded earlier open them as follows:

Note: For all settings in this subsection refer to the Outlook Mailboxes list recorded earlier in the Full Migration Tasks subsection.

- Open Microsoft Outlook and navigate to the Account Settings as follows:
  - Outlook 2010: Select File menu, Info tab, then select Account Settings button, then select Account Settings from the dropdown.
  - Outlook 2007: From the Tools menu select Account Settings.
  - Outlook 2003: From the Tools menu select E-mail Accounts.
- Select the Primary Exchange account then click Change.
- Click the More Settings button and in the Microsoft Exchange settings window select the Advanced tab.
  - In the Mailboxes section highlight any user names that are from the old system (broken) and click Remove.

        - In the Mailboxes section click Add, enter the name of the user who's mailbox is to be opened and then click OK.
        - Repeat this process for each users mailbox to be opened.
    - Click OK to close the Microsoft Exchange settings window and in the Change … window click Next then click Finish. Close the Account Settings window.

- ☐ If Public Folders\Favorites were recorded earlier configure them as follows:

    Note: For all settings in this subsection refer to the Public Folder Favorites list recorded earlier in the Full Migration Tasks subsection.

    - Open Microsoft Outlook and navigate to the Public Folders, All Public Folders in the All Folder List.
    - Select each folder to appear in the Public Folders\Favorites container, right-click on the item and select Add to Favorites from the menu.

- ☐ Fix all Outlook E-mail Rules as follows:
    - Open Microsoft Outlook and select Rules and Alerts from the Tools menu (Outlook 2003 and 2007) or Select Manage Rules and Alerts from the Rules dropdown on the Home menu (Outlook 2010).
    - If any broken Rules exist message from Microsoft Office Outlook should pop-up indicate that One or more rules contain errors. Delete or modify these rules. Click OK to close the window.
    - In the Rules and Alerts window any broken Rule will be highlighted in Red and will have the word (Error) appended to the end of the Rules name.
        - Open each broken Rule and step through the options by clicking the Next button to identify where the Rule is broken.
        - Correct any values that are indicated and then click Finish to close and save the Rule.
        - Repeat this process until all Rules in error have been fixed.
    - Click OK to close the Rules and Alerts window.

- ☐ Additional tasks to perform on this workstation as outline by the Client technical Contact:
    - ______________________________
    - ______________________________

Windows Mobile 6 Device

Note: The steps outlined here are only for users who have a Windows Mobile 6 device to be connected to the Exchange server. If they do not have a Windows Mobile 6 device to be configured skip this section.

- ☐ To connect a Windows Mobile 6 device to an Exchange Server over-the-air configure the Windows Mobile 6 device as follows:
    - On the Home screen select Start then ActiveSync.
    - On the ActiveSync page select set up your device to sync with it.
        - On the Edit Server Settings page in the Server address field enter remote.*company.xxx* then select Next.
        - On the User Information page enter the User name, Password, and Domain, select the Save password check box. then select Next.

        - On the Options page select the check boxes for each data item to be synchronized with Exchange Server.
            - To change settings for any data item select that data item, select Menu \ Advanced and adjust settings as required then click Next to return to the data item selection list.
            - Repeat the above process for each data item to configure.
        - Select Finish to complete the configuration.
    - The Windows Mobile device will try accessing the Exchange Server mailbox with the user credentials entered earlier, create a partnership and begin the synchronization process.

- ☐ Test the configuration of the Windows Mobile 6 Device by reviewing new email in the users Inbox on the device and by sending a test message from the device.

Final Check

Note: There is a User Profile Component General Reference list in the Resources section that may be very valuable if troubleshooting a broken or miss-migrated profile component.

- ☐ Configure some of the nuisance settings in Outlook as follows:
    - Open Microsoft Outlook.
    - Navigate to the Folder List in the Navigation Pane on the left and select the Journal folder.
        - On the Microsoft Office Outlook prompt pop-up for Journal tracking check the box Please do not show me this dialog again and then click No.
    - For Outlook 2007 and older only: Select Options from the Tools menu, select the Other tab and then click on the AutoArchive button.
        - Clear the checkbox Run AutoArchive every… to disable AutoArchive.
    - For Outlook 2010: Select File menu, Option then select Advanced from the menu on the left.
        - Select the AutoArchive Settings button.
        - Clear the checkbox Run AutoArchive every… to disable AutoArchive.
- ☐ Test e-mail flow outbound and inbound as follows:
    - Open Microsoft Outlook and compose a new e-mail message for testing purposes.
    - Address the email to any e-mail account you have access to and that is not hosted by this Exchange server.
    - Reply to the test email sent to your external e-mail account and verify it is returned to the user.
- ☐ Open Internet Explorer and verify access to the Companyweb site.
- ☐ Verify access to Microsoft.com (or any outside web site).
- ☐ Open Windows Explorer and verify access to data files in the My Documents folder (XP Pro) or Documents (Vista and Windows 7).
- ☐ In Windows Explorer verify all network shares that should be mapped to local drives for this user based on their group membership have been mapped. Refer to the Discovery section - Active Directory / Group Policies subsection.
- ☐ In Windows Explorer verify access to data files in each network drive available.
- ☐ Open the Printers folder from Control Panel or from the Start menu and set the default printer to be the one recorded earlier in the Workstation Migration Preparation section of this checklist.
- ☐ Test each printer in the folder as follows:

Note: Do not test virtual printers. e.g. Microsoft Document Writer or Acrobat Distiller.

- In the Printer folder, right-click on the printer and select properties from the menu.
- Click the Print Test Page button and when the process completes click Close on the test page pop-up and then click OK to close the Printer Properties.
- Verify the test page was in fact printed. Attach the test page to the back of this checklist.
- Troubleshoot printing issues as required.
- Delete any printers that have been removed or are no longer in service if possible.

Fine Tuning

☐ Verify Windows auto update is set to disabled if this machine is managed and if it is not set it to Automatic (recommended) and accept the default frequency.

- Windows XP: Open the System Properties and select the Automatic Updates tab.
- Windows Vista: Open Control Panel \ Security \ Windows Update \ Change settings.
- Windows 7: Open Control Panel \ System and Security \ Windows Update \ Change settings.
- Verify Windows auto update is set to disabled if this machine is managed and if it is not set it to Automatic (recommended) and accept the default frequency.

☐ Physically label the CPU with the Workstation name if it is not already labeled.

☐ If there are no other tasks to perform turn the machine over to the user.

- Turn the Workstation Migration notice over and prop it up near the keyboard on the desk with the Workstation Migration is Complete! side showing.

Note: If Passwords sharing is an issue consider placing the page under the keyboard with only the Workstation Migration is Complete! Portion showing.

- Be sure to ask the user to "look around" their workstation to see if everything seems to be in order and that they have the required programs and network access.

Other

☐ ____________________

☐ ____________________

☐ ____________________

Cleanup

☐ Migrate all unresolved issues for this workstation migration to either the Project Fine Tuning or Spin-Off checklists in this binder.

☐ Update the Migration Tracking Sheet with all required information for this workstation migration including tech name, date, time, etc.

☐ Place this checklist into the front sleeve of the Network Migration Project binder.

Notes / Issues:

- ☐ ____
- ☐ ____
- ☐ ____
- ☐ ____

NOTICE: Workstation Migration in Progress!

Please do not attempt to use this computer as we are in the process of migrating it to the new network.
If you have any questions or concerns please contact your in house Technical Contact.

Thank you,

The KPEnterprises Network Migration Team

NOTICE: Workstation Migration is Complete!

This machine has been migrated to the new network and is available for use.

Your new Logon ID is: ______________________

Your new Password is: ______________________

Please do not remove this notice.

Thank You,

The KPEnterprises Network Migration Team

17. Remote Migration

Company:________________________ **Date:** ________________________

Full User Name: ________________ **Technician:** ________________

Logon ID: ______________________ **Machine Name:** ______________

Password: ______________________

Start Time: ________ **Finish Time:** ________

Note: Anytime during the migration whenever prompted for the user's name always enter the full correctly spelled name and proper initials. e.g. Phil McCracken - PM

Note: Anytime during the migration it is assumed that whenever prompted by the User Access Control (UAC) that Windows needs your permission to continue the request will be acknowledged with Continue.

RWW and OWA Setup

☐ Send the remote user the new Security Certificate to install from the new Server as follows:

- Log on to the new server or any workstation on the new domain and then log on to the administrators OWA email account at https://remote.*company.xxx*/owa.
    - Compose a new email message to the remote user who's system is being configured.
    - Attach the file *newservername*\public\downloads\install Certificate Package.zip.
    - In the Subject field enter the words For your eyes only.
    - In the body of the email enter:

        This information will be required to connect to the new Small Business Server.

        Thank you

        The KPEnterprises Network Migration Team.
    - Send the email, log off of the administrators email account then close the Internet Explorer tab.

☐ Download and install the new Security Certificate on the remote workstation as follows:

- Establish a connect to the remote machine with LogMeIn via the Continuum management portal, the user's personal LogMeIn account or join.me.
- Log on to the OWA email account for the remote user who's system is being configured at https://remote.*company.xxx*/owa.
    - Open the email from the administrator titled For your eyes only.
    - Save the attached file to the default directory. Note the directory where the file is being downloaded/saved to here: ________________________
    - Open Windows Explorer and navigate to the download location of the Install Certificate Package.zip.
    - Right-click on the Install Certificate Package.zip and select Extract all from the menu.

        Note the directory where the file is being downloaded/saved to here: ________________

        ____

    - In Windows Explorer navigate to the location of the extracted files and double click on the Install Certificate application.
    - If there is a pop-up requesting confirmation Do you want to run this program click Run.
    - On the Certificate Installation window select Install the certificate on my computer then click Install.

      Note: Watch for and approve any pop-up including the UAC that may require confirmation that it is OK run this program and to install this certificate.
    - When the Certificate Installation wizard has finished click Close.

☐ Set up Favorites as follows:

- Open Internet Explorer and surf to the new Remote Web Workplace site at https://remote.*company.xxx* and log on using the remote users credentials.
- Add the RWW site to the users Favorites by pressing the Alt+Z keys on the keyboard.
- Surf to the clients new Outlook Web Access page at https://remote.*company.xxx*/owa and add it to the users Favorites by pressing the Alt+Z keys on the keyboard.

Outlook using RPC over HTTP Setup

Note: For the procedure outlined below it is assumed that both Microsoft Outlook 2003 or newer and the new Server Security Certificate are already installed on the remote users workstation.

Note: The new Server Security Certificate should already have been installed while performing the steps outlined in the RWW and OWA Setup section at the top of this Remote Migration checklist.

☐ Establish a connect to the remote machine with LogMeIn via the Continuum management portal, the user's personal LogMeIn account or join.me.

Setup New Outlook 2010 or 2007 Profile

Note: The steps in this subsection are only for creating a new Outlook 2010 or 2007 Profile.

If the installed Outlook version is 2003 skip down to the subsection titled Setup New Outlook 2003 Profile.

Note: If the user has previously used Outlook to connect to the SBS Exchange server from this workstation, skip this subsection and proceed to the subsection below entitled Configuration of Existing Outlook Profile.

☐ Run Microsoft Outlook.

- If prompted for a New Profile name enter the users full Name then click OK.
- If prompted with the Outlook 20xx Startup Welcome page click Next.
- On the E-mail Accounts page asking would you like to configure an E-mail account, accept the default of Yes and click Next.
- On the Auto Account Setup page:
    - Enter the user's full name in the Your Name field.
    - Enter the exact email address for the current user in the E-mail Address field.
    - Enter the users password in the Password and retype Password fields then click Next.
    - If prompted with a Microsoft Outlook popup requesting permission to Allow this website to configure the users email server settings check the box Don't ask me about this website again then click Allow.

- On the Windows Security popup enter the users password, check the box Remember my credentials or Remember my password then click OK.

  Note: The user name may be presented as username@company.xxx but will likely need to be changed to *domain\username*.

  e.g. zdtminc\philm

- If presented with the Add new E-mail Account wizard page verify all configurations where completed then click Finish.
- If prompted by an Add E-mail Account popup indicating You must restart Outlook for these changes to take effect click OK.
- When prompted for the User Name enter the full, correctly spelled, first and last name, and capitalized initials, for the current user then click OK.
- When prompted with the Welcome to Office window, accept the defaults (Outlook 2007) or select Don't make changes (Outlook 2010) then click OK.
- If prompted with the Microsoft Office Outlook junk mail page check the box Please do not show me this dialog again then click Close.
- If prompted to save RSS Feeds is presented click No.

- Once Outlook has completed loading do not close Outlook until the Exchange cache is fully synchronized.

The message "All Folders are up to date" will be displayed in the status bar in the lower right corner of the Outlook window.

Setup New Outlook 2003 Profile

Note: The steps in this subsection are only for creating a new Outlook 2003 Profile.

Note: If the user has previously used Outlook to connect to the SBS Exchange server from this workstation, skip this subsection and proceed to the subsection below entitled Configuration of Existing Outlook Profile.

☐ Open the Microsoft Office Outlook Profiles applet (Mail icon) from Control Panel \ User Accounts.

☐ If the Outlook Profiles applet (Mail icon) does not appear in the Control Panel \ User Accounts folder it is because the Outlook Installer has never been run for this user. Proceed as follows:

- Open Microsoft Outlook and on the Outlook 2003 Startup wizard Welcome page click Cancel.
- On the Outlook 2003 Startup cancelation confirmation page click Yes.
- Open the Microsoft Office Outlook Profiles applet (Mail icon) from Control Panel \ User Accounts.

Note: The Mail icon may not show up until the folder view is refreshed. Press F5 key on the keyboard.

☐ In the Mail Setup window click on the Show Profiles button.

☐ In the Mail Profile list window Click the Add button and in the New Profile wizard enter the users first name for the Profile Name then click OK.

- On the E-mail Accounts page select Add a new e-mail account and click Next.
- On the Server Type page select Microsoft Exchange Server and click Next.
  - On the Exchange Server Settings page in the Microsoft Exchange Server field enter the local name of the Exchange server as documented in the Discovery Section - Domain Names, IP's subsection. e.g. *servername.domainname*.local.

    Example: zdtmsbs.zdtminc.local

- Clear the checkbox Use Cached Exchange Mode.
- In the User Name field enter the users domain logon name but do not click Check Name.
- On the Exchange Server settings page click More Settings.

  Note: The Outlook client will not be able to connect to or authenticate with the SBS Exchange server.

  - When the Microsoft Office Outlook logon warning pops up click OK.
  - Close the Microsoft Exchange Server use name check window when it pops up by clicking Cancel.
  - In the Microsoft Exchange Server settings window select the Connection tab.
    - On the Connection tab, in the Exchange over the Internet section check the box to Connect to my Exchange mailbox using HTTP and then click the Exchange Proxy Settings button.
    - On the Exchange Proxy Settings page in the Use this URL to connect to my proxy server field enter the FQDN for the SBS server as documented in the Discovery Section - Domain Names, IP's subsection. e.g. *publicname.domainname.com.*

      Example: remote.zdtminc.net
    - Check the box to Connect using SSL only.
    - Check the box Mutually authenticate the session when connecting with SSL.
    - In the Principal name for the proxy server field enter the FQDN for the SBS server preceded by MSSTD: e.g. msstd:publicname.domainname.xxx.
    - Example: msstd:remote.zdtminc.net
    - Check the box On slow networks, connect using HTTP first, then connect using TCP/IP.
    - In the Proxy authentication settings section select Basic Authentication from the dropdown menu.
    - Click OK to close the Proxy Settings window, click OK to close the More Settings window
  - On the Exchange Settings window click Next then click Finish.

☐ In the Mail Profile list window click the dropdown arrow to the right of the Always use this profile field and select the newly created profile name from the list.

☐ Click OK to close the Mail applet and then close the Control Panel.

Configuration of an Existing Outlook Profile

☐ Open the Microsoft Office Outlook Profiles applet (Mail icon) from Control Panel \ User Accounts.

☐ In the Mail Setup window click on the Show Profiles button.

☐ If there are multiple profiles select the Outlook profile this user uses for connecting to their office email and then click on the Properties button.

- In the Mail Setup window click on the E-mail Accounts button.
- Office 2003 only: In the E-Mail Accounts Wizard select View or change existing e-mail accounts and click Next.
- Highlight the Microsoft Exchange Server account and click Change.

- On the Exchange Server Settings page in the Microsoft Exchange Server field enter the local name of the Exchange server as documented in the Discovery Section - Domain Names, IP's subsection. e.g. *servername.domainname*.local.

  Example: zdtmsbs.zdtminc.local

- Clear the checkbox Use Cached Exchange Mode.
- In the User Name field enter the users domain logon name but do not click Check Name.
- On the Exchange Server settings page click More Settings.

Note: The Outlook client may not be able to connect to or authenticate with the SBS Exchange server. If not proceed as follows:

  - When the Microsoft Office Outlook logon warning pops up click OK.
  - Close the Microsoft Exchange Server use name check window when it pops up by clicking Cancel.

- In the Microsoft Exchange Server settings window select the Connection tab.
  - On the Connection tab, in the Exchange over the Internet section check the box to Connect to my Exchange mailbox using HTTP and then click the Exchange Proxy Settings button.
  - On the Exchange Proxy Settings page in the Use this URL to connect to my proxy server field enter the FQDN for the SBS server as documented in the Discovery Section - Domain Names, IP's subsection. e.g. *publicname.domainname.xxx*.

    Example: remote.zdtminc.net

  - Check the box to Connect using SSL only.
  - Office 2003 only: Check the box Mutually authenticate the session when connecting with SSL.
  - Office 2007 and 2010 only: Check the box Only connect to proxy servers that have this principal name in their certificate.
  - In the Principal name for the proxy server field enter the FQDN for the SBS server preceded by MSSTD: e.g. msstd:*publicname.domainname.xxx*.

    Example: msstd:remote.zdtminc.net

  - Check the box On slow networks, connect using HTTP first, then connect using TCP/IP.
  - In the Proxy authentication settings section select Basic Authentication from the dropdown menu.
    - Click OK to close the Proxy Settings window, click OK to close the More Settings window and on the Exchange Settings window click Next then click Finish.

☐ In the Mail Profile list window click the dropdown arrow to the right of the Always use this profile field and select the newly modified profile name from the list.

☐ Click OK to close the Mail applet and then close the Control Panel.

Outlook Final Check and Synchronization

☐ Open Microsoft Outlook and in the Connect to window enter the users domain logon ID in the format *internaldomainname\username* and their password then click OK.

☐ Configure some of the nuisance settings in Outlook as follows:

- Navigate to the Folder List in the Navigation Pane on the left and select the Journal folder.
- On the Microsoft Office Outlook prompt pop-up for Journal tracking check the box Please do not show me this dialog again and then click No.

- For Outlook 2007 and older only: Select Options from the Tools menu, select the Other tab and then click on the AutoArchive button.
- Clear the checkbox Run AutoArchive every… to disable AutoArchive.
- For Outlook 2010: Select File menu, Option then select Advanced from the menu on the left.
- Select the AutoArchive Settings button.
- Clear the checkbox Run AutoArchive every… to disable AutoArchive.

☐ Test e-mail flow outbound and inbound as follows:

- In Microsoft Outlook compose a new e-mail message for testing purposes.
- Address the email to any e-mail account you have access to and that is not hosted by this Exchange server.
- Reply to the test email sent to your external e-mail account and verify it is returned to the user.

☐ Verify that Exchange Synchronization is Enable now as follows:

- Open Microsoft Outlook and navigate to the Account Settings as follows:
- Outlook 2010: Select File menu, Info tab, then select Account Settings button, then select Account Settings from the dropdown.
- Outlook 2007: From the Tools menu select Account Settings.
- Outlook 2003: From the Tools menu select E-mail Accounts.
  - In the E-Mail Accounts window select View or change existing e-mail accounts and click Next.
- Select the Exchange account and click Change.
  - Check the box to Use Cached Exchange Mode then click Next.
  - On the Microsoft Office Outlook warning message indicating that you must exit close and reopen Outlook for the changes to take effect click OK.
  - Click Finish, close any open windows and then close Microsoft Outlook.

☐ Run Microsoft Outlook, log in and verify folder synchronization is processing.

- Do not close Outlook until the Exchange cache is fully synchronized.

The message "All Folders are up to date" will be displayed in the status bar in the lower right corner of the Outlook window.

Note: If there are problems with Outlook synchronizing with the Exchange server, one quick solution is to verify that the Microsoft Exchange is the only account in the Outlook profile. If it is, delete the Outlook profile and rebuild it from scratch starting at the Outlook using RPC over HTTP Setup section.

VPN Connection

Note: Do not set up a VPN connection unless this user has been authorized to connect to the network remotely using VPN.

Note: Once a VPN connection is created and established any remote session (LogMeIn, join.me, etc.) to the users workstation or laptop will be lost. Simply re-establish the connection to proceed with the next steps. The same re-connection will be required when the VPN is disconnected.

☐ Establish a connect to the remote machine with LogMeIn via the Continuum management portal, the user's personal LogMeIn account or join.me.

Setup VPN Connection – XP Pro

- ☐ Navigate to the Control Panel \ Network and Internet Connections \ Network Connections container.
  - Delete any VPN connection to the old SBS Server.
- ☐ Click on the Create a new connection link in the Task list on the left or select New Connection from the File menu.
  - In the New Connection Wizard click Next, select Connect to the network at my workplace then click Next.
  - Select Virtual Private Network connection then click Next.
  - In the Company Name field enter the name for the connection and click Next. Usually this is the acronym for the company name. e.g. ZDTM Inc.
  - In Host name / IP filed enter the public name for the SBS server as documented in the Discovery section - Domain Names, IP's subsection and then click Next.

    Note: This is most likely remote.*company.xxx*
  - On the Connection Availability page select Anyone's use then click Next.
  - On the Completing the New Connection page check the box to Add a shortcut to this connection to my desktop and then click Finish.
- ☐ In the Connect *vpnconnectionname* window enter the users domain logon ID and Password, check the box to Save this user name and password for the following users then click Connect.

  Note: Do not select the Anyone who uses this computer option.

Setup VPN Connection – Vista and Windows 7

- ☐ Navigate to the Control Panel \ Network and Internet \ Network Connections container.
  - Delete any VPN connection to the old SBS Server.
- ☐ Navigate to the Control Panel \ Network and Internet \ Network and Sharing Center container.
  - For Windows Vista click on the Set up a connection or network link in the Task list on the left.
  - For Windows 7 click on the Set up a new connection or network link in the Change your network settings section.
    - On the Choose a connection option page select Connect to a workplace then click Next.
    - If the wizard prompts Do you want to use a connection that you already have select No then click Next.
    - Select Use my Internet connection (VPN).
    - In the Internet address field enter the public name for the SBS server as documented in the Discovery section - Domain Names, IP's subsection.

      Note: This is most likely remote.*company.xxx*
    - In the Destination name field enter the name for the connection. Usually this is the acronym for the company name. e.g. ZDTM Inc.

    Note: Do not select the Allow other people to use this connection option.
    - On the user name and password page enter the users domain logon ID and Password, check the box to Remember this password then click Connect.

Map Network Drives

Note: For all drive mappings refer to the Discovery section - Active Directory / Group Policies subsection and the domain logon.bat file.

- ☐ Open Windows Explorer and navigate to My Computer (XP Pro) or Computer (Vista and Windows 7).
  - Delete any drive previously mapped to the old server by right-clicking on them and selecting disconnect from the menu.
- ☐ Based on the group membership and requirements for this user set up persistent drive maps as follows:
  - In Windows Explorer select Map Network Drive form the Tools menu or Tool bar.
    - Select the appropriate drive letter for this mapping then type in the full UNC path to the required share.
    - Check the box Reconnect at logon then click Finish.
    - In the Connect to window enter the users domain logon ID in the format *internaldomainname\username* and their password, check the box Remember my password then click OK.
    - Verify access to the content of the share and then close the Explorer window.
  - Repeat the above process for each drive to be mapped.
- ☐ Close all open windows and then disconnect the VPN connection by right-clicking on the connection icon in the system tray and selecting Disconnect from the menu.

Windows Mobile 6 Device

Note: The steps outlined here are only for users who have a Windows Mobile 6 device to be connected to the Exchange server. If they do not have a device to be configured skip this section.

- ☐ To connect a Windows Mobile 6 device to an Exchange Server over-the-air configure the Windows Mobile 6 device as follows:
  - On the Home screen select Start then ActiveSync.
  - On the ActiveSync page select set up your device to sync with it.
    - On the Edit Server Settings page in the Server address field enter remote.*company.xxx* then select Next.
    - On the User Information page enter the User name, Password, and Domain, select the Save password check box. then select Next.
    - On the Options page select the check boxes for each data item to be synchronized with Exchange Server.
      - To change settings for any data item select that data item, select Menu \ Advanced and adjust settings as required then click Next to return to the data item selection list.
      - Repeat the above process for each data item to configure.
    - Select Finish to complete the configuration.
  - The Windows Mobile device will try accessing the Exchange Server mailbox with the user credentials entered earlier, create a partnership and begin the synchronization process.
- ☐ Test the configuration of the Windows Mobile 6 Device by reviewing new email in the users Inbox on the device and by sending a test message from the device.

Fine Tuning

☐ Inform the client that they need to leave their machine on and Outlook open until the "All folders are up to date" message is indicated by Outlook in the status bar at the bottom of the Outlook window.

☐ Provide instructions for the user on where the shortcuts to RWW, OWA and the VPN connection are and how to use them.

☐ If there are no other tasks to perform turn the machine over to the user.

☐ Disconnect from the remote machine.

Other

☐ ____________________

☐ ____________________

☐ ____________________

Cleanup

☐ Migrate all unresolved issues for this workstation migration to either the Project Fine Tuning or Spin-Off checklists in this binder.

☐ Update the Migration Tracking Sheet with all required information for this workstation migration including tech name, date, time, etc.

☐ Place this checklist into the front sleeve of the Network Migration Project binder.

Notes / Issues:

☐ ____________________

☐ ____________________

☐ ____________________

☐ ____________________

18. Migration Tracking Sheet

List all local and remote workstations or users to be migrated as documented in the Active Directory / Group Policies subsection of the Discovery. Enter the order of migration of workstations and users as dictated by LOB, migration, uptime requirements etc.
Be sure to note the level of user profile migration. Tracking the time taken for migration of any machine or user is critical for future planning.

	Order	Level	Workstation	User(s)	Tech	Date	Time	Disposition
☐								
☐								
☐								
☐								
☐								
☐								
☐								
☐								
☐								
☐								
☐								
☐								
☐								
☐								
☐								
☐								

19. Shortages

Record here all hardware, software or information shortages for the entire project. Inform the proper person to get the shortage resolved. Always follow up with an email. Always check the status frequently.

- ☐ ____________________
- ☐ ____________________
- ☐ ____________________
- ☐ ____________________
- ☐ ____________________
- ☐ ____________________
- ☐ ____________________
- ☐ ____________________
- ☐ ____________________
- ☐ ____________________
- ☐ ____________________
- ☐ ____________________
- ☐ ____________________
- ☐ ____________________
- ☐ ____________________
- ☐ ____________________
- ☐ ____________________
- ☐ ____________________
- ☐ ____________________
- ☐ ____________________
- ☐ ____________________
- ☐ ____________________
- ☐ ____________________
- ☐ ____________________

20. Pack-Up / To-Do Checklist

Pack-Up

- ☐ Server
- ☐ Server power chords
- ☐ All documentation for server and related hardware
- ☐ Server Operating System software
- ☐ UPS and data cable
- ☐ All software packages used for installation
- ☐ ____________________
- ☐ ____________________
- ☐ ____________________
- ☐ ____________________
- ☐ ____________________
- ☐ ____________________

To-Do

- ☐ Change Server IP required before shutdown and move to site? YES / NO
- ☐ Disable DHCP required before shutdown and move to site? YES / NO
- ☐ ____________________
- ☐ ____________________
- ☐ ____________________
- ☐ ____________________
- ☐ ____________________
- ☐ ____________________
- ☐ ____________________
- ☐ ____________________
- ☐ ____________________

21. Fine Tuning

Record here all items and issues requiring fine tuning or follow-up of some sort. Be detailed so anyone can do the follow-up. If the item or issue is extensive enough consider whether it should be put on the Spin-Off Project Checklist so that it gets its own Service Ticket.

- ☐ ______
- ☐ ______
- ☐ ______
- ☐ ______
- ☐ ______
- ☐ ______
- ☐ ______
- ☐ ______
- ☐ ______
- ☐ ______
- ☐ ______
- ☐ ______
- ☐ ______
- ☐ ______
- ☐ ______
- ☐ ______
- ☐ ______
- ☐ ______
- ☐ ______
- ☐ ______
- ☐ ______
- ☐ ______
- ☐ ______
- ☐ ______

22. Spin-Off Projects and Issues

Record here all issues born from any part of this project that are not within the scope of this project as defined. All items listed here must be entered into the Service Tracking System as a new Service Ticket for this client.
Check off each item as it is properly addressed.

- ☐ ______
- ☐ ______
- ☐ ______
- ☐ ______
- ☐ ______
- ☐ ______
- ☐ ______
- ☐ ______
- ☐ ______
- ☐ ______
- ☐ ______
- ☐ ______
- ☐ ______
- ☐ ______
- ☐ ______
- ☐ ______
- ☐ ______
- ☐ ______
- ☐ ______
- ☐ ______
- ☐ ______
- ☐ ______
- ☐ ______

23. Project Completion

The Project Completion is simply the official wrap up of the migration project itself, a double check of all checklists and some tasks related to editing of the document to keep it up to date.

- ☐ Review each of the following Checklists and verify all items have in fact been correctly checked off to completion. Address any discrepancies immediately.
  - System Build
  - Network Migration Preparation
  - Network Migration
  - Sub-System Migration
  - Migration Tracking Sheet
  - Shortages
  - Pack Up / To Do Checklist
  - Fine Tuning
  - Spin-Off Project
- ☐ Have a brief sit-down meeting with the Client Technical Contact to discuss the migration. How it went, timing, expectations vs. reality, overall satisfaction. Take detailed notes.
- ☐ If any items have been missed they must be entered into either the Fine Tuning Checklist or the Spin-Off Project Checklist.
- ☐ All comments and observations should be noted in either the Retrospective section or the Project Notes section of this binder so that they will be properly addressed during the Retrospective.
- ☐ Migrate all applicable notes from the technicians and from the various sections of this document to the Project Notes section of this binder so that they will be properly addressed during the Retrospective.
- ☐ Double check the File Tuning Checklist and verify that all items listed have either been completed, re-assigned to the Project Spin-Off Checklist or have been turned into a Service Ticket for this client.
- ☐ Double check the Project Spin-Off Checklist and verify that all items listed have been turned into a Service Ticket for this client.
- ☐ Review and verify each section of this project for content that should be changed corrected or incorporated into the original Network Migration Project Template document.
- ☐ Present all revision suggestions to the Project Manager for approval during the Retrospective.

STOP: Complete the Project Retrospective before continuing.

- ☐ Strip all pages (not tabs) from the Network Migration Project binder and file them along with all other related project documents together in an expandable manila folder at KPEnterprises office file cabinet. Label the folder with the company name followed by Network Migration 200x

Project Complete!

24. Retrospective and Revision History

Review Process

Record here any additional notes for issues and items that need to be covered during the post project review. The project review should be objective and focus on both the root cause of things gone wrong and the successes in new methods and strategies.

- ☐ Organize the note from this section and the Project Notes section into a list that is prioritized by impact to the overall project.
- ☐ Instruct everyone who worked on this project to make a list of the top five to ten items they feel impacted the project (positively or negatively) and how. Ask them to be objective and remind them this not just about negative impact.
- ☐ Schedule a meeting time for the Retrospective within one week of the project completion. Schedule the meeting for a time when all people involved can attend.

  Note: Do not let the meeting get postponed or pushed off more than once or critical ideas and knowledge will be lost!
- ☐ During the review check off each item as it is properly addressed. Take detailed notes.
  - Review all proposed content changes, corrections or incorporations to the original Network Migration Project Template document.
  - Review all strategies used (New and Old) and document methods that worked and that need work.
  - Make specific notes on what policies or procedures must change to avoid the same downfalls or to ensure the same success.
- ☐ Based on the finding of the Retrospective, adjust company policies in need of revision.
- ☐ Based on the finding of the Retrospective, revise all necessary checklist and procedures in the Network Migration Project Template document
- ☐ Based on the finding of the Retrospective, revise all documented strategies used for network migrations. (Migration Strategies section of the Network Migration Project Template document)
- ☐ Properly record all document revisions in the Document Revision History Section of the Network Migration Project Template document.
- ☐ Update the Revision Number on the first page of the Network Migration Project Template document based on the nomenclature detailed in the Using This Document section of this document.

Notes:

- ☐ ______________________________
- ☐ ______________________________
- ☐ ______________________________
- ☐ ______________________________
- ☐ ______________________________
- ☐ ______________________________

Document Revision History

2011.09.01.01
Document released to public

25. Project Notes

26. New Network Documentation

General

This is where all Network Documentation should culminate during and after the migration.
One of the final steps in the Network Migration is to merge the Old Network Documentation with the New Network Documentation. If everything is correctly organized and merged you can simply move all of this information into a single binder and label it "Network Documentation".

Note: You will find a form for all the documents listed below except those that appear in Italics.

Procedures

Documentation of all procedures relevant to the system. The more critical the component the more extensive the documentation of the procedure should be.
Procedures found here may be simply marked up whitepapers specific to common network tasks.

Net Specs

- Network Map
- Internet Domain Registration Information
- Router Configuration Form
- Firewall Configuration Form
- IP Address Allocation Record
- Hard Coded IP Address Record
- Network Timing Diagram
- Shared Resources Record
- Shared Resources Permission Record
- UPS Power Distribution Form
- Group Policy Object Record

Machines Specs

- Machine Specification Sheet
  For every Server, Workstation, Laptop, Printers, Copiers, NAS, SAN, CDP, Phone System, Time Clock, Surveillance System, etc.

Users & Passwords

- User Names, Logon ID and Passwords Records
- Email Addresses Record
- POP or MAPI Account and Credential Records
- Security and Distribution Group Membership Record
- Password Policy Form

Products

- Line of Business Application Record
- *License / Key / Code Documents for all LOB's, applications and software of any kind.*
- *Service Agreements, Support Packs, Care Packs, etc.*

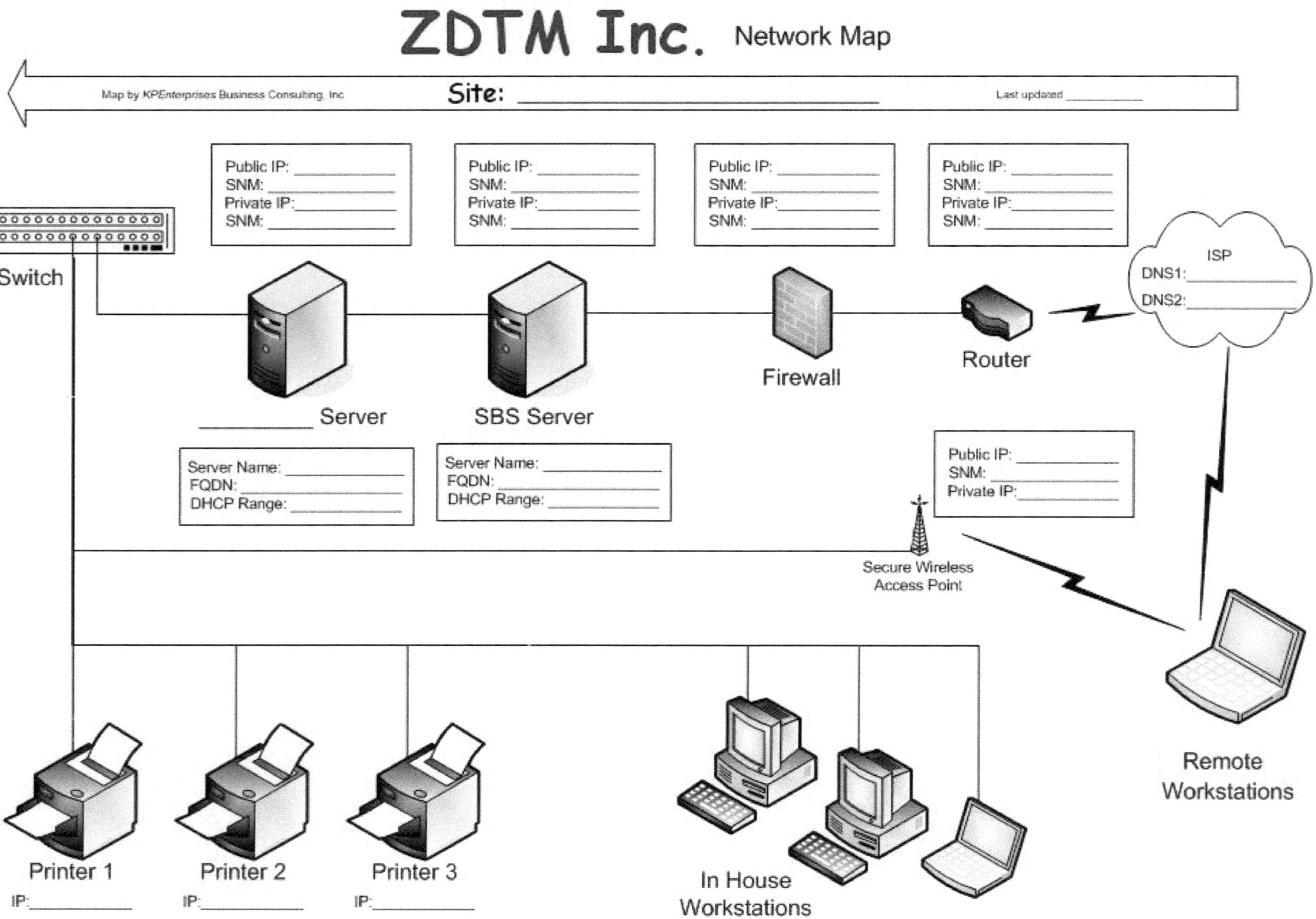
ZDTM Inc. Network Map
Map by KPEnterprises Business Consulting, Inc
Site: ____
Last updated ____
Switch
Public IP: ____
SNM: ____
Private IP: ____
SNM: ____
____ Server
Server Name: ____
FQDN: ____
DHCP Range: ____
Public IP: ____
SNM: ____
Private IP: ____
SNM: ____
SBS Server
Server Name: ____
FQDN: ____
DHCP Range: ____
Public IP: ____
SNM: ____
Private IP: ____
SNM: ____
Firewall
Public IP: ____
SNM: ____
Private IP: ____
SNM: ____
Router
ISP
DNS1: ____
DNS2: ____
Public IP: ____
SNM: ____
Private IP: ____
Secure Wireless Access Point
Remote Workstations
Printer 1
IP: ____
Printer 2
IP: ____
Printer 3
IP: ____
In House Workstations

Internet Domain Registration Information

Company: ______________________

Last Updated: ______________________

Organization: ______________________

Domain Name: ______________________

Domain Name: ______________________

Registrar (e.g., Network Solutions): ______________________

Registrar Website: ______________________

Admin Account Number / Username: ______________________

Password: ______________________

Admin Contact: ______________________

Admin Email: ______________________

Admin NIC Handle: ______________________

Tech Contact: ______________________

Tech Email: ______________________

Tech NIC Handle: ______________________

Billing Contact: ______________________

Billing Email: ______________________

Billing NIC Handle: ______________________

Primary Domain Name Server: ______________________

Secondary Domain Name Server: ______________________

Notes:

____

____

Router Configuration

Company: ____________________

Last Updated: ____________________

Router: ______________________________

Serial Number: ____________________ Firmware Version: ____________

Username: ____________________ (case sensitive)

Password: ____________________ (case sensitive)

Router Managed by : ____________________

Contact: ____________________ / Ph: ____________________

Security information needed for Contact: ____________________

ISP: ____________________

Contact: ____________________ / Ph: ____________________

Security information needed for Contact: ____________________

PPPOE or other username: ____________________

Password: ____________________

Telco Circuit Number: ____________________

Router Gateway: ____________________ / 255.255.255.____

Router WAN / Un-trusted Address: ____________________ / 255.255.255.____

Router LAN / Trusted Address: ____________________ / ____________________

ISP-assigned DNS1: ____________________ DNS2: ____________________

Summary of Settings and Terminology: ____________________

____

Notes:

____

____

____

____

____

Firewall Configuration

Company: ____________________

Last Updated: ________________

Firewall: ________________________________

Serial Number: ______________________ Firmware Version: _____________

Username: _________________________ (case sensitive)

Password: _________________________ (case sensitive)

Firewall Managed by: ____________________________

Contact: __________________________ / Ph: ____________________________

Security information needed for Contact: ____________________________________

Firewall Gateway: ____________________________________ / 255.255.255.______

Firewall WAN / Un-trusted Address: _______________________ / 255.255.255.______

Firewall LAN / Trusted Address: _________________________ / ________________

Summary of Settings and Terminology: ____

____

The following ports are opened:

Service	Port #	From Public IP	To Private IP
Email	25	______________	______________
POP mail	110	______________	______________
HTTP	80	______________	______________
HTTPS	443	______________	______________
SharePoint 03	444	______________	______________
SharePoint 08	987	______________	______________
RWW (https)	4125	______________	______________
RDP	3389	______________	______________
Ping	n/a	______________	______________
DNS	53	______________	______________
PPTP	1723	______________	______________
GRE	47	______________	______________
______	______	______________	______________
______	______	______________	______________

IP Address Allocation

Company: ____________________

Last Updated: __________________

This is an overview of how IP Addresses ranges are allocated in the organization.

Network and Subnet: ______________ / ______________

IP Address Range From To	**Range Description**
	Network Equipment
	Servers
	Printers
	DHCP Range - used by desktop machines. These are allocated by the: Server Router Other: __________
	RAS IP's allocated by:
Hosts file contains:	For use by:

Hard Coded IP Addresses

Company: ____________________

Last Updated: ____________________

The devices listed below have a dedicated IP address.

Network and Subnet: ________________ / ________________

IP Address(s)	Use Description

Network Timing Diagram

Company: ____________________

Last Updated: ____________________

List all scheduled events on the network. Backups, Images, Defrags, Data copies or Sync's, Exchange maintenance, normal business hours, etc.
An X or filled in box represents the event runs the entire hour. An / represents the event runs for ½ hour. You can color the upper left half in to represent the first half hour and the lower right half for the second half hour. Another option is to use the four corners of the square as ¼ hour indicators.

Scheduled Event	00 am	1 am	2 am	3 am	4 am	5 am	6 am	7 am	8 am	9 am	10 am	11 am	12 pm	1 pm	2 pm	3 pm	4 pm	5 pm	6 pm	7 pm	8 pm	9 pm	10 pm	11 pm

Shared Resources

Company: ____________________

Server Name: ____________________

Domain Name: ____________________

Last Updated: ____________________

Data Shares, Shared Printers* and Network Printers

Description	UNC Path	Physical Location	Access Groups	Permission
Example: Public Data	\\sbsserver1\public	D:\Public Data	Everyone	Full control

Network Printers

Description	Port Type	IP Address	Access Groups	Permission
Example: HP 4600TN	JetAdmin	192.168.16.25	Sales	Full control

* A "Shared Printer" is one that is physically attached to a computer (server or desktop) and shared on the domain. This is managed very much like a data share. This is different from a Network Printer, which is connected directly to the network. Generally speaking, users can print directly to Network Printers. If you have a large enough printer demand, you may manage a Network Printer through a server, in which case it appears to users as a Shared Printer. This is becoming less useful as printer memory and self-management increases.

Shared Resource Permission Record

Company: ____________________

Domain Name: ____________________

Last Updated: ____________________

Read Only = RO
Read Write = RW

Shared Resource	Group Name																			

UPS Power Distribution

Company: ____________________

Last Updated: ____________________

UPS 1: ____________________

Make: ____________________

Model: ____________________

Device / New Battery installed on: ____/____/____

Outlet 1: ____________________	Watts: ________
Outlet 2: ____________________	Watts: ________
Outlet 3: ____________________	Watts: ________
Outlet 4: ____________________	Watts: ________
Outlet 5: ____________________	Watts: ________
Outlet 6: ____________________	Watts: ________
Outlet 7: ____________________	Watts: ________
Outlet 8: ____________________	Watts: ________
Outlet 9: ____________________	Watts: ________
Outlet 10: ____________________	Watts: ________

UPS 2: ____________________

Make: ____________________

Model: ____________________

Device / New Battery installed on: ____/____/____

Outlet 1: ____________________	Watts: ________
Outlet 2: ____________________	Watts: ________
Outlet 3: ____________________	Watts: ________
Outlet 4: ____________________	Watts: ________
Outlet 5: ____________________	Watts: ________
Outlet 6: ____________________	Watts: ________
Outlet 7: ____________________	Watts: ________
Outlet 8: ____________________	Watts: ________
Outlet 9: ____________________	Watts: ________
Outlet 10: ____________________	Watts: ________

Rules

#1 The server with the highest power consumption goes on the UPS with the highest Wattage rating.
#2 The monitor and KVM for the primary server must be on the same UPS as that server.
#3 Where possible, keep the router and firewall on the same UPS as the primary server.
Note: This is only useful if the primary server plugs directly into the firewall.
#4 Label the UPS(s) with their number.
#5 Label both ends of all cables plugged into the UPS(s).

Group Policy Object Record

Company: ____________________

Server Name: ____________________

Domain Name: ____________________

Last Updated: ____________________

Group Policies in use on this domain.

For all intricate GPO's that are listed here, attach a report of the GPO to this page.
(Right-click the GPO, select Save Report, save as html, print the html file)
Note: Do not list Default GPO's that have not had any of their settings changed or are not disabled.
Note: There is no need to list the Domain Password Policy GPO a it has its own form.

Group Policy Name: ____________________
☐ Enabled ☐ User Config disabled ☐ Computer Config disabled ☐ All Settings Disabled
Notes: ____________________
____

Group Policy Name: ____________________
☐ Enabled ☐ User Config disabled ☐ Computer Config disabled ☐ All Settings Disabled
Notes: ____________________
____

Group Policy Name: ____________________
☐ Enabled ☐ User Config disabled ☐ Computer Config disabled ☐ All Settings Disabled
Notes: ____________________
____

Group Policy Name: ____________________
☐ Enabled ☐ User Config disabled ☐ Computer Config disabled ☐ All Settings Disabled
Notes: ____________________
____

Group Policy Name: ____________________
☐ Enabled ☐ User Config disabled ☐ Computer Config disabled ☐ All Settings Disabled
Notes: ____________________
____

Group Policy Name: ____________________
☐ Enabled ☐ User Config disabled ☐ Computer Config disabled ☐ All Settings Disabled
Notes: ____________________
____

Group Policy Name: ____________________
☐ Enabled ☐ User Config disabled ☐ Computer Config disabled ☐ All Settings Disabled
Notes: ____________________
____

Machine Specification

Company: ______________________

Last Updated: ____________________

Machine Was New: _______________

Computer or other Machine Configuration Specifications

Machine: ________________________________

User: ___________________________________

Machine Description: ________________________________

Serial Number: ________________________________

CPU: / Slot Type: ________________________________

RAM: ________________________________

RAM slots: ________________________________

Operating System: ________________________________

TCP/IP Address: ________________________________

Hard Drive 0: ________________________________

Hard Drive 1: ________________________________

Hard Drive 2: ________________________________

NIC 1: ________________________________

NIC 2: ________________________________

Video Notes: ________________________________

Sound Notes: ________________________________

Other ________________________________

Other ________________________________

Notes:

____

____

____

____

____

____

____

User Name, Logon ID and Password Record

Company: ______________________

Domain Name: __________________

Page: ______ of ______

Full Name	Logon ID	Password
Local administrator – Server		
Domain Administrator		
SQL SA		
IT Management Account		
Local administrator - Workstation	Administrator	
Default Domain User password	%Username%	

User Name, Logon ID and Password Record

Company: ______________________

Domain Name: ______________________

Page: ________ of ________

Full Name	Logon ID	Password

Email Address Record

Company: ____________________

Domain Name: @____________________

Primary SMTP domain? Y / N

User Name	Email address(s)

POP and MAPI Account Record

Company: ____________________

Last Updated: ____________________

User's Full Name	Email Address	Logon ID Password	Security / Account Notes:	Incoming Mail Server and Port	Outgoing Mail Server and Port
Example: *Jacob Plumber*	*Jake@* *Handyman.net*	*JakePlumber* *Pipe1234*	*SPA required* *In and Out server use same creds*	*pop.mailman.org*	*smtp.mailman.org*

Security and Distribution Group Membership

Company: ____________________

Domain Name: ____________________

Last Updated: ____________________

User Name	Group Name																			

Password Policy

Company: ____________________

Server Name: ____________________

Domain Name: ____________________

Last Updated: ____________________

Password Policy will be configured? Y / N

Enforce password history: _______ Passwords will be remembered.

Maximum password age: ________ Days until password expire.

Minimum password age: _________ Days until password can be changed.

Minimum password length: _______ Characters required for password length.

Password must meet complexity requirements: Enabled / Disabled

Store passwords using reversible encryption: Enabled / Disabled

Account Lockout Policy will be configured? Y / N

Account lockout duration: ________ Minutes account will remain locked out.

Account lockout threshold: _______ Failed logon attempts will lock the account out.

Reset account lockout counter after: ___________ Minutes.

Company Password Policy

Please Note: Your password is case sensitive!

- We have adopted the following password security policy for our company.
- User passwords will expire every ____________ days. You will get several warnings prior to when your password expires, and you will be required to change your password.
- All passwords are must be at least ___________ characters long, and can include any letters, numbers, and the following characters: ~ ` ! @ # $ % ^ & ( ) - _ { }
- The system will remember your last: _________ passwords so you will not be able to immediately reuse the same passwords.
- Should you attempt to log on _________ times with an incorrect password, you will be locked out of the network for _________ minutes.
- Should you forget your password, you will need to contact the system administrator to gain access to the network.

Line of Business Application Record

Company: ____________________

Last Updated: ____________________

Application or Product Name: ____________________

What platforms will this application run on: ____________________

The current and most recent version of this application: __________ / __________

The current and most recent service pack for this application: ______ / ______

The most critical server requirements for this application are: (SQL for example)__________

____

The most critical workstation requirements for this application are: ____________________

____

Support Contract is from: Publisher / Third Party / Other: ____________________

Support Provider contact information:

Name: ____________________

Website: ____________________

Email address: ____________________

Phone number: ____________________

Phone number: ____________________

Support contract for the applications expires on: ____________________

Support method is: Open / Per Incident / Per Hour / Other: ____________________

Installation / Configuration / Migration Notes:

27. Index to the Network Migration Project

R

S

T

U

V

W

X

Z

Appendix B

Procedure-Based Index

This index is based on the Big Checklist (Appendix A). It identifies the sections and page numbers for specific procedures found within that checklist.

This is particularly useful if you wish to identify a procedure in isolation from a migration as a whole. For example, if you wish to move a database, you will need documentation forms, checklists, and related items, all of which are scattered throughout "The Big Checklist" in Appendix A.

At some level, mastery of the process as a whole consists of mastery of each of the minor processes that make up the whole. With that in mind, we present some guidelines for picking out the pages most relevant to specific projects.

To use this Appendix, first identify the products you wish to migration. Second, pull out the pages identified for those products. And, third, pick out the appropriate pages from the "Apply to All" section. Of course you'll need to tweak and tune the pages to create *your* product-specific checklist. You may wish to separate these procedures and create a whole checklist for this product or procedure.

Apply to All

Pages that apply to all process-specific migrations:

- Section 1 Using This Document (all pages)
- Section 2 Pre-Discovery (selected pages)
- Section 3 Project Description and Scope
- Section 4 Discovery (selected pages)
- Section 5 Planning and Timeline
  Note: This is a critical section for any project
- Section 6 Migration Strategies
- Section 7 Resources
- Section 8 Communication and Training
- Section 11 Troubleshooting and Repair Log
- Section 18 Migration Tracking Sheet
- Section 19 Shortages
- Section 20 Pack-Up / To-Do Checklist
- Section 21 Fine Tuning
- Section 22 Spin-Off Projects and Issues

Migration Topics / Pages

Accounting or Finance Packages

Note that we did not include a specific example in the checklist. Your process for the Accounting Package of choice should be fleshed out in this section.

The most common accounting package is QuickBooks, but there are plenty of others out there as well. In most companies the accounting package is only used by a few people. So you will have to coordinate your move with just those folks.

This is a perfect example of a process that can take advantage of RDP or virtualization. You can create a connection to the "new" service that runs in a virtual machine or RDP environment for the few users who need the accounting system. This allows the users to do most of their work in the "old" environment and access the new system in the virtual environment until their desktop is migrated to the new server/domain.

Antivirus Solution

We give an example of using Trend's Worry Free managed service offering. You'll need to adjust for your preferred product.

Backup Software, Devices and Methods / Backup Solution

We give an example using Symantec Backup Exec. You'll need to adjust for your preferred product.

The BES 4.5 product is not compatible with SBS 2008. Please note that we've posted BES 4.5 instructions for SBS 2003 on the ZeroDownTimeMigration.com web site. You will have access to this when you register you book online.

This is an example of the changing environment that makes migrations complicated!

Notes: In some sense, the transfer of non-database files is very straight forward. You can use RoboCopy or one of a dozen commercial products to synchronize files. The most important part of the process is to be *extremely rigorous* about documenting what you're doing. Know what you've done and what you haven't done. Know where you put things!

Appendix C

Online Materials

This book includes several online components.

First, you need to register to the book at www.zerodowntimemigration.com. On the front page, simply click on the Register the Book link. Note: This takes some time because we need to authenticate your purchase. Please allow up to 72 hours for us to process your request if it occurs over a weekend.

Once you register the book you will receive access to the ZDTM Registered Owners content. This includes electronic versions of the checklist (Appendix A plus older 2003 and 2008 checklists), plus additional materials, such as:

- Excel Spreadsheets for quotes, from Chapter 4
- Visio diagram of common network configuration
- PowerPoint Presentation: Pre-Migration Introduction
- PowerPoint Presentation: Post-Migration Welcome

In addition, we will have a forum area exclusively for Registered Owners. We hope you'll help keep the big checklist up to date with vendor-specific procedures, etc.

One of the most important pieces of knowledge is the "Our Favorite Whitepapers" section. We'll have that online for Registered Owners only and welcome your additions, corrections, etc.

This book was delayed by a series of new product releases and documentation updates from Microsoft. Eventually we decided that we can't expect that to ever stop. So we sealed up the writing process and shipped the book.

But we hope the online Registered Owners section of Zerodowntimemigration.com will help you (and us) keep up to date.

If you have questions, comments, or suggestions, you can always contact us at

Warning About Used Books

When you register your book online, you agree that the book is no longer returnable for a refund. We simply have to assume that anyone who registers the book is going to download the electronic content and use it. Therefore, the book cannot be returned once the e-version has been downloaded.

That also means that the owner of a used copy of the book does not have access to the electronic version.

If you bought this book used, and you want electronic versions of the checklists, you need to ask the seller for a refund so you can buy a new copy of the book.

We are sorry that this policy is necessary, but we have had a few "bad apples" buy the book and then intentionally violate the copyright. As you can imagine, this book took thousands of hours of labor to produce. Even a casual user will save dozens of hours of labor by using these checklists and resources. So, while the price is not cheap, we believe it is fair.

Thank you for your support and understanding.

KarlP@greatlittlebook.com manuel@conceptualageconsulting.net

Other Great Little Books

From Great Little Book Publishing Co., Inc.

Managed Services In A Month

Karl W. Palachuk

This book has helped hundreds of small business consultants take the leap into managed services. This great little book focuses completely on the step-by-step process, with examples and templates from the real world.

Service Agreements for SMB Consultants

A Quick-Start Guide to Managed Services

Karl W. Palachuk

Much more than service agreement template! Thousands of business from all over the world have used this "Quick Start Guide" to define their business, their clients, and their offerings.

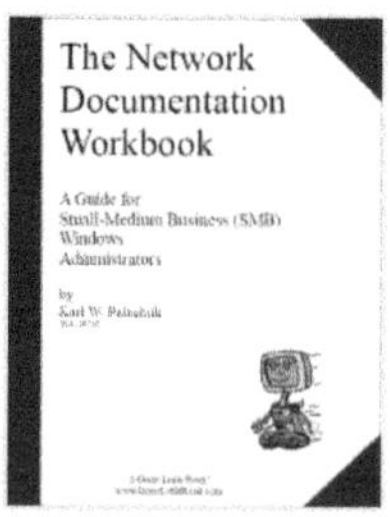

The Network Documentation Workbook

A Guide for Small-Medium Business Windows Administrators

Karl W. Palachuk

Our best seller ever is now an e-book you can download today. Filled with all for the forms and procedures to take you consulting business to the next level!

Relax Focus Succeed®

A Guide to Balancing Your Personal and Professional Lives and Becoming More Successful in Both

Karl W. Palachuk

Put a little more fun and a lot less stress in your life with the award-winning book.

And More . . .

These and other books by Karl Palachuk and other SBS/SMB consultants are available every day at www.smbbooks.com. SMB Books strives to be a great resource for Small Business Consultants who are looking to improves themselves and their businesses.

We welcome your feedback. Please email karlp@greatlittlebook.

www.ingramcontent.com/pod-product-compliance
Ingram Content Group UK Ltd.
Pitfield, Milton Keynes, MK11 3LW, UK
UKHW051456290926
15471UKWH00008B/1227

9 780981 997872